The Anthem Handbook of Screen Theory

The Anthem Handbook of Screen Theory

Edited by Hunter Vaughan and Tom Conley

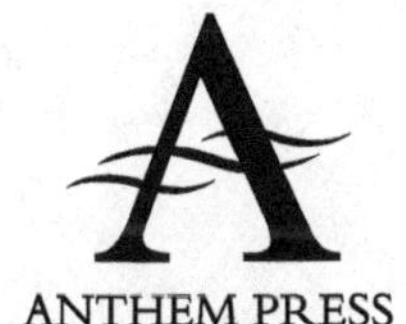

Anthem Press
An imprint of Wimbledon Publishing Company
www.anthempress.com

This edition first published in UK and USA 2020
by ANTHEM PRESS
75–76 Blackfriars Road, London SE1 8HA, UK
or PO Box 9779, London SW19 7ZG, UK
and
244 Madison Ave #116, New York, NY 10016, USA

First published in the UK and USA by Anthem Press 2018

British Library Cataloguing-in-Publication Data
A catalogue record for this book is available from the British Library.

Library of Congress Cataloging-in-Publication Data
Library of Congress Control Number: 2020941410

ISBN-13: 978-1-78527-523-4 (Pbk)
ISBN-10: 1-78527-523-2 (Pbk)

This title is also available as an e-book.

CONTENTS

FIGURES

PREFACE

Welcome, readers, to *The Anthem Handbook of Screen Theory*! We cordially invite you to step inside, meander around and explore. Hopefully, as you open this collection, doors will open on both sides of the page, and we will enter into a conversation. We may not always agree, and we may not always even speak the same language, but we are all here because we (1) believe that critical thinking is important; (2) understand the sociocultural importance of screen media in the unfolding of the twenty-first century, and in the formation of the century that preceded it; and (3) are ready to explore new horizons and to carve new folds in the brain that meet the challenge of a world, of media apparatuses, and of social configurations that have changed radically since film theory was canonized some thirty years ago. As you will find central to the concerns of this book, from Francesco Casetti's Introduction essay to Tom Conley's Postface, we have entered into a highly mediated digital era that throws notions of the "filmic" and the "cinematic" largely into question, the traditional boundaries of medium specificity blurred by the convergent nature of this new wonderland of wireless signals, mobile screens and virtual windows. An era, simply put, of screens: screens in our town-squares and on our wrists, in our classrooms and on our dashboards, screens in outer space, underwater and in our pockets—a world of screens that problematizes the conventional notions both of the moving image and of the social function of cultural practice. These pages may not solve such debates, but we aim to equip readers to take part in them.

The contemporary film and media student emerges at a unique moment: the proliferation of digital technology is increasingly turning individuals into daily content providers and empowering global populations through communications networks, while also aiding the transnational flow of a borderless mainstream screen culture and, at the same time, prompting the emergence of local, small nation and counter-cinemas. Because of the heightened role that image culture plays in today's individual lives, community activisms and global economies, and because new technologies such as smart phones have democratized the means of textual production, theory is needed more than ever to nurture our complex understanding—and *use*—of screen media and to challenge the horizons of our sociopolitical and philosophical engagement of the world.

We live in a cinematic—and increasingly post-cinematic—civilization, in which *no one alive today was alive before the birth of moving images*. Let us pause to really consider that. Our entire extant species has lived its entire life and will live its entire life in coexistence with a virtual universe that bends time and space and offers human beings a crystalline range of liminal screen experiences, from Nickelodeon theaters to online avatars. And, more than ever, these experiences and lives are linked by networks of fiber-optic cables and satellite signals, a wired planet whose messages and debates unfold in the form of push notifications, graphics interchange formats (GIFs) and echo chambers. In an age of drone strikes and smart thermostats, remote-operated fracking drills and camera-driven interstellar exploration—in a pluralistic screened world where transgender communities have televisual spokespersons and racial violence persists across multimedia outlets via the crowd-sourced content of smart-phone videos, we need more than ever to understand how our screens produce and communicate meaning.

Engaging equally with lofty concepts and popular discourses, *The Anthem Handbook of Screen Theory* asks its contributors and readers to embrace and to be responsive to the activist potential of critical thinking, to bring ideas out of the ivory tower and to render them applicable, clear and—perhaps most of all—relevant. This is the primary goal of this book's unique approach: abandoning the practice of anthologizing canonical essays, we want a diverse group of active scholars, representing a mixture of established and emerging voices in the field, to bring critical thinking and cultural studies into the present. While we genuinely hope the reader will pursue the primary writings of Germaine Dulac, Sergei Eisenstein, André Bazin, Laura Mulvey, Lev Manovich, bell hooks and others, and while the essays here will be freckled with references to and summaries of the names and works that have shaped our intellectual history, we believe these original icons are already readily available. In order to move beyond the types of anthology already on offer, we aim here to bridge intellectual histories with contemporary practices, so that each entry here explains the background and exemplifies the pertinence of specific theoretical fields, while also thinking innovatively about how these theories can adapt to the changing landscape of contemporary screen media, global politics and philosophical thinking.

Screen theory has been equally informed by the technological developments and aesthetic innovations of screen culture as by the social upheaval and geopolitical chaos of its times. As such, it is necessary to view it in both "diachronic" and "synchronic" terms: *diachronic* in that it vertically follows the building of thought as historical moments stack upon one another, and *synchronic* in that each articulation of theory is itself connected horizontally across a contemporary moment, situated within a network of conflicted and conflicting political, sociological, technological and cultural forces. In other words, screen theory is both an evolution and a morphology, the current state of which—at any moment—is unique to that moment's artistic and ideological context. With the rise of Communism and Fascism in the early twentieth century, and the spread of global capitalism in the past decades, theory was interwoven into the fight for and against political superstructures. Theory spoke the early poetry of high Modernism and the fractured pop culture of the postmodern, the intervening postwar years fraught with the existential anxiety of a human condition traumatically scarred by the Holocaust, Hiroshima and Nagasaki. The 1960s witnessed the advent of structural and Marxian solutions to dilemmas of social revolution, while since the 1970s theory has peered deeper into these structures in order to contextualize and defend the individual identities that composed this revolution, the echoes of which resound through Pasi Väliaho's deft updating of Marxist thought as well as Theresa Geller's portrait of gender and sexuality theory, Camilla Fojas's exploration of issues of race and ethnicity, and my own call for an environmentalist approach that sees beyond the human.

Theory has been inundated by the great paradigms of twentieth and twenty-first-century thought, including psychoanalysis, semiotics, structuralism and post-structuralism, feminism, environmentalism, cultural studies, and digital theory. As Brendan Kredell, Mary Desjardins and Codruţa Morari illuminate, we must continuously update our toolkit not only according to the arrival of new screen stories, but also for new audiences and modes of viewership, new constructions of stardom and new terms of authorship. As such, we strive here to adapt crucial theories of the image to an age that has moved beyond film, to this multimedia existential range that makes room for transnational distribution, YouTube celebrity, multilingual interfaces and Twitter presidents. And, as Elisabeth Bronfen, James Tweedy and Trond Lundemo so aptly map out, respectively, our conceptualization of the world must increasingly accommodate a cultural permeability that allows genres to slip between media, meanings to transverse national boundaries and signal configurations to recode between technological formats.

Yet, in an era when scholarship is largely guided by a focus on industry history and practice, one might pose the simple question: "why theory?" That is a fair question, as would be: "why think?" The heyday for Grand Theory ended in the late 1960s, and with it a certain resistant idealism for the power of critical thought. As the planet tipped toward global capitalism, theory seemed less and less utilitarian, yielding less monetized value in an increasingly corporatized system of higher education. But in a world challenged by ideological fragmentation, social change and discursive diversity, critical thinking is more valuable and necessary today than ever—we hope you will find in these pages convincing arguments not only for the relevance of theory, but for its applicability, its relevance, even for its essential necessity.

While the word "theory" evokes a certain metaphysical or intangible quality, critical and cultural theory grows from an active and activist nature and can have a concrete impact on the morphology of artistic practices, social attitudes and political action. Thoughts produce actions, and vice versa. Nadine Boljkovac, Warren Buckland and Daniel Yacavone will assist our understanding of how the eye and mind make sense of the moving image's construction of worlds, from visual realism to puzzle narratives to the abstractions of formalist experimentation, and in doing so, will help us explore how the texts we view shape our brains and thought patterns, and consequently, our values and beliefs. Ways of understanding our screen experience have transformed in synchrony with the evolving nexus of ideology, philosophy and visual culture: with theory we seek to understand how that virtual universe can impact and shape our thoughts, hoping to illuminate how screen culture, which seems increasingly immaterial in the digital age, has material resonance in a world of blood, mineral and petroleum. From William Rothman's philosophical insights to Laura U. Marks's political commentary, this collection is imbued with the influences of both humanist philosophy and dialectical materialism, the two woven together (and sometimes in rich debate) to explore how screen texts both shape and reflect our worldviews from the metaphysical to the quotidian.

Sadly, all collections must be selective, and there are certainly omissions in these pages; we have aimed for a progressive approach that, while including most traditional methods, moves beyond them. There is no essay, for example, and perhaps most notably, on psychoanalysis. While some of the essays in this collection engage with psychoanalytic theories (which were crucial especially for the emergence of 1960s apparatus theory as well as feminist film theory and theories of gender and sexuality in the 1970s, as is expertly detailed in Tom Conley's and Theresa Geller's essays herein), and though psychoanalytic concepts and methods persist in the work of certain writers, and psychological approaches to the moving image are still widely popular in cognitive theory (see William Brown's contribution), paradigms of screen theory have shifted so far away from psychoanalysis that its place now seems more fitting for a historical perspective than a contemporary field. Moreover, the Freudian and Lacanian lynchpins of twentieth-century psychoanalysis, however much they informed us to certain dynamics of human behavior and communication, proved over time to be lacking in terms of their accessibility and applicability to social diversity.

Nonetheless, we hope to do justice here to the great contributions of psychoanalytic approaches, as they have interwoven key threads into the shaping of cinema and its theorization. In addition to the role that desire plays in our tangling of individual and cultural behaviors, the lasting legacy of psychoanalysis concerns most crucially the importance of the subject, which emerged as *the* fulcrum of modern philosophy, political theory and social sciences, centering on the triadic convergence between individual self-identity, social agency and projective identification with representational texts. The philosophical root of colonialism, sexism and environmental destruction, the subject–object binary has intrinsically offered *the* central conceptual battlefield for the last four centuries of Western thought, a struggle played out microcosmically in the arena of screen theory amidst the great political and social changes of the last hundred years. From the Romantically poetic espousal of artistic potential identified by early theorists such as Jean Epstein, to the *auteur* theory of the 1950s and 1960s that isolated the director as the visionary genius of a film, to the apparatus theories of Jean-Louis Baudry, Daniel Dayan and Jean-Louis Comolli, the semiotics of Kaja Silverman, and the politicized gender and sexuality theory of Laura Mulvey, Linda Williams and Robin Wood, to the complex raced and sexed and queered identity approaches of cultural studies in the 1980s (see Stuart Hall, Judith Butler and others), to the postmodern, digital and post-human approaches of the last two decades, the subject—as locus of textual action and meaning, as abstract positioning of consciousness within the film world, and as person or social group with social agency—has been at the core of film and media theory.

While such central concepts will play out in these pages, this is not the book for merely summarizing past theory—exactly why we have chosen to leave certain frameworks at the periphery. Instead, we hope these pages include a solid introduction to the texts and methodologies that shaped the first century of screen theory, while opening important doors to the present and future of its many vistas. As psychoanalysis gives way to cognitive theory, as formalism and realism must interplay in reflection of the convergence of various media through digital technology, as theories of gender and sexuality adapt to new social dynamics and issues of race and ethnicity shift with rapidly changing political structures, and as notions of identity must accommodate the age of environmentalism and artificial intelligence—so must we continuously adjust our conceptual language and understanding.

We have bundled essays into three groups, each bundle a possible theme for a third of a typical academic semester. These do not in any way follow a chronological or historical arrow: each essay does cultivate its own screen theory within the larger genealogy of cultural and intellectual history, but we deemed it more rewarding for readers to explore the content according to themes, themselves moving in outward rings like ripples emanating across a conceptual ocean. Unlike many collections that begin with the specifics of film and media form and move toward the larger social and global dynamics and networks that produce and bear the impact of visual culture, we are going to begin with the vast and move toward the particular: from the political, social and ethical fields through which screen texts circulate, to the industrial frameworks and technological conditions under which they are made, to the ways in which viewers make sense of them perceptually, philosophically and logically.

Part I, "What We Are," focuses on the connection between human identity—race, class, gender, sexuality, nationality, ecology—and screen meaning. It begins with Pasi Väliaho's "The Brain's Labor: On Marxism and the Movies," which offers an updated vision on the fundamental Western philosophical and sociological approach—Marxism, which ultimately asserts that there is a hegemonic class that maintains and exerts power through exploitation and repression—that underpins nearly all resistant theoretical models of sociocultural study. This sets the groundwork for other specific approaches to screen culture and identity, including Camilla Fojas's essay, "Racial Being, Affect and Media Cultures," on race and ethnicity and Theresa L. Geller's "Thinking Sex, Doing Gender, Watching Film," which, in looking at feminist and queer theory, maps out arguably the most historically fruitful field of identity-based screen theory, if not film cultural studies as a whole. In "'Complicated Negotiations': Reception and Audience Studies into the Digital Age," Brendan Kredell explores theory's recent turn toward the sociological exploration of reception theories, while James Tweedie's "World Cinema and Its Worlds" discusses how screen practices are tied to the machinery of national culture and contemporary issues of globalization. Extending this geopolitical beyond the anthropocentric and to more environmental concerns, Hunter Vaughan's "Screen Theory Beyond the Human: Toward an Ecomaterialism of the Moving Image" concludes this section by positioning our screen practices within a larger natural world, urging readers and writers alike to consider the environmental and ecological ramifications of our image culture.

Having established the larger context in which screen practices take place, we then turn to the practices themselves. Part II, "What Screen Culture Is" (to co-opt a phrase from Dudley Andrew) addresses the formal specificities of screen technology, as well as the industry functions that have been integral to its growth, popular appeal and cultural machinations. In "Apparatus Theory, Plain and Simple," Tom Conley explores the basis of structural inquiries into how film's basic machinery and its consequent conventions have broader significance. The mechanics and machinations of the moving image, however, are only parts of a larger industrial network, one that functions according to different dynamic conventions and systems of production, marketing and consumption, a Catherine wheel of creative and cultural forces introduced in Codruţa Morari's "Properties of Film Authorship." Authorship is one of many industry functions that have long been deeply rooted in major local and global screen cultures, and is deeply intertwined with stardom and genre—all three of which experienced critical renaissance in the 1960s structuralist approaches to screen industries; in "'Deepest Ecstasy' Meets Cinema's Social Subjects: Theorizing the Screen Star," Mary R. Desjardins brings theories of stardom and the star system into the digital age, while Elisabeth Bronfen's "Rethinking Genre Memory: Hitchcock's *Vertigo* and Its Revision" explores ways in which meaning circulates through repetition and difference across genres, across media, across cultures and across time. This is followed by Trond Lundemo's "Digital Technologies and the End(s) of Film Theory," which lays out the complex ramifications of our recent transition from analog to digital practices; arguing a point that in many ways underpins this entire collection, Lundemo speaks for our collective in noting that screen theory, as the late Anne Friedberg precipitously argued, must today view cinema and film as part of a larger screen genealogy that is now moving beyond those formats. We live in a digital age: we must theorize for a digital age.

This technological and screen cultural shift also marks a shift in our internal systems of meaning (philosophy, psychology) and our collective systems of meaning (semiotics, storytelling), as is explored in Part III, "How We Understand Screen Texts." How film signification has been—and can be—theorized is the focus of Daniel Yacavone's "The Expressive Sign: Cinesemiotics, Enunciation and Screen Art," which pushes beyond the traditional linguistic base of semiotics to explore how entire cinematic worlds are constructed. Yacavone's essay explores how we make sense of screen texts, much as Warren Buckland does in the subsequent piece, "Narratology in Motion: Causality, Puzzles and Narrative Twists," which addresses this primarily through narrative theories of how films tell stories and produce meaning. But narrative assembly, patterning and logic is only one part of the equation: after all, there is a human brain that must make sense of it, which is the topic of William Brown's "He(u)retical Film Theory: When Cognitivism Meets Theory," exploring one of the two major recent trends in psychological and philosophical screen theory. Robert Sinnerbrink's "Philosophy Encounters the Moving Image: From Film Philosophy to Cinematic Thinking" explores the flip side to cognitive theory, in pursuit of illuminating a dialectic that perhaps all writers in this collection chase: how screen culture has shaped not only our society, arts and industry, but also our very brains. This focal point of the book as a whole may belie a bias of the project as a whole, one that leans toward the opening of theory to the beauties and significance of uncertainty, flux and impermanence, which govern the world as they do the mind as well as the moving image—a connection that is brought home to roost in Nadine Boljkovac's "Screen Perception and Event: Beyond the Formalist/Realist Divide," which dissolves the traditional binary between these regimes in a study of the osmotic flow of screen meaning.

We have also solicited three intervention essays from among the most influential theorists of the past half-century, including an exploration of theory in the "post-" era by Francesco Casetti, a state of raced media identity in the global union by Laura U. Marks, and a career-in-review in which William Rothman guides us down the rabbit hole of what it means to be a screen philosopher. These essays complement the larger sections both in theme and in tone, but—like each contribution here—can also stand alone as compelling and complete snapshots of where theory is today, how it got here and where it is going. While it would be impossible for any one volume to touch every base, play every note and provide exactly the same number of blueberries in every muffin, we have aimed here to bring readers a collection that makes theory both rounded and pertinent, one that offers both precision and range, historical overview and contemporary relevance. Our contributors have been asked to do justice to the theory of the past, challenged to render the present more accessible, and encouraged to think outside the box in envisioning new horizons for the future—we can only ask the same of our readers.

Hunter Vaughan
Coconut Grove, Florida

ACKNOWLEDGMENTS

Arching over years and across continents, this collection has been a collaborative passion project from start to finish: we are grateful to everyone who has helped to make it possible. We are deeply indebted to the dynamic group of theorists, thinkers, writers, visionaries and poets of the moving image who informed and inspired the pages herein. The shape that this book has taken owes much to the generosity of our contributing authors—we thank them not only for their uncommon patience and perseverance but also for the innovation they bring to screen theory. We would also like to thank Tej Sood, Abi Pandey, Nisha Vetrivel and the team at Anthem Press, whose careful attention and direction were invaluable to this endeavor.

In addition …

Hunter Vaughan: I would like to embrace with gratitude those who still believe that critical thinking and cultural ethics hold a place in today's world—may that torch continue to burn, scorching those who would obscure its light. I am grateful to Tej Sood for entrusting me with this project and extend my warmest appreciation to Tom Conley, my comrade in the trenches and a perpetual source of great inspiration and support. Special thanks to Meryl Shriver-Rice for her insights, insistences and care—this book is one of many spinning in the orbit of ideas interwoven into our cobblestone strolls and wandering discussions.

Tom Conley: I wish to thank everyone who has taken part so selflessly and generously in a project whose worth and wealth are born of collective endeavor. Without Hunter Vaughan's perseverance, commitment and vision, may I add, the *Handbook* would not have seen the day. We owe boundless gratitude to him.

Introduction

POST-, GRAND, CLASSICAL OR "SO-CALLED": WHAT IS, AND WAS, FILM THEORY?

Francesco Casetti

Today, film theory is at a crossroad. On the one hand, its body of concepts is growing thanks to the emergence of new perspectives and new situations to be taken into account. On the other hand, some of its traditional keywords are being strongly criticized, especially by the exponents of the so-called philosophy of film, because of their alleged inconsistency and inefficacy.

The growth of theory responds to a multifold impulse. First of all, the process of digitalization and media convergence, with their huge impact on film, urge theory to reckon with new questions and to dialogue with other disciplines equally interested in the same facts. The increasing use of new devices and platforms, from computers to smart-phones and to headsets like Oculus Rift, changes our perspectives on the film apparatus and recalls aspects that are more familiar to media studies. Film's migration into domestic spaces, urban squares or theme parks calls for an ecological sensibility that was formerly largely unknown in the field (although the configuration of movie theatres could have certainly already suggested that cinema is an environmental art). The development of new forms of vision, from 3-D to virtual reality, reshapes our approach to film reception and asks for a wider attention to processes that are currently undertaken by neurosciences. Film theory confronts unprecedented situations and adjusts its own methods and goals. As a consequence, it shares with other disciplines concepts like digitization, scale, network, hybridity, cybernetics, embodied cognition and the Anthropocene.[1]

At the same time, the availability of never-explored archives provides the opportunity to gain a better grasp on the topics discussed in the past. This is true for the Western canon: one thinks of Abel (1988), an anthology on the first wave of French film theory, Andel and Szczepanik (2008), a collection of early Czech film theory, and more recently, Kaes, Baer and Cowan (2016), an anthology of German film theory until 1933. It is equally true for traditions that fall outside of it, as shown by current explorations of early Asian debates by Nornes and Gerow (2009), Bao (2015) and Fan (2015), which provide a much better sense of the issues at stake in the field and their transnational circulation. This archival work elicits a global reconsideration of film theory: the latter not only discovers the wealth of its lineages, but is also encouraged to reread its canonical texts[2] beyond the borders of an aesthetic approach still persistent in some reconstructions (see Rodowick 2014).[3]

Film theory flourishes, either in retracing its own past or in facing cinema's future. And yet it is under attack. A group of scholars, predominantly Anglo-American, and generally followers of the analytical philosophy, claim that most of the concepts that film theory uses are weak, inaccurate and groundless. They lack internal coherence and they do not appropriately explain how cinema works. Hence, such scholars claim, we need a philosophical approach that can offer both a rigorous scrutiny and a redefinition of the traditional issues.[4] There is no doubt that the presence of a sort of meta-theory, aimed at questioning the nature and the basis of what we usually call film theory, is extremely useful.[5] Many concepts have been, and are, merely the outcome of fashionable approaches. Unfortunately, in opposition to a tradition that saw the Italian philosopher Giovanni Papini, praised by William James in 1907 for his polemical flair, ask the cinema to infuse philosophy with its own questions and philosophy to respond with its full competence (see Papini 2017), the "new" philosophers of film tend to interpret their task in a prevalent antagonistic mode. Concepts under scrutiny are generally dismantled and often dismissed, and when redefined, it is in a new light, often alien to their history. The consequence is an attempt—often unexpressed—to legitimize film philosophy as a discipline that overrules and supersedes film theory: as if the former were able to provide a "truth" that the latter cannot completely attain.

But what is the "truth" of a theory? The exactness of its concepts or the necessity that makes them appear? Its internal coherence or the very fact that it is an answer to an emerging question? The "truth" of film theories—as for literary, theatrical or artistic theories, so different from scientific ones—is deeply connected with their endless attempt to move "toward" their object with steps that are always reflecting the spirit of the time; in this sense their "truth" overlaps with their historical significance and effectiveness. Formal scrutiny of their claims fails to grasp their core. Put in another way, discourses are "events," as Foucault used to say;[6] they occur at one moment and at one place, and they respond to rules of construction that change over time. An analysis outside their context risks misunderstanding them—or not capturing their potentiality. Film theories are no exception: they are discourses that respond to the pressure of their time, and we can grasp them only in the force-field in which they move.[7]

It is in this vein that I'd like to propose a reconsideration of what we intend by *film theory*. If we assume (again, with Foucault 1972) that film theories are also "discursive formations" that keep together a variety of statements otherwise dispersed, then we can detect under the same term at least four different kinds of aggregation, each of them emerging in a distinct period, making a distinct array of connections, obeying a distinct set of rules, aiming at distinct tasks, and, inevitably, swiveling on a distinct idea of "truth." Film theory is not one; historically speaking, it is at least a fourfold reality that reflects different styles of thought.

The first contributions with a "theoretical" ambition appeared around 1907, in coincidence with the stabilization of cinema as theatrical spectacle. I put the term between quotation marks: indeed, early "theories" do not possess those characteristics to which the great reflections on film from the mid-1920s onward have accustomed us. For example, they do not develop from systematic work carried out in books and essays. Instead, they are usually sporadic interventions, related to current events or cultural polemics, and are printed in daily newspapers, promotional journals, illustrated papers and works of fiction. Trade journals have sometimes organized more focused debates: in the United States *The Moving Picture World* offered ongoing considerations about cinema's social role and critics' duties. And yet only in the mid-1910s do we find book-long reflections that try to study in depth one or another aspect of a multifaceted phenomenon. The authors of these early interventions were not individuals whose research dealt entirely or even predominantly with cinema; rather, they were often journalists, intellectuals or writers on a wide variety of subjects, for whom cinema was only one of many interests. Again, we find exceptions: Thomas Bedding, Stephen W. Bush and Louis Reeves Harrison in the United States or Ricciotto Canudo and later Louis Delluc in Europe, were *film* critics; but the bulk of debate was constituted by contributions from nonspecialized individuals. There was not a "discipline" as a frame of reference that clearly outlined how and why cinema should be examined; instead contributions responded to a range of different motivations, from simple curiosity about a recent invention to observations of the effects that films have upon social life. Finally, this discursive production did not often call itself theory, and when it did, it was not without reticence. Such is the case with Victor Oscar Freeburg, who in 1918 claimed for himself the "role of theorist and philosopher," and at the same time recognized the primacy of producers in dealing with cinema (Freeburg 1918, 263), as well as with Arturo Sebastiano Luciani, who in 1919 assigned theoretical status to his ruminations, and at the same time acknowledged that they can raise suspicion—a suspicion that he tried to dissolve by practically incorporating his ideas in a sample of film script inspired by Judith's story (Luciani 1919, 2).[8]

The four characteristics of early film "theories"—their sporadic occurrence, quasi-anonymous writers, lack of a clear "method," and hesitation toward self-identification—find their roots in the main question that these discourses had to deal with: in short, they shared the need to provide an image of cinema that facilitated its social comprehension and acceptance. Cinema at first sight appears a puzzling and even a scandalous fact. How can one grasp an apparatus that seems to capture the fleeting moment and ensure the permanence of life? How can one justify a machine with a gaze that goes beyond human capacities? How can one adapt to something that glorifies ubiquity, simultaneity, speed and details? And how can the enormous success of cinema be explained? The early "theories" respond to the demand for a practical and shared definition of a phenomenon that seems to challenge our expectations and our habits. In this sense, early "film theories" are similar to those personal *accounts* that we formulate to make sense of our daily actions, and that ethnomethodology describes as a key component of our social lives (see Garfinkel 1967). Accounts epitomize the ways members of a community signify, describe or explain the properties of a specific social situation in order to clarify and share its meaning. Likewise, early theories seek to make what at first might appear ambiguous and strange into something comprehensible and graspable: they show what cinema is and how we encounter it, what distinguishes it and how we can react to it, what it can offer us and why we must accept it. The result of all of this is a "public image" of cinema, which functions to both define and legitimate.

I want to add that early film "theories" also had a dark side. Not all the accounts were aimed at making film an acceptable object; there was no lack of negative interpretations and disqualifying assessments. As a counterpart of a "cinephiliac theory," we can find a cinephobia that tries to display its own reasons (see e.g., the Kinoreform section in Kaes, Baer and Cowan 2016).

In the mid-1920s, we have the gradual emergence of a new "discursive formation." What takes shape is the so-called classical film theory. A turning point is the extremely influential *Visible Man* by Béla Balázs, originally published in 1924 (Balázs 2010). According to Balázs, film is an already established reality; its relevance makes it worthy of a deeper investigation. But aestheticians are lazy in welcoming new objects into the precinct of art, hence the need to create a new field of investigation. Film theory is such a new field. Its first task is "to explore film's *possibility in principle*"; consequently, it can move forward "by fixing on definite goals and calculating all their implications," and finally it can test "the pathways leading to these goals" (Balázs 2010, 5 and 6 respectively). Hence the great metaphors that Balázs uses to define theory: "It is the road map for those who roam among the arts, showing them pathways and opportunities"; or "[it] is, if not the rudder, then at least the compass of an artistic trend" (Balázs 2010, 3 and 5 respectively).

Six years later, Rudolph Arnheim, with his even more influential *Film* (often read and quoted in the amended and less interesting version of 1957, even though the original was immediately translated into English: see Arnheim 1933) performs a more radical move: instead of highlighting the elements that make cinema a relevant art, like the revitalization of our visual skills, the presence of close-ups and the representation of landscape, he directly focuses on the rules that govern film. Arnheim starts from an axiom: "In order that the film artist may create a work of art it is most important that he should consciously stress the peculiarity of its medium." (Arnheim 1933, 46). The medium of cinema finds its peculiarity in its ability to perfectly reproduce an object, yet transform it in a purely visual representation. Hence a second axiom: "It is due to divergencies between film picture and nature that it is possible for a work of art to emerge from a film camera." (Arnheim 1933, 46). From these two axioms stems a full array of norms that define an appropriate and effective film practice. As a consequence, what in Balázs was the map or the compass orienting film practice and criticism, in Arnheim becomes the rule of law that leads toward a correct film-making and a consistent film appreciation.

The main characteristics of classical film theory largely stem from this new orientation. First, theory is a foundational discourse: its purpose is to provide the "principles" on which the new art is based—the "specificity" that it obeys. Second, debate becomes more systematic: it is now centered on few well-defined issues to be explored. Third, theory is a recognizable field of research, different from personal accounts or simple reviews. Fourth, the function of legitimizing cinema as art is addressed not to public opinion, but to the intellectuals who can appreciate its basic norms and its inner way of working: theory is a business for specialists. However paradoxical it may seem, the great contributions of the 1940s and 1950s, notably André Bazin's (2005, originally 1958) and Edgar Morin's (2005, originally 1956), also follow this line. There are key elements that define cinema as such (the restitution of the real in Bazin, the creation of an imaginary in Morin); there is a net of concepts that sustains the basic ideas (in Bazin, the redefinition of film language in "indexical" terms; in Morin, its redefinition in terms of a "reason"); and there are methods of reading films that develop in cine-clubs (Bazin) or in academic environments (Morin).

I just add two remarks. Classical film theory takes advantage of the long-lasting period of stability that film has enjoyed between the end of 1910s and the end of 1960s. Despite some occasional variation, film's modes of representation—as well as its modes of production—are steady, and taken as intrinsically characteristic of cinema. Film theorists can analyze them as they were film's essence, when, as Jonathan Crary states, "what were most often identified as essential were temporary elements of larger constellations whose rates of change were variable and unpredictable" (Crary 2013, 38). Second, at the core of classical theory, undoubtedly there is an aesthetic concern. Yet, there is no lack of different interests. For example, Bazin and, even more, Morin display a persistent anthropological background. Classical theory looks compact, but it is far from being immobile.

At the beginning of the 1970s, a new "discursive formation" appears. It is the well-known Grand Theory, as Bordwell and Carroll (1996) call it with utmost contempt.[9] Without going into details, suffice it to say that Grand Theory is underpinned by a two-fold aspiration. Through the convergence of three main fields of reference—semiotics, psychoanalysis and Marxism—it wants to provide a unified framework for interpreting cinema's way of working in connection with the rules that govern language, the inner psychic processes and the general mode of commodities production. And through a deconstruction of cinema's way of working, it aims at unfolding its ideological consequences—including the fact that spectators perceive on the screen a representation as if it were reality and follow the represented events as if they were mastering them.

In a certain sense, Grand Theory does not deflect from the path already traced: there is a set of axioms and their application to film at large. Yet the trajectory looks unidirectional: instead of asking theory to explore and evaluate a wide set of occurrences, now a scheme is applied without distinction. In this sense, Bordwell's and Carroll's critique—Grand Theory had come to be characterized by ambition, abstraction and ambiguity—sounds reasonable. What they miss is the context (or, better, they reduce the context to a French–American rivalry): if early "theories" reflected an epoch of novelty and classical theory an epoch of institutionalization, then Grand Theory responds to an epoch of film's supposed omnipotence, the sense that Hollywood mode of production dominates cinema and that cinema dominates our culture in its inner fibers. Hence Grand Theory's obsession with providing a conceptual framework able to orchestrate a critical response to an alleged massive attack, everywhere and anytime. Grand Theory's original sin is not its arrogance; it is its paranoia.

Once again, two remarks. The fear of film's omnipotence is nevertheless productive: if it takes a paranoid connotation in Baudry (1976 and 1986) or in a journal like *Cinéthique*, then it also elicits concepts that are crucial, starting from the ideas of subject position and film apparatus. In this vein, we are still indebted with the way in which Mulvey (1975) unfolds the dialectics between the pleasure that film gifts us and the trap in which it frames or with the way in which Metz (1982) explores the complicity between film's procedures and our psychic processes. Second, such a fear of film's omnipotence emerges in the wrong moment: at the beginning of the 1960s, Hollywood is in distress, and other media are taking the lead. The Grand Theory—as well as its critics—do not perceive that enemy, if there is one, is elsewhere. The paranoia is misplaced.

What Bordwell and Carroll hail in their condemnation is the advent of another kind of film theory based on small-scale research and more rigorous procedure. A piecemeal theory that drops excessive ambitions is seen as fruitful.[10] The request for such a new form of theorizing responds to a desire of control: scholars must avoid concepts that lack of solid foundation; they must abstain from explications referring to an overly wide range of phenomena; and they must follow rigorous procedures of verification. In this sense the new approach is far from being a natural or innocent choice: it largely depends on the ideal of natural sciences—and yet an ideal that at the time was criticized by different branches of epistemology, including the so-called epistemological anarchism (see Feyerabend 1975), and that collides with the recurring attempt to develop theories that encompass different fields. In any case, according Bordwell and Carroll, research must be limited and practical. Theory (with capital T) must cede its place to a post-theory.

During the 1990s and 2000s, post-theory was rampant. However, the landscape was far from being homogeneous: there was a new discipline, cognitive psychology, that tried to take the lead, but there were also active discourses still indebted to Grand Theory and its filiations (including parts of gender studies), as well as approaches that resumed a sort of "ontological" orientation, as most of the contributions about the advent of digital would do, for reasons of their claim that the end of the indexical image is the end of cinema. In a sense Bordwell and Carroll's program ends up in a marketplace where everyone can find the commodity she likes. In the spirit of a perfect neoliberal age, film theory too becomes a shopping mall. And yet, this chaotic situation (a theory of Babel …) is what makes possible the extensions, contaminations and innovations that theory enjoys nowadays.

It should be a mistake to consider film "theories" (between quotation marks), classical film theory, Grand Theory and post-theory as "discursive formations" belonging to the past. History is not necessarily a sequence of events in which the newer buries the older: it is not even a chronological chain, but a set of relations in which there is an endless back and forth between past and present.[11] This is peculiarly true for these different stages of film theory: they leave behind them a sort of wake whose waves are breaking on our shores. It is not by chance that many of their key words are still in use in film studies: our current vocabulary is deeply indebted to them. In this sense, the film theory that we are practicing nowadays is a field that lies on four geological strata; or, if you prefer, a four-layered cake that we must eat appreciating its many flavors (the flavor of theory is something that Balázs already noticed).[12] The book that my few pages are intended to preface would reflect this configuration of the field, with keywords that emerged in different stages, sometimes in the far past, sometimes as recent eruptions, but both displaying their potentialities in the present. I like to imagine it as a tectonic book.

Why reconsider film theory and make use of it for contemporary needs? How can certain concepts be retained and revived? If "theories" between quotation marks faced a novelty, if classical theory confronted an institutionalization, if Grand Theory responded to a fear, if post-theory established a free market of methods, then today the challenge comes from a dilemma. Is the deep transformation that cinema is experiencing a way to preserve its identity and to rediscover its possibilities or a step toward its dissolution into a wider landscape? I am supportive of the first hypothesis (Casetti 2015), but the second should not be excluded: going beyond its usual extent or even trying to reboot itself, cinema can collapse.

The aforementioned growth of the conceptual body that today characterizes film theory reflects this dilemma: our vocabulary recaptures concepts that frame what film could be or would have been and at the same time encapsulates concepts that belong to other disciplines. It is the case with the three main trends that characterize film studies nowadays: a neo-aesthetics, often indebted with philosophers like Deleuze orRanciére, that focuses on cinema as a special region of Art or Thought; a reconsideration of spectator's sensorial and affective activity, often tied with neuro-sciences; and an interest in the place of cinema within media landscapes and physical territories, tuned with environmental studies. The result is reassuring and alarming at once—reassuring in safeguarding a field whose borders are increasingly porous, and alarming in a concession to the vantage points of competing approaches. Theory's expansion—like film's—can become a dispersion.

The impulse for a meta-theory echoes the same dilemma. No doubt that a critical scrutiny of theory's vocabulary can be extremely useful: it can offer the opportunity to understand concepts' resilience and endurance. In this sense, it is a contribution to make the field wider, but also solid and tuned with the current situation.[13] Yet no test comes without a price. If the scrutiny becomes a systematic revision, if the stratification of concepts is dropped, then the "cleansed" vocabulary risks no longer speaking film theory's language. In this case, the operation is an involuntary contribution to the dismissal of film and its history from our present. A redefinition becomes a foreclosure.

Cinema's uncertain destiny puts theory under stress, but it also allows the theory to acquire an agility it has never had before. Theory can fully become what it has always been: an endless Penelope's web, ceaselessly made and remade but always aimed at one goal, to capture film's nature. Cinema still needs discourses able to understand and explain its own presence. Its present status amplifies this request—and makes its query even more worthy.

Notes

1 A contribution widely representative of the problems and concepts raised by post-cinema is Shaw and Weibel (2003).

2 An impulse to reread canonical texts comes, among others, from the special issues of two journals: "A Return to Classical Film Theory?" *October* 148 (Spring 2014); and "What's New in Classical Film Theory?" *Screen* 55, no. 3 (Autumn 2014).

3 Rodowick's is an extremely useful and influential contribution, and yet, it narrows film theory to an aesthetically based discourse. My claim here is that film theory, included the classical film theory, was not exclusively an aesthetic discourse.

4 At the origin of this movement is Carroll (1988a and 1988b); see also Allen-Smith (1997) (in particular the "manifesto" by Gregory Currie, "The Theory That Never Was: A Nervous Manifesto").

5 "One of the characteristics of philosophy as a discipline is its questioning of its own nature and basis. The philosophy of film shares this characteristic with the field in general. Indeed,

a first issue that the philosophy of film must address is the grounds for its own existence. This involves not only the question of what the field should look like, but also that of whether it has any reason to exist at all." (Wartenberg 2015).

6 See in particular Foucault (1972).

7 On the historical nature of film theory, see the Niemeyer and Hochscherf (2016) and the special issue of *Historical Journal of Film, Radio and Television* that they edit.

8 For the ambivalent attitude toward theory until the 1920s, see also Seldes (1924). And yet there is no lack of clear praises: suffice it to recall what Vachel Lindsay states: "Somewhere in this enormous field, piled with endowments mountain high, it should be possible to establish the theory and practice of the photoplay as a fine art." (Lindsay 1922, 30). By the end of the 1920s the term will become a shared currency.

9 Most of the criticism expressed in Bordwell and Carroll (1996) is anticipated in Carroll (1988a). The term Grand Theory is borrowed—consciously or unconsciously—from *The Sociological Imagination* by C. Wright Mills (1959) where it designates "a systematic theory of the nature of man and society" as expressed in particular by Talcott Parsons.

10 "Currently, then, we are in need of piecemeal theorizing, in need of theories about film rather than Film Theory. [...] Perhaps some of the fruits of our piecemeal theories will be organizable into larger, systematic and theoretical constellations." (Carroll 1988a, 232). Žižek (2001) would ironize about the modesty of the Carroll's and Bordwell's "modest proposal."

11 Benjamin's "dialectical image" captures precisely this back and forth between the past and the now. See Benjamin (1999), in particular Section N.

12 "Aesthetic theory is nothing more than a thoughtful savouring in the attempt to feel and enjoy the hidden product of an inner life." (Balázs 2010, 7).

13 Malcolm Turvey often underscores the claim that keywords need not only to display their glorious past, but also to confirm their current convenience: see for example the "Roundtable on the Return to Classical Film Theory" in the aforementioned special issue of October (Spring 2014, pp. 5–26) and his recent "Epstein, Sound, and the Return to Classical Film Theory," *Mise au point*, 8, 2016, URL: http://map.revues.org/2039.

References

Abel, Richard, ed. 1988. *French Film Theory and Criticism. A History/Anthology, 1907–1939*, 2 vols. Princeton: Princeton University Press.

Allen, Richard, and Murray Smith, eds. 1997. *Film Theory and Philosophy*. Oxford: Oxford University Press.

Andel, Jaroslav, and Petr Szczepanik, eds. 2008. *Cinema all the Time: An Anthology of Czech Film Theory and Criticism*. Prague: National Film Archive.

Arnheim, Rudolf. 1933. *Film*. London: Faber & Faber. Originally *Film als Kunst* (Berlin: Ernst Rowohlt Verlag, 1932).

Balász, Béla. 2010. *Visible Man, Or the Culture of Film*. In *Béla Balász: Early Film Theory*, edited by Erica Carter, 1–90. New York; Oxford: Berghahn Books. Originally *Der sichtbare Mensch oder die Kultur des Films* (Vienna: Deutsch-Österreichischer Verlag, 1924).

Bao, Weihong. 2015. *Fiery Cinema: The Emergence of an Affective Medium in China, 1915–1945*. Minneapolis: University of Minnesota Press.

Baudry, Jean-Louis. 1976. "The Apparatus: Metapsychological Approaches to the Impression of Reality in the Cinema." *Camera Obscura* 1 (Fall): 104–26. Originally "Le Dispositif," *Communications*, 23 (1975), 56–72.

———. 1986. "Ideological Effects of the Basic Cinematographic Apparatus." In *Narrative, Apparatus, Ideology*, edited by Philip Rosen, 286–98. New York: Columbia University Press. Originally "Cinéma: *effets idéologiques* produits par l'appareil de base," *Cinéthique*, 7–8 (1970): 1–8.

Bazin, André. 2005. *What is Cinema?* Berkeley: University of California Press. Originally *Qu'est ce que le cinema? 1. Onytologie et Language* (Paris: Edition du Cerf, 1958).

Benjamin, Walter. 1999. *The Arcades Project.* Cambridge, MA: Belknap Press of Harvard University Press.

Bordwell, David, and Noël Carroll, eds. 1996. *Post-Theory: Reconstructing Film Studies.* Madison: University of Wisconsin Press.

Carroll, Noël. 1988a. *Mystifying Movies. Fad and Fallacies in Contemporary Film Theory.* New York: Columbia University Press.

———. 1988b. *Philosophical Problems of Classical Film Theory.* Princeton: Princeton University Press.

Casetti, Francesco. 2015. *The Lumiére Galaxy.* New York: Columbia University Press.

Crary, Jonathan. 2013. *24/7. Late Capitalism and the Ends of Sleep.* London: Verso.

Fan, Victor. 2015. *Cinema Approaching Reality: Locating Chinese Film Theory.* Minneapolis: University of Minnesota Press.

Feyerabend, Paul. 1975. *Against Method: Outline of an Anarchistic Theory of Knowledge.* Atlantic Highlands, NJ: Humanities Press.

Foucault, Michel. 1972. *The Archaeology of Knowledge.* New York: Harper & Row.

Freeburg, Victor Oscar. 1918. *The Art of Photoplay Making.* New York: Macmillan.

Garfinkel, Harold. 1967. *Studies in Ethnomethodology.* Englewood Cliffs, NJ: Prentice-Hall.

Kaes, Anton, Nicholas Baer and Michael Cowan, eds. 2016. *The Promise of Cinema. German Film Theory 1907–1933.* Oakland: University of California Press.

Lindsay, Vachel. 1915. *The Art of the Moving Picture.* New York: Macmillan, revised edition 1922.

Luciani, Sebastiano Arturo. 1919. "Lo scenario cinematografico." *Cronache d'attualità* 2, no. 15 (August 10): 1–3.

Metz, Christian. 1982. *The Imaginary Signifier: Psychoanalysis and Cinema.* Bloomington: Indiana University Press. Originally *Le significant imaginaire: Psychanalyse et cinéma* (Paris: UGD, 1977).

Morin, Edgar. 2005. *The Cinema, or, the Imaginary Man.* Minneapolis: University of Minnesota Press. Originally *Le cinéma ou l'homme imaginaire: Essai d'anthropologie sociologique* (Paris: Minuit, 1956).

Mulvey, Laura. 1975. "Visual Pleasure and Narrative Cinema." *Screen* 16, no. 3 (Autumn): 6–18.

Niemeyer, Katharina, and Tobias Hochscherf. 2016. "Early Film Theory Revisited: Historical Perspectives." *Historical Journal of Film, Radio and Television* 36, no. 2: 127–32.

Nornes, Abé Mark, and Aaron Gerow. 2009. *Research Guide to Japanese Film Studies.* Ann Arbor: Center for Japanese Studies, University of Michigan.

Seldes, Gilbert. 1924. "An Open Letter to the Movie Magnates." *The Seven Lively Arts.* New York; London: Harper and Bros, 323–42.

Papini, Giovanni. 2017. "The Philosophy of Cinematograph." In *Early Film Theories in Italy. 1896–1922*, edited by Francesco Casetti, Silvio Alovisio and Luca Mazzei, 47–50. Amsterdam: Amsterdam University Press.

Rodowick, D. N. 2014. *Elegy for Theory.* Cambridge: Harvard University Press.

Shaw, Jeffrey, and Peter Weibel. 2003. *Future Cinema. The Cinematic Imaginary after Film.* Cambridge, MA: MIT Press.

Wartenberg, Thomas. 2015. "Philosophy of Film," *The Stanford Encyclopedia of Philosophy* (Winter), Edward N. Zalta (ed.), URL: http://plato.stanford.edu/archives/win2015/entries/film/.

Žižek, Slavoj. 2001. *The Fright of Real Tears: Krzysztof Kieslowski between Theory and Post-Theory.* London: BFI.

Part I

WHAT WE ARE

Chapter One

THE BRAIN'S LABOR: ON MARXISM AND THE MOVIES

Pasi Väliaho

Karl Marx died in 1883. He was buried in a Victorian cemetery in Highgate, North London. Still today, a small but regular flow of tourists from across the globe visits the grave, where the British communist party built a tombstone with a portrait bust in 1954 (Figure 1.1). Some of them bring flowers, some even burst to sing aloud "The Internationale" in front of the cenotaph. But, very rarely do these visitors happen to cross another grave, which is located off the beaten track at the far side of the cemetery, next to the fence that borders Swain's Lane and the mock Tudor houses from the 1920s. This is where we encounter the grave of William Friese-Greene, a British entrepreneur and early pioneer in the development of moving picture technology in the United Kingdom (Figure 1.2). Friese-Greene passed away in 1921.

Surely, it is merely a coincidence that these two individuals came to share the same cemetery. The spatial proximity of Marx's and Friese-Greene's earthly remains nonetheless suggests resonations and overlaps between the two key historical forces of modernity these two individuals were part of, and in many ways epitomized. In this respect, a visit to the Highgate cemetery today brings about a certain sentiment of loss, even nostalgia. On the one hand, we remember the individual who gave his name to one of the defining political worldviews and philosophies of the twentieth century, a worldview that is increasingly undermined by the triumph of the current neoliberal form of capitalism. On the other hand, we are reminded of a person who, even if he holds merely a minor position in the (pre)histories of cinema written today, contributed to the birth of a medium that is now losing its status as the leading global cognitive and cultural technology. Digitalization and neoliberalism—those are the predatory forces (tightly married to one another, one could argue) that have been eroding the subjects of this essay: films and Marxism.

But how are we to map cinema in relation to Marxist thought? Marx, as is known, was a philosopher and political economist of German Jewish origin, famous for his theory of historical materialism—stipulating, to put it crudely, that a society's means of production determine its makeup. He was above all a theorist of the industrial age, a sharp critic of the forms of capital accumulation and exploitation of labor force that various amalgamations of human and machine performance and the emergence of mass-production methods gave rise to in the nineteenth century. His analyses emphasized material relations of

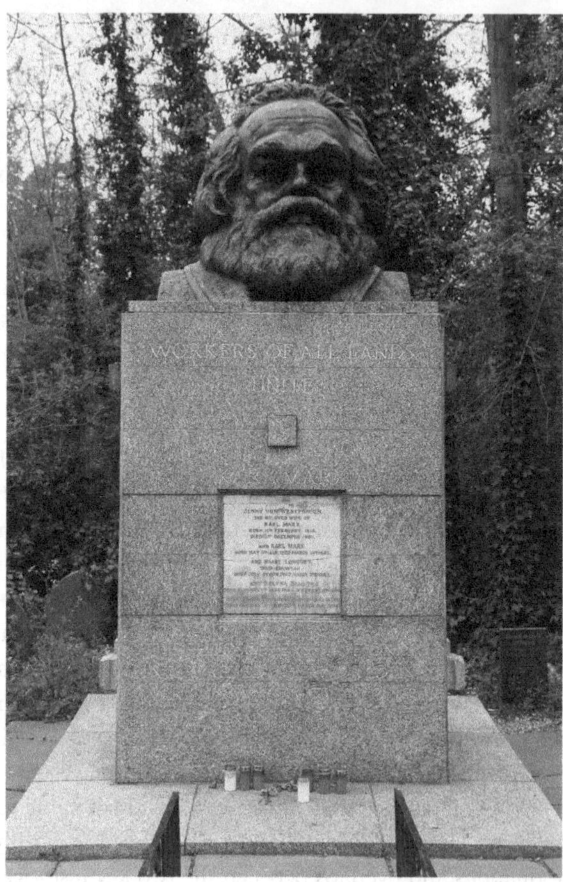

Figure 1.1 Karl Marx's grave at Highgate cemetery. Photograph by the author.

doing and making of which, he argued, everything else—philosophical ideas, religions, moralities, aesthetic judgments—were mere sublimations. Marx announced that historical materialism was a matter:

> Not of setting out from what men say, imagine, conceive, nor from men as narrated, thought of, imagined, conceived, in order to arrive at men in the flesh; but setting out from real, active men, and on the basis of their real life-process demonstrating the development of the ideological reflexes and echoes of this life-process. (Marx and Engels 1998, 42)

With this in mind, when pacing from Marx's grave to Friese-Greene's, the idle visitor to the Highgate cemetery can draw parallels between capitalism and the beginnings of movies in several ways. She or he can, for instance, view cinema as part of the technological system of production and circulation that supported the rise of industrial and consumer capitalism—of railways and automobiles that brought about new velocities, of semi-automated industrial machines that required workers to adjust to their monotonous

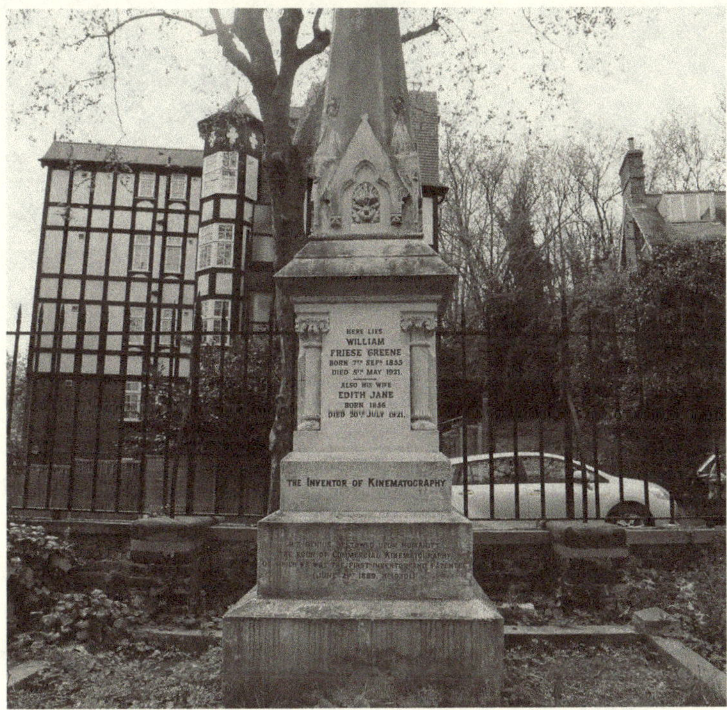

Figure 1.2 William Friese-Greene's grave at Highgate cemetery. Photograph by the author.

rhythms. Cinema and new transport technologies both exemplified how, as Marx pointed out, "capital [...] drives beyond every spatial barrier." Marx noted that capitalism is in the first instance a question of managing time, of "the annihilation of space by time," which becomes "an extraordinary necessity for it" (1993, 524). In this respect, when thinking about the immediate historical precursors of the movie machine, the visitor may also remember, among other things, the French physiologist Etienne-Jules Marey's chronophotographic experiments with the dynamics of human and other animals, which disclosed an organic link between the recording of movement and time, and the control and administration of bodies. In Marey's experiments, which fed into the so-called rationalization of labor in Taylorism, cinema began as a machine for calculating the body's expenditure of energy and for optimizing *how* one is to move one's body when performing a particular task. Cinema thus began as the capture and organization of the time of living labor (see Crary 2013, 62).

The history of cinema aligned early on with the epistemic and pragmatic concerns of industrial labor and capital accumulation. Not surprisingly, one of the first films made by Auguste and Louis Lumière—the Frenchmen known for their invention of the *cinématographe*—portrayed a group of workers (mostly females) marching out the gate to the brothers' factory in the Lyon suburbs, having apparently ended the day's work of manufacturing the photographic plates and paraphernalia that Auguste and

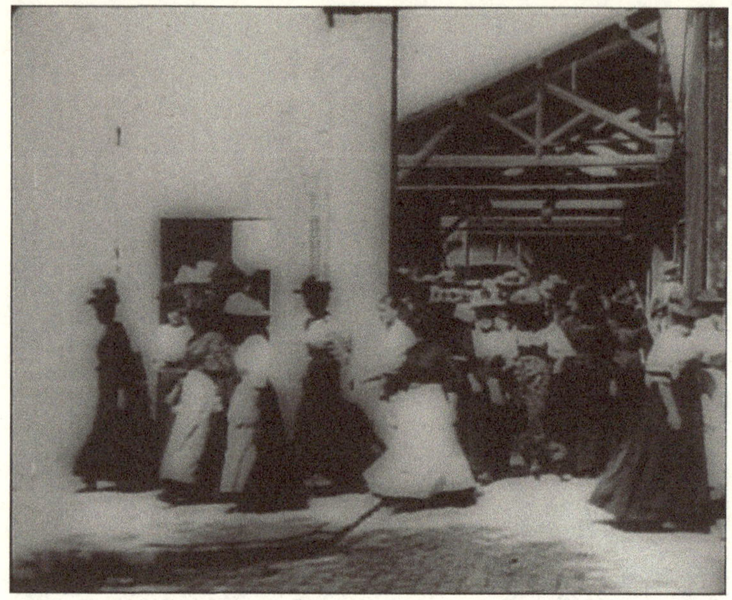

Figure 1.3 *Workers Leaving the Lumière Factory* (*La Sortie de l'usine Lumière à Lyon*, 1895). Frame capture.

Louis were, and still are, famous for (Figure 1.3). In this instance, cinema wanted to impose its presence at the moment the day's work was over; it appeared, not inside the factory, but when individual narratives could restart after having escaped the factory's confines, the evening involving the promise of a chance encounter or just the repetition of ordinary routines. Cinema, the Lumière brothers' *Workers Leaving the Lumière Factory* (*La Sortie de l'usine Lumière à Lyon*, 1895) suggests, has ever since its beginning been an art of the masses, of the anonymous crowds that flock in and out the gates of factories as well as office buildings.

The gate in *Workers* marks a threshold between two critical poles: production and consumption. Labor, the film reminds us, is what keeps the movies going—the labor of both manufacturing and consuming. What Marx was acutely aware of was that labor is a world-changing process: it transforms one thing into another, a piece of metal into a spoon, a piece of cloth into a shirt, nitrocellulose (and other materials) into celluloid film and so on. However, by labor power, Marx noted (1990, 283), we not only act upon external nature and change it, but also simultaneously change our own nature. Labor produces us: it is a dynamic, temporal process of "becoming," if you will. So is the labor of making and watching films.

How might making and watching films shape us and the world in which we live in? This is the conundrum that has preoccupied Marx-inspired film theory and practice since the early twentieth century. On one side, Marxist critics have often denounced the cinema as an industry of dreams, the primary purpose of which is to allow moments of escapism for capitalism's alienated individuals. Siegfried Kracauer (1995, 326) asserted in the 1920s how the masses had become "addicted to distraction" that the movies offer them, captivated by auditory and visual "stimulations of the senses that succeed one another with such rapidity that there is no room left between them for even the slightest contemplation." Theodor W. Adorno (1995, 25), for one, complained that "every visit to the cinema leaves me, despite all my vigilance, stupider and worse." Adorno's critique focused on cinema (and other modern media) as "culture industry" and social regimentation, which, rather than changing prevailing historical and material conditions, only reinforces them, producing individuals "without autonomy of substance of their own" (Adorno 1995, 15).

On the other side, however, cinema has also given us a powerful, often utopian promise of contributing to the class struggle, of allowing the working class to assert their autonomy and to capture the means of production into their own hands. Cinema's emancipatory potential was perhaps most extensively and acutely taken up in the newly founded Soviet Russia of the 1920s, where links between cinema and labor became articulated not only in terms of alienation, but also in terms of social change. "Of all the arts for us cinema is the most important," Vladimir Lenin famously exclaimed in 1922, about five years after the Bolshevik revolution (Taylor 1979, 26). By this he meant, to be sure, cinema's significance as a propaganda machine, its power to get the message across, so to speak, to as many people as possible, literate as well as illiterate. Yet more importantly, Lenin was alluding to cinema's key role in the process of social transformation, in mobilizing the masses in the class struggle as well as in giving birth to the new communist society. We know the role that several film directors (who were simultaneously also early theorists of film) played in this process, from Lev Kuleshov and Dziga Vertov to Sergei Eisenstein. Film was seen as a primary means to give rise to the revolutionary collective consciousness, and even as a "cyborg" system in which the hardware of cinema could merge with the wetware of our bodies and minds and thus give rise to a "new, perfect man" (Vertov 1984, 17).

Overall, we might now be in a better position to plot a path from Marx to cinema and back. Pacing from Marx's grave to Friese-Greene's can indeed take several intellectual directions. On the one hand, Marx's critique of capitalism has provided conceptual background for a wide range of theories of cinema as a capitalist machinery of exploitation and appropriation. On the other, his thinking has also been essential to explorations of cinema's political potential, the medium's promise to give birth to a new society, even a new type of human. The intention of what follows is to mainly follow the former path, and to investigate some of the key concerns of critical Marxist theorization of films. The following paragraphs will explore critiques of cinema as an industry of money and dreams, of "girls and guns," as Jean-Luc Godard put it. The chosen path will take us from Marx's critique of commodity to the development of modern film theory in the 1960s and 1970s and the critique of mainstream spectatorship, in particular, as well as to recent reassessments of Marxist thought in the so-called post-cinematic age. It will obviously leave several alternative paths unexplored concerning the development of political cinema, for instance, including the Soviet filmmakers noted above as well as the decolonial projects of the 1960s and 1970s such as the "Third Cinema" manifesto driven by a desire to create "a subversive culture capable of contributing to the downfall of capitalist society" (Getino and Solanas 1969, 107). At the end of the essay, however, we will pause on some perhaps now obscure concepts and images from the first half of the twentieth century so as to understand what an emancipatory politics of cinema might mean.

Capitalism's Phantasmagoria

In 1889, six years after Marx was buried, Friese-Greene filed a patent for his apparatus of making "animated photographs," a patent that, we are told, "contained many of the features of the future movie camera proper" (Chanan 1996, 89). Very soon after filing the patent, Friese-Greene, at least according to his own account, sent a description of his invention to Thomas Alva Edison in the United States. Historians can only speculate whether Friese-Greene's invention was of essential inspiration to the kinetoscope, a motion picture exhibition device developed by Edison and his employee William Dickson. But what historians can confirm is that with Edison, if not with Friese-Greene, a long story of moving images meant for mass consumption began; a story of entertainment parlors equipped with various kinds of apparatuses, from kinetoscopes (Figure 1.4) designed for individual observers to vitascopes (Figure 1.5) amassing, like the Lumière brothers' cinematograph, large numbers of spectators transfixed on the screen, each displaying varying cinematic contents to trigger the consumers' pleasure nerves.

What can be said about these contents? About the parents feeding the baby on a summer's day, the gardener being tormented by a boy or the little child tormenting a goldfish, that the Lumière brothers' famous first commercial cinema show at the Grand Café in Paris, on the December 28, 1895, put on display? Likewise, where shall we place the boxing cats, or the Sioux Indians performing a ghost and a buffalo dance, that populated the visions of those who paid a nickel for the opportunity to peep into Edison's kinetoscopes? One crucial point to note is that, from early on in the movies, images became treated as commodities: as products of mass labor meant to be exchanged on the "market," that is to say, within networks of circulation and reception. As Walter Benjamin (1968) observed in the 1930s, in the age of "mechanical reproduction" (photography and cinema), images have acquired the status of commodities in the sense of ephemeral copies to be traded without any essential difference between them, losing thus their historical religious functions (as objects of worship) and artistic values (as aesthetic experience).

Benjamin was indebted to the critique of commodity—this "very strange thing" (Marx 1990, 163)—that Marx put forward in the volume one of *The Capital* (1867). Marx was puzzled by how the objects of utility that individuals manufacture can become abstracted from their immediate, practical uses and be attributed with other kinds of properties and values. Most notably, he wanted to understand how labor power is turned into exchange value when its products are traded for each other or for money. Commodities are precisely objects that have become abstracted as items of exchange, objects that thereby crystallize the economic structure of capitalism. Today, perhaps more than ever, our lives are saturated by such things—Apple iPhones, Gucci handbags, Levi's jeans, you name

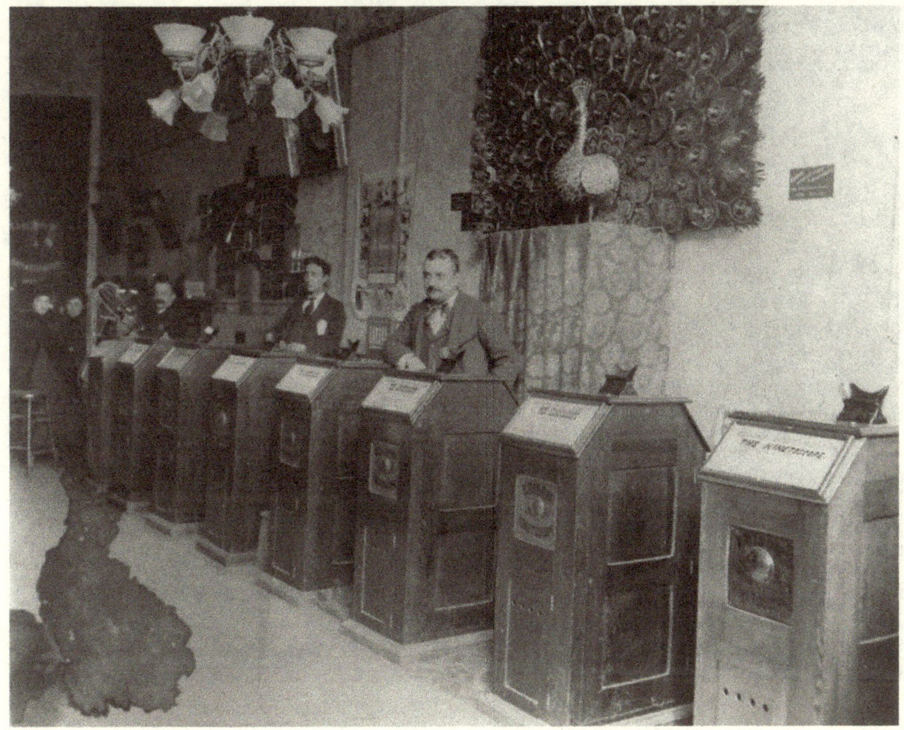

Figure 1.4 Kinetoscope and phonograph parlor in San Franscisco, 1895. Natural Park Service/Edison Historic Site.

it. What is crucial is that these products have come to mediate and structure our social relations, exchanges of looks, gestures, smiles and words. The commodity, Marx (1990, 165; 1991, 72) wrote, "is nothing but the definite social relation between men themselves which assumes here, for them the fantastic [*phantasmagorische*] form of a relation between things." Commodities thus, in Marx's terminology, "reify" social relations, meaning that our relationships with ourselves and with others around us become expressed in terms of traded things. The power of commodities lies precisely in this objectification of the human world.

The English translation of *Capital* somewhat occludes the media's historical underpinnings of Marx's analysis. The original German word Marx used to describe the work of commodities—*phantasmagorische*, "phantasmagorical"—we should note, bears the trace of a popular entertainment form from the turn of the eighteenth and nineteenth centuries. Phantasmagoria was a type of magic lantern spectacle that dealt with ghostly apparitions and everything otherworldly (Figure 1.6)—and as such also a veritable visual innovation of its times (see Mannoni 2000, 136–75). Magic lanterns mounted on wheels, and always hidden behind a screen, projected images that grew or diminished as quickly as they appeared and disappeared. Not only solid objects but also smoke were used as projection surfaces to create vibrating, eerie visual impressions. These projections

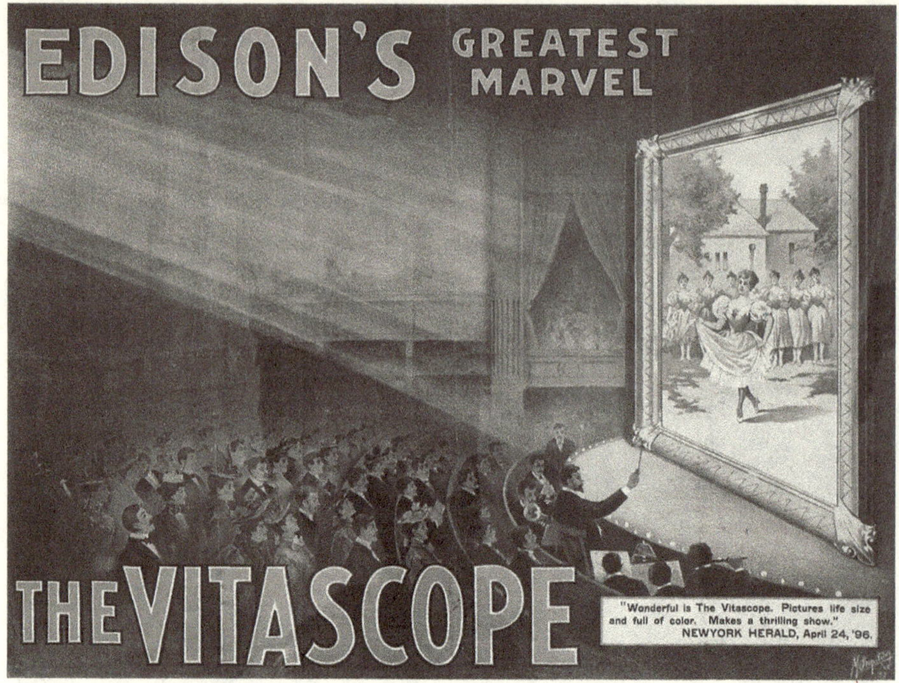

Figure 1.5 Publicity poster for Edison's Vitascope, Metropolitan Print Company, c. 1896. Library of Congress.

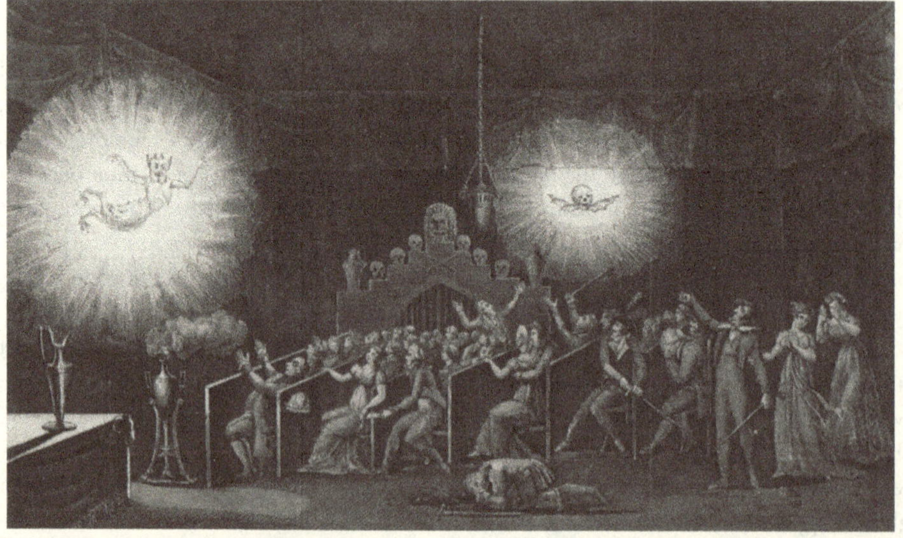

Figure 1.6 Etienne-Gaspard Robertson's phantasmagoria at the Cour des Capucines in 1797. Frontispiece of Etienne-Gaspard Robertson, *Mémoires récréatifs, scientifiques et anecdotiques*, vol. 1 (Paris, 1831).

would mediate between the living and the dead, as a phantasmagoria showman going under the pseudonym Paul Philidor claimed:

> I will bring before you all the illustrious dead, all those whose memory is dear to you and whose image is still present for you. I will not show you ghosts, because there are not such things; but I will produce before you enactments and images, which are imagined to be ghosts, in the dreams of the imagination or in the falsehoods of charlatans. (Quoted in Mannoni 2000, 144)

Phantasmagoria projections were situated somewhere between illusion and reality, the brain's internal phantoms and the external world. They wanted to burst out the traditional picture frame, which separates between them and us, appearing to "abandon their material supports and enter our world" (Elcott 2016, 47).

Marx's choice of words ought to be considered in relation to this media's historical background. His critique was that commodities turn material, that is to say, real relations into mere appearances, or rather, that appearances acquire the status of the real. Capitalism, Marx observed, rules by overshadowing reality: by producing projected illusions—those otherworldly creatures that commodities are—that we (the spectators) take as factual. Marx (1990, 165) continued: "In order, therefore, to find an analogy [to commodity] we must take flight into the misty realm of religion. There the products of the human brain appear as autonomous figures endowed with a life of their own, which enter into relations both with each other and with the human race."

Earlier, Marx had, together with Friedrich Engels, used another media metaphor to argue how ideology distorts our vision and understanding of the world. "In all ideology," Marx and Engels (1998, 42) pointed out, "men and their relations appear upside-down as in a *camera obscura*." Ideology produces a distorted and illusory relation with the world just like the *camera obscura* (if not corrected with a lens mechanism) misrepresents the world outside (see Kofman 1998, 1–20). In *The Capital*, this notion of illusion and misrepresentation is made more elaborate with the reference to the magic lantern's shadows. The question is no longer how the world is reflected but rather how it is projected, that is to say, produced. Projection is production, and Marx's point of critique was that capitalist exchange produces mere brain phantoms, simulacra abstracted from their referents in the material world (Andriopoulos 2013, 44–45). The activity of projecting apparitions of ghosts in the dark crystallizes, in other words, the ontology of capitalist economy.

Readers might already be wondering, and for good reasons, what all this has to do with cinema. At least, the close resonances between Marx's understanding of the commodity form and the cinematic image as a projected illusion should now be dawning. Indeed, capitalist economy can be understood through the history of the movie machine and its various precursors. The moving image is, by definition, a phantom, partially a product of our own brains—a fleeting image without substance, which only exists in the act of projecting and beholding as a blend of material and mental image. And it is these mental products that, it can be argued, drive the economy. "Trade follows film," as the Hollywood mantra goes, suggesting how the circulation of interchangeable visual materials—stars and starlets, guns and girls—reinforce the capitalist market system by habituating individuals to its demands. What these products obscure is the larger totality of social relations, hence they diminish the possibility of collective consciousness and action. Rather than increasing the individual's autonomy, they do exactly the opposite. On this basis, Bernard Stiegler has recently asserted that consumer capitalism, cinema included, marks another phase in the "thwarting of spirit" and general proletarianization that started with the industrial revolution. "The consumer," he writes, "is the new proletarian figure, and the proletariat, very far from disappearing, is a condition from which it has become nearly impossible to escape" (Stiegler 2011, 35).

The Couch and the Screen

How does cinema succeed in turning us into capitalism's subjects, into spiritless proletarianized consumers (if Stiegler is right)? This was one of the key concerns of the formation of what is called modern film theory after the Second World War. It was in this context that Marx's critique of capitalism became systematically applied in the analysis of cinematic spectatorship, driven especially by the epistemological and ontological dilemma concerning the real and the virtual that the concept of commodity involves—a dilemma that has directed critical thinking about the media systems that support capitalist social formations to the present day. Consider, for instance, how Marx's argument that ideology and/or the image distorts real, material conditions, and replaces them with illusory representations, is essential to Jean Baudrillard's (1995) concept of the simulacrum and his analysis of the televising of the Iraq War in the early 1990s in terms of misrepresentation. Likewise, Guy Debord's treatment of societies of the spectacle from the 1960s—focusing on Hollywood cinema and the commercial television, in particular—was drawn on Marx's critique of commodity. The world of spectacle, Debord (1995, 26) wrote, is "the world of the commodity ruling over all lived experience," indeed, a world where social relations and individual desires have become dictated by images.

The analysis of cinematic spectatorship under capitalism was initiated in the France of the 1960s and 1970s, among Parisian intellectuals and film critics, who married Marx's thought with psychoanalysis. In the dethroning of the idols of consumerism and patriarchy that took place during and after May 1968, including the idols of the silver screen, what Marx had argued about the commodity form and capitalist exchange became viewed in relation to what psychoanalysis had divulged about the intricacies of psychic life (see e.g., Goux 1990). For instance, Félix Guattari (2009), who alongside his friend and cowriter Gilles Deleuze, became famous for reinterpreting Marx's ideas about social production (labor) in terms of desire, wrote about cinema as "The Poor Man's Couch." Guattari compared the movie experience to going to see one's analyst: both events are particular ways of disciplining who we believe and imagine we are. Both the silver screen and the analyst tinker with our innermost desires and drives, mold them according to their own (and the society's) purposes. Another analogue for commercial and mainstream cinema, for Guattari, was drugs. What the spectator expects from the movies, Guattari wrote:

> is the confection of a certain type of drug that, though technologically more sophisticated than the ordinary joint or pipe, nonetheless functions by transforming the mode of subjectivity of those who use it: one captures the energy of desire in order to turn it against itself to anaesthetize it, to cut it off from the external world in such a way that it ceases to threaten the organization and values of the dominant social system. (Guattari 2009, 259)

Here, Marx's critique of capitalism's phantasmagoric nature returns, in a slightly disguised form, in the parallel that Guattari drew between the druggy's internal visions and the moviegoer's hallucinations. For Guattari, the spectator's elementary relation with the screen is animated by desire, and the movie machine comes across as capable of fixing, blocking and structuring our desires or alternatively liberating them. For Guattari, then, the power of cinema lies in how it either locks us within the society's drug-infused and ideologically loaded visions or rather is capable of directing us outside them.

Whilst Guattari might have been somewhat unorthodox in his critique of mainstream psychoanalysis, he did iterate several of the concerns of his contemporaries, regarding the dialectic of the screen and the society (the former reproducing the latter in its molding of the spectator), and of lifting the veil over the mechanisms that produce us as docile subjects—in a manner similar to the protagonist of John Carpenter's *They Live* (1988), who realizes when he puts on a pair of special sunglasses that the world is actually ruled by capitalist aliens disguised in human form. The critic's role, one might assume, was to offer people a pair of such glasses.

"The Poor Man's Couch" was originally published in the special issue of the journal *Communications* (1975) on psychoanalysis and cinema in which several essays constitutive of modern film theory, or "screen theory," came out, ranging from Raymond Bellour's "Symbolic Blockage" to Julia Kristeva's "Ellipsis on Fright and the Seduction of the Specular" and Christian Metz's "The Imaginary Signifier." But the one that most vividly continued the critique of capitalism's and/or cinema's illusory nature was Jean-Louis Baudry's (1975; 1992) essay on the *dispositif*, or "the apparatus," a concept that still persists in film and media theoretical debates.[1]

Both media technological metaphors prominent in Marx come into play in Baudry's essay: the *camera obscura* as a distorted vision of reality and the magic lantern as the production/projection of brain phantoms. The first key point of Baudry's analysis was to demonstrate that the illusion of transparency most (commercial) films want to give us the illusion that we are as if looking through the screen to reality itself, not at the screen—is precisely what it is: an illusion. Moreover, it is an illusion mediated by ideology. Baudry (1974) wanted to expose the cinema's economically and politically driven mechanism of perceptual distortion, which substitutes reality for the products of fantasy, to expose the cinema as an ideological "apparatus" that works to support capitalist economic and social structures. Cinematic images came across in Baudry's analysis as "sublimates" in the sense that Marx described it: "the phantoms formed in the brains of men are also, necessarily, sublimates of their material life-processes, which is empirically verifiable and bound to material premises" (Marx and Engels 1998, 42).

But how does cinema function as "a brain phantom," or sublimation, machine? Baudry's aim was, secondly, to understand cinema as a "psychic apparatus" the operating principle of which, he argued, closely resembles dreaming. Fleeting and fragile but in appearance all-powerful projections of light and shadow on the silver screen compared in Baudry's analysis with the dream images that the psyche projects onto the mind's internal canvas, if you will, when asleep. The implications of this analogy were twofold. On one hand, Baudry argued that cinema's reality-effect was nothing but the result of the particular psychic disposition to which cinema submits its spectators—merely "a hallucinatory psychosis of desire," a state, as Baudry (1992, 699–701) explained, "in which mental perceptions are taken for perceptions of reality." On the other hand, Baudry (1992, 707) expanded that "the entire cinematic apparatus is activated in order to provoke [...] a simulation of a condition of the subject, a position of the subject, a subject and not reality." Going to the movies was thus a psychic drilling of sorts, to comply with the demands and values of the ruling classes.

Overall, Marx's observations about capitalism's phantasmagoria paved the way for critical assessments of the spectator's engagement with the silver screen in the "academic" study of film. What became prominent was the understanding of cinema as a subjectifying machine, which is driven by the moviegoer's impulses to fulfill their desires and which produces perceptual hallucinations in conformance with the ideologies of the day (see Comolli and Narboni 1992). The task of the film theorist, like the task of critical theorist in general, was to expose cinema's libidinal economy, to disclose why and how cinema's phantom projections can have their powerful grip on us.

To Look Is to Labor

The claims and assumptions of the screen theory of the 1970s have subsequently been criticized, even debunked as overstatements, particularly by more historically and empirically nuanced approaches. Yet the question of the production of subjectivity—or "the calibration of spectators," to borrow Jonathan Beller's (2006, 285) words—is still what concerns, in one way or another, most critical theoretical writing about film and other media. The idea that cinema adjusts and positions our bodies and minds to meet capitalism's overproduction of commodities has provided a firm background upon which critical theory has established its analyses of the image-worlds we live in.

In this regard, Beller's investigation of the visual economy of cinema can be considered one of the most prominent recent reinterpretations of Marx's thought. Beller (2006, 2) articulates what the Lumière brothers' *Workers Leaving the Factory* already showed or at least implied that "to look is to labor." Here, the spectator is not someone who, powerless, becomes caught in a hallucinatory psychosis in the movie theatre's darkness but is someone who is engaged in social production—someone who works, produces value and whose work is appropriated and capitalized on.

Beller points out particularly the economization of our senses and mental capacities in the age of moving images. "From a systemic point of view," he writes:

> cinema arises out of a need for the intensification of the extraction of value from human bodies beyond normal physical and spatial limits and beyond normal working hours [...]. It realizes capitalist tendencies toward the extension of the work day (via entertainment,

> email), the deterritorialization of the factory (through cottage industry, TV), the marketing of attention (to advertisers), the building of media pathways (formerly roads), and the retooling of subjects. (Beller 2006, 13)

Beller's aim is thus to update Marxist critique into the age of global circulation of images on all sorts of screen platforms. Going to the movies, watching television, liking on Facebook, playing video games and so on are all activities that require our psychic investment, particularly our capacities of paying attention—the capacities to gaze, to focus, to be distracted, to switch from one shot or "window" to another in milliseconds. Furthermore, they are activities that are capitalized on by the producers of whatever these shots or windows contain as well as their frames themselves—the global media conglomerates. To put it bluntly, while we watch a film, zap between channels, lurk online, we do not simply "pay" attention; rather, we sell, unknowingly perhaps, our powers of paying attention to the industry in exchange (in most cases) of pleasure. This affective and cognitive economy of the cinema and other moving image media resembles, Beller (2006, 112) suggests, what Marx argued about labor and the extraction of surplus value: queuing to the movies, perched on their sofas in front of the telly or navigating online, spectators are at work in various kinds of "deterritorialized" factories, plugged into systems of global production of value for media companies and their investors. The result of this development, Beller notes, is the alienation of ourselves from what we see in front of us. "The separation and expropriation of labor from the laborer, the alienation of labor, is a precursor introduction to the separation and expropriation of vision from the spectator" (Beller 2006, 7–8).

For Beller, the attention economy we are so familiar with today started with the invention of cinema, with Edison, the Lumière brothers, Friese-Greene and so on. It was the movies that first produced images as "units" exchangeable on the editing table. It was the movies that most vehemently turned looking into a surplus-generating activity across the globe. This, one might surmise, was based on the fact that paying attention is a temporal process, just like the cinematic image is. Cinema demands our time: it captures our durations—in a manner similar to the capitalist who extracts the physical or psychological durations of his/her laborers—with particular affective and cognitive rewards in return.

This is of course the reality of almost all the media we encounter and interact with today. Jonathan Crary (2013, 84) has suggested that contemporary capitalism, materialized in "smart" phones, iPads, laptops and so on, "is not simply a continuous or sequential capture of attention, but also a dense layering of time, in which multiple operations or attractions can be attended to in near-simultaneity, regardless of where one is or whatever else one might be doing." Crary points out a totalitarian colonization of individual experience taking place today, which the Hollywood moguls of cinema's golden age (or likewise Josif Stalin's bureaucrats) could only dream of. Virtually every smallest moment of our lives has now been made an object of capital accumulation to the point that, Crary argues, we have become "dispossessed of time." The only limit for exploitation seems to be the moment when we fall asleep and thus cross the threshold from production to unproductivity. "Sleep is the only remaining barrier, the only enduring 'natural condition' that capitalism cannot eliminate," Crary (2013, 74) suggests. Today, we can perhaps assert some level of autonomy amidst the commodification of experience by capitalism's phantasmagoric screens only when the mind begins its own internal phantasmagoric activity. The virtual worlds we enter when falling asleep, rather than material conditions of production, have become sites of struggle and resistance.

Yet the question remains as to how independent our dreams in fact are from the contents consumed during waking life; how indeed dreaming can "always evade [...] appropriation," as Crary (2013, 98) assumes. Expanding Baudry's analogies between the movie experience and dreaming, for instance, one might become ever so suspicious about the arguable autonomy of sleep from the powers of accumulation. How often have we not woken up with a dim awareness of the fleeting images of the dream we were just having, which blended the movie stars and starlets of our adoration, or locations and events from our favored films, with personal experiences and memories? Where, in other words, does the production of surplus actually find its limit (see Fisher 2009, 8–9)?

"Vacation from the Self"

Marxist investigations of film and media, to sum up, have more often than not focused on the critique of the virtual realities of capitalism and their technological supports: the movie theatre's hallucinatory darkness, the monotonous lure of the television screen, nervously interactive "touchpads." The themes that run through these critiques relate most often to the effects of dispossession and alienation that the media, on the large societal and existential scale (individual audiovisual contents matter very little here), have on their beholders.

Let me finish this essay, however, on a somewhat different note, with an early piece that the Hungarian Marxist philosopher György Lukács (2008) wrote on the aesthetics of cinema in 1913. Lukács's essay presents an extraordinary early appreciation of film's transformative potential, a view that this "classical Marxism's most prominent twentieth-century aesthetician," as Lukács has been described, later abandoned when he chose to subscribe to social realist aesthetic doctrines imported from the USSR (Aitken 2001, 195). In the early 1910s, Lukács was concerned with the aesthetic specificity of film and came up with a conception of the medium that was both critical and utopian, as Tom Levin (1987) points out. Lukács sketched a vision of cinema as an art of the event, of pure happening. Cinema, above all, breaks the shackles of theatrical representation bound to "destiny." On the editing table, Lukács observed (reiterating the amazement of several early critics of cinema), the logic of cause and effect was not valid anymore; rather, things became mutable, continually transforming themselves as the film unfolded. Thus, cinema mixes the "fantastic" with the perception of reality. Ultimately, cinematic production and organization of images is not bound by the spatiotemporal boundaries of experience, but is based on the only rule that "everything is possible" (Lukács 2008, 217).[2]

Surely, as we have seen, such mutability and exchangeability are the key qualities of commodities too. In one way, indeed, Lukács can be considered describing the process of alienation that happens in the lived experience of capitalism (see Levin 1987, 40). Cinema, Lukács (2008, 217) argued, hollows out the subject, presenting "a life without a soul, pure surface." But on the other hand, this is precisely the opportunity for a new kind of experience and a new kind of subjectivity to emerge. Liberated from the world of laws and meaning, the spectator becomes childlike, "irresponsible" (Lukács 2008, 220). The spectator, to quote Levin (1987, 43), "enjoys a 'vacation from the self.' "

Lukács's (2008, 218) key observation was that cinema is able to make the real possible, or, rather, it confounds the categories of reality and possibility. Cinema injects what we see, hear, think and do, with potentiality. This is cinema's perhaps most beautiful poetics. It is something that, one could argue, was explored in the poetic realist films made in France in the 1930s, by directors such as Jean Renoir, Jean Vigo and Marcel Carné. Consider, for example, Vigo's *L'Atalante* (1934). The film tells the story of a newly married couple, Jean and Juliette, who travel to Paris on a river barge, which Jean is the captain of, along with the first mate Père Jules and the cabin boy. The film focuses on struggles in love and faith. Above all, *L'Atalante* is about dreams of liberation, of breaking away from the restrictions of conventional life as well as one's social background—dreams that nonetheless threaten to sink in the industrial landscape of smoking chimneys in the outskirts of Paris, which the camera studies on several occasions. Against these pictures of production and accumulation, however, the film is mostly concerned with opening reality to the fantastic. This happens for the first time in the scene where Juliette studies Père Jules's weird collection of objects in the barge, which includes an old phonograph, a huge seashell, oriental fans and a puppet. In a cupboard, she even finds Père Jules's ultimate fetish piece (Figure 1.7): a pair of hands preserved in a jar of brine (the hands used to belong to Père Jules's friend, or as we are led to conjecture, lover, before he died). Here, *L'Atalante* seeks to carve the mysterious out of the everyday. However fetishistic, these objects are nonetheless not commodities in Marx's sense, or at least their value for Père Jules is of another kind than exchange value—they are intimate (something his existence depends on) as well as otherworldly but not monetized.

Generally speaking, the film wants to portray existential and social relations that, if not escape, at least challenge being captured into circuits of production and consumption, and that are situated at the margins of social order. These relations can be strongly erotic (yet not pornographic), like for instance in the scene where Jean and Juliette, separated, both masturbate at the same time in their beds. But it is above all when Jean, tormented, plunges into the river and sees Juliette's image in front of him that the film affirms the couple's preternatural relation. The latter sequence presents itself, to be sure, as mere fantasy, but, as Lukács (2008, 216–17) noted, fantasy is not opposed to "living life," it is only a new aspect of it, an aspect that is not overburdened by destiny and meaning.

L'Atalante ends with an aerial shot of the barge continuing its journey on the river—we don't know where. Before this, we have seen Jules escort Juliette back to the barge where Jean is waiting, hiding in the cabin, and their reunion results in a passionate embrace. The final scene of the film is ambivalent. On the one hand, it implies the enclosure of Juliette and Jean into a fantasy of nuclear family—the elemental reproductive unit in capitalism and the core of private property, for Marx and Engels—staged below the deck "in an indeterminate zone in a network of commercial waterways," as Tom Conley (2006, 268) puts it. The couple has rejoined, the confusion is over, and the demands of the company the barge crew is working for have proven superior over the short-lived

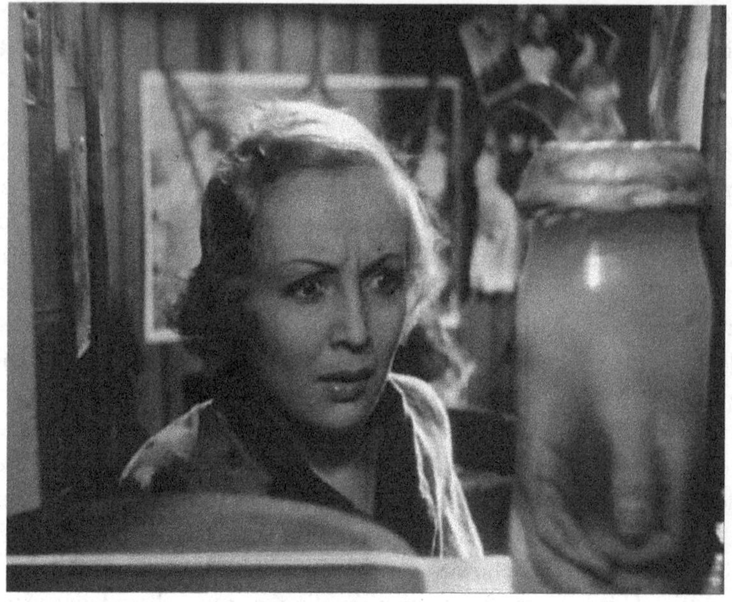

Figure 1.7 *L'Atalante* (dir. Jean Vigo, 1934). Frame capture.

promise of happiness. But on the other hand, we are also left with the fragile feeling of an alternative ending. The strong emphasis on movement in the final shot—movement in a very visceral, proprioceptive sense that is conveyed by a jerky camera mounted on an aeroplane—suggests adventure over order, the future's openness over the repetition of routines and traditions. And maybe Juliette's return to the barge marks the beginning of a fantasy, not of a nuclear family, but of a different way of being together. Enclosed in the boat, sailing toward an unknown future, is a heterogeneous community of things and beings, which includes, alongside Jean and Juliette, at least the cabin boy, Père Jules as well as the latter's fetish objects, and potentially many more.

L'Atalante was made in 1934 within a tumultuous political environment in France, predating the establishment of the left-wing Popular Front government within a couple of years. For the first time in 1936, France had a socialist prime minister, Léon Blum. During this short-lived period of socialist utopia, several of the improvements in working conditions we (still) take for granted were made. New labor laws limited work to 40 hours per week, and the right to strike was created, for instance. As Dudley Andrew (1995, 348) describes, "the Popular Front had put in question the ideology of labor […] The country declared life to be larger than production." Perhaps this is what *L'Atalante* also wanted to portray: that life is larger than production. Or, to put it in terms of *L'Atalante's* somewhat romantic overtones, that love (in its various manifestations) is larger than production. One could speculate that the film's ethos was, at some level at least, realized in the Popular Front, that the film in a sense anticipated the kind of social cohesion that the Popular Front sought to achieve by attempting to clamp down on exploitation. This doesn't mean that the film represented what was to come; no film is a fortuneteller. It instead suggests that *L'Atalante* (among many other films of the period, to be sure) sought, for its part, to unlock people's imagination to the possibility of change. It contributed to composing a shared sensibility of emancipation, to reimagining what it means to be in this world.

Perhaps it is here, more generally speaking, that we should locate the cinema's political potential. As Lukács observed, cinema is capable of offering "vacation from the self," of releasing us, even if momentarily, from our edified and regulated relations with ourselves and with the world, and thereby disclosing the future as something that has not (yet) been determined, something that we can reaffirm as ours. Of course, not every film achieves this—in fact, only a few do. And individual films work differently in different social and political situations. *L'Atalante* means something else to us today than it meant to its spectators in France in the mid-1930s. Overall, however, cinema's aesthetic and political stakes relate to whether it can edit and alter our imaginations of what can be, rather than just sinking us back to our repetitive nightmares. Films do not merely re-present reality; they can also foreshadow it. That is their beauty. How do films, as vehicles for the imagination, become driving forces of history? This is where the Marxist question concerning the emancipatory powers of cinema can be located.

Notes

1 For recent assessments of Baudry's notion of *dispositif*, see e.g., Kessler (2009); Kessler, Chateau and Moure (2016); Bellour (2009, 83–89). A different, even if related, way of thinking about the *dispositif* derives from Michel Foucault's work. See in particular Agamben (2009).

2 Lukács was not alone in his assessment. The French art historian Elie Faure (1973, 16–36), among others, put forward similar arguments about cinema's "plastic" powers to reshape reality in the early 1920s.

Works Cited

Adorno, Theodor. 1995. *Minima Moralia: Reflections on a Damaged Life*. Translated by E. F. N. Jephcott. London: Verso.

Agamben, Giorgio. 2009. "What Is an Apparatus?" In *What Is an Apparatus? and Other Essays*, edited by Werner Hamacher, translated by David Kishik and Stefan Pedatella, 1–24. Stanford: Stanford University Press.

Aitken, Ian. 2001. *European Film Theory and Cinema: A Critical Introduction*. Edinburgh: Edinburgh University Press.

Andrew, Dudley. 1995. *Mists of Regret: Culture and Sensibility in Classic French Film*. Princeton: Princeton University Press.

Andriopoulos, Stefan. 2013. *Ghostly Apparitions: German Idealism, the Gothic Novel, and Optical Media*. New York: Zone Books.

Baudrillard, Jean. 1995. *The Gulf War Did Not Take Place*. Translated by Paul Patton. Bloomington: Indiana University Press.

Baudry, Jean-Louis. 1974. "Ideological Effects of the Basic Cinematographic Apparatus," translated by Alan Williams, *Film Quarterly* 28, no. 2: 39–47.

———. 1975. "Le Dispositif: Approches métapsychologiques de l'impression de réalité." *Communications* 23, no. 1: 56–72.

———. 1992. "The Apparatus: Metapsychological Approaches to Illusion of Reality in Cinema." In *Film Theory and Criticism: Introductory Readings*, edited by Gerald Mast, Marshall Cohen and Leo Braudy, 4th ed., 690–707. Oxford: Oxford University Press.

Beller, Jonathan. 2006. *The Cinematic Mode of Production: Attention Economy and the Society of the Spectacle.* Hanover, NH: Darmouth College Press.

Bellour, Raymond. 2009. *Le Corps du cinema: Hypnoses, émotions, animalités.* Paris: P.O.L.

Benjamin, Walter. 1968. "The Work of Art in the Age of Mechanical Reproduction." In *Illuminations: Essays and Reflections*, edited by Hannah Arendt, translated by Harry Zohn, 217–51. New York: Schocken Books.

Chanan, Michael. 1996. *The Dream that Kicks: The Prehistory and Early Years of Cinema in Britain.* London: Routledge.

Comolli, Jean-Luc, and Jean Narboni. 1992. "Cinema/Ideology/Criticism." In *Film Theory and Criticism: Introductory Readings*, edited by Gerald Mast, Marshall Cohen and Leo Braudy, 4th ed., 682–89. Oxford: Oxford University Press.

Conley, Tom. 2006. "Getting Lost on the Waterways of *L'Atalante.*" In *Cinema and Modernity*, edited by Murray Pomerance, 253–72. New Brunswick: Rutgers University Press.

Crary, Jonathan. 2013. *24/7: Late Capitalism and the Ends of Sleep.* London: Verso.

Debord, Guy. 1995. *The Society of the Spectacle.* Translated by Donald Nicholson-Smith. New York: Zone Books.

Elcott, Noam. 2016. "The Phantasmagoric *Dispositif:* An Assembly of Bodies and Images in Real Time and Space." *Grey Room* 62 (Winter): 42–71.

Faure, Elie. 1973. *Fonction du cinema: L'Art de la société industrielle.* Paris: Denoël/Gonthier.

Fisher, Mark. 2009. *Capitalist Realism: Is There No Alternative?* Winchester: O Books.

Getino, Octavo, and Fernando Solanas. 1969. "Toward a Third Cinema." *Tricontinental* 14 (October): 107–32.

Goux, Jean-Joseph. 1990. *Symbolic Economies: After Marx and Freud.* Translated by Jennifer Curtiss Cage. Ithaca, NY: Cornell University Press.

Guattari, Félix. 2009. "The Poor Man's Couch." In *Chaosophy: Texts and Interviews 1972–1977*, edited by Sylvère Lotringer, translated by David L. Sweet, Jarred Becker and Taylor Adkins, 257–67. Los Angeles, CA: Semiotext(e).

Kessler, Frank. 2009. "The Cinema of Attractions as Dispositif." In *The Cinema of Attractions Reloaded*, edited by Wanda Strauven, 57–69. Amsterdam: Amsterdam University Press.

Kessler, Frank, Dominique Chateau and José Moure. 2016. "The Screen and the Concept of Dispositif – A Dialogue." In *Screens: From Materiality to Spectatorship – A Historical and Theoretical Assessment*, edited by Dominique Chateau and José Moure, 264–71. Amsterdam: Amsterdam University Press.

Kofman, Sarah. 1998. *Camera Obscura of Ideology.* Translated by Will Straw. Ithaca, NY: Cornell University Press.

Kracauer, Siegfried. 1995. "The Cult of Distraction." In *The Mass Ornament: Weimar Essays*, translated and edited by Thomas Y. Levin, 323–28. Cambridge, MA: Harvard University Press.

Levin, Tom. 1987. "From Dialectical to Normative Specificity: Reading Lukács on Film." *New German Critique* 40 (Winter): 35–61.

Lukács, György. 2008. "Pensées sur une esthétique du cinema." In *Le Cinéma: Naissance d'un art, 1895–1920*, edited by Daniel Banda and José Moure, translated by Pierre Rusch, 214–22. Paris: Flammarion.

Mannoni, Laurent. 2000. *The Great Art of Light and Shadow: Archaeology of the Cinema.* Translated by Richard Crangle. Exeter: University of Exeter Press.

Marx, Karl. 1990. *Capital: A Critique of Political Economy*, vol. 1. Translated by Ben Fowkes. London: Penguin.

———. 1991. *Das Kapital: Kritik der Politischen Ökonomie*, Erster Band. In *Gesamtausgabe*, 10. Band. Berlin: Dietz Verlag.

———. 1993. *Grundrisse: Foundations of the Critique of Political Economy.* Translated by Martin Nicolaus. London: Penguin.

Marx, Karl, and Friedrich Engels. 1998. *The German Ideology.* New York: Prometheus Books.

Stiegler, Bernard. 2011. *The Decadence of Industrial Democracies: Disbelief and Discredit*, vol. 1. Translated by Daniel Ross and Suzanne Arnold. Cambridge: Polity.

Taylor, Richard. 1979. *The Politics of the Soviet Cinema 1917–1929*. Cambridge: Cambridge University Press.

Vertov, Dziga. 1984. "The Resolution of the Council of Three, April 10, 1923." In *Kino-Eye: The Writings of Dziga Vertov*, edited by Annette Michelson, translated by Kevin O'Brien, 13–21. Berkeley: University of California Press.

Chapter Two

RACIAL BEING, AFFECT AND MEDIA CULTURES

Camilla Fojas

While much of film theory has explored the function of representation, image and stereotype, there is renewed focus on the "being" and affective life of race within visual culture. Critics explore the conditions of racialization in which a subject does not fully accede to humanity—forms of what Mel Chen calls animacy specifically in relation to Asian objects and bodies—and how racialization exposes subjects to conditions of precariousness and risk of death. The history of racial stereotype might be explored through this lens, through the calcification of type as a form of denaturing or what Homi Bhabha calls the "'fixity' in the ideological construction of otherness" or a fixed form of representation that denies the play of difference (312). The most abiding racial and ethnic stereotypes are of figures that are deemed uncivilized, subhuman or disposable subjects: Mexican bandits, Latina spitfires, Latino buffoons, Pacific Islanders in grass skirts, mammies, uncle Toms, maids of all races, bloodthirsty Native Americans, hypersexual squaws, inscrutable Asians, lotus blossoms and dragon ladies. In all of these depictions, race is a sign of nonbeing or lesser being. In this chapter, I explore various tributaries of film theory and racial being through recent critical interventions that capture many of the tropes of film and media theory and point to new ways of imagining and depicting racialized figures.

Visual culture participates in the transformation of political cultures, a link made all the more powerful and complex by the recent emergence of new digital modes of screen production and reception and a social responsibility raised to heightened value in times—such as now—of great social tension. Films such as *Get Out* (2017) are imbued with the charged political events and violence against black bodies that inspired Black Lives Matter while television shows that feature nuanced black characters and storylines, like Shonda Rhimes's *Scandal* (ABC 2012–18), are bolstered by the political efforts of Black Twitter—the same digital means that helped foment a revolution in the Arab world.

One of the founding organizers of Black Lives Matter, Alicia Garza, makes apparent the connection of this movement with Latinx politics, particularly around the carceral complex that includes prisons and extends to detention centers for migrants. William Nerriccio and Frederick Aldama explore digital activism as part of Latinx visual culture and make the case for this in #browntv (forthcoming), noting, for instance, the importance of sites like #not1more, for the cause of migrant justice. Native cinemas, in the American Pacific and across the Americas, address issues of settler colonialism and the forces of genocide while telling stories of their own histories and lineage while, for example, resisting colonial depictions in films like *The Descendants* (2011), *Aloha* (2015) and *Moana* (2016). And the activism around the persistent invisibility and whitewashing of Asians, along with the controversial practice of yellowface, has inspired a generation of Asian American artists and activists in Hollywood to struggle for better roles, better compensation and new venues for self-expression. Artists and activists move beyond mainstream images and stereotypes to engage creative ways of addressing racial inequities across various media, modes and platforms.

Spectatorship and Race

The various permutations of the "gaze"—male (Laura Mulvey), colonial (Edward Said), white (Frantz Fanon and Toni Morrison), medical (Michel Foucault)—brought forms of intimate encounter to visual spaces. There is a rich history of reexamining spectatorship as it relates to bodies of color, that is, as it specifies those aligned with the active gaze and those deemed objects of the gaze. Much of this analysis is drawn from feminist interventions in film theory through psychoanalysis, perhaps best known in the work of Mulvey, who noted first that the body of female characters is rendered a passive object of the male gaze, and soon after revises this to note that the female viewer's gaze oscillates between active and passive identification.

The racialized subject, object of a colonial gaze, is similarly oscillating and unstable. In work that precedes Mulvey's and is more squarely located in psychoanalysis, Frantz Fanon finds that the black gaze emerges from colonial policy and practice and that the unconscious—that place of contradictions and chaotic extremes inaccessible to the conscious mind—is itself colonized, signaling the intransigence of the socialized inequities of racialization. For Fanon black spectatorship is a vexed issue. He argues in *Black Skin/ White Masks* that identifying with blackness means accepting a devalued and denigrated position. He challenges his 1952 readership to the following experiment; "Attend showings of a Tarzan film in the Antilles and in Europe. In the Antilles, the young Negro identifies himself *de facto* with Tarzan against the Negroes. This is much more difficult for him in a European theater, for the rest of the audience, which is white, automatically identifies him with the savages on screen. It is a conclusive experiment. The Negro learns that one is not black without problems" (152–53, n. 15).

Fanon's point here is taken up as a central wing of identity politics by the generation to follow. Manthia Diawara and bell hooks count among critics who emphasize resistance and opposition in visual modes of identification. Diawara uses the term "resisting spectator" to denote those who resist mainstream images of blacks. This insight might be extended to include all racialized and nonhegemonic depictions. The resistant eye turns "passive identification into active criticism" in a manner that "both informs and interrelates with contemporary oppositional filmmaking" (853).

In an attempt to reframe our understanding of the viewing experience according to popularly accessible contexts, much recent work revises the history of film theory through textual and contextual readings of classical-era films and spectatorship. Jane

Gaines specifies racial dynamics in looking relations and cautions critics against "textual detachment" or the abstraction from historical and social context, particularly of race and class. She argues that the psychoanalytic frame takes gender as a point of departure and risks universalizing all looking relations according to a white, Western, middle-class model. Writing in 1986, she finds that "the basic tenants of contemporary feminist film theory—that the (male) spectator possesses the female indirectly through the eyes of the male protagonist (his screen surrogate)—is [*sic*] problematized in a film in which racial difference structures a hierarchy of access to the female image" (75). She finds psychoanalysis unable to account for race. Likewise, Jacqueline Stewart rethinks the classical model of viewing relations by examining urban black viewing practices. The conditions and spaces of viewing for black audiences during the silent era created critical interpretive communities of "reconstructive spectatorship" in which viewers engage with and respond to racist images to revise them. Thus the "creation of literal and symbolic spaces in which African Americans reconstructed their individual and collective identities in response to the classical system's moves toward narrative integration and in the wake of migrations fragmenting effects" (653). Black audiences experienced the communal experience of racial pride that interrupted the flow of the classical filmic narrative and disrupted the images and representations of black lives.

Early film criticism reflected the racial discourses of films of the classical era in instrumentalizing racialized bodies in the production of theory. William Nerriccio, in his analysis of past film criticism of *Touch of Evil*, shows how Stephen Heath and other film critics used the film and its "Mexicans" to establish and formalize film theory. This is reflected in industrial conditions as the film industry colonized geographical space to project an imperial image in Hollywood. Charles Ramírez Berg notes that the imperial expropriation of Native Californio land to build the first major studios was inflected in the colonial portrayals of Latinx characters in early film. And this social and racially defined inequity was reflected in the industrial practices of early Hollywood. During the heyday of the classical Western, particularly those depicting the settling of the West, the marginalization of Asians and their association with forms of labor, generated Western storylines that placed Asian workers in the background.

From the earliest cinematic images, race signifies an alien condition, either foreignness or a sign of primitive backwardness, of a state out of joint with the present. And race is often associated with place, with territories beyond the US borders or marginal zones. In the case of Asian, Native, Arab and Latinx characters, those in the "racial middle" within the polarized racial schema of the United States, race is associated with foreign language and origin. Native American characters and storylines originated in early Westerns as bloodthirsty threats to the settlement of the United States. Likewise, Latinx characters, mostly bandits and greasers, derived from Western-themed "dime novels" that presented colonial ideas about those native to the southwest as uncivilized—ideas that were used to justify the US conquest of former territories of Mexico and the genocide of its native inhabitants. Ward Churchill describes the depictions of racialized others, particularly Native Americans, in Hollywood as the cinematic fantasies of the "master race." These depictions of Native Americans enable the perception that Natives are of another time and extinct in a manner that rids the United States of the "moral or psychic obligation to confront the fact of Native America, as either an historical or topical reality" (699). He argues that criticism of mainstream images must be engaged dialogically and "only a concerted effort to debunk Hollywood's mythology can alter the situation for the better" (703).

Classical Hollywood depicts Asians in much the same way as Latinx characters: as perpetual foreigners and migrant labor. They are agents of the "yellow peril" or the idea that Asian immigration in the nineteenth century was a threat to the United States and they are simultaneous, a "model minority" or the standard against which all other ethnic and racial minorities are measured and fall short. The yellow peril and the model minority are the two most persistent and abiding stereotypes about Asian Americans. Peter X. Feng notes that this contradictory positioning of Asian Americans in US visual media cultures underscores a crisis in the definition of American identity (1).

While visual cultural analysis is methodologically diverse and multidisciplinary, much of the focus on race and imagery in early film criticism was attuned to the role and work of image and representation. And this work, the first wave of criticism, forms the basis for subsequent analyses mentioned earlier. An early text about race in cinema is the groundbreaking *The Negro in Film* by Peter Noble published in 1948. Fifteen years later, the acclaimed work of Donald Bogle, *Toms, Coons, Mulattoes, Mammies and Bucks* problematizes the striving for positive representation, which only represses and conceals the social issues within communities of color. A number of surveys of black images in film emerged in the 1970s, including Edward Mapp's *Blacks in American Films* (1972) and Thomas Cripp's *Slow Fade to Black* (1977). Similar surveys of the presence and visibility of long stereotyped and erased communities were more prevalent in a post-civil rights context along with the emergence of "multicultural" curricular reform.[1] Race is shaped by visual culture, which in turn is shaped by industrial conditions, and the history of participation of people of color in Hollywood film and television is one of restriction and exclusion.

During and after the civil rights era, issues related to racial relations emerged in popular culture in television shows like *Chico and the Man* (1974–78), *All in the Family* (1971–79) and *The Jeffersons* (1975–85) and by the 1980s and the rise of independent cinema, peoples of color began telling their own stories from their own point of view. The consolidation of multiculturalism by the late 1980s enabled the creation of the niche "ethnic" and "urban" markets that identified audiences for films like *Stand and Deliver* (1988), *Do the Right Thing* (1989), *Double Happiness* (1994) and *Smoke Signals* (1998).

Fears about racialized others intensified after the events of September 11, 2001. The increase in negative sentiment about immigration and a heightened state surveillance impacted popular depictions of migrants, refugees and those with heritages that might be traced back to the Middle East. After 2001, there was a marked increase in the depiction of Arabs as villains along with the practice of casting non-Arabs to play these roles. The Hollywood film and media industry's practice of transracial casting underscores a representational indifference of those in the racial middle. And the anxieties about "evil Arabs" were readily transposed onto undocumented migrants and alien others who represented a threat to the national order through the (imagined) twin villanies of undocumented immigration and terrorism. Tim Jon Sammerling argues, there is no more enduring image of "evil" than the distorted image of Arabs in popular culture. These depictions raise the question about whether the image of the racialized other as a threat to the domestic order might be remedied by a positive or more humane portrait. Though there is a continual struggle for more nuanced depictions of racialized subjects across US popular culture, many critics agree that positive representations that contests stereotype are not a remedy for racial inequities. Peter X. Feng argues that there is no absolute positive or negative representation but that representations are deployed, interpreted and contextualized in a positive or negative manner. He argues that the identity of the cultural producer does not guarantee the type of representations produced. Sut Jhally and Justin Lewis argue as much about "The Cosby Show," noting that the Cosby family success implies that all other African Americans who do not ascend to the middle-class are failures. Henry Gray finds that the show, as Janice Peck notes about the Oprah Winfrey show a decade later, occludes the painful realities besetting African American communities in the 1980s. Positive representation may have negative implications, and for this reason, Gray turns to new ways of framing image and representation in relation to race and racism, providing a new take on the pitfalls of representation and authenticity through the concept of concern.

Working on a metatheoretical level, Gray engages Bruno Latour's query about the failures of critique to posit matters of concern over matters of fact in issues related to race. Ella Shohat and Robert Stam issue a similar resistance to the issue of veracity in stereotypical images, shifting from the idea of images as false or negative to questions about whom such images serve, particularly within the logic of Eurocentrism. For Gray, the analysis of image and representation is a point of entry for an "assembly" of "feelings, attachments, identities, sentiments, policy, violence" around mediated accounts of race and difference (254). By shifting from the accuracy of fact, we might rethink the role of representation from veracity to the ways it arranges and mobilizes affect, feelings, belonging and a sense of identification.

Rejecting the critical focus on representation, Sara Ahmed argues that race is constituted through affect. She examines the role of affect in the production of racialized meanings or how emotions give value to racialized bodies. These emotions may function as forms of social power and become impetus for collective action. Similarly, Gray explores the inchoate and conflicting concerns racialized images elicit that may range from pleasure to disgust, provocation and attraction. Thus, we might explore where these concerns coalesce, upon what physical sites, bodies, territories and how they constitute social worlds—in this way, we might interpret the racial logics and affects as practices that generate and promulgate inequity. Gray and Ahmed elucidate the role of sentiment and affect in the practice and emotional life of racism in mediated worlds. Taking this a step further, Sharon Holland, in a study that resonates with Celine Parreñas Shimizu's work on Asian/American women's hypersexualization, argues that the "attachments" of race are erotically charged and libidinally vested. The depiction and experience of race is charged with a conflicting and often contradictory array of attunements, investments and affects. And these feelings and attractions, desires and attachments are what make racialized storylines and characters and place key and intractable elements of visual culture.

Getting In to *Get Out*

The history and context of race in visual culture is varied, and this is but a short survey of some of the major tropes and conditions of racialization along with some of the various ways that critics have addressed this issue. Some of the contemporary conditions besetting peoples of color in the United States, and globally, might be better elucidated in relation to contemporary cinema—and in direct resistance to the strictures and limits of representation across other modes and mediums of visual culture.

Get Out—a surprise critical and commercial hit from Jordan Peele, one of the creators and stars of Comedy Central's *Key and Peele* sketch comedy show—engages many of the issues related to visual cultures of race and racism: it addresses the condition of being/non-being and race in a manner that coincides with activist challenges to various forms of genocide like #blacklivesmatter and #nomoredeaths while it cites other popular cultural texts, like *Scandal*. It tacitly refers to the social context of black lives while exploring ideas of the black gaze, looking relations, and agency within the complex of racialized affects, including pain and grief, attendant to, what Linda Williams identifies as one of the body genres, horror. Briefly, the film is about a black man, Chris Washington, who leaves for a trip with his white girlfriend to visit her family that lives in a remote suburban location in a wooded area of the eastern United States. The promotional materials describe the film in terms of the tension of mixed race intimacies; "When Chris (Daniel Kaluuya), a young African-American man, visits his white girlfriend's (Allison Williams) family estate, he becomes ensnared in the more sinister, real reason for the invitation. At first, Chris reads the family's overly accommodating behavior as nervous attempts to deal with their daughter's interracial relationship, but as the weekend progresses, a series of increasingly disturbing discoveries lead him to a truth that he could have never imagined" (Figure 2.1). Before they leave the city, Chris asks, ominously, whether Rose's family knows if he's black and she responds, "No, should they?" This opens the first of many chasms between them and activates the narrative intrigue, with her liberal "post-racial" attitude minimizing his experience of the cultural determinism of race (Figure 2.2).

Get Out recalls all scary movies that begin with a light-hearted trip from the city to the woods in which you get the sense that not all occupants of the car will make it back on the return journey. Indeed, the situation moves artfully from cheery to eerie as each character seems to be hiding something and much of this concealment has racial overtones or overt racial significance. All of the black characters he meets in his girlfriend's home seem to be hollow and affectless in a manner that is alien and alienating. The horror emanates from the realization that these characters have been taken over, occupied, coopted and possessed by dead white people. They are the living dead. This real and cinematic death is symbolic: it recalls the denaturing of racialized bodies across the history of visual culture. This scenario reflects how racialized positions are ceded by whites for various kinds of gain in a manner most apparent in times of economic crisis.[2]

The film is part of a cultural history of black effacement through visual modes. In his essay "My Black Death," conceptual artist Arthur Jafa examines his sense of obliteration and diminishment in relation to the imagined ideoscapes of science fiction and

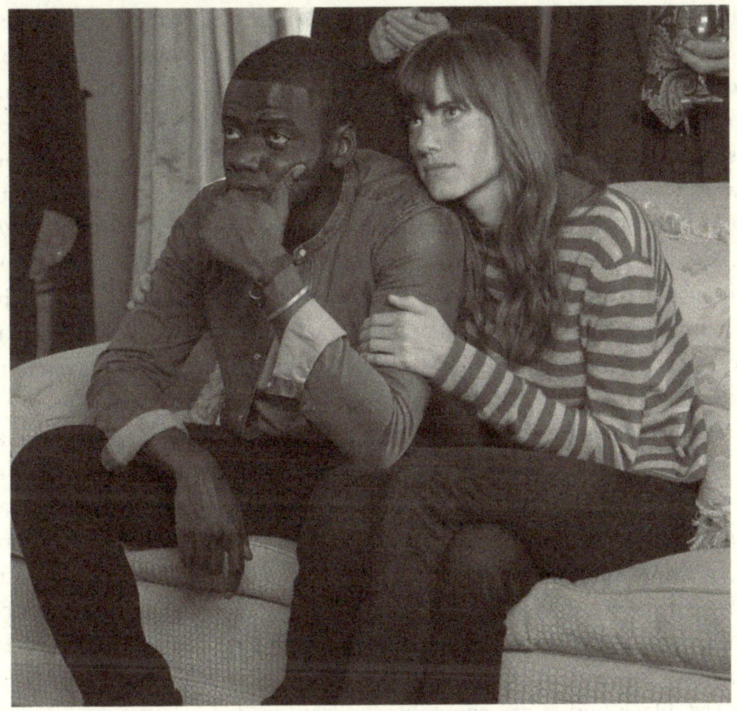

Figure 2.1 Rose and Chris. *Get Out* (dir. Jordan Peele, 2017). Frame capture.

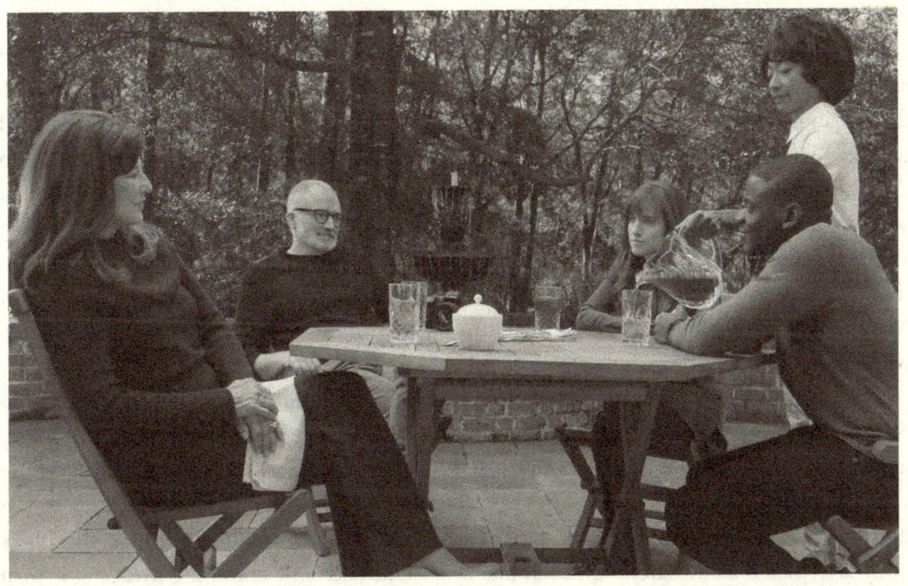

Figure 2.2 Rose's family meet Chris. *Get Out* (dir. Jordan Peele, 2017). Frame capture.

fantasy genres. Jafa describes his preadolescent experience of watching Stanley Kubrick's *2001: A Space Odyssey* (1968) as baffling and disorienting in a way that exemplifies the transformative power of art. He experiences the aesthetic whiteness of the film, literally and symbolically, in the archetypical Euro-American characters and the whiteness of the physical spaces, as the absence and suppression of blackness. This complete whiteout suggests a disavowal of the threat of blackness, an "anxiety-ridden preoccupation with blackness," and overwhelming "fear of blackness" (162). Indeed the story of *2001* begins in Africa, identified as the primitive origins of humans, and marks the development of civilization into the habitation of space as a completely white domain. The characters occupy a blindingly white spaceship that traverses the black abyss of space. And the story takes place at a time of black political visibility during the civil rights movement marked by the presence of the Black Panthers and the Black Power movement.

Jafa notes his interpretive experience of the film as one that encodes racial anxieties into fears about the decline of white civilization and the subsequent removal of all visual evidence of the black threat circulating in mass culture. I draw upon his critical insight in relation to *Get Out* for two reasons. First of all, the conditions of racialization in both instances, in 1968 and 2017, have changed little, but in *Get Out,* the critique of race and racism is reflexively engaged in the storyline without irony or cynicism. And, second, the role of space in both films is key to understanding how race in visual culture acts as an abyss, as a powerful vacuum of meaning as empty as it is overdetermined.

In *Get Out*, black bodies are cooptable "objects" ceded to extend white lives in an enhanced physical form, which, in the discourse of the film, is defined as black bodies so that, when the older white relative in Chris's girlfriend's family dies, her soul lives on in the "help"—in perhaps a reflection on the Oscar nominated film *The Help*, in which a white protagonist tells and writes the story of black women, a similar story of the cooptation of black lives to accrue cultural and actual capital (Figure 2.3). And the film engages the vexed issue of transracialism in the embodiment of blackness as a form of denaturing. White lives signify Black Death. And whites are represented as terrible and terrific through the "black imagination," which for bell hooks, "emerges as a response to the traumatic pain and anguish that remains a consequence of white racist domination, a psychic state that informs and shapes the way black folks 'see' whiteness" ("Representing Whiteness," 88). The film arises out of a social context in which black lives are continually subject to terror, violence and death, notably in the shooting death of Trayvon Martin, the murder of Michael Brown, and mistreatment and suicide of Sandra Bland while in police custody.

The film is also a powerful intervention into genre filmmaking. Genres, as Thomas Schatz argues, persist because the major issues it addresses remain unresolved. Genre, like trauma, is a machine of repetition, addressing, in this case, the trauma of white supremacy. It shifts the terms of horror, inverts them, so that, as Jafa describes it, the monstrous and terrifying black body is resignified. In mainstream storylines, the black body is depicted as threatening much like other characters of color, the invading brown immigrant, the yellow peril, the rapacious Indian, and the terrorizing Arab. And the white woman of Hollywood lore across genres is pure and innocent, often deemed a passive victim of a man of color—from *Birth of a Nation* (1915), *The Searchers* (1956),

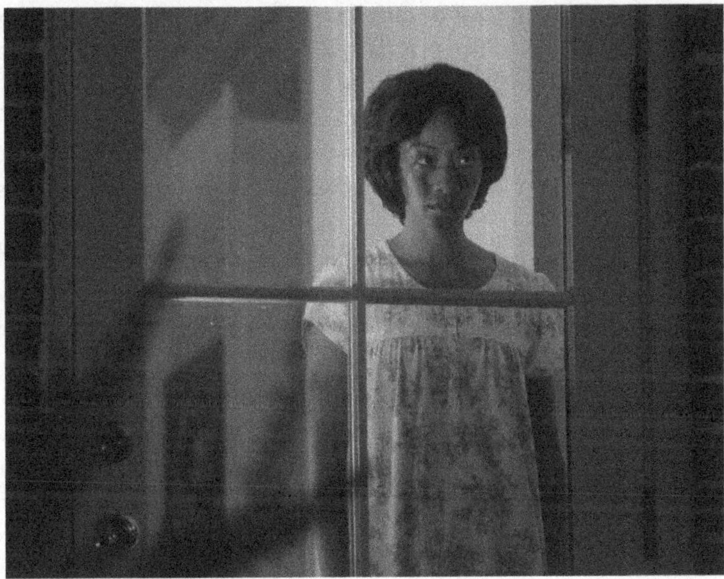

Figure 2.3 Georgina in *Get Out* (dir. Jordan Peele, 2017). Frame capture.

Touch of Evil (1958), to *Traffic* (2000). Yet in *Get Out*, all of the typical racial codes are inverted, the white woman is the true face of duplicity and evil, and black characters are complex and heroic under the threat of white terrorism. It reflexively engages with the tropes of the genre while highlighting the racialized anxieties that animate the horror film. It reflects on spectatorship and the dynamics of looking within a critique of the disembodying forces of white supremacy. It does this while capturing the attentions of the most mainstream popcorn loving audiences in the popular date movie genre of the scary movie.

Get Out's director, Jordan Peele, is a member of the mixed race comic duo Key and Peele—both are biracial and make light of being mixed and of racial divisions and conflicts in popular culture. They are committed to the community of mixed race artists and activists and were a featured act at *Mixed Roots Film and Literary Festival* of mixed race art and culture that took place in Los Angeles in 2012. This attention to the conflicts and issues related to interracial intimacies is thematized in the film in the black protagonist's relationship to his white girlfriend. While she is liberal and understands his social predicament, evident as she advocates for him when they are stopped by police, her good intentions, like those of her white liberal family members, often veil racially charged ideas. For instance, she fetishizes black men, which Chris discovers when he happens upon a box of pictures of her boyfriend past, all are African American—thus contradicting Rose's assertion that he is her first black boyfriend.

Moreover, the film is immersed in the logic of the racial fetish. A fetish stands in for and covers over difference. Difference is terrifying for a hegemonic subject for the way it exposes the lack of the other. The racial fetish represents an attempt to control difference, to manage and overcome it by denying it, thereby protecting against lack and loss of power and control. Thus the fear of racialized others is controlled through possession and through the disavowal of difference. The white characters in the film acknowledge their fantasies about the physical superiority of blacks, and then subsume this difference by literally possessing their bodies as lovers or as body snatchers. Rose's father, Dean, in reference to his travels, describes the "privilege to be able to experience another person's culture," a privilege and entitlement of whiteness that Chris will discover has a more sinister resonance.

Like the work of recent critics on the complexity of racial sentiment, the film shows how racism operates as envy and love and desire as much as through negative affect, like disgust and fear. Peele complicates white desire and shows how vexed the rapport to racialized others is for whites, while he also shows the impact of this dynamic on black characters which is experienced as trauma and inertia. At Rose's parents' house, the white, save one Japanese—signaling the erroneous perception that Asians are "honorary whites," guests of a party to raffle off access to Chris in some variation of Bingo, the guests say things like "Black is in fashion." Later, when musing on why blacks are targets for bodily possession, a character muses that maybe it is because they are "stronger, faster, cooler."

The film literalizes part of what bell hooks describes as "eating the other" as a form of appropriation basic to desire (hooks, "Eating the Other"). The lack in the white subject, and in whiteness, is filled by consuming and thus obliterating the racial other. This dynamic resonates with the racial atmosphere of the United States in which people of color are those most exposed to death. Chris must break out of the spell to resist being consumed by the white supremacists in his midst: Peele makes Chris's consciousness—being "woke"—and seeing things clearly, a matter of life and death.

Race is defined visually. Recent work that breaks from this rigid determinacy is equally drawn from the scopic register in the agency and language of the look and the structuring of point of view. This agency emanates from the power of self-representation, of control over image and story as a means of realigning inequities. Chris's role as photographer of the African American communities in which he circulates allegorizes that of Peele himself, the director of the film. The film displaces the white gaze as a controlling center and the shifts racialized discourses about black bodies. It is this gaze or Chris's "eye" as an artist that the white character in the film, the art dealer Jim Hudson, wants to appropriate for himself. The film raises a challenge to the white appropriation of black bodies, aesthetics, affects and points of view.

Jordan Peele and Keegan-Michael Key, in their comedic work, target racial categories and reverse them to reveal common racial perceptions and ultimately, the instability of racial categories. In one of their most popular sketches, "Substitute Teacher," they flip the classroom of the typical urban problem film in which the white teacher tries to manage an inner-city classroom—as in *Dangerous Minds* (1995). In this feature, the teacher, Mr. Garvey (played by Key), is of color. The classroom is white. Mr. Garvey is ready to impose strict discipline on wayward youth. He chides the class for their failure to recognize and correctly pronounce their own names. Their names however lack the creative invention to which he is accustomed in which Denise, to him, is Dee-Nice. They are punished for not knowing the correct, racially defined, codes. Likewise in *Get Out*, the codes of horror film are inverted. Chris's point of view has primacy that underscores the experience of the terror and terrorism of whiteness and white supremacy. The story begins by flipping the racial codes of suburbanization—a consequence of white flight from cities—and shows how the white suburbs is a terrifying place for people of color. The latter is evident in a confusing encounter in which a black man, Andre Hayworth, is pursued and terrorized by a white car while lost in the suburbs. He is abducted and becomes part of the nefarious white plot to take over black bodies.

The film is a horror reprise of *Guess Who's Coming to Dinner* (1967), often deemed the first interracial storyline in Hollywood—though there are some significant precursors.[3] And the racial conflict of this plotline plays out in a far creepier white liberal post-Obama context that cites aspects of the horror films that include *Invasion of the Body Snatchers* (1956 and 1978), *Rosemary's Baby* (1968), and *Night of the Living Dead* (1968) while drawing on tropes of racial fetishism, postracial and transracial fantasies, and the psychic and physical dispossession of chattel slavery. While it cites key filmic texts, it is also about one of the major precepts of film theory, the status of the racialized gaze and the dynamics of looking. The story invests all of its symbolic energies in Chris's (Daniel Kaluuya) gaze, underscored by his work as a photographer. He carries his camera and takes pictures to signal his agency and interpretive power as, it could be argued, a stand-in, at times, for the director. His peering look is not a controlling gaze, like that of a Hitchcockian paranoid lead, or objectifying, but is rather that of a seeker, someone who, confused and bewildered, seeks clarity and knowledge. In the main publicity still of the film, his is the gaze of traumatic inertia, of being unable to act against overwhelming forces.

This image of his frozen gaze recalls a moment in the Mexican film *Miss Bala* (2011) about a teenage girl held hostage by a drug lord and forced to obey his will. In one scene, she is accepting her ill-gotten prize in a beauty pageant and is unable to speak; instead, her response is a frozen yet emotionally wrought gaze signaling an oppression from which she is unable to escape. Her stricken stare recalls several other kinds of oppressed gazes. In *Dragon: The Bruce Lee Story* (1993), the fictional Bruce Lee is on a date with a white woman in a theater watching the yellowface character in *Breakfast at Tiffany's*; as the audience, including his date, laughs, he sits frozen, his expression both bewildered and humiliated. In the scene of his traumatized stare in *Get Out*, Chris is frozen in pain after being hypnotized by his girlfriend's mother, Missy, who is a psychiatrist ostensibly seeking to help him cease smoking cigarettes. She hypnotizes him without his consent and taps into his sadness and guilt, confirming his misapprehension, formed as a child, that he was responsible for his mother's death. She then controls him through his pain and makes him sink into what she calls the "sunken place" where each African American character's consciousness is submerged to wrest control of their conscious mind and occupy their bodies. In this way, the white characters control all aspects of the black characters they coopt.

During the hypnosis session, Missy delves into Chris's psychic pain, which he experiences as falling through space in a manner that recalls Jafa's essay on Black death. There is a key congruence between space as outer space and the abyss of blackness in visual culture. In *Get Out*, space renders the expansiveness and unboundedness of black pain. And it is this pain that cannot be fully contained by the white characters. The black

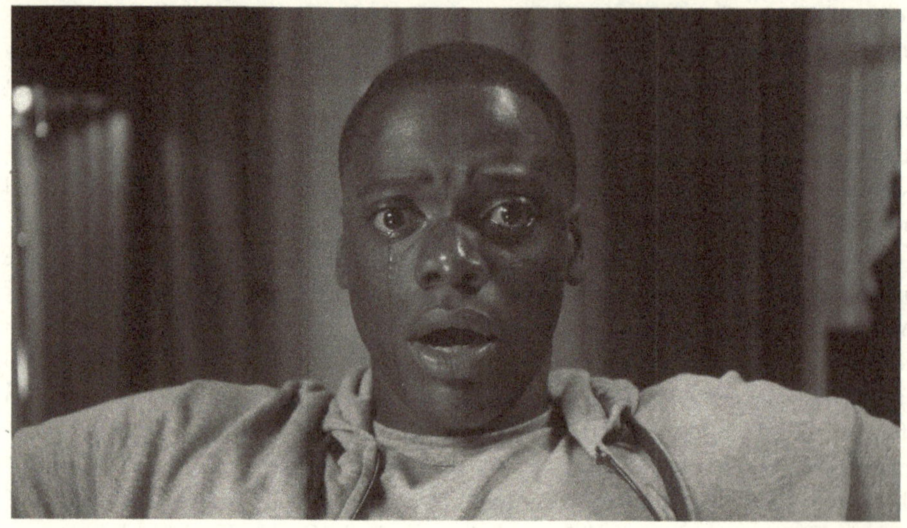

Figure 2.4 Chris's frozen gaze in *Get Out* (dir. Jordan Peele, 2017). Frame capture.

characters exhibit a body snatched-like affectlessness. Their bodies are ceded but their emotional life remains inaccessible (Figure 2.4). Pain is a key trope that immobilizes Chris and ultimately mobilizes him no sooner setting in motion the racial critique of the story. Sara Ahmed reflects on the power of pain to align people and become a "demand for collective politics" (39). Each possessed character has a momentary lapse in their possession that exposes brief flashes of pain and anguish. Chris identifies their turmoil, and through it, he registers an affinity that is akin to alliance. He connects to them through their pain.

Zadie Smith explores the film along with an infamous and highly criticized painting about Emmet Till called *Open Casket* by white artist Dana Shutz, which was featured in the Whitney Biennial the same year that *Get Out* was released. The subtitle of Smith's piece, "Who Owns Black Pain?" conveys what she identifies as the question at the crux of both cultural artifacts. Of the film she writes; "I will not easily forget the lengthy close-ups of suffering black faces; suffering, but trapped behind masks, like so many cinematic analogues of the arguments of Frantz Fanon." She finds the black characters "frozen in attitudes of trauma, shock, or bland servility, or wearing chilling fixed grins. In each case the eyes register an internal desperation. *Get me out!*" The film evokes the range of conflicting and inchoate affects simmering in the audience unconscious and, unlike horror features of yore, it puts the viewers squarely in the moral, emotional and psychic world of the black protagonist.

The emotions of the black characters provoke action and suggest political potential, which coalesces when the submerged being of black characters emerges as pain and anguish. Black pain is the origin of collective action; it links the various characters together in a way that leads to Chris's liberation.

Get Out is also a story about grief and the mourning of black lives. As Chris and Rose drive into the woodsy area where her parents live, they hit a deer and leave it maimed.

Chris is deeply affected by this. His reaction is complicated by being profiled by police on the scene as well as by Rose's defense of his civil rights. But his reaction becomes meaningful when we learn that he has not been able to forgive himself for his inaction as a child, when his mother does not return home after being struck by a hit and run driver and eventually dies. He believes he should have searched for her and saved her. This scene repeats again and again, first with the deer, then when he hits Georgina and revises his traumatic history by saving her—which does not go well. When Georgina and Walter meet their deaths, Chris is frozen in a state of shock, imbued with grief for the lives lost before and after he entered the woods. The story cites a social context in which African Americans are disposable targets for the police. In the final scene, as Chris struggles with Rose, and police-like sirens and lights flash, Rose assumes the posture and demeanor of an innocent white victim and the "cop" turns out to be Rod, Chris's friend who is not a cop but a member of the Transportation Security Administration (TSA). The audience, attuned to the context of ongoing police violence, knows the typical outcome of this scenario. By not making Rod a cop, the story does not simply enact a reversal that resignifies police. Rather, it associates white violence with terrorism to be "handled" by a federal agency. And it cites the famous line from Shonda Rhimes's television show with Kerry Washington as Olivia Pope, a crisis manager in Washington, who punctuates tough situations with the assertion that "it's handled." Citing the show signals recognition of a large community of activist consumers of African American storylines who promote the show and discuss it over social media to amplify its effects.

Hollywood storylines and characters offer a limited view of the diversity in the United States for mainstream audiences. Critics of screen cultures continue to grapple with the vexing issues of representation of race and ethnicity across a range of theoretical and methodological approaches, including issues around the valence of image and representation, spectatorship, community engagement and activism and industrial conditions of employment and authorship. *Get Out* is a key example of a film that critically and dialogically engages mainstream images and impacts the emotional resonance of race by shifting our point of view and transforming prevailing discourses around race. This dialogic engagement with mainstream depictions of race is but one of many points of intervention into the mediated social life of race. Some of the alternative modes and means of representation and discourse apparent in digital culture—YouTube, blogs, vlogs, Twitter, and so on—may be used to contest the dominant images of racialized peoples or enter into a debate about them.

The key to open access media like YouTube is that, in the potential for particularity in representations and performances, we get to see the foibles, interests, desires and anxieties of actual people who are often performing characters. These characters might be more nuanced and particular than their mainstream counterparts. Alternate media create a new field of representation and discussion to contest the hegemonic or controlling gaze of mainstream media. For instance, the blog, *Angry Asian Man*, started in 2001 by Philip Yu, the blog *Angry Asian Man* is a space to discuss, argue and rant about issues related to the Asian American community. Yu does not allow the public to comment on his posts though he can be contacted via email and discussion ensues on platforms like Facebook. The blog is an aggregator of anti-Asian issues as they arise.

Critical media workers and producers are working out a new cultural paradigm for peoples of color. And hashtags like #nomoredeaths or #blacklivesmatter enable communities to form and communicate to resist the violence besetting those marginalized in a culture of emboldened white supremacy. Critical producers and consumers of mainstream media might engage the conflicts and emotional life of these social events and integrate them into storylines that act on audiences in ways that are not immediately apparent but that have long-term effects and impact on their social, political and affective life.

Notes

1 See e.g., George Hadley-Garcia in *Hispanic Hollywood: The Latins in Motion Pictures* published in 1990 and Frank Javier Garcia Beruman with *The Chicano/Hispanic Image in American Film* published five years later, and like work by critics of African Americans in film, these texts survey instances of the participation of people of color in the industry. Surveys of Native Americans in film include Jacqueline Kirkpatrick *Celluloid Indians: Native Americans and Film* (1999) and *Hollywood's Indian: The Portrayal of Native Americans in Film* (2003) by Peter Rollins and John O'Conner. Jack Shaheen's *Reel Bad Arabs: How Hollywood Villifies a People* (2001) is also a documentary film by Sut Jhally and featuring Shaheen produced in (2006) and *"Evil Arabs" in American Popular Film: Orientalist Fear* by Tim Jon Semmerling (2006). Critical surveys of Asian Americans include Peter X. Feng's edited collection *Screening Asian American* from 2002 and *Asian Americans in the Media* by Kent Ono and Vincent Pham (2009).

2 See Fojas, *Zombies, Migrants, and Queers: Race and Crisis Capitalism in Pop Culture* (Urbana Champaign: University of Illinois Press, 2017).

3 See *Mixed Race Hollywood*, ed. Mary Beltrán and Camilla Fojas (New York: NYU Press, 2008).

Works Cited

Ahmed, Sara. 2004. *The Cultural Politics of Emotion.* New York: Routledge.

Beltrán, Mary, and Camilla Fojas. 2008. *Mixed Race Hollywood.* New York: New York University Press.

Berg, Ramírez. 2003. "Colonialism and Movies in Southern California, 1910–1934." *Aztlán* 28, no. 1: 75–96.

Bogle, Donald. 2001. *Toms, Coons, Mulattoes, Mammies and Bucks: An Interpretive History of Blacks in American Films.* New York: Continuum.

Churchill, Ward. 2000. "Fantasies of the Master Race: Categories of Stereotyping of American Indians in Film." In *Film and Theory: An Anthology*, edited by Robert Stam and Toby Miller, 697–703. Oxford: Blackwell.

Diawara, Manthia. 1999. "Black Spectatorship: Problems of Identification and Resistance." In *Film Theory and Criticism: Introductory Readings*, edited by Leo Braudy and Marshall Cohen, 845–53. New York: Oxford University Press.

Feng, Peter. 2002. *Screening Asian Americans*, edited by Peter X. Feng. New Brunswick, NJ: Rutgers University Press.

Gaines, Jane. 1986. "White Privilege and Looking Relations: Race and Gender in Feminist Film Theory." *Cultural Critique* 4: 59–79.

Gray, Herman. 2013. "Race Media and the Cultivation of Concern." *Communication and Critical/Cultural Studies* 10, no. 2–3: 253–58.

hooks, bell. 2012. "Eating the Other: Desire and Resistance." In *Media and Cultural Studies: Keyworks*, edited by Meenakshi Gigi Durham and Douglas Kellner, 366–80. Malden: Wiley Blackwell.

———. 2014. "Representing Whiteness in the Black Imagination." In *The Race and Media Reader*, edited by Gilbert B. Rodman, 85–93. New York: Routledge.

Jafa, Arthur. 2014. "My Black Death." In *The Race and Media Reader*, edited by Gilbert B. Rodman, 157–63. New York: Routledge.

Jhally, Sut, and Justin Lewis. 2014. "White Responses: The Emergence of 'Enlightened Racism'." In *The Race and Media Reader*, edited by Gilbert B. Rodman, 108–19. New York: Routledge.

Nericcio, William. 1992. "Of Mestizos and Half-Breeds: Orson Welle's *Touch of Evil*." In *Chicanos and Film: Representation and Resistance*, edited by Chon Noriega, 47–58. New York: Garland.

Semmerling, Tim Jon. 2006. *Evil Arabs in American Popular Film: Orientalist Fear*. Austin: University of Texas Press.

Shohat, Ella, and Robert Stam. 2011. "Stereotype, Realism, and the Struggle over Representation." In *Critical Visions in Film Theory: Classic and Contemporary Readings*, edited by Timothy Corrigan, Patricia White and Meta Mazaj, 800–822. Boston, MA: Bedford/St. Martin's.

Smith, Zadie. 2017. "Getting In and Out: Who Owns Black Pain?" *Harper's Magazine* (September 23) (accessed August 15, 2017).

Stewart, Jacqueline. 2003. "Negroes Laughing at Themselves? Black Spectatorship and the Performance of Urban Modernity." *Critical Inquiry* 29: 650–77.

Williams, Linda. 1991. "Film Bodies: Gender, Genre, and Excess." *Film Quarterly* 44, no. 4: 2–13.

Chapter Three

THINKING SEX, DOING GENDER, WATCHING FILM

Theresa L. Geller

I would argue [feminist film theory] has been the most influential form of narrative critique in the past two decades. (Nichols 1993, 64)

What is needed in feminist film studies now is not less theory (although this seems to be the prevailing trend) but more. (Doane 2004, 1234)

Judith Butler has been called upon time and again to explain the motivation for her seminal work, *Gender Trouble: Feminism and the Subversion of Identity*. One particularly telling rationale for her project appears in *Undoing Gender*: "I wanted something of gender trouble [...] to disturb—fundamentally—the way in which feminist and social theory think gender [...] one has to understand the sea-change that took place when feminist studies turned from being the analysis of 'images' of women [...] to being an analysis of sexual difference at the foundation of cultural and human communicability" (2004, 207–8). And yet, few commentators on *Gender Trouble* saw it as a reaction to "the analysis of 'images' of women," as Butler herself notes. Certainly, no discipline at the time of *Gender Trouble*'s writing more exemplified the analysis of images of women than film theory. Feminist film theory established the terms by which images of women became the central epistemological question of the 1970s and 1980s in film and related disciplines. That a Hegelian philosopher took as her starting point the analysis of "images of women" speaks to how transdisciplinary the analysis of images of women was at the time. Feminist film theory, like Woman herself, refused to stay domesticated, confined. As Janet McCabe explains in *Feminist Film Studies: Writing the Woman into Cinema*, "the body of work called feminist film theory and criticism has played a crucial—and often controversial—role in the emergence of film studies as an academic discipline; in turn, film studies shaped feminist concerns as well as granted feminist research a space to flourish" (2004, 1). This body of work was so far-reaching that by 1990, it played a crucial role in the advent of queer theory, a term coined by one of the founding scholars of feminist film theory, Teresa de Lauretis (1991). In this chapter, I will explore the fraught and intertwining histories of feminist film studies and queer theory, as they represent the predominant routes by which film theory explores sexuality and gender, while also troubling, or in Butler's language, "resignifying," both concepts.

"Images of women" analysis emerged as a result of second-wave feminism—a truism replayed in many "women and film" and "feminist film theory" collections. The way images shape gender, particularly sociocultural perceptions of femininity, was a logical extension of concerns raised by the women's liberation movement in the United States and the second-wave feminist movements finding momentum across Western Europe in the 1960s and 1970s. While many women were critical of cinema's representation of femininity, almost from the birth of cinema itself, they did not form a consistent body of knowledge. Rather, they were observations made by women artists and writers for whom, over the decades, the cinema was a vital art form. For instance, the poet H.D. (Hilda Doolittle) published eleven essays for the film journal *Close Up*, in which she interrogated the commodification of the female body in silent cinema and provided an early instance of star studies in her ruminations on Greta Garbo (Hopewell 2005). Indeed, first-wave feminists found in this definitively twentieth-century medium a unique forum for political engagement, from the avant-garde films of feminist activist and critic Germaine Dulac to the myriad women journalists penning newspaper columns on motion pictures and "personality sketches" of their stars, often connecting movies to the suffragette movement in implicit and explicit ways (R. Abel 2006).

Women were not simply commentators on the fledgling medium; they also played a significant role in the early days of film production before it solidified in the studio system. Dulac, in France, is often identified as the first feminist filmmaker, expressing her political beliefs in cinema, most notably with the scathing *La Souriante Madame Beudet* (1922), a domestic melodrama from the perspective of an intelligent woman trapped in an unhappy marriage to her imbecile husband. Melodrama, in fact, was the genre of choice for many of the early women filmmakers in Hollywood as well, including the prolific Lois Weber, whose controversial films addressed birth control (*Where Are My Children?* [1916], *The Hand That Rocks the Cradle* [1917]) and poverty and wage equity (*Shoes* [1916]), though most of her film work homed in on the complexities of married life, often from the woman's point of view, exemplified by her masterpiece, *The Blot* (1921), which arguably transformed the melodramatic tropes of the time with her formal and narrative innovations (Parchesky 1999). Even before Dulac and Weber, Alice Guy Blaché paved the way as the first and arguably only female filmmaker from 1896 to 1906, directing or supervising nearly six hundred films in her career that spanned decades, continents (France and the United States, specifically) and genres, including socially critical melodramas and female-centered action films.[1]

Notably, both experimental and mainstream women filmmakers found ways to criticize rigid normative gender roles and cinema's role in reproducing them. Most famously, it was another filmmaker, Dorothy Arzner, who took this critique directly to her audience near the end of her long career in Hollywood (1919–1943). Arzner, the most prolific woman filmmaker in her 15 years spent as a studio director, was ideally suited to observe the gender-specific effects of classical narrative cinema. In her penultimate film, *Dance, Girl, Dance* (1940), Arzner orchestrates a scene in which ballet dancer, Judy O'Brien, confronts a mixed audience of men and women, rich and working class, who is mocking her as her she performs a serious dance for them as part of a burlesque show. The men of the audience crassly shout for her to take off her clothes. Rather than running offstage,

Judy stops the performance, walks to the very front of the proscenium, arms folded, and scolds her audience for their prurient reasons for attending a burlesque: "I know you want me to tear my clothes off so you can look your fifty cents' worth [...] What's it for?" Judy demands. "So you can go home when the show's over, strut before your wives and sweethearts and play at being the stronger sex for a minute? I'm sure they see through you. I'm sure they see through you just like we do!" This explicit attack on male voyeurism, and its founding relationship to (hetero-)masculinity, would eventually be theorized by feminist film scholars and form one of the core tenets of film theory, due in no small part to scholarship on Arzner specifically. However, Arzner was far from alone in her observations; Maya Deren may have been living just down the street from the studios in Los Angeles where Arzner was making her films, but Deren, who made her first short film the same year Arzner was to make her last, 1943, was worlds away artistically, making experimental films for what Hollywood spent on lipstick, as she famously put it. Nevertheless, informing the films that would bequeath her the title, "Mother of the American Avant-Garde," was this same insight about "the latent Peeping Tom in the audience" (Geller 2006).[2]

While many women filmmakers, journalists and social critics raised the "images of women" question throughout the history of cinema, it would take the mass movement of the next wave, the second wave, to produce a systematic analysis, challenging it, testing and contesting its terms in the process of its institutionalization. The story goes something like this: the confluence of sixties-era liberation movements with the widespread engagement with revitalized Marxist theory and the academic dissemination of "theory" in the form of structuralism, poststructuralism and, especially, psychoanalysis, coincided with the advent of film studies in the academy. From this confluence of factors, the question of representation became politically central in a vast range of scholarship. However, the centrality of this question to the very origins of the second wave is rarely acknowledged. As Imelda Whelehan details:

> The so-called "second-wave" in feminism is [...] the result of a dawning recognition that the system itself seemed to have an inbuilt propensity for institutionalizing gender (as well as other) inequality. The second wave is therefore distinct [from the first wave] in recognizing the possibility that there might not be a solution to women's continued oppression short of a revolution. (2005, 3–4)

Whelehan and others date the emergence of the second wave from 1968 when the first steps toward revolution began with the critique of "images of women" in the form of the highly publicized protest of the Miss America pageant and the now-notorious Freedom Trash Can in which women tossed bras and girdles.

Indeed, the very concept of patriarchy defined by Kate Millett in one of the first manifestos of this revolution, *Sexual Politics*, is situated in a work of cultural criticism that dramatically redefined the political. In developing a theory of politics that takes as central the power inequities that define gender relations under patriarchy, Millett occasionally referenced cinema in her analysis of her representative authors (D. H. Lawrence, Norman Mailer, Jean Genet). Yet, more significantly, Millett modeled radical criticism that refused to hold the author sacrosanct, insisting that feminist critique should interrogate aesthetic forms for their reproduction of patriarchal relations and the reification of woman. More to the point, a central lesson of *Sexual Politics* has been the feminist methodology to challenge the politics of a work directly, ideologically, rather than from behind the screen of formalism: "Critics who disagree with Lawrence, for example, about any issue are fond of saying that his prose is awkward […] It strikes me as better to make a radical investigation which can demonstrate why Lawrence's analysis of a situation is inadequate, or biased, or his influence pernicious, without needing to imply that he is less than a great and original artist" (1970, 12). This question of formalism is a lesson we continue to learn in film theory, whether it is praising a filmmaker for his/her formal genius without adequately engaging his/her film's politics (from D. W. Griffith's 1915 *Birth of a Nation* to James Cameron's 2009 *Avatar*; or, Kathryn Bigelow's "embedded" military film, *The Hurt Locker* [2008]) or using formalist excuses to disparage (or refuse to fund or screen at festivals) the work of women filmmakers (e.g., Arzner as a metteur-en-scene), or more recently, promoting formalist analysis to put feminist criticism back in its (silent) place.

Central to the revolutionary tenets of second-wave feminism was a radical rethinking of the sexual politics of the media—film and television were self-evident problems from the beginning. In 1963, Betty Friedan published *The Feminine Mystique*—a book that literally changed the lives of thousands of women. Friedan argued explicitly that movies and television shaped women's lives in limiting and destructive ways (80, 133, 366, 368, 369). This pivotal work sparked the Women's Liberation Movement, encouraging women to reexamine cultural texts and to question the images and the stories conveyed. Although this was a rather naïve sociological view of media, it catalyzed a body of research that would come to form the basis of early feminist film criticism. Major feminist works that emerged in the mid-seventies specifically focused on stereotypical images of women in Hollywood and European cinema; the feminist film critics "looked at how best to interpret gender and representation in relation to patriarchy […] explor[ing] sexist content of cinema narratives as well as how the media constructs women as sex objects" (McCabe 2004, 7). These works of feminist film criticism originated the "images of women" analytic, principally Molly Haskell's *From Reverence to Rape: The Treatment of Women in the Movies* (1974), which prefigured central themes that would dominate film theory's approach to gender and sexuality to this day. Haskell's book introduced a comparative approach to genre studies, with special attention to the women's film and to femininity as a social construction shifting and morphing in different historical contexts. Joan Mellen's sweeping analysis, *Women and Their Sexuality in the New Film*, also published in 1974, bolstered the emergent field of feminist film criticism with her broad-stroke examinations of images of women in European film. And, Marjorie Rosen's *Popcorn Venus: Women, Movies, and The American Dream*, published the same year, complemented Haskell's and cemented the field by interrogating the contradictory position of the female star—an early precursor to the body of criticism identified as Star Studies that became a major area for the analysis for sexuality (Steve Cohan, Richard Dyer, Brett Farmer) and gender (Christine Gledhill, Jackie Stacey, Miriam Hansen, Daisuke Miyao). Sexuality and gender would eventually grow more and more distinct with the rise of lesbian and gay film studies, a split, at times, only slightly less contentious than what took place within the feminist movement itself, with its infamous distancing from the "lavender menace" in 1970 called for by Friedan in her position as the president of the National Organization of Women (NOW). However, lesbian issues were ratified as central to NOW's platform the following year—a testimony to the rapid adaptability and accountability of the early years of the movement. Second-wave feminism's responsiveness to challenges from lesbians and women of color, notably leaders in the movement from the beginning, reflect a historical intersectionality glibly disavowed in today's dismissals of "white feminism."

Notably, this early scholarship reflected the impact of radical feminist thought—a significant influence often overlooked in the teleological accounts of feminist film studies. If the "images of women" paradigm was shaped by early feminist critiques of patriarchal culture, the radical feminist project of reclaiming and valuing women's work, creative and otherwise, was the first real step in this direction. In this radical feminist praxis, discovering women writers, artists and filmmakers became a priority. An early indication that film could be an important forum for feminist debate was Robin Morgan's 1970 anthology, *Sisterhood is Powerful: An Anthology of Writings from the Women's Liberation Movement*, which included "a list of films 'recommended either for their insights into women's problems or into the society that creates problems'" (Chaudhuri 2009, 7). Screening women's films became an extension of consciousness-raising; made up of small cell-like groups, consciousness-raising was the central apparatus by which women were revolutionized, discovering in these spaces the myriad ways in which "the personal was political." Frequently organized by members of such groups, women's film festivals brought women together to discover films by women, like Arzner and Deren, and begin a discussion that would found "the entire project of feminist film criticism," a discussion centered on "the question of the relation between aesthetics and politics," a question, Mary Ann Doane suggests, "that has never been thoroughly addressed" to this day (Doane 2004, 1231).

Festivals like the New York International Festival of Women's Films (1972) and the Toronto Women and Film Festival (1973), not to mention the hundreds of smaller, local film screenings held by feminist groups, fostered the intellectual environment for women to discuss and develop theses about "images of women" and "women's cinema." Indeed, there were direct and apparent links between feminist film festivals and the canonical works that founded feminist film studies: "In Britain, Laura Mulvey and Claire Johnston joined the London Women's Film Group, which started in 1971 and was devoted to screening films by women. They also helped to organize the first women's film festival in Edinburgh in August 1972 [...]. The festivals coincided with the launch of the first feminist film journal, *Women and Film*" (Chaudhuri 2009, 7–8). Today it is hard to imagine how these festivals found audiences, especially as most feminist film festivals died off in the intervening years. But the sweep of the Women's Liberation Movement was vast before the backlash of the 1980s (e.g., most of that states had already ratified the Equal Rights Amendment before the right mounted a feminist backlash). The wide support for the ideals of feminism was evident not only in the proliferation of feminist film festivals but also in the ways the movement impacted mass culture. Feminism was a positive topic in the media *before* the explosion of feminist scholarship in the academy; notably, in March 1971, not one but *three* major network television series embraced feminism explicitly: Marlo Thomas, an outspoken supporter of the Equal Rights Amendment, made sure her TV series *That Girl* ended its run not with a wedding, despite being engaged for the length of the series, but rather by bringing her fiancé to a Women's Liberation meeting in the series' final episode. That same month, the first television show to star an African American woman, *Julia* (starring Diahann Carroll), aired "The Gender Trap" (3:25), described in *TV Guide* as "the women's lib bug hits Julia." Lastly, and possibly most famously, and certainly most ambivalently, *All in the Family*, aired "Gloria Discovers Women's Lib" (1:11) that same month.

Three decades later, another network situation comedy would pointedly equate women's studies as an academic discipline with the origins of feminist film theory. In the NBC series, *Parks and Recreation,* second-wave feminism is celebrated, if atavistically so, in the show's lead, Leslie Knope, forming a through-line for the character that her faith in second wave ideals founds her perpetual ambition wedded with unwavering optimism. Yet, when the series includes a storyline of Andy Dwyer attending college and matriculating in a Women's Studies course, it is not Leslie's liberal feminist heroes (Gloria Steinem, Madeleine Albright, Hillary Clinton, et al.) that are cited, but feminist film theorist Laura Mulvey. In the episode, "Lucky" (2012; 4:18), loveable lunkhead Andy is studying for his Women's Studies final with his spouse, April Ludgate, who quizzes him: "Who was Laura Mulvey?" To which he responds, "Laura Mulvey was a feminist film critic who wrote a major essay that helped shift the orientation of film theory to the psychoanalytic framework!" This astute summation of Mulvey's "Visual Pleasure and Narrative Cinema," in an episode written by Nick Offerman and in the context of an introduction to Women's Studies course, is an accurate representation of the impact of this groundbreaking work. Along with memorizing Susan B. Anthony's birthplace, knowledge of what many argue are the origins of feminist film theory is now canonical in Women's Studies according to this episode, which also offers an altogether different male character, one not in the Women's Studies class, talking about the male gaze in his hesitation to "objectify" Andy's Women's Studies professor.

The male gaze and the "shift in orientation of film theory to the psychoanalytic framework," did indeed mark a turning point in thought about gender, sexuality and representation worthy of recognition on network television. Since its publication in 1975 (although written in 1973), "Visual Pleasure" has been anthologized countless times across disciplines, from art history to women's studies, and in volumes focused on feminist film theory specifically, it is not unusual to find Mulvey's influence described thus: "No other single article in the feminist film theory canon has impacted so widely as Mulvey's seminal essay;" (McCabe 2004, 29) or "In many ways, one might say that feminist film history begins in 1975 with Laura Mulvey's essay [...] Certainly, it could be argued the essay generated cinema/feminist studies' historical turn in *response to* Mulvey's focus on the 'male gaze' and her declaration of visual pleasure as essentially masculine." (Callahan 2010, 9). These are not overstatements of the case—to this day, no film textbook that even gestures towards film theory can fail to acknowledge Mulvey's centrality to the field. Moreover, Mulvey's seminal work and the writings of her British colleagues, Claire Johnston and Pam Cook, who both published on the work of Dorothy Arzner the same year Mulvey published "Visual Pleasure," were distinct from the Americans writing on film at the same time (discussed above) in that the former were much more intensely theoretical than their more sociological colleagues in the United States. They also came out of the unique context of consciousness-raising groups in the United Kingdom and the women's film festivals to which they gave rise, which introduced feminists to long-ignored works by women directors such as Arzner and Ida Lupino. These festivals inspired a boom of independent women filmmakers (including Mulvey herself) and film collectives such as London Women's Film Group.

While Mulvey would return to the ideas of "Visual Pleasure" to revise and nuance her central thesis several times, many feminist anthologies and critical approaches to feminist film theory nonetheless begin with this essay or the ideas presented therein.[3] In her polemic, she uses psychoanalytic concepts to examine how visual pleasure is derived from narrative cinema in its structuring of woman's "to-be-looked-at-ness" for the spectator, positioned as a male through the operations of suture. We are sewn into the position of the camera or the male on screen who perceives the woman either as a mystery to be solved in the narrative, as exemplified by the films of Alfred Hitchcock, or as a fetishized object of spectacle, as in the films made by Josef von Sternberg starring Marlene Dietrich. Mulvey summarizes:

> In "Visual Pleasure and Narrative Cinema," I argued that the eroticized cinematic look was constructed textually, inscribed on the screen through its cinematic organization, point of view, privileged screen space, and so on, and that this way of looking is gendered "male," in keeping with Freud's naming of the pleasure of looking, voyeurism, as active, and therefore, metaphorically masculine. This masculinization of the look also responded to the feminization of the spectacle, which had emerged with particular strength in mass entertainment and its commodification [...]. I also argued that this gendered gaze produced contradictions, especially for the female character, whose position would be aligned with the male gaze or self-consciously detached from it or oscillating between both. (Mulvey 2010, 20)

An entire body of knowledge built up around these core tenets, adopting psychoanalytic theory whole cloth, negotiating it or contesting it outright, but Mulvey's argument about the gendered structures of narrative cinema helped found not just a huge body of scholarship but an entire discipline itself. To all extents and purposes, "poststructuralist gender trouble" began in film studies. As Mary Ann Doane summarizes, "Given film studies' emergence in the late 1960s and early 1970s and its relative youth and disciplinary instability, its encounter with influential movements of semiotics, structuralism and poststructuralism was characterized by an ease quite foreign to those in the established traditions" (2004, 1230). In other words, when Butler speaks of feminist studies turning to the "analysis of sexual difference at the foundation of cultural and human communicability," to a very large extent, she is describing the revolutionary work of feminist film theory. Almost two decades before *Gender Trouble* was published, feminist film theorists had already undertaken the work of overturning the "images of women" paradigm with the widespread incorporation of "theory" into its midst. Primarily, psychoanalytic theory provided the critical terms for the interrogation of both "representation" and "woman" as static, self-evident concepts.

As much of an intervention as *Gender Trouble* was, it was certainly not the first "cultural translation" of French poststructuralism, nor the first "to subject these theories to a specifically feminist reformulation" (Butler 1999, ix). Essentially, in a single year (1975), feminist film criticism pivoted from the "analysis of 'images' of women" to a complex and fraught engagement with "French theory." Having left the reflectionist assumptions of "images of women" analysis far behind, poststructuralist feminist film theory flourished in such journals as *Screen*, *Camera Obscura* and *m/f*. Film scholars like Teresa de Lauretis reworked semiotics and narrative theory for the cinema from a committedly feminist position as early as 1980 in *Alice Doesn't*, followed up by her even more expansive work, *Technologies of Gender* (1987), which engaged a wide range of critical theories to produce a "feminist theory of textual production," and, like Butler, de Lauretis turned not only to the writings of Michel Foucault and Louis Althusser, but also to the scholarship of radical women of color like Gloria Anzaldua, Cherrie Moraga, Gloria Hull and Barbara Smith, to thoroughly route gender essentialism, forwarding in its place, a different "subject of feminism," one which is the effect of a set of technologies that intersect and collide with the technology of the cinema (92). Yet, the ways feminist film theory really laid the groundwork for *Gender Trouble* were in its lengthy engagement with psychoanalysis, which feminist film theory had thoroughly developed in the intervening years between Mulvey's and Butler's key works.

Kaja Silverman, Tania Modleski, Elizabeth Cowie, Mary Ann Doane and so many more took up with a vengeance Christian Metz's famous query about how psychoanalysis might well contribute to the study of the cinematic signifier (1983, 21). Yet, unlike how they have been represented in recent years (see below), this was far from unitary or uncontested. Psychoanalytic theory provided feminist film critics arguably the most useful theory for mapping out the production of desire. Moreover, psychoanalysis—in feminists' hands—explained in great detail the production of sexual difference. If one is not born but becomes a woman, as Simone de Beauvoir announced, planting the first seeds of second-wave feminism, psychoanalysis elaborates that becoming as an effect of familial and cultural meanings. As Jacqueline Rose richly elaborates in *Sexuality in the Field of Vision* (1986), "The question of identity—how it is constituted and maintained—is [...] the central issue through which psychoanalysis enters the political field. This is one reason why Lacanian psychoanalysis came into English intellectual life, via Althusser's concept of ideology, through the two paths of feminism and the analysis of film (a fact often used to discredit all three)" (5). Yet, before the systematic and well-orchestrated discrediting of this field of inquiry that Rose only saw a glimmer of in the mid-eighties, feminist film theory would articulate the most complex and nuanced theory of the psychic development of gendered subjectivity to date—one that continues to inform a wide range of critical theories to this day, from the queer theory of Tim Dean, Judith Butler and Lee Edelman to the critical race and postcolonial theories of Homi Bhabha, Claudia Tate and Hortense Spillers. Its continued relevance has everything to do with the key question of the relationship of aesthetics to politics and how to formulate that relation.

Central to this relation is the study of the unconscious. We should recall that *before* Butler rejected the "images of woman" analysis, Mulvey authored "a polemical response against existing accounts of the woman-as-image [...] drawing on psychoanalytic and existing feminist theories […] as 'a political weapon' to psychoanalyze 'the way the unconscious of patriarchal society has structured film form'" (McCabe 2004, 29). This engagement with film's formal mechanisms "moved the debate on spectatorship further than other critics working in this area at the time—including Metz and [Raymond] Bellour—by taking the discussion off into an entirely new and feminist direction" (McCabe 2004, 29). This shift to the spectator not only deepened what is glibly referred to as "apparatus theory," but also complicated and enriched narrative approaches in film theory. Linda Williams (1981), for example, historicized Mulvey's discovery of cinema's structuring of narrative around masculine activity and agency back to Eadweard Muybridge's early films, mapping a trajectory for the cinematic engendering of plot that construes woman as an impediment to the narrative long before the establishment of what Noël Burch calls the Institutional Mode of Representation. Others, like E. Ann Kaplan, extended Mulvey's argument, teasing out her theory in "Is the Gaze Male?," which addressed the early resistances to psychoanalysis within feminist film circles by explaining its import:

> One could argue that the psychic patterns created by capitalist social and interpersonal structures (especially the late-nineteenth-century forms that carried over into our century) required at once a machine (the cinema) for their unconscious release and an analytic tool (psychoanalysis) for understanding […] If this is so, it is extremely important for women to use psychoanalysis as a tool, since it will unlock the secrets of our socialization within (capitalist) patriarchy. (2010, 35)

Although contested since its first introduction to film studies (challenged early on by Julia Lesage, B. Ruby Rich and Judith Mayne, for example), the effectiveness of this tool was undeniable, spawning important scholarship that provided correctives and expansions to that method, both in clarifying distinctions in narrative form, like Judith Mayne's exploration of the woman's film (1987), or Barbara Creed's work on the horror film (1993), and in pursuing the specificity of spectatorship, with interventions authored by bell hooks, Jane Gaines, Jacqueline Bobo, Michele Wallace, Lola Young, and more recently, Janell Hobson and Corinne Columpar.

In short, no other academic discipline offered as rich and expansive a field for the discussion of patriarchal relations as film studies did for women and men alike—Stephen Heath, Robin Wood, Bill Nichols and Dana Polan all contributed substantial scholarship to this critical paradigm. And yet, like all parts of the feminist movement, it became the target of intense backlash—what would later be identified as "the Paradigm wars" (Gaines 1993). As feminist film criticism received a swell of interest from academic presses and universities, the now infamous crisis in the academic job market was beginning to get attention, along with the culture wars generally. So it was of little surprise that feminist film theory, in particular, came under attack. While methodologies were constantly debated within and across disciplines, this was different. As Gaines's designation implies, it was a war—a war waged against the particular paradigm affiliated with *feminist* film theory, though of course, few called attention to the gendered terms of their attack.

There were certainly bitter divides within the field of gender studies itself. Feminism was still in the throes of the essentialism debates as well as reeling from the porn wars, with the AIDS crisis bringing into stark perspective the importance of a precise and thoughtful parsing of what sexuality means (distinct from gender), as Gayle Rubin's "Thinking Sex" demonstrates only too well with its diagrammatic analysis of the "golden circle" of sexuality and those left outside of it.[4] The Women's Movement had from its very inception fraught debates about how to define both the project of and the subject of feminism because of the multiple frameworks that made up the second wave: socialist feminism, liberal feminism, radical feminism, difference feminism, lesbian feminism and others. Indeed, in the first issue of the journal *m/f* (1978), in which many key articles founding feminist film theory were first encountered, these debates were already being rehearsed: "some theoretical formulations of women as a specific social group entail positions with which we must disagree. One such formulation is in terms of essential femininity. This can take two forms; either the idea of transhistorical oppression of women at all times, or the idea of an 'original' femininity that is repressed or suppressed" (Copjec 1990, 22). In other words, throughout the history of the second wave, feminist scholarship staged such disagreements to hone its terms and aims. Yet, the tenor of these debates was distinctly different than the paradigm wars that took place in film studies.

Two decades after Mulvey, Pam Cook, Claire Johnston and others, building on the work of Christian Metz, Jean-Louis Baudry and Raymond Bellour, "helped shift the orientation of film theory to the psychoanalytic framework," substantial questions about that framework had accumulated from those working within its purview. Yet, these were still self-identified film theorists (Stephen Heath, Mandy Merck, et al.). Apart and distinct from this position was a movement to reject "theory" whole cloth, coming to a head in David Bordwell and Noël Carroll's infamous *Post-Theory* (1996), which made its endgame clear in its subtitle, "Reconstructing Film Studies." The aim was to rout the prevailing paradigm of "theory," replacing it with what has become the "historical turn"—a turn that has also meant a turn *away* from feminist *theory*, a coincidence nowhere acknowledged by the architects of the "reconstruction," in large part because, as Bill Nichols notes in his anatomization of Bordwell's work, "conveniently, it seems, there have not been any women nor feminist theories [...] that need to be cleared away" (1993, 64). Instead, Bordwell, Carroll and Stephen Prince, primarily, target psychoanalysis—the core methodology of feminist film theory for over two decades. The editors of *Post-Theory* proclaim, in what can only be retroactively understood as a hegemonic struggle over the institutional direction of the discipline, "Film Studies is at a historical juncture which might be described as the waning of Theory," and "Theory" here means (Lacanian) psychoanalytic cine-structuralism (1). Todd McGowan graciously translates their position as a resistance to "a universal and totalizing theory of the filmic experience," as psychoanalysis is thought to be by its detractors (2004, 27). Yet, McGowan's defenses of psychoanalysis miss the point (and insinuate that feminists did not actually get Lacan "right," missing the point that feminist analysis necessitated getting Lacan "wrong"). McGowan's footnote, however, is more to the point: the post-theory resistance to the psychoanalytic model served the interests of replacing it with an empirical model, which has, in intervening years, come to dominate film departments, conferences and publications, so that by the dawn of the new millennium "theory as such has given way almost completely to historicism and empirical research" (xii, n. 1).

Since its publication, *Post-Theory* has generated a range of critiques because of the near-total success of its central project, which may have even surprised its authors, as Marco Abel notes: "Attacking what they call Grand Theory [Lacanian psychoanalysis, structuralism, poststructuralism, and ideological critique such as Althusserian Marxism] Bordwell, Carroll, and their 'conspirators' forcefully argued against the allegedly fanciful, esoteric […] theoretical encounters with cinema that dominated film studies from the early 1970s on" (2006, 132). Post-theorists, on the other hand, "promote a turn to scientific empiricism […] [and] see themselves replacing the abstractions of film theory with the concreteness and specificity of empirically demonstrable, scientific knowledge" (M. Abel 2006, 133). One might well note that the language of empirical science can be equally "esoteric" and "elitist" and certainly as theoretical as "the Theory" (for a fictive comparison, one might think of Andy Dwyer explaining Laura Mulvey versus the arcane scientific language of the nerds on *The Big Bang Theory*). Indeed, the problematic and contradictory terms of the post-theorists' arguments have been thoroughly interrogated by some of film theory's leading scholars, including Slavoj Žižek and D. N. Rodowick. And yet, as these debates raged, *feminist* film theory became the receding horizon against which these (masculine) territory wars raged. Exemplary of this is the way Mulvey is (or is not) evoked in these debates—a whipping girl in McGowan and D. N. Rodowick before him, for her failure to implement Lacanian psychoanalysis correctly and even more heavily disparaged, if in coded language, in *Post-Theory* precisely for her Lacanian methodology.[5] Even in the defenses of theory, as in Rodowick's "An Elegy for Theory," feminist film theory is nowhere acknowledged as an origin; women disappear, fading from the history of film theory, becoming itself a version of Stanley Cavell's "melodramas of the unknown woman" (Rodowick 2011, 1123).

An elegy for *feminist* film theory has not as yet been written. Rodowick cites no women and mentions only one, Judith Mayne, in passing, among those who began to be reflexive about Theory (citing himself as the first) (1111–12). There is only an odd use of "her" to avoid sexist language when contesting *Post-Theory*: "Unlike the scientist, the humanist must examine phenomena that may be shifting before her very eyes. She must account for change in the course of its becoming, while she herself might be in a process of self-transformation" (1117). Of course, this is not a generic proposition—this is precisely what feminist theory did and continues to do, exemplified by Mulvey's own research over the years, from her first piece on the Miss World contest to her research on new media technologies in *Death at 24x a Second: Stillness and the Moving Image* (2006) and her historical criticism on marginal artists like Tina Modotti and Jimmie Durham to her recent edited volume, *Feminisms: Diversity, Difference, and Multiplicity in Contemporary Film Cultures* (2015), a collection that stresses the multiplicity of methods and texts available in feminist film theory today, despite the rhetoric of postfeminism that seems, particularly after the last US election, as spurious as declarations of postracism in Obama's America.

While postfeminism remains one key conceptual device for understanding media representations after the backlash against feminism, this has still assumed that there is something "there" in texts that reflect women's postfeminist lives. Instead, we might inquire after the postfeminist state of the field that is part and parcel of its "reconstruction." Some film studies scholars have offered pointed reflections about what I am calling "post-theory feminism." In the works from which I draw the opening epigraph, both Mary Ann Doane and Bill Nichols confront the legacy of the "success" of *Post-Theory*'s condemnation of "the Theory," specifically noting the feminist baby tossed out with its supposedly totalizing bath water. In "Aesthetics and Politics," Doane comments on the already stinging theme of mummification concerning film feminism in 1989 and the conditions under which she revisits the field in 2004: "New approaches in film history have focused on women's role in the early cinema [...]. And new media have produced novel questions about virtual sexualities and identities. All this is well known [–...]. Yet what seems to be lost in the flurry of this activity are some basic questions and, even more crucially, the desire to pursue basic questions, a desire that often goes by the name of *theory*" (1230). Post-theory feminist scholarship avoids accusations of doing (the) Theory by turning to "history and the archive [...] with a logic of the local, the specific, the individual [...]. There are no limits to the objects that can be subjected to analysis, but there is a general assumption that the objects are 'out there' just waiting to be studied and all we have to do is expand our range" (Doane, "Aesthetics and Politics," 2004, 1230). In other words, post-theory feminism negotiates film studies' subsequent reconstruction by toeing the line of the empirical, stepping back from the risk of theory. For Doane, this is a notable loss and, in fact, may be a return to a reflectionist theory of art that sidesteps questions about the relationship of aesthetics to politics, a relationship originally bound up with that early second-wave conceit, "the personal is political."

If Doane calls for more theory, she does not necessarily provide the terms by which this might be accomplished or the factors that impede it. She correctly assesses that the prevailing trend is away from theory in large part because "current film feminisms often ally themselves with the logic of the local and its corresponding suspicion of abstraction. And this, to my mind, is a grave error" (2004, 1231). Yet, it is an "error" that is enforced by dissertation committees, editorial boards and academic presses as a result of the "paradigm wars" that had all but settled on its winner—historical research, the archive over theory. Both Modleski and Nichols reveal the real collateral damage of these wars—feminism. *Post-Theory*, but others as well, aimed to disarm feminists of the "political weapon," in Mulvey's terms, that psychoanalysis provided feminists for exposing the technologies of patriarchal power, like cinema. Modleski is one of the few to call out the editors explicitly for their antifeminist motivations: "some major film scholars like David Bordwell and Noël Carroll who apparently felt left in the dust by psychoanalytic critics, particularly feminist ones, began insisting on the appropriateness of a different methodology of the study of film, cognitive philosophy. That cognitivism, with its emphasis on awareness, reasoning and judgment, was meant not to supplement psychoanalytic theory, with its emphasis on the psyche and the unconscious, but to replace it" was clear (20). While Rodowick interrogates Bordwell and Carroll's preoccupation with scientific rigor, Modleski calls it out for what it is: "Bordwell himself had long been denouncing the very enterprise of interpretation, frequently singling out examples from feminist work to ridicule. Indeed, some might be tempted to say that his and his cohorts' concern with hard, solid, empirical data and with the workings of reasoning and judgment are very male defenses against the messiness brought to the critical task by women who have focused on the often unsavory contents of the psyche and the unconscious" (2002, 20).

In short, denigrating "theory" worked to finally foreclose (and repress) the real content to which feminist film theory directed much energy and utilized psychoanalytic tropes to explain: sexual difference.

What remains most often unsaid about "the Theory" is the way it made gender, specifically femininity, a central concern, if not *the* central question, of cinema studies; or, as Stephen Heath sums up, "theoryfilmanalysis" is that which conjoined psychoanalytic concepts "with a film in the interests of the interpretive elaboration of issues around (mainly) sexual difference" (1999, 35). Although its critics, as we have seen, situate film theory's dogmatism in the theories of structuralist semiotics and psychoanalysis, these theories were, in fact, critical tools used to nurture the infancy of feminist poststructuralism, which found fertile ground in the youthful discipline of film studies long before it made gender trouble in queer theory. If cine-psychoanalysis became hegemonic, it often did so in tandem with questions raised by the Women's Movement. This core piece all but disappears in the post-theory position *and its counter-arguments.* For example, the editors of *m/f*, which "produced some of the most rigorous and powerful work feminism has to offer," saw their scholarship in neo-Marxist psychoanalysis as an "ethical project," one committedly anti-essentialist yet one foregrounding the question of women's desire in a patriarchal culture (Copjec 1990, 17). Indeed, long before the reconstruction, it was the feminists who had a bone to pick with apparatus theory, particularly "the Theory" elaborated by Christian Metz, Jean-Louis Comolli, Jean-Louis Baudry, et al., who turned to metapsychology to analogize the psychic operations of the cinematic machinery, because these theorists elided sexual difference in their taking up of psychoanalysis. Cine-psychoanalysis empowered feminists to boldly lead the charge in film theory, exemplified by Jacqueline Rose, who laid down the gauntlet at the Cinematic Apparatus conference in 1978: "Sexuality, and specifically sexual difference [...] need to be centered in the analysis and consideration of cinema if those concepts from psychoanalysis are to have any meaning [...] and if that movement away from a classical semiology is to have proper effects" (218). Of course, the response to this line in the sand was to reject psychoanalysis entirely rather than confront the bedrock of sexual difference and the gendered politics that subtend it.

It took two decades, but Bordwell and his "conspirators" were able to cordon off the question of sexual difference entirely (and thus the question of woman's desire became unspeakable) by using neoformalism as a political weapon to silence the "vacuous overgeneralization" of "ideological criticism" (Nichols 1993, 55). As Nichols argues, "The value of this designation [ideological criticism] lies less in its descriptive accuracy than in its rhetorical agency: it helps make room for a presumably open-ended, nonmonolithic, nonideological theory and criticism that will restore those qualities of nuance and detail, complexity and contingency, that ideological preoccupation neglect" (1993, 54). However, as Nichols continues, this is far from the case, as the price for such "nuance" is the complete erasure of the specificity of the spectatorial subject; more to the point, postfeminist post-theory passing for poetics "allows for no history, no subjectivity [...] [it] neglects differences that make a difference, achiev[ing] coherence by excluding history and subjectivity" (1993, 64). While the hegemony of the reconstruction all but silenced any *theorization* of gender within the field, history and subjectivity were restored to film studies through the emergent scholarship of queer theory. Butler (but others as well, including Elizabeth Grosz, Eve Sedgwick and Rubin) took up the ethical project of feminist poststructuralism, turning to key thinkers central to feminist film theory, especially Lacan and Foucault, to not only confront the bedrock of sexual difference but tear out its foundation to reveal the disavowed homosexual desire beneath it. Indeed, the psychoanalysis-heavy, poststructuralist feminist theory of *Gender Trouble*, which directly engaged Jacqueline Rose, Mary Ann Doane and Stephen Heath, was only retroactively identified as queer theory. While the feminist paradigm was vilified covertly by arguments aimed at the ahistoricism of psychoanalysis, Butler deftly mined Freud and Lacan to produce one of the most important histories of the gendered subject ever written.

Queer theory returned to the "analysis of sexual difference" but rejected the compulsory heterosexuality at its core. In her feminist reformulation of poststructuralist theories, Butler "sought to counter those views that made presumptions about the limits and propriety of gender and restricted the meaning of gender to received notions of masculinity and femininity," and "to criticize a pervasive heterosexual presumption in feminist literary theory" (Butler 1999, viii). Of course, this presumption was equally in evidence in feminist film theory, with noteworthy exceptions like Teresa de Lauretis, Judith Mayne and Mandy Merck. If the Women's Liberation Movement ignited feminist film theory, the Gay Liberation Movement mobilized analyses of sexualities that challenged heteronormativity. Early forerunners in lesbian and gay film criticism employed image analysis of gay men and lesbians in the media much like the first stages of feminist film criticism. Vito Russo's *The Celluloid Closet: Homosexuality in the Movies* (1981) was published the same year as the "Lesbians and Film" issue of the radical film journal, *Jump Cut*, in an homage to Caroline Sheldon's very early work in the field, "Lesbians and Film: Some Thoughts," included in Richard Dyer's edited volume, *Gays and Film* (1977). In these early collections, stereotype analysis tended to be the focus; yet, this quickly grew into dense analyses of cinema frequently published in the gay and lesbian press. The early work of Dyer, Thomas Waugh, Parker Tyler and Robin Wood formed the foundations of gay film criticism, particularly Wood's essay, "Responsibilities of a Gay Film Critic" (1978).[6]

While Wood and Dyer both found political and critical homologies with feminism, lesbian film criticism had to confront feminist film theory directly: "Feminist film theory based on sexual difference has much to gain from considering lesbian desire and sexuality. Women's desire for women deconstructs male/female sexual dichotomies, sex/gender conflation, and the universality of the oedipal narrative" (Straayer 1990, 50). That this was published the same year as *Gender Trouble* reflects a critical strain within feminist theory larger than what is usually narrowly attributed to Butler alone. Indeed, queer theory essentially exploded on the scene in 1990, impelled in large part by the AIDS epidemic and the community and activism that formed in response to the crisis. For example, the collective Bad-Object Choices were rethinking concepts like "desire, gaze, spectatorship, and representation" from a queer perspective, and organized a conference on queer film and video, "How Do I Look?" (1989), with keynotes presented by feminist film scholars Teresa de Lauretis and Judith Mayne. The following year, Richard Dyer published *Now You See It: Studies on Lesbian and Gay Film* (1990), the next year *Inside/Out: Lesbian Theories, Gay Theories* (Fuss 1991) brought together several chapters of film scholarship from writers such as D. A. Miller, Lee Edelman, Patricia White and Judith Mayne; by 1993, queer theory had solidified itself as a leading form of ideological criticism in film and media studies with Alexander Doty's *Making Things Perfectly Queer: Interpreting Mass Culture* and the edited volume, *Queer Looks: Perspectives on Lesbian and Gay Film and Video.* Queer theory emerged as a safe haven for scholars committed to the political use of theory while sectors of film studies grew increasingly unfriendly to them. Many of the next generations of feminist film scholars turned to queer theory to pursue questions that were once native to feminist film theory.[7]

One reason queer theory was particularly seductive was that it found its complement in a new film movement. The same year that *Gender Trouble* was published, several films were in production that would explode on the scene to form a movement: New Queer Cinema (NQC). Just like the films generated by the second wave that gave feminist concepts an aesthetic form, NQC translated political ideals into a common style, "Homo Pomo," as B. Ruby Rich identified it: "There are traces in all [the film and video] of appropriation and pastiche, irony, as well as reworking of history with social constructionism very much in mind [...] these works are irreverent, energetic, alternately minimalist and excessive. Above all, they are full of pleasure" (Rich 2004, 54). NQC shared with the feminist film movement an aesthetics infused with political urgency, even if the contexts were very different. The urgency of the AIDS crisis mobilized activists to turn to art to mobilize the movement. Groups like Gran Fury, a branch of ACT UP, utilized the immediate impact of graphics to translate political concepts, most famously the Silence=Death campaign, while Damned Interfering Video Activists (DIVA) TV documented the movement and used such documentation to deconstruct the mystification of the crisis in mainstream media.

Activist artists then turned to the more extensive medium of film and video armed with the tools forged in the fires of resistance politics. Tom Kalin, a cofounder of ACT UP, debuted his feature, *Swoon* (1992), an experimental narrative that revisits the story of Richard Loeb and Nathan Leopold, Jr., who had murdered a child and whose trial had made national headlines. Kalin's film exemplified NQC's spurning of positive images for a more radical interrogation of cinematic homosexual desire, in this case, returning to a story twice told on film, first in Alfred Hitchcock's *Rope* (1948) and then in *Compulsion* (1959). This film, and so many like it, is "queer" not because it is about homosexuals but rather because it queered (cinematic) representation and identity in form and content. Exemplifying the shorthand that queer is a *doing* rather than a *being*—a verb rather than a noun—NQC incarnated queer theory's "theoretical approach to rethinking human sexuality [...] [and] the social, cultural and historical factors that define and create the conditions for such orientations and behaviors" (Benshoff 2004). NQC films such as *Swoon*, Todd Haynes's *Poison* (1991), Gregg Araki's *The Living End* (1991) and Gus Van Sant's *My Own Private Idaho* (1991) explored and exploded the association of criminality with homosexuality traced back through mainstream cinema's killer queers, from decades of one-note bad guys to more ambivalent and complex representations, like *Silence of the Lambs* (Jonathan Demme, 1991) and *Cruising* (William Friedkin, 1980), but filtered through the cinematic legacy of New German Cinema, specifically Rainer Fassbinder, and the writings of Jean Genet and theoretical work of Michel Foucault and Guy Hocquenghem. Lesbians were not exempt from criminality, with women's refusal of heteropatriarchy finding release in illicit transgressions, exemplified in *Heavenly Creatures* (Peter Jackson, 1994), *Bound* (the Wachowskis, 1996) and *I Shot Andy Warhol* (Mary Harron, 1996) and the long history of lesbian vampire films preceding NQC. Indeed, the vast majority of these films are produced by Christine Vachon and her aptly named independent production company, Killer Films.

The feminist film movement emerging in the early 1970s shared a similar tenor of urgency with NQC—indeed, Rich was there to document that earlier movement, too: "Is there any way to convey the sense of risk and courage that accompanied those early screenings, back when scarcely any films by women had been seen, received, or apprehended as such?" (Rich 1998, 21). While there were vast differences between NQC and the feminist film movement of the seventies, there were also notable overlaps; both were committed to independent filmmaking and favored avant-garde or experimental filmmaking and the documentary form. Although separated by two decades, the movements shared a dedication to innovative filmmaking that eschewed positive images for a theoretically engaged praxis. One of the most influential films from the feminist movement is Chantal Akerman's *Jeanne Dielman, 23 Quai du Commerce, 1080 Brussels*, released the same year as Mulvey's "Visual Pleasure" and arguably as influential. Embodying Mulvey's call to refuse a visual pleasure premised on sadistic voyeurism, Akerman's three-hour *tour de force* is a restrained study of a widow going through her regimented daily routine, and its unraveling measured in nearly imperceptible changes from it, ending in an unexpected eruption of violence. The film star Delphine Seyrig, an outspoken leader in the feminist movement in her own right and a contributor to the movement, adapted Valerie Solanas's *SCUM Manifesto*; she was the leading actor in European feminist cinema, having worked with Ulrike Ottinger and Marguerite Duras as well as Akerman. She was also instrumental in founding a distribution company for women's films. Seyrig's Dielman is a nearly silent performance of a mother raising her son by having Johns come to her apartment for sex while her son is out. This is treated with the same respectful distance and care as the real-time scenes of her peeling potatoes. Akerman's distant, static camera and methodical pacing introduced a loving, noninvasive cinema that refused the spectator the comfort of identification with the main character.

Akerman's feminist counter-cinema was formally and narratively innovative in ways that emboldened feminist and queer filmmaking alike and provided a shared film language for the interrogation of sex, sexuality and gender. Indeed, these lines blur in films indebted to *Dielman*, such as Todd Haynes's women's films, most notably, *Safe* (1995) and the works of Thai director Apichatpong Weerasethakul. Just as Butler's book on "feminism and the subversion of identity" is identified with the advent of queer theory (without ever mentioning the word queer), the innovations of queer filmmaking are similarly indebted to feminist origins—both cinematic and theoretical. Queer filmmakers have been inspired by the formal inventiveness and narrative experimentation of individual filmmakers like Akerman, Sally Potter, Yvonne Rainer, Lizzie Borden, Carolee Schneeman and Mulvey herself (also a filmmaker), but possibly more significantly, lesbian, gay, bisexual, transgendered queer (LGBTQ) art activists have benefitted from the distribution and exhibition structures created out of the separatist agenda of radical feminism, including film festivals and independent production companies formed to promote the work of women. While today's feminist filmmakers are at home working in queer vernacular, exemplified by films like Dee Rees's *Pariah* (2011), about a teenage lesbian of color, and *Appropriate Behavior* (2014) by Iranian-American filmmaker Desiree Akhavan, some gay male directors have carried on the flame of (and a torch for) feminist filmmaking and the theory that inspired it.

Few films model queer-feminism better than *I Am Love* (*Io Sono l'amore,* Luca Guadagnino, 2009). Metonymic of the origins of second-wave feminism, and the remarkably influential film theory to which it gave rise, *I Am Love* centers on what director Guadagnino himself identifies in the DVD commentary as the "patriarchal roots of capitalism." Such an intellectually ambitious project is not surprising from the "analytical" director and his committedly feminist partner, Tilda Swinton, since Guadagnino has publicly bemoaned the loss of "film language," or, as he explains it, "the capacity of a film to interpret reality and create different visions of it for those watching—not simply showing people or emotions, but going further, creating a sort of social consciousness about an issue" (Zahm 2015). Notably, the social issues presented in *I Am Love* are ultimately inseparable from the feminist interpretation of reality it pursues and foregrounds—one indebted to the ways gender and sexuality studies revolutionized our understanding of film language and the feminist and queer filmmakers who both challenged its patriarchal and heteronormative syntax while crucially expanding its vocabulary. In *I Am Love*, these twinned and entwined epistemologies are embodied by Tilda Swinton, the androgynous Brechtian actor who has worked with feminist filmmakers like Lynn Hershman Leeson and Sally Potter, while coming to cinematic notoriety as the longtime muse of gay activist and avant-garde filmmaker, Derek Jarman, who died of AIDS. Guadagnino and Swinton collaborated for 11 years on *I Am Love*, producing a film that figures the critical trajectories of gender and sexuality in the history of film theory, specifically returning to the question of women's desire in a domestic melodrama about a bourgeois housewife cut from the filmic cloth of *Dielman*.

That *I Am Love* is named after a bit of dialog from *Philadelphia* (1993) is significant; certainly the fact that the latter film was the first mainstream film to address the suffering and the humanity of people with HIV is crucial to analyzing Luca Guadagnino's postmodern melodrama, with its openly gay director and its lead actor, Pippo Delbono, a renowned political activist whose own experience living with HIV has informed his performance art and theater for decades. *Philadelphia*, in that it represents queer affect, particularly grief and loss, is a compelling intertextual relay, one complicated and deepened by other citations, including several Hitchcock films, and especially those of Douglas Sirk—two particularly favored directors in feminist film criticism. Indeed, the plot of the film mirrors that of Sirk's *All That Heaven Allows* (1955), with its story of an older woman, Emma Recchi (Swinton) falling in love with a younger man associated with the fecundity of the earth. Yet, *I Am Love* is not a simple retread of a generic formula. Set in Milan as it is, the film evokes the history and theory of second-wave Italian feminism (famously associated with the Milan Women's Bookstore, whose leadership included Teresa de Lauretis). The Italian feminists insisted it was impossible to have a feminist movement in Italy that did not base itself on the analysis of women's work in the home and no genre better encapsulated this work, "The Work of Love," than the domestic melodrama. Notably, in her foundational book, *The Work of Love*, Giovanna Franca Dalla Costa references a famous melodrama of the 1950s; she states: "Under capitalism, love, far from being 'a many splendored thing,' is the heaviest of ideological mystifications imposed on a labor relation, namely housework, in order to force women into performing this work without getting paid" (Dalla Costa 2008, 43). Yet, what sheds light on this mystification in the film is not Emma's affair with her young lover; rather, what catalyzes her change from instrument of the "work of love" *qua* housewife to subject of love, to love itself (*I am Love*), is her daughter's queer resignification of love. It is not the introduction of her future lover, but rather her daughter's awakening desires that are the catalyst for change in the Recchi home. Emma, on an errand to pick up the drycleaning, discovers a card meant for her son from daughter Betta. On the front of the card, simply the printed word—in English—"LOVE." Inside are the details of Betta's love for another woman. The impact of Betta's "love" is underscored by the non-diegetic voice of Betta reading the words written on the card. In this, we experience the visual and aural excess of melodrama that aims at a consciousness-raising by proxy in the spectator, ultimately symbolized in Betta's direct address to the camera through an odd use of parallel editing, which intercuts Betta speaking the words of the card Emma is reading, breaking the fourth wall and speaking them directly to the spectator. Emma's transformation is wrought through the counterforce of queer desire. "Love," as it is (literally) envisioned in the film, is the expression of female desire outside the patriarchal family, which ultimately mobilizes Emma to abandon the imprisonment of the domestic sphere altogether. Through Betta, Emma (and the viewer) are offered a new queer-feminist social consciousness, "within a frame of reference no longer patriarchal or male-designed, but made up of perceptions, knowledge, attitudes, values and modes of relating historically expressed by women for women—creating a female genealogy or a female symbolic" (de Lauretis 1990, 6).

Coda

Today, feminist scholarship is often found "reclaiming the archive," which includes a return to feminist film criticism's earliest roots in research on women's filmmaking and its historical significance. But unlike, say, the late Claire Johnston's early work on Dorothy Arzner (1975), this new scholarship rarely takes the theoretical leap that characterized early feminist film scholarship. Without the frisson of theory, especially its urgency about changing the future even as it looks back, one cannot help but wonder if the fruits of political filmmaking from Akerman and Potter and to Haynes and Guadagnino would have ever been seeded, to begin with, and what cinema has been lost in the "waning of Theory." In other words, as more and more studies of women in the history of media industries, stardom and the like emerge, it is essential that we return to Johnston's central question—the question of film history itself:

> Why do feminist film critics place considerable emphasis on the role women have played, however marginal, in film history? […] Do feminist film critics simply want to introduce

> women into film history? Film historians have until very recently confined themselves to the accumulation of "facts" and the construction of chronologies […] The historicism and pseudo-objectivism of this approach leaves little room for theory of any kind. Indeed, it is commonly believed that the pursuit of theory must inevitably be at the expense of "facts." Merely to introduce women into the dominant notion of film history, as yet another series of "facts" […] would quite clearly be sterile and regressive […] Women and film can only become meaningful in terms of a theory. (Johnston 1975, 140)

While some of the strongest work in queer theory today foregrounds psychoanalytic theory—for instance, Lee Edelman's impactful polemic, *No Future: Queer Theory and the Death Drive* (2007) which provides brilliant readings (one might say, ideological interpretations) of Hitchcock's films (like the feminists before him: Mulvey, Wood and Modleski)—feminist film studies has been told such methods of inquiry, such desires, are unseemly, and that we would do well to return to the 'facts' of film history. Yet, as the feminist and queer cinema discussed here demonstrates, illicit transgressions and the resistance to (disciplinary) domestication are paradigmatic of radical politics and the social consciousness it creates. Put differently, what is needed now, as Doane succinctly sums up, is *more theory* to make feminism and film history meaningful once again.

Notes

1 For complete filmographies and related scholarship, see the Women Film Pioneers Project. https://wfpp.cdrs.columbia.edu/pioneers/.

2 See Geller, "The Personal Cinema of Maya Deren: *Meshes of the Afternoon* and Its Critical Reception in the History of the Avant-Garde."

3 Here are just some of the books and journal issues that not just include "Visual Pleasure and Narrative Cinema," but either begin with it or organize its chapters in response to it, or found their sections on "Feminist Film Theory" on it, in chronological order: *Women and the Cinema: A Critical Anthology* (1977); *Women & Film: Both Sides of the Camera* (1983); *Issues in Feminist Film Criticism* (1990); *The Sexual Subject: A Screen Reader in Sexuality* (1992); *Feminism and Film* (1997); *Feminist Film Theory: A Reader* (1999); *Feminism and Film* (2000); Special Issue of *Women's Studies Quarterly*—Looking Across the Lens: Women's Studies and Film (2002); *Feminist Film Theorists: Laura Mulvey, Kaja Silverman, Teresa de Lauretis, Barbara Creed* (2006); *Feminist Film Studies: Writing the Woman into Cinema* (2004). And even when "Visual Pleasure" is not the touchstone, other anthologies will nonetheless begin with her other writings—both *Reclaiming the Archive: Feminism and Film History* (2010) and *Feminisms in the Cinema* (1995) open with chapters authored by Mulvey.

4 See Cindy Patton, *Inventing AIDS* (New York: Routledge, 1990); Gayle Rubin, "Thinking Sex," in *The Lesbian and Gay Studies Reader*, ed. Henry Abelove (New York: Routledge, 1993); Paula Treichler, *How to Have Theory in an Epidemic: Cultural Chronicles of AIDS* (Durham: Duke University Press, 2006).

5 One might well note that despite many trained feminist film theorists writing on and arguing with Mulvey's thesis, the editors of *Post-Theory* imported a female philosopher with no background in psychoanalysis or film studies—despite their own proclamations about the import of an authentic film scholarship—to attack feminist film scholarship.

6 I discuss the import of this particular piece in "Is Film Theory Queer Theory? Or, Everything I Know About Queerness I Learned at the Movies."

7 For example, Geller, "Queering Hollywood's Tough Chick: The Subversions of Sex, Race, and Nation in *The Long Kiss Goodnight* and *The Matrix*."

Works Cited

Abel, Marco. 2006. "Own Your Lack!: New Lacanian Film Theory Encounters the Real in Contemporary Cinema: Lacan and Contemporary Film by Todd McGowan; Sheila Kunkle." *South Atlantic Review* 71, no. 1 (Winter): 132–40.

Abel, Richard. 2006. "Fan Discourse in the Heartland: The Early 1910s." *Film History: An International Journal* 18, no. 2: 140–53.

Bad Object-Choices, ed. 1989. *How Do I Look?: Queer Film and Video.* Seattle: Bay Press.

Becker, Edith, Michelle Citron, Julia Lesage and B. Ruby Rich. 1998. "Lesbians and Film." In *Out in Culture: Gay, Lesbian, and Queer Essays on Popular Culture*, edited by Corey K. Creekmur and Alexander Doty, 25–43. Durham, NC: Duke University Press.

Benshoff, Harry, and Sean Griffin, eds. 2004. *Queer Cinema: The Film Reader.* New York: Routledge.

Bordwell, David, and Noël Carrol, eds. 1996. *Post-Theory: Reconstructing Film Studies.* Madison: University of Wisconsin Press.

Butler, Judith. 1999. *Gender Trouble: Feminism and the Subversion of Identity.* New York: Routledge.

———. 2004. *Undoing Gender.* New York: Routledge.

Callahan, Vicki, ed. 2010. *Reclaiming the Archive: Feminism and Film History.* Detroit: Wayne State University Press.

Chaudhuri, Shohini. 2009. *Feminist Film Theorists: Laura Mulvey, Kaja Silverman, Teresa de Lauretis, Barbara Creed.* London: Routledge.

Copjec, Joan. 1990. "'Editorial' m/f no. 1." In *m/f: The Woman in Question*, edited by Parveen Adams and Elizabeth Cowie, 21–24. Cambridge, MA: MIT Press.

Creed, Barbara. 1993. *The Monstrous-Feminine: Film, Feminism, Psychoanalysis.* London: Routledge.

Dalla Costa, Giovanna Franca. 2008. *The Work of Love: The Role of Unpaid Housework as a Condition of Poverty and Violence at the Dawn of the 21st Century.* New York: Autonomedia, 43.

de Lauretis, Teresa. 1987. *Technologies of Gender: Essays on Theory, Film, and Fiction.* Bloomington: Indiana University Press.

———. 1990. *Sexual Difference: A Theory of Social Symbolic Practice.* Bloomington: University of Indiana Press.

———. 1991. "Queer Theory: Lesbian and Gay Sexualities – An Introduction." *Differences* 3, no. 2 (Summer): iii–xviii.

Doane, Mary Ann. 2004. "Aesthetics and Politics." *Signs: Journal of Women in Culture and Society* 30, no. 1: 1229–35.

Doty, Alexander. 1993. *Making Things Perfectly Queer: Interpreting Mass Culture.* Minneapolis: University of Minnesota Press.

Dyer, Richard. 1990. *Now You See It: Studies on Lesbian and Gay Film.* London: Routledge.

Edelman, Lee. 2007. *No Future: Queer Theory and the Death Drive.* Durham: Duke University Press.

Friedan, Betty. 1963. *The Feminine Mystique.* New York: W.W. Norton.

Fuss, Diana, ed. 1991. *Inside/Out: Lesbian Theories, Gay Theories.* New York: Routledge.

Gaines, Jane. 1993. *Classical Narrative Cinema: The Paradigm Wars.* Durham: Duke University Press.

Geller, Theresa L. 2004. "Queering Hollywood's Tough Chick: The Subversions of Sex, Race, and Nation in *The Long Kiss Goodnight* and *The Matrix.*" *Frontiers: A Journal of Women Studies* 25, no. 3: 8–34.

———. 2006. "The Personal Cinema of Maya Deren: Meshes of the Afternoon and Its Critical Reception in the History of the Avant-Garde." Edited by Linda Rugg. *Biography – Special issue: Self-Projection and Autobiography in Film* 28, no. 1 (Winter): 140–58.

———. 2013. "Is Film Theory Queer Theory? Or, Everything I Know About Queerness I Learned at the Movies." *Camera Obscura: Feminism, Culture, and Media Studies* 84 (December): 59–67.

Haskell, Molly. 1974. *From Reverence to Rape: The Treatment of Women in the Movies.* Chicago: University of Chicago Press.

Heath, Stephen. 1999. "Cinema and Psychoanalysis: Parallel Histories." In *Endless Night: Cinema and Psychoanalysis, Parallel Histories*, edited by Janet Bergstrom, 25–36. Berkeley: University of California Press.

Hopewell, Katherine. 2005. "The Leaven, Regarding the Lump." *Feminist Media Studies* 5, no. 2: 163–76.

Johnston, Claire. 1975. *The Work of Dorothy Arzner: Towards a Feminist Cinema.* London: British Film Institute.

Kaplan, E. Ann. 1983. *Women and Film: Both Sides of the Camera.* London: Methuen.

Martha, Gever, John Greyson and Pratibha Parmar, eds. 1993. *Queer Looks: Perspectives on Lesbian and Gay Film and Video.* New York: Routledge.

McCabe, Janet. 2004. *Feminist Film Studies: Writing the Woman into Cinema.* London: Wallflower.

McGowan, Todd, and Sheila Kunkle, eds. 2004. *Lacan and Contemporary Film.* New York: Other Press.

Metz, Christian. 1983. *Psychoanalysis and Cinema: The Imaginary Signifier.* New York: Palgrave.

Millett, Kate. 1970. *Sexual Politics.* New York: Avon Books.

Modleski, Tania. 2002. "On the Existence of Women: A Brief History of the Relations between Women's Studies and Film Studies." *Women's Studies Quarterly, Special Issue: Looking across the Lens: Women's Studies and Film* 30, no. 1/2: 15–24.

Mulvey, Laura. 1975. "Visual Pleasure and Narrative Cinema." *Screen* 16, no. 3: 6–18.

———. 2006. *Death 24x a Second: Stillness and the Moving Image.* London: Reaktion.

———. 2010. "Unmasking the Gaze: Feminist Film Theory, History, and Film Studies." In *Reclaiming the Archive: Feminism and Film History*, edited by Vicki Callahan, 17–31. Detroit: Wayne State University Press.

Mulvey, Laura, and Anna Backman Rogers, eds. 2015. *Feminisms: Diversity, Difference and Multiplicity in Contemporary Film Cultures.* Amsterdam: Amsterdam University Press.

Nichols, Bill. 1993. "Form Wars: The Political Unconscious of Formalist Theory." In *Classical Hollywood Narrative: The Paradigm Wars*, edited by Jane Gaines, 49–78. Durham: Duke University Press.

Parchesky, Jennifer. 1999. "Lois Weber's 'The Blot': Rewriting Melodrama, Reproducing the Middle Class." *Cinema Journal* 39, no. 1: 23–53.

Rich, B. Ruby. 1998. *Chick Flicks: Theories and Memories of the Feminist Film Movement.* Durham: Routledge.

———. 2004. "The New Queer Cinema." In *Queer Cinema: The Film Reader*, edited by Harry Benshoff and Sean Griffin, 53–60. New York: Routledge.

Rodowick, D. N. 2011. "An Elegy for Theory." In *Critical Visions in Film Theory: Classic and Contemporary Readings*, edited by Patricia White and Meta Mazaj Timothy Corrigan, 1109–26. Boston, MA: Bedford/St. Martin's Press.

Rose, Jacqueline. 1986. *Sexuality in the Field of Vision.* London: Verso.

Russo, Vito. 1981. *The Celluloid Closet: Homosexuality in the Movies.* New York: Harper & Row.

Sheldon, Caroline. 1977. "Lesbians and Film: Some Thoughts." In *Gays and Film*, edited by Richard Dyer. London: British Film Institute.

Straayer, Chris. 1990. "The Hypothetical Lesbian Heroine in Narrative Feature Film." *Jump Cut* 35: 50 57.

Whelehan, Imelda. 2005. *Modern Feminist Thought: From Second Wave to "Post-Feminism".* Edinburgh: Edinburgh University Press.

Williams, Linda. 1981. "Film Body: An Implantation of Perversions." *Cine-Tracts* 3, no. 4 (Winter): 19–35.

Wood, Robin. 1978. "Responsibilities of a Gay Film Critic." *Film Comment* 14, no. 1 (January–February): 12–17.

Zahm, Olivier. 2015. "Luca Guadagnino, an Interview." *Purple Magazine*, no. 24 (Fall/Winter).

Chapter Four

"COMPLICATED NEGOTIATIONS": RECEPTION AND AUDIENCE STUDIES INTO THE DIGITAL AGE

Brendan Kredell

Introduction

In reviewing the literature in reception and audience studies over the last few decades, one is struck by a common distinction drawn by authors surveying the state of the field before them. In short, this distinction is often distilled to two signifiers, film studies and cultural studies, themselves meant to stand in for complex ways of conceptualizing the relationship between the media text and the viewer. Will Brooker and Deborah Jermyn describe this as

> a journey in Film Studies, from the primacy of the "spectator" as a hypothetical subject position constructed by the filmic text, to an increasingly expansive recognition of the "audience," as actual, empirical viewers belonging to distinct socio-historical contexts. This gradual shift in focus owes much to the more traditionally ethnographic approach of Cultural Studies, which was steadily accusing a seminal body of work on "real" audiences and their relationships with media texts over the same period. (Brooker and Jermyn 2003, 127)

Here Brooker and Jermyn offer an account of the field framed in terms initially laid out by Miriam Hansen some fifteen years earlier; she described the relationship between the "textually-constructed spectator" and the "empirical moviegoer" as the distinction between the "hypothetical point of address of the film as a discourse," on the one hand, and the individual spectator, on the other (Hansen 1989).

Importantly, however, Hansen argued that we err in approaching these as discrete objects of study. Referring to the imagined spectator and the empirical moviegoer, she asserted that

> positing these terms as distinct, alternative levels of argument seems to me symptomatic of the development of film studies as a discipline, of the increasing division of labor between film theory and film history. Not only do we need to conceptualize spectatorship as a process that mediates between the two levels, as a historically constituted and variable matrix; we also

> need to complicate the issue with a third term—one that accounts for the social, collective, experiential dimension of cinematic reception. (Hansen 1989, 169)

While Hansen's intervention comes at a formative point in the evolution of reception studies within the broader field of cinema and media studies, its enduring importance lies in her insistence that studies of reception be at once historical and theoretical—that studies which reproduce a binary distinction between "film theory" and "film history" are ill-suited to address the "historically constituted and variable matrix" that is spectatorship. Herein, I seek to explore the practice of reception studies, guided by Hansen's productive and yet cautionary definition. Though the distinction may seem a semantic one to the reader, I am mindful of the difference between "reception theory" and "reception studies"—the latter, it seems to me, is much more keeping within the spirit of the kind of theoretically- and historically -informed research that Hansen calls for, and as we shall see, reception-oriented scholars have (with some notable exceptions) broadly embraced this call since the publication of Hansen's essay.

To begin, then, let us consider what precisely we are doing *when we do* reception studies. Are we trying to account for how individual spectators made sense of particular films? Are we trying to figure out the experience of a modal spectator, whoever that might be? Or is our concern more generally with groups of spectators—audiences—and how they responded to films? And what to make of the films themselves? Should we focus our attention on the process by which the film constructs a position for its viewer to occupy? Or, alternatively, might we relegate the actual films themselves to a secondary status, as in Richard Maltby's suggestive analogy: "the history of the American cinema is not the history of its products any more than the history of railroads is the history of locomotives" (Maltby 2007).

Herein lies the first important distinction that arises when we turn our attention to considering the relationship between film and its viewer. In simple terms, it would appear to be a problem of unit: whether the questions we ask concern the individual film spectator, or whether we are more interested in the way that those spectators form into larger groups—audiences—that respond collectively. Yet as Hansen reminds us, this is a false dichotomy; when viewing films, we are always at once individuals and members of a crowd. What is more, at the individual level, we need to distinguish between the theoretical spectator—what scholars have often referred to as the film's "subject"—and the historical viewer herself. Thus I begin surveying the field of reception studies to first consider each of these axes—the textually defined spectator, the individual moviegoer and the collective cinema audience—separately, with the ultimate goal of working toward the kind of synthetic model that Hansen advocates for.

Spectatorship Approaches

> The reader is a man without history, without biography, without psychology; he is only that someone who holds gathered into a single field all the paths of which the text is constituted.
>
> —Roland Barthes (Barthes and Heath 1977)

Beginning in the late 1960s, scholars began to develop theoretical frameworks for understanding the relationship between a film and its viewers, drawing significantly from existing literature in the fields of psychoanalysis, semiotics, feminist theory and structural Marxism. When authors refer to the "film studies" tradition, it is this body of literature to which they point. While more recent work has strayed from the path paved by these theorists, the legacy of this research is easily located in contemporary research. Work in this tradition often seeks to ask not only *what* but *how* films mean to viewers—what structures of meaning are individual viewers bound up within, to what extent do those structures shape or even determine the response of the viewer to film and what, if any, capacity does the individual viewer have to construct her own meaning from the film text?

Consider the famous phrase of Roland Barthes: "the birth of the reader must be at the cost of the death of the Author" (Barthes and Heath 1977, 148). By insisting upon the centrality of the reader—or the spectator—Barthes helped to usher in a sea change in thinking about the cinema. The death of the author is not only the birth of the reader but in some manner of speaking, so too is it the birth of reception studies. Of course, there are important precursors to consider: in literary theory, for instance, reader-response criticism has important roots in the early twentieth-century work of I. A. Richards and Louise Rosenblatt. But Barthes's essay is published at a moment when reader- (and viewer-) oriented approaches start to cohere. Wolfgang Iser and Hans-Robert Jauss (the founders of the Constance School) theorize a model of reading around the figure of the "implied reader," who exists within bounds defined for them by the work itself; this text-centric model would influence structuralist film theory in the years to come (Iser 1974).

Spectatorship theory emerged in the early 1970s, taking as its primary concern the process by which cinema addressed its viewer. Jean-Louis Baudry, a key figure in its development, described a model of the "basic cinematographic apparatus": a camera, a projector, a screen and a spectator (Baudry and Williams 1975). In this instance, the spectator is not a historical person, but rather a *position* within the structure of cinema. Baudry's apparatus theory began from the presumption of an "ideal spectator," the term used to define the viewer as the subject of the film's textual address. Broadly speaking, this work built upon foundations in psychoanalysis, semiotics and structural Marxism. While apparently in dialogue with contemporaries in literary theory such as Iser, Jauss and Stanley Fish, we can also trace the notion of the ideal spectator back to Plato's foundational allegory of the Cave.

In particular, a trio of French writers—Jacques Lacan, Roland Barthes and Louis Althusser—was especially influential on the development of spectatorship theory during the 1970s. Lacan's influence was largely based on his integration of Freudian psychoanalytic concepts with structural linguistics. His lectures on subjectivity and the unconscious became very influential within cinema studies, as scholars such as Christian Metz argued that the experience of the cinema offered an appeal to the unconscious, working to create the illusion of a unified subject position (Metz 1974, 1975). Barthes's work positioned the reader/viewer at the center of scholarly inquiry. His monograph *S/Z* (1970) proved immediately influential on the spectatorship approaches of the 1970s; the method of textual analysis that Barthes developed in that book offered a model for film scholars interested in the process by which a film "hailed" its viewer. From Althusser, theorists borrowed the notion that the cinema functioned as an "ideological apparatus," following from Althusser's influential extension of the classical Marxist concept of the "state apparatus" (Althusser 1971). He contended that the apparatuses of power that worked to communicate ideology and reproduce the dominance of the state were invisible to the individual. Althusserian film scholars argued that cinema worked to bind itself to the spectator and subliminally convince him that his[1] desires should be the aligned with the agenda of the state. From this, a theory of film spectatorship was born, one that is often associated with the journal *Screen*, in whose pages many of the key English-language essays by authors like Stephen Heath and Colin MacCabe were first published (Heath 1976; MacCabe 1985).

Spectatorship and Identity

While this approach was enormously influential in poststructuralist film theory, it also came under critique almost immediately from scholars who regarded the model as too passive and only able to account for a white, male, heteronormative spectator position. Laura Mulvey problematized the assumptions underpinning the emergent theory by considering the gendered nature of spectatorship (Mulvey 1975). She argued that Hollywood cinema constructed a binary between female characters, who exist to be looked at, and male viewers, who in her phrase serve as "bearers of the look." In her account, the male gaze is the fundamental structural principle of Hollywood filmmaking, such that it is embedded in the form and structure of cinema itself. Her response was to call for a radical break, championing avant-garde filmmaking that rejected "narrative pleasure" outright. Her goal, as she provocatively phrased it, was that by "analyzing pleasure or beauty [we] annihilate it."

Mulvey sparked considerable debate within the then-emergent field of feminist film criticism, such that we can trace the influence of her essay over the course of decades (Doane 1982; Modleski 1998; Sassatelli 2011). Of note here is that her intervention marks an important point at which identity intercedes in the debates around spectatorship. While Mulvey's argument is couched in the then-dominant terms of psychoanalytic film theory, her conclusion—that gender difference was a structuring force in Hollywood cinema—presages much of the research into spectatorship and reception that would follow. While the methodological approaches have not always been rooted in psychoanalysis, scholars following Mulvey have argued for the existence of a variety of discrete, identity-based spectator positions. A short—and necessarily incomplete—list of research in this tradition would include the works of Manthia Diawara and Jacqueline Stewart on Black spectatorship (Diawara 1999; Stewart 2003), bell hooks and Jacqueline Bobo on a specifically Black female spectatorship (Bobo 1995; hooks 1999), Michele Aaron on queer spectatorship (Aaron 2004), and Ella Shohat and Robert Stam on intersectionality (Shohat and Stam 2014), among many others.

Cognitive Approaches

In the decade after the introduction of spectatorship theory, some scholars began to turn instead to cognitive approaches to explain the relationship between film and audience. To apply a reception-based approach to theorists and theories discussed elsewhere in this collection, scholars such as David Bordwell, Noël Carroll and Edward Branigan generally shared with the spectatorship theorists the notion of an ideal spectator but disputed the notion that the spectator was a passive receiver of ideological communication. To the contrary, according to this view, the viewer is a goal-oriented film consumer, and different modes of cinema make different kinds of appeals to the explanatory schema she possesses. Like spectatorship theory, cognitive models are text-based and frequently presume an ideal spectator. The key point of departure is the theoretical assumptions used to model reception. Whereas early theories of spectatorship were grounded in psychoanalysis and semiotics, the cognitivists cohered around a loosely confederated research agenda that sought to foreground the cognitive process by which rational viewers made sense out of film texts. By design, this approach resisted the totalizing theoretical models advanced by the spectatorship theorists. Per Noël Carroll, cognitivism resists classification as a general theory and is better understood as a series of working theories, united by a shared interest in research in neurology and cognitive psychology about how the brain processes visual and aural information (Carroll 1996).

For at least some of the cognitivists, the appeal of this approach lies in its ability to ask and answer specific questions about the nature of reception. In later work, David Bordwell would take to calling this the "empirical-experiential" approach to cinema studies. Following from Carroll, he calls for research into questions that

> are neither simply items of fact nor vast philosophical teasers; they are rooted in empirical issues but have, inevitably, broader conceptual implications. Examining such middle-range problems amounts to what Noël Carroll calls "piecemeal theorizing," the focus on "small-scale, delimited questions." (Bordwell 2010, 12)

The Empirical Moviegoer: The Spectator as Ticket Buyer

While the debate over the spectatorial position in film theory ensued, film historians struck out on their own, developing alternative methodologies and channels of inquiry. What emerged was a fundamental divide over the concept of film viewers. For psychoanalytic and cognitive film theorists alike, the "spectator" was an imaginary construct of the film text, perhaps reflective of the lived experience of actual filmgoers but by no means grounded in the social and historical contingencies of an individual act of film watching. Historians, on the other hand, embraced the contingent: they began to mine the available information about film reception, including published reviews, advertisements, box office receipts and other archival materials, all in an effort to better understand and describe the ways in which historical filmgoers actually viewed film. In sum, they reversed the premise of Barthes's description of the reader: for them, the reader is a person *with* history, biography and psychology, and the goal was to develop a framework for understanding how history inflected the ways in which film audiences viewed the cinema.

Just as the pioneering spectatorship scholars produced theory that was criticized as being overly totalizing, similarly early reception scholars were susceptible to the opposite charge. Following the innovative work of Carlo Ginzburg in developing the idea of microhistory (Ginzburg 1980), film historians turned toward the study of the very specific details of cinema culture, often focusing on a particular city (or even a particular neighborhood or theater). Douglas Gomery and Robert C. Allen were two of the pioneers of exhibition microhistories (Allen and Gomery 1985). In their work (both individually and as collaborators), we find a keen attention to geographical detail; for example, both argue that much can be learned about the origins and evolution of the exhibition industry by paying careful mind to the siting of theaters and the urban contexts in which they existed. Yet for as insistent as they were about the historical contingencies of cinema, their microhistories were equally agnostic about the role of ideology and the textual operations of individual films; they set out to answer questions about cinema that were primarily social in origin. In sharp contrast to the prior ambitious efforts to develop unifying theories, film historians insisted that the specificity and contingency of their research precluded the possibility of grand narratives. Allen, for instance, cautioned that "easy generalizations serve to hide complex histories" and that "the extent to which these findings can be generalized […] is a moot question."

The fissure between text-centered theoretical approaches and context-centered historical approaches has been a source of frustration for a number of contemporary scholars. Richard Maltby writes that "the larger picture—the understanding of cinema's social agency in the twentieth century once promised by 1970s theories of ideology—continues to evade us" (Maltby 2007). His resolution is to propose a dichotomy between film histories and cinema histories; the former he distinguishes as those concerned primarily with "textual relations"—the relationship between the film and its viewer—while the latter is oriented away from the text and toward the cultural and social systems of meaning in which the film exists.

Audience Studies

Running parallel to this developing strand of inquiry in cinema studies is a tradition of audience-focused research located within the field of communications studies. This approach has typically taken as its premise that there are meaningful correlations between demographic distinctions and film consumption habits. To that end, researchers tend to focus on the third term of Hansen's description: the "social, collective, experiential dimension of cinematic reception." This frequently means that sociologically defined groups form the base unit of analysis: teen audiences, black women, college-educated viewers and so on.

The seminal audience research in communication studies predates the initial spectatorship debates in cinema studies; importantly, we see precursors not only in the scholarly literature but also in industry-funded research. As Eric Smoodin has shown, it was unclear in the formative years of cinema studies as to which direction the field was moving in (Lewis and Smoodin 2007). Key early works like the Payne Fund Studies of the late 1920s and early 1930s, George Gallup's audience research reports of the 1940s (Ohmer 2006) and Leo A. Handel's *Hollywood Looks at Its Audience* (Handel 1950) indicate the degree to which understanding audience preference was a business imperative for Hollywood studios and its would-be censors alike. With that said, a full accounting of the place of the audience in communication studies falls outside of the scope of this chapter. Interested readers would do well to consult one of the excellent histories of this research (Morley 1992; Webster 2014).

However, one particular strand of audience studies merits discussion, given its wide influence across media studies. Beginning in the 1960s, researchers at the University of Birmingham's Centre for Contemporary Cultural Studies (CCCS)—led first by Richard Hoggart and later by Stuart Hall—began to research cultural consumption and media. The agenda developed at CCCS—often referred to collectively as "The Birmingham School," or more generally as "British cultural studies"—represented a rejection of the idea of the consumer as a passive receiver of media messages. In this sense, it was a response to both Marxist critiques of the culture industry (Adorno 1975) as well as the psychoanalytically derived ideal spectatorship models described above. In Hall's landmark "Encoding/Decoding" essay, he proposed a model in which media producers retain a kind of agenda-setting power that enables them to construct cultural frameworks. However, he also argued for the possibility of active viewers who are able to "decode" their own meanings from the media they consume (Hall 1980).

This model would become the foundation of a robust research program carried out by the Birmingham School, one that would prove influential internationally via the work of scholars such as John Fiske, Ien Ang, David Morley and Charlotte Brunsdon, among others (Morley 1980; Brunsdon 1981; Ang 1985; Fiske 2011). The cultural studies approach remains influential in contemporary research into media audiences and has been influential within the field of reception studies. It should also be noted here that the development of the cultural studies approach also signaled something of a rupture—at least temporarily—between scholars of cinema and television. Much of the foundational work within cultural studies—including all of the seminal studies cited above—focused primarily on television audiences; given the importance that *Screen* theory scholars placed on the apparatus of the cinema itself, it is unsurprising that these two approaches would seem irreconcilable. More contemporary work in the field has attempted to mend the fences of medium-specificity and develop a unified understanding of media reception studies (Staiger 2005).

Toward a Synthesis: Reception Studies

As we can see, the intellectual precursors for reception studies can be traced back by decades. With that said, "reception studies," styled as such, is a relatively recent invention. Many of the books that helped to define the field—including key monographs by Janet Staiger, Miriam Hansen, Henry Jenkins, Judith Mayne and Jackie Stacey—were all first published in the early 1990s (Hansen 1991; Jenkins 1992; Staiger 1992; Mayne

1993; Stacey 1994). While it is impossible to reduce the diversity of this body of work to a simple, pithy conclusion, Janet Staiger offers us a useful way of conceiving of what reception studies is, what it is not—and in a broader sense, what the stakes of the intervention were for her and her cohort. "Reception studies is not textual interpretation," she writes. "Instead, it seeks to understand textual interpretations as they are produced historically." Put differently: "reception studies considers the process of producing interpretations rather than providing them" (Staiger 1992, 9). Along the same lines, Judith Mayne signals a break with a prior generation of film scholars; in her work, she proposes that we move beyond the seemingly intractable debates between, as she characterizes it, "subjects" (the interest of 1970s film theory) and "viewers" (the real people who attend cinemas). She describes the "complicated negotiations" between these two approaches as "the horizon of film spectatorship" (Mayne 1993, 9), echoing Hansen's earlier call that reception-oriented scholars attend both to the textually constituted subject and the historically specific viewer.

By refocusing critical attention away from grand questions of agency and cognition and by rooting itself in the historical particularities of lived experience, reception-oriented scholarship potentially offers us a pathway by which to navigate between the Scylla and Charybdis of Hansen's definition, wary of the ahistorical tendencies of idealizing the spectator while equally cautious of the descent into infinite particularity that Gomery and Allen observe when they caution that the very notion of an "audience" is, "in any sociological or historical sense [...] really only an abstraction generated by the researcher, since the unstructured group that we refer to as the movie audience is constantly being constituted, dissolved, and reconstituted with each film-going experience" (Allen and Gomery 1985, 156).

Reception Studies into the Digital Age

Janet Staiger once wrote, "the job of a reception historian is to account for events of interpretation and affective experience" (Staiger 2000a, 1). Bearing this in mind, the onset of the digital era of cinema unsettles both the theoretical construct of the spectator and the methodological frameworks used to study film viewers historically. Reception-oriented scholars confront an archival and epistemological problem when researching media texts: the nature of reception studies is that we are seeking traces, documents of experience that are inherently ephemeral. Even when we can hold up tangible artifacts of reception—a film review, for instance, or reports about box office gross—it is a struggle to say with certainty how accurately the moments of reception that we can document correspond with the various "events of interpretation" surrounding that particular media text. Much of the methodological innovation in reception studies is borne from this tension: left only with the traces of cinemagoing, how can we best reconstruct the "affective experience" such that we can speak meaningfully about the ways in which audiences engaged with a given film?

Approaches to answering this question are both methodologically and theoretically diverse, but we can recognize certain recurring moves made by reception-oriented scholars. Consider, as an example, a reading that Staiger offers of *Ferris Bueller's Day Off* in her essay "The Places of Empirical Subjects in the Event of Mass Culture" (Staiger 2000b). Her aim is stated plainly at the outset of the essay:

> How can we use a film such as *Ferris Bueller's Day Off* to consider and reconsider Louis Althusser's theories of ideology, aesthetics, institutions such as schools and family, and mass culture? (Staiger 2000b, 115)

I use this example because it aptly illustrates a negotiation of the tensions that Hansen observed at the outset of this essay. Staiger clearly positions her argument within an existing theoretical framework. Responding to an earlier reading of the same film by Chip Rhodes (Rhodes 1994), Staiger identifies a tension between the individual and the subject in Althusserian theory and uses it to offer a reading of *Bueller* that investigates how "identities mobilized [...] in the interaction with this mass culture text matter for considering any interpretation of the ideological effects" of the film (Staiger 2000b, 121).

However, as the title of the essay indicates, the method by which Staiger does so is very much rooted in the individual experience of specific moviegoers. Performing such an analysis requires consideration of the material traces of film reception, but as Staiger notes, this proves particularly problematic when the questions we seek to answer involve marginalized people or groups whose voices are historically excluded from discourse about mass culture.

> The words of peoples without dominant voices are seldom recorded permanently for the researcher to locate later [...] What the researcher must often do is resort to very contaminated evidence or convoluted and speculative analysis. (Staiger 2000b, 118)

Her analysis of *Bueller* relies on such "contaminated evidence": 13 reviews of the film published in the popular press at the historical moment of its release. This turn to discourse analysis is common among reception-oriented scholars; faced with an overwhelming absence of the material traces of spectatorship, scholars often resort to those accounts which do survive—often in the form of print reviews in newspapers and magazines—in order to infer something about the way that the film was received by audiences upon its release.

Some scholars have used this approach to define a filmgoing public more narrowly; one vein of research has explored the reception of Hollywood and "race" films in the African American press, for instance (Tracy 2001). But, as Staiger observes, the constraints of the archive—our ability to access the traces of film reception—ultimately constrain the kinds of questions that we can ask as researchers. With that in mind, it is incumbent upon reception-oriented scholars of the twenty-first century to take advantage of the fact that more data about the act of viewing are available for the researcher than ever before. Indeed, scholars examining the contemporary media environment face the opposite challenge posed to those who investigate reception in earlier eras: the surplus of information available forces the researcher to make decisions about assigning value. Rather than confronting questions of contaminated evidence, we instead must consider how the assumptions we make in weighing one kind of evidence over another affect the conclusions that we reach in our analyses.

On the one hand, we see scholars make a clean break from the interpretative debates that consumed early spectatorship studies. By approaching reception as an empirical question rather than a philosophical or psychological one, it becomes possible to take advantage of the same technologies that make data abundant in enabling new techniques of analysis and modes of argumentation. Deb Verhoeven has described this as the "computational turn" (Verhoeven 2012) in media studies; her Kinomatics project (see http://kinomatics.com/)—a collaborative research endeavor with scholars in economics, geography and data analysis—points the way toward one potential future for reception studies in the digital era. Verhoeven and her colleagues have approached the question from the macro level, building a global database of theatrical show times and box office data and using the tools and methods associated with big data analysis to identify patterns and flows within those datasets.

As this example illustrates, at the wide end of the lens, we can see reception studies entering into productive interdisciplinary inquiry with fields such as cultural geography and economics. Unsurprisingly, then, the same impulse to interdisciplinarity is evident when zoomed in: at the micro level, we can see the continued influence of ethnographic methods in reception studies and the embrace of methodological innovations associated with the digital humanities. Here, rather than forgo questions of meaning-making, new research methods allow the reception scholar unprecedented access to what Staiger called the "process of producing interpretations." Matthew Hughey's work on the "white savior film" (Hughey 2014) represents one example of the sociological influence in reception studies; through critical analysis of nearly three thousand film reviews and a series of focus groups and interviews, Hughey traces the construction of "color blindness" in popular American cinema.

The current flurry of methodological innovation results in large part from the underlying confluence of the two fields of media anthropology (Rothenbuhler and Coman 2005) and digital ethnography. Media anthropologists and ethnographers have developed innovative approaches for studying audiences (Mankekar 1999; Larkin 2008), while separately, a tradition of digital ethnography grew up alongside the internet and locating its roots in science, technology and society studies (Murthy 2008; boyd 2014). As recently as the early 2000s, it was possible to speak of media separately from digital culture, but reception studies—or at least media ethnographies—now must begin from a synthetic approach (Gómez Cruz and Ardèvol 2013).

For example, the rise of blogs and social media platforms mean that we must adapt our methods of data collection and analysis to the torrent of information about reception now available to contemporary scholars. We are now able to track conversations about how actual film viewers are responding to films, rather than having to rely on critical reviews, box office receipts, or other proxy measurements. Only gradually are scholars beginning to exploit the possibilities afforded by these new sources of information about film reception, but the potential is clear. Industry lore has it that early television executives would make decisions about national programming by speculating about how a given show would "play in Peoria"; now scholars can answer that question. By taking advantage of geocoded social media posts, it becomes possible to track the discourse among all viewers in a specific geography. Indeed, such an approach could be used to construct reception studies that investigate how viewers at individual cinemas on opposite sides of the town responded differently to the same film.

Of course, these approaches need not be mutually exclusive; as the reception archive expands seemingly infinitely and in all directions, the challenge for scholars is to think about how existing modes of scholarship—articles, monographs, and so on—and existing modes of presentation for digital research—data journalism, interactives, and so on—can productively co-exist. For some, this means working collaboratively in order to produce studies at a staggering scale: witness Ernest Mathijs and Martin Barker's "World *Hobbit* Project," which studied the reception of Peter Jackson's trilogy of films by means of surveying 36,000 respondents in 34 languages (Barker and Mathijs 2016).

My own work employs digital tools and methods to focus on much more narrowly defined communities and geographies. In earlier work, I have shown how the growth of the American art-house cinema during the 1990s and 2000s closely tracked with urban gentrification during the same time period (Kredell 2011). To do so, I built exhibition maps of art-house sites in American cities during that era and then compared those maps to census tract-level data as to which areas of cities were gentrifying, and when. More recently, I have explored using the techniques of data-scraping and geographic information system (GIS) analysis to reconstruct maps of video rental preference at the neighborhood level throughout a metropolitan area (Kredell 2016). By overlaying these maps with community-level data, it is now possible for researchers to develop a more robust portrait of the moviegoing audience than ever before.

At the same time, and developing out of the tradition of reception studies, scholars aligned with fan studies have demonstrated the instability of the seemingly static categories of "producer" and "consumer." Following from Henry Jenkins's seminal notion of "textual poaching" (Jenkins 1992), fan studies researchers have expanded the frame of reception studies to consider how the act of consumption can itself be productive, and an important avenue for understanding how identity and community are formed through media (Gray, Sandvoss and Harrington 2007). Indeed, judging by the extent to which fan textual production—as the title of an influential journal within the field puts it, "Transformative Works and Cultures"[2]—has become a central focus of fan studies research, it may be fair to say that reception studies and fan studies have diverged from a common path, or at the very least that the latter has matured as a subfield in its own right.

In sum, I would suggest that the challenge confronting reception-oriented scholars moving forward is in developing methodological frameworks that allow us to best utilize the explosion of digital traces of reception now available to us, while at the same time keeping our approaches grounded in a firm theoretical understanding of the relationship between media text and viewer. Examples such as those I have offered above illustrate how the boundaries between film theory and social science research are blurring in an era of abundant data. Given this abundance, it is tempting to follow the trail of evidence further and further into the realm of the historically specific. Now more than ever, it is important to remember Hansen's rejection of the spectator/viewer binary that I have used to frame this essay. While it is possible to reconstruct the act of viewing with a degree of precision unavailable to prior generations of scholars, the fundamental tension between imaginary subject and empirical viewer remains as important to reception studies today as it did before the rise of the Internet. Reception-oriented scholars can and should avail themselves of new approaches to working with data as they seek to, in Staiger's terms, "understand textual interpretations as they are produced historically." Yet, we should not mistake the greater clarity with which we can apprehend the act of reception for the development of a new kind of media spectator with agency unencumbered by the textual constraints and frameworks of her forebears. Judith Mayne described the work of reception studies as understanding the "complex negotiations" between text and viewer; while the terms of those negotiations may have shifted somewhat since she wrote those words, the fundamental concept remains the same.

Notes

1 The use of masculine-gendered pronouns here is intentional, as scholars in this early period frequently discussed spectatorship by invoking explicitly masculine terminology: the castration complex, the Oedipal complex, etc. The critiques offered by Laura Mulvey and a subsequent generation of feminist film theorists, described at greater length below, were developed in large part in response to this masculine-centric perspective.

2 http://journal.transformativeworks.org/.

Works Cited

Aaron, Michele. 2004. *New Queer Cinema: A Critical Reader.* New Brunswick, NJ: Rutgers University Press.

Adorno, Theodor. 1975. "Culture Industry Reconsidered." *New German Critique* 6: 12–19.

Allen, Robert C., and Douglas Gomery. 1985. *Film History: Theory and Practice.* New York: Alfred A. Knopf.

Althusser, Louis. 1971. "Ideology and Ideological State Apparatuses (Notes towards an Investigation)." In *Lenin and Philosophy and Other Essays*, 127–86. New York: Monthly Review Books.

Ang, Ien. 1985. *Watching Dallas: Soap Opera and the Melodramatic Imagination.* London: Methuen.

Barker, Martin, and Ernest Mathijs. 2016. "Introduction: The World Hobbit Project." *Participations: Journal of Audience & Reception Studies* 13, no. 2: 158–74.

Barthes, Roland, and Stephen Heath. 1977. "The Death of the Author." *Image, Music, Text.* New York: Hill & Wang, 142–48.

Baudry, Jean-Louis, and Alan Williams. 1975. "Ideological Effects of the Basic Cinematographic Apparatus." *Film Quarterly* 28, no. 2: 39–47.

Bobo, Jacqueline. 1995. *Black Women as Cultural Readers, Film and Culture Series.* New York: Columbia University Press.

Bordwell, David. 2010. "The Part-Time Cognitivist: A View from Film Studies." *Projections* 4, no. 2: 1–18. doi:10.3167/proj.2010.040202.

Boyd, Danah. 2014. *It's Complicated: The Social Lives of Networked Teens.* New Haven, CT: Yale University Press.

Brooker, Will, and Deborah Jermyn. 2003. *The Audience Studies Reader.* London: Routledge.

Brunsdon, Charlotte. 1981. "'Crossroads' Notes on Soap Opera." *Screen* 22, no. 4: 32–37.

Carroll, Noël. 1996. *Theorizing the Moving Image.* Cambridge: Cambridge University Press.

Diawara, Manthia. 1999. "Black Spectatorship: Problems of Identification and Resistance." In *Film Theory and Criticism*, edited by Leo Braudy and Marshall Cohen, 845–54. Oxford: Oxford University Press.

Doane, Mary Anne. 1982. "Film and the Masquerade: Theorising the Female Spectator." *Screen* 23, no. 3–4: 74–87.

Fiske, John. 2011. *Television Culture*. 2nd ed. London: Routledge.

Ginzburg, Carlo. 1980. *The Cheese and the Worms: The Cosmos of a Sixteenth-Century Miller*. Baltimore: Johns Hopkins University Press.

Gómez Cruz, Edgar, and Elisenda Ardèvol. 2013. "Ethnography and the Field in Media(ted) Studies: A Practice Theory Approach." *Westminster Papers in Communication and Culture* 9, no. 3: 27–46.

Gray, Jonathan, Cornel Sandvoss and C. Lee Harrington. 2007. *Fandom: Identities and Communities in a Mediated World*. New York: New York University Press.

Hall, Stuart. 1980. "Encoding/Decoding." *Culture, Media, Language*. London: Routledge, 128–38.

Handel, Leo A. 1950. *Hollywood Looks at Its Audience; A Report of Film Audience Research*. Urbana: University of Illinois Press.

Hansen, Miriam. 1989. "Untitled." *Camera Obscura* 7, no. 2–3: 169–74.

———. 1991. *Babel and Babylon: Spectatorship in American Silent Film*. Cambridge, MA: Harvard University Press.

Heath, Stephen. 1976. "Narrative Space." *Screen* 17, no. 3: 68–112.

Hooks, Bell. 1999. "The Oppositional Gaze: Black Female Spectators." In *Feminist Film Theory: A Reader*, edited by Sue Thornham. New York: NYU Press.

Hughey, Matthew W. 2014. *The White Savior Film: Content, Critics, and Consumption*. Philadelphia, PA: Temple University Press.

Iser, Wolfgang. 1974. *The Implied Reader: Patterns of Communication in Prose Fiction from Bunyan to Beckett*. Baltimore: Johns Hopkins University Press.

Jenkins, Henry. 1992. *Textual Poachers: Television Fans & Participatory Culture, Studies in Culture and Communication*. New York: Routledge.

Kredell, Brendan. 2011. "Redeveloping the City, Redeveloping the Cinema: Film and Urban Culture at the Turn of the Twenty-First Century." PhD diss., Screen Cultures Program, Northwestern University.

———. 2016. "The Geography of Taste: A Study of Netflix Rental Patterns." European Network of Cinema and Media Studies Conference, Potsdam, Germany, July 29.

Larkin, Brian. 2008. *Signal and Noise: Media, Infrastructure, and Urban Culture in Nigeria*. Durham: Duke University Press.

Lewis, Jon, and Eric Loren Smoodin. 2007. *Looking Past the Screen: Case Studies in American Film History and Method*. Durham: Duke University Press.

MacCabe, Colin. 1985. *Theoretical Essays: Film, Linguistics, Literature*. Manchester, UK: Manchester University Press.

Maltby, Richard. 2007. "How Can Cinema History Matter More?" *Screening the Past* 22.

Mankekar, Purnima. 1999. *Screening Culture, Viewing Politics: An Ethnography of Television, Womanhood, and Nation in Postcolonial India*. Durham, NC: Duke University Press.

Mayne, Judith. 1993. *Cinema and Spectatorship*. London: Routledge.

Metz, Christian. 1974. *Film Language; A Semiotics of the Cinema*. New York: Oxford University Press.

Metz, Christian. 1975. "The Imaginary Signifier." *Screen* 16, no. 2: 14–76.

Modleski, Tania. 1998. *The Women Who Knew Too Much; Hitchcock and Feminist Theory*. London: Routledge.

Morley, David. 1980. *The Nationwide Audience: Structure and Decoding*. UK: British Film Institute.

———. 1992. *Television, Audiences, and Cultural Studies*. London: Routledge.

Mulvey, Laura. 1975. "Visual Pleasure and Narrative Cinema." *Screen* 16, no. 3: 6–18.

Murthy, Dhiraj. 2008. "Digital Ethnography: An Examination of the Use of New Technologies for Social Research." *Sociology* 42, no. 5: 837–55.

Ohmer, Susan. 2006. *George Gallup in Hollywood*. New York: Columbia University Press.

Rhodes, Chip. 1994. "Ideology Takes a Day Off: Althusser and Mass Culture." *Studies in 20th Century Literature* 18, no. 1: 39–54.

Rothenbuhler, Eric W., and Mihai Coman. 2005. *Media Anthropology*. Thousand Oaks, CA: Sage.

Sassatelli, Roberta. 2011. "Interview with Laura Mulvey: Gender, Gaze, and Technology in Film Culture." *Theory, Culture & Society* 28, no. 5: 123–43.

Shohat, Ella, and Robert Stam. 2014. *Unthinking Eurocentrism: Multiculturalism and the Media*. 2nd ed., *Sightlines*. London, New York: Routledge, Taylor & Francis Group.

Stacey, Jackie. 1994. *Star-Gazing: Hollywood Cinema and Female Spectatorship*. New York: Routledge.

Staiger, Janet. 1992. *Interpreting Films: Studies in the Historical Reception of American Cinema*. Princeton, NJ: Princeton University Press.

———. 2000a. *Perverse Spectators: The Practices of Film Reception*. New York: New York University Press.

———. 2000b. "The Places of Empirical Subjects in the Event of Mass Culture: Jeannie Bueller and Ideology." In *Perverse Spectators: The Practices of Film Reception*, 115–24. New York: NYU Press.

———. 2005. *Media Reception Studies*. New York: New York University Press.

Stewart, Jacqueline. 2003. "Negroes Laughing at Themselves? Black Spectatorship and the Performance of Urban Modernity." *Critical Inquiry* 29, no. 4: 650–77.

Tracy, James F. 2001. "Revisiting a Polysemic Text: The African American Press's Reception of Gone With the Wind." *Mass Communication and Society* 4, no. 4: 419–36. doi:10.1207/S15327825MCS0404_6.

Verhoeven, Deb. 2012. "New Cinema History and the Computational Turn." World Congress of Communication and the Arts Conference, University of Minho, Portugal.

Webster, James G. 2014. *The Marketplace of Attention: How Audiences Take Shape in a Digital Age*. Cambridge, MA: MIT Press.

Chapter Five

WORLD CINEMA AND ITS WORLDS

James Tweedie

In a 2001 essay introducing the already vast literature on globalization, Mauro Guillén asks, tongue partially in cheek, "Is Globalization Civilizing, Destructive or Feeble?" Guillén presents globalization as a problem rather than a stable and coherent field, as a paradox best approached indirectly, through the wide range of responses that it generates. How, he asks, can the process of global integration in the economic and cultural spheres be perceived simultaneously as a powerful force of modernization, a step toward an Americanized world, a mortal threat to existing ways of life and a mere rhetorical flourish or vacuous academic trend with few real-world consequences? How can globalization be viewed as the pathway to "boundless prosperity and consumer joy" (135), a formula for homogenization and inequality, and nothing at all?

Instead of accounting for the inherent contradictions in the literature on globalization, most scholars have focused on a particular subset of the field, managing those incongruities by excluding them from their frame of analysis and leaving the outliers for another discipline. In the intervening years, the contradictions have only multiplied, with an intensified version of technological utopianism and corresponding resistance movements now assuming a more prominent role in the cultural politics of globalization.

The primary problem with studies of world cinema or global media is not the images or industries in the foreground of that scholarship but, rather, the acceptance of a commonplace but unsustainable definition of the "world." To consider the range of problems that fall under the rubric of globalization, we have to first address the foundational question formulated recently by Pheng Cheah, "What is a world?"[1] A slight alteration of the perspective or analytical frame can distort that object beyond recognition, especially when the focus changes from the abstractions of mathematized financial markets or utopian internationalism to the concrete reality of skyscrapers, factory labor and environmental devastation. As John Urry argues, "The emergent global order is one of constant disorder and disequilibrium," and its effects are "non-linear, large-scale, unpredictable and partially ungovernable" (2000, 208). Any study that engages with a phenomenon on the scale of the world immediately encounters what Horst Rittel and Melvin Webber call "wicked problems," with no definitive framework, no clear stopping points, an inexhaustible number of possible solutions and questions that yield only additional questions rather than the desired answers.[2]

In this essay, I will argue that the study of globalization and cinema is riddled with the same contradictions as other academic disciplines and that a survey of that subfield reveals an equally complex array of irreconcilable responses ranging from celebrations of the global impact of Hollywood cinema to dire predictions about the development of a global monoculture to heartening accounts of resistance and revival in film industries around the world. While this essay will sketch just a brief introduction to that expansive and burgeoning field, it will highlight the unique perspective on the process of globalization offered by the study of film and media. Debates about globalization have reactivated perennial divisions in the field. Is film studies concerned with the history and economics of media industries or the images on the screen, with political economy or aesthetics? Does an initial choice of paradigms and methodology necessarily exclude the others? Underlying these debates are distinctions between cinema as an image and films as physical objects, intellectual property or commercial goods produced and consumed under particular material conditions. What I hope to show below is that the fundamental instability of its subject makes cinema and media studies a privileged vantage point on the contemporary world system.[3] The field has been organized around the conflicts that continue to define and constrain the study of globalization, even if the emergence of moving pictures long predates the popularization of that keyword and critics have deployed the slightly different rhetoric of their times. Cinema and media studies has always straddled the line between conceptual opposites because it contemplates a subject that has always been both global and local, and both art and commerce. The field has for a century transformed philosophers, literary and art critics, historians and sociologists into *compagnons de route* who confront different facets of the ontological question posed most famously by André Bazin, "What is Cinema?"[4]

Film and media studies scholars have also engaged with both optimistic claims about the positive effects of world cinema, most of them emanating from Hollywood, and denunciations of a destructive or feeble cinema that usually amounts to wholesale dismissals of popular culture as either an irresistible force or a parade of passing fads. As they constantly reframe their own object of study and focus alternately on aesthetics or industries or identity, scholars have adapted to their multifaceted field by experimenting with the type of methodological pluralism that remains one of the most important intellectual legacies of cinema and media studies and that has only recently begun to reorient the study of globalization away from its primary focus on politics and economics. Like the images that appear on silver screens and televisions in every country, like the stars who have become icons worshipped around the world, like the film industry that from the beginning has stretched across geopolitical borders, cinema and media studies has always been a global phenomenon. Rather than describe something new about the state of the contemporary film and media industries, the academic and popular interest in globalization has allowed the field to rediscover a global history that extends back to the late nineteenth century and continues into—and beyond—our contemporary moment.

Always Global

A discussion about the links between globalization and cinema may seem almost redundant because the production, distribution and exhibition of films have been global enterprises from the beginning. Just seven months after their first public screening in Paris at the end of 1895, the Lumière brothers unveiled their Cinématographe to audiences in New York and the *Times* was describing it as "The Sensation of Europe—Exhibited before all the crowned Heads and hailed universally as the Greatest Marvel of the 19th Century" (Puttnam 2000, 19–20). By the end of the nineteenth century, the Lumière company was sending filmmakers like Alexandre Promio abroad to demonstrate the new invention and record actualities, adding those early "foreign films" to a catalog of images captured more conveniently in France. As Tom Gunning suggests, "early cinema" was already a "global cinema" marked by the "encyclopedic" ambitions of pioneering figures, from the Lumière brothers to the cinematic collector Albert Kahn and his Archives de la Planète.[5] Cinema, Gunning writes, offered a "new consciousness of the global" (2016, 13) made accessible through these roving camera crews and filtered through modern technology. These films appeared in small theaters like Nickelodeons or, as in the case of an early global hit like *A Trip to the Moon* (*Le Voyage dans la lune*, 1902) by Georges Méliès, they played at the World's Fairs, amusements parks and fairgrounds that were becoming an alternative exhibition space where that emerging global consciousness could be cultivated (Solomon 2011, 17).

According to the most enthusiastic critics like Vachel Lindsay, cinema's highest ambition was to become nothing less than a form of "hieroglyphics" (1916, 171) that could communicate across all existing language barriers. In the first three decades of its existence, the celebration of cinema's potential as a visual "Esperanto," and a "universal language" exceeded even our grandest contemporary aspirations to the merely global.[6] With the benefit of hindsight and during an era less inclined to believe in universality, Miriam Hansen (and the many colleagues and students inspired by her work) characterized cinema as the "first global vernacular" (1999, 68), with equal attention to both the transnational quality of cinematic modernity, its capacity to travel across borders and appeal to audiences around the world, and the vernacular forms it assumed in each location. In its first decades, Hansen suggested, cinema was already staging negotiations between the global and the local that would eventually become a staple of the academic discourse on economic and political globalization.

At the same time, however, this aspiration to the exalted condition of a universal or global mode of communication could only be realized through the expansion of national film industries across existing borders and territories. As Gunning argues, cinema "followed global pathways opened up by worldwide capitalism, colonialism, and imperialism" (11), and universalism often served as a shield for more aggressive economic and political ambitions. Combining the language of warfare ubiquitous at the time with the more mundane realm of business strategy, Ian Jarvie describes Hollywood's activity in the North Atlantic between 1920 and 1950 as nothing less than an "overseas campaign" designed to realize an overarching "grand strategy" (1992, 9) and assert American influence in Europe. He points out that this close connection to imperialism and fear of domination made "motion pictures [...] an early focus of the arguments about whether free trade in popular culture was a Good Thing or a Bad Thing" (1). Victoria de Grazia highlights the intimate connection between American geopolitical ambitions and the economic fortunes of corporations in what she calls a "market Empire," "a great imperium with the outlook of a great emporium" (2005, 3). Cinema was the perfect device to export this "irresistible empire" around the world, and "no American industry was more self-consciously rivalrous about its role in shaping international cultural trends, none more engaged in reaching out, responding to, and shaping consumer tastes abroad, none more aggressive in taking on the barriers and obstacles to its installation in other societies" (288). But film was also the most "disruptive" industry because it "presented itself at one and the same time as commodity and cultural artifact, it overrode national boundaries, eluded political controls, infiltrated local community, insinuated itself into private lives, and was suspected of penetrating the unconscious" (288). Because it provides an ideal mechanism for a technologically enhanced form of cultural imperialism, cinema has long been a flashpoint for critics hoping to counteract this seemingly irresistible force and protect national boundaries, local community and the other casualties of an empire built on both traditional forms of power and the appeal of images.

Cinema occupied an equally important position in cultural politics during the post–World War Two era when culture acquired enormous significance as a key weapon in the Cold War's ideological competition. As Walter Wanger wrote in 1950, the economic incentives of the American studios were virtually indistinguishable from the political, diplomatic and economic goals of the US government. He argued that the studios "have done a great service in not only selling America but also American products. As long as 25 years ago, merchants in Europe began to protest to their respective governments against the influence of Hollywood films on their businesses. Many studies have established the fact that audiences which see American housing, clothes, furniture, automobiles and radios show an understandable preference for American products" (446). The American film industry was one of the most cosmopolitan institutions in the world, he argued, with talent drawn from around the globe, and the studios assembled an unprecedented information-gathering network that exceeded the capabilities of the government itself. For this reason, he concluded, "Hollywood will be recognized as the logical capital of the Marshall Plan for ideas—Hollywood, with its array of statesmen and humanitarians like Walt Disney, John Ford, Ethel Barrymore, Bob Hope, Darryl Zanuck, Al Capp, Irving Berlin and Milton Caniff-Donald Duck as World Diplomat!" (452). The "Good Neighbor Policy" of the 1930s and 1940s also conscripted Hollywood into the service of international diplomacy, this time with calls for a "harmonious political, economic, cultural and emotional hemispheric union" with Latin America (Pérez-Melgosa 6), though most critics now view the products of that era as "charming and unselfconscious vehicles for U.S. cultural imperialism" (91). Postcolonial theory looks back at the hybrid corporate and diplomatic initiatives of mid-century through, in Benedict Anderson's famous image, the other end of a telescope (Anderson 2), and it views these light-hearted musicals, cartoons and other popular fare as yet another exercise of political and economic power.

Hollywood was not only an advertisement for the American consumer lifestyle then being exported around the world but was also a laboratory for various arguments celebrating the material and intangible benefits that would supposedly follow in the wake of global trade. The trade groups established by the major American studios, beginning with the MPPDA and now the MPAA, have been effective advocates for an idealized world united through its fascination with Hollywood movies and for policies that would make that economic and cultural dream a reality on the ground. "We operate a small State Department," said Jack Valenti in 1985, again underscoring the intimate relationship between mass culture and politics, between the emporium and the imperium. At a time of burgeoning trade deficits in the United States and Cold War soft diplomacy, he characterized the motion picture industry as "America's secret weapon—the supreme visual force in the world, dominating screens in theaters and in living rooms."[7] Among the principal themes sounded by the MPAA have been the importance of the major film studios to the American economy, their status as world leaders in the motion picture business, and the need to protect those economic interests through domestic and international channels, including international trade agreements. In testimony before the US Trade Deficit Review Commission in 2000, Valenti said: "'Hollywood' is a global industry; it provides a home to artists from the world over to tell universal stories. Perhaps more important for the purpose of today's proceedings, America's audiovisual industry is a global industry because the magic of Hollywood is eagerly sought after by consumers in over 100 countries around the world."[8] While the MPAA's focus has shifted over time and online piracy has joined foreign import and screen quotas on the top of its agenda, the representatives of the major Hollywood studios remain active participants in the development of American trade policy and vigorous promoters of an overwhelmingly positive vision of what happens when images cross borders (though only under conditions favorable to the bottom line at the studios). The threat of piracy and illegal downloading aside, it would be difficult to find a more optimistic account of the effects and possibilities of globalization than the one emanating from the key players at the mainstream Hollywood studios. For this reason, the long history of the global film industry is often framed as a harbinger of globalization itself.

Those apologies for the global media industry have reemerged with increasing intensity in recent years, though they feature new players, with Walt Disney and John Ford replaced by Steve Jobs and Mark Zuckerberg and Silicon Valley overtaking Hollywood in the vanguard of a technologically updated variation on the theme of universalism. Now the tech sector has become the most hotly contested terrain in this decades-long conflict between often self-serving expressions of an abstract ideal and its messy realization on the ground. Zuckerberg began working on the project that would eventually make him a billionaire when the Harvard *Crimson* argued that photos of students should be placed online in order to show the world a "happy face" and encourage more social interaction (Kirkpatrick 2011, 28). Sounding like a younger version of Lindsay or Wanger, Zuckerberg went one giant leap further and tried to create not just a tool for a particular group of students but a "universal facebook" (28) whose user base now exceeds two billion people worldwide. The claims of universality sound familiar to anyone versed in the history of cinema, as do charges of cultural imperialism, with the idealistic new media of a decade ago inheriting the mantle of the early Hollywood studies and becoming the twenty-first century's corporate giants and empire-builders.

The postwar critique of the global media market also echoed its precursor in the first decades of the twentieth century. Worldwide trade in cinema and other audiovisual media has been a grave concern for the majority of countries where imported cinema is the norm and domestic industries are under constant pressure from better-financed rivals, especially Hollywood. Tariffs, quotas and other import restrictions remain the primary tools for governments and film industries faced with the threat of cultural imperialism. The so-called cultural exception to global trade agreements underscored the difference between cultural products and more utilitarian goods, with the former distinguished by their crucial role in affirming the identity and ensuring the continuity of particular communities organized around a common culture. As Jonathan Buchsbaum argues, a more recent focus on "diversity" (2006, 19) has displaced the "exception" of the 1990s, with filmmakers and governments devising new strategies to finance and sustain that diversity in the face of the overwhelming economic clout of the blockbuster. In his review of *Star Wars: Episode 1—The Phantom Menace* (George Lucas, 1999), Anthony Lane comments on the irony that one of the film's major plot points—a more powerful political body forcing interstellar trade agreements down the throats of its beleaguered partners—would feature in a major Hollywood production poised to dominate box offices around the globe. He writes that the "Federation, the object of principled scorn throughout the movie is a massive corporate body that happily tramples over the protests of elected governments in its bid to expand, and will not rest until wearily compliant leaders sign on the dotted line; 'The Phantom Menace', on the other hand is being distributed by 20th C Fox, a charming family business that ventures only where it knows it will be welcome, and likes nothing better than to close a deal with a cup of coffee and a smile" (80).

The most influential critique of the trade and labor practices in the contemporary global media landscape is articulated in the two editions of *Global Hollywood* (Miller et al. 2001). The collective of authors foregrounds the role of labor in the production of films and television programs, and they argue that contemporary moving image producers deploy the same corporate strategies as other globalized industries: outsourcing to reduce labor costs, exploitation of overseas workers, exacerbation of inequality and a race to the bottom in labor and environmental standards. That book and the larger intellectual movement that it represents have tried to remove the façade of liberal values that constitutes Hollywood's preferred self-image and reveal its implication in some of the most disturbing trends in the global economy. In examining globalization as the exercise of unequal power relations, the authors of *Global Hollywood* reveal the influence of postcolonial theory outside its more familiar contexts, with the narrative disseminated by the major US studios and distributors becoming a tale of domination rather than the studio yarn focused on the inevitable triumph of universal stories desired around the world. At the same time, other scholars have constructed competing stories of globalization, with "Global Bollywood," "Global Nollywood," or a series of new waves displacing American cinema from its central position in the study of film and media.[9] Each of these narratives contains its own subplot of resistance to the dominance media producers in the West, though these industries also participate in another dynamic of economic and cultural domination within their domestic and regional film economies. What's feeble about the dominant discourse of economic and political globalization is its inability to tell several contradictory stories at once, especially when confronted with images that never quite fall in line with the familiar narratives of economic progress or global integration, on the one hand, and steadfast resistance on the other.

Always Local

Cinema has been one of the most prominent examples—positive, negative and ambivalent—of the globalization of culture, suggesting that "world" or "global" cinema merely adds a redundant adjective to a technological and cultural phenomenon that has always had its sights on the world. But it also seems redundant to highlight the locality of film because photographic media have been concerned from the very beginning with the bodies, objects and spaces located in front of the camera. For the Lumière brothers and early film pioneers, this meant the everyday life near at hand in Lyons and elsewhere in France and then the very different localities explored by their roving teams of cameramen. For studio films, the local reality consisted of actors arrayed before the camera or sets constructed by workers at the studios in and around New York, then Hollywood, or at Joinville outside of Paris or Film City in Mumbai. The locality of cinema became even more pronounced after WWII when neorealists used more portable equipment developed for filming newsreels and brought film production out of the studio and back into the streets. This rediscovery and reinvention of cinematic realism has recurred at regular intervals in the history of cinema. The French New Wave perfected a more spectacular variation on the theme with real-world settings serving as the stage for plots modeled on the most artificial modes of cinema: use the world as a stage and therefore make the immediate surroundings of the filmmakers into the raw materials of cinema. What cinema globalized through the trade in motion pictures was always a vision of a particular world assembled or observed in close proximity to the camera.

Because of that link to the locality recorded by the camera and the primacy of domestic funding and production systems, the nation-state has remained a key reference point in film and media studies, as evident in the national markers in festival programs and the sheer volume of scholarly work focused on national cinemas. Even in those contexts, however, transnational funding arrangements have destabilized the earlier consensus that categorized a film according to the citizenship or residency status of a director, and recent scholarship has underscored the crucial role of cinema in questioning or troubling the identity of the nation-state itself. Neither a recent condition nor a symptom of the millennial interest in worldly connections, that dissatisfaction with the analytical category of the nation has been evident for decades, even in the foundational texts that developed the basic concept of national cinema. Suspicious of the more superficial political and economic framework habitually used to study the nation-state, Siegfried Kracauer organized *From Caligari to Hitler* around a quest for the "German soul" (3), the "deep layers of collective mentality which extend more or less below the dimension of consciousness" (6), and he viewed cinema as one of the most revealing lenses onto that psychological realm. But he also rejected the "concept of a fixed national character" (8), concentrating instead on the "collective dispositions or tendencies" (8) actualized at a particular time under the influence of political, economic and social forces. For Kracauer, the screen in Weimar Germany offered a valuable perspective on history precisely because it turned away from the more overt signs of nationhood and made visible the "secret history" (11) of the German people with the Nazi era in the offing. With his emphasis on the psychological history of a collectivity, Kracauer framed his study of

German national cinema in the 1920s and 1930s as a challenge to more conventional approaches to the study of nationhood.

One of the most influential and frequently cited theoretical essays in cinema and media studies, Andrew Higson's "The Concept of National Cinema" (first published in 1989) reveals a more profound skepticism about the deeply ingrained but often thoughtless conventions that link films and the nation-state. Viewed as a text organized around a partial worldview or "cultural identity" (Higson 139) and featuring particular character types and their languages, as an industrial phenomenon supported by a range of government subsidies and other cultural policies, as an object exhibited and consumed in a specific geographical context and as a creation of critical conventions and consensus, almost any film is, in a fundamental sense, a product of national cinema (132–33). But as Higson also insists, what counts as a national culture varies radically when the focus shifts from production to consumption so that the work emanating from a domestic film industry is not always the dominant cinema at the box office or in the consciousness of audiences (137). He instead posits a more flexible understanding of the nation that extends beyond "the films produced by and within a particular nation state" (139) and emphasizes the point of consumption and the "overall institution of cinema" (139) in a national context rather than the origin of the work itself. Higson rethinks national cinema as a concept that must be reconciled with the border-crossing potential of moving images and a challenge to models that assimilate film into a conservative and exclusive notion of cultural heritage. As Chris Berry and Mary Farquhar suggest in *China on Screen: Cinema and Nation*, a new generation of scholarship should be organized around the more flexible category of the "national" rather than a monolithic and unchanging state. They write: "Instead of taking the national for granted as something known and unproblematic—as the older national cinemas model tended to—our larger analytical framework puts the problem of what the national is—how it is constructed, maintained, and challenged—at the center" (3). In the most vibrant recent scholarship on national cinema, the identity and coherence of the nation remain open questions, as films and media industries respond to challenges from forces beyond and within the borders of the state.

Other scholars have framed their subject at a larger scale than the nation while also resisting the tendency to adopt the abstractions and obscurantism so often inherent in the rhetoric of globalization. While they recognize the value of extending the field of world cinema beyond a collection of discrete national units viewed in isolation, Nataša Ďurovičová and Kathleen Newman argue for a "transnational framework" situated "above the level of the national but below the level of the global" (2009, ix) in order to acknowledge the "persistent agency of the state" (x) in a supposedly global age. In a world that still consists of nations, they suggest that "national cinema" can survive not as "recalcitrant essentialism but rather as a forthright political project, whose aim is to resist, as best possible, the totalizing logic of a 'global film culture'" (xi). Within this context, they identify a range of artistic and scholarly movements that use the transnational as a form of resistance against both the constraints of nationalism and the homogenizing forces of globalization, including the "small nations" model examined and theorized by Mette Hjort and the border crossing sensibility facilitated by a common language in Hispanophone and francophone cinema.[10] Balancing the specificity evident in the "physical" (23) dimensions of cinema and the theoretical demands of a global and postcolonial age, Lúcia Nagib calls for a "polycentric" conception of the world in "world cinema" and stresses that all film cultures "can generate their own, original theories" when scholars place them on an "equal footing" (2011, 1) instead of replicating within an academic domain the inequities of the global economic and geopolitical order. As Annette Kuhn and Catherine Grant point out, "It is surely no coincidence that those areas of the world most prominently involved in transformations in the global cultural economy are precisely the ones that have given rise to many of the debates on transnational film cultures" (2006, 5). They also search for a scale that allows for both "inclusivity and distinctiveness" (1) that acknowledges the "interconnectedness and interdependence" (2) of film cultures around the world, while refusing to reduce cinema and media to cultural manifestations of a global political economy and thereby obscuring the signs of rebellion often visible on the screen.

In their volume on *Global Indigenous Media*, Pamela Wilson and Michelle Stewart foreground questions of recognition and sovereignty in a media ecology more attuned to the language of flows, networks and globalization. Reversing the more standard, top-down movement from massive institutions and large-scale processes to the local level, they argue that "local control over media has often fostered political and economic sovereignty, while also helping to forge international networks" (21). Françoise Lionnet and Shu-mei Shih identify a similar phenomenon in their study of "minor transnationalism," which remains "less scripted and more scattered" (2005, 5) than the all-encompassing and normalizing category of the global would seem to permit. As Dudley Andrew argues, cinema is characterized by a form of "jet lag" or "décalage" (60), especially during a period when globalization has become a ubiquitous slogan and images can travel around the world on fiber optic cables at the speed of light. Cinema, Andrew suggests, has always been out of step with the times, as the illusion of presence created by projected images belies the fact that each step of the production, distribution and exhibition process takes time and occurs at a particular place, inserting a gap between the "here and there" and "now and then" (60). Although it operates primarily at the level of cables and satellites rather than the images that pass through them, recent work on media infrastructure likewise focuses on the material gaps and local conditions that the discourse of globalization habitually elides. As Nicole Starosielski (2015) writes, undersea cable networks transmit images at almost unimaginable speeds, but the lines themselves operate in a real-world environment that constantly poses obstacles to the flow of information, from the moment the paths were negotiated and selected to the adverse conditions encountered underwater to the crucial spaces where they return to land and connect to existing communications networks. "The fluidity of our information sphere is made possible only by this historical fixity of communications infrastructure [...]. These slow, fixed, disconnected spatial practices are the hidden layers that support contemporary global networks" (20).

All of these scholars suggest that it's difficult or impossible to operate at the level of generality assumed by many accounts of globalization when the subject is a series of images recorded at a particular location or the overseas workers who process and perfect those images or the audiences who respond to them or the communications infrastructure that transmits them on physical cables running under concrete and water. Even film and media scholarship produced at opposite ends of a spectrum between aesthetics and infrastructure overlaps as it calls for closer engagement with local conditions that films make visible or that corporate and governmental agencies hide from view during the construction of a "seamless" global network. The challenge in the study of globalization has been to think about grand, overarching themes without becoming so enamored of that totalizing paradigm that it's impossible to think of anything else. The solution proposed by the images and infrastructure is the stubborn fact that the aspiration to a universal or global communications system has always passed through the most local of realities captured by the camera or more literally in the physical conditions of dissemination or reception. Before global-local became an academic slogan, it accurately described the vertiginous, scale-jumping experience of watching cinema that remained grounded in reality but also flowed around the world.

Global *Gomorrah*

Matteo Garrone's 2008 film *Gomorrah* (*Gomorra*)—an adaptation of the best-selling "nonfiction novel" by Roberto Saviano—tells the story of the contemporary Neapolitan mafia by examining its impact on the lives of individuals in Naples and its aspirations to a global empire. The film displays with stunning clarity some of the most troubling aspects of a world order normally visible through a glass, darkly. No longer a parochial organization involved in extortion and drug dealing, the Camorra, known informally as "the System," has become a multinational enterprise that operates alongside the legal business interests of global capitalism. As Richard Porton argues, based on his reading of Saviano, "the Camorra sees itself not as an adjunct of the Italian State [like the Sicilian mafia] but as a malleable multinational corporation" (2009, 12) with historical connections to Naples but a global criminal and business network. If the primary locus of the traditional gangster film has usually been the neighborhood—the place where a young man makes his fortune, ascends to a position of domination and perishes after the inevitable fall—*Gomorrah* views that home turf as merely a base of operations for a business empire, as the corporate headquarters of a criminal enterprise. While the American gangster film has almost always displayed a romantic and nostalgic streak for the streets of ethnically and racially segregated cities of yesteryear, from Coppola's Little Italy to the Harlem and South Central Los Angeles of 1970s Blaxploitation, the bosses in *Gomorrah* have as little affection for their old neighborhood as the CEO of a corporation currently housed in a suburban office park and contemplating relocation to an offshore tax haven.

Garrone's film explores the various levels within this hierarchical structure and the effects of the "system" on the neglected and superfluous localities left behind. It concentrates on the unglamorous reality of small-time, low-level mobsters who operate within the poor and hopeless environment of the largest Neapolitan housing project. These characters alternately live within and terrorize Scampia, a complex infamous for both its pervasive criminality and the spectacular failure of its modernist design and social engineering. Constructed in the 1960s and early 1970s and badly damaged after decades of neglect and an earthquake, Franz Di Salvio's Vele di Scampia, a series of seven high-rises whose triangular profile resembled sails on the skyline, now houses roughly half its original population. Three of the "sails" have been demolished. The structure has become a potent symbol of the breakdown of idealistic modernist social housing, whose utopian aspirations too often remained aesthetic gestures and collapsed because of their failure to address the political and economic causes of inequality, because their democratizing designs rarely translated into the actual practice of democracy. The plot that unfolds in *Gomorrah* is therefore implicated in a setting on the verge of ruins, with the global economic order viewed as a consequence of the disintegration of utopian modernism. What makes the film such a compelling commentary on the condition of globalization is the way abstract economic forces manifest themselves in the most mundane environments: in the gray hallways and basements of the housing projects or the makeshift factories assembled in a warehouse in an undisclosed suburban location.

After a spectacular opening sequence involving a gangland assassination under the blue light of a tanning booth, *Gomorrah* descends into much more mundane matters and unfolds in restrained images reminiscent of Italian neorealism from the immediate post-WWII era and its subsequent revivals. The film follows the relatively sedate affairs of Don Ciro, who, with all the charisma of the stereotypical accountant, doles out payments to the families of imprisoned mobsters. It narrates the story of Totò, a child who witnesses a drug transaction and eventually finds himself conscripted into the gang, where his youth and apparent innocence become tools in the service of reprisal and retribution around the neighborhood. On the other hand, the film reveals the moral dilemmas of the more cosmopolitan Roberto, whose budding career in a waste management company is curtailed by his misgivings about the effects of dumping toxic waste in agricultural fields. If the ostensible home territory of the Camorra remains the poverty-ridden projects of Naples, Roberto's world extends into airport lounges, luxury hotels and massive construction sites with a multinational, multilingual labor force. Once-fertile fields stage a final confrontation between Roberto and his boss (played by Toni Servillo) but instead of the common cinematic satisfaction provided by a return to roots in the land and the subsequent feeling of nostalgia, *Gomorrah* sees only inedible fruit and soil contaminated for generations. If postcolonial theory viewed capitalism through the looking glass, through its racialized rationalizations for exploitation and inequality, *Gomorrah* presents the history of Italy through the lens of the "Southern question," with the relatively underdeveloped, agricultural South colonized by northern business and political interests and simultaneously exploiting workers who migrate to Italy from the developing world.

The film also recounts the dilemmas of a tailor, Pasquale, who is hired to train Chinese workers making name-brand knockoffs in an Italian sweatshop and who, like all the major characters in the film, finds himself immersed within a massive network of economic connections and rivalries governed at the local level through the administration of disproportionate and spectacular violence. More than any other industry, the domain of high fashion evokes the jet-setting lifestyles of supermodels and their emulators among the rich and famous, but in *Gomorrah*, haute couture and its underside, the unregulated factories churning out counterfeit goods, also fall within the global webs woven by the mob. Like the characters in the conspiracy films studied by Fredric Jameson in *The Geopolitical Aesthetic*, the low-level functionaries and pawns in *Gomorrah* are unable to determine their position within an "unmappable system" (1992, 4) and therefore discover that every action designed to assert their independence and secure their wellbeing results in punishment visited on them from out of the blue, almost like a form of divine intervention. Gayatri Chakravorty Spivak suggests that the concept of a world always emerges from a process of "worlding" (1985, 243) that conjures up a historically specific model of the globe and obscures the ideological assumptions that made it possible in the first place. *Gomorrah* traces a map of the world that consists, on the one hand, of fragments of everyday misery glimpsed in rundown high-rises or farms laden with debt and toxic sludge, and, on the other, the glorious promises of multinational corporations and transnational organizations like the European Union. What the film reveals is the irreconcilable contradiction between the elusive future of globalization and the present reality of enduring poverty and inequality.

When characters assert their agency within the world system and try to cash in on its promises, they are rewarded only with explosions of violence. In between the contradictory visions of globalization, between the attempts to live out its heavily marketed fantasies and the impossibility of their universal realization, reside the various forces charged with reconciling those contradictions, most notably, in *Gomorrah*, the mob. In 1948, Robert Warshow framed the classical Hollywood gangster film as a commentary on an American Dream defined primarily as the accumulation of wealth. He argued that the gangster's "business" combines a type of "rational enterprise"—illegal activities designed to yield windfall profits—and "irrational brutality" (2007, 14). With success and violence so intimately intermingled, these films suggest that in "the deeper layers of the modern consciousness, *all* means are unlawful, every attempt to succeed is an act of aggression" (15). In the variation on the gangster film visible in *Gomorrah*, the rational enterprise of globalization depends on the exercise of brutality on the local level. As we descend the economic hierarchy, raw and deadly manifestations of power replace the rule of law and the response to the question raised by Guillén—"Is Globalization Civilizing, Destructive or Feeble?"—is a radical foreclosure of all access to a reality beyond bare subsistence and survival, with the confining walls of a warehouse or the hallways of a decaying apartment block now constituting the totality of the visible world. Instead of providing answers, in other words, the mob insists that its victims stop asking so many questions.

Set within this complex environment where global forces exert a profound influence on everyday life but remain inaccessible in their totality, *Gomorrah* deploys a series of seemingly contradictory strategies that establish its roots in both the traditions of realist or documentary film and the tale of multinational corporate intrigue. Featuring dialogue in the local Neapolitan dialect and many untutored actors from the housing projects and surrounding neighborhood, the film strives for the type of authenticity and rootedness in a community that founded the neorealist ethic and aesthetic. Aspiring to the most local of cinemas, Garrone encouraged his actors not to recite the dialogue as written but to insert their own expressions and manners of speech, transforming the script into a co-authored document that changed with the performance of each take. The "making-of" footage reveals the permeability of the "sets," with actors, crew members and equipment hastily assembled on city streets, people gathering to watch and participate in the film-making process and the "sails" of Scampia looming over them. At the same time, the

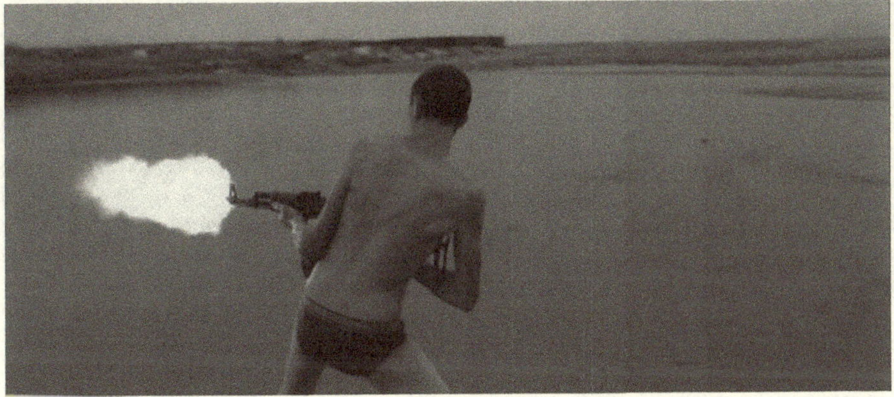

Figure 5.1 *Gomorrah*

film resists the label of "realism" because it engages just as intensely with other traditions and rejects the ghettoizing tendencies in world cinema that have made realism the official style and only cinematic export for much of the periphery, even in countries that produce more popular genre cinema for domestic or regional consumption. Garrone remains only a partial devotee of realist cinema and cobbles together images from seemingly distinct aesthetic traditions, ranging from the guilty pleasures of the ultraviolent gangster genre to the more sedate pedagogy of a documentary on globalization.

In *Gomorrah*, as in revisionist mafia narratives like *The Sopranos*, characters delight in comparing themselves to their counterparts in the movies, seeing themselves as participants in a network that includes both their own bodies and the images that display the perverse heroism of the fictional gangster. Operating at one of the lowest and most precarious rungs in the global hierarchy, these characters take momentary pleasure in the promise of connection and continuity with a cinematic and televisual world that provides the raw materials for their own idiosyncratic vision of the globe. With its signature poster image of teenage gangsters shooting guns in their underwear or the mobster bathed in the blue light of a tanning bed, *Gomorrah* also contributes to the repertoire of stunning images of mob violence that another generation of aspiring mobsters will mimic years or decades down the line (Figure 5.1). As Fabrizio Cilento points out, social media postings from young Milanese Mafiosi show them imitating the poses of the characters in *Gomorrah*, suggesting that the overall critique of the damage wrought by the mob can be undermined by the allure of images that celebrate the countercultural appeal of criminality or revel in destruction itself.[11]

These moments of aesthetic precision and control insert the film within the generic conventions and global cinematic imperatives that it otherwise condemns and seeks to revise. And while the film wears its imperfections as a badge of honor, with jittery camerawork and arbitrarily framed images a sign of its commitment to capturing life on the run, at other moments the insistent framing and careful composition begin to resemble the technical perfection of Edward Burtynsky, whose photographs of factories

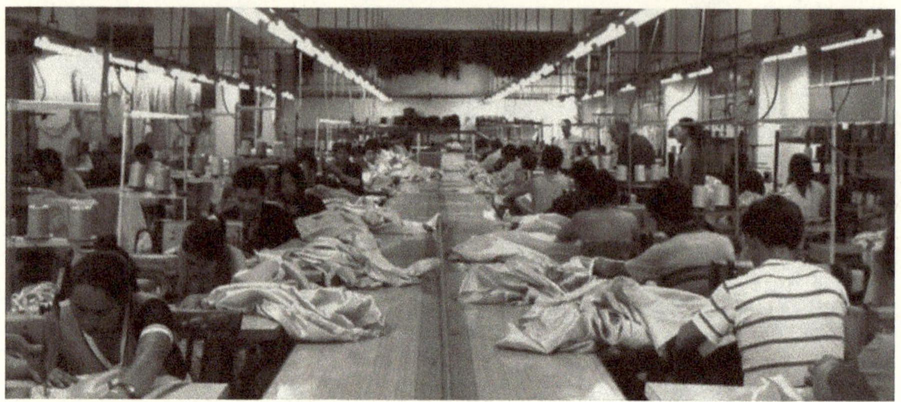

Figure 5.2 *Gomorrah*

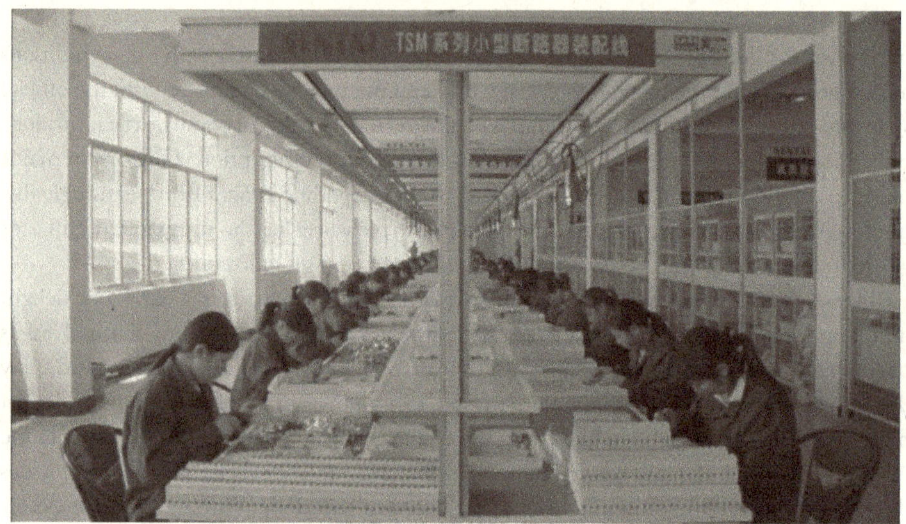

Figure 5.3 *Manufactured Landscapes*

and waste sites are displayed in Jennifer Baichwal's documentary about those images and locations, the descriptively titled *Manufactured Landscapes* (2006) (Figures 5.2 and 5.3). *Gomorrah* is "global art cinema" as described by Rosalind Galt and Karl Schoonover, a "mongrel" (6) form that draws on several traditions at the same time and bridges the conceptual divide between realism focused on the object before the camera and the more formalist attention to the visual image.

In addition to these allusions and responses to neorealism, modernist art practices, and, of course, the gangster film, *Gomorrah* also contributes to the revival of the increasingly globalized genres of film noir and dramatized literary reportage. As Cilento argues,

"Garrone's work is revelatory of how today film noir is not a uniquely American cinematic phenomenon, but rather a transnational and transgeneric one, capable of crossing national boundaries and dramatizing the crisis of urban peripheries." But, as Cilento adds, the historical variations on film noir itself were always already "heterogeneous, polyglot, and indeed cosmopolitan," as they were produced under the influence of movements as diverse as expressionism, French and Italian variations on the theme of realism and popular Hollywood genre cinema. *Gomorrah* draws on multiple, seemingly contradictory archives in order to represent both the everyday life of a community in Naples viewed through the lens of neorealism and the global aspirations of that community, even as that world remains tentative and inaccessible except through highly aestheticized images and allusions to other films.

Globalization becomes cinema through the exploitation of moving images to market a corporate vision of the world. The selection of one future among all the other possibilities and the celebration of its "civilizing" potential have established the discourse of globalization as its own dream factory, with nothing less than participation in global modernity hanging in the balance. In films like *Gomorrah,* the fantasy is contrasted with its aftermath and the destruction that follows in its wake, even if the film also reveals the enormous power of the fantasy itself, especially when it permeates an environment where dreams often seem like the only source of hope. Film scholars have for decades studied the industrialized production of dreams, including the initial variations on the theme of globalization (or its *forme fruste*) visible in the late nineteenth and early twentieth centuries. What film studies contributes to the study of globalization is the capacity to explore the charisma and allure of the fantasies that promise to liberate the masses from the sails of Scampia into a castle in the sky. At the same time, if cinema can venture into the image, inhabit its luxuries and indulge in its logic and appeal, filmmakers can also venture into the world, as when Garrone and his collaborators narrow in on the particularity of the Neapolitan social environment depicted on the screen or the conditions of a global trade in goods and images and their effects on local communities, individual lives and the environment represented as literally as possible by toxic soil. To understand globalization requires that we engage with all of those interwoven worlds, to account for their paradoxical simultaneity, to realize that illusions emanating from the globalizing media industry and the inescapable reality of everyday life are always bound up with and implicated in each other.

An impossibly complex realm has been the purview of film and media studies for over a century, and its long history makes it one of the most promising avenues into the study of globalization. Since the early twentieth century, critics and film industry executives have argued that "trade follows the film" (Lowry 1925, 12) because goods follow in the wake of images that create familiarity and desire. Others have argued that film instead follows the flag into overseas markets already made accessible through diplomatic or military means. Political, economic and academic movements are also multidirectional, and while the study of globalization remains the playfield of economists and political theorists, it would not exist without its own ongoing media campaigns and their unceasing production of desire for a more modern and interconnected world, without first convincing an audience that their vision of the globe is real and promising rather than destructive or feeble. The discourse of globalization is yet another dream factory that has merged with the world it created and the one it displaced. In that sense and so many others, globalization has followed in the footsteps of cinema.

Notes

1 See Pheng Cheah, *What Is a World?: On Postcolonial Literature as World Literature* (Durham: Duke University Press, 2016).
2 Horst W. J. Rittel and Melvin M. Webber, "Dilemmas in a General Theory of Planning," *Policy Sciences* 4 (1973): 155–69.
3 On "world systems" theory, see e.g., Immanuel Wallerstein, *World-Systems Analysis: An Introduction* (Durham: Duke University Press, 2004).
4 See André Bazin, *What Is Cinema?* vol. 1, ed. and trans. Hugh Gray (Berkeley: University of California Press, 1968).
5 See Paula Amad, *Counter-Archive: Film, the Everyday, and Albert Kahn's Archives de la Planète* (New York: Columbia University Press, 2010).
6 Miriam Hansen, *Babel and Babylon: Spectatorship in American Silent Film* (Cambridge: Harvard University Press, 1994), 77.
7 Clyde H. Farnworth, "Jack Valenti's State Department," *The New York Times*, December 18, 1985.
8 See Testimony of Jack Valenti, Chairman and CEO, Motion Picture Association of America, Before the United States Trade Deficit Review Commission, March 13, 2000. http://govinfo.library.unt.edu/tdrc/hearings/13mar00/jvalenti.pdf.
9 See Anandam P. Kavoori and Aswin Punathambekar, eds., *Global Bollywood* (New York: NYU Press, 2008); Matthias Krings and Onookome Okome, eds., *Global Nollywood: The Transnational Dimensions of an African Video Film Industry* (Bloomington: Indiana University Press, 2013); James Tweedie, *The Age of New Waves: Art Cinema and the Staging of Globalization* (New York: Oxford University Press, 2013).
10 See Nataša Ďurovičová and Kathleen Newman, eds., *World Cinema, Transnational Perspectives* (New York: Routledge, 2009).
11 See Fabrizio Cilento, "Saviano, Garrone, *Gomorrah*: Neorealism and Noir in the Land of the Camorra," *Fast Capitalism* 8, no. 1 (2011).

Works Cited

Amad, Paula. 2010. *Counter-Archive: Film, the Everyday, and Albert Kahn's Archives de la Planète*. New York: Columbia University Press.

Andrew, Dudley. 2010. "Time Zones and Jet Lags: The Flows and Phases of World Cinema". In *World Cinema, Transnational Perspectives*, edited by Nataša Ďurovičová and Kathleen E. Newman. New York: Routledge, 59–89.

Bazin, André. 1968. *What Is Cinema?* vol. 1, edited and translated by Hugh Gray. Berkeley: University of California Press.

Buchsbaum, Jonathan. 2006. "'The Exception Culturelle Is Dead,' Long Live Cultural Diversity: French Cinema and the New Resistance." *Framework* 47, no. 1: 5–21.

Cheah, Pheng. 2016. *What Is a World?: On Postcolonial Literature as World Literature*. Durham: Duke University Press.

Cilento, Fabrizio. 2011. "Saviano, Garrone, *Gomorrah*: Neorealism and Noir in the Land of the Camorra." *Fast Capitalism* 8, no. 1. https://www.uta.edu/huma/agger/fastcapitalism/8_1/cilento8_1.html.

de Grazia, Victoria. 2005. *Irresistible Empire: America's Advance through Twentieth-Century Europe.* Cambridge: Harvard University Press.

Ďurovičová, Nataša, and Kathleen Newman, eds. 2009. *World Cinema, Transnational Perspectives.* New York: Routledge.

Grant, Catherine, and Annette Kuhn, eds. 2006. *Screening World Cinema.* New York: Routledge.

Guillén, Mauro. 2001. "Is Globalization Civilizing, Destructive or Feeble? A Critique of Five Key Debates in the Social Science Literature." *Annual Review of Sociology* 27: 235–60.

Gunning, Tom. 2016. "Early Cinema as Global Cinema: The Encyclopedic Ambition." In *Early Cinema and the "National"*, edited by Richard Abel, Giorgio Bertellini and Rob King. New Barnet, UK: John Libbey.

Hansen, Miriam. 1999. "The Mass Production of the Senses: Classical Cinema and Vernacular Modernism." *Modernism/Modernity* 6, no. 2: 59–77.

Higson, Andrew. 1989. "The Concept of National Cinema." *Screen* 30, no. 4 (Oct. 1): 36–47.

Jameson, Fredric. 1992. *The Geopolitical Aesthetic: Cinema and Space in the World System.* Bloomington: Indiana University Press.

Jarvie, Ian. 1992. *Hollywood's Overseas Campaign: The North Atlantic Film Trade, 1920–1950.* New York: Cambridge University Press.

Kavoori, Anandam P., and Aswin Punathambekar, eds. 2008. *Global Bollywood.* New York: NYU Press.

Kirkpatrick, David. 2011. *The Facebook Effect: The Inside Story of the Company That Is Connecting the World.* New York: Simon and Schuster.

Krings, Matthias, and Onookome Okome, eds. 2013. *Global Nollywood: The Transnational Dimensions of an African Video Film Industry.* Bloomington: Indiana University Press.

Lane, Anthony. 1999. "Star Bores." *The New Yorker* (May 24): 80.

Lindsay, Vachel. 1916. *The Art of the Moving Picture.* New York: Macmillan.

Lowry, Edward G. 1925. "Trade Follows the Film." *Saturday Evening Post* (November 7): 12.

Lionnet, Françoise, and Shu-mei Shih. 2005. *Minor Transnationalism.* Durham: Duke University Press.

Miller, Toby, et al. 2001. *Global Hollywood.* London: British Film Institute.

Nagib, Lúcia. 2011. *World Cinema and the Ethics of Realism.* New York: Continuum.

Pérez-Melgosa, Adrián. 2012. *Cinema and Inter-American Relations: Tracking Transnational Affect.* New York: Rutledge.

Porton, Richard. 2009. "Inside 'The System': An Interview with Matteo Garrone." *Cineaste* 34, no. 2: 12–15.

Puttnam, David. 2000. *Movies and Money.* New York: Alfred A. Knopf.

Rittel, Horst W. J., and Melvin M. Webber. 1973. "Dilemmas in a General Theory of Planning." *Policy Sciences* 4: 155–69.

Solomon, Matthew. 2011. "Introduction." In *Fantastic Voyages of the Cinematic Imagination: Georges Méliès's Trip to the Moon*, edited by Matthew Solomon. Albany: SUNY Press.

Spivak, Gayatri. 1985. "Three Women's Texts and a Critique of Imperialism." *Critical Inquiry* 12, no. 1: 243–61.

Starosielski, Nicole. 2015. *The Undersea Network.* Durham: Duke University Press.

Tweedie, James. 2013. *The Age of New Waves: Art Cinema and the Staging of Globalization.* New York: Oxford University Press.

Urry, John. 2000. *Sociology beyond Societies: Mobilities for the Twenty-First Century.* New York: Routledge.

Wanger, Walter. 1950. "Donald Duck and Diplomacy." *Public Opinion Quarterly* 14, no. 3: 443–52.

Warshow, Robert. 2007. "The Gangster as Tragic Hero." In *The Gangster Film Reader*, edited by Alain Silver and James Ursini. Pompton Plains, NJ: Limelight Editions.

Chapter Six

SCREEN THEORY BEYOND THE HUMAN: TOWARD AN ECOMATERIALISM OF THE MOVING IMAGE

Hunter Vaughan

Due to its proximity to the renewal of new art and communication forms and their placement at the vanguard of politically engaged fields, film and media studies has proudly asserted itself as a leading academic voice of sociopolitical commentary. Today, as screen culture is diversified across new technologies and media and moves us beyond the filmic, screen theory remains the chosen arena of innovation for thinkers and activists coming from other fields. There remain those, myself included, who agree with David Rodowick's claim that the real accomplishment of cinema studies "is to have forged more than any other related discipline the methodological and philosophical bases for addressing the most urgent and interesting questions, both aesthetic and cultural, of modernity and visual culture" (2001, 1403). However, the more optimistic among us would like to encourage more focus on adding "ethical" to the important types of questions, and to continue to push film and media studies to engage with the pressing issues of the day, even to have the foresight and honesty to acknowledge what will be the pressing issues to come. Therefore we must now ask: What is the defining problem that civilization is and will be facing in the years to come?

The environment. Climate change, global warming, sea level rise, natural resource use and scarcity, the epic climax of this long slough of humanity's carbon footprint. As Sean Cubitt claims with casual poignancy, ecopolitics is the last master narrative (2005, 9). Identity difference and geopolitical struggle will mean nothing if this planet becomes uninhabitable, which most scientific and critical studies point to in an increasingly near future; we are today starting to reap the harvest of what Marx referred to as "metabolic rift," a term McKenzie Wark has resurrected to refer to the lasting geological, atmospheric and elemental impact of human industry as we wade out of prehistory and into the endgame era commonly known as the Anthropocene (2015, viii). Awareness of and concern for ecological issues have risen greatly in the past two decades, and the past half-century has seen an intellectual and activist evolution from environmentalist writing to ecocriticism, alongside a trending wave of environmentally focused films, media texts and screen studies. As Nadia Bozak claims in her 2013 *The Cinematic Footprint: Lights, Camera, Natural Resources*, this newly emerging critical approach "makes it possible to engage a set of heretofore divergent lines of inquiry: moving-image technology, environmental erosion, and the hydrocarbon culture they all, together and separately, define" (147).

In this essay, I will a history of cultural ecocriticism, in particular highlighting the emergence of studies of media and the environment over the past two decades, and offering examples of how this approach might be applied to different types of screen text. Moreover, I will push here—as I have done elsewhere in my analysis of classical Hollywood (2016), digital media and incentivized production, and as others have addressed regarding a range of media platforms from telecommunications to video games, as demonstrated by the staggering range of contributions to Starioselski and Walkers's 2016 *Sustainable Media*—for the transition of screen-centric ecocriticism to what I call "ecomaterialism." Moving away from the conventional focus on representation, ecomaterialism will push instead to assess the environmental impact of media practices, turning from the aesthetics of showing nature to the way in which cultural production, distribution, consumption and waste impact our ecosystems and define our use of natural resources, the acceleration of global warming and the institution of a new mode of ecological imperialism that ranges from the mining of Congolese precious metals to the assembly of smart technology in Chinese sweatshops to the dumping of toxic e-waste in Kenyan villages.

However, the genealogy of ecocriticism dates back centuries, as the species-old cultural navigation of the natural world was forced by the impact and aesthetics of the industrial revolution to consider the heightened potential of humanity's detriment to the micro and macro ecosystems of which we are a part. Let us now look at that intellectual history.

Many ecocritical accounts look to the nineteenth-century poets and natural philosophers—Wordsworth, Shelley, Whitman, Thoreau, Emerson—as the prototypes for the literary and artistic eco-warrior, championing the transcendental idyll and scrawling odes to the daffodils that danced beneath an ominous horizon of black factory smoke, artists and critics at the breach of industrial modernity. Such writers are only part of a larger literary history addressed in *The Country and the City* (1973), in which Raymond Williams embarks on a literary history to chart the relationship between rural and urban spaces in the collective imagination. Heralding the emergence of ecocriticism, Williams notes how Virgil's antique dichotomy between the peace of country life and the disturbance of war grew in time, especially through the post-Renaissance, into a Foucaldian binary of exploitation that was integrated into the growing schism of capitalism: "an unreflecting celebration of mastery—power, yield, production, man's mastery of nature—as if the exploitation of natural resources could be separated from the accompanying exploitation of men" (37).

The connection between power and exploitation Williams reveals across literary history is also central in the twentieth-century development of environmentalist thought and activism. In *Eco-politics*, Verena Andermatt Conley argues that the environmental discourse of the 1990s owes much to the rhetoric of the 1960s political and intellectual movements, with a rejection of the classical subject–object binary being central to critiquing the treatment of women, non-Western cultures and, today, nature itself (1997, 1). It is no surprise that the decade of great social revolution, artistic subversion and ideological rupture produced the seminal texts of the environmental movement, with works like Rachel Carson's 1962 *Silent Spring* responding to the postwar boom's exponential reliance on plastics, preservatives and pesticides. Though Carson's generation developed a newfound sense of casual environmental awareness in tandem with what Conley argues to have been a paradigmatic shift in social politics and philosophical thought, and while ecological activism and awareness would become increasingly mainstreamed—over the 1970s, Greenpeace would evolve from a fringe antinuclear campaign to a household name and *Time Magazine*, the bastion of mainstream news, would reach widely with a 1989 cover story on climate change titled "Planet of the Year: Endangered Earth"—it would not be until the turn of the millennium that issues such as global warming would spur a wave of popular productions and criticism focusing on problems of the environment and sustainability.

In many ways growing as film studies had originally grown in the academy—from the umbrella of literary and cultural studies and in the cradle of English and other liberal studies departments—what has come to be termed *ecocriticism* in film and media studies is only the youngest offspring of environmental studies' belated encroachment into the humanities. Following in the footsteps of Lawrence Buell (1996), Cheryll Glotfelty and Harold Fromm (1996) and others' ecocritical remapping of literary criticism, film and media criticism unleashed a torrent of production to meet the popular releases of films like *The Day after Tomorrow* (2004) and *An Inconvenient Truth* (2006) and the subsequent advent of a genre popularly referred to as "ecocinema." Along this trajectory, we can witness an accelerated example of the growth of a topic in film and media theory: beginning with the first wave of texts focusing primarily on establishing an agenda and exploring problems of representation, followed quickly by a second wave that branches this agenda into other methodologies such as philosophy and industry studies, followed at last by a turn toward issues of practice and materialism.

Indicative of the dominant methodologies in our field, most of the monographs and collections that provide an ecocritical approach to film revolve around history and representation, focusing on how media has spoken the environmental movement, and how films have shown the nonhuman natural world and humanity's relationship to it. Alison Anderson's 1997 *Media, Culture, and the Environment* was a few years ahead of the curve, placing ecocriticism within the rising critical analysis of globalization, arguing that environmentalism is a global problem that must be understood "within the context of global capitalism, new systems of mass communication, and the rise of consumer culture" (1997, 75–76). Tracing a philosophical genealogy from Locke and Hobbes, up to the moving-image's central status in the advent and theorization of modernity and on through the postmodern visual politics of television, Anderson's fundamental claim that nature is a cultural construct would resonate through the first wave of ecocritical texts on film and media.

Books such as David Ingram's (2000) *Green Screen: Environmentalism and Hollywood Cinema*, Sean Cubitt's (2005) *Eco Media*, and Pat Bereton's (2005) *Hollywood Utopia: Ecology in Contemporary American Cinema* helped to lay the groundwork for ecocriticism, taking this fundamental argument—that nature is a cultural construct—and drawing it out across different national cinemas and film genres. These studies assess not only how moving-image culture constructs nature, but also how this connects to tendencies in film aesthetics and marketing (i.e., problems of spectacle and excess; formations of subjectivity; film industry practices such as film genres and merchandising) and the larger intellectual and political context of environmentalist history and activism. For example, in a chapter on "Wilderness Landscapes," Ingram makes connections between the romanticization of films such as Robert Redford's (1992) *A River Runs Through It* and the director's campaigns in the 1980s and 1990s for forest preservation. The film offers a perfect example of the complex contradictions of mainstream representations of nature: ostensibly a film about men appreciating the glory of nature, the plot actually offers a story of the mastery over nature; and, perhaps more powerfully, the connotations of this anthropocentric worldview is bolstered through its formal construction of subjectivity and spectatorial positioning. These messages, of course, contradict the director's off-screen conservationist agenda.

Much Hollywood ecocriticism revels in similar "symptomatic readings" (Moore 2015) of the contradictions and hypocrisies of mainstream practices; in this vein, Ingram offers a blueprint of major tropes in filmic representations of nature and then pokes holes in these genres through historical extra-filmic analysis. Beginning with a critique of the hypocrisies of Disney's renaissance, Ingram argues that Disney's environmental initiatives surrounding *The Lion King*'s release, coupled with the film's own Elton John-soundtracked glorification of nature, were part of a larger media campaign that reaped billions of dollars from sweatshop labor and other dubious practices. In "Indians and Primly Purity," he reveals the role of Haitian sweatshops in fueling the first-world profit of Disney's *Pocahontas*; "Garden and Wilderness" explores the dark irony of the fact that *Ferngully: The Last Rainforest*, a film about the dangers of overdevelopment, was in fact produced by FAI Insurance Life, a coal company that made their fortune through doing exactly that.

Similar connections between representation, politics and industry drive the other formative texts of ecocriticism, which attempted to expand the object of study. Though not all films are specifically about the environment or natural world, our relation to nature has always been fundamental to defining ourselves as a species and civilization. Cubitt argues, "At any historical juncture, the meaning of what it is to be human is constructed from the relationship between nature and technology" (2005, 135). Echoing Mulvey's notion of the "male gaze" and Conley's connection between environmentalism and identity politics, Cubitt argues that the representation of nature, by humans, through means of technical reproduction, has rendered nature as an object that cannot itself signify. As such, as mentioned above, a pro-nature film like *A River Runs Through It* is run through by a contradictory message that pits humans against nature, then glorifies the human's reckless abandon in becoming one with nature (Paul (Brad Pitt) slipping into the rapids in pursuit of the fish on his fly) as long as the conclusion is his mastery over it (soaked and exhausted, he triumphantly holds the caught and dying fish alight at the end of the scene, a large white-toothed smile on his face as the fish slowly flops its final drowning gasps). This mastery is instilled more subtly in the film's forms of representation, which position the viewers to identify with the human subjects and in spatial and connotative opposition to the object-world of nonhuman nature.

Brereton's *Hollywood Utopia* and Robin L. Murray and Joseph K. Heumann's *Ecology and Popular Film* extend this type of symptomatic reading to a wide array of films, aiming in the latter's words "at ecological themes underpinning obvious readings" (2009, 4). Hoping to anchor media ecocriticism to larger goals and needs for environmental thought and policy, Brereton attempts to contextualize film criticism within Andrew Dobson's framework for "ecologism," according to a philosophical basis (limits to growth), ethical perspective (ecocentrism) and social vision (a sustainable society) (2005, 16; for more, see Dobson, 2004). Less interdisciplinary and more focused on film history and textual analysis, Murray and Heumann establish a central ecological question for moving-image cultural history: "When, how, and why does disaster become a spectacular image?" (2009, 32). Looking at films as diverse as early Lumière silent shorts of the Baku oil fields, Parc Lorentz's 1938 *The River*, and the blockbuster *The Day after Tomorrow* in terms of their historical context and representational connotations, Murray and Heumann have established the standard for ecocritical approaches to film, which they have extended through an ongoing engagement especially with the environmental analysis of genre cinema.

Indeed, much ecocritical scholarship has sprouted around the application of environmentalist concerns to previously established areas of inquiry: from *Transnational Ecocinema* to *Eco-Trauma Cinema*, the newly fashioned lens of ecological concern has reinvigorated and found new connections and depth for areas of film and media study including national and global film theory, psychoanalytic theories of trauma representation and more. Reflecting its taxonomical dexterity, ecocriticism can be viewed as arising in tandem with the advent of a particular type of film, often referred to as "ecocinema," though it has become a very fashionable tool for exploring a multitude of genres. Looking at films as diverse as blockbuster feature fiction films like *Deep Impact*, television essay films such as Josh Fox's *Gasland* and less commercial media phenomena like the Cochabamba water war films, ecocinema refers to films that explicitly address environmental concerns, often aimed at taking an informative but ideological stance on ecological issues such as climate change or natural gas fracking. The binding drive to assert the agency and importance of nonhuman nature often promotes more experimental aesthetic and representational practices, such as can be found in Ron Fricke's *Baraka* (1992) and even Al Gore and Davis Guggenheim's (2006) *An Inconvenient Truth*. As a practicing filmmaker, Scott MacDonald puts it: "The job of ecocinema is to provide *new kinds of film experiences* that demonstrate an alternative to conventional media spectatorship and help to nurture a more environmentally progressive mindset" (2013, 20). However, this genre must also be seen to include more conventional mainstream films like Steven Zaillian's (1998) *A Civil Action* and Gus Van Sant's (2012) *The Promised Land*, mainstream films that explore what Kaapa and Gustafsson refer to as "green politics in a capitalist ecosystem" (2013, 32), a popularization of the topic that has both diminished the radical praxis and aesthetics of the genre and, conversely, expanded the audience of this important message by millions.

Stephen Rust, Salma Monani and Sean Cubitt's 2013 edited collection, *Ecocinema Theory and Practice*, does an excellent job of introducing the ecocinema genre as a collection of texts, practices and disciplinary problems and providing a range of perspectives on such films and how to theorize and even teach the field. As much as ecocinema and ecocriticism have triggered a wave of enthusiastic media activism and scholarship, there are dissenting voices regarding the ideological and aesthetic rhetoric of such films. Much of this could be seen to revolve around the problem of subject–object relations implicit in the pointed camera—a danger that Bart Wellig, connecting representations of nature to the gender inequity of the commodifying male gaze and the fetishized female body, refers to elsewhere as "ecoporn" (2009, 53). Couching a similar argument in specifically rhetorical terms, David Ingram takes issue with the "prescriptive moralism" of environmentalist films, as opposed to the more subversive dialogic or polyphonic approach of the Bakhtinian carnivalesque (2013, 57). Some of the problems of both representing and writing about the environment stem from its position of resistance and also from the difficulty in establishing methods for this resistance. Andrew Hageman sagely connects the contradictions held in many ecologically minded films as the growing pains of a new genre that could well be applied to the theoretical field as well: "Every film contains contradictions—points at which their ecological representations and messages break down. Such breaking points must not be read as signs of failure to be lamented, but as indices of the contradictions within the ideology that determines our current ability to think and represent ecology" (2013, 65).

Adrian Ivakhiv echoes this last point in the language of film-philosophy, arguing that two major twentieth-century shifts—cinema and ecology—have not yet been *thought together* in a sustained way (2013, 87). In his 2013 book, *Ecologies of the Moving Image*, Ivakhiv attempts just this, adapting Deleuze's image-semiotics, which in turn were crafted from Peirce and Bergson, to develop an "ecophilosophy" to help reconceive our relations with moving images (viii). Ivakhiv's triple-layered framework of image ecologies is a complex blueprint for theorizing the ecological ramifications and expressivity of cinema; however, though in his introduction Ivakhiv points to the material conditions and political-ecological resonances surrounding a film during its production and for years following its release, it remains a strongly theoretical work. Indeed, most works in the formative decade of ecocriticism hint at the necessity to include a thorough analysis of the material reality of screen culture as an industrial set of practices and then proceed instead to focus on problems of representation and theory.

Case Study 1: *Baraka* (1992)

Documentary cinema has been the primary domain for ecocinema, as its industrial processes and mode of address make possible and even encourage filmmakers to confront audiences with complex new information and challenging ways of viewing the world. Aimed at a spectator that wants more than just to be entertained and financed with the expectation of lower profit return, the realm of documentary film has traditionally given life to controversial social messages and innovative expressive forms. Both more didactic and more dialogical, documentary cinema intertwines categorical and rhetorical regimes to convey information about the world and the human experience, and as such has been harnessed by the environmentalist movement over the past three decades in an attempt, from short-form messaging of NGOs such as Greenpeace to the experimental films of Ron Fricke, to make us question our impact on nature and to challenge how we understand our relationship with the nonhuman world.

Before the genre of ecocinema erupted in the mid-2000s, before films like *An Inconvenient Truth* and *Gasland* catapulted eco-documentaries to commercial success, Academy recognition and the extended viewership of premium cable, Fricke's (1992) *Baraka* bore avant-garde testament to the problematic relationship between human civilization and the natural world. Filmed in 70 mm Todd-AO format over 14 months and in 24 countries across six continents, *Baraka* contains no dialogue, using imagery and a non-diegetic score of percussion and didgeridoo to document the many rituals of a variety of species: from monkeys in a hot spring to assembly-line conveyer belts whisking chicks to have their beaks burnt shut in a chicken factory, from Buddhist monks to fighter jets, from tribal rituals to strip mines, *Baraka* manages without a word to convey a very strong indictment of advanced human industrialization, celebrating the simplicity of ancient customs and the nonhuman in an environmentalist critique of human modernity. By rejecting the inevitable process of inclusion and alienation produced through language and by denying any narrative impetus or specific preferred rational meaning, *Baraka* challenges the communicative and rhetorical basis of mainstream feature filmmaking, hinting at the possibility of an ecocinematic turn from anthropocentrism to ecocentrism.[1] The film's clear mediation on behalf of the nonhuman and non-industrial is further strengthened by its rejection of conventional modes of cinematic subject-formation and positioning: not only does it refuse to construct patterns of identification with the industrial peoples, but it also subverts the ethnographic myth of objectivity by allowing its subjects to look back into the camera, breaking the fourth wall and creating a sort of inspective loop in which the spectator's wonder at the world is then itself turned into an object of inquiry.

And, yet, its subversive tendencies are largely anthropocentric. Due to its mobilized location shoot, encyclopedic range of representations and formalist attempt to deny privileged subject positions, *Baraka* is often cited as a film that exceeds the traditional structure of national cinema, exemplifying the practices and goals of a global cinema. It denies the privilege of any particular identification, defies the typical finance and marketing process tied to any localized practice and attempts to uproot the apparatus from any specified terrain. It may be a global cinema, but one must ask: Is it planetary? That is, what of the earth itself? In his analysis of the film and the "global culture industry," Martin Roberts points out the lack of an image of Earth from space, that is, an actually global representation (1998, 75). However, Roberts's analysis is of the film's situation within debates on world cinema; an ecocritic would need to address this issue in terms of the film's planetary view, which is fundamentally neutral. On the surface, the film's representations of the treatment of the earth (through mining) and animals (through industrial farming) are certainly critical, though this relies on a particular hermeneutics: technically, the film only presents us with things as they are and other than the seemingly accusatory gaze of one or two tribal humans, there is no certainty that the film is in fact criticizing human practices. Moreover, while it does represent natural settings and nonhuman animals as independently existent, and while it uses montage methods to spatially integrate the viewer within the natural setting (as opposed to only viewing it from a detached distance), the film certainly does not give any clear understanding of the concrete impact of human practice on the ecosystems involved.

Lastly, and perhaps most importantly for an ecocriticial reading, we should question the film's practices from an ecomaterialist standpoint. What Roberts refers to as "coffee-table globalism," (66) this film exemplifies how the contact zone of our global imaginary has expanded and even democratized, but what of its carbon footprint? Indeed, the impressive scope of the film's production belies thousands of miles traveled in airplanes and thousands of feet of celluloid, invasive camera crews in a mode of runaway shoot that has proven historically to alter local biospheres and ecosystems. The horizon of ecocriticism, as I will explore in the second half of this essay, must expand to the material questions of film and media practice and culture.

Baraka is an example of what might be called a global or transnational ecocinematic text, or ecofilm; and, as that test case is meant to illuminate, most approaches to ecocinema reside primarily within the critical register of representation. However, as Kaapa and Gustafsson argue in *Transnational Ecocinema*, "While textual discussion of transnational ecofilms is a crucial starting point for challenging the dominant paradigms of ecocinema, future studies need to consider their production and circulation in depth" (2013, 38). Like many others who make this argument, though, the authors do not necessarily pursue this methodological shift, offering a challenge to the next set of scholars—well, we are here, and that time has come.

Though it is unclear if this marks a shift in the field in general, there have emerged a handful of works that do focus more on what I call an "ecomaterialist" approach, turning from the analysis of representation and toward issues of production cultures and film practices, looking less at how we show things than at the environmental and natural resource ramifications of how we make, distribute, watch and dispose of media texts and their contingent materials. Such works include, and will no doubt continue to be influenced by, Bozak's *The Cinematic Footprint* and Richard Maxwell and Toby Miller's *Greening the Media*, both of which came out in 2012. As Bozak argues, to a degree, cinema and ecological thought have always been intertwined, at least implicitly. "An ecological cinema is nothing new. Cinema has always demonstrated an awareness of its industrial self and therefore a connection to the environment, the realm from which it derives its power, raw materials and, often enough, subject matter. But because its biophysical layer is so inextricably embedded within film's basic means of production, distribution, and reception, its effects remain as overlooked as they are complex" (2012, 11). As the title indicates, Bozak's book looks in particular at the "relations between the consumption of natural resources and film's ontological, aesthetic, and political dimensions."

Beginning with the ontology of film itself, Bozak discusses how cinema is an energy-based art: though mostly intangible and invisible, its uses of energy are extensive and important. The captured and projected is, ultimately, the "transduction of radiant energy"—in other words, the image is produced by the imprint left by light and is projected as the transparent partition of cast light. This ontological argument is continued elsewhere by Mathilde Nardelli and Karl Schoonover (2013) in terms of film as waste, and is only a starting place for looking at the way that natural resources factor into film production, distribution and exhibition, all of which depend heavily on the energy sector for their technological and transport apparatus.

This material relationship between media and the environment informs the rather broad spectrum of Maxwell and Miller's *Greening the Media*, a work that expands well beyond Bozak's primary focus on "peripheral examples: documentary cinema, experimental films, Third and Fourth cinema, photography and installation art" (2011, 11), offering a more comprehensive study that touches on problems of energy, waste and governmental policy, while addressing not only exceptional cinematic cases but also the mainstream of Hollywood, television and other media. An explicitly Marxist approach to the environmental impact of the media—through an incisive citation of Marx's observation that "industrial progress was 'progress in the art, not only of robbing the labourer, but of robbing the soil'" (1906, 555–56)—*Greening the Media* extends Conley's poststructuralist connection between the social movements of the 1960s and the environment by arguing that industrial capitalism produces a devaluation of worker, indigenous culture and nonhuman nature alike (2012, 89).

This address of Marx's ecological relevance is crucial in developing what I call an ecomaterialist approach that both updates the conventional notion of materialism, a methodological and conceptual move that has taunted and inspired many recent works in and peripheral to the field, from political ecology to media archeology, to object-oriented ontology (OOO). Most approaches to reconceptualizing "materialism" involve a drive to deconstruct the subject–object hierarchy founded in the classical Cartesian philosophy that still dominates most basic worldviews of the value difference between human life and non-human nature. In *Vibrant Matter*, Jane Bennett evokes Foucault's theories of power and Deleuze and Guattari's "machine assemblages" to draw our thinking to the "vitality of matter and the lively powers of material formations," insisting on the ethical necessity of such a turn, "my hunch is that the image of dead or thoroughly instrumentalized matter feeds human hubris and our earth-destroying fantasies of conquest and consumption" (2010, vii, ix). Helping to illuminate her argument that human agency has always been only "an interfolding network of humanity and nonhumanity" (31), the very term "materiality" applies a sense of flattened playing field for Bennett, "draws human attention sideways, away from the ontologically ranked Great Chain of Being and toward a greater appreciation of the complex entanglements of humans and nonhumans" (112).

Bennett's eliding comments on energy make her philosophical approach less abstractly challenging than, say, the object-oriented ontology (OOO) developed by writers such as Steven Shaviro (2014), and align her with works such as Timothy Morton's (2013) *Hyperobjects*. However, it would take extrapolations of self-styled "media archaeology" and "media ecology," such as Jennifer Garbys's *Digital Rubbish* (2013) and Jussi Parikka's (2015) *A Geology of Media* to integrate this challenge of materialism and materiality into studies of media and image culture. In what she refers to as a "natural history" of electronics, Gabrys essays a "paleontological" record of dead electronics and the fossil forms in which they persist, evidence of the "materiality of electronics," "often lost between the apparent 'virtuality' of information, the increasingly miniature scale of electronics, and the remoteness of electronic manufacture and disposal" (2013, vi).

Parikka's self-described "media history of matter" takes on a similar mission, engaging fossil and zombie media with questions of deep time to unearth "the specificity and agency of mediatic matter" (2015, 103); differentiating *media materialism* from Marx's *historical materialism*, Parikka argues that technology must be viewed as an active ontological and epistemological agent, that media—as structures of metal, plastic, energy exchange, chemical reaction—have carved a huge geopolitical and philosophical impact. Reframing Bennett's theory of vibrant matter in more specifically ecological and medial terms, Parikka writes, "In philosophical terms, the geological becomes a way to integrate in a material and non-human-centered way the constitutive folding of insides and outsides and the temporal regimes involved in media culture" (21). *Ecomaterialism* as envisioned in this essay embraces the Deleuzean aspect of this claim and these philosophical attempts to unhinge the concept of materialism: the complex enfolding of insides and outsides, the deconstruction of the subject–object hierarchy, the inter-temporality and deep time of media archeology. However, I would also incorporate this into a Marxist materialism and environmental studies notion of natural resource use, one that is grounded in the praxis of capital and exploitation, by acknowledging the planet itself as the participant in industrial productivity that is ultimately alienated completely from the product and its profits; as such, and in light of the very real concrete impact of the human endeavor on the natural ecosystem, we must shift the focus of ecocriticism to the concrete material consequences of media practices. We must move beyond the identity politics of the human, and ecocriticism must move beyond the methodological problems of representation. Maxwell and Miller point us in just such a direction when, in the opening pages of their work, they demand of the larger domain of media studies, "The field has largely neglected the physical environment. Can it be nudged toward a materialist ecology?" (2012, 9).

Extending this Marxist logic through the formation of early Hollywood and into the digital age, Maxwell and Miller assess the various ways in which, "For decades, Hollywood and the electronics sector followed a grotesque economic model that ravaged the environment in the name of entertainment, enlightenment, growth, and progress" (71). Born from the mass production techniques that catapulted the industrial revolution into the era of hypercapitalism, the moving-image and communications—that is, the "culture"—industries were bound to the same philosophy of labor, financial investment in techno-scientific research and anthropocentric standards and practices for the development and use of plastics and other potentially toxic products and substances as the other major industries to develop at the in the late nineteenth and early twentieth centuries. Going into great statistical detail of the media industries' energy demand and pollution production—"Powering Media Is a Dirty Business"—Maxwell and Miller take notice of the political policies (such as the US Toxic Substance Control Act, which allowed PCBs between 1976 and 2025) that helped to enable a grossly pollutant set of production and waste disposal practices (27).

However, in light of the recent popular concerns regarding global warming and other environmental impacts of human industry, Hollywood and the media industries have taken strides to green their practices. In equal parts environmental conscience, public-image-shaping and practical economy, the MPAA introduced a Best Practices Guide for Green Production and helped to assemble a Solid Waste Task Force, a network of companies that help to recycle production materials and eliminate solid waste; studios have introduced environmental and sustainability executives and departments and productions have begun to calculate their carbon footprints to monetize environmental impact and atone via the carbon offset market. Movies stars like Leonardo DiCaprio slum it in Priuses and make vanity projects on global warming, while taking private jets around the world and making $20 million for starring in a film decrying international labor exploitation. Obeying the logic of democratic pandering, media vehicles like Ecorazzi.com have popped up to incorporate green awareness into the ever-mirroring evolution of the star system. From Disney's greenwashing to NewsCorp's Global Energy Initiative, Hollywood and the media industry' move toward green practices is a complex machine that does not apparently challenge the fundamental ideological paradigms of excess, waste, spectacle and exploitation that have built their empire, but is based more on image rebranding and, much like its dealing with sexuality in the past, the industry's desire to maintain self-regulation and avoid government intervention. As Maxwell and Miller put it: "A social and environmental duty to care for other living creatures is absent from the rhetoric [...]. This is all at once a business plan, an element of the company's environmental policy that markets its corporate responsibility, and an attempt to elude democratic regulation" (83–84).

Case Study 2: *Titanic* (1997)

Winning 11 Oscars and taking in over two billion dollars in international profits, James Cameron's 1997 *Titanic* is a polar opposite test cast to *Baraka*: a blockbuster effects-driven spectacle directed by an established fiction feature film director and starring two up-and-coming stars, it was commercially mainstream and the darling of the Academy. Framed according to a parallel narrative structure that moves between the titular ship's 1912 maiden and sole voyage and a present-day attempt by a diving crew to wrest its artifacts for one particular survivor, the film is the play of two love stories: that between Rose and Jack (or Kate and Leo) and that between James Cameron and cinematic technology. Indeed, between the great early transport symbols of modernity (the train, the car, the ship) and the contemporary ubiquity of digital technology for atomizing and mapping our natural environs (sonar, GPS, automated drone and advanced audiovisual recording and signal processing technologies), *Titanic* stretches from port to bow of the industrial mediatized human quest to conflate, comprehend and conquer its natural surroundings. And, while the legend of that ship explicitly evokes the hubristic inclination of industrial modernity to tame the sublime scope of nature through grandiose constructions, the film lacks any irony regarding how its present-day narrative of deep-sea excavation follows this very genealogy, using elaborate transport vehicles and electronic mapping to defy all limitations to the human mastery of nature.

Though contextualized within a period-piece historical melodrama as opposed to a science-fiction future melodrama, *Titanic* rings with the climate change awareness and panic that begin to emerge in the late 1990s and early 2000s, as films like *The Day after Tomorrow* (2004) made more plot-central the rising social anxieties about the eventual environmental consequences of our civilization's practices. The building of the ship—the towering symbolism of humanity's triumph over the expanse and vicissitudes of the natural world, an icon of the industry and class exploitation that made it both desirable and possible—incited the wrath of the eco-gods who rained down their punishment from the frozen depths in the form of an iceberg. However, as indicated in my closing notes on *Baraka*, it is important that ecocriticism move beyond the limitations of representation, beyond the issue of negative and positive depictions and even beyond the question of ideology and subject-positioning, to an ecomaterialism of moving-image culture, an analysis of the concrete ecological ramifications of how we make, consume and dispose of our media texts and events.

The *Titanic* itself was not the centerpiece of the film's marketing and myth leading up to its release; instead, it was but an emblem for the grandiose production of the film itself, a marketing discourse typical of the romanticization of excess central to Hollywood's regime of spectacle. Repeatedly ballooning over budget in its quest for bigger and better effects, James Cameron's *Titanic* became the latest and largest in a long line—dating back at least to David O. Selznick's 1939 *Gone with the Wind*—of blockbuster destruction spectacles defined specifically by the excess of their means, a set of practices itself implying an indifference to resource use and waste while in pursuit of some "greater" calling: the box office, the Oscar statue. Much of the filming took place not in the Atlantic Ocean (where the film is set), but in two large water tanks built off the Pacific, in the village of Popotla in Baja, Mexico, on a 40-acre lot purchased by 20th Century Fox just for this production; one tank held 17 million gallons of water, the other held 5 million, the water being culled directly from the ocean, polluted during its cycling through the production and then pumped back into local waterways.

Maxwell and Miller highlight the film as testament to the transnational cultural production intended by the North American Free Trade Agreement (NAFTA), and the film's generation of certain levels of local industry and interest earned director James Cameron the Order of the Aztec Eagle from the grateful Mexican government (2012, 69). However, while it did bring a heightened visibility to northern Mexico as a site of cheap labor for American productions, to which Hollywood could easily relocate materials and equipment, there was also a very negative "unseen" impact on the local biosphere—"unseen" in that it was not part of Fox's marketing campaign for the film, nor part of the narrative being told in the trade papers, such as *Variety*, that feigned outrage and incredulity at the film's excesses in order to implicitly reaffirm Hollywood's grandeur. Popotla was cut off from the sea and local fisheries by a massive movie wall that was built to keep local citizens away, and Fox's chlorine treatment of the water on set led to the pollution of surrounding seawater, decimated the local sea urchin industry, thereby reducing overall fish levels by a third (70).

None of this was, of course, part of the film's marketing discourse: it focused on the Titanic-esque production history and the Titan-esque feats of the director, the visual grandeur of the film's effects and production design and the sweeping romance of the central love story. The text itself may be a model of dramatic structure and classical continuity technique, but the true story of the film takes place over two years in the mid- to late 1990s; what should be of central concern to film theorists is not the film's representational romanticization of an ill-fated moment in civilization, but the concrete importance of the film's material reality: the natural resources that were used to get the film shot and onto the screen, the ecosystem impact that the shoot had on its environs and the social contract of spectacle that prizes the myth of excessive production above all else. And, while *Titanic* certainly speaks to the apotheosis of an industrial-age modernity and also of a classical Hollywood mode of excessive production and regime of spectacle, its special effects innovations also point us toward a new horizon of cultural technology and a new network of the ecological ramifications of media practice beyond the traditional cinematic apparatus.

When Alison Anderson argues that the green movement is historically part of a new relationship between activist organization and the public, she refers to the role that television and visual politics play in the new order of social change on two levels: both the ability of a group like Greenpeace to spread its message via communications media and also the power of visual expression in impressing upon the public the crimes being committed against nature through audiovisual representation and rhetoric (1997, 22). However important this rhetorical and representational evolution is, an ecomaterialist approach would demand that we consider the concrete ecological impact of the new technologies that have coincided with the growth of the green movement over the last decades.

Having gained much traction and bursting into popular familiarity and concern at around the same time (the *Time* cover story was 1989 and Steven Spielberg's *Jurassic Park* gave the audiences of 1993 a sneak preview of the digital film revolution to come), the green movement and the digital turn are often viewed as coinciding historically. As hinted at earlier, in fact, the two are often seen to be, if not causally linked, at least ontologically and ideologically intertwined—"ontologically" in that their mode of being can be understood as coexistent and even symbiotic, "ideological" in that they are both often politicized against traditional practices and viewed in tandem as working toward a cleaner, more efficient and more democratized future, with digital technology purportedly requiring less material input, operating with more energy economy and producing less tangible products (such as film itself) and waste. Adrian Ivakhiv notes that the recent tightening of the ties that bind moving-image culture and discourse on the environment is part of a historical genealogy: "Cinema arose alongside the industrialization of material production—that is, alongside the unleashing of creative capacities that had been stored on or beneath the surface of the planet for millennia. Digitalization is simply the latest phase of the development of the bio-social-technical apparatus that has undergirded industrialization" (2013, 338).

Many argue optimistically that this dependency and excess are lessening with the advent of digital technology; however, Bozak and others reveal the dangers of this shift, from preproduction through the waste disposal phase. While new smart technologies appear to get smaller and more efficient, their size belies a vast array of production resources and a tangled web of geopolitical conflict. In *Digital Rubbish*, Jennifer Gabrys calculates that "to produce a two-gram memory microchip, 1.3 kilograms of fossil fuels and materials are required" (2013, 26).[2] Moreover, the rare precious metals used in these technologies are the object of a new world political order, from basic strategies of import-export policy to violent guerilla warfare (such as the civil wars sparked across and surrounding in the Democratic Republic of Congo between paramilitaries battling over the nation's reserves of Coltan, a precious metal used in capacitors for laptops and other smart technology).

Even the heightened use of digital technology during the production phase, from art films like *Russian Ark* to blockbusters like *Avatar*, which has carried with it an often exaggerated public relations campaign for green practices, poses new demands on the earth's resources and increases pollution through the energy required by digital servers and the cooling warehouses that run and store them. As Bozak claims, "Behind the phantom image composed of touchless binary code is a pulsing, energy-hungry data processing center" (2013, 146). This extends well beyond the scope of traditional film studies and theory, and—like so many developments of the last 20 years, and as many essays in this collection demand—pushes us to acknowledge that film and cinema are part of a larger network of media that we engage with daily and that consequently demands new and more interdisciplinary critical frameworks. As demonstrated in Nicole Starosielski's *The Undersea Network* (2015) and the *Sustainable Media* collection, Maxwell and Miller's *Greening the Media* and Sean Cubitt's work from *Ecomedia* to *Finite Media* (2017), the mission of ecomaterialism is quickly adapting to the range of media that define our cultural values and social habits.

Ecomaterialist scholars such as Bozak and Maxwell and Miller shift our attention beyond the phases of development and production, to those of distribution, exhibition and disposal of the vast network of digital and smart technology necessary to consume the texts of the digital era, an era increasingly governed by a seemingly hyper-advanced technology whose "guiding principle is planned obsolescence," a paradigm that is itself horribly anachronistic and negligent of the geopolitics and environmental impact of waste (Bozak 2013, 179). Building upon nineteenth-century Western ethics of waste and lingering remnants of postcolonial cultural terrorism, this cultural world of excessive digital waste has given rise to the era of the digital dumping ground, in which "the richest regions of the world use those of the poorest as dumping grounds for noxious electronic junk" (2012, 104). E-waste and scrap hardware are shipped to villages in Kenya, Nigeria, Brazil, China and elsewhere, where a rising labor class made up predominantly of preteen girls forage and melt down hardware to extract precious metals, a highly toxic process that presents clear and immediate danger as well as allowing for toxins to seep into the local soil and water supply, polluting the ecosystem for generations to come. As we can see from the preproduction industrial development phase to the new modes of digital production to the waste disposal of smart modernity, in Jussi Parikka's words from *A Geology of Media*, "despite 'the digital' carrying continuously the immaterial connotations of information, it is and always has been grounded and also territorialized" (2015, 111).

In other words, digital media have heightened the dangerous myth of immateriality connected to audiovisual culture, a network of practices that we can see is far from immaterial but, instead, makes use of concrete resources and has tangible impact on the earth, natural environments and humanity as well. Just as the more conventional cinema before it, new media are both the subject and object of a new environmental frontier: they can be used to express and represent ecological issues, while at the same time the way they are made and used has profound ecological repercussions. While this is not a call to the extreme opposite of classical subjective philosophies, such as can be found in the fascinating recent movement toward OOO and speculative realism found in the works of Shaviro and others, it is certainly necessary to grant more concern to our impact on the nonhuman world and to reconsider our evaluation of the role played by the machinery of our culture. As McKenzie Wark (2015) points out, a recent history of ecology and climate science is a history of its media; and, this story must include the flip side to how such technology and media show us the world—it must include how such methods use nature as well. Just as new technologies have produced a new phase of environmental problems, they have also helped to generate and disseminate information about these problems.

In other words, there is a growing symbiosis that implores us to include our media of analysis into our environmental thinking, just as the prominence of environmental issues and awareness makes it no longer possible to neglect the material natural impact of our cultural practices. To use Bozak's words, "as the digital revolution and the green revolution continue to converge and the more that information about the depth of our reliance on nature's power becomes available, the more difficult to *not* see how the energy economy and the image economy (and the information economy more broadly) are inextricably intertwined. It is necessary to consider both, together and separately, for each current comes together—collides, really—in the fluctuating space of the cinematic image" (2013, 190). But, as is clear, these issues stretch well beyond cinema or what is traditionally thought of as "cinema" or "film," and the rising tide of environmental interest across the humanities and social sciences is helping to tear down the barriers of any monodisciplinary approach to theorizing film and media. Just as digital media and online platforms are changing the format of how environmental messages are constructed and disseminated, so must the qualitative approaches of screen studies and the empirical methods of communications and anthropology find new reconciliations, to bring us ways of understanding environmental media that account for aesthetics and rhetoric, ethics and materiality. Hopefully, by recasting the lens of theory in relation to the natural world, we will learn that being human, and that human culture, are not conditions and exercises that exist through the use of and despite the limitations of the natural world, but instead that our endeavors are parts of a nature that we indelibly affect with every act, every scene, every image.

Notes

1 Paula Willoquet-Maricondi refers to this turn as a "paradigm shift" that is occurring, from environmentalist films such as *A River Runs through It* to ecocinema films such as *Riverglass*, in which we challenge the conventional view of nature as an object within the human narrative and, instead, consider its own perspective in an inter-subjective context that we share (2010, 45–47).

2 For more information, see Jan Mazurek, *Making Microchips: Policy, Globalization, and Economic Restructuring in the Semiconductor Industry* (Cambridge, MA: MIT Press, 1999).

Works Cited

Anderson, Alison. 1997. *Media, Culture, and the Environment.* New Brunswick, NJ: Rutgers University Press.

Bennett, Jane. 2010. *Vibrant Matter.* Durham: Duke University Press.

Bozak, Nadia. 2012. *The Cinematic Footprint.* New Brunswick, NJ: Rutgers University Press.

Brereton, Pat. 2005. *Hollywood Utopia: Ecology in Contemporary American Cinema.* Chicago: Intellect Books.

Buell, Lawrence. 1996. *The Environmental Imagination.* Cambridge: Harvard University Press.

Conley, Verena Andermatt. 1997. *Ecopolitics.* New York: Routledge.

Cubitt, Sean. 2005. *Eco Media.* Amsterdam: Rodopi.

Dobson, Andrea. 2004. *Citizenship and the Environment.* Oxford: Oxford University Press.

Garbys , Jennifer. 2013. *Digital Rubbish.* Ann Arbor: University of Michigan Press.

Glotfelty, Cheryll, and Harold Fromm, eds. 1996. *The Ecocriticism Reader.* Athens: University of Georgia Press.

Gustafsson, Tommy, and Pietari Kääpä. 2013. *Transnational Ecocinema.* Chicago: Intellect Books.

Hageman, Andrew. 2012. "Ecocinema and Ideology: Do Ecocritics Dream of a Clockwork Green?" In *Ecocinema Theory and Practice*, edited by Salma Monani, Sean Cubitt et al., 63–86. New York: Routledge Press.

Ingram, David. 2000. *Green Screen: Environmentalism and Hollywood Cinema.* Exeter: University of Exeter Press.

Ivakhiv, Adrian. 2013. *Ecologies of the Moving Image.* Waterloo, ON: Wilfred Laurier Press.

Marx, Karl. 1906. *Capital Vol. 1.* Translated by Samuel Moore. New York: Modern Library.

Maxwell, Richard, and Toby Miller. 2012. *Greening the Media.* Oxford: Oxford University Press.

Mazurek, Jan. 1999. *Making Microchips: Policy, Globalization, and Economic Restructuring in the Semiconductor Industry.* Cambridge, MA: MIT Press.

Morton, Timothy. 2013. *Hyperobjects.* Minneapolis: University of Minnesota.

Moore, Ellen Elizabeth. 2015. "Green Screen or Smokescreen? Hollywood's Messages about Nature and the Environment." *Environmental Communication* 10: 539–55. doi:10.1080/17524032.2015.1014391.

Murray, Robin L., and Joseph K. Heumann. 2009. *Ecology and Popular Film.* New York: SUNY Press.

Nardelli, Matilde. 2013. "The Sprawl of Entropy: Cinema, Waste, and Obsolescence in the 1960s and 1970s." *Necsus* 1, no. 2: 431–46.

Parikka, Jussi. 2015. *A Geology of Media.* Minneapolis: University of Minnesota Press.

Roberts, Martin. 1998. "'Baraka': World Cinema and the Global Culture Industry." *Cinema Journal* 37, no. 3 (Spring): 62–82.

Rodowick, David. 2001. "Dr. Strange Media." *PMLA* 116, no. 5: 1396–404.

Rust, Stephen, Salma Monani, and Sean Cubitt. 2013. *Ecocinema: Theory and Practice.* New York: Routledge.

Sancton, Thomas A. 1989. "Planet of the Year: Endangered Earth." *Time* (January 2).

Schoonover, Karl. 2013. "Documentaries without Documents? Ecocinema and the Toxic." *Necsus* 1, no. 2: 431–46.

Shaviro, Steven. 2014. *The Universe of Things: On Speculative Realism.* Minneapolis: University of Minnesota Press.

Starosielski, Nicole. 2015. *The Undersea Network.* Durham: Duke University Press.

Vaughan, Hunter. 2016. "500,000 Kilowatts of Stardust." In *Sustainable Media*, edited by Nicole Starosielski and Janet Walker, 25–37. New York: Routledge.

Wark, Mackenzie. 2015. *Molecular Red.* Brooklyn: Verso.

Wellig, Bart. 2009. *Ecosee*, edited by Sidney I. Dobrin and Sean Morey. Albany: SUNY.

Williams, Raymond. 1973. *The Country and the City.* New York: Oxford University Press.

Willoquet-Maricondi, Paula, ed. 2010. *Framing the World: Explorations in Ecocriticism and Film.* Richmond: University of Virginia Press.

Chapter Seven

"WE WILL EXCHANGE YOUR LIKENESS AND RECREATE YOU IN WHAT YOU WILL NOT KNOW": TRANSCULTURAL PROCESS PHILOSOPHY AND THE MOVING IMAGE

Laura U. Marks

And you see the mountains, considering them solid, but they are passing by like the floating of clouds.

—Qur'an 28:88

Viewing a thing from the outside, considering its relations of action and reaction with other things, it appears as matter. Viewing it from the inside, looking at its immediate character as feeling, it appears as consciousness.

—Charles Sanders Peirce[1]

The triumph of consciousness comes with the negative intuitive judgment […] a conscious feeling of what might be, but is not.

—Alfred North Whitehead[2]

This essay invites those of us who think with cinema to try on a process approach. Let's try seeing the world as an open, ever-changing whole, a matrix of motile relations from which all kinds of entities take shape, differentiate and create new relations. This is what we see when we switch from a metaphysics of substance to a metaphysics of process.[3] As we'll see, film theory is already doing process philosophy, avowedly or not. I will introduce some concepts from process metaphysics that show how objects crystallize from processes; characterize becoming as an interrupted flow; privilege relations over fixity; treasure singularity; and critically examine how entities individuate in a milieu. All these concepts lend well to thinking alongside movies. The essay will draw on European and North American process thinkers, highlighting the work of Alfred North Whitehead. I will also bring in the thoroughly modern thought of the seventeenth-century Persian philosopher Sadr al-Din al-Shirazi, or Mulla Sadrā, and the relational philosophy of Martinican philosopher-poet Édouard Glissant.

My cinematic thinking companion, two works by African American filmmaker Arthur Jafa, test the possibility of viewing someone or something—in particular, Black people and Blackness—as not a figure, subject/object or thing but as a process of becoming. Jafa's 2013 documentary *Dreams Are Colder Than Death* both witnesses and elicits creative individuations, within and despite a murderous milieu. Jafa's film draws in arguments from Black intellectuals, including Saidiya V. Hartman, Hortense Spillers and Fred Moten, which enable me to test and hone the aptness of process concepts of singularity, individuation and relation. All these ingredients, refined with cinema's unique process capacities and seasoned with a dash of neo-Marxism, will finally give rise to some process-based concepts of radical social creativity, which will constitute—to use a term of Whitehead—this essay's satisfaction.

Cinema Studies and Process Philosophy

In his enjoyably curmudgeonly manner, Graham Harman writes, "The current fashion is to view substances as rigid, static, reactionary, patriarchal, and oppressive, while dynamic fluxes and flows strike the educated public as innovative, liberating, interactive, holistic, and fresh."[4] This remark suggests that cinema studies, if it hasn't already embraced and surpassed process philosophy, is thoroughly behind the curve. Nevertheless, a default substantialism, the belief that the basic entities of being are substances, still populates many of our movies and methods. As Nicholas Rescher points out, thinking in terms of substances raises all kinds of problems. How do you explain the way an acorn becomes a tree? How can you determine whether a sock that has been mended until it's all new material is still the same sock? Process metaphysics considers that processes, not substances, are fundamental: substances are just effects of processes. So the fundamental stuff of the universe consists not of substances—acorn, tree, sock—but of the processes by which an acorn becomes a tree, the process of mending by which a sock becomes a different sock.[5]

Cinema studies' substantialism is easy to understand, as most movies are about people who do things in places—a chain of discrete entities, or substances. Yet it's easy to acknowledge that processes are real when we ask how people change, what constitutes a place, how things come to be and pass away. In this simple shift of perspective, the focus changes from objects to processes, "figure" to "ground." Movies fall into a fascinating new relief. Our most time-honored approaches, looked at from this angle, can be seen as studies of process. And the Process Studies Institute in Claremont, CA, has been holding a film festival since 2001. Given the radically interdependent nature of all that exists, the festival organizers point out, "We are each responsible for contributing as much as we can toward the common good."[6]

All art forms can fruitfully be considered in terms of process. Recorded, time-based media have special vocabularies to trace the processual lives of things, for they suggest in time both how individuals become completely singular or realized and how they break down and give rise to other individuals. Cinema and its theories have mostly dwelt on the separateness and otherness of individual entities, especially human individuals. But cinema as a time-based medium also shows the processes that give rise to individuals, the ways they are formed by their milieu and how they become part of the milieu for others. And cinema also turns away from humans to show processes in nature, industrial processes, ecological change, the fantastic becomings of animation and any number of other processes of transformation.

In fact, cinema studies has been doing process philosophy for years without specifically acknowledging it. Moving images by their nature partake in processes, collapsing the wave into a particle, teasing the particle into a wave. Narrative theory, for example, shows its process roots in Hegelian dialectics, a ceaseless dynamic of confrontation and synthesis between opposed entities. Psychoanalytic film theory examines the struggle, often violent, between a self and the disavowed others that constitute it. Phenomenology pays as much attention to the relationships that give rise to perception and meaning as it does to perception and meaning themselves. Feminist film theories draw attention to the relations and processes that generate meaning and subjectivity. Similarly, queer, postcolonial and race-critical theories critique the fixity of representation and put figure-ground relationships into process; for example, to disrupt movies' reliance on solo heroes by showing the relational web that engenders and supports individuals. Critical race theory, as this essay will show, dissolves the fiction of the sovereign subject and replaces fixed identity with relationality. Sometimes it appears that new fashion for process philosophy, and other philosophies that turn away from the human, is appropriating the findings of these identity-based critical theories. My method in what follows works against that tendency.

Process philosophy "proper" has sprung up all over the humanities in recent years. Film and media scholars are drawing from the minor but deep process strand of Western philosophy, a strand that includes Gilles Deleuze, Gilbert Simondon, Whitehead, Gottfried Wilhelm Leibniz and Baruch Spinoza. Deleuze and Deleuzian film scholars describe cinema as the intensifying counterpart to a flowing, individuating world, the closest approximation of the universe according to Bergson. Peirce's semiosis, a world of swirling signs in constant communication and transformation, also contributes to the process nature of Deleuze's cinematic philosophy.[7] The theory of affect, which has inspired and been developed by cinema scholars too numerous to cite, is also a theory of process, analyzing the field of affective relations that remake and recombine bodies, human and nonhuman, filmic and spectatorial. Phenomenologies of cinema and media pay attention to how the apparatus perceives, or "prehends," to use Whitehead's term, the pro-filmic reality.[8] We can also think of editing and postproduction as prehensive events resulting in satisfaction. A number of film scholars have moved along a trajectory over the years from Deleuze or phenomenology to theories of affect to process philosophy.[9]

Ecological film theory too recognizes the usefulness of process philosophy. Most process philosophies hold that every entity in the universe—human, molecule, tree, civilization—is ontologically equal, even if some are more complex than others. This recognition shifts the focus from humans to honor the life of every entity and recognize the relations among all beings. Studies of the material ecology of cinema itself, the carbon footprint of filmmaking, exhibition, distribution and archiving, take seriously the ecological relationships incurred at every stage of the cinematic event.[10] A process-ecological approach, such as that developed by Adrian Ivakhiv, allows us to study not only how movies represent ecology, but the interdependency of humans and the natural world and the processes, at scales larger and smaller than the human, through which our relationships unfold.[11]

In my use, the word *cinema* keeps intact the definition of recorded moving images, and it denotes any kind of time-based, moving-image media, recorded or rendered, from large-screen films to digital video to smartphone apps. Cinema is always live, and therefore, an event and a process, occurring in time in an assemblage with place and audience.[12] Numerous media theorists draw on process philosophy and actor-network theory to redefine media in terms of relations and assemblages rather than specific mediums.[13] For my purposes in this essay, the assemblage engendered by the single-channel audiovisual moving image, the world it encounters, and the beholders who receive it abundantly rewards a process analysis. Process philosophy does, however, have a particular appeal for analyzing non-theatrical digital media. Timothy Scott Barker draws on Whitehead, Deleuze and Michel Serres to emphasize the multiple temporalities and performative encounters of interactive media.[14] Azadeh Emadi brings Sadrā and Deleuze to understand the intensive, non-chronological temporality of the pixel, arguing that digital video has the potential to render the reality of existence more truthfully because its pixels, as a unified internal multiplicity, change and move in infinite time, forming a perceptual unit of moving image.[15]

A Note on "Western" and "Non-Western," Philosophy and Theory

Whitehead writes that his "philosophy of organism" has stronger links with Indian and Chinese thought than with European or West Asian (by which I think he means Arabic) philosophy.[16] Harman rather sarcastically dismisses the legacy: "Non-Western cultures are frequently praised for being less beholden to petrified enduring substances and their ostensible counterpart, subject-predicate grammar."[17] Ivakhiv notes that process-relational thought has a deep and global history: "in the pre-Socratic Greek philosopher Heraclitus and in the later Hellenistic Stoics, in Nagarjuna and the Madhyamika philosophers of India, and in Shuang Zhu and the T'ian-t'ài and Hua-Yen Buddhists in China," as well as a long list of European and North American thinkers beginning with Giordano Bruno, Spinoza, and Leibniz.[18] Yet while opportunities for intercultural concept-making often get mentioned in passing, they are rarely explored.

Process philosophy's transcultural siblings include cyclical ontologies, such as those of Zoroastrianism, Taoism and Buddhism.[19] They include thought systems that emphasize interconnectedness across time and species, which Aboriginal philosophies exemplify. Interestingly, theological process studies—which was developing Whiteheadian ideas while film scholars were still trying to get their heads around Lacan's *objet petit "a"*—has a history of addressing non-Western approaches in pursuing Whitehead's positioning of God as the entity that incorporates all actualizations.[20] Some in media studies are making good on Whitehead's casual observation; for example, Sha Xin Wei, in his process model of interactive media art, identifies the philosophical roots of process philosophy with Laozi and Zhuangzi as well as Heraclitus, Marx, Foucault and Whitehead.[21] Process philosophy also has strong meeting points with panpsychism, the belief that some kind of soul or mind is in everything, whether because everything has spirit, as in many Aboriginal philosophies, Jainism and Shintoism, or because the universe is a single entity from which all things emanate or differentiate, as in the somewhat more Western views descended from Neoplatonism. Sadrā, for example, is a panpsychist because he equates being and consciousness.[22]

Though he is by no means alone in such omissions, Ivakhiv's list cited above neglects the transformative contribution of Arabic and Islamic thought to process philosophy, let alone the conceptual bridges it built between Greek and European thought.[23] Moreover, the source from which both Arabic and European philosophy diverged, eventually (sooner in the Arabic case) to rediscover process philosophy, is a single thinker, Avicenna (Ibn Sînā). Western philosophy is only recently devising concepts of becoming, individuation and intensity that resemble those developed by Islamic systematic philosophies of process centuries ago. Therefore, while I'd like to see all kinds of intercultural work on process philosophy, the one I will take up has not only conceptual resonance but a strong historical foundation.

The most fully developed of these is the work of seventeenth-century philosopher Sadr al-Dîn Muhammad al-Shîrāzî, or Mulla Sadrā (1571–1640). Sadrā's process philosophy developed the Peripatetic (Greek-Islamic) synthesis of Avicenna, Sunni and Shi'a rationalist theology, the Illuminationism of Suhrawardi and the Sufism of Ibn 'Arabi. These shared concerns of modern Euro-American and modern Islamic philosophy with conceptions of being as a process are gradually being recognized.[24] Eastern Islamic thought continued in a process vein after Sadrā, for example, in the work of Shi'i philosopher and mystic Shaykh Aḥmad al-Aḥsā'ī (1753–1826), whose thought Farshid Kazemi is working to bring into contact with cinema.[25] I wish to incorporate Islamic process philosophy with a minimum of fuss, given that it constitutes part of the expanded Western philosophical legacy.

The Martinican poet and philosopher Édouard Glissant argues, inflecting concepts of Deleuze and Guattari, that identity is inextricably relational, a rhizomatic process of becoming. Glissant's Mondalité or worldliness is an avowedly fragmentary knowledge, based on irreducible difference and open to the outside. He argues that Caribbean-style relational thinking must replace the Mediterranean-based thought systems based on origins, filiation and legitimacy.

Both Sadrā and Glissant respond directly to the Greek sources claimed by Western philosophy. Their thought gives us an opportunity to reconsider the category of Western philosophy and to either expand it, to include Islamic and African-diasporic philosophy, or to suspend it as a category. Arabic and Islamic philosophy tends to be excluded from non-Western philosophical surveys because they are not exotic enough, and from Western surveys because, although modern European philosophy is in large part founded on Arabic philosophy, this connection is usually minimized or repressed. Glissant's philosophy of relation is a truly "American" philosophy, arising from the history of the Americas: the survivors of slave ships and plantations attained relational epistemology, an understanding of the totality by way of the part that is denied to those who think in generalizations.

Glissant would refuse to be categorized a systematic philosopher, even along the anti-discursive lines of Whitehead and Sadrā. He rejects "theoretical thinking" for its tendency to reduction and dogmatism and cautions that methods lead to laziness. Instead of examples, he gives long, poetic lists. Glissant's thought regrounds (I would write "re-racinates," were he not so opposed to roots) the process philosophies of Whitehead and

Sadrā, examining "Relation" on social, political and ecological scales that center on the Caribbean and relate to the totality. Alexander Weheliye points out that white European thinkers get "conceptual carte blanche" while the same arguments coming from minorities are relegated to their ethnographic locality. For example, Giorgio Agamben's concept of "bare life" is based on the extreme example of the concentration camp, rather than the more "ordinary" slavery, and then elevated to a concept neutral of any racial or ethnic history.[26] By such sleights of hand, certain thinkers are elevated as philosophers, while others are considered local, partial theorists.

Arthur Jafa's Process-Relational Cinema

Arthur Jafa, whose works will singularize this essay's thought process, is the acknowledged master of African American cinematography, who has filmed for Black auteurs including Julie Dash, Spike Lee and John Akomfrah. Throughout his oeuvre, Jafa has developed means to show Black figures in states of emergence and relation, often by making the "background" alive with movement, vibration and presence. For example, to shoot some scenes of Dash's *Daughters of the Dust* (1991), which portrays an African American extended family in the late nineteenth century, Jafa used a hand-crank camera, which allows the frame rate to vary. As the scenes of the family moving together on the beach gently quickens and slows, the film suggests an intensive temporality. For this innovative and stunning work, he won Best Cinematography at Sundance. Jafa wrote in 1992 that the hand-crank camera is "a more appropriate instrument with which to create movement that replicates the tendency in Black music to 'worry the note'—to treat notes as indeterminate, inherently unstable sonic frequencies rather than the standard Western treatment of notes as fixed phenomena."[27] Through cinematography and digital editing, Jafa continues to develop what he calls "black visual intonation."

Many Black scholars critique visual media for their tendency to objectify what it sets before our eyes, and hence to commodify and fetishize. They look instead to Black sonic experimentation for liberatory aesthetics. The critique certainly holds for representations that manage Blackness into that which can be safely consumed as an object or unproblematically "identified" with.[28] By contrast, the effect of Jafa's visual experiments is to emphasize that images, like people, arise from a relational field that draws in both history and the viewer.

Jafa made *Dreams Are Colder Than Death* (2013) for German television company ZDF on the fiftieth anniversary of Martin Luther King's "I Have a Dream" speech. Black intellectuals and artists in the United States, talking with Jafa and Greg Tate, respond in many ways to the question of what Blackness means, with recurrent themes of the still-volatile inheritance of slavery; Black community and creativity; the constant threat to Black life. We do not see their faces as they speak, and the camera does not look into their eyes. Instead, it approaches them askance, caressing the skin of fingers, the silhouette of eye and eyelid, a burst of hair. The figures are often backlit, illuminated by lens flares; lens flares transfigure the silhouette of filmmaker Charles Burnett's silhouetted head in a burst of shimmering rose-gold hexagons. When Jafa does show the faces of his interlocutors, they are silent and statuesque. In these ways, the cinematography defers subjectifying the speakers, in the sense of identifying their being with their psychic interiority. Instead, it suggests that their ideas cannot be separated from their living bodies and the atmosphere in which they are immersed.

Dreams Are Colder Than Death, as I will describe, is full of life, in large part through its seemingly casual documentary sequences. Historical photographs, including documents of foulest violence, accompany the speakers—and so do renderings of distant planets, galaxies and spacecraft. Melvin Gibbs's minimalist score, a low, pulsating drone occasionally punctuated with a soft resonant beat, underscores feelings of latent energy—and latent threat.

Subjects? Objects? in a Relational Field

The subject of Jafa's films, what it is and how it feels to be Black in the United States, immediately raises questions about the aptness of process approaches, the vogue for which constitutes part of the larger nonhuman turn in contemporary critical theory. The general eclipse of theories of the subject has a weightlessness that smacks of disavowal. With object-oriented philosophy, the psychological interiority that people are no longer supposed to have has been transferred to nonhuman entities. A whiff of disavowal extends to process philosophy too, in which humans have no special privilege over other atoms jostling around in the universe. It seems weird to celebrate a flattened ontology, be it the relational one of process philosophy or the object-oriented one, when the Western liberal notion of the subject endures not-quite-deconstructed, legal systems based on it remain intact, and Black people continue to be treated as objects in the American law enforcement, prison and entertainment industries. Yet, modern liberal individualism's theory of the free and self-determining subject relies on a fictional substantialism produced by disavowing material and economic relationships.[29] Saidiya V. Hartman shows that after Emancipation, freed slaves were required to adopt the responsibilities of the liberal individual, "displac[ing] the nation's responsibility for providing and ensuring the rights and privileges conferred by the Reconstruction Amendments and shift[ing] the burden of duty onto the freed."[30] In short, modern American law constructs subjects by disavowing the economic, social and historical relations that actually constitute them.[31] Treated as objects, not yet subjects, why would Black people be interested in a philosophy that dissolves both object- and subjecthood in a field of relational processes?

Jafa's short film *APEX* (2014) consists entirely of hyper-volatile figures. In this devastating seven-minute high-speed montage with pounding electronic dance music, still images flash by in a half-second, just enough to brand themselves on a viewer's eyeballs. Some of them touch the most painful wounds of African American history, including the infamous photograph of a lynched Black man tied to a tree, and a woman lying on a bed with her arms cruelly bound behind her. Also flashing by are— a futuristic Grace Jones; a satanically grinning black Mickey Mouse; a man with a gleaming grill on his teeth who looks psychotic but (if the viewer pauses the video to check) is just wall-eyed. These pictures alternate with creepy extreme close-ups of microscopic insects. *APEX* feels dangerous to watch, as though the images have the power to infect the viewer, or as though they already have.

The violence and uncanniness of *APEX*'s hyper-objectified images explode the categories of figure and object. They show Black people spectacularized in their reduction to things, that is, fetishized. A fetish is a seeming object that is volatile because it is composed of relations to entities and events from the past, its "outside." Fetishism disavows relations—sexual, economic and historical—by pressing them into the object. There the relations threaten to remanifest, to show how you the viewer are connected to the thing you are beholding. This is why fetishes feel so threatening.

Black philosophers, including some who speak in *Dreams Are Colder Than Death*, ask what kind of interiority a human object, the chattel slave, might possess. Moten compares the slave to Marx's impossible notion of a commodity that speaks—or more precisely, screams. A chattel slave is a being consigned by law and language to the status of a thing, but whose living voice corrodes those systems from within. What appears to be objects maintain a private reserve that is effectively performative.[32] In the same way, Jafa's images in *APEX* embody a radioactive agency that will destroy any safe, separate, "positive" figurations of Blackness.

The nonhuman turn needs a shot in the arm from Black anti-humanism, which critiques ideals of humanity and individuality that have never fully admitted Black and other people. If the theory of the subject be cast aside, let it be with the contemptuousness of Afrofuturism. To appropriate Kodwo Eshun's words, Blackness now "deliberately fails all these Tests [of humanity], these putrid corpses of petrified moralism; it treats them with utter indifference; it replaces them with nothing whatsoever."[33] Given this context, process philosophy's treatment of relational becoming can be adequate to thinking with and through apparent objects that tremble with potentiality, without lapsing into what we could call ontological flatness. Every object, seen from inside, is a subject, and the heart of every subject pulses with relations. We'll see that for Whitehead, Sadrā and Glissant—with differences, of course—things connect internally to the entire universe. A seeming object has potentially infinite internal connections to the universe that other entities may or may not recognize. What appear to be objects are processes of relation.

Saccadic Flows

Some worry that process implies "going with the flow," a mushy world in which everything blurs with everything else, incapacitating the conflict and confrontation that politics necessitates.[34] However, process philosophy has a saccadic side, in which flow takes form and requires conflict. Processes consist not of mush or the *informe* but saccadic, completely actualized steps. Harman divides process philosophy into schools that dissolve all into flows, including Gilbert Simondon and Deleuze, and those that retain objects, like Whitehead. However, even in those approaches that radically de-emphasize the object, processes have their own structures, including likely outcomes, while they remain open-ended.[35] They are becomings that cannot be reversed. Keith Robinson argues that Whitehead and Deleuze differ most fundamentally in their understanding of the relationship between creativity and continuity. For Whitehead, creativity gathers, synthesizes and unifies. "In this activity the actual occasion is produced, the new is disclosed, and its achievement becomes objectively immortal, 'saved' by passing into the 'consequent nature' of God. For Deleuze, in contrast, the essential movement of time in creativity breaks and disrupts any gathering, disjoins synthesis, and opens thought to an unknown future."[36] It's possible to dispute this assessment by pointing to Deleuze's career-long interest in the univocity of being, the force of differentiation that is itself a form of continuity (which, we will see, closely resembles Sadrā's concept of Being).[37] But for both philosophers, as Robinson emphasizes, creativity works through continuous actualizations, quantum breaks in the flow of becoming.

Cinema studies already deploys the quantum-like steps of process approaches in triadic systems based on Charles Sanders Peirce's semiosis. Deleuze characterizes the cinema in terms of Peirce's triadic structure of experience, which he translates as affection, action and reception. Cubitt himself proposes that cinema consists of the triad pixel, cut and vector, which he synthesizes from Deleuze's Peircean triad and Lacan's triad of the unconscious, namely imaginary, symbolic and real.[38] Ivakhiv's process-relational analysis of cinema is grounded in the interrelated triad of social (anthropomorphic), material (geomorphic) and perceptual. The model of enfolding-unfolding aesthetics that I propose analyzes perceptibles as nodes in a process whose sources is the immanent infinite.[39] In this triadic process, the images our bodies receive unfold from information, which, in a given manner of enfolding, enfolds the infinite. In what I call the "affect of unfolding," when a change of state occurs, you feel it.

Whitehead's Process Universe: Intensifying Atomistic Becomings

Whitehead's universe is an interconnected, open whole in a constant, atomistic process of transformation.[40] At the simplest level, these processes are undergone by things he terms both *actual entities* and *actual occasions*, depending on whether one focuses on the thing in space or in time. In the process of its own coming together, an entity selectively feels (prehends) the sea of data in which it swims, privately synthesizes these feelings, transforming them into a coherent, complex feeling, or *satisfaction*, and passes into immortality, in turn becoming new data for other entities in the universe.[41] At the same time, other entities in the vicinity are coming into being by responding differently to the data.

Echoing Peirce, quoted in the epigraph of this essay, Whitehead argues that every experience has two poles: how it feels from the inside (the subjectivating pole), and how it appears from the outside (the objectivating pole). The process of coming together begins with the subjective experience of the universe's infinite, swirling data and of the pure potentials or *eternal objects* that can be activated (in Whitehead's term, *ingress*) in one of these comings-together. Thrillingly, Whitehead asserts that every entity in the universe prehends every other entity. The catch is that this prehension can be positive or negative. For example, I negatively prehend the color of the socks of my next-door neighbor. How, then, does the emergent entity "decide" what to take in? First, though causal efficacy, a feeling of influence related to self-preservation, such as plants feel when they grow toward the light or people feel when they hear vague noises in the dark. Causal efficacy determines what data will be felt and taken up as the entity comes together. Then a more disinterested observation, which Whitehead calls presentational immediacy, kicks in to assess the data.[42]

The actual occasion then privately unifies the diverse data into a single, cohesive and determinate entity. This involves what Whitehead calls the *aesthetic supplement.*

> There is an emotional appreciation of the contrasts and rhythms inherent in the unification of the objective content in the concrescence of one actual occasion. In this phase perception is heightened by its assumption of pain and pleasure, beauty and distaste. It is the phase of inhibitions and intensifications. It is the phase in which blue becomes more intense by reason of its contrasts, and shape acquires dominance by reason of its loveliness. What was received as alien, is recreated as private.[43]

As the emergent entity or occasion is still choosing how to prehend the data that will determine its final form, it undergoes a private process of testing, intensifying some contrasts and inhibiting others. Like going on a date or cooking soup, the emergent entity privately feels, tastes and adjusts what it is becoming.

The process of coming together concludes in satisfaction, a state in which the actual entity has (positively or negatively) prehended every item in its universe and is ready to become an objective element of the universe, completely singular, for others to enjoy.

An actual entity can be as large as a civilization or as small as a quark. Relatively enduring composites of actual entities are termed *nexûs* and *societies*; for example, a person is a society. It's tempting to say that the tiniest entities constitute the proper realm of inquiry, begging an infinite regress of explanation. But since actual entities, according to Whitehead, are any things that have experience, and that "function in respect to [their] own determination," this kind of infinite regress is not necessary.[44] We are free to characterize atoms, people and nations as actual entities, even if they are in turn composed of other actual entities.

While an actual entity can't detect the subjective process of coming-to-being of other actual entities, it does feel the final, "satisfied" form of their encounters with the world. In this way, each actual entity nests within it something of how prior actual entities experienced the world. This is the basis of interrelatedness in Whitehead's cosmology. "The plant sings of the glory of God," Deleuze writes in his gloss of Whitehead, "and while being filled all the more with itself it contemplates and intensely contracts the elements from which it proceeds."[45] As for Leibniz, a monad may potentially increase its "clear area" to infinity; in Whitehead, the aim is for ever-richer, mutually positive prehensions. He argues that this creative process tends toward order, or the heightened intensity that occurs when all the entities in a nexus are capable of feeling one another in all their complexity.[46] Yet there are always elements that don't come into in a given synthesis—negative prehensions linger at the threshold of actualization.

Whitehead's universe, an ever-differentiating sea of actualization, maps well onto movies. It accounts for the web of relations in which entities feel and respond to each other. It describes how interactions mutually and differently transform people and things. Whitehead's actualization-packed cosmology would be exciting to take a spin on psychological dramas, screwball comedies, action movies, mysteries, parallel-worlds films (in which the parallel courses of events result from divergent prehensions), and of course the genre of connected-universe movies that includes *The Red Violin* (François Girard, 1998),

Syriana (Stephen Gaghan, 2005) and *The Tree of Life* (Terrence Malick, 2011). The philosophy of organism also describes the unique encounters that occur within and with the cinema. As James Williams defines it, the Whiteheadian event is "a fragile and passing harmony of convergence and divergence. The event is then a disjunctive many that enters into harmony without losing the disjunctive processes relating to its emergence."[47] This coming together can characterize any shot or scene, the film as a whole, or indeed the event of a given audience viewing a given film. A close-up concentrates and realizes the convergent and divergent potentials of a given moment. So does a car chase. So does the assemblage of a movie with a murmuring audience, a rioting audience, or an individual viewer's aroused, transfixed or distracted response.

Jafa's films are alive with Whiteheadian atomistic comings-together. Vibrating atmospheres, slight shifts of focus, many small elements coming together in the shot, all suggest a hypersensitive field of minute prehensions. In its attentive shots taken in Black neighborhoods and meeting places, *Dreams Are Colder Than Death* witnesses encounters that synthesize prehensions into fully actualized wholes. Almost all the shots are in rhythmic slow motion, which choreographically unifies seemingly unrelated movements. People are enmeshed in habitats of neighborhoods, city and country roads, bus stops, yards and curbs and trees stirring in the wind. Many shots are hazy, with lens flares and motes of dust catching the light. All these techniques make the space around people vibrate with palpable energy that seems to come from both within and without them, like a force field of potentials for prehension. Often Jafa uses a very shallow focal range so that only one plane of the image is in focus, and subtly shifts focus over the face or the space being observed. In contrast to the usual deployment of focus pull, I find the effect is to show people emerging, taking shape, as though there is always more to them that can be seen—concrescences that are not completed.

It is the voices we hear, thanks to Jafa's editing, that make the images concresce into "satisfied" units by bringing the invisible—memory and knowledge—into prehension. At one point Hartman, whom we have seen in her Brooklyn neighborhood, is saying, "I know at any moment my life could end because of an act of gratuitous violence. I know so many people who have died. Almost all the boys who I had crushes on are like, all *dead*." Her voice accompanies a shot from behind, on a verdant street, of a strong young man in a white T-shirt, who as he walks makes a casual flourish of gang-like hand gestures. Perhaps his gesture is for the camera's benefit, but Hartman's words touch on the precariousness of this young man's life. Just as Hartman is saying, "Part of Blackness is that intimacy with death," three skipping children cross the young man's path. The slow motion captures the smallest child's joyous leap in the air. Now, this unit of the film feels, to use Whitehead's language, like a fully satisfied—actual and complete—entity, bringing together the threat, the bravado, the history of violence and the children's carefree joy into a single complex feeling of life that is intimate with death.

Sadrā's Universe: Individuation in an Intensifying Flow

Sadrā, like the European Scholastics, inherited from Avicenna a sophisticated substantialist metaphysics in which a single "Being" can be predicated of the many without losing its unity.[48] Sadrā submits this concept to a process critique, arguing that Being is predicated of all things through modulation.[49] He argues that Being, *wujûd*, is a unified reality graded in degrees of intensity, which encompasses all things in a transformative flow (*al-sarayān al-wujûd*, the flow of Being).[50] Existence is a process of modulation or individuation (*tashkīk al-wujûd*, the modulation of being; individuation, *tashakhkhus*, from *shakk*, to doubt). God is the most real and most intense being, and everything else has degrees of intensity; but all beings, from humans to rocks, are capable of becoming more real and more intense. While for Avicenna and Aristotle substances are unchanging, Sadrā argues that substances undergo internal change, which he terms *substantial motion* (*al-harakat al-jawhariyya*).[51] Citing *Qu'ran* 56: 60–61, "We will exchange your likeness and recreate you in what you will not know," he argues that the divine source transforms individuals through substantial motion.

We saw that entities in Whitehead's universe are singular, for no two actual entities have the same experience. In Sadrā's universe, too, becoming is necessarily singular. We think of things as belonging to categories, such as rock, tree and animal, but, Sadrā argues, this is merely a mental convenience. In fact, Sadrā writes, anticipating Whitehead, things are "structures of events" that move from general and indeterminate to definite and concrete.[52] It's easier to see the form than the becoming—because, as Sadrā argues, the form can be cognized, the becoming only intuited.[53] In his great untranslated work *Al-Asfar*, the *Four Journeys* (summarized in English by Fazlur Rahman), Sadrā explains how entities individuate, gaining reality and intensity and losing their names. Taking to the furthest degree, a long series of Arabic interventions in the Platonic essence-existence distinction and in Aristotle's matter-form distinction, he replaces these with a genus-differentia distinction. Genus lacks reality; only the differentia that arise in the entity's movement from potential to actual, are real.[54] The flow of being intensifies the specificity of a thing and makes it *more* like itself.[55]

Sadrā's process philosophy shows the unreality of categories and abstractions, while the flow of being, which cannot be grasped conceptually but can only be sensed through experience, is real. "Existences are the principal realities," Sadrā writes, "whereas quiddities [...] have never smelled the perfume of real existence."[56] This preference for the non-cognitive feeling of becoming brings Sadrā's thought close to Whitehead's—and also to Jafa's films, which fight the death-grip of clichés in order to witness the emergence of things too singular to name.

As *Dreams Are Colder Than Death* begins, King's famous speech echoes under Spillers's voice declaring emphatically, "Two hundred years ago Black people didn't have a prayer" against brutality, lynching and rape at the hands of white people. We hear her over photographs of Black men who have been lynched and hanged, surrounded by the white perpetrators—and then over a mysterious picture of parallel, gleaming strands that call to mind cells of some kind. Now, Spillers says, Black Americans are "the head of international courts, president of the United States, CEO of American Express, you name it!" We see numerous outdoor shots of Black people, each preciously distinct: a woman wearily tosses her honey-colored hair as she walks; a father carries his daughter on his shoulders; a young man stands in a parking lot, carefully attired in gangsta getup of baggy clothes, bandanna and baseball cap, his long shadow cast on small figures moving in the distance; spillers herself in her yard, embraced by hazy air and brilliant greenery. "But the price of that is to lose this precious insight that connects you to something human and bigger than black folk, white folk [. . .] We are losing that connection because we are buying this other shit." Later Melvin Gibbs states, "We're expected to play a role [. . .] we're almost like computer code that way. We have this thing, like Black man X Y Z, and that thing almost operates by itself. Because there's always the real you, and then there's this puppet." When Blackness gets reified into named forms, Spillers and Gibbs are arguing, even when they are forms of seeming success, this cuts off their connection to a source of life, drains their energy and makes them less real. What Spillers calls "this precious insight that connects you to something human" refers, in Sadrā's terms, to presential knowledge, a knowledge beyond names—the grasp of the flow of being.

Jafa's film participates in substantial motion by seeing and hearing beyond what is physically present and beyond clichés, in what we could call imaginal perception. In a piquant challenge for contemporary materialist thought, in Sadrā's philosophy matter is nothing in itself. Matter is pure potentiality, actualized at every moment by the flow of being.[57] "Every body and every bodily thing whose being is in any way connected with matter is constantly renewed in its ipseity and impermanent in its being and its individuality."[58] However, perception can see *through* matter to its becoming.

For Sadrā, as for Whitehead, perception is partial, since every entity only perceives some aspects of other entities. And like those thinkers, Sadrā emphasizes that the more spiritually advanced a being is, the better it can perceive the flow of being as it differentiates in all things. Presential knowledge (*'ilm hudûrî*), or knowledge of things in their extreme singularity, comes closest to the flow of being.[59]

Glissant's Relational Synthesis

Like Whitehead and Sadrā, Glissant in his later work insists that things are most real, and most active and actualizing, in their singularity, arguing that generalization, the bad habit of Mediterranean thought, blocks the world's only real energy source, singular entities, which he terms particulars. And as in their process philosophies, in Glissant's entities, both are irreducibly singular and enmeshed in relations. "Relation exists, especially as the particulars that are its interdependent constituent have first freed themselves from any approximation of dependency." The unattainable horizon of the Whole beckons in Glissant's philosophy, as in Sadrā's and Whitehead's, "the finally realized totality of all possible particulars"—a totality that is constantly changing because it consists of changing relations.[60] The more that it is singular, the more an entity can activate potential relations. Glissant's terms "participation and confluence" resonate with Whitehead's language of prehension, ingression and concrescence. While the entities analyzed in Whitehead's philosophy can be any size—particles, civilizations—Glissant gives preference to a social and political scale: the community, the culture, the plantation.

Glissant celebrates opacity, for it safeguards the singularity of every entity and guarantees the fruitfulness of their encounters. "The more the other resists in its thickness or fluidity [. . .], the more its reality becomes expressive, and the relation fruitful."[61] Western thought, Glissant points out, can no longer claim that knowledge is transparent; but it is not able to deal with the new opacity of knowledge. Now, he writes, that mirror is clouded by "a whole alluvium deposited by populations," inscrutable, more often than not despised, yet insistently present. The motif of silt, which recurs in *Poetics of Relation*, indicates deeply deposited knowledge, especially that possessed by those who have been torn away from their ancestral culture, which forms the ground of relational knowledge of the entire world. Like Leibniz's monad, Glissant's relational thinker has only the dimmest awareness of things beyond its immediate environment, with which it is nevertheless inextricably connected. Thus, thought must begin with the world at hand: the wandering thinker who strives to know the totality of the world "plunges into the opacities of that part of the world to which he has access."[62] From a node in an ever-changing network, an individual is able to detect relations to the whole: Deleuze and Guattari's concepts of nomad and rhizome resonate in Glissant's writing.

In its historicity, Glissant's philosophy provides a truthfulness that systematic philosophy lacks. Glissant argues that the African diaspora originated not only in Africa but also in the terrible and transformational abysses that the millions of slaves deported from Africa underwent: the "womb-abyss" of the slave ship, the depths of the sea. These abysses remain as unconscious knowledge, the basis for a knowledge of the whole and relation within the whole. Movingly, Glissant argues that this openness need not be fearful, perhaps because enslaved people have already undergone a dreadful encounter with the unknown, "We know ourselves as part and as crowd, in an unknown that does not terrify."[63] The historicity of his thought is also the reason for Glissant's measured optimism: after slavery, colonization, decolonization and the initial disappointment of the United Nations, he observes the increasing durability of creole cultures, "whose very nature is to vary tremendously within Relation."[64]

This relational philosophy, and the privileged position it ascribes to enslaved and creole people, describes the universe of *Dreams Are Colder Than Death*. Resonating with Glissant's characterization of the slave ship as a womb-abyss, Moten refers, rather, to Kant, "The fantasy of flight produces a radical disruptive imaginative capacity. The hold of the ship was a language lab. The reason we think it was iconic of brutality is not because it shut down our capacities of reason, imagination, erotic, but because all those were still online." Over a shot of cold-looking waves breaking on a rocky coast, Spillers reminds listeners that Africans were involved in the slave trade: the elders betrayed the youth by selling them into slavery, "an Oedipal crisis buried in the Middle Passage." Through montage, Jafa folds these histories into the present being of the people his film cherishes, volatilizing the relations to the past and the whole that are latent within them. The unafraid openness that Glissant advocates resonates with these words of Rich Blint, "I think there's something about the end of safety that Black folks have to court."

Individuation and Milieu

For the same reasons, those relations singularize the entity. All process philosophies conceive of a force of differentiation that flows through individuals from the universe, or at least the larger milieu. Things transform from within in response to a pull from without. At the objectless end of process philosophies, Simondon holds that individuation is ontologically prior to individuals, and individuals are simply effects of individuation, the way a wave is the result of the movement of the sea.[65] In Whitehead, the actual entity has a lot of choice about how it will concresce from its milieu, though it doesn't last long after the process has completed. Glissant's particularities connect from within deeply interrelated milieus. "Things of the community, without being diminished, [...] would be the initiation to totality without renouncing the particular."[66] In Sadrā, substantial motion, a flow of divine energy, transforms individuals from within, making them more real *and* more like themselves.[67]

In his work on cinema, Deleuze characterizes the action-image in terms of mutually transformative relations between action and milieu. In milieu-driven genres like the Western (the "large form"), the milieu expands and contracts as though breathing, inspiring the characters. In action-driven genres like the comedy of manners (the "small form"), tiny differentia in the action produce vast differences in the situation.[68] Deleuze emphasizes the completeness or satisfaction of these events, "Everything is individuated: the milieu as a particular space-time, the situation as determinate and determining, the collective as well as the individual character."[69] This model, enriched by our other process thinkers, effectively characterizes cinema's capacity to explore the mutually creative relations of individual and milieu.

In *Dreams are Colder Than Death*, individuations take place in two milieus, framing and internal. In the framing milieu, especially in public places, constant danger assumes causal efficacy, in Black people's prehensions of the world. The film demonstrates that historical threats of lynching and murders of civil rights leaders such as King and Fred Hampton continue in the American epidemic of murders of unarmed Black people: it documents a protest of the 2013 murder of Trayvon Martin, the event that instigated the Black Lives Matter movement. In the internal milieu, throughout the film, Jafa creates African American-only spaces for his subjects. The speakers are framed by their homes, the interiors, yards and the streets of their neighborhoods. Other shots come from Black neighborhoods with nary a white (or other non-Black) person in sight: busy streets, parks, a basketball court, a parking lot, someone's front yard. The effect, I find, is to temporarily create the world of which Malcolm X dreamed, in which Black communities maintain economic and social autonomy. In these mini-utopias, there are no police, no imposition of government force. The people we see come together in a relatively free space.

Thus the temporary free spaces Jafa carves out in the film witness a greater openness to the world, including the luxury of perceiving for the pleasure of it, Whitehead's presentational immediacy. Not without tension and sadness, these scenes reveal the opulence of potential becoming when immediate dangers are absent and experience can embrace more of the world. Jafa and his apparatus are part of the milieu: his mobile camerawork and use of variable slow motion enhance its breath-like quality.

Spillers's first words accompany a scene of boys jumping not into but out of a swimming pool, spinning backwards, in sheaves of droplets, and landing on their feet. Jafa's virtuosic postproduction, reverse motion at variable slow speeds, intensifies their pleasure to joy and impossible athleticism.[70] In one brief scene, as Moten is speaking of the distinction between Blackness and Black people, the camera comes into a backyard where a seated woman is laughing at two pretty dogs that have leapt up on the table. In the next shot, this woman, who has light skin, blond hair and blue eyes, looks toward the receptive camera in calm, supremely composed self-recognition as Black.

In one of *Dreams Are Colder Than Death*'s moments of saccadic becoming, the camera, peering through leafy branches, observes an encounter while we hear Gibbs is explaining "playing the puppet." A teenaged girl wearing a Wendy's uniform passes through a group of boys on a basketball court. In movements whose precise choreography the slow motion reveals, two of them get into her space, she slaps one boy's hand away, but he insistently taps her arm and reaches for her ass. A taller, bearded youth reaches to touch her, and as in that brief moment she continues to resist, the boys all turn away, laughing. A second later, the girl is moving on, toward the camera, a flutter of recomposure on her face as she puts her earbuds back in. She passes her hand over her face, perhaps to protect it from Jafa's camera, which finally observes her from a distance as she crosses the street. Gibbs is saying, "That's always the psychic drain—time to deal with the puppet." The actions of the girl, the boys, the basketball court, the trees and Jafa's observing camera come together into a single unit. In Sadrā's terms, all the parties in the encounter undergo substantial motion, subtly differentiating and becoming more real. Jafa's use of slow motion emphasizes the interconnected energy of the whole group, the milieu of neighborly sexual aggression they create. It draws attention to the occasion's aesthetic supplement, its phase of inhibitions and intensifications: the infinitesimal decisions each participant, including the camera, makes as to how the encounter will play out.

Through these and other shots, Jafa suggests a kind of creative coming from within, not just within individuals but with the community. It is the "precious insight that connects you to something human" that Spillers asserts is African American people's most powerful possession, a force of individuation from within that connects to the widest possible milieu without. As Glissant argues, the more the particulars are free from dependency, the more relation exists.

Creativity and the Great Refusal

For those who study cinema and other creative forms, it's especially intriguing that all three philosophers privilege art as the best means to feel the universe's flow of differentiation—where art is the capacity to cultivate unnamed diversity and connectivity. Sadrā argues that while the intelligence is best at gaining a sense of the universe as One, the imagination best at attaining a sense of the universe as infinite: thus art is best at touching the delicate singularities of the world without crushing them.[71] "What are perceived by the five senses," Sadrā wrote, "are luminous hidden images existing in another world."[72] Art is able to perceive these luminous images that are more real than matter. For Glissant, the world's endless, unpredictable differentiation constitutes the motor of universal energy, and poetic thought safeguards this diversity.[73] The poetics of relation, as Sheila Petty points out, produces an aesthetics that values interactions within the work and intersections with the outside influences of its time.[74] Glissant celebrates works of art, from William Faulkner's novels to Bob Marley's music, which draw together reverberations from the entire world, in what he calls *echos-monde*.

The most compelling actualizations of Black process and individuation in *Dreams Are Colder Than Death* occur in Black-only spaces. But individuation draws from the larger milieu as well, from the dangerous spaces defined by American law and the dominant white imagination. The danger of being turned into a thing, or a puppet, is ever present. In the face of this threat, Blackness may cohere as the "representing" subject of the politics of identity.[75] Or it may take the risk of continuing to individuate in the expanded milieu. As Moten argues, Blackness constitutes a radical creativity that corrodes racist deep structures that both rely on and disavow it.[76]

Differentiation in the presence of danger gives rise to seeming monsters, freaks, uncategorizable performances. In the film, Hartman recounts that in the early days of Emancipation, Black leaders tried to quell the anarchic energy of Black people, condemning them as fallen women or thugs.[77] But now as well, she argues, Black people are producing modern forms of culture that appear initially as "monstrous." Hartman's words are heard over shots of a man gyrating, holding a bottle in a paper bag, his head not visible in the frame, and a close pan of a stripper's body prone on the nightclub stage, deftly twitching her rump in sequined G-string. Twerking, of course, has thoroughly entered the clichéd cultural lexicon, but throughout the film, Jafa's montage of words and performances emphasizes Black creativity and inventiveness in the face of threat. What appear to be "freaks" and "monsters" are truly novel actualities.

The film suggests that it is possible to draw on a deep energy source beyond local intimacy and beyond the murderous milieu. Artist Nicole Fleetwood, whose troubling collages of Black figures we see, delightedly recalls what went on at her grandmother's one-room church. "They knew how to *generate energy*." If an old woman started to go into a trance, the congregation would interrupt the sermon, her grandmother would go to the piano and someone else to the drums, and "they would rock out for another hour! One of my aunts would start speaking in tongues." Jafa matches Fleetwood's story with pictures of a little church, Black congregations—and distant galaxies. These, and the spaceship-like animations that flash into the film a couple of times, evoke the Afrofuturist idea that since the Middle Passage, which constituted a kind of alien abduction, African-diaspora people came from and belonged to somewhere else than the present.[78]

Beyond the *écho-monde* Glissant describes, these images reach to other universes. Jafa's montage suggests that the ladies at Fleetwood's grandmother's church were making contact with some extraterrestrial energy source. This evocation of a place beyond Earth, as well as Hartman's and Moten's statements on creativity, resonate with a rather odd definition of evil that Whitehead proposes. Evil, he writes, is novelty that arises at the wrong time or place, so that the responses to it consist mostly of inhibitions. "Insistence on birth at the wrong season is the trick of evil."[79] This definition characterizes acts that are so creative their milieu cannot sustain them. "But," Whitehead writes, "the advance, when it does arrive, will be richer in content, more fully conditioned, and more stable." The great leap, the apparently unsustainable "break," makes contact with a reality that is truer than the present actuality. Sadrā terms this reality the imaginal world, which is glimpsed in prophetic visions.

Refusing present actuality in favor of an unlikely but truer reality is a heroic act. A process basis for critical theory arose when neo-Marxist critical theorist Herbert Marcuse took up and ran with a concept of Whitehead's, the "great refusal."[80] When an entity refuses the most evident prehension, refuses to take up the most evident data in its environment in favor of a more rare and unlikely one, its creativity increases and it attains a more vital truth. Actualizing just a hint from the environment leads to more powerful novelty. A negative prehension negates the immediately present and opens to the possible.

The great refusal attempts the riskiest actualizations. Marcuse argued it is capable of overthrowing the status quo, which relies on what he called the "Performance Principle," a self-sustaining mimicking of reality that represses novelty.[81] Developing Guattari's work in his process revision of Marxism, Franco Berardi argues that proliferation of singularities replaces dialectical revolution as the new political task. To support them, he argued, we must create nontemporary autonomous zones, even in the face of racist and fascist aggression.[82] These statements by neo-Marxist theorists become individuated and actualized in Black life and Black philosophy. In the African American experience, the great refusal draws on powers that contradict the oppressive majority of experience, to create something really new that has the potential to endure.

In *Poetics of Relation*, Glissant returns twice to the figure of a silent man who walks, seemingly without end, on the black beach. He "exhausts no territory; he sets roots only on the sacred of the air and evanescence, in a pure refusal that changes nothing in the world."[83] The man who walks is Glissant's most radical image of one who will have no part of the compromised relationships of the present, who cultivates the as-yet-unconsidered meanings deposited like silt in the sand. Drawing on Glissant's celebration of errantry, a rhizomatic creative path that rejects filiation, Hartman advocates waywardness, "the refusal to be governed. It is the next phase of the general strike, the flight from the plantation and refusal of slavery and the demeaning conditions of work, this time it happens in the slum. It is a social experiment and an effort to elaborate new forms of existence."[84]

The great refusal enacts the most difficult and most powerful actualization because it prehends what is most distant. The difference between the "evil" of failed becoming and the creativity of successful becoming is that the individuating entity is able to draw enough energy into and through itself, from that distant source, to actualize it. In cinema, the great refusal has its moment of total negative prehension—refusing to recognize any of the habitual signs in its milieu. It dwells in the virtual, in the moment before satisfaction is possible. But the great difference is that it *does* recognize some rare, unlikely sign, far-flung in its environment—and it is around that prehension that the occasion actualizes. Jafa witnesses this moment of the great refusal and its satisfaction in the emergence of singular figures that hum with the presence of an unseen community.

Notes

1 Charles Sanders Peirce, "Man's Glassy Essence," Collected Papers of Charles Sanders Peirce, ed. Charles Harthshorne and Paul Weiss (Cambridge: Belknap Press of Harvard University, 1960), 6, 268.

2 Alfred North Whitehead, *Process and Reality: An Essay in Cosmology*. Corrected edition, ed. David Ray Griffin and Donald W. Sherburne (New York: Free Press, 1978), 273.

3 One can say "substance ontology and "process ontology," but I use the term "metaphysics" with the Deleuzian motivation to avoid the fixity of ontology.

4 Graham Harman, "Whitehead and Schools X, Y, and Z," in *The Lure of Whitehead*, ed. Nicholas Gaskill and A. J. Nocek (Minneapolis: University of Minnesota, 2014), 235.

5 Nicholas Rescher, *Process Metaphysics: An Introduction to Process Philosophy* (Albany: State University of New York Press, 1996).

6 Whitehead International Film Festival, home page and 2016 Selection Criteria page. Consulted July 27, 2016.

7 As John Mullarkey notes, Deleuzian film theorists tend to diverge between virtualist and actualist tendencies, depending on whether they rely more on Deleuze's cinema books or other parts of his oeuvre. John Mullarkey, *Refractions of Reality: Philosophy and the Moving Image* (Basingstoke: Palgrave Macmillan, 2009), 107.

8 What Vivian Sobchack terms the film's body accounts for how a given kind of camera or audio device is able to see and hear the world. This concept extends into an understanding of prehensive encounter of camera and world and its completion or satisfaction. Jeffrey Langille, "How is it that there is always something new?" MFA thesis, School for the Contemporary Arts, Simon Fraser University, 2014. I supervised Langille's thesis.

9 One of the most interesting such trajectories is Steven Shaviro's, who has moved over two decades from being one of the first to propose a cinema of the body, to develop theories of cinematic and post-cinematic affect, to a full-fledged philosophical encounter with Spinoza, Whitehead, Kant, and object-oriented philosophy Steven Shaviro, *The Cinematic Body* (Minneapolis: University of Minnesota Press, 1994); *Without Criteria: Kant, Whitehead, Deleuze, and Aesthetics* (Cambridge, MA: MIT Press, 2009); *Post Cinematic Affect* (Winchester: Zero Books, 2010); *The Universe of Things: On Speculative Realism* (Minneapolis: University of Minnesota Press, 2014).

10 See e.g., Matthew Fuller, *Media Ecologies: Materialist Energies in Art and Technoculture* (Cambridge, MA: MIT Press, 2005); Sean Cubitt, *Finite Media: Environmental Implications of Digital Technology* (Durham, NC: Duke University Press, 2016); Kenneth Rogers, *Petromedia: Oil Culture and Media Culture*, in progress; and Hunter Vaughan, *500,000 Kilowatts of Stardust: An Eco-Materialist Reframing of* Singin' in the Rain, in progress.

11 Adrian Ivakhiv, *Ecologies of the Moving Image: Cinema, Affect, Nature* (Waterloo: Wilfrid Laurier University Press, 2013).

12 On the film-audience assemblage see Kennedy, *Deleuze and Cinema*. On assemblages of film production, the film itself, and reception, see Janet Harbord, *The Evolution of Film: Rethinking Film Studies* (Cambridge: Polity, 2007); and Kjetil Rødje, *Images of Blood in American Cinema: The Tingler to The Wild Bunch* (London: Ashgate, 2015).

13 For example Siegfried Zielinski, *Deep Time of the Media: Toward an Archaeology of Seeing and Hearing by Technical Means*, trans. Gloria Custance (Cambridge, MA: MIT Press, 2006); Jussi Parikka, *Insect Media: An Archaeology of Animals and Technology* (Minneapolis: University of Minnesota Press, 2010).

14 Timothy Scott Barker, *Time and the Digital: Connecting Technology, Aesthetics, and a Process Philosophy of Time* (Hanover: Dartmouth College Press, 2012).

15 Azadeh Emadi, *Motion Within Motion: Investigating Digital Video in Light of Substantial Motion* (Ph.D. thesis, Auckland University of Technology, 2014); "Pixelated view: investigating the pixel in light of Substantial Motion," in *Proceedings of the 19th International Symposium of Electronic Art*, Sydney, ed. Kathy Cleland, Laura Fisher, and Ross Harley (Sydney: ISEA International, the Australian Network for Art & Technology and the University of Sydney, 2013). I was one of Emadi's doctoral supervisors.

16 Whitehead, *Process and Reality*, 7. I think Whitehead excludes Arabic philosophy because of its Aristotelian lineage. However, Arabic grammar does complicate subject-predicate logic, partly because it uses the verb *wajada*, to be found, instead of a copula such as "is."

17 Harman, "Whitehead and Schools X, Y, and Z," 237.

18 Ivakhiv, *Ecologies of the Moving Image*, 42–43.

19 See e.g., Abe Masao's comparison of Whitehead's philosophy and Mahayana Buddhism in *Zen and Western Thought*, ed. William R. LaFleur (Honolulu: University of Hawaii Press, 1989).

20 Masato Ishida, "The Sense of Symmetry: Comparative Studies of Whitehead, Nishida, and Dogen," *Process Studies* 43, no. 1 (2014): 4–34; Michel Weber, "A Process Interpretation of Aztec Metaphysics," *Process Studies* 44, no. 1 (2015): 48–62; Li Yijing, "Masao Abe's Dynamic Sunyata and Buddhist Thought," *Process Studies* 44, no. 1 (2015): 120–41.

21 Sha Xin Wei, *Poeisis and Enchantment in Topological Matter* (Cambridge, MA: MIT Press, 2013).

22 Sajjad H. Rizvi, *Mulla Sadrā and Metaphysics: Modulation of Being* (London: Routledge, 2009), 85.

23 As Parviz Morewedge points out, Islamic philosophy from Shihab al-Dîn al-Suhrawardî (1153–1191) on—which is to say, eastern Islamic philosophy—abandoned substantialism for process. Parviz Morewedge, "The Neoplatonic Structure of Some Islamic Mystical Doctrines," in *Neoplatonism and Islamic Thought*, ed. Parviz Morewedge (Albany: SUNY Press, 1992); see also Lenn Evan Goodman, *Avicenna* (New York: Routledge, 1992), 62.

24 See e.g., Anna-Teresa Tymieniecka, ed., *Islamic Philosophy and Occidental Phenomenology on the Perennial Issue of Microcosm and Macrocosm* (Dordrecht: Springer, 2006); Laura U. Marks, "A Deleuzian *Ijtihad*: Unfolding Deleuze's Islamic Sources Occulted in the Ethnic Cleansing of Spain," in *Deleuze and Race*, ed. Arun Saldhana and Jason Michael Adams (Edinburgh: Edinburgh University Press, 2013), 51–72; Rizvi, *Mulla Sadrā and Metaphysics*. Sadrā's thought profoundly influenced subsequent philosophy in the eastern Muslim world. It remains central to official philosophy in present-day Iran, though, as Seyyed Hossein Nasr notes, educated Iranians' interest began to turn to European philosophy in the early nineteenth century, due to Persians' "cultural inferiority complex vis-à-vis the West that still continues in many non-Western circles." Nasr, *Islamic Philosophy from Its Origin to the Present: Philosophy in the Land of Prophecy* (Binghamton: State University of New York Press, 2006), 251–52. Some of Sadrā's work began to be translated into Western languages in the late nineteenth century, and scholars in English and French have increasingly turned to his work since the 1980s, but only a few of his writings are translated, and very little of the work of thinkers who followed Sadrā in the eastern Islamic world has been translated. Thus, although I am championing Sadrā's work as an important contribution to process philosophy, a note of caution is necessary until Western scholarship can catch up with the philosophers who developed and critiqued his work.

25 Farshid Kazemi, "A Cinematic Cosmos in Process: Shaykh Aḥmad al-Aḥsā'ī, *Hūrqalyā*, and Cinema," in progress.

26 Alexander Weheliye, *Habeas Viscus: Raializing Assemblages, Biopolitics, and Black Feminist Theories of the Human* (Durham, NC: Duke University Press, 2014), 5–12.

27 Arthur Jafa, "69," in *Black Popular Culture*, ed. Gina Dent (Seattle: Bay Press, 1992).

28 See e.g., Saidiya V. Hartman and Frank B. Wilderson III, "The Position of the Unthought," *Qui Parle* 13, no. 2 (Spring/Summer 2003): 183–201; Fred Moten, *In the Break: The Aesthetics of the Black Radical Tradition* (Minneapolis: Minnesota University Press, 2003); and Alexander Weheliye, *Phonographies: Grooves in Sonic Afro-Modernity* (Durham, NC: Duke University Press, 2005). See also the classic work on female vocal resistance to fetishization, Kaja Silverman, *The Acoustic Mirror: The Female Voice in Psychoanalysis and Cinema* (Bloomington: Indiana University Press, 1988).

29 See Étienne Balibar, "Subjection and Subjectivation," in *Supposing the Subject*, ed. Joan Copjec (London: Verso, 1994).

30 Saidiya V. Hartman, *Scenes of Subjection: Terror, Slavery, and Self-Making in Nineteenth-Century America* (Oxford: Oxford University Press, 1997), 118.

31 To some degree the critiques of Hartman, Wilderson, Moten and others can be extended to other historical slave-based economies. But the African American situation is unique because of this concurrence of the slave economy and the rise of modern European philosophy.

32 Moten, *In the Break*, 9–12, 263n1. Moten is writing about a "commodity" that screams: Frederick Douglass's aunt Hester, screaming as her owner whips her, which Douglass writes about in

his 1845 *Narrative of the Life of Frederick Douglass*. Moten resists placing too much hope in this performative agency, like Hartman, who calls attempts to celebrate the agency of oppressed groups "obscene." Hartman and Wilderson, *Qui Parle*, 185.

33 Kodwo Eshun, "Operating System for the Redesign of Sonic Reality," in *Audio Culture: Readings in Modern Music*, ed. Christoph Cox and Daniel Warner (New York: Continuum, 2004), 157–59.

34 See e.g., Sean Cubitt, *The Practice of Light* (Cambridge, MA: MIT Press, 2014), 12; Grant Kester, *The One and the Many: Contemporary Collaborative Art in a Global Context* (Durham, NC: Duke University Press, 2011), 54; and Peter Hallward, "Édouard Glissant between the Singular and the Specific," *The Yale Journal of Criticism* 11, no. 2 (Fall 1998): 441–64.

35 Nicholas Rescher, *Process Metaphysics: An Introduction to Process Philosophy* (Albany: State University of New York Press, 1996).

36 Keith Robinson, "The Event and the Occasion: Deleuze, Whitehead, and Creativity," in *The Lure of Whitehead* (2014), 207.

37 See e.g., Gilles Deleuze, *Difference and Repetition*, trans. Paul Patton (New York: Columbia University Press, 1994), 35–42, and "Twenty-Fifth Series on Univocity," *The Logic of Sense*, trans. Mark Lester with Charles Stivale, ed. Constantin V. Boundas (New York: Columbia University Press, 1990), 177–80.

38 Sean Cubitt, *The Cinema Effect* (Cambridge, MA: MIT Press, 2004).

39 See e.g., Laura U. Marks, "Noise in Enfolding-Unfolding Aesthetics," in *The Oxford Handbook of Sound and Image in Digital Media*, ed. Amy Herzog, John Richardson and Carol Vernallis (Oxford University Press, 2014); "Enfolding-Unfolding Aesthetics, or the Unthought at the Heart of Wood," in *Technology and Desire: The Transgressive Art of Moving Images*, ed. Rania Gaafar and Martin Schulz (Karlsruhe; London: ZKM; Intellect Books), 151–61; *Enfoldment and Infinity: An Islamic Genealogy of New Media Art* (Cambridge, MA: MIT Press, 2010), chapter 1; "Information, Secrets, and Enigmas: An Enfolding-Unfolding Aesthetics for Cinema," *Screen* 50, no. 1 (Spring 2009): 86–98.

40 To make the ideas more clear, I have occasionally rendered some of Whitehead's specialized terms in simpler language. For his term *actual entity* I substitute *entity*; for *prehension* I substitute *feeling* or *taking in*; for *concrescence* I substitute *coming together*.

41 Whitehead, *Process and Reality*, 26.

42 Whitehead, *Process and Reality*, 176, 172. On causal efficacy and presentational immediacy, see also Pierfrancesco Basile, *Leibniz, Whitehead and the Metaphysics of Causation* (Basingstoke: Palgrave Macmillan, 2009) and Shaviro, *The Universe of Things*.

43 Whitehead, *Process and Reality*, 213.

44 Indeed it constitutes both misplaced concreteness and the "bifurcation of nature" into what is experienced and what is "true," that Whitehead critiques and Isabelle Stengers examines further in "A Constructivist Reading of *Process and Reality*," *Theory, Culture, & Society* 25, no. 4 (2008): 91–110.

45 Gilles Deleuze, *The Fold: Leibniz and the Baroque*, foreword and translation by Tom Conley (Minneapolis: University of Minnesota Press, 1993), 78.

46 Whitehead, *Process and Reality*, 83.

47 James Williams, "Event," in *Gilles Deleuze: Key Concepts*, ed. Charles J. Stivale (Durham: Acumen, 2005), 84.

48 Many strains of Islamic philosophy emphasize that the universe unfolds from God and go to pains to identify different manners of unfolding, from the gradations of emanation in Islamic Neoplatonism to the occultations of Isma'ili Shi'ia theology.

49 Rizvi, *Mulla Sadrā and Metaphysics*, 51.

50 The Arabic word *wujûd*, meaning "what is found," is more suggestive than the English *being* or the German *Sein*, though some scholars carefully compare it to Heidegger's *Dasein*, e.g., Alparslan Acikgenc, *Being and Existence in Sadra and Heidegger: A Comparative Ontology* (Kuala Lumpur: International Institute of Islamic Thought and Civilization, 1993); Nader El-Bizri,

The Microcosm/Macrocosm Analogy: A Tentative Encounter between Graeco-Arabic Philosophy and Phenomenology," in Tymienicka, 3–23; Seyyed Mohammed Khamenei, "Time, Temporal, and Temporality," in Tymienicka, 129–36; and Muhammad Kamal, *From Essence to Being: The Philosophy of Mulla Sadra & Martin Heidegger* (London: Islamic College for Advanced Studies Publications, 2010).

51 Chittick 122; also translated as transubstantiation, transsubstantial motion, and essential motion.

52 Sadr al-Dîn al-Shîrâzî, *Asfâr* 1, 14–19; cited in Fazlur Rahman, *The Philosophy of Mullâ Sadrā (Sadr al-Dîn al-Shîrâzî)* (Albany: State University of New York Press, 1975), 97.

53 Rahman, *The Philosophy of Mullâ Sadrā*, 30.

54 Rahman, *The Philosophy of Mullâ Sadrā*, 50–51.

55 Mullâ Sadrā, *The Book of Metaphysical Penetrations*, trans. Seyyed Hossein Nasr, ed. Ibrahim Kalin (Provo, UT: Brigham Young University Press, 2014), 45.

56 Sadrā, *The Book of Metaphysical Penetrations*, 37.

57 *Asfâr* 1:3, Rahman, *The Philosophy of Mullâ Sadrā*, 114. For more on substantial motion see Christian Jambet, "Essential Motion," in *The Act of Being: The Philosophy of Revelation in Mullâ Sadrâ* (New York: Zone, 2006), and Emadi, *Motion Within Motion*, 50–56.

58 Sadr al-Dîn al-Shîrâzî, *The Wisdom of the Throne* I §13, quoted in James Winston Morris, *The Wisdom of the Throne: An Introduction to the Philosophy of Mulla Sadra* (Princeton: Princeton University Press, 1981), 119–20. This statement refers to Qur'an 56: 60–61, "We will exchange your likeness and recreate you in what you will not know."

59 *Asfâr* III: 297–98; in Rizvi, *Mulla Sadrā and Metaphysics*, 89.

60 Édouard Glissant, *Poetics of Relation*, trans. Betsy Wing (Ann Arbor: University of Michigan Press, 2010), 142, 32.

61 Édouard Glissant, *L'Intention poétique* (Paris: Seuil, 1969), 23; my revision of Halliward's translation.

62 Ibid., 111, 190, 20.

63 Ibid., 6–9.

64 Ibid., 142.

65 Gilbert Simondon, "The Genesis of the Individual," trans. Mark Cohen and Sanford Kwinter. In *Incorporations*, ed. Jonathan Crary and Sanford Kwinter (New York: Zone Books, 1992), 296–319.

66 Glissant, *L'Intention poétique*, 55.

67 He wrote that *wujûd* "exists in all things according to that thing such that in the intellect, it is intellect; in the soul, it is soul; in nature, it is nature; in the body, it is body, in substance, it is substance; and in accident, it is accident." Mullā Sadrā, *The Book of Metaphysical Penetrations*, 45.

68 Deleuze, *Cinema 1*, 145–46, 160–64, 169–73.

69 Ibid., 142.

70 I must note Billy Woodberry's criticism of this shot, namely that it connotes the nasty fact that after desegregation, some southern whites poisoned swimming pools with bleach or ink. In conversation at the Robert Flaherty Seminar, June 2016.

71 Philosophy here corresponds to the intelligible realm, visions to the imaginal realm. Mullā Sadrā, *The Elixir of the Gnostics*, trans. W. C. Chittick (Provo, UT: Brigham Young University Press, 2003), Part 1, §39, 9. See also Jambet, "Essential Motion," 87, and Marks, "Noise in Enfolding-Unfolding Aesthetics," 2015.

72 Sadrā, *The Wisdom of the Throne*, §3, in Morris, *The Wisdom of the Throne*, 134. For the relevance to cinema of Sadrā's concept of the imaginal realm, see my essay "Real Images Flow: Mulla Sadrā Meets Film-Philosophy," *Film-Philosophy*, 20, "A World of Cinemas" special issue, ed. David Martin-Jones (2015): 24–46.

73 Glissant, *L'Intention poétique*, 30–32.

74 Sheila J. Petty, "African Frameworks of Analysis for African Film Studies," in *De-Westernizing Film Studies*, ed. Saër Maty Bâ and Will Higbee (London: Routledge, 2012), 76.

75 As John Akomfrah of Black Audio Film Collective says of the group's emergence in the early 1980s in Britain, "We did not have the luxury to be hostile to a question of identity because our very moment of becoming is tied to the question and the politics of identity." To avoid getting slotted, he says, the collective turned to the question of memory—another way to expand the milieu for individuation. "An Absence of Ruins: John Akomfrah in conversation with Kodwo Eshun," in *The Ghosts of Songs: The Film Art of the Black Audio Film Collective*, ed. Kodwo Eshun and Anjalika Sagar (Liverpool: Liverpool University Press, 2007), 132.

76 Fred Moten, "The Case of Blackness," *Criticism* 50, no. 2 (2008): 212. Moten is writing of Frantz Fanon's struggle, in *The Wretched of the Earth*, to defend Algerians against racist colonial stereotypes.

77 Hartman and Moten respond to W. E. B. DuBois's anxious late-nineteenth-century exhortations that Black people conform to white, Christian and bourgeois respectability. See also Fred Moten, "Uplift and Criminality," in *Next to the Color Line: Gender, Sexuality and W. E. B. Du Bois*, ed. Alys Weinbaum and Susan Gilman (Minneapolis: University of Minnesota Press, 2007), 317–49.

78 Afrofuturism, a term coined by Mark Dery in a set of interviews with Tricia Rose, Samuel R. Delany, and Greg Tate in 1994, took form as a movement on a listserv founded by Alondra Nelson in 1998 and conference in 1999, though references to science fiction in African diasporic culture long predate these. The literature on the movement is voluminous: see e.g., Kodwo Eshun, *More Brilliant Than the Sun: Adventures in Sonic Fiction* (London: Quartet Books, 1998); Alondra Nelson, ed., "Future Texts," special issue of *Social Text* 71, 20, no. 2 (Summer 2002); George E. Lewis, ed., "After Afrofuturism," special issue of *Journal of the Society for American Music* 2, no. 2 (May 2008); André M. Carrington, *Speculative Blackness: The Future of Race in Science Fiction* (Minneapolis: University of Minnesota Press, 2016).

79 Whitehead, *Process and Reality*, 223.

80 Duston Moore, "A Whiteheadian Critical Theory," in *Applied Process Thought 1: Initial Explorations in Theory and Research*, ed. Mark Dibben and Thomas Kelly (Frankfurt: Verlag, 2008), 172–76.

81 The concept compares to Félix Guattari's "event-centered rupture," a perilous moment of creative differentiation. Félix Guattari, *Chaosmosis: An Ethico-Aesthetic Paradigm*, trans. P. Bains and J. Pefanis (Sydney: Power, 1995), 81–82.

82 Franco Berardi, *After the Future*, ed. Gary Genosko and Nicolas Thoburn, trans. Arianna Bove et al. (Chico, CA: AK Press, 2011), 118–20.

83 Glissant, *L'Intention poétique*, 208.

84 Saidiya V. Hartman, quoted at "Make a Way out of No Way," event at Arika, Glasgow, September 2014. http://arika.org.uk/events/episode-6-make-way-out-no-way. See also Saidiya V. Hartman, "The Belly of the World: A Note on Black Women's Labors," *Souls* 18, no. 1 (2016): 166–73; and *Wayward Lives, Beautiful Experiments* (Norton, forthcoming).

Part II

WHAT SCREEN CULTURE IS

Chapter Eight

APPARATUS THEORY, PLAIN AND SIMPLE

Tom Conley

Apparatus theory claims to study the "machineries" of the seventh art. Dealing not so much with cameras, projectors, film stock, the design of iPads, editing programs and applications than the relations that viewers sustain with the medium, it lays stress on psychic and social mechanisms that shape the experience of cinema. Considered in a broad sense, it accounts for the power that film holds in respect to the world in which it operates or is deployed. Adepts of apparatus theory consider how cinema is viewed, what it does to the imagination, and in what ways it gets consumed, remembered, classified and even forgotten. For enthusiasts of cinema trained in psychoanalysis, apparatus is understood as a complex process of libidinal exchange between the perceiving spectator and the various screens on which moving images are perceived and registered, which include both the surfaces on which films are projected and the psychic devices that sift the impressions we gather from the experience of viewing a film.[1] For the sociologist and historian of the seventh art, apparatus can refer to a broadly defined economic sphere in which of film is construed to play a significant role in the construction, management and practice of everyday life, in short, as a mechanism having purchase on the lives and minds of collective groups of moviegoers. For those who would call themselves "ordinary" or garden-variety viewers of cinema, apparatus theory deals with how enthusiasts and cinephiles control, mediate or even politicize their passion for film.[2]

For the sake of brevity it can be said, *grosso modo*, that in its purview of the mental economies that drive the medium the theory gives rise, first, to a critical appreciation of cinema and, second, to a *creative doubt* prompting us to be aware of why and wherefore cinema functions in our sentient lives.

The contexts in which the idea of apparatus takes shape tell much about what it was, how it has evolved and, perhaps, where it is and how it works today. Officially born in France in the turmoil and conflict of May 1968, it reflected on the political and aesthetic virtues of theory—in other words, on how film, which otherwise belonged to the industry of capital, could be interpreted to acquire political and philosophical mettle enough to work contrary to consumerism. In harking back to classical Greek, in other words, in investing the history of language into the world of moving images, its proponents melded *theoria*, signifying contemplation and speculation, with *theoros*, a term designating "spectator." Etymology showed how spectacle and spectator were interrelated or even consubstantial. It indicated that theory belonged to a long and rich tradition, reaching back to Plato's cave in the *Republic*, in which projection was at the core of sensation, perception and, most of all, ideological control. The architects of apparatus theory—and Jean-Louis Baudry counted among the most visible—found in both language and philosophical dialogue what they needed to show how cinema is tied to biological and political forces that shape and determine cognition and experience. For the same theorists, it was immediately evident that *apparatus* (in French, *appareil de base*) was more or less synonymous with *dispositif*, in their eyes an untranslatable term designating a mechanism or a filmic "device" responsible for the creation and dissemination of filmic effects, notably those leaving the impression—but only the impression—that the moving image is a reliable transmitter of a sense of reality. Better than any other medium of communication, said to transfer images of reality with little distortion or aberration, cinema was what could reliably "represent" the world at large. Nonetheless, in tandem with its reference to the spatial "disposition" of things and to a "mechanism," the term bore inflections of polemology or the science of strategic and tactical operations.[3] As they did with *dispositif*, critics related *apparatus* to *ideology*, understood not as what Webster declares it to be—a set of beliefs or a credo to which individuals or groups adhere—but, in affiliation with the teachings of Louis Althusser, a welter of *imaginary* relations that human subjects hold with agencies producing material objects, rules of law and, most of all, both passive and active consciousness (including perception), and also what shaped the more difficult and almost unfathomable realm of the unconscious.

When cinema was studied from two angles, one being the history of film in its economic development and the other in how it conditions mental life, cinema was understood as a component belonging to a greater "ideological apparatus." It is easy to see how and why. In the 1960s and 1970s, when cinema was cultivated through dedicated viewing—before the era of the cellphone, the laptop, the DVD, the net-stream, etc., when spectators were obliged to "go to the movies"—its projected images made viewers spending 80 minutes or more in a darkened theater believe that, if only because they bought into the allure of its fantasy and in return for their investment, what it put before their eyes was alluring enough to let disbelief be suspended and the images felt to belong to a real, natural and convincing world or, simply, for contractual reasons, in the purchase of a ticket and the anticipation of pleasure and relief from life outside of the theater that the operative principles—the economy of capital and consumerism—had to go without saying.[4] Thus when seen as a vehicle of ideology, the cinematic "apparatus" was felt to have untold virtue for agencies or seeking to control subjects and subjectivity.

The same theorists arched back to the ostensive origins of cinema to see if, at a moment in its gestation or its birth, it was innocent or at the very least untethered to ideological moorings. Was there, as Noël Burch long ago wondered, a "primitive" moment in its development? A moment in which its images were simply recording, and not yet fashioned to construct and, in collusion with other industries, its viewers' sense of where they are and what they are doing in the world, or even an illusion of "identity"? Or else, could it be asked how, either consciously or unbeknownst to its first creators, in an "ideological" phase of its development, its force of attraction became channeled for the ends of exploitation, hence of subjection and control?[5] And then too, it was wondered if, from the moment of its ostensive genesis, there was at stake an economy of attractions shared among viewers and makers. In looking afresh both at early cinema and at how historians set it in narratives of development and exploitation, theorists of apparatus retained a strong political motivation that ran counter to the aims of the industry. Even if the answers to the queries were negative, in other words, even if, in fact, ideological apparatus was synonymous with the seventh art when the Lumière Brothers filmed *Sortie d'usine* (Workers Exiting a Factory), the return to the origins drew attention to apparatus in general and, at the same time, it invested a political aesthetic into the philosophy and history of film. In doing so, it transformed early objects of capital into aesthetic forms, effectively appreciating them as *dispositifs* in the history of ideological production and setting them in a context at a far remove from what they had been.

Hindsight also shows how the emergence of apparatus theory was tied to a will, first, to call in question the ideology of the *auteur* and, second, to harness speculation on cinema to an egalitarian ethic consonant with the militant work in the wake of May 1968, a moment almost a decade following the birth of the *nouvelle vague* and that too was not long after Hollywood witnessed the dismantling of the studio system. Critics and filmmakers affiliated with *Cahiers du Cinéma* who had embraced auteur theory began to question why they previously had embraced a cult of the "self," the "signature" or even the "worldview" or "vision" of artist-directors—John Ford, Howard Hawks, Alfred Hitchcock and a host of others—who had worked within a ruthlessly exploitative industry. Moving away from embrace of American cinema and tending toward affiliation with the French Communist Party (the PCF), the new generation of theorists wondered if the genius that an earlier wave of writers associated with *Cahiers du Cinéma* had championed owed to that of a "system" of capital in which their own criticism had been imbricated.[6] Much like what Michel Foucault had been addressing in studies of Raymond Roussel and in reflections on space in new modes of fiction, they asked, first, if indeed an "auteur" is an ideological commodity and, second, if its emergence belonged to a history of much longer duration.[7]

Marking a shift from the cult of the director to the study of apparatus, the new generation at the desk of the *Cahiers* launched a collectively written article advocating a close and protracted analysis of John Ford's *Young Mr. Lincoln,* a feature that 20th Century Fox launched in 1939, the year that witnessed the isolation of the United States from the beginnings of World War II. At its very outset, the stakes of the article were clear: editors proposed a *reading,* which implied a close study of the relation of the classic film as a labor of *writing* requiring attention to contradictions and differences between the graphic matter as read and as seen in the film, between the sound track as it could be read and visualized in the field of the montage and staging or *mise-en-scène* and between what was given—as if unconsciously—in the field of the image and what could be grasped, even if fleetingly, in its lexical dimension.

They proposed their reading to be a mode of "scanning," of attending to iconography, of drawing attention to allusion, and to how film is a rewriting of inherited "facts" belonging to the time and place both represented, whether in respect to its reception in 1939, or even in its exhumation and reprise in *Cahiers* in 1970, the date and context of the publication itself. No less notable was the attention that the editors drew to 1939. Studied on the heels of May 1968, the film invited a comparison of the aftermath of the conflicts in Paris to the disastrous effects of the signing of the Hitler–Stalin Pact, an event synchronous with the appearance of Ford's feature that led to the catastrophe of the War and that further hastened the onslaught of the Holocaust. Reference to 1939 had the effect of a critical eye cast upon the history of auteur theory. Prior to the new piece in *Cahiers*, in his seminal "Evolution of Film Language," an essay of several pieces that discerned signature of directors through their uncommon use of deep-focus cinema within conventions born in (or imposed by) the sound era, Bazin had noted how, much as 1913 had been for literature, 1939 had been an *annus mirabilis* for classical cinema . It was then that the seventh art, he asserted, reached its perfection.[8] With the great effects of the long take and deep focus, genial directors obtained a perfect equilibrium of sound, space and narrative. On the one hand, Renoir's *La Règle du jeu* capped everything the director had been getting at from *La fille de l'eau*, in 1924, up to *Une partie de campagne*, in 1937. On the other, John Ford found an optimum balance in a narrative of literal and figural displacement in *Stagecoach*, a film bearing the facture of silent cinema (reaching back to the same director's *Straight Shooting* of 1917) while making the most of the incomparable space of the Monument Valley.

As if working both with and against Bazin in selecting Ford at a watershed date and with attention to a film in the shadow of *Stagecoach*, the anonymous editors of the collective engaged a study of the ideology of naming and nomination. Ford's feature did *not* herald the early years of an *Abraham* Lincoln but of an anonymous figure, an everyman and an anybody, a genial but wily figure whose name would resemble the "no one," the name with which Odysseus had identified himself when facing the monocular Cyclops in the dark cavern in Homer's epic. Who was Mr. Lincoln? As the budding apparatus critics noted, he could be comparable to the anonymous "Mr." of Frank Capra's *Mr. Deeds Goes to Town*, or by extension, to Mr. Smith of *Mr. Smith Goes to Washington*. Ideology dictated that ordinary viewers of cinema could identify with these and other anonymous subjects, like themselves, in the time of the New Deal. Were they of progressive bent? Did they lean toward the films of Warner Brothers and identify with Roosevelt, who championed restricting the powers of "Republicans and Big Business." Yet also, would they have been aware of Hollywood's isolationist stance amidst "new threats of internal and international crisis," what the editors called "the fairly gloomy context of the *Young Mr. Lincoln* undertaking."[9] Noting how 20th Century Fox supported the Republicans and Big Business, and how the studio had sanctified Lincoln for the sake of putting him at the origin of their economic programs, the editors showed how the feature, despite being a piece of hagiography and an "ideological undertaking," was riddled with contradiction.

Without rehearsing how the editors deploy structural analysis based on Lacanian psychoanalysis to show how the "film's ideological project" is led astray where rifts in form and logic ripple "the deceptively calm surface" (529), it suffices to apply their own apparatus theory to details of which—perhaps for their lack of familiarity with English, their desire to jump to conclusions, or their failure to read closely—they were unaware or did not study—but that nonetheless confirm what they propose. At stake there was—and perhaps still is—the matter of naming, what "the editors" make glaringly clear when, in the aura of a collective, they refuse to append their own names to what they undertake. After noting how the front-credits of Ford's film establish the ideological operation of what follows, they divide the feature into 15 successive units. Beginning with the first, the "electoral speech" (503–7), what in their eyes amounts to a "repression of politics" (506), they aim at showing how the beginning of the film, "castrating Lincoln of his historico-political dimension," seeks to create a legend, "and even more to rid it of its historical roots in order to liberate its universal and eternal meaning" (507). They skip over the passage from the last piece of the front credits, a quotation of a poem attributed to author "Rosemary Benét," inscribed in smaller characters in the lower right corner of the frame. Written in epigraphic majuscule to resemble characters incised on a tombstone, in a very long take (01:29–01:45) that promotes a slow and ponderous reading of the words, the penultimate line of the poem reads (in contrast to the litany of five "dids" in the stanza of eight lines, "DO YOU KNOW HIS NAME?" (01:32), before the final line asks, as if in tendering a lure to the viewer, "DID HE GET ON?".

Prior to this sequence, the title of the film (00:26–00:32) notes only the protagonist's surname, leaving the Christian moniker aside. With "Mr.," however, there is an advocacy of commonality and an invitation to follow a narrative of what might be called a "mistery" or, for psychanalysts who listen closely to the writing of speech, to a "Mr.-ry". The point is reinforced where the poem has already underscored that the hero's mother is dead and that it is her voice that speaks through the scripture as it is seen. A sort of *ex-voto,* in the lines shown in the previous shot, the absent (and silent) voice of the dead mother asks, having only referred to "Abe", "you wouldn't know about my son?" The remark, which would prompt viewers to wonder if the mystery can be glossed, à la Lacan—with whom the editors identified—as "missed her he." Thus began, in the ideological machinery, a relation with death or an inaugural absence of a missing mother. Without noting how or why the epigraphy might or might not be related to the first shot, the editors skipped over to John T. Stuart's words that were denouncing "the corrupt political who are in power" (503) before attending to those introducing the "local candidate whom he is sponsoring: the young Mr. Lincoln" (503–4).

In reaching back to what the editors had been getting at, it is worth looking closely at the first nine shots of the film (that for sake of transition include the last of the title-cards):

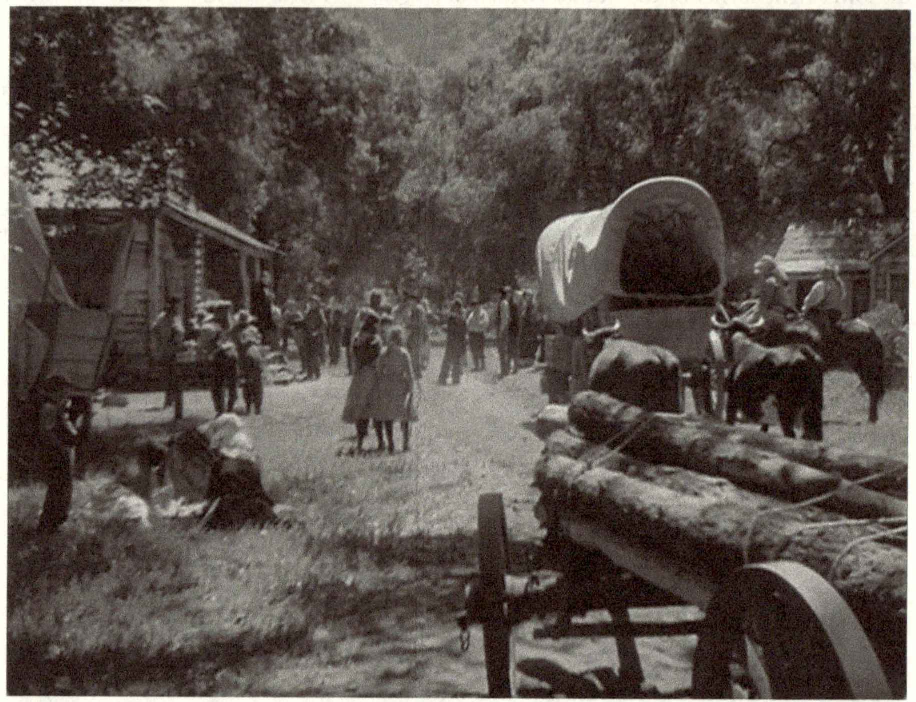

- Shot 1: final credit on which the time and place are incised: "New Salem, Ill. 1832" (1:50–52) before fading in black to
- Shot 2: a scene in deep focus in which in the background people gather in front of the veranda of a building seen very obliquely, toward which, on a path in the middle ground, followed by two oxen, a covered wagon moves. To the left of the center of the frame and its field are what appear to be two girls or young women, their backs facing the scene, who seem to be looking at what is beyond. In the foreground, slanting into the frame as if to aim at something that cannot be located, an open wagon bears a load of logs. By way of the retinal suspension or memory of the writing of the front-credits, viewers might wonder if these are the logs that children recall from the myth of the president who was raised in a log cabin and that are invariably associated with the myth of the child who had read voraciously in candlelight. After repeated viewings (thanks to apparatus unavailable to the editors in 1969–70) the spectator notes a minuscule character, dressed in black, standing on an upper step to the veranda (1:55:2:03). Cut to
- Shot 3: The man in black, now in the middle ground, standing on the veranda, his left arm raised, addresses seven spectators (not counting the camera), seen from the back, whose mass occludes sight of the right side of the veranda (2:03–17). Cut to
- Shot 4: a medium close-up of the man, his right arm raised, who continues to denounce the dirty politics in Washington. In the middle ground a man, his face not seen, listens while smoking a corncob pipe (2:17–20). Cut to

- Shot 5: the setting of shot 2, the man, calling himself John T. Stuart, now promising to get the vermin out of Washington (2:20–35). Cut to
- Shot 6: the setting of shot 4, Stuart continuing his speech, now praising—*without naming*—the man from New Salem to whom (off, to the right) he gestures, asking him to come forward (2:35–52). Cut to
- Shot 7: medium close-up of a young man leaning back on a chair, his feet on a balustrade (off), engrossed in a book he reads, as if oblivious to the words being spoken. He gets up slowly, almost maladroitly, ambles to his right (the camera pans), moves from shadow into light, stands in the place Stuart evacuates, gazes outward, and begins to speak softly and affirmative, "Gentleman" (2:52–3:15). Cut to
- Shot 8: medium close-up of the young man, in bright light against the darker background of the building, his long-sleeved shirt open, wearing suspenders, his hands in his pockets. "And fellow citizens." He stops, looks down, and up again. "I presume you all know who I am." Softly, he adds, "plain Abraham Lincoln. I've been solicited by many friends to become a candidate for the legislature." He pauses, reflects, then adds, "my politics are short and sweet [...] the old woman's dance." He pauses again, now more affirmatively: "I'm in favor of an internal improvement system and a high protective tariff." He pauses. "These are my sentiments and political principles." He pauses. "If elected I should be thankful [...] if not, it'll be all the same." He smiles, bends twice in slight curtsies of gratitude (3:15–4:09). Cut to
- Shot 9: medium close-up of two smiling, freckled children, a girl and a body, who look and listen in rapt admiration (4:09–10).

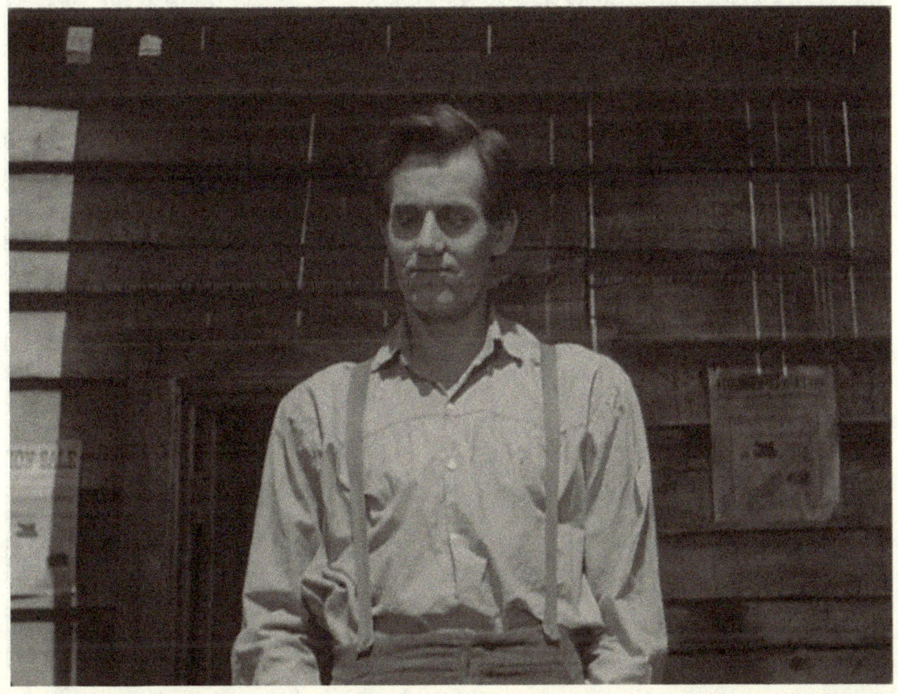

Surely the *conscious* ideological apparatus is manifest in the eighth and very long and single shot of 69 seconds in which Lincoln tells us who he is, what he is aiming to do, and how he thinks. The editors of *Cahiers* were quick to note that "Lincoln's youth is in fact *rewritten* by what has to filter through the Lincolnian myth" (507). They overlooked the fact that the *unconscious* ideological apparatus is manifest in paronomasia, what in the image seems to be a carefully orchestrated pun that occurs at the moment Lincoln is compelling to tell spectator who he is when he accords himself a proper name:

> I presume you all know who I am [...] plain Abraham Lincoln.

The remark calls in question the position of the spectator who must ask if indeed the person in view represents Abraham Lincoln or if he must be judged like the Lincoln of *The Birth of a Nation*, or Steven Spielberg's avatar of 2012, as a "genuine imitation" or a fetish object that is a sign of joyous disavowal. A point of difference between the mythic figure embossed on American pennies issued since 1909 (and replacing the Indian head counterparts as if to be rid of Native American just as the Buffalo nickel gave way to a portrait of Thomas Jefferson) is seen in the protruding nose, bathed in bright light, that anyone familiar with Fonda since his first film (*Spendthrift*, 1933), knows is prosthetic. A Freudian analyst in 1939, the very year when Freud was forced to flee Vienna, would see in the figure a "glanz" on the nose—a fetish.[10] So prominent in the shot that it is almost in *trompe l'œil*, Lincoln's nose resembles those of the Marx Brothers. The man speaking is both *plain* Abraham Lincoln and *playin'* Abraham Lincoln.

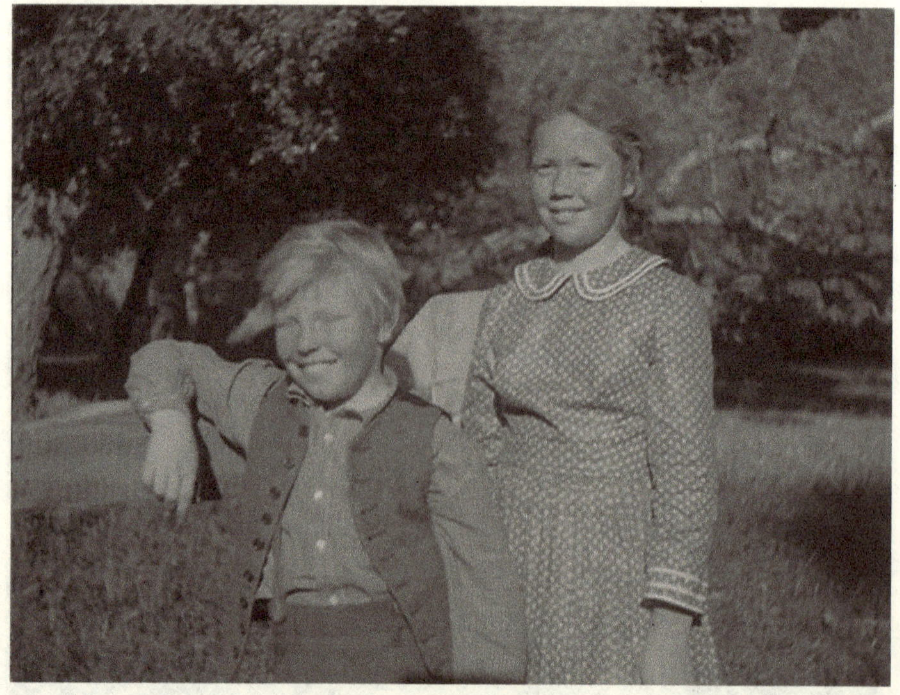

From the moment the paronomasia calls the character's identity into question, *apparatus* becomes both visible and audible. Hence the rhetoric of the ninth shot: portraying the children admiring the man who is "plain" Abraham, the boy and the girl become emblems of the ideal viewer the film is constructing. Children, puerile and docile, entranced by the effect of what is before their eyes, look both at the character playing Lincoln and, from the angle of the spectator gazing upon them, at the movie itself, considering the simulacrum as if what they were seeing were the paradox of an authentic representation, a paradox calling in question the veracity of words heard and the images seen. The astute viewer would note how Lincoln's "aura" suspends disbelief and turns history into myth: hence the machinery of ideology. The unnamed editors of *Cahiers du Cinéma*—editors, themselves playing hide-and-seek, maybe presuming readers all knew who they were—became, simply and plainly, astute agents of ideology. Pretending to be everyone and anyone, they transformed a film affiliated with an *auteur* and a founding name in the history of Hollywood into a political work riven with contradiction. Belonging to an *apparat* (and themselves, as it were, apparatchiks), the editors made an irrefutable case for showing how consciousness of apparatus is at the core of critical spectatorship. In hindsight, when the analysis is revisited almost fifty years after its publication, the writing might seem overdrawn, the appeal to Lacanian idiolect tiresome, and the conclusions either overblown or crafted—albeit correctly—to impugn American foreign policy at the time it waged a senseless, costly and traumatizing war in Vietnam. Surely too, where it works on law and transgression in the final pages, the collective reaches conclusions familiar to students of Ford's cinema.[11] Yet, its political investment gets at how media are in and of ideology, and how what is purveyed in a film that otherwise belongs to an archive says something about the machineries that control the imagination and, no less, about cognition itself.

Further history of apparatus theory indicates how and why. In 2009 Jean-Louis Comolli (if not one of the article's authors, at least an avowed affiliate of the collective when it emerged in 1970) published a searing study of the contemporary condition of media in the age of spectacle. So seamless, so overwhelming, so stupefying are films and televisual events of our moment, he argues, that they colonize and control perception and sensation in ways that heretofore had been unimaginable. We are now witnessing audiovisual works whose formatting "of seeing and hearing, of feeling and dreaming" effectively constrains our ability to think. Like the proponents of apparatus theory of yesterday, critical or emancipated spectators of both today and the future will be those whose task is to protect us from the effects of spectacle.[12] The critical spectator of today must "fend off [a] longing to be blinded by the flickering lights, and to be engorged by the accumulation of visual and acoustic effects."[13] In the same volume, Comolli reprints *verbatim* several decisive essays and reflections on apparatus and depth of field, published in 1972, that now are, he adds, "all the more active for having been so successfully repressed, for belonging to a grey zone which we do not want to know about, for disturbing us more than seducing us, for having fallen under a contemporary malediction that a 'theory' of the cinema can be useful and practical. It is true that the spectacle abhors 'thought', and even in expelling all forms of thought from its temple" (53). So pernicious is the spectacle that *alienation*, what in the earlier writing had been decried in the moment of workers' struggles for equality, is now cherished. In the current age of spectacle, whose crushing effects are far more pervasive than they had been in the time when apparatus theory was born, alienation gathers extraordinary critical mettle. It alerts the spectator to how mental and physical machineries construct and disseminate spectacle. Formatting of media today aims at depriving viewers and participants of their alienation, a condition that gives rise to critical agency.

In his work that returns to the matter of depth of field, Comolli revisits André Bazin's embrace of the long take and extreme depth of field in the major essays, including "The Evolutions of Film Language," comprising *What is Cinema!?* Showing how their idealistic tenor was a function of ideology, he notes that nonetheless they suggest how a critical view of spectacle is afforded when the viewer looks at the image as the construction of an *illusion* of spatial depth and, from a different angle, as a flat surface on which visible and audible forms are in play. For Comolli, in contrast to Bazin for whom the redemptive worth of cinema was visible in what was set before our eyes, ideology emerges from the apparent differences and contradictions within the frame. A *cache* or a limiting form, the frame becomes the site where differences—hence signs of alienation—are set forward, and where the *lure* of simultaneously believing while disbelieving what is seen becomes a critical point of reference. In reprinting essays that had been loosely affiliated with apparatus theory, he adds that contrary to a good deal of film history that relegates the fortunes of depth-of-field to the scientific development of sensitive film stock in the age of analogue cinema or today, when it goes without saying in the realm of digital process, its use and abuse are better explained through the lens of ideology. When, at the beginning of the Great Depression, sound film became a norm, in collusion with theater and an emerging star system, the apparatus of industry imposed an erasure of depth of field. It "liquidated montage as a general principle of cinematic writing" (241). Histories of cinema that argue for progress and development through miracles of technology, he suggests, both then (in 1972) and now (in 2017), fail to note how silent cinema was already riddled with signs of sound, and how its editing and montage afforded on the part of the spectator a valuable sense of distance—or alienation—with respect what it put on display. With the advent of sound film, especially when sound and motion could be located in the visual field, identification with the image became a norm. When depth-of-field "returned" to sound film as it had in the work of Welles and Ford, attention was drawn to the apparatus. When the latter is made manifest in cinema, a critical or "emancipated" consciousness gives rise to a political aesthetics in the very condition of viewing. The return to classical or early cinema, what otherwise would be a continuum of film history or "cinephilia," acquires uncommon agency. It is here where history and theory meet and where, together, they are of formidable virtue. For whatever its fortunes have been, however abstruse its arguments or its idiolect, plain and simple, apparatus theory remains an invaluable critical tool.

Notes

1 A forerunner is Jean-François Lyotard's aptly titled *Dispositifs pulsionnels à partir de Marx et Freud* (Paris: Christian Bourgois, 1984), in which «dispositif» describes how works of art, notably those of «immaterial» composition, acquire political agency through the conceptual processes they embody.

2 In this respect, a crucial (and only very lately translated) work is Jean Louis Schefer's *L'Homme ordinaire du cinéma* (Paris: Gallimard/Cahiers du Cinéma, 1985), its title underscoring a

commonly shared and often everyday experience of film by allusion from Georg Simmel to Michel de Certeau.

3 No doubt theorists had been using *dispositif* in ways related to the definition given in *Le Dictionnaire Robert*: from the Latin *dispositus* it could mean setting into action, as in the formula (once used by Roland Barthes), "tu proposes, et je dispose", a slogan meaning "your wish is my command." It would be the "[m]anner by which the parts, the organs of an apparatus are arranged [*disposés*]," or "the mechanism itself," as well as the "sum of means arranged in conformity with a plan," the latter "a map, a blueprint, or a plan of action."

4 See Francesco Casetti on Erich Feldmann, "Going to the Movies," in *The Lumière Galaxy: Seven Key Words for the Cinema to Come* (New York: Columbia University Press, 2015), 141.

5 Noël Burch, *La Lucarne sur l'infini: Naissance du langage cinématogrphique* (Paris: Nathan, 1991).

6 In the history of the debates within the frame of *Cahiers du Cinéma*, it happened that André Bazin, its founding father, whose studies of Welles and Renoir had been crucial for the articulation of auteur theory, was compelled to put a brake on excess of his acolytes in an article that argued for correlating styles of various directors with the "genius of system" in which they worked.

7 Michel Foucault, *Raymond Roussel* (Paris: Éditions Gallimard, 1963); "Le langage de l'espace" (in *Critique*, no. 203, 1966: 378–82), reproduced in Daniel Defert and François Ewald, eds., *Michel Foucault: Dits et écrits*, vol. 1 (Paris: Éditions Gallimard, 1994), 407–12; "Qu'est-ce qu'un auteur", in Defert and Ewald, *Michel Foucault*, 789–821. The deeper history of the emergence of the "author" at the threshold of print-culture is taken up in Cynthia Brown, *Poets, Patrons and Painters* (Ithaca: Cornell University Press, 1996); that of the "writer" is the topic of Alain Viala, *Naissance de l'écrivain: Sociologie de la littérature à l'âge classique* (Paris: Éditions de Minuit, 1985).

8 For Roger Shattuck, in his classic *Banquet Years* (1955), 1913 witnesses Paul Valéry's return to poetry in the composition of *La Jeune Parque*; the publication of Apollinaire's *Alcools*; the first volume of Proust's *À la recherché du temps perdu*; Marcel Duchamp's experiments in the visualization of language and form in motion; Erik Satie's renditions of spare musical harmonies. The imminence of war in a fragile and volatile world, he remarked, prompted extraordinary creative drive. So also, implies Bazin, was 1939, when Renoir, Welles and Ford develop deep-focus cinema on the eve of an inalterably imminent war.

9 "John Ford's *Young Mr. Lincoln:* A Collective Text by the Editors of *Cahiers du Cinéma*," translated and reprinted in Bill Nichols, ed., *Movies and Methods*, vol. 1 (Berkeley: University of California Press, 1976), 493–529 (498). The essay first appeared in *Cahiers du Cinéma*, no. 223 (1970).

10 He or she might be prompted to see in the Fonda figure what might be a Jewish Abraham Lincoln. It is not by a stretch of the imagination that a Jewish Lincoln would be, in Ford's writing of the myth of the hero, comparable to what Michel de Certeau makes of Freud's devastating "joke," the construction of an "Egyptian Moses" in his last work, *Moses and Monotheism* (*Standard Edition*, vol. 23, 7–137, notably on fragments, 42–43) that in fact doubles the analyst's displacement and migration to England, in "Ce que Freud fait de l'histoire," chapter 9 of *L'Écriture de l'histoire* (Paris: Éditions Gallimard, 1975), chapter 9, in English as: "What Freud Makes of History," in *The Writing of History*, translated by Tom Conley (New York: Columbia University Press, 1992).

11 Among others, Jean Douchet, *L'Homme cinéma* (Paris: Écriture, 2013); Andrew Sarris, *The John Ford Movie Mystery* (Bloomington: University of Indiana Press, 1975); Lee Clark Mitchell, *Westerns: Making the Man in Fiction and Film* (Chicago: University of Chicago Press, 1996); Jean-Louis Leutrat, *Le Western: Archéologie d'un genre* (Lyon: Presses de l'Université de Lyon, 1987); *Le Western: Quand la légende devint réalité* (Paris: Éditions Gallimard, 1995); with Suzanne Linandrat-Guigues, *Westerns* (Paris: Klincksieck, 2007).

12 Comolli argues that the *critical* spectator is close in character to Jacques Rancière's concept of the *emancipated* spectator in his book of the same title, *Le Spectateur émancipé* ((Paris: La Fabrique, 2003), in English as *The Emancipated Spectator* (London: Verso, 2009)).

13 *Cinema against Spectacle*, edited and translated by Daniel Fairfax (Amsterdam: Amsterdam University Press, 2015), 52.

Chapter Nine

PROPERTIES OF FILM AUTHORSHIP

Codruţa Morari

A Resilient Notion

In the new millennium, five major English-language books and anthologies have returned to the question of film authorship (Gerstner and Steiger 2003; Wexman 2003; Grant 2008; Sellors 2010; Kozloff 2014) putting into new light the richness of film studies classics such as John Caughie's *Theories of Authorship: A Reader* or Andrew Sarris's *The American Cinema: Directors and Directions*. To this day, virtually every guide to film studies presents an entry on the topic. Studies on national cinema, including Hollywood, tend to devote substantial space to "directors and directions." Monographs and biographies in this vein abound; director series published by academic presses have proliferated. For all the profusion, there is general agreement that film authorship is a powerful myth and the film author a decidedly problematic construction. Nonetheless, even the most recent and sophisticated auteur studies do not fully embrace the constructionist assumption nor completely reflect the many theoretical misgivings well known to film studies scholars. For all the debates about the constitution of film authorship, embodied authors are more present than ever in film reviewing, film criticism, film studies as well as in film festivals and the film industry in its various countenances.

The notion of the film author is intimately linked to the larger endeavor to establish cinema as an art and movie going as a legitimate cultural practice. "The auteurist idea at its most basic (that movies are primarily the creation of one governing author behind the camera who thinks in images and sounds rather than words and sentences) is now the default setting in most considerations of moviemaking, and for that we should all be thankful," assessed Kent Jones in 2014. "We'd be nowhere without film auteurism, which boasts a proud history: the lovers of cinema did not just argue for its inclusion among the fine arts, but actually stood up, waved its flag, and proclaimed its glory without shame" (Jones 2014, 41–42). The long and illustrious history of this notion dates back to European film reviewing and criticism of the 1920s. It was, however, not until the post-Liberation years, and well into the 1950s, that the notion became institutionalized in film criticism, first in France and particularly in the pages of *Cahiers du cinéma*, then in England, with *Sequence*, *Movie* and *Sight and Sound*, and subsequently on an international scale.

The *Cahiers* phase during which the famous *politique des auteurs* was formulated marks the first significant chapter of auteurism. In the beginning of the 1960s and during the 1970s, a decided shift from the stress on the author as the source of meaning to an emphasis on the spectator forced a reevaluation of the term's foundations and functions. Starting with the *cinestructuralist* movement of the British intellectual left that sought to uncover the structuring principles of individual films while retaining the artist, critics proceeded to emphasize the ideological and historical factors implicated in the construction of authorship. The author was seen as a subject position, either an instance of politics or pleasure (Jean Narboni and Jean-Louis Comolli), an effect of the text (Roland Barthes, Christian Metz and Stephen Heath), or simply an authenticating factor for the circulation of texts (Michel Foucault, whose notion of the "author function" would inspire Timothy Corrigan's discussion of the "commerce of auteurism"). Under the aegis of the "death of the author," this episode prompted a further shift in the poststructuralist years of the 1980s, namely to a reborn author who was commercially conditioned and theoretically refurbished. The author now assumed various guises, a historically and culturally shaped entity (cultural studies), determined by economic, technological and historical-materialist determinations (David Bordwell, Janet Staiger and Kristin Thompson), gendered (Laura Mulvey and Tania Modleski), or a function of an increasingly globalized world (Jeong and Szaniawski).

To this day, auteurism retains a great amount of its cultural capital, even after the author has been declared dead and replaced by cine-structures, texts and readers. From its initial reputation as a scandalous proposition, the notion of *auteur* has evolved into an often-invoked and, in many minds, inflationary appellation. Its use today, in the assessment of filmmaker Olivier Assayas has become codified, no matter how many detractors consider it to be reactionary and retrograde (Assayas 2001, 177). Despite challenges and misgivings about the collaborative nature of film production, self-branding and marketing, or alternative modes of production both within and outside the film industry, the category of authorship has proved to be inordinately resilient. In the age of mass media, given its plurality of voices that so often are hard to localize, authorship matters more than ever, argues Janet Staiger, especially "to those in non-dominant positions in which asserting even a partial agency may seem to be important for day-to-day survival or where locating moments of alternative practice takes away the naturalized privileges of normativity" (Staiger 2003, 27).

Proto-Auteurism

So strong is the influence of auteurism that scholars have often retroactively assigned the status of authors to early inventors and operators (see Pinel 1994 and Séguin 1999). Tom Gunning (1991, 42) points out that the cinema of attraction promoted machinery, as did "other technological wonders such as the widely exhibited X-rays or the phonograph. [...] It was the Cinématographe, the Biograph, or the Vitascope that were advertised on the variety bills in which they premiered," rather than the name of a human agent or the title of a show. The notion of film authorship would come to dominate the discourse of film criticism and later film theory, especially in assessments of Hollywood productions where the relations between the industrial frame and artistic volition were often so fraught. To the commercial value of big studio productions, authorship "added the promise of certain spectatorial pleasures, the cachet of cultural respectability, or cult status." Together with the centrality of genre and star, authorship became a valuable form of product recognition used to market films.

During the first twenty years of cinema's history, films seemed to be, above all, determined by their technology. The collective nature of film production, much less its instrumentation that relied on mechanical reproduction, made it difficult to assign authorship, authority or agency to a single individual. Early critics who sought to apply interpretive models used for the other arts, especially for literature and painting, were hard-pressed to discern who the rightful author of a film should be. Disagreeing about whether the credit should be given to the director, the scriptwriter, or perhaps even the producer, they concurred at best that the artistic medium of film needed an individual author with a controlling vision that granted a film its unity and coherence. Jean Epstein, Germaine Dulac, Louis Delluc, Ricciotto Canudo and Léon Moussinac all defended the artistic potential of the medium and urged people working within the industry to develop a personal form of filmmaking—even in spite of variances of opinion as to who exactly constituted the dictating force on any given set. Scriptwriters often discredited directors, describing the latters' endeavors as the mere application of technique and the deployment of technology rather than the creation of original art. The discourses that circulated in French film criticism in the 1920s are crucial for any appreciation of how the *politique des auteurs* came into being and how auteurism would become such an essential and influential discourse.

The thought that an industrialized practice such as film might also be seen as an artistic creation in many minds posed a challenge and a provocation. The valorization of the film *auteur* would bring aesthetic legitimation to a medium that was widely seen as a vehicle of mass diversion. The film critic and director Jean Epstein emphasized the filmmaker's vision in the process of cinematographic creation, linking it to the property of *photogénie*, which would serve as a founding stone of art cinema: "Mechanically speaking the lens alone can sometimes succeed in revealing the inner nature of things in this way," he wrote in 1926. "This is how, by chance in the first instance, the *photogénie* of character was discovered. But the proper sensibility, by which I mean a personal one, can direct the lens towards increasingly valuable discoveries. This is the role of an author of film, commonly called a film director" (Epstein 2012, 296).

Politique des auteurs/Auteur Theory

In discussions of film history, much attention has been devoted to the *politique des auteurs* and the critical practice that it engendered. The tale has been told so often that it has taken on the status of a myth: in France of the 1950s and 1960s, a group of Parisian young men of a certain generation came together and gave rise to the new and strong voice of a postwar era that the journal *L'Express* called Nouvelle Vague. Claude Chabrol, Jean-Luc Godard, Eric Rohmer, François Truffaut began as cine-club animators and film critics, pursuing a calling that emerged from their spectatorial practices of watching films all day and discussing them into the night. They criticized what François Truffaut (1954) termed "a certain French tradition," turning to Hollywood and especially American B-movies. Their articles, appearing in the monthly journal *Cahiers du cinéma*, eschewed academic discourse; with willful élan and subjective panache, they lingered on memorable scenes and privileged moments. Their written responses to films, observed film scholar Paul Willemen, were highly impressionistic, "in T.S. Eliot's terms, an 'evocative equivalent' of moments which, when encountered in a film, spark something which then produced the energy and the desire to write" (1994, 235). These critics believed that the principle of authorship, in the words of Jean-Luc Godard, "having acknowledged that a film by Hitchcock, for example, is as important as a book by Aragon, film authors, thanks to us, have finally entered the history of art" (1972, 146). The *Cahiers* critics were praised by the eminent Andrew Sarris for paving the way to redeem Hollywood from the critical dismissal when it was compared to European art cinema.

A director's singularity served as the central point of focus for this critical method that insisted that mise-en-scène only, as the true language of cinema, revealed the auteur's signature and that this was a matter of aesthetic values and not of sociological resonance. Though mentored by André Bazin, these critics were denied the master's endorsement in matters of *auteur policy*. Bazin (2001) praised them for eschewing a limited focus on the subject matter of films and for promoting appreciation of an author's unique personal style (the magic word was "mise-en-scène"). Nonetheless, maintained Bazin, the *politique* was bound to fail because its scope did not extend to aesthetic theory; it failed to account for how individual signatures, once integrated into a larger system and network of meaning, assumed a decidedly relational dimension.

The principal concern of the *politique*'s exponents was not the legitimation and recognition of French directors. Hollywood studios, the oft maligned site of industrialized fantasy production, would become the primary ground on which the young critics would carry out their campaign. In the words of Derek Schilling, they sought to revive "the romantic notion of artistic genius in a domain largely defined by economic and institutional pressures. However constraining the circumstances, they affirmed, an *auteur* manages to convey themes and obsessions which compose an inviolable signature" (2007, 78–79). The *politique des auteurs* formulated standards of evaluation, a critical method that would assure cinema a place within the established arts. To grant Hollywood productions the status of art was a bold move—and a decidedly discriminating one as well. For by linking the medium's industrial hegemony to the West's aesthetic, the *politique* critics excluded from consideration vast stretches of filmic possibility and far reaches of film history.

The stakes of film authorship become particularly apparent in the complicated—and controversial—transformation of a critical tool, *la politique des auteurs*, into what Andrew Sarris and many Anglo-American critics in his wake would call the "auteur theory." Sarris praised the French critics for showing that "[t]he art of the cinema is the art of an attitude, the style of a gesture. It is not so much *what* as *how*. The *what* is some aspect of reality rendered mechanically by the camera. The *how* is what the French critics designate somewhat mystically as mise-en-scène [...] The whole point of a meaningful style is that it unifies the *what* and the *how* into a personal statement" (1996, 36). Kent Jones would later comment that "[w]hen Andrew Sarris Americanized the *politique*, he made a crucial adjustment by turning a declaration of artistic liberty into both a system of evaluation (the auteur 'theory') and a crusade to change the way that cinema was thought of and discussed. An auteur was no longer an artist who spoke 'in the first person,' as Rivette put it, and who had actually crafted a formidable body of work, but any director who had produced *evidence* of authorship, i.e. the ability to think in visual terms" (2014, 42).

In their redemptive approach to luminaries like Alfred Hitchcock, Howard Hawks and Otto Preminger, the *Cahiers* critics hailed these Hollywood auteurs for maintaining a singular vision and a directorial integrity despite material constraints and pressures from studios. Their very status as auteurs rested in their resistant energy, their remarkable ability to create film art that transcended the impersonal workings of the industrialized instrumentality from which their features issued. The auteur, in this understanding, retained his inimitable signature and artistic integrity no matter where he worked and regardless under what conditions. As such, auteurs distinguished themselves from filmmakers who remained subservient to the industrial machine and functioned as impersonal metteurs-en-scene. The opposition between artists and artisans has left indelible marks in the perception of film authorship—so much so that other discourses have been practically dismissed, even though the relationship between artistic creation and professional endeavor has a long and complex history, particularly in France. Auteurism's prism remains narrowly focused on films and filmmakers; its focus needs to be expanded beyond a mere fixation on aesthetic factors if one is to appreciate the profound ways in which films also reflect—and reflect on—the realities of working artists.

The Death of the Author and Auteur-Structuralism

The ascription of a single, unified and identifiable author of a film or a body of films has become inextricably bound to the status of film as an expressive form. Even though the medium would assume a firm institutional shape as a collaborative, commercial and narrative enterprise already in the 1910s, it would not be taken seriously as a legitimate art until it generated its own version of authorship. The *auteurist* movement became a significant factor not only for film theory but also for the twentieth-century history of ideas. Nonetheless, its great success, seen in hindsight, seems paradoxical due to what Colin MacCabe has identified as two "massive contradictions" (2003, 40). The first relates to the complicated quality of film production and the legal determinations that regulated this complex process, including new copyright laws. By its very nature, filmmaking is, in John Caughie's words, a "collective, commercial, industrial and popular" enterprise (1981, 13). The multiple agencies involved in the making of a film are so diverse and the process so intricately divided among a multitude of specialist trades and professions that "for all practical purposes" (Stillinger 1991, 174) film authorship seems impossible to assign (see Bennett 2005). Yet the victory of *auteur* theory was so considerable that this concern about any film's collective constitution would seem to be at best a quibble.

The second contradiction stemmed from the proclamation of the death of the (literary) author by the critic Roland Barthes, whose intervention written in 1967 was echoed in Michel Foucault's 1969 conference at Collège de France, "What Is an Author?" which emphatically begins with Beckett's question, "What does it matter who is speaking?" Even though cutting-edge work in linguistics, psychoanalysis and the social sciences increasingly was coming to stress the social construction of subjectivity, *auteur* theory continued to rely on a conception of unified agency, that is, a stable subject. The auteurist persuasion remained quite resilient in film and visual studies, even as the author met with the demise in other branches of humanities. "One prefecture of French culture," quipped Robert Carringer, "was reinventing the idea of authorship while another one was trying to kill it off" (Kozloff 2014, 7). In fact, the social upheavals that led to the events of May 1968 had a substantial impact on the discourse and the practice of the Nouvelle Vague. Under the guidance of Jean-Louis Comolli, *Cahiers du cinéma* published a special issue that reevaluated the *politique des auteurs*. The editors questioned the concepts of "mise-en-scène" and "signature," deploring the inflated usage of these terms particularly in discussions of American cinema (Fieschi et al., 1965). Indeed, the debate about the death of the author occurred only a few months before *Cahiers*'s reconsideration of the *politique* and, in so doing, it took leave from the journal's venerable legacy of cinephilic ocularcentrism. In the same vein, Claude Lévi-Strauss (1966 (1962)) declared that "the goal of the human science is not to constitute man, but to dissolve him," formulating what would be seen as the "slogan of the decade" for the France of the 1960s (see also Culler 1975 and Burke 1998).

Lévi-Strauss's structuralist methodology had a strong impact on European discourses in the humanities and social sciences and would soon find its way into film studies. At the end of the 1960s, leftist intellectual circles in Great Britain became sensitive to film's cultural rise and sought to introduce the study of cinema into university curricula, turning both to Lévi-Strauss and classical auteurism. The most notable result of this combination is Peter Wollen's *Signs and Meaning in the Cinema* (1972), which addressed and integrated theoretical challenges in an expansive understanding of authorship. Tracing a theoretical path from the idealized construction of a filmic author to a structuralist critique of authorial subjectivity, Wollen distinguished between a ciné-structuralist idea of film authorship and the auteurist cult of personality. The director should not be seen as an "individual" who "expresses himself or his own vision in the film" but should instead be viewed as a subject whose "preoccupations" allow for "unconscious, unintended meaning" that can be decoded. The author's signature becomes the unifying principle of the film, a center of focus and source of meaning. This revised understanding of auteurism involved a "tracing of a structure (not a message) within the work, which can then *post-factum* be assigned to an individual, the director, on empirical grounds" (Wollen 1981, 146). "It is wrong," maintained Peter Wollen, "in the name of a denial of the traditional idea of creative subjectivity, to deny any status to individuals at all. But Fuller or Hawks or Hitchcock, the directors, are quite separate from 'Fuller' or 'Hawks' or 'Hitchcock,' the structures named after them, and should not be methodologically confused."

The insistence on the socially constructed subjectivity of authorship gave rise to multiple variations in poststructuralist discourses. The place of the author in the production apparatus, the patriarchal discourse of the male film director that informs a film's shape and dynamic and the dominance of the category of authorship as an aesthetic Western (especially European) tool which often is hard-pressed in approaches to non-Western cinemas, have been central questions in film studies in the wake of poststructuralism. The example of Olivier Assayas's feature *Irma Vep* will allow us to probe the pertinence and richness of this discursive legacy.

The Author, the Star and the Making of a Genre Film: *Irma Vep* (Olivier Assayas, 1996)

Olivier Assayas's feature from 1996, *Irma Vep*, provides substantial confirmation about just how much authorship still matters. To be sure, as a film critic Assayas seemed to have closed discussion on the subject when in *Cahiers du cinéma* he attacked both the codified application of the term and its decisive victory within film criticism. According to the French *auteur*, it was the only discourse that sustained the scandalous energy of the May 1968 uprising. *Irma Vep* is, however, anything but a lament, a eulogy or an example of nostalgic auteurism. Instead, the film commingles cinephilic investment and an embrace of film history, witty anecdotes and the exploration of those mythical forces that made cinema a site of attraction and derision during the twentieth century.

Set in Paris at the end of the twentieth century, the film spirits us to a production set charged with a remake of *Les Vampires* a popular ten-episode crime serial written, directed, produced and distributed by Louis Feuillade at Gaumont from 1915 to 1916. The original installments follow a journalist and his friend as they try to unmask a gang of male thieves known as The Vampires. *Irma Vep* borrows its title from the muse of this gang. Originally played by the actress Musidora, *Irma Vep* became an icon of French femininity and a factor essential to the story's tremendous success. The remake of *Les Vampires* is assigned to René Vidal, a former Nouvelle Vague film *auteur* who is now mocked by journalists, his crew and his fellow filmmakers, and whose lapsed reputation seems to be barely enough to sustain the project. As enacted by Jean-Pierre Léaud, perhaps the Nouvelle Vague's most recognizable face, René Vidal is an eclectic artist who still believes in romantic concepts such as truth and beauty and hopes for the regeneration of his country's struggling cinema, whose current situation resembles the one indicted by François Truffaut in his famous polemic, "A Certain Tendency of French Cinema." Reluctant to remake a classic, René agrees to the project only if Musidora's role be played by "graceful and mysterious" Maggie Cheung, a Hong Kong actress whose work René came across in a "very cheap cinema in Marrakech." Having just finished filming an action movie in Hong Kong, the inimitably professional Maggie joins a disorganized and chaotic group of people whom she fails to understand, language being far from the only obstacle. Tensions between the *auteur* and the crew lead to many misunderstandings and ultimately to the director's nervous breakdown. Vidal is to be replaced by José Murano, whose different vision of French film history and the Feuillade materials requires first of all that Irma Vep be played by a French actress.

Feuillade's *Les Vampires* was tremendously successful with wartime audiences and Musidora's star status made her the incarnation of French femininity. The serial's undeniable popularity did not prevent film critics from attacking Feuillade for pandering to the masses and taking recourse to the trivial likes of the *feuilleton* genre. Considering Feuillade's films as mere popular entertainment, commentators excluded him from the circle of film auteurs who might grant French cinema a strong international standing. *Les Vampires* gained its fame primarily from the allure of a gripping genre and the appeal of an auratic star—and not from a gifted filmmaker's distinctive vision of the cinematograph. For this reason, Assayas's choice of Feuillade to dramatize the magnificence of early filmmaking within the "larger project of reasserting national patrimony" (Hudson 2006, 220) might seem to be odd, even mistaken. Indeed, in her thorough analysis of Feuillade's place in film history, Louise Shea (2009) demonstrates how the director's vast *oeuvre* of over eight hundred films was consistently snubbed by contemporary critics who were committed defenders of the seventh art, including exponents of proto-auteurism eager to establish film as a legitimate and noble practice.

Feuillade's subsequent rehabilitation owes a great deal to the Surrealist movement that saw *Les Vampires* not as a popular attraction, but the work of a lyrical dreamer and avant-garde visionary. After Breton, Aragon and Desnos praised *Les Vampires*, Henri Langlois attempted to restore Feuillade's early prints for the Cinémathèque and both ensure and promote his legacy. Assayas reenacts the variance in Feuillade's early reception by staging Vidal's appropriation of the avant-garde Feuillade against Murano's vision of *Les Vampires* as popular entertainment. Playing out the tension between the author and the film, Assayas significantly picks two clips from *Les Vampires* to present the two sides of Feuillade that made him such a complex and controversial figure in French cinema history.

The first clip is selected by Vidal in order to introduce Maggie to the serial and the character of Irma Vep. He selects a sequence from episode six in which Musidora, dressed in her famous catlike costume, breaks into a hotel room, the same sequence that Maggie will later reenact in the sleepwalking scene at the hotel. In the seven-hour serial, Musidora wears this costume only for about fifteen minutes (Callahan 1998, 89) but its brief appearance did not keep Robert Desnos (1926) from a rhapsodic appreciation of the silent film female star. As Vidal turns on the VCR, he turns off the sound, emphasizing the importance of silence and suggesting that it is the nonnarrative quality of the film that appeals to him. Vidal's take on Feuillade ignores *Les Vampires*' status as a popular melodrama and relies on its Surrealist celebration as an avant-garde production. In short, he wants to update it, nevertheless facing the crew's objections that a remake is superfluous, that the original itself was already boring; it is at best significant as a relic of history and a mark of a certain time and genre. In his broken English, Vidal insists to Maggie that only she can assume the film's female lead: "I think not a French actress can play Irma Vep. After Musidora, it's impossible, it's blasphemy. But I tell them maybe I have an idea. You. You can be Irma Vep because you have the grace. I tell them I can do the film if you play the film. Big discussion, why you ask a Chinese actress? But I'm sure nobody else can do it because I saw you in this film [he points to the tape of an action Hong Kong film he's watching]. You are mysterious like Irma Vep, you are beautiful like Irma Vep, and also you are magic like her, and also very strong, and it's very important, you are modern. I want a modern Irma Vep." Rehearsing a Surrealist recuperation of the early film director, Vidal also seems to suggest that Hong Kong genre cinema might help to revitalize the French classic. At the same time, we can read in this attitude that Hong Kong cinema offers an alternative to Hollywood as a model for global cinema.

The second clip from Feuillade is associated with the author's replacement, José Murano, after he has been asked to take over the project. Seen watching a scene from episode three in which Irma Vep performs at Le Cabaret Chat Huant, Murano can only imagine a French actress in the role of Musidora. As he confesses to Laure, Maggie's understudy, "Irma Vep is Paris, it's Paris underground, popular Paris, Arletty, Irma Vep is not Fu Manchu." If René's conception of the project depends on Maggie Cheung's performance, it is precisely this performance by *une Chinoise* that puzzles Murano—played by Lou Cassel, the director in Fassbinder's famous film about filmmaking *Beware of a Holy Whore.* While Vidal's appropriation of Feuillade not only stresses the prototype's artistic appeal but also suggests the ways in which its updated rendering might turn to Asian and Hollywood cinema, Murano's resolutely insists on its Frenchness.

Feuillade's example assumes a prominent role in analyses of the different conventions in classical French and Hollywood cinema, most notably in David Bordwell's 1985 discussion of the economic, technological and institutional determinations of authorship. For Bordwell (1985), Feuillade's style, built on long takes and in-depth staging, offers a comprehensive alternative model to Hollywood and enacts France's response to Griffith and a nascent classical Hollywood narrative. More generally, in the study of film style and cinematic modes of production, Bordwell, along with Janet Staiger and Kristin Thompson advance a more thoroughgoing conception of authorship that factors in formal and technological determinations. These factors come in addition to the ideological ones invoked by Jean-Louis Comolli, Jean Narboni and Stephen Heath in their model of authorship derived from Christian Metz, on the one hand, and Louis Althusser, on the other. For Bordwell, the budgetary framework of a film is important insofar as it informs the technological choices and the aesthetic conventions of a period; in his view, though, the interrelations between these practices are contingent, not matters of causality à la Althusser, as he expressed it in "Ideology and Ideological State Apparatuses." Bordwell's model of authorship informs a reading that would oppose Feuillade's style to Hollywood practice of the teens as it would oppose contemporary Hollywood to Hong Kong and to French auteurist cinema. To be sure, such a binary eschews the classic auteurist discourse that placed art cinema and popular culture at opposite extremes. Assayas aligns himself with Bordwell and the latter's emphasis on Feuillade's "Frenchness" (as opposed to Hollywood conventions) when he writes that the director "participates in France, in a critical way, to the definition of cinematic narrative syntax, that is firmly embedded in the Lumière Brothers's virgin reality and that helps to postulate a fictional space where one would see reverberate, without the artificiality of magic, the imaginary incursions inaugurated by Méliès" (Assayas 2006, 116–17).

The rich footage cited by Assayas invokes another discourse on authorship that was present in the critical writings of the late 1960s. In addition to the two sequences from Feuillade's masterpiece, the French author includes a short scene from *Classe de lutte/Class of Combat* (a wordplay on "lutte de classe" or class struggle), a militant film realized in 1969 by the film collective Medvenkine, named after the Russian director who utilized cinema in the service of the masses and the Revolution. In the heat of the events of May 1968, established French filmmakers including Chris Marker and Jean-Luc Godard broke with the ideology of the individual artist and engaged in class struggle, for instance, with factory workers. After René's dismissive criticism of the film in progress, the crew meets for dinner at the Director of Photography's house, where a videotape brings back images from those days of revolutionary glory. Assayas selects a sequence from the beginning of *Classe de lutte* that defines cinema not as "a form of magic, but a technique and a science, a technique born out of a science and put to the service of one will: the workers' will of liberation." The juxtaposition of this sequence and the crew's commitment to their own work not only reflects on the ideological construction of the notion of authorship but also points to the aporia of an artistic revolution that led to the demise of the author. The film author as the ordering intelligence of the film continues, despite past experience and better knowledge, to persist in contemporary discourses.

Irma Vep reflects on film authorship in a variety of ways. Assayas complicates the relationship between *auteur* and *star*, suggesting that the former empowers the latter, who in turn embodies the film's meaning. The oneiric sequence when Maggie, dressed in her latex costume, enters a guest's room in the hotel and steals a necklace displays how the star becomes the medium for the director's project. To the logic of the film within a film, Assayas adds a dream within a dream in which Maggie Cheung truly becomes Irma Vep. In his analysis of *Irma Vep*, Tom Conley goes so far as to suggest that this sequence can be understood as a subtly staged response to Laura Mulvey's feminist theory of visual pleasure and narrative cinema. Maggie's hotel wanderings bring her to the room of a woman engrossed in a transatlantic conversation with her American lover. "Before the theft, for a moment, we observe Maggie observing the woman in her *molle nudité*," notes Conley (2000, 426). "The staging of her gaze cast upon the integrally naked woman complaining about her love life brings forward a reversal of Laura Mulvey's famous theory of narrative desire which aligns the pleasure gained from suspending disbelief in a story with male scopophilia. The corpulent object viewed by a svelte starlet poured into plastic armor collapses the theory of the gaze." If *Irma Vep* has any significant erotic charge, it is the attraction that Zoe, the costume designer, feels for Maggie Cheung; men seem to be completely oblivious to the star's physical appearance, or for that matter to Musidora's.

Unlike Godard's *Le Mépris* where the star and the producer are dispensed with so that the scriptwriter's collaboration with the director might take its fateful direction, *Irma Vep* points to the star's understanding of the director's vision as well as her equal sensitivity both to artistic imperatives and industrial constraints. Maggie is the bigger defendant of the coexistence of genres and quite familiar with commercial trends. When the French TV journalist insists (in stilted and heavily accented English) that French cinema, meaning auteur cinema, is "boring" and unappealing to a public drawn to action movies and star-studded global productions, she argues for diversity. She sets herself apart from Schwarzenegger and Van Damme and from her own action roles where all the work was done by stunt persons and seems to be the only one on the set truly receptive to and appreciative of René's work. The journalist speaks of a difference between cinema as entertainment and cinema as art. This variance for him is not one between popular cinema and auteur cinema, but rather between Hollywood and France.

Assayas's film is intriguing in the way it faces off two directors with opposite visions of what cinema is and might be. It comes as a surprise that José Murano, not René Vidal, turns out to be the example par excellence of the narcissistic filmmaker described by the journalist, someone convinced that French cinema should cultivate a cinephilic public organized around connoisseurship, and not attempt to reach out to a wider audience. For Murano, competition comes both from the West and the East, and French cinema's response within this global struggle should be its very Frenchness, its very elite appeal to a sophisticated and appreciative public, in other words, an approach quite similar to what Timothy Corrigan (1991) has spoken of as "the commerce of auteurism." In spite of multiple revisions, argues Corrigan, auteurism has not changed much over time; from Astruc to Peter Wollen to Stephen Heath and David Bordwell, the auteur has been conceived as a structuring and authoritative principle of cinematic enunciation. The most significant change, according to Corrigan, came in the 1980s and 1990s with the commercial performance of the author, in other words, the social implementation of the "business of being an auteur" (1991, 102).

A film-within-the-film, *Irma Vep* received critical acclaim for its endeavor to reflect on the history of French cinema, from its origins to its future in an increasingly globalized world and transnational market. The film complicates the relationship between the author and the star. The final sequence takes us into the projection room where the crew, the production team and Murano watch René's rushes. The unsteady camera, maneuvered nervously in a style that evokes the rest of Assayas's film, focuses closely on Irma Vep dressed in her cat-woman latex costume as she nimbly traverses the roofs of the city. Arrows radiate from Irma Vep's eyes as retro special effects, creating geometric forms on the celluloid, ambiguous marks that can be interpreted as either scars or x-ray projections, inscriptions on the film stock that reveal the workings of history, past and future. Alternating close-ups and jittery shots of a shoulder-held camera, the final sequence bears witness to Assayas's own style and signature. The inscribed *auteur* has fled to the country, and the production's *star* flies to New York to meet with Ridley Scott. What is left is the *film* itself, René's *Irma Vep* giving way to Assayas's final credits.

Irma Vep is compelling in the way that it complicates the models of authorship that we have discussed. While Murano seems to exemplify the commerce of auteurism, Vidal finds a tragic, but heroic end to his quest. Vidal's disappearance to a country retreat and his failure to finish the homage to French film history is also a noble act of resistance to a market of mass consumption. Any illusion that *Les Vampires*, a representative of a national cinema's former glory, might be remade so that France might confirm and strengthen its place in the film world, is compromised from the beginning. Instead, the film leaves the door open for a different interpretation, namely that Assayas attempts to reconcile authorship with genre and stardom as well as a national cinema with a global market.

New Directions: Authorship, Cinephilia and the Promise of Democratic Emancipation

The relationship between Vidal and Murano in Assayas's *Irma Vep* enacts a crucial opposition between different cinephilic audiences, the global art cinema fans following in the steps of classical cinephilia and the French cinema connoisseurs, nostalgic followers of unaltered French (or European) cultural products. *Irma Vep* thus displays the inherent connection between auteurism and cinephilia, a relationship that is constantly changing and, because of its intrinsic dynamic, forces a productive reevaluation of the category of film auteur. Despite numerous responses to and revisions of auteur theory, there remains dissatisfaction with such an elitist concept, enthroned by a form of film connoisseurship deemed to be apodictic and exclusionary. The assignment of the latest James Bond movie to Sam Mendes, an author in his own right, provides yet further proof that the frontiers between auteur cinema and popular culture have become more and more porous. The next and last part of this essay will turn to the problem of auteurist elitism and the challenges such an exclusionary concept offers in the face of the popular practice of movie going. A productive and stimulating path to take in new studies of the author is the examination of different cinephilic practices, groups and forums for patterns of "electing" auteurs and reshaping the cinephilic "Pantheon."

Noël Burch, a witness to the development of *Cahiers' politique des auteurs*, sorely lamented "the establishment of a pantheon as proof for the artistic legitimacy of cinema, the cult of films (*oeuvres*) removed from socio-historical contingencies," claiming that such gestures "institute cinephilia as a cultural practice that is masculine, individualist and elitist" (Burch, 2007, 86). In 2009, Laurent Jullier, an advocate of a more inclusive "postmodern" cinephilia, waged a further attack against *Cahiers* auteurism (see also Jullier 2010). He sought to rekindle awareness that "there is still the cult of Great Men (the *auteurs*), esotericism, aestheticism, sexism and especially 'disgust for the taste of others' in the words of Pierre Bourdieu" (Jullier 2009, 202). Jullier took exception with Jean Douchet's petition in support of the *Cahiers du cinéma* during the journal's acute financial crisis, particularly with the claim that "the cinema concerns us all in a pressing way: artists, philosophers, writers, filmmakers, critics, actors, directors of festivals." The statement, asserted Jullier, "lacks only one category of people: those who are not part of this 'little world', that is to say, common mortals!" He went on to say that "one sees it clearly when one talks to a Parisian critic: they still conform to the Baudelairian model of *the one who knows* (how to appreciate modernity), who stands apart from the *vulgar taste* of the public."

Indeed, the elitism and club culture of *auteurism* have often been denounced in the name of democracy and egalitarianism. What started as a method to democratize the access to art and to legitimate movie going as a cultural praxis, yielded to the exclusionary elitism of tastemakers with their critical pantheons and stylistic orthodoxies. The *politique des auteurs* was political insofar as it valorized the preferences of cogniscenti and granted them authority in matters of aesthetic judgment. One wonders, however, whether it might be possible to imagine a form of auteurism that possesses an egalitarian dimension. In closing, I would like to ponder this question from a perspective that goes beyond cinema and into the thick of one of the most animated contemporary debates, that between a post-Kantian and post-Enlightenment vision of art, on one side, and the sociological perspective on the social distinction, on the other. This debate has been staged in the writings of the philosopher Jacques Rancière and the sociologist Pierre Bourdieu, whose contributions figure within an apparently irresolvable dialogue.

For the philosopher of equality, Jacques Rancière, auteurism and cinephilia were able to democratize cinema by linking "the cult of art to the democracy of entertainment and emotions" and in that way "challenging the criteria for the induction of cinema into high culture" by taking recourse to a tradition that opposes "minor arts" to already constituted cultural legitimacies (Rancière 2011a, 7). If we turn to Rancière's deliberations on aesthetics and politics (2004b, 2009), however, we can go further in the understanding of such cinephilic claims, for here he evokes the postulate of equality not only to explain how aesthetic judgments are performed by viewers, but also how these aesthetic judgments bring viewers together, that is, how they both constitute and function within communities. Assuming equality among individual viewers, Rancière shifts the focus from the celebration of film as an artistic experience that maintains a rarefied approach to artistic objects and communities while managing to avoid any populist eschewal of discursive elitism.

Because it displaces the customary duality between "form" and "matter," between intelligence and sensation, auteurist mise-en-scène, claims Rancière, offers the cinephile a means to access an inviting world. As understood and elucidated by the *Cahiers* critics and cinephiles, mise-en-scène was historically and conceptually bound to the socio-political changes that came after World War II. This understanding of mise-en-scène as a form of aesthetic judgment central to a cinephilic community fits into an aesthetic project that grants film a special status. As an object of sense experience, cinema is part of a world that, because it is enriched by thought, has been transformed in a singular way. The power of mise-en-scène enables us to "extricate a portion of the sensory realm [*le sensible*] from its ordinary connections and inhabit it by a heterogeneous power" that suspends the dualities of ordinary sense experience (Rancière 2004b, 24). At stake here are not only the separations "between appearance and reality, but also between form and matter, between activity and passivity, understanding and sensibility" (Rancière 2009, 30). Because it possesses the power to overcome these hierarchies, mise-en-scène exemplifies how cinema can be art and confirms cinephilia's potential as the frame or "thought of the new disorder" (Rancière 2009, 13).

For all its constructive resolve, Rancière's proposition occasioned considerable resistance. In the eyes of Pierre Bourdieu (1986), this is an "illusory" approach, for political and intellectual disparities exist in the social order. Despite its keen awareness of discord and tension, Rancière's equality, from Bourdieu's perspective, amounts to a form of consensual reduction. Rancière has come under further attacks for defending the universality of aesthetic judgment. Critics of cinephilia who take a Bourdieusian approach (Burch 2007; Jullier 2010) object to how Rancière defends the universality of aesthetic judgment and seeks to build a cultural practice on such a foundation (Rancière 2004b; Bourdieu 1986; Nordmann 2006). Rancière submits that aesthetic judgments are universal because anyone who is graced with cognition is capable of making them. For this reason, there is something *egalitarian* about the capacity for aesthetic judgment in Kant's account and in the tradition of philosophical aesthetics that it generated; this *egalitarian* universalism enacted in classical cinephilia's auteuristic constitution is what Rancière seeks to defend. Rather than denouncing the possibility of equality as "illusory," he firmly believes that artists and spectators should endeavor to deliver on its promise. His aesthetic theory attempts to spell out more clearly how such a promise of equality might be articulated and practiced.

The optimistic promise of equality makes Rancière's theory both alluring and nonetheless tenuous in our present discussion of authorship. Much turns on the definition of cinephilia as a matter of passion that activates the autonomous voice of spectators able to identify an author's mise-en-scène as a unique artistic signature. Bourdieu's *Questions de Sociologie*, for example, responds *avant la lettre* to the cinephilic defense of mise-en-scène as an intuitive relationship to the world: "Intellectuals spontaneously understand the relationship to a work of art as a mystical participation in a common good, without rarity. My entire book [*The Distinction*] argues that access to a work of art requires instruments that are not universally distributed" (Bourdieu 1993, 2). In other words, Bourdieu argues that no encounter with a work of art, in our context cinema, takes place outside a system of predefined, embodied codes that only reveal the act of "dispossession."

Unlike Bourdieu, Rancière prefers to use the premises of equality rather than expertise or connoisseurship as a point of orientation. Cinema constitutes the ideal art to explore the consequences of such a postulate: "Precisely because cinema is not a language, because it does not define an object of knowledge belonging to a systematic order of reason, learning it suits particularly well the application of the method of intellectual emancipation—'to learn something and to relate it to all the rest by this principle.'—We *learn* cinema by widening our circle of perceptions of affects and of significations organized around several films" (Rancière 2011b, 210). Auteurism and cinephilia thus foster intellectual emancipation; cinephiles follow "the artist's emancipatory lesson, opposed on every count to the professor's stultifying lesson" (Rancière 1991, 70–71). Each of us, argues Rancière, is potentially an artist, impatient to be more than a dabbler and eager to grant our work a means of expression, wanting not only to feel things but to share what we feel and think with others. In this way, the argument for the artist's singular visionary sensibility gains a new impetus and a renewed suggestiveness. The *auteur* in this understanding is not so much a master of time and space as an animating force for heightened appreciation and different experience.

Works Cited

Althusser, Louis. 1971. "Ideology and Ideological State Apparatuses." *Lenin and Philosophy, and Other Essays*. Translated by Ben Brewster. London: New Left Books, 127–88.

Assayas, Olivier. 2001. "Que d'auteurs, que d'auteurs. Sur une politique." In *La Politique des auteurs. Les Textes*, edited by Antoine de Baecque and Gabrielle Lucantonio. Paris: Cahiers du cinéma.

———. 2006. "Louis Feuillade." In *Louis Feuillade. Maître du cinéma populaire*, edited by Gauthier and Francis Lacassin, 116–17. Paris: Découverte Gallimard Arts.

Bazin, André. 2001. "De la politique des auteurs." In *La Politique des auteurs: Les Textes*, edited by Antoine De Baecque and Gabrielle Lucantonio. Paris: Cahiers du cinéma.

Bennett, Andrew. 2005. *The Author*. London: Routledge.

Bordwell, David, Janet Staiger and Kristin Thompson. 1985. *The Classical Hollywood Cinema: Film Style and Mode of Production to 1960*. New York: Columbia University Press.

Bourdieu, Pierre. 1986. *The Distinction: A Social Critique of the Judgment of Taste*. Translated by Richard Nice. London: Routledge & Kegan Paul.

———. 1993. *Sociology in Question*. Translated by Richard Nïce. London: Sage.

Burch, Noël. 2007. "Cinéphilie et Masculinité." In *De la beauté des latrines: pour réhabiliter le sens au cinéma et ailleurs*. Paris: L'Harmattan.

Burke, Seán. 1998. *The Death and Return of the Author: Criticism and Subjectivity in Barthes, Foucault and Derrida*. Edinburg: Edinburg University Press.

Callahan, Vikki. 1998. *Zones of Anxiety. Movement, Musidora, and the Crime Serials of Louis Feuillade*. Detroit: Wayne State University Press.

Caughie, John. 1981. *Theories of Authorship: A Reader*. London: Routledge.

Conley, Tom. 2000. "Revamping Irma: Immodest Reflections on French Cinema and Globalization." *Sites: The Journal of Twentieth-Century/Contemporary French Studies* 4, no. 2: 417–33.

Corrigan, Timothy. 1991. *A Cinema without Walls: Movies and Culture after Vietnam.* New Brunswick: Rutgers University Press.

Culler, Jonathan. 1975. *Structuralist Poetics: Structuralism, Linguistics and the Study of Literature.* London: Routledge.

Desnos, Robert. 1926. "Fantômas, les Vampires, les Mystères de New York." *Le Soir* (February 26).

Epstein, Jean. 2012. "On Certain Characteristics of Photogénie." Translated by Tom Milne. In *Jean Epstein, Critical Essays and New Translations*, edited by Sarah Keller and Jason N. Paul. Amsterdam: Amsterdam University Press.

Fieschi, Jean-André, Jean-Louis Comolli, Michel Mardore, André Téchiné, Gérard Guégan and Claude Ollier. 1965. "Vingt ans après. Le cinéma américain, ses auteurs et notre politique en question." *Cahiers du cinéma* 172: 18–31.

Gerstner, David A., and Janet Staiger, eds. 2003. *Authorship and Film.* New York; London: Routledge.

Godard, Jean-Luc. 1972. *Godard on Godard: Critical Writings.* Translated by Tom Milne. New York: Viking Press.

Grant, Barry Keith, ed. 2008. *Auteurs and Authorship: A Film Reader.* London: Blackwell.

Gunning, Tom. 1991. *D.W. Griffith and the Origins of American Narrative Film: The Early Years at Biograph.* Urbana: University of Illinois Press.

Hudson, Dale. 2006. "'Just Play Yourself, Maggie Cheung': *Irma Vep*, Rethinking Transnational Stardom and Unthinking National Cinemas." *Screen* 72, no. 2: 213–32.

Jeong, Seung-hoon, and Jeremi Szaniawski, eds. 2016. *The Global Auteur: The Politics of Authorship in 21st Century Cinema.* New York: Bloomsbury.

Jones, Kent. 2014. "Critical Condition: From the *Politique des Auteurs* to the *Auteur* Theory to Plain Old *Auteurism*, How Clear of a Picture of Actual Movies Are We Receiving?" *Film Comment* 50, no. 2: 41–42.

Jullier, Laurent, and Jean-Marc Leveratto. 2010. *Cinéphiles et cinéphilies: Une histoire de la qualité cinématographique.* Paris: Armand Colin.

Jullier, Laurent. 2009. "Philistines and Cinephiles: The New Deal." *Framework* 50, no. 1–2: 202–5.

Kozloff, Sarah. 2014. *The Life of the Author.* Montréal: Caboose.

Lévi-Strauss, Claude. *The Savage Mind.* 1966. Translated by George Weidenfeld. London: Nicholson.

MacCabe, Colin. 2003. "The Revenge of the Author." In *Film and Authorship*, edited by Virginia Wright Wexman. New Brunswick: Rutgers University Press.

Nordmann, Charlotte. 2006. *Bourdieu/Rancière. La Politique entre sociologie et philosophie.* Paris: Editions Amsterdam.

Pinel, Vincent. 1994. *Louis Lumière inventeur et cinéaste.* Paris: Nathan.

Rancière, Jacques. 1991. *The Ignorant Schoolmaster: Five Lessons in Intellectual Emancipation.* Translated by Kristin Ross. Stanford: Stanford University Press.

———. 2004a. *The Philosopher and Its Poor.* Edited by Andrew Parker, translated by John Drury. Durham: Duke University Press.

———. 2004b. *The Politics of Aesthetics: The Distribution of the Sensible.* Translated by Gabriel Rockhill. New York: Continuum.

———. 2009. *Aesthetic and Its Discontents.* Translated by Steven Corcoran. Cambridge: Polity.

———. 2011a. *Les Écarts du cinéma.* Paris: La Fabrique.

———. 2011b. "Questions for Jacques Rancière around His Book *Les Écarts du cinéma*: Interview Conducted with Susan Nascimento Duarte." *Cinema: Journal of Philosophy and the Moving Image* 2: 196–97.

Sarris, Andrew. 1996. *The American Cinema: Directors and Directions 1929–1968.* New York: Da Capo Press.

Schilling, Derek. 2007. *Eric Rohmer.* Manchester: Manchester University Press.

Séguin, Jean-Claude. 1999. *Alexandre Promio ou les énigmes de la lumière.* Paris: L'Harmattan.

Sellors, C. Paul. 2010. *Film Authorship: Auteurs and Other Myths*. London: Wallflower.

Shea, Louise. 2009. "From Louis Feuillade to Johnny To: Olivier Assayas on the Future of French Cinema." *French Forum* 34, no. 3: 121–36.

Staiger, Janet. 2003. "Authorship Approaches." In *Authorship and Film*, edited by David A. Gerstner and Janet Staiger. New York: Routledge.

Stillinger, Jack. 1991. *Multiple Authorship and the Myth of the Solitary Genius*. Oxford: Oxford University Press.

Truffaut, François. 1954. "Une certaine tendance du cinéma français." *Cahiers du cinéma* 31.

Wexman, Virginia Wright, ed. 2003. *Film and Authorship*. New Brunswick, NJ: Rutgers University Press.

Willemen, Paul. 1994. *Looks and Frictions*. Bloomington: Indiana University Press.

Wollen, Peter. 1972. *Signs and Meaning in the Cinema*, 3rd rev. ed. Bloomington: Indiana University Press.

———. 1981. "The Auteur Theory." In *Theories of Authorship: A Reader*, edited by John Caughie. London: Routledge.

Chapter Ten

"DEEPEST ECSTASY" MEETS CINEMA'S SOCIAL SUBJECTS: THEORIZING THE SCREEN STAR

Mary R. Desjardins

Film stars—performers whose names, likenesses, biographies and appearances circulate as commodities outside of the films they appear in—are often featured in histories and theories of fame or religion that account for the phenomenon of persons renowned among a great number of people or across wide temporal dimensions. Within film theory, the film star is usually discussed in relation to the sociology and phenomenology of film viewing, theories of enunciation and authorship, the role of film and film actors in the marketplace of capitalist economies (i.e., in industrial production and mass circulation of commodities), as well as in relation to theories of spectator identification, audience (even national) adulation and fan fascination. These theoretical lenses are not mutually exclusive and, in fact, theories focused on one of these contexts usually implicitly or explicitly address questions pertinent to the others.

Theorists working within film studies or "star studies" contexts since the 1970s typically identify and examine stardom as a discursive construct—that is, as constructed out of a variety of media representations that produce and are produced by culturally and historically situated meanings—and much of what follows in this essay explores their theories. However, early film theorists concerned with defining the aesthetic and phenomenological and, in some cases sociological, qualities of film form often used the acting or appearance of stars in films, and their own responses to them, to describe not only what is cinematically specific and sociologically important about that form, but also what makes film viewing such a powerful, affective experience.

The Star and the Power of the Filmic Image

Many film theorists writing in the 1920s explored cinematic specificity against the aesthetic properties of literature, theater, painting and photography. These writers believed that the camera was an instrument of knowledge and identified the close-up shot as exemplary not only of film's uniqueness as an art form but also as a significant mode of communication about the world. French theorist Louis Delluc, credited by French theorist and film director Jean Epstein as the originator of the term *photogenie,* wrote that "the cinema will make us all comprehend the things of this world as well as force us to recognize ourselves" (Delluc, 139). Although both painting and photography can represent people and objects in close-up, film's ability to register the mobility, and thus the temporality, of people and objects in close-up could reveal, according to Hungarian librettist, screenwriter and theorist Béla Bálazs, "the most hidden parts in our polyphonous life, and teaches us to see the intricate details of life as one reads an orchestral score" (Bálazs, 55). For Epstein, *photogénie* is the term which describes how film "enhances the moral value" of objects and "souls," and it is the specifically *mobile* "aspects of the world, of things and souls" that see their "moral value increased by filmic reproduction" (Epstein, "On Certain Characteristics," 314–15). All three theorists isolate the movements of actors in film and, in particular, in close-ups of actors' faces, as catalysts or vehicles for the most powerful experience of comprehension of the world and of the self. Close-ups of the actor's face, in which subtle movements of facial expression, or what Bálazs terms "microphysiognomy," communicate that which "could not otherwise be seen with the naked eye or in everyday life" (Bálazs, 65) and can "confer life in its highest guise: personality" (Epstein, "On Certain Characteristics," 317).

Delluc and Epstein theorize the power of filmic movement and of the close-up in relation to actors (mobile bodies on film), but do not discuss them in terms of their agency as authors of the film. Bálazs does provide detailed analyses of actor performances, but like the other two theorists, designates other figures as making the choices in filming that initiate a "dramatic concern," an engagement of the "mobile" and "personal" aspects of things in which objects seem alive and beings and objects alike "acquire a higher moral value." Epstein suggests that directors are stagers of cinema's revelations of "increasingly valuable discoveries" (Epstein, 315–17), and Bálazs identifies the director or "[another] man behind the camera" (Bálazs, 90) as the agents responsible for the artistic composition of films.

However, as pointed out by Noel King in conversation about "cinephilia" (love of cinema) with fellow critic Paul Willemen, Bálazs makes explicit in one section of his theory what is more implicitly present in the work of Delluc and Epstein—namely, that the pleasure experienced invoked by watching actors on film can be the result of those moments in which the spectator believes he or she sees something "that is impossible to program into the representation," some aspect of the biography or subjectivity of the actor coming through (Willemen, 240–41).[1] And for Delluc, Epstein and Bálazs, not just any actors inspire these moments of pleasure: the exemplary actors for all three theorists tend to be *stars*, performers who had been judged by critics as superior actors and whose names, likenesses, and personalities had been commodified and circulated as unique or extraordinary by other mass media by the time these early theorists were publishing their work. Charlie Chaplin, Lilian Gish, Asta Nielsen, William S. Hart and Sessue Hayakawa are frequently singled out as figures of fascination and as sources of cinema's power enabling the pleasures of film viewing and perhaps inspiring the urge to theorize. Indeed, at times, especially in the writings of Delluc and Epstein, details of stars' faces or performances seem to offer the potential for the viewer to have a near-religious experience. For Delluc, Hayakawa and Chaplin, are "expressions of beauty" and Hayakawa, in particular, is a "natural force" whose face is a "poetic work" (Delluc, 138–39). Close-ups allow Epstein to "consume" faces, they are "in" him "like a sacrament," and Hayakawa's movements are "pure *photogénie*" instances of "harmony" (Epstein, "Magnification," 239; "The Senses I (b)," 243).

While the work of French theorist Roland Barthes re-oriented film criticism toward structuralist and semiotic analyses, his "On the Face of Garbo" (first written in the 1950s and translated into English in the 1970s) looks as much back to theories of *photogénie* to theorize the star as it looks forward to the ideological critiques of star mythologies that characterize much of star studies since the 1970s. Barthes uses descriptors like "ecstasy," "perfection," "essential beauty," "mystical feelings," "deified face," "descended from heaven," to define what makes Greta Garbo's face the "archetype of the human face" (Barthes, 261–62). Although Barthes suggests that Garbo's face and how it was used in film was characteristic of a particular historical period—he infers, through comparison and contrast to Rudolph Valentino and Audrey Hepburn, that he identifies her face with the "deepest ecstasy" of star faces from silent-era and early sound-era film—his contemplation suggests that her stardom cannot be separated from the magic of myth. The mythic power of Garbo as a star, condensed in her face, is her reconciliation of "two iconographic ages" in a cinematic moment in which archetypes or "essential beauty" yield to "existential" beauty. In other words, Garbo's face represents a timeless archetypicality that can only emerge in myth—or in the era of silent cinema!—while Hepburn's face represents a particularity and a social context (e.g., social themes about women, such as "woman as a child") and the viewer's pleasure in it may be dependent on historical contingencies.

Barthes's essay is still widely reprinted and referenced, but his affinity for exploring photogenie-like aspects of visual representation has had a less direct influence on star studies than his structuralist and semiotic analyses that theorize how images and discourses convey ideology. However, notions of *photogénie* and *cinephilia* still play roles in examinations of the affective impact of the star. Epstein's focus on the facial close-up serves as a point of departure for Amy Lawrence's (2010) study of film star Montgomery Clift, in which she explores how Clift fans articulate, through religious inflections and expressions, their passionate response to the actor's beauty, devotion to acting and mental and physical suffering (due to his chemical addictions, pain and disfiguration from an automobile accident, his semi-closeted sexuality and his conflicted relationship to Hollywood's star machinery).

Lawrence points out that both Epstein's definition of photogenie and contemporary notions of "cinephilia" conceptualize spectatorial fascination with cinema's transformation of things and beings (via close-ups or other formal means) in terms of an investment in the filmic detail—"the moment, the trace, the gesture" (Lawrence, 25). Lawrence agrees with Mary Ann Doane's argument that the libidinal charge of this spectator-screen relation is most localizable in details of an actor's performance, such as gesture, body position and facial expression.[2]

Lawrence's own critical approach "highlight[s] the differences between [Clift's] […] experience (creating work within a specific historical moment)" and the myths that have reduced Clift's star persona to either victim or saint, which she identifies as "what audiences have done […] with works created by, for, and about him" (Lawrence, 6). Like Epstein, cinephiles, and fans of Clift, Lawrence displays a fascination with details of performance and the power of the close-up. However, while Epstein and Delluc identify their fascination with film actors as evidence of photogenie's power, they credit directorial choices as responsible for staging its presence. Lawrence, on the other hand, argues that formal analysis and historical contextualization of Clift's performance choices throw into relief the actor's agency in cinematic production, contributing to an important component of his star persona, but also mitigating the victimhood versus sainthood antinomies that reduce other aspects of the persona to a restrictive binary framework.

Sociology and the Collective Production of the Star

Associations between the terminology of divinity and stardom resurface in theoretical work on the film star throughout the history of "star studies"—e.g., Edgar Morin titles one of the chapters in his 1957 study *The Stars* "Gods and Goddesses," and another "Stellar Liturgy." Richard Dyer's (1986) follow-up book to his 1979 book *Stars* is titled *Heavenly Bodies*. However, much of the theoretical work on stars produced in the second half of the twentieth century is more likely to position those terms as metaphors for how stars have had an extraordinary impact on, or interrelation with, social formations. Morin, a French sociologist whose work moves across interdisciplinary boundaries, states that "when we speak of the *myth* of the star, we mean first of all the process of divinization that the movie actor undergoes, a process that makes him the idol of crowds." The process of divinization involves the way the actor who is a star "absorbs some of the heroic—that is, divinized and mythic—substance of the hero or heroine of the movies, and who in turn enriches this substance by his or her own contribution" (Morin, 30). Morin argues that the "cinematic imagination" of the society that creates and receives the movie hero is "middle class" in nature and, therefore, responds to film narratives and characters that enable the viewer "to live one's own dreams and to dream one's life," but which still draws the imaginary close to the real (Morin, 11–13). Stars are the figures within whom (heroic) role and performance mutually define one another; they are the "new mediators between the fantastic world of dreams and man's daily life on earth" (Morin, 25–28). The star provides the "image and model" of the mask of individuality, which in a capitalist society, is a "product of a dialectic of participations and affirmations of the self." Stars release in the individual "a flux of such affirmations and participations," from "mimetisms" of star gestures, attitudes and fashion to "amorous participations" (Morin, 136–42).

The Italian sociologist Francesco Alberoni, in his 1963 study, *The Powerless Elite*, delineates the role stars play in modern society in relation to the contemporary status of democratic societies as mass-mediated social formations. He argues that while once "the daily demands for orientation of community life" were met by family and neighborhood, now they tend to be "met at the level of a more general community life." In these kinds of societies, mass media takes on the role of presenting to the public "persons who belong to the extended community and who become an object of interest, identification, and collective evaluation." The capacity and skill of these people acquire a "charismatic dimension" thanks to a collective consensus—in other words, through collective interest, identification and evaluation, they become stars (Alberoni, 75–76). While stars become stars out of collective interest, that interest is less the product of media manipulation than of the media's presenting certain figures to the public as "candidates" for election to stardom (Alberoni, 74).

Alberoni identifies the star as a "powerless elite," arising in sociopolitical contexts in which there is "a social mechanism of separation, which [...] holds that the 'stars' do not occupy *institutional positions of power*" (Alberoni, 65). While the career trajectory of Ronald Reagan, the film star who became the president of the United States in 1980 might present a qualification of Alberoni's theory (Reagan was a *former* film star when he was elected first to the governorship of California and then to the presidency), the case of Indian film stars becoming leaders of political parties and getting elected to the Indian Parliament certainly challenges some points of this argument. In his 2004 study of the politics of south Indian cinema, M. Madhava Prasad uses the examples of several male stars who led political parties and/or were elected to political office to demonstrate how particular convergences of cinematic, political and geographical elements came together to produce the star as a political leader. He argues that the cinema became a site of strong political investment when the ideological gaps in the Indian project of nationalism and the reorganization of the states according to the dominant languages converged with aspects of regional film production, in particular, production of action and mythic genres. The popular male star leads of these films became representative of linguistic communities, setting the stage for affirmation of their leadership in politics.

Recent scholarship suggests that Indian cinema provides productive contexts from which to explore the film star's relation to society and politics. Neepa Majumdar has also theorized the relation of stardom to Indian nationalist politics in her 2009 study, *Wanted Cultured Ladies Only! Female Stardom and Cinema in India, 1930s–1950s*. Majumdar argues that although the Indian film industry (and the press) between the 1930s and the 1950s expressed a certain desire to import from Hollywood "a 'finished' concept of stardom as a technology of publicity," the meanings of stardom were highly contested because of the dissonance between this Hollywood technology of stardom (with its reliance on publicizing the private lives of stars) and the discourses of improvement characterizing both British colonialism as well as Indian nationalist thought. This discourse imagined and produced a different kind of female star from the Hollywood star, a star whose persona was "dictated by the needs of a nationalist moral space occupied by performing women" of a cultured, educated background.

Film production in Germany's Nazi-era, in which nationalized industries controlled the employment of creative labor as well as aspects of textual production, has also been the subject for theorizations of the star and politics. It is well known that film stars played a significant role in the cultural and racial imaginary of Germany's Third Reich society and, in particular, in the imaginaries of its leaders. Anecdotes about Marlene Dietrich's refusal to return to Germany from Hollywood after the Nazi takeover continue to circulate as evidence of one star's unwillingness to serve as a German ideal under this political regime. Erica Carter, in her 2004 book *Dietrich's Ghosts: The Sublime and the Beautiful in Third Reich Film*, theorizes the place of the "German ideal," specifically Kantian ideals of beauty and the sublime in how stars functioned in film production and in society during Germany's Nazi era. Fascism organized the idea of the *Völk* under the godhead of the Fuhrer and attempted a "regulation of the mass" through a "recuperation of popular films" according to "idealist aesthetic values, refracted through völkisch [i.e., ethno-nationalistic] ideology" (Carter, 143). Carter suggests that respected stage and film star Emil Jannings, whose body functioned as an "expressive vehicle of a 'blood and soil' aesthetic [...] [through an acting style] organized around climatic moments of static pose and symbolic gesture," embodied a "masculine völkisch sublime" in the star system of Third Reich film (Carter, 131).

While the arguments of Prasad, Majumdar and Carter suggest that the sociological and aesthetic work of film stardom can be enmeshed, in certain contexts, with the nationalist and political ideas of citizenship, governance and leadership, the work of British film theorist Richard Dyer has had, since the late 1970s, perhaps the greatest impact on how star studies regards the social dimensions of stardom. According to Dyer, Alberoni "ignores the ideological significance of the stars" because his argument relies on the assumption that "because a star cannot become a crucial decision-maker (and remain a star)," he or she is "without political significance" (Dyer, *Stars*, 7). In both *Stars* (1979) and *Heavenly Bodies: Film Stars and Society* (1986), Dyer employs multiple disciplinary and theoretical frameworks (e.g., semiotics, Marxism), historical and material evidence (e.g., fan magazines, photos, films) and methodologies (e.g., close analysis of print texts, performance signs and narrative) to argue for an ideological analysis of stardom, one which would demonstrate the political significance of stars by identifying the "structured polysemy" of the star image and by examining how this image is related to "contradictions in ideology—whether within the dominant ideology or between it and other subordinate/revolutionary ideologies" (Dyer, *Stars*, 30). The concept of "structured polysemy" is derived from semiotics, one which Dyer uses to describe how a star image is a discursive construct with a "finite multiplicity of meanings." Some of these meanings are, in particular, media incarnations and contexts, suppressed or displaced, or function as "magic reconciliation[s]" of the apparently contradictory elements of ideologies (Dyer, *Stars*, 3, 30). Thusly, stars are a source of fascination because "they enact ways of making sense of the experience of being a person in a particular kind of social production (capitalism), with its particular organization of life into public and private spheres." They "represent how we think that experience is," or sometimes in a more utopian vein, they represent "how lovely to feel that it is" (Dyer, *Heavenly Bodies*, 17).

Dyer's work draws on relevant historical contexts (e.g., history of consumerism, of sexuality, etc.), film performances, film and star publicity and promotion (including fan magazines and publicity stills and portraits), and even rumor and gossip, to read the star image and identify the role it plays in the history of film production and in both dominant and subcultural social formations. The theory of the social subject (both star and audience) and the methodologies (evident in the use of a variety of material sources and intertexts for analyzing the structured polysemy of a star image) laid out in *Stars* inspired many different star-study projects, including Dyer's own analyses of Marilyn Monroe's image in relation to 1950s notions of female sexuality, of Paul Robeson's image in terms of how it was understood through assumptions and fantasies about racial identity, and of Judy Garland's image in relation to the existence and lived experience of gay subcultures—all case studies in his *Heavenly Bodies*. *Stars* and *Heavenly Bodies*, as well as

Dyer's article "Entertainment and Utopia" (1985) and book *White* (1997), have influenced projects on the social or sociopolitical dimensions of stardom as diverse as Andrea Weiss's *Vampires and Violets: Lesbians in Film* (1993), Jackie Stacey's *Star Gazing: Hollywood Cinema and Female Spectatorship* (1994), Gaylyn Studlar's *This Mad Masquerade: Stardom and Masculinity in the Jazz Age* (1996), and Diane Negra's *Off-White Hollywood: American Culture and Ethnic Female Stardom* (2001).

Weiss agrees with Dyer that "audiences can't make media images mean anything they want to, but they can select [what works for them] from the complexity of the image" (Dyer quoted in Weiss, 35). She argues that the complex, contradictory aspects of certain female stars' images were appropriated by women in the growing lesbian subcultures of the 1930s and "played an influential role in defining the distinctive qualities of that subculture" (Weiss, 35). Stacey uses Dyer's contention that the pleasures of "escapist" Hollywood film need to be understood in relation to specific contexts in her theorization of how female spectators negotiate their relationships to films and film stars through social and cultural activities that enact the contradictory demands of femininity in a patriarchal culture. In studying stardom and the construction of masculinity in the 1920s American film, Studlar uses multiple cultural intertexts "to illuminate the process by which a star is embedded in culture." Much like Dyer's analysis of the star image of Marilyn Monroe, Studlar demonstrates how cultural and social contexts figure into a star's construction and promotion to an audience already invested in "controversies, dilemmas, or spectacles that are already in cultural circulation" (Studlar, 8–9). Negra, using Dyer's ideas about how stars can reinforce ideology through repeating, reproducing or reconciling aspects of its beliefs and attitudes argues that Hollywood films and publicity selectively activate associations of ethnicity with certain white European and American female stars for a variety of purposes, such as demonstrating Hollywood's (and America's) inclusivity or responding to perceived threats to American ideals supporting the hegemonies of white masculinity.

Producing Stars and Spectators as Subjects

The influence of Dyer's work on star studies is registered in specific citations of his work or adoption of his methodologies, but it can also be seen in the way so many star studies of the last twenty-five years reject or qualify aspects of "apparatus theory" or psychoanalytically inflected theorizations of spectatorship and subjectivity. These theories, which rely on positing a relationship between film spectatorship, classical narrative and psychic mechanisms—from Lacanian mirror stage narcissism to voyeurism and fetishism—that allegedly construct the gendered subject, were predominant in poststructuralist theory of the 1970s and 1980s that analyzed the subject effects of classical Hollywood film.[3] They contend that the spectator is positioned by the film text, as its narrative, visual and aural elements (and, in apparatus theory, its conditions of projection) facilitate the spectator's regression to earlier states of subjectivity, to a moment when the self first experienced a unified wholeness with the maternal body, or more precisely, a fantasy of that state. Pleasure is derived from the way film viewing enables a voyeuristic sense of separation from (and thus control over) the projected image. This theory posits castration as characterizing the development of human subjectivity (presuming male subjectivity as universal), with the classical film text providing fetish objects and processes for disavowing what is actually the spectator's "split subjectivity," that is, his powerlessness and separation from the maternal body. In these theoretical models, stars can function as ego-ideals for identification and/or as fetish objects whose overvaluation aids in the process of disavowal. Many of these works are also informed by Marxist theories of ideology so that the film and the star not only function as fetishes within the psychic mechanisms awakened by the viewing experience but also as commodity fetishes that circulate in specific material and social contexts. The subject positioned by viewing pleasure is not only "unified" psychically, but also ideologically.

Jackie Stacey's *Star Gazing* is a response to some of the feminist theories of the female spectator that, based on psychoanalytic theories of identification and object choice within a framework of a masculinity/femininity binary, "masculinize active female desire" (Stacey, 27). This masculinization is the outcome of an alleged relation that the female spectator has with the image—unlike the male who has separated from the mother in the completion of the oedipal phase of subject formation, the female is not separated from the maternal body. She can neither experience the mastery over the image that separation allows nor disown/disavow when she sees lack; in this system, she is the lack, she is the image. Only through a "flaunting" or masquerading of femininity can the female spectator achieve that distance. Stacey problematizes this theoretical model by investigating women as social subjects: specifically, how women have asserted their agency as consumers in material practices of investment in star images, such as copying, imitating and resembling favorite stars. These activities represent the female fan's aspiration to achieve the courage, confidence and independence that they attribute to their favorite star. Stacey's argument, written in response to what she saw as limitations in psychoanalytic theories of spectatorship and their influence on star studies, echoes some of the observations made by film critic Molly Haskell in her 1973 book *From Reverance to Rape: The Treatment of Women in the Movies*. Haskell also imagines an active female viewer or fan of female stars: "whatever the endings that were forced on Bette Davis, Joan Crawford, Carole Lombard, Katharine Hepburn, Margaret Sullavan, or Rosalind Russell, the images we retain of them are not those of subjugation or humiliation; rather, we remember their intermediate victories, we retain images of intelligence and personal style and forcefulness" (Haskell, 31). John Ellis, in his 1982 study *Visible Fictions*, conceptualizes the power of the film star in contexts informed by psychoanalysis—he recognizes that film viewing awakens psychic mechanisms—but bypasses the necessity of the masculine/feminine binary that Stacey identifies as the dead-end for theorizing an active female spectator that isn't masculinized. Ellis argues that the filmic image is characterized by "the photo effect," the fact that what is present in the image is actually absent, unavailable to the film spectator because it was only present in the pro-filmic moment of the film's shooting. The filmic presence of stars, "at once ordinary and extraordinary, available for desire" because "unattainable," reinstates the paradox of the photo effect (Ellis, 91). Ellis considers this desire for the unattainable as available to both male and female spectatorial subjects—the photo effect, which has the present-absent paradox as the only condition for its effect, activates psychic mechanisms which "participate in the construction of polyvalent desires of both male and female viewers" (Ellis, 97). Stars promise the experience of cinema to viewers; in turn, a star's film "completes" or brings together the scattered images of the star that exist in extratextual materials that circulate to promote the cinema.

In their examinations of fan texts, star studies scholars Michael De Angelis and Mary Desjardins have explored specific star images that facilitate the "polyvalent" desires of spectator-subjects, or which enable the fantasy of transcending gendered or sexed binaries. De Angelis's 2001 study *Gay Fandom and Crossover Stardom: James Dean, Mel Gibson, and Keanu Reeves* theorizes the power of certain stars for gay male fans may reside in those stars' "crossover" appeal, "in which a star's popularity with 'straight' audiences also accommodates a strong gay male following" (De Angelis, 4). De Angelis employs "fantasy theory" (psychoanalytic theory based on work by Laplanche and Pontalis and used by a number of scholars theorizing melodrama to contend that the pleasure and power of fantasy is the setting out of desire rather than its fulfillment) in his analysis. He describes and examines a type of fan fantasy in which a star's ultimate sexual orientation is not determinant. Fantasy's appeal is based on the sustained fan engagement in "the *process* of negotiating identities and overcoming obstacles" (De Angelis, 5). In *Recycled Stars: Female Film Stardom in the Age of Television and Video* (2015a), Desjardins argues that the 1991 experimental video *Meeting Two Queens*, which uses images from films starring Greta Garbo and Marlene Dietrich to suggest a possible love relation between the two stars, is pleasurable to an audience of diverse sexual and fan orientations in its use of rhetoric and fantasy scenarios recognizable from melodrama that do not restrict pleasure to a straight/gay polarization. The fan's extra-cinematic knowledge (through gossip or historical accounts, for instance) of the stars' biseuxal or gay sexualities is acknowledged by the video's scenarios, but the structure of the video into settings of desire that never end in fulfillment, offers a conceptualization of stardom as powerful in its appeal to plural and fluid identities.

While some scholars have found ways to complicate the psychoanalytic-based theories of spectator/fan relations to film stars, there are other theorists who have posited a relation between stardom and subjectivity via a focus on the star and/or viewer as *social subjects* explainable in terms of specific social contexts for agency, authorship and labor. This focus obviously is indebted to Dyer's work, but also intervenes into specific aspects of film history and creates new historiographic frameworks (i.e., theorizations of how histories are told). Richard DeCordova's (1990) study *Picture Personalities: The Emergence of the Star System in America* is certainly a key text in these regards. He argues that "the impression of reality that the cinema produces is [...] only that—although the objects and events presented in film are present to the eye they are at the same time [...] absent." DeCordova identifies the historical mechanisms and specific discourses in which the star "emerged as a particularly privileged site at which this relationship between presence and absence could be negotiated and turned into a matter of pleasure and fascination" (DeCordova, 145–46). Examining critical press evaluations, industry promotion and publicity, and fan magazines from the 1900s to the 1920s, he argues that the social subjectivities of actor and fan were enmeshed in a process in which "as the actor is increasingly individualized." Around 1909–10, film companies started crediting and advertising actors by name, a move that DeCordova argues supported "an expansion of the actor's identity through writing that reveals what she or he is 'really like' behind the screen." The fan is engaged, and the star is born as the actor is "assigned a personality, a love life, and perhaps even a political persuasion" (DeCordova, 21).

Richard Dyer argues that cinematic and extra-cinematic factors interact to construct the *star persona* in terms of three registers of identity: the physicality of the actor, the roles he/she plays in films and the image and biography as circulated in media outside the film text. Dyer and DeCordova delineate the power of film stardom to interpolate spectators or audiences as social subjects as emerging out of the tensions among these registers, especially between the film roles played by the star and the star's biographical narrative. DeCordova argues that the parallel historical trajectories of early film stardom (i.e., the expansion of actors' identities from what is known about their film roles to what is known about their personal biographies) and of modernity's constitution of private identity in terms of what is known about a person's "sexual identity" are characterized by a fascination with, and drive to uncover, some ultimate "truth" (perhaps ultimately "revealed" by scandal). This theorization of stardom as emerging from processes of discursive revelations and/or investigatory impulses is compatible with aspects of Dyer's position that stars relate to beliefs or experiences that are "deep and constant features of human existence" (Dyer, Stars, 3) and with Ellis's emphasis on the presence-absence dialectic behind viewer's pleasures in stars. It is also compatible with or even influenced many of the aforementioned analyses of the historical status and/or fluidity of star-fan relationships, such as those by Studlar, Weiss, De Angelis and Desjardins.

Barry King's very influential essays, such as "Articulating Stardom" (1985) and "Stardom as an Occupation" (1986) deploy the idea of the "star persona" in a different manner, one which is less interested in how the tensions among components of the persona relate to psychic mechanicisms or historical constructions of "truth." Instead, they discuss how actors adapt to the capitalist/commodity producing environments of the Hollywood studio and post-studio systems through a formation of star personae that can be exercised as "monopolies." Although King formulates stardom "as a specialization based on film acting," in distinguishing the difference between the actor and the star, he argues that a film actor subsumes the self—"a personal identity, operative behind all roles and settings"—into a character in a limited social setting. Film stars labor as actors, but remain "the same in a variety of contexts, locations, and environments," which makes them "transfilmic entities" (King, "Stardom as an Occupation," 158). This transfilmic status has potential value for both actor/star and system (Hollywood film production): the actor as star can negotiate for contractual benefits on the basis of his/her monopoly of his/her image, and the system uses the transfilmic status of the image to promote its film commodities. King posits the possibility for agency and autonomy for the star but emphasizes that the star is not the sole creator of his or her image (e.g., during the studio system era, studios invested heavily in crafting performance style, altering physical features and creating publicity about their actors under contract) nor is he or she in control of the conditions of the capitalist contexts of their production and circulation. King's "cultural materialist" approach identifies a limited agency for the star.

In her *Negotiating Hollywood: The Cultural Politics of Actors' Labor* (1995), Danae Clark approves of the approaches of both DeCordova and King, but argues that what is needed is a theory (and history) that "introduces the notion of struggle into the scene of actors' labor" (Clark, 3). Clark conceptualizes actors in terms of "labor power," and examines how the Hollywood studios in the 1930s (the era many consider as the "golden age" of star production) used processes she identifies as "shifting," "fragmenting," and "binding," to position actors in subordinate positions within the hierarchy of the system as a way of countering acting labor's struggles to unionize. For example, the studios shifted the focus from the process of production to positioning stars as commodity fetishes; they fragmented actors' agency by typecasting and by privileging certain actors (stars) over others; they bound actors to the system by positioning them as "family" to ensure loyalty to the company. Clark claims her theorization is an interrogation of the "very premises upon which 'star studies' traditionally rests," and that her goal is to "destabilize the concept of 'star' " (Clark, ix). Clark's critical framework has been influential, but often within studies still committed to examining stars over other acting labor. Adrienne L. McLean's *Being Rita Hayworth: Labor, Identity, and Hollywood Stardom* (2004) is a study that takes Clark's theorization of the social and constructed subjectivity of the actor as worker very seriously, but not only does McLean focus on a very major star of the Hollywood studio period rather than the acting collective, she also seeks to understand "*how* that labor is performed and at whose cost" (McLean, 9). Consequently, McLean explores Hayworth as worker and image in terms of the star's talent and aspirations as evident in such material practices as craft and professionalism. In addition, while McLean is invested in aspects of industry discourse and systems of commodification characteristic of the studios in which Hayworth labored, she also positions Hayworth's work and image in relation to women's history of work inside and outside the home—that is, within the general type of historical contexts favored in Dyer's approach to theorizing the social valences and relevance of certain star images and personas over others.

Marlene Dietrich and the Projects of Film Theory

Few film stars have figured into so many different theories of film and stardom as Marlene Dietrich, whose career spanned multiple decades within national and transnational contexts in a variety of genres, film styles, and forms of art and entertainment. Recent scholarship has demonstrated an interest in analyzing the power of Dietrich's star image in relation to the power evoked by her face and/or her legs visualized in films and photos, or her voice in sound recordings. Lutz Koepnick's (2007) essay "Dietrich's Face," returns to some of the terms of *photogenie*, although via Barthes ("The Face of Garbo") rather than the French theorists of the 1920s. Contrasting the image of Dietrich's face to Garbo's, Koepnick argues that it represents "a deliberate adaptation to, by testing and managing, the various machines of cinematic fantasy production" (Koepnick, 53). Garbo's face "embraced the fleetingness of modern time as the condition for touching the eternal," while Dietrich's immortality is related to the constant transformation of the morph, the posthuman. In a move that is compatible with Barry King's theory of stars' agency in how they exercise monopolies of their images, Koepnick finds evidence for the adaptability of Dietrich's face not just in the cinematic uses of the face itself—for example, in how director Josef von Sternberg used it as an element within his visual universe—but also in how Dietrich intervened and managed the manner in which her face would be presented in films and publicity photos to sustain a decades-long career.

For much of the period between 1970 and 2000, film scholars who used the example of Dietrich's star image did so from an interest in appraising auteur style (of von Sternberg, not typically of Dietrich) or in theorizing the way classical Hollywood film functions as an ideological and psychic apparatus that produces a particular kind of subject. *Cahiers du Cinema*'s collectively written ideological critique, "Josef von Sternberg's *Morocco*" (1970), analyzes how the erotic mythology of the woman in classical Hollywood film functions to mask the film's ideological underpinnings. In the essay's reading of *Morocco*, Dietrich represents the epitome of the fetishistic eroticization that defines a star as star. The *Cahiers* editors employ auteurist, psychoanalytic and ideological (Marxist) theories to conclude that the film's use of Dietrich as an object of exchange within its narrative and as an image within the "plastic effects" of its mise-en-scene—such as masks and veils—constitutes the filmic image itself as gauze or screen, creating a fetishistic appeal that contributes to the construction of a patriarchal, capitalist spectator-subject.

Claire Johnston, whose 1974 essay "Women's Cinema as Counter-Cinema" serves as a mediating link between the *Cahiers* essay and Laura Mulvey's highly influential "Visual Pleasure and Narrative Cinema," argues that the implications of the *Cahiers* analysis is that classical Hollywood cinema constructs a binary of male/nonmale in which the fetishization of the female functions as a phallic replacement. In Johnson's argument, the way Dietrich's image was conceptualized in von Sternberg's films is evidence of film as a collective phallocentric fantasy. Mulvey's argument deepens and complicates these theorizations of the Dietrich image. She links the camera, the filmic character and the (masculine) spectator of classical cinema as offering positions of looking that sadistically control and spectacularize the female image. Although her point that von Sternberg's imaging of Dietrich exemplifies fetishization is in line with the arguments made by others, Mulvey argues that the Dietrich character is not mediated for the spectator by the controlling gaze of the male protagonist. Instead, Mulvey argues provocatively that the spectator has access to "direct erotic rapport" with Dietrich.[4]

In her 1988 book *In the Realm of Pleasure: Von Sternberg, Dietrich, and the Masochistic Aesthetic*, Gaylyn Studlar continues the dialogue about the power and meaning of Dietrich's image within a psychoanalytic context. She argues that the pleasures of looking in these films are structured around masochistic, rather than sadistic pleasures. The male character/spectator submits to the gaze of the female/Dietrich, in longing for a pre-Oedipal relation to the mother, before scenarios of maternal castration and lack dominate the formation of subjectivity. In a subsequent development of her theory (her 1990 article "Masochism, Masquerade, and the Erotic Metamorphoses of Marlene Dietrich"), Studlar argues that Mulvey does not explore the implications of her own point that von Sternberg's films allow Dietrich "direct erotic rapport" with spectators. Studlar instead claims that Dietrich—the performer *and* the von Sternberg character—"possesses an aloofness that suggests a distanciation from her constructed image, a refusal to invest in her 'femininity'" (Studlar, "Masochism," 243). In other words, the star has some agency in authoring meaning through her resistance to patriarchal positioning.

Judith Mayne, in a 1989 essay, "Marlene Dietrich, *The Blue Angel*, and Female Performance," argues that if "resistance" is the appropriate term to define the Dietrich image it is because "resistance is fully part of the narrative and visual imagery that comprise the Dietrich persona" (Mayne, 42). This resistance is most clearly evident in Dietrich's enactment of characters that move among multiple modes of performance. In other words, resistance is an effect of the self-consciousness of performance itself, especially in the ironic imitations of the conventions of femininity enacted by Lola Lola of *The Blue Angel* and Christine of *Witness for the Prosecution*. As Erica Carter points out in her 2004 study of Dietrich's star performance style in relation to the neo-Kantian aesthetics of Third Reich cinematic stardom, Dietrich's "anti-realist" acting style and her "studied erotic poses" and "knowing winks" disturbed those ideals of beauty in their signaling of identity as performed. Consequently, Dietrich became a figure of great ambivalence for German critics during the Nazi era (Carter, 155).

The Future of Star Studies in Film Theory

Taken together, the analyses of Dietrich from the late 1970s to the 2000s suggest a movement away from understanding her star persona as an inert, passive image entirely constituted by a collective phallocentrism toward an understanding of the Dietrich star persona as performed, contributing to the enunciation of the films' meanings and multiple positions available for spectators. Some analyses also gesture toward a *historiographic* understanding of the Dietrich star persona as developed and replayed over time, across different genres, national contexts and historical moments—status of the star that has theoretical implications for how we write film history. Many recent studies of film stars—who, in the twenty-first century, still play an important role in how film industries in many parts of the world fund and promote films—are compatible with the recent critical moves I've just discussed as important to the theorization of Dietrich's image.[5] However, although these recent studies are in continuity with moves toward theorizing star agency and multiple subject positions for spectators, there is a growing interest in exploring the permeability of the line between stars and audiences as star promotion increasingly shifts from production companies to stars themselves and fans engage in user-generated media.

Paul MacDonald commented in 2003 that "although stars may be thought of as a phenomenon of the old media world, the presence of stars on the internet represents the extension of the star system in the new media universe" (MacDonald, 43). Yet, new digital technologies and new media (such as video games and social media) have had an impact on how some stars are created and maintained as images, or how they are incorporated into fan communities within a digital culture characterized by "copying, sampling, animating, imitating, hybridizing, morphing, re-enacting, re-mixing, and re-membering" (Notaro). The launching of the scholarly journal *Celebrity Studies* in 2010 not only signals how film stars are now likely to be studied within the more general notion of "celebrity," but also how theory has moved to a consideration of social media such as Twitter, and social activity such as charitable philanthropy and eco-activism, as the sites in which film stars are likely to be encountered, identified with and/or critiqued by audiences and theorists.

Film stars had appeared in "new" media before the development of online communication and social media in the late 1990s and 2000s: film stars (at least in the American context) had confirmed, contested and expanded aspects of their personas in emergent media since the advent of commercial radio in the 1920s and television in the late 1940s and early 1950s. More significantly, the typically domestic reception of radio and television, as well as their capacity to transmit images and/or sound "live" (simultaneous with reception) challenged or reworked the presence-absence dialectic as stars could share time and space with the audience, "appearing" in a viewer's home simultaneous with their performance in studio. In these earlier modes of media convergence, film stardom had to be renegotiated in terms of domesticity and intimacy to gain or maintain audience fascination (Mann; Desjardins, *Recycled Stars*). This renegotiation became especially crucial to the maintenance of film stardom as the emergence of American commercial television in the late 1940s and early 1950s coincided with the break-up of the studio system and the long-term contract practices that had controlled so much acting labor and star promotion (including the strategic deployment of "revelations" about a star's private life) since the early 1920s.

Many of the scholars theorizing film stardom as well as the diverse categories of celebrity in the age of user-generated social media centralize questions about star and fan agency as well as about the viability of earlier terms by which theorists and audiences alike understood stardom, such as the "presence-absence" dialectic of star-spectator relations (Ellis) and the "extraordinary-ordinary" dialectic that informed many star personas (Dyer). In 2001, early in the history of "online communities," Steven Cohan theorized the continuing status of Judy Garland's "special relation to ordinariness" in relation to the complex and contradictory positions and fantasies of her fans communicating via the internet (Cohan, 134). He focuses on two online sites devoted to Garland (a biographical and career "database" webpage and an e-mail LISTSERV that enables participation of subscribers in discussions) that either remove aspects of the star's persona associated with a "gay sensibility" or dismiss the relevance of nonnormative aspects of her persona (androgyny, pathos, "normal" without being normative) to contemporary fan—gay or straight—subcultures. Cohan's examination provides evidence for the historical and ideological status of stardom as grounded in public and reiterative processes of fans who construct, confirm and/or contest the meanings of star personas, especially those meanings that have implications for how stars texts support or question dominant social formations.

Scholars have also looked to more recently emergent user-generated media, such as YouTube and Twitter, to explore what aspects of star construction and fan participation remain in continuity with or depart from practices codified by earlier media forms and industries. "Video mash-ups" (videos which combine preexisting video clips from a variety of sources into a single video text) using images of stars from films, newsreels, television, publicity photos and so on, abound on YouTube, a site on which users can upload and tag videos and provide and receive commentary from other users of the site. Creators upload video mashups of star imagery in honor or memoriam of favorite stars, to show off taste preferences by celebrating star fashion, to study performance style or thematic resonances of a star's film work, or to comment on or reveal aspects of a star's private life, such as in the video mashups that juxtapose clips of Loretta Young and Clark Gable from their films with television interview clips of their "secret daughter" Judy Lewis in which she comments on how Young hid the truth of Lewis's parentage from the public for over sixty years. Such user-generated media practices in many ways confirm that the nearly century-old fascination with film stardom has been partially based on the "surface and depth" play within star discourses—that is, the possibility that "truth" or "authenticity" resides in a "private" sexuality (partially) hidden from public consumption (Desjardins, *Recycled Stars*). In addition, these practices are evidence that stars still have use-value to the public to the extent that their biographies, however mediated, seem relevant to real social concerns.

Although there have been notable exceptions, YouTube has been more frequently employed by fans than by stars themselves to comment on or shore up star texts. Conversely, Twitter—a social messaging service that allows users to write and/or read short texts in real time—has been used extensively by stars to stay in the forefront of public consciousness. Stars' use of this social media exemplifies the challenge for contemporary stars to sustain "a viable self in a welter of interactions" enabled and demanded by a proliferation of new media outlets (King, "Embodying an Elastic Self," 60). Sarah Thomas argues that despite the way Twitter allows for limited, but temporally fluid conversation between stars and fans/followers and thus the sense that barriers of distance have been breached between these subjects, it enables stars to adapt "different strategies of public presentation according to the pressures of management and audience reception" (Thomas, 249). In other words, stars who communicate with the public via "tweets" (the "microblog" texts of Twitter) have tended to use the form for image management in ways not dissimilar to earlier modes of star constructions of the alleged "authentic self." Thomas emphasizes that this communication is a mediation that is performed to appear unmediated.

While most scholars studying fan and/or star-construction practices on social media have so far concluded that these new media have not created a rupture with past understandings of stardom (even as the pool of celebrity grows and the sites for discourse proliferate), scholars who have examined the "digital" star and the "synthespian" (virtual actor or "vactor") have tended to see both continuities with and departures from what were considered the grounds of stardom, acting labor, spectator relationships with visual media and narrative and even of ontological conceptions of the human body. Mary Flanagan, writing in 1999 about the emergence of video game character Lara Croft as a "digital star," suggests that star figures who do not rely on physical bodies have the potential to dissolve "conventional ideas of the self through the destabilization of the subject," perhaps even offer alternative subject positions, even though the current visualization of Croft's body is characterized by a hypersexuality and the game lacks "feminist content" (Flanagan, 91). Flanagan uses the concept of "becoming" as theorized by Gilles Deleuze to argue that the basis of fan's fascination with Croft resides in the way her figure becomes a site for doing or "becoming," providing pleasure for the user/player in the data-driven events of losing, winning, moving, fighting. The implication here is that pleasure/knowledge/empowerment derived from interaction with a "becoming" figure is on a different ontological level than identification with a film actor/star who is presumed to have an identity based in a physical, gendered body and biographical narrative.

Yet, biography does figure into Flanagan's definition of digital stardom. She compares the historical film star with the digital star partly on the basis of a stardom constructed out of inauthentic biographical narratives—for example, the star texts of both Theda Bara and Lara Croft are made up of impossible and multiple fictions. However, she contrasts the two kinds of stardom by arguing that Bara's fictional biography (e.g., an Egyptian origin) is "fixed" (determined by a film studio), while Croft's is open to fan contribution and multiple realities, and these contributions represent another way the digital star invites user interactivity. Flanagan's argument ignores the kinds of "interactivity" Stacey identified as enacted by female fans of film stars in active processes of fantasy and imitative behaviors. Even though Flanagan acknowledges that both film and digital stardom rely on the separation of the public and private and the historical and the fictional biography, her analysis underestimates the implications of the film star system's awakening of a hermeneutic drive that spurred the fan or viewer to desire what was hidden under the biographical narrative of the star. In other words, the logic of the film star system founded on the tensions between the star performance and the star biography and in the implicit acknowledgment that star biographies were, if not inauthentic, at least only partially true or adequate, requiring a "real" person behind the fiction and a kind of active reading between the lines on the part of the fan. This active reading process, informed by the fan's place within a social formation characterized by contradictions, still offers the potential for alternative subject positions even if these are accessible at the level of the "extra-cinematic social," rather than the level of the ontological that Flanagan identifies for user play with digital stars.

The emergence of digital actors, also referred to as "synthespians" or virtual actors, has moved film production and film theory toward the possibility of a new category of film stardom, one that designates a hybrid conjoining of a "real" carbon-based human and a digital creation (Notaro; Gunning; King, "Articulating Digital Stardom"; Wojcik; Desjardins, "Performance, Labor"). The use of living actors' bodies (or images of dead actors once photographed in analog cinematic processes) as raw material for digital "motion capture" to create a new, "synthetic" actor or image has been employed to supply extras, supporting players and even animated versions of major stars in contemporary motion pictures. Anna Notaro notes that this move not only testifies to a trend toward "convergence mode" of filmmaking, animation and game development, but also to the possibility that one figure of the familiar "triads" through which critics and audiences have understood cinematic agency (director, actor, viewer) may no longer be human. Is this just another way of posing questions about the origins of cinematic pleasure and meaning, which Delluc, Epstein and Bálazs explored in terms of the spectator deriving pleasure and knowledge through the experience of the "microphysiognomy" of the star/actor personality as orchestrated by a director? In his discussion of the motion-capture use of actor Andy Serkis's body to create the synthespian "Gollum" in *The Lord of the Rings* film trilogy (2001–3), Tom Gunning sees continuity between earlier analog forms of "capturing" the motion of human actors, such as rotoscoping and chronophotography, and current digital processes of using the human body as raw data for the creation of immaterial bodies.

Some scholars share the beliefs of Notaro and Gunning that synthespians pose new questions about the relationship of the acting body to cinematic characters and illusions of reality, as well as maintain continuity with previous practices of star construction and promotion. While the synthespian is created out of the raw data captured from the human body and the carbon-based star actually materially embodies the star image, King and Desjardins emphasize that the synthespian's similarity to the film star relies on the possibility of promotion of its image as a commodity and its reliance on a group of laborers (whether these be computer technicians, make-up artists, costume designers or acting teachers) in shaping a performance and an image (King, "Articulating Digital Stardom"; Desjardins, "Performance, Labor"). Whether a film uses the motion capture process to create a synthespian who is an animated visualization of a carbon-based star, such as Tom Hanks in *The Polar Express* (2004), or a whole cast of synthespians not obviously visually referencing major stars, as in *Final Fantasy: The Spirits Within* (2001), or a secondary character synthespian playing opposite carbon-based actors/stars, as in *The Lord of the Rings* trilogy, the virtual actor will surely continue to be one contender for stardom, whether we call it film stardom or digital stardom, for some time. What remains to be seen is how those theorizing film stardom will continue to find in synthespians connections to, and departures from, the popular, industrial, and critical understandings of film stardom of the last hundred years.

Notes

1 Although there are shared motivations between theories of director as auteur and theories of stardom and acting—namely, the identification of whom or what is responsible for filmic meanings or controlling agency over formal choices in filmmaking—as the conversation between Noel King and Paul Willemen suggests, what might be the source of the viewer's love for cinema is somehow wrapped up with what the actor or star consciously or unconsciously "reveals" on screen.

2 Lawrence is referencing Mary Ann Doane, *The Emergence of Cinematic Time* (Cambridge, MA: Harvard University Press, 2002), 226.

3 These studies are too numerous to list here, but many were influenced by the writings of Christian Metz, especially his *The Imaginary Signifier: Psychoanalysis and the Cinema* (Bloomington: Indiana University Press, 1982). Kaja Silverman, in *The Subject of Semiotics* (New York: Oxford University Press, 1983), provides a good summary and analysis of a variety of applications of post-structuralist theories to film analysis.

4 Laura Mulvey later qualified aspects of her argument about spectatorial pleasure and classical Hollywood narrative, and delineated a space for an active female spectator as "transvestite." See, "Afterthoughts on 'Visual Pleasure and Narrative Cinema' inspired by King Vidor's *Duel in the Sun* (1946)," reprinted in Laura Mulvey, *Visual and Other Pleasures* (Bloomington: Indiana University Press, 1989).

5 For more theorizations of Dietrich's star image, see Gerd Gemunden and Mary Desjardins, eds., *Dietrich Icon* (Durham, NC: Duke University Press, 2007).

Bibliography

Alberoni, Francesco. 1963. *The Powerless Elite*. Milan: Vita e Peniero. Excerpted as "The Powerless 'Elite': Theory and Sociological Research on the Phenomenon of the Stars." In *Stardom and Celebrity: A Reader*, edited by Sean Redmond and Su Holmes, 65–77. Los Angeles: Sage, 2007.

Bálazs, Béla. 1970. *Theory of the Film: Character and Growth of a New Art*. New York: Dover.

Barthes, Roland. 1973. "The Face of Garbo." *Mythologies*. London: Paladin. Reprinted in *Stardom and Celebrity: A Reader*, edited by Sean Redmond and Su Holmes, 261–62. Los Angeles: Sage, 2007.

Cahiers du Cinema Collective. 1990. "Josef von Sternberg's *Morocco*." In *Cahiers du Cinema, 1969–1972*, edited by Nick Browne, 174–86. Cambridge, MA: Harvard University Press.

Carter, Erica. 2004. *Dietrich's Ghosts: The Sublime and the Beautiful in Third Reich Film*. London: BFI.

Clark, Danae. 1995. *Negotiating Hollywood: The Cultural Politics of Actors' Labor*. Minneapolis: University of Minnesota Press.

Cohan, Steven. 2001. "Judy on the Net: Judy Garland Fandom and the 'Gay Thing' Revisted." In *Keyframes: Popular Cinema and Cultural Studies*, edited by Matthew Tinkcom and Amy Villarejo, 119–36. London: Routledge.

De Angelis, Michael. 2001. *Gay Fandom and Crossover Stardom: James Dean, Mel Gibson, and Keanu Reeves*. Durham, NC: Duke University Press.

DeCordova, Richard. 1990. *Picture Personalities: The Emergence of the Star System in America*. Urbana: University of Illinois Press.

Delluc, Louis. 1988 (1917). "Beauty in the Cinema." In *French Film Theory and Criticism, Volume I: 1907–1929*, edited by Richard Abel, 137–39. Princeton: Princeton University Press.

Desjardins, Mary. 2015a. *Recycled Stars: Female Film Stardom in the Age of Television and Video*. Durham, NC: Duke University Press.

———. 2015b. "Performance, Labor, and Stardom in the Era of the Synthespian." In *Production Studies, the Sequel! Cultural Studies of Global Media Industries*, edited by Miranda Banks, Bridget Conor and Vicki Mayer, 11–22. New York: Routledge.

Dyer, Richard. 1979. *Stars*. London: BFI.

———. 1986. *Heavenly Bodies: Film Stars and Society*. New York: St. Martin's Press.

Ellis, John. 1982. *Visible Fictions: Cinema: Television: Video*. London: Routledge & Kegan Paul.

Epstein, Jean. 1988a (1921). "Magnification." In *French Film Theory and Criticism, Volume I: 1907–1929*, edited by Richard Abel, 235–41. Princeton: Princeton University Press.

———. 1988b (1921). "The Senses 1 (b)." In *French Film Theory and Criticism, Volume I: 1907–1929*, edited by Richard Abel, 241–46. Princeton: Princeton University Press.

———. 1988c (1924). "On Certain Characteristics of *Photogenie*." In *French Film Theory and Criticism, Volume I: 1907–1929*, edited by Richard Abel, 314–18. Princeton: Princeton University Press.

Flanagan, Mary. 1999. "Mobile Identities, Digital Stars, and Post-cinematic Selves." *Wide Angle* 21, no. 1: 76–93.

Gunning, Thomas. 2006. "Gollum and Golem: Special Effects and the Technology of Artificial Bodies." In *From Hobbits to Hollywood: Essays on Peter Jackson's Lord of the Rings*, edited by Ernest Mathijs and Murray Pomerance, 319–49. Amsterdam: Rodopi.

Johnston, Claire. 1979. "Women's Cinema as Counter-cinema." In *Sexual Strategems: The World of Women in Film*, edited by Patricia Erens, 133–43. New York: Horizon Press.

King, Barry. 1985. "Articulating Stardom." *Screen* 26, no. 5. Reprinted in *Star Texts: Image and Performance in Film and Television*, edited by Jeremy G. Butler, 125–54. Detroit: Wayne State University Press, 1991.

———. 1986. "Stardom as an Occupation." In *The Hollywood Film Industry*, edited by Paul Kerr, 154–83. London: Routledge & Kegan Paul.

———. 2003. "Embodying an Elastic Self: The Parametrics of Contemporary Stardom." In *Contemporary Hollywood Stardom*, edited by Thomas Austin and Martin Barker, 45–61. London: Arnold.

———. 2011. "Articulating Digital Stardom." *Celebrity Studies* 2, no. 3: 247–62.

Koepnick, Lutz. 2007. "Dietrich's Face." In *Dietrich Icon*, edited by Gerd Gemunden and Mary Desjardins, 43–59. Durham, NC: Duke University Press.

Lawrence, Amy. 2010. *The Passion of Montgomery Clift*. Berkeley: University of California Press.

MacDonald, Paul. 2003. "Stars in the On-line Universe: Promotion, Nudity, Reverence." In *Contemporary Hollywood Stardom*, edited by Thomas Austin and Martin Barker, 29–44. London: Arnold.

Majumdar, Neepa. 2009. *Wanted Cultured Ladies Only! Female Stardom and Cinema in India, 1930s–1950s*. Urbana: University of Illinois Press.

Mann, Denise. 1992. "The Spectacularization of Everyday Life: Recycling Hollywood Stars and Fans in Early Television Shows." In *Private Screenings: Television and the Female Consumer*, edited by Lynn Spigel and Denise Mann, 41–64. Minneapolis: University of Minnesota Press.

Mayne, Judith. 1989. "Marlene Dietrich, *The Blue Angel*, and Female Performance." In *Seduction and Theory: Readings of Gender, Representation, and Rhetoric*, edited by Dianne Hunter, 28–46. Urbana: University of Illinois Press.

McLean, Adrienne L. 2004. *Being Rita Hayworth: Labor, Identity, and Hollywood Stardom*. New Brunswick, NJ: Rutgers University Press.

Morin, Edgar. 1957. *Les stars*. Paris: Éditions du Seuil. Reprinted as *The Stars*. Translated by Richard Howard. Minneapolis: University of Minnesota Press, 2005.

Mulvey, Laura. 1975. "Visual Pleasure and Narrative Cinema." *Screen* 16, no. 3: 6–18.

Negra, Diane. 2001. *Off-White Hollywood: American Culture and Ethnic Female Stardom*. New York: Routledge.

Notaro, Anna. 2009. "'Reality in the Performance': Issues of Digital Technology, Simulation, and Artificial Acting in Simone." *Refractory: A Journal of Entertainment Media* 15. www.http://refractory.unimelb.edu.au/2009/06/25 (accessed February 21, 2016).

Prasad, M. Madhava. 2004. "Reigning Stars: The Political Career of South Indian Cinema." In *Stars: The Film Reader*, edited by Lucy Fischer and Marcia Landy, 97–114. New York: Routledge.

Studlar, Gaylyn. 1988. *In the Realm of Pleasure: Von Sternberg, Dietrich, and the Masochistic Aesthetic*. Urbana: University of Illinois Press.

———. 1990. "Masochism, Masquerade, and the Erotic Metamorphoses of Marlene Dietrich." In *Fabrications: Costume and the Female Body*, edited by Jane Gaines and Charlotte Herzog, 229–49. New York: Routledge.

———. 1996. *This Mad Masquerade: Stardom and Masculinity in the Jazz Age*. New York: Columbia University Press.

Thomas, Sarah. 2014. "Celebrity in the 'Twitterverse': History, Authenticity, and the Multiplicity of Stardom." *Celebrity Studies* 5, no. 3: 242–55.

Weiss, Andrea. 1993. *Vampires and Violets: Lesbians in Film*. New York: Penguin Books.

Willemen, Paul. 1994. *Looks and Frictions: Essays in Cultural Studies and Film Theory*. Bloomington: Indiana University Press/BFI.

Wojcik, Pamela Robertson. 2006. "The Sound of Film Acting." *Journal of Film and Video* (Spring). Reprinted in *Annual Editions*, edited by Heather Addison and Charles Berg, 31–39. Dubuque, IA: McGraw Hill Contemporary Learning Series, 2007–8

Chapter Eleven

RETHINKING GENRE MEMORY: HITCHCOCK'S *VERTIGO* AND ITS REVISION

Elisabeth Bronfen

As Barry Keith Grant notes in the introduction to his *Film Genre Reader*, "Stated simply, genre movies are those commercial films which, through repetition and variation, tell familiar stories with familiar characters in familiar situations." Precisely because, as he adds, "they encourage expectations and experiences similar to those of similar films we have already seen," genre films proved to be significant in establishing popular cinema "as a cultural and economic institution, particularly in the United States, where Hollywood studios early on adopted an industrial model based on mass production" (Grant 1986, xi). Indeed, since the heyday of silent cinema, the notion of categorizing films according to certain types allowed Hollywood to standardize their production so as to market their films more effectively. The designation of genres, "each with its recognizable repertoire of conventions running across visual imagery, plot, character, setting, modes of narrative development, music and stars," made it possible for the studios to target their audience by both predicting and catering to their expectations (Cook and Bernink 1999, 138). When genre criticism, in turn, emerged within film studies in the mid-1960s, it served to articulate its dissatisfaction with auteur theory by recalling that conventions and formulas had, from the start, been at the heart of the Hollywood system. Rather than treating cinema exclusively as part of the "high art" of modernism, and, in so doing, privileging the artist as the seminal force behind a given film or set of films, critics such as Tom Ryall brought the notion of genre back into the discussion so as to once again engage the specifically popular dimension of cinema.

A dynamic and mutually determining relation between three equally constitutive forces is key, Ryall argues, to understanding genre films—the artist and his or her embeddedness within the studio system, the actual film product and the targeted audience with its knowledge and expectations. Thus, while generic rules, patterns, and styles help manage the creation, production and viewing of popular cinema, at issue for film theory is precisely more than merely a taxonomic system that determines which films fit a given category. Indeed my own rethinking of genre—for which, in the second part of this essay, I will offer a cross-mapping of the cultural afterlife of Hitchcock's *Vertigo*—hinges on the wager that a hermeneutic praxis is equally at stake. Using the notion of genre to examine films that share certain kinds of narrative structures, I shall contend that figural constellations or visual styles allow critical interest to shift to questions of repetitions and variations among the chosen set of films. These, in turn, are primarily detected in the process of watching (and reading) films (Bronfen 2009). While acknowledging the originality of the director, the critical discussion can move beyond focusing on his or her idiosyncratic mode of artistic expression so as to include the position not only of the original audience but also all subsequent critical readings. If, in what follows, I repeatedly return to the idea of cinema as a cognitive space where cultural concerns are addressed and negotiated transhistorically, it is worth recalling that genre theory originally brought the issue of audience identification and recognition into play so as to draw attention to the conditions of Hollywood studio production and mass market consumption. At the same time, it also wanted to foreground the relation popular culture has to ideology, by focusing on the social practices of the historical moment out of which a set of films emerged and the concerns these films helped shape for an implied spectatorship.

Moreover, in that it proposes a dynamic and mutually dependent relation between artist, film and spectator, as well as between film production, audience consumption and ideology, genre theory brings not only the issue of adaptability into play but also the notion of cultural memory. Given that genre formulas and conventions *cater to* but also *bank on* audience expectations, they can be seen as remembering and rewriting prior patterns of narrative structure and dramatic modalities so as to adapt generic patterns and styles to fit the contemporary moment, with its specific aesthetic tastes, technical possibilities and cultural concerns. How much leeway, however, is there regarding the transformation of conventions and how much stability must be maintained so that a genre can be recognized as recalling predecessors and passing on past cultural knowledge? So as to engage these two perspectives on genre, Rick Altman (1987) has suggested that "we can as a whole distinguish between generic definitions which depend on a list of common traits, attitudes, characters, shots, locations, sets and the like—thus stressing the semantic elements which make up the genre—and definitions which play up instead certain constitutive relationships which might be called the genre's fundamental syntax" (Grant 1986, 30). The semantic perspective (referring to the genre's building blocks) is inclusive and allows for variations and changes over time but, because of its broad applicability, has little explanatory power. The syntactic relation (referring to overarching stable structures), in turn, involves distinct, more exclusive patterns even as its explanatory force is more precise.

Rather than choosing between these two perspectives on genre, Altman proposes that the relationship between them constitutes the "very site of negotiation between Hollywood and its audience, and thus between ritual and ideological uses of genre" (Grant 1986, 35). By remembering and refiguring conventional narratives, genre films may change the semantic signals they emit, but they can be effective only if the syntactic expectations determining their structure remain stable. Or put another way, the repeated deployment of substantially the same syntactic strategies allows for modification on the level of the elements used to keep the genre alive and meaningful over time. It is, then, precisely by conceiving genre not as a static system with rigid rules that determine which films to include and which to exclude in a certain set, but rather as a provisional structure, as a flexible category in process, albeit based on shared thematic (*parole*) and formal (*langue*) criteria, that genre theory can foreground notions of adjustment, modification and realignment. Or put another way, to draw attention to the way popular cinema emerges from and acts upon a specific sociohistoric context is precisely why genre should not be reduced to a consideration of studio interests, along with the production and distribution system they command. Rather, as Steve Neale suggests, it is best conceived in terms of "systems of orientations, expectations and conventions that circulate between industry, text and subject" (1990, 19).

Precisely in order to foreground the spectator as critical reader in assessing the transhistorical force of genre films, I have proposed thinking of Hollywood as a conceptual space for aesthetic refigurations, and, in the specific case of war films, as generating a serial process of recyclings that address the specific cultural concerns of different historical moments (Bronfen 2012). Given that media specificity keeps reshaping the visual style of cinema even as the attitudes of the viewing (and reading) subject engaging with it change with time, these systems are necessarily protean. They not only tap into cultural conventions but thrive on transformation and differentiation by virtue of appropriation and adaptation, which is to say by working *with* as well as *against* conventions that keep the recognizable over-arching structure intact. As Ralph Cohen argues, "since each genre is composed of texts that accrue, the grouping is a process, not a determinate category. Genres are open categories. Each member alters the genre by adding, contradicting, or changing constituents, especially those of members most closely related to it" (in Neale 1990, 217).

Given the focus I have placed on the transhistorical aspect of genre cinema, it is fruitful to add Mikhail Bakhtin's concept of genre memory to the discussion. For Bakhtin, genre forms, conceived as key organs of memory that embody the systems of value of the historical period in which they originated, implicitly impose this perspective on subsequent texts (Burgoyne 2010). Precisely because they resuscitate visual and narrative formulas from the past so as to refigure these conventions for the present, genre forms function as principle vehicles for shaping social experiences and transmitting these from one generation to the next. As Morson and Emerson explain, genre forms make up such a seminal part of cultural memory because they serve as residues, as "congealed events" and "crystallizations of earlier interactions," even while, with each new deployment, they accumulate more density regarding the aesthetic formalizations they transmit. As they move through time, they carry with them the "layered record of their changing use." Furthermore, because genre forms are "so often adapted from previous genres, they may carry the potential to resume their past usage and so to redefine a present experience in an additional way." As such, they "remember the past, and make their resources and potentials available to the present" (Morson and Emerson 1990, 292f).

What genre memory thus adds to the discussion is the notion that as conventions regarding figural constellations, thematic concerns, narrative structures and visual styles are refigured over time, so as to be applicable to each new contemporary moment, past formalizations always also implicitly resurface. Indeed, it is useful to recall that the term is derived from the Latin *genus* (birth, origin) as well as *gegnere* (to beget, produce). By conceiving genre as an organ of memory, attention is not only drawn to the way that, by shaping ideological concerns for an ever changing contemporary moment, genre reproduces past experience so as to translate cultural intensities even while engendering new aesthetic formalizations. Rather, in that with each new figuration semantic density is accrued while the syntactic structure that is recalled is also maintained, and in the process, the new aesthetic formalizations that emerge change our collective cultural image repertoire. This brings the audience, to whose knowledge, expectations and desires genre films cater, into play in yet another way. Thomas Schatz also treats genre film as an evolutionary form of collective cultural expression. His point of reference, however, is Lévi-Strauss's conception of myth as offering imaginary resolutions for antagonisms that can not be resolved in social reality. Arguing for the socio-cultural significance of genre formulas, he, in turn, emphasizes the specific function genre films perform for American society at large, in that they offer a "ritualization of collective ideals, the celebration of temporarily resolved social and cultural conflicts, and the concealment of disturbing cultural conflicts behind the guise of entertainment, behind what Michael Wood terms "the semitransparent mask of a contradiction" (in Grant 1986, 97).

Even though any engagement with genre film must take into account that as a popular medium cinema thrives on audience expectations, it should not only be treated as a highly commercial product, predetermined by convention, with certain demands imposed on it by the cinematic system. Rather, as Schatz insists, genre films offer "a distinct manifestation of contemporary society's basic mythic impulse, its desire to confront elemental conflicts inherent in modern culture while at the same time participating in the projection of an idealized collective self-image" (in Grant 1986, 99). The variations and transformations attributed to genre as an organ of cultural memory are, thus, necessary so that each new generation of films can respond to the shifts in the communities to whose mythic desire they respond. Genre specificity, in turn, is predicated on how they deal with sociocultural issues, ambiguities and conflicts: "What emerges as a social problem (or dramatic conflict) in one genre is not necessarily a problem in another" (Schatz 1981, 25). Thus, while courtship and marriage may be problems in romantic comedies and melodramas, they are more rarely negotiated in detective genres, with its focus on issues of law and order. While the psycho-thriller, in turn, engages the dark side of American individualism and self-reliance, most often leading to a repudiation of society, romantic comedy and melodrama think through what it takes to be integrated again into the space of social consensus.

If, then, each genre possesses its own dramatic modalities, figural constellations and thematic resolutions to the ideological concerns they negotiate, I propose rethinking the ritual force Schatz attributes to genre film so as to ask how it is that cultural conventions determine that a particular thematic concern such as law, order and destructive individualism should be negotiated in the detective genre and not in romantic comedies. Or put another way, what does the privileging of certain thematic issues say about the possibilities and limits of a particular film genre? What happens to our reading of a film or a set of thematically related films when cultural concerns they share are shaped by tapping into various literary genres—shifting between comedy, tragedy and romance? Do formal similarities override thematic analogies? As Jacques Derrida notes, precisely because the law of genre has a controlling influence "which draws the genre into engendering, generations, genealogy, and degenerescene," it touches on more than merely formal issues: "it covers the motif of the law in general, of generation in the natural and symbolic senses, of birth in the natural and symbolic senses, of the generation difference, sexual difference between the feminine and masculine genre/gender" (1980, 221).

I have chosen as my case study Hitchcock's *Vertigo* and its cultural afterlife precisely because it cannot readily be assigned to only one genre, straddling as it does the gothic and the melodrama with self-reflexive visual irony. What, then, are the consequences of designating *Vertigo* as a psycho-thriller rather than a dark comedy and how do subsequent films, recycling Hitchcock's narrative, rethink this categorization? Might the inclusion of genre memory (and generation difference) in a discussion of the ritual function of popular cinema not also allow us to think about genre films in terms of hybridity? And finally, what might be gained when the dynamic flexibility critics have come to associate with genre falls mainly on the spectator, as the third position in a triad linking him or her both to the film text (as a densely layered aesthetic formulation) and to the community (be it the film industry or the social world to which the film offers a mythical response)? What might be gained by focusing not only on the ideological function genre films serve but also the reading effect they produce? Might this allow for the re-inclusion of some aspects of auteur theory, particularly a focus on mise-en-scène and artistic ingenuity, into genre theory's concern with audience expectations and the cultural memory transported by narrative conventions?

Deploying the notion of genre as an interpretive scheme or engaging critically with individual films offers a particularly promising way to rethink the concept over and beyond issues of taxonomies. Conceived in terms of a heuristic praxis, genre and genre memory transform into categories that allow the critic to track not just the transformation of a thematic concern. Rather—as my comparative reading of three films—*Vertigo*, *Phoenix* and *Gone Girl*—is meant to illustrate, this transformation also involves the process by which generic definition itself (detective film, melodrama, romantic comedy) becomes hybridized over time, as subsequent directors refigure a predecessor text and, in so doing, repeat thematic elements with a generic difference. The question of identification on the part of the reader takes on a new function when the fixed rules that determine which films are to be included or excluded in a genre are no longer the decisive point. My wager is that having determined a set of texts as making up a genre owing to a shared thematic concern, the question instead becomes how thinking these films as a series effects an individual reading of each as well as an engagement with the genre(s) that structure them.

In *Vertigo*, Scottie (James Stewart), a retired San Francisco police detective, falls in love with an allegedly suicidal woman whom a former acquaintance, Gavin Elster, has hired him to protect. Unbeknown to him he has in fact been cast as the prime witness to a murder plot, in which Judy (Kim Novak) is simply performing the role of Madeleine Elster. During the inquest, Scottie will testify that Elster's wife jumped to her death when, in reality, her husband strangled her before throwing her off a church tower. Knowing that his vertigo would prevent him from making it to the top of the winding staircase, Judy had led him to follow her into the church, so that he, seeing a body falling, would assume it was hers. When, purely by accident, Scottie meets Judy again, still unaware of the deception played upon him, he compels her to allow him to recreate her in the image of the dead Madeleine whom he is still in love with. If, like so many of noir's femmes fatales, she agreed to take part in Elster's murder plot purely for pecuniary reasons, when she meets Scottie *again*, an ambiguous desire for this melancholic man is aroused. Complying once more to a makeover will prove fatal to her.

In *Phoenix*, Nelly Lenz (Nina Hoss) having survived a concentration camp and brought by a friend to a clinic, asks the surgeon to restore her disfigured face such that she will look exactly the way she did before she was arrested. Her sole reason for staying alive is to seek out Johnny (Ronald Zehrfeld), her German husband. When she finds him, he too will force her to consent to his recreating her in the image of the woman whom he believes to have died in a camp, only in Petzold's recycling of *Vertigo* the deception cuts both ways. While Nelly is the one who, in contrast to Hitchcock's heroine, initiates her resuscitation, she willingly deceives herself about the loyalty of her former husband. Johnny, in turn, is everything but an innocent pawn in the game of others, guilty himself of a double crime. On the one hand, he wants to use this impersonation act so that, by claiming his wife has returned from the camp, he can come into Nelly's post-Nazi inheritance. On the other hand, while this is intentionally conceived as an illegal act, he is also morally unjustified to make this claim. He had divorced Nelly a few days before betraying her to the Gestapo. Thus, in contrast to *Vertigo*, the recreation of a dead woman serves to sustain the heroine's erotic desire, while it is the hero who is in it only for the money.

Finally, in *Gone Girl*, Amy (Rosamund Pike) choses to punish her husband Nick (Ben Affleck) for his infidelity by staging her death and casting him as her implicit murderer. In yet another twist on the *Vertigo* narrative, she, like Judy's Madeleine, had merely been impersonating the role of "cool girl" for her clueless husband, even after they were forced to leave Manhattan and move to his rural hometown, living off her estate there. In contrast to the other two films, however, Amy is the sole director of the psycho-drama of her disappearance, compelling her husband to play a role she has scripted for him. She is, in turn, not only completely autonomous in the staging of her own resuscitation, but, once she returns from her presumed death, she also dictates the terms of their remarriage.

In all three films, then, the transformation of a woman into an idealized image is at issue, deliberately produced in each case to satisfy the desires of the hero (Scottie's necrophilia, Johnny's postwar financial ambition, Nick's pending criminal indictment). Regarding narrative management, and thus speaking to the mythic resolution genre film affords, the resilient survival of the heroine addresses the larger cultural concern regarding cold-war paranoia, German postwar repression or media saturation in the early twenty-first century. The heroine's metamorphosis, however, also allows the films to think about the specificity of the cinematic medium, by equating a woman, allegedly returned from the dead, with a portrait that is refracted in the process of being produced—in *Vertigo* the painting in a museum which serves as the model for Judy's impersonation of Madeleine Elster, in *Phoenix* the photograph used by the surgeon to restore Nelly's face and in *Gone Girl* the flashbacks pertaining to Amy's diary entries exposed as fictions deliberately produced to lead the police astray. In all cases, the woman who is repeatedly transformed into an image of herself references the cinematic image.

On the story level, furthermore, this self-reflexivity draws attention to the fact that the heroes are in love not with an actual woman but a role she is performing—be this the reserved Madeleine haunted by her predecessor "Mad Carlotta," the unnerved Nelly traumatized by her camp experience or Amy's "cool girl" thwarted in her sense of self-perfection. By debunking the presence of these three heroines on screen as an artifice, aimed at duping the hero, each film deliberately challenges the very magic of transformation it deploys so as to captivate the audience. We are meant to take note that the woman who returns from the dead is not who she pretends to be, even while we are drawn into the charismatic force of her cinematic presence. In her impersonation of a woman, resuscitated from the dead, each heroine thus not only plays to the desire of the hero but, in that she brings the past with her, she also functions as an embodiment of genre memory. Her appearance *again* on screen is pointedly layered; it has accrued meaning, recalling her previous appearance as well as the images (the painting, the photograph, the diary self) her impersonation gave shape to. And yet, drawing attention to the artifice of her recreated cinematic image as a comment on the fact that she was, from the start, nothing other than a screen for her lover, first and foremost brings into play the question of his response once he is forced to acknowledge his own willful self-deception.

At stake in my reading these films as a series is, thus, the shift they perform as they accrue an ever more dense genre layer. While a superficial taxonomy would declare all three to be psycho-thrillers, the narrative resolutions they offer can as fruitfully be seen in relation to traditional literary genres, playing with an uncanny interface between melodramatic romance and tragedy. In order to elaborate on this interplay, it is, however, necessary to delineate the theoretical interest I bring to rethinking genre takes its cue from the intermedial conversation Stanley Cavell proposes when, in *Pursuits of Happiness*, he argues that the comedy of remarriage not only constitutes a particular genre within classic Hollywood but also emerges as "an inheritor of the preoccupations and discoveries of Shakespearean romantic comedy" (1981, 1). Given that his conception of overcoming divorce in remarriage is predicated on a miraculous metamorphosis of death and survival, he finds a precedent for this narrative structure in *The Winter's Tale*. If, in turn, Shakespeare's translation into the medium of Hollywood film is the lynchpin of the genre he proposes, the seminal role cultural memory plays refers to Cavell's specific sense of an inheritance earned by the American films. Although he tracks the resurfacing of a Shakespearean dramatic structure in classic Hollywood, he is not interested in writing the history of the comedy of remarriage. Rather, at issue for him is the way this genre constitutes a particular direction of responses to problematics established by and thus inherited from Shakespeare's dramatic texts.

In other words, while thematic features and their variations allow him to claim that a set of films constitutes a particular facet of the romantic comedy—a couple can come together *again* only once the hero's understanding of the heroine has been transformed owing to her own achievement of self-knowledge—at issue for him is proposing the logic of this set, "The idea is that the members of a genre share the inheritance of certain conditions, procedures and subjects and goals of composition," with each representing a study of these conditions, "something I think of as bearing the responsibility of the inheritance" (Cavell 1981, 28). Along with common thematic features, important for the proposition that they constitute a genre is the way that, read as a series, they also bring what is distinct about each into focus. As each film investigates the particular set of preoccupations and discoveries it inherits from the Shakespearean imaginary, it makes these more explicit even while doing so in a manner that also distinguishes each film from the other films in the set. Thought of as a constant process of rendering certain inherited conditions ever more explicit, with each new film making their relation to the concerns they shape more explicit as well, the critical gaze loops back and forth among the members of the genre as these, in turn, can be seen reflecting upon one another and their relation to each other.

Cavell, having discovered a resurfacing of Shakespeare in classic Hollywood, thus conceives this shared common inheritance (and in this he agrees with the ritual function Schatz attributes to popular cinema) in terms of myth: "The members of a genre will be interpretations of it," he argues, "revisions of it, which will also make them interpretations of one another. The myth must be constructed, or reconstructed from the members of the genre that inherits it, and since the genre is, as far as we know, unsaturated, the construction of the myth must remain provisional" (1981, 31). For my own discussion of Hitchcock's *Vertigo* and its interpretation and revision by *Phoenix* and *Gone Girl*, I take from Cavell the idea that in each case certain preoccupations of *The Winter's Tale* resurface as well, much as my own rethinking of genre also hinges on the significance of proposing a complex relation: On the one hand the relation that unfolds among the three films once they are seen as members of a set and, on the other, the relation the three cinematic texts can be shown to entertain with Shakespeare's late romance. While all three share a thematic concern, namely the possible reconciliation of a couple based on a metamorphosis of death and revival, the point of reading them as a generic series is to ask why only *Gone Girl* ends in remarriage while reconciliation both in *Vertigo* and *Phoenix* proves impossible. To say that they, nevertheless, make their own claim to a Shakespearean inheritance, thus brings into play the genre against which his late romances define themselves, namely tragedy.

Let us recall the mythic restoration which the remarriage of Leontes and Hermione at the end of *The Winter's Tale* affords is not only predicated on a theatricalized reanimation of the statue of the dead woman on the part of her trusted servant Paulina, but also on the fact that we recognize in this narrative resolution a counterfigure to the staged corpse of Desdemona in the closing scene of *Othello*. Indeed, if the successful resurrection of Hermione is predicated both on her husband's conviction that his jealousy caused her death as well as on the mournful self-questioning this recognition entails, the marriage regained draws its affective force from our remembering that Desdemona was not afforded such a second chance at life. The dramaturgic discovery in Shakespeare's late romance I propose as being significant for *Vertigo* and its revisions is not only the restorative desire revolving around the recreation of a woman out of death—on the part of the hero and the cinematic mise-en-scène—but also the challenge to a tragic imperative it performs. In contrast to Shakespeare's dark comedy, *Much Ado About Nothing*, which also ends in the reanimation of a woman declared dead in response to her lover's accusations of infidelity, and fatality is not prevented in the last minute. Rather, the magical redemption *The Winter's Tale* affords is predicated on the wager that having acknowledged Hermione's death to be the logical consequence of her husband's desire, the play's dramatic resolution calls upon us to notice the difference between consciously repudiating tragedy rather than merely forestalling it.

How, then, is the interplay between a tragic imperative and its repudiation refigured in *Vertigo* and its revisions? In Hitchcock's psycho-thriller, Scottie's response to discovering that Judy and Madeleine are identical sets the lethal repetition compulsion underwriting his necrophilic desire into motion again. Having dragged her to the scene of the crime, she performs the fall she had initially been witness to, with her dead body sprawled across the church roof, repeating but also putting closure on the series of feminine corpses she had incorporated into her impersonation. In *Phoenix*, the moment of anagnoresis leads to Nelly's walking out on her awestruck husband, while in *Gone Girl* this recognition opens up the possibility of remarriage which *The Winter's Tale* proposes, albeit in a far more cynical tone. I propose thinking these three responses in terms of the genre transformation they perform because they touch on a compelling point in Cavell's theory of genre. The source of hope in Shakespearean tragedy (and thus its ability to transform into romance), he suggests, resides in the fact that the fatality it puts on display is *not* unavoidable. According to Cavell, the reason consequences furiously hunt down the characters is because—and this is precisely the argument of *Vertigo*—they go on doing the very thing that produced these consequences in the first place. A challenge to the tragic impulse, in turn, entails "the courage, or plain prudence, to see and to stop" (1987, 81). The distinction between tragedy and romance is that while the former insists that fate is inescapable, the latter can imagine a move beyond inevitability.

The discovery of *The Winter's Tale*, one might say, is that restitution is sustainable when the very repetition compulsion on which the return of the heroine from the realm of death is predicated, can be interrupted, perhaps abandoned altogether, perhaps rechanneled. For it not to require any further repetition of fatality—as in *Vertigo*—the woman who has returned must be conceived as significantly different from the woman lost, which is to say different from her reduction to an artifice produced to screen the hero's narcissistic desire. *The Winter's Tale* further proposes that what initially sustains the possibility of tragedy is Leontes's refusal to see his wife as distinct from the image he has of her, which is to say the fantasy of infidelity he, for whatever reason, feels compelled to ascribe to her. To avert tragedy, in turn, hinges not only on the heroine's ability to make herself intelligible in her singular separateness but also on a willingness, on the part of the hero, to see and listen to this challenge. Indeed, if, as Cavell argues, tragedy "grows from fortunes we choose to interpret, to accept as inevitable" (1987, 89), then *The Winter's Tale* calls upon us to ask what Leontes initially gains by making this choice, inflicting suffering upon Hermione, and, in turn, causing both her disappearance from the world and his own long period of grief and mourning. The magic of Hermione's reanimation, redeeming from death, as it does the wife Leontes had cast aside, allows the play to discover a way to avert the inevitability of loss.

If then, in Shakespearean romance, hope involves the repudiation of a fatalistic interpretation, trusting instead in the idea that metamorphosis of death and life is possible, the fact that, in tragedy, this turn is not taken does not mean it isn't an option. The refusal is a choice Shakespeare's characters are shown to make. As Cavell insists, the death this genre conventionally requires "is inflicted, it need not have happened. So a radical contingency haunts every story of tragedy." At the same time, precisely because no one seems to know what could have prevented death, "a radical necessity haunts every story of tragedy." Death strikes us as necessary "but we do not know why; avoidable, but we do not know how" (1987, 112). *The Winter's Tale* offers its response to the conundrum found in *Othello* by harnessing the spirit of contingency. If death need not have happened, then Leontes's sustained period of mourning, filled with critical introspection, can undo the ill suspicion that proved tantamount to "killing" his wife by virtue of his false accusation. Significantly, the woman whose statue is reanimated may resemble Hermione, but she, too, has been transformed by the wide gap of time since the couple was first separated. The point is not only that Leontes can claim his wife *again*, but that she accepts the repudiation of his previous decision to declare her infidelity as inevitable. The stage is set for recognition of mutual humanness.

What the resurfacing of Shakespeare's late romance in Hitchcock's *Vertigo* draws our attention to, in turn, is the fact that this possibility is refused. Given that, here too, the couple is reunited, why can Scottie not live with the knowledge that Judy has an agency of her own regarding the necrophilic fantasy he forces her to perform? What satisfaction does his blindness to her being a separate human being afford? While the production of Judy's dead body undoes the metamorphosis of death and revival, read in conjunction with *The Winter's Tale*, we are called upon to ask: Why does Hitchcock so blatantly stage the privileging of a tragic interpretation that renders consequences unavoidable? Why does the death of a beautiful woman emerge here as both a psychic necessity for the necrophiliac lover and an aesthetic necessity for the director, whose cameo appearance introduces us to the original murderer? (Bronfen 1992). And how does the redemptive interpretation found in Shakespeare's late romance resurface in the films that interpret his revision of *Winter's Tale*? Why does *Phoenix* refuse the restitution of a marriage regained, although Nelly succeeds where Judy fails, forcing her husband to see her for what she is, the wife he betrayed twice over? Why, in turn, does *Gone Girl* revise the psycho-thriller, by refusing a tragic interpretation at all costs?

By reading this set of films in relation to the way each refigures the thematic concern they inherit from Shakespeare, I am not interested in making a claim to any concrete intertextual borrowing on the part of the three directors. Reformulating Cavell's notion of genre, my own theoretic interest is that, having discovered a shared thematic concern among all four texts, what the consequences of this relation for a critical engagement with them might be. While the cross-mapping I am proposing is predicated on structural and thematic analogies, the heuristic challenge is to isolate what makes each distinct. By relating similar events in different texts to each other, the murky interface between tragedy and romance can be drawn into focus. My theoretical interest, in other words, is not to reduce the preoccupations of *Vertigo* and its revisions to those of *The Winter's Tale*. Rather, given the discovery of their genre relation, the question becomes why the concerns of *Vertigo* are worked out in a particular shape and those in *Phoenix* and *Gone Girl* in another. Indeed, what are the concerns of each of the films and what shapes do they take?

The point of conjunction, of course, is the moment when Paulina calls out her stage directions to Hermione, "tis time. Descend. Be stone no more. Approach./ Strike all that look upon with marvel. Come,/ I'll fill your grave up. Stir. Nay, come away. Bequeath to death your numbness, for from him/ Dear life redeems you" (5.3.99–103). In Hitchcock's interpretation of this scene of resuscitation, Judy, finally ceding to Scottie's desire that there be absolutely no difference between her impersonation of Madeleine and the image of her he has preserved in his mind, goes into the bathroom of her apartment to adjust the final discrepancies. In contrast to Hermione, she needs no external stage directions, when, cast in an eerie green fog, she once again steps across the threshold and, now a perfect replica of the dead woman, walks toward him with the same cautious stride she had commanded before her forestalled fall. Hitchcock's irony, debunking the very metamorphosis he stages, consists in the fact that Kim Novak's performance of the resuscitated Madeleine emphasizes a contained, statuary walk, in stark contrast to Judy's vitality.

Then, to indicate that the couple has magically re-entered a heterochronic space, suspending them between past and present, the room disappears as they embrace and, as a rear projection, we see the stable in front of the Spanish mission again, where Scottie held Madeleine in his arms for the last time. Significantly, Scottie notices the phantasmagoric change in scenery as the camera begins a 360-degree pan around the couple. For a moment, he looks up before returning to the passionate embrace, at the culmination of which the couple is back in Judy's hotel room. The fulfillment of his fantasy is staged as a gap in time, in which the past screens out the present, not—as in *Winter's Tale*—a closure of this gap. The fact that Judy remains oblivious to the hallucinatory change in décor, in turn, suggests that we are meant to recognize her as a skilled impersonator, drawing her deluded lover into the repetition of a fantasy scene, in which she, once more, directs his desires. While Scottie wants to be duped by the illusion that a dead lover can return to him, she knows this to be pure theater. At the same time, given that the mise-en-scène positions Judy/Madeleine at the center of the 360-degree turn and pinned down energetically by Scottie's embrace, it also anticipates the tragic interpretation of inevitability that will accompany her necrophilic lover's anagnoresis.

The fact that, following upon this embrace, she asks him to help her fasten the necklace he is sure to recognize from the portrait in the museum, with both standing in front of a mirror to boot, could well be read not as an unconscious slip but rather a dexterous sleight of hand. In the serial production of this ideal woman, for whom there is no referent, Judy seems to be unintelligible as a separate person. By placing the telltale necklace around her neck, she compels Scottie to recognize her separateness from his fantasy screen woman. Her appeal is that he might love her for what she is, an impersonator consciously and willingly playing to his desire. If this possibility serves as the source of hope in *Vertigo*, the fact that Scottie chooses instead to read his fortune as tragic is all the more poignant. His own actions condemn him to reassume the position of mourning lover. In his preferred interpretation, the production of the feminine corpse can be the only logical conclusion to a series of feminine impersonations in which the heroine, even while accruing meaning, only always existed as an embodied image. To insist that her own fate can only be a repetition of the woman she impersonated pointedly counteracts the agency ascribed to Judy. Given that her attempt at undermining the fatal repetition compulsion proves futile, attention is drawn to the fact that within this particular logic, in which (like Hermione) she is initially redeemed from death, she cannot be heard. In contrast to Shakespearean romance, what is ultimately regained is her loss to death.

One might read Scottie's violent response as a refusal to accept that he is not the mastermind behind a scene of resurrection and instead merely repeating the recreation of a woman that Elster had already stage-managed to dupe him. Or one might read his insistence that he must reenact the crime, regardless of all consequences, as a reflection on the logic of cold war culture, in which inevitability was the code for justifying a variety of potentially fatal political choices. Or one might bring Hitchcock's reflection about the deadly force of the cinematic image into play, so that the inexorable drive towards a repeated production of female corpses on the part of his hero, marked as such, adds ironic distance to the psycho-thriller genre. In all cases, the challenge which the final image of Judy's dead body offers is one that underscores the seductive charm of a tragic interpretation of fortunes precisely because this emerges as a necessity that could have been avoided.

In *Phoenix*, the moment of magical resuscitation repeats and revises Hitchcock's mise-en-scène. As in *Vertigo*, Nelly has consented to be part of Johnny's makeover and, having moved into his cellar apartment, shown herself not only capable of imitating the handwriting of her former self but also walking the way he remembers Nelly to have done, ironically in the shoes he once bought her in Paris. Like Judy, she resists certain aspects of the look he is imposing on her, saying that for her to return from a concentration camp wearing an elegant red dress and fancy shoes wouldn't be plausible. Johnny's retort that people avert their gaze from those who, returning from the East, bear traces of their suffering, is part of Petzold's ideological argument regarding a collective repression of guilt in postwar Germany. Johnny invokes denial when he assures her that they will only succeed in convincing others that she is really Nelly if she puts on exactly the same happy mien that she was known for before the war. Despite her sustained uncertainty, Nelly ultimately gives in to all of Johnny's directions because it was the image she had of him that kept her alive in the camp. She is convinced that she needs his gaze to assure her that she has survived, that she is, indeed, still alive, that she can continue to exist.

Nelly's transformation, thus, involves a far more intersubjective act than is the case in *Vertigo*. In contrast to Judy, she is precisely not in it for the money, but rather, given her emotional dependence on Johnny, she is the willing accomplice in a confidence game that touches above all on the ethics of forgiveness. If the metamorphosis they engender together confirms the avoidance of knowledge both crave, what *Phoenix* takes from *The Winter's Tale*, in turn, is that by redeeming the heroine from death, the man responsible for her disappearance from the world of the living is to be redeemed from his sin. Leonte's performative speech act of "killing" Hermione by having her imprisoned for an imaginary infidelity runs analogous to Johnny's performative killing when, after having divorced Nelly, he denounced her to the Gestapo. Significant for the difference in shape this concern takes is that in the wide gap of time since they were separated, he has felt no remorse.

As in *Vertigo*, the final touch in the metamorphosis involves Nelly coloring her hair and putting on makeup in precisely the same way she used to. Upon returning to the cellar apartment in anticipation of her change, Johnny, also, is taken by surprise at the perfect resemblance. The camera tarries with him, drawing attention to his confusion while Nelly begins walking toward him. Only after she has asked him, with fervor in her voice, whether he recognizes her, does the reverse shot reveal her to us as well. Nelly is now the one who, like Scottie, yearns for the embrace, seeking to undo the gap of time. Johnny, however, denies her (and himself) this kiss, and instead chooses to break the spell. Rather than conceiving the proximity she desires as a way of transcending guilt, Johnny perceives it as a threat to the successful refusal of his own guilt. Recognizing her is precisely what, at all costs, he tries to avoid.

As in *Vertigo*, the narrative resolution hinges on how he will respond when this repudiation of knowledge can no longer be sustained. During the party he has organized for a small group of friends in celebration of what they are staging as her return on a train from the East, Nelly asks him to accompany her on the piano. Only now is he forced to notice the one thing unique about his wife—the timbre of her singing voice. She continues with her song even after he stops playing, having noticed the number tattooed on her left arm. The fact that Nelly has allowed the sleeve of her dress to slip up is unequivocally intentional—exposing herself in a way he cannot refuse to see. For her, as for Hermione, the gap between her former and her current self is literally written on her body. Yet, while this anagnoresis makes a tragic interpretation impossible, *Phoenix* also refuses the magic of redemption. Nelly suddenly breaks off her song and departs, leaving her dumbstruck husband behind. Having educated him, she has the courage, or plain prudence, to leave the scene of his macabre resuscitation. As she moves further and further into the vanishing point of the image, her figure becomes ever more blurred, until, once she has fully disappeared from sight, the screen goes black. What we get is a waking up, not only from the couple's shared fantasy (her hope to restore love after betrayal, his to obliterate a love he betrayed) but we also awaken from the illusion of the cinematic image. The only redemption *Phoenix* can give shape to is that of a definitive separation. While no one must die, impossible also is the hope Leontes expressed to Hermione at the end of *The Winter's Tale*, that they might "leisurely/ Each one demand and answer to his part/ Performed in this wide gap of time since first/ We were dissever'd" (5.5.153–56). In the context of postwar Germany, to have survived means to refuse the illusion that any redemption for those guilty of betrayal should be possible.

In proposing *Gone Girl* as yet a further revision of *Vertigo*, my theoretical interest turns to how, in the media saturation of the early twenty-first century, our cultural fascination with feminine self-sacrifice can be recast as the source for feminine empowerment given that, when Amy returns from her presumed death, she flaunts her wounds. After having staged her own murder, she ended up in the beach house of a former lover. There, while watching Nick on TV, confessing his remorse and pleading with her to come home, she is as taken in by his desire for her resuscitation as her predecessors. The difference, however, is that Fincher's mise-en-scène leaves no doubt that they both recognize this media stunt, organized to feed the hunger of the audience that has become deeply invested in the outcome of her story, to be a con game they can share. Amy will mutilate herself so as to claim that, having been raped by the man who has been sheltering her, she was justified in killing him in self-defense. Reversing the logic of *Phoenix*, the reporters who have been camping outside the home of the Dunne's take notice of Amy precisely because, as she emerges from her car, her body is covered in blood. Having pointedly staggered toward her husband, as bewildered as his predecessors, she throws herself into an embrace he cannot avoid even while he does not desire it. While the cameras frantically record this reunion, he can only whisper into her ear, "you fucking bitch," prompting her, in turn, to faint in his arms. So as to underscore the theatricality of this scene of feminine resurrection, the camera moves into a counter-tilt.

Shakespeare's *The Winter's Tale* thus resurfaces in this film in the way it casts Amy's return as the reanimation not of a statue but rather of all the still photographs of her that the news coverage had been circulating while the search was still on. And yet, if in *Gone Girl* everything also hinges on a metamorphosis of death and life, this transformation offers a poignant deconstruction of the gendering of the formula. As in *Vertigo*, a flashback reveals Amy's cunning ploy, so that the narrative resolution can focus not on what happens to her, but on how Nick will respond once he discovers her dupery. Her voiceover begins by declaring, "I am so much happier now that I am dead. Technically missing, soon to be presumed dead, gone." While we see her driving along a highway, tossing her writing tools out the window, she recasts Hermione's accusation: "Nick Dunne took my pride, and my dignity and my hope and my money. He took and took and took from me until I no longer existed. That's murder. Let the punishment fit the crime." In contrast to the other flashbacks, supporting the immaculate image of "cool girl" she had constructed for herself, this one offers a satiric revision of the production of the feminine corpse, in that it flaunts the meticulous planning that went into faking her murder. This recollection ironically segues into an image anticipating her death by drowning, as she finishes her narrative of justified retribution: "when they find my body they will know Nick Dunne dumped his beloved like garbage and she floated down past all the other abused, unwanted inconvenient women." Her proleptic vision, of course, plays to genre memory, so that implicitly she is also floating past all the other feminine corpses of the psycho-thriller genre, including Judy, sprawled out on the church roof.

The seminal revision that *Gone Girl* offers of the feminine corpse as a trope for the cinematic image thus consists in the fact that Amy is not only the one to come up with and execute her imaginary killing. Rather, her voiceover commentary underscores the control she has over this multiply the refracted visual production of her own dead body. As the sole author of her presumed demise, she not only redeems herself from death but, in so doing, also redeems Nick from the law such that she assures his complete dependence on her. Her excessive empowerment is further underscored in that she is reanimated as a genre hybrid: Her parents' Amazing Amy fused with the scheming con woman, who resumes her role as "cool girl" by turning the logic of the psycho-thriller into that of the comedy of remarriage orchestrated entirely on her own terms. Because she knows how to control the publicly disseminated images of herself, she has the media on her side. The reversal of the logic proposed by *Vertigo* is such that she is the one to compel her husband to participate in this dark restitution. In that he has no choice but to consent we also, however, find a revision of Scottie's refusal to acknowledge Judy's part in the resurrection drama they performed together, causing her to fall to her death. By taking both her death and her reanimation into her own hands, Amy is not only able to make herself intelligible to the man who had cheated on her but has also forged a situation in which he can do nothing other than accept this challenge. Nick cannot but see his wife for what she is in all her cruel yet ethically justified manipulation. She will not let him disappear and, instead, insists on a TV interview in which they publicly reconfirm their marriage vows. There is an inevitability in the narrative resolution that *Gone Girl* offers but not of a tragic kind. Precisely because he has no choice, it lies in his power to accept this shared confidence game, in which both "can demand and answer to their part," as Leontes proposes. Fully cognizant of the impersonation, having mutually consented to it, they have achieved the conversation that will sustain them as a couple.

By refusing an avoidance of tragedy, *Vertigo* offers an interpretation of *Winter's Tale* in which the hero persists through to the end in not seeing the heroine, while we are privy to this blindness. In *Phoenix*, an aversion of tragedy, based on the fact that the hero is finally forced to acknowledge the separateness of the woman he thought was his creation, in turn, is tantamount to refusing restitution. What is renewed to life, along with Nelly's recreated face, is a knowledge of past suffering that will not be caught in an image. If both films play through the lethal aspect of the cinematic image, Hitchcock's sleight of hand is to celebrate what he also discloses, allowing all his magic to culminate in the shot of a final female corpse, while Petzold's pathos is to move toward a zero point of cinematic phantasmagoria. Fincher's comedy of remarriage, in turn, proposes that an avoidance of tragedy is predicated on a mutual recognition involving a rhetoric of denial. His couple knows that their relation is based on images they project *on*, and roles they play *for* each other.

If each of these films reshapes its responses to preoccupations voiced in Shakespeare's *Winter's Tale* by readjusting the formula, what my cross-mapping sought to perform is that, by reading these texts as a series, my own critical commentary loops back and forth between the Shakespearean romance and its resurfacing in popular cinema. The theoretic aim is to open up a relation among different texts even while showing the distinction with which each addressed a shared problematic. The transformation of the heroine, her metamorphosis of death and life, and as such her equation with the cinematic image, emerges as the lynchpin for a discussion of the psycho-thriller as a genre that can either challenge or give in to a tragic imperative. Given that the heroine's metamorphosis also emerges as a trope for genre memory, the resolutions discovered not only offer a multifarious response to the question of feminine agency within this logic, ranging from self-sacrifice or deliberate disappearance to taking control of the very images that control one. Invariably, to factor genre memory into a discussion of the adaptability of genre sheds new light on the preoccupations and discoveries of *The Winter's Tale* as well, transformed as it is in the process of its cinematic reformulation.

Bibliography

Altman, Rick. 1987. *The American Film Musical.* Bloomington: Indiana University Press.

Bronfen, Elisabeth. 1992. *Over Her Dead Body. Death, Femininity and the Aesthetic.* Manchester: Manchester University Press.

———. 2009. *Crossmappings. Essays zur visuellen Kultur.* Zürich: Scheidegger und Spiess.

———. 2012. *Specters of War. Hollywood's Engagement with Military Conflict.* New Brunswick, NJ: Rutgers University Press.

Burgoyne, Robert. 2009. *Crossmappings. Essays zur visuellen Kultur.* Zürich: Scheidegger und Spiess.

———. 2010. *Film Nation. Hollywood Looks at U.S. History.* Revised Edition. Minneapolis: Minnesota University Press.

Cavell, Stanley. 1981. *Pursuits of Happiness. The Hollywood Comedy of Remarriage.* Cambridge, MA: Harvard University Press.

———. 1987. "The Avoidance of Love: A Reading of King Lear." *Disowning Knowledge in Seven Plays of Shakespeare.* Updated Edition. Cambridge: Cambridge University Press.

Cook, Pam, and Mieke Bernink. 1999. *The Cinema Book*, 2nd ed. London: BFI.

Derrida, Jacques. 1980. "The Law of Genre." *Glyph* 7: 202–32.

Grant, Barry Keith. 1986. *Film Genre Reader.* Austin: University of Texas Press.

Morson, Gary Saul, and Caryl Emerson. 1990. *Mikhail Bakhtin. Creation of a Prosaics.* Stanford: Stanford University Press.

Neale, Steve. 1990. "Questions of Genre." *Screen* 31, no. 1.

———. 2000. *Genre and Hollywood.* London: Routledge.

Ryall, Tom. 1998. "Genre and Hollywood." In *The Oxford Guide to Film Studies*, edited by John Hill and Pamela Church Gibson. Oxford: Oxford University Press.

Schatz, Tom. 1981. *Hollywood Genres: Formulas, Film-making, and the Studio System.* New York: Random House.

Filmography

Gone Girl (2014). Dir. David Fincher
Phoenix (2014). Dir. Christian Petzold
Vertigo (1958). Dir. Alfred Hitchcock

Chapter Twelve

DIGITAL TECHNOLOGIES AND THE END(S) OF FILM THEORY

Trond Lundemo

For well over two decades, film studies has posed the question as to what the conversion to digital has meant for cinema. The answers have ranged from proclamations of the end, or in a more anthropomorphic phrasing, the 'death' of cinema, to assertions of the resilience of cinema in digital code. Twenty years ago, but with lingering prescience, Thomas Elsaesser summed this up in saying that cinema 'will remain the same, and it will be utterly different' (Elsaesser 1998, 204). The digital has brought about pervasive changes in shooting, editing, distribution and marketing as well as screening contexts. Still, 35mm film remains the reference standard for image resolution, and there is an astounding resilience of the classical mode of editing, of the star and genre systems and the cinematic projection mode. The industry of cinema persists despite its apocalyptic detractors, because, as Elsaesser recently noted, it is '"business as usual," because, as usual, it was (a) business' (Elsaesser 2016, 184). Yet, digital technologies have radically reconfigured cinema, notably in the arena of inscription, screening and reception.

But if we instead ask exactly how digital technologies have changed film scholarship, the 'same but different' answer is less satisfying. Even harder to answer is the question of how the digital has impacted film theory. Some strands of cognitivist and reception theory may have remained the same, insofar as moving images engage people, and induce feelings and emotions and create meaning according to similar cues and schemata as before. But the ontologies of cinema have changed in every way. Film theory today asks not only 'What is Cinema?', but also 'where' and 'when' is cinema (Hagener 2008; Hediger 2012). The proliferation of screens and the near-ubiquity of moving images, with all the promises of an accrued relevance of film theory this should entail, has instead created a crisis where an entire discipline seems to have lost its compass. One indication of this reconfigured territory of film theory is found in the hurried renaming of film studies departments and organizations into different conjunctive alliances: the largest international association of screen studies, Society of Cinema Studies (SCS), became the Society of Film and Media Studies (SCMS) in 2002 and the NECS quickly renamed itself European Network for Cinema and Media Studies (but keeping the old acronym) after it was formed in 2006. Film studies departments all over the world have had to print new business cards during the last decades. Their names now carry conjunctions, most often 'film and media' or 'cinema and culture'. These renaming gestures may often be motivated by extradisciplinary measures, such as the implementation of corporate structures in universities, but the result seems to be the same: film scholars and students are no longer certain of what 'film' or 'cinema' means.

Where the disciplinary boundaries of film studies may have been challenged, digital technologies announce possible renewal and renovation. In this sense, the digital turn has posed more fundamental challenges to cinema studies than it has to scholarship in other arts and media: texts are produced and disseminated in ways very different than before the computer, and music is composed, recorded, arranged and listened to with very different tools – yet there are few discussions about the 'end' of music or literature. There are of course obvious reasons for this, if only because the end of the nineteenth century witnessed a technological framement defining the new medium. For this reason, its demise is countenanced where the context in which it was brought to life has given way to another of a very different character. Critics and theorists tolled the knell at fairly regular intervals: André Gaudreault and Philippe Marion recently identified eight ways in which cinema has 'died' throughout its history (Gaudreault and Marion 2015). In spite of or because of this, film studies has often pronounced itself to be the best horizon from which to approach issues of digital media. However, film theory has so far offered little evidence to hold up this claim.

Given how digital technologies have borne impact upon film theory, now manifest, two recent orientations are worth considering. On the one hand, film theory has found it necessary to widen its scope and approach different kinds of screens and venues for the display of moving images. This is, of course, necessary in order to remain relevant for the contemporary development of media environments, and I will return to some of the responses to this threat of obsolescence or unemployment later. On the other hand, digital technologies have prompted careful rereadings of classical and marginalized film theory, turning theory itself into a historical object. If we don't know what (nor when or where) cinema is any longer, then we also don't know what film theory is. This retrospective orientation may be seen as a defensive strategy, as it allows us to speak about film theory when we still (believed we) knew what it was.

However, the ongoing publication of previously unavailable or untranslated texts by Hugo Munsterberg, Sergei Eisenstein, André Bazin, Jean Epstein and Christian Metz, often together with new critical essays, are not signs of a primarily regressive attitude. To be fair, most of these volumes aim at excavating forgotten and neglected dimensions of classical texts and rediscovering earlier theoretical endeavours at a time when we believed that we knew what cinema was – for a time when we don't know this any longer. Furthermore, rereading Eisenstein or Bazin may serve not to establish what cinema *was*, but rather to destabilize its ontology. Just as the current death of cinema spurred Gaudreault and Marion to historicize its many deaths throughout history, today's ontological crisis reveals that Bazin and Eisenstein were not so sure what cinema was either: why else ask 'What is cinema?' The current retrospective trend is less about assessing a relatively stable model of classical cinema than about reconnecting with film theory at a time it was itself engaged in processes of reconfiguring cinema during media transitions.

Eisenstein and Bazin were often engaged in identifying cinema among other arts and as such part of a comparative aesthetics orientation of film theory, as Etienne Souriau phrased it (Souriau 1952, 113). Especially Eisenstein's later works trace montage as a universal principle throughout art history, where cinematic specificity resides in the ability to synthesize and transcend the boundaries of spatial and temporal art forms (Eisenstein 1991; 2016). Bazin identifies photographic and cinematic ontology in the automatic and mechanical 'transfer of reality', which is where cinema breaks off from other arts (Bazin 1958). The texts become new in the different media context of the digital and allow for an excavation of marginalized modes of thinking and forgotten passages. The retrospective tendency aims, for this reason, at rereading theoretical approaches to media configurations of the past in the light of how the digital engages a reconsideration of the history of the seventh art. The current new media have spurred an archaeology of media reconfigurations.

Media Archaeology

What does it mean to say that digital technologies have led film theory into an archaeological approach? Media archaeology is a notoriously fragmented and diverse field of studies, on the verge of becoming a floating signifier in contemporary media studies. Jussi Parikka and Erkki Huhtamo have shown how different the approaches under this label can be, and range from the excavation of marginal, forgotten and even imaginary technologies to the attempts at establishing a coherent disciplinary framework (Huhtamo and Parikka 2011; Parikka 2012). This multiplicity of orientations may indeed be the strength of media archaeology, as claimed by Parikka and Huhtamo, as it is heterogeneous and non-normative, a travelling discipline straddling existing disciplinary boundaries. Thomas Elsaesser suggests that media archaeology may serve the purpose of coming to terms with the crisis emerging with the radical changes of moving images with digital technologies and is, for this reason, a symptom and a form of therapy. On a more critical note, Elsaesser points out how the situation may also be understood as an ideology. Media archaeology offers a remedy to the sense of unstoppable change and innovation by promising to preserve the past, and thereby fetishizes memory and rescues material from obsolescence (Elsaesser 2016). In the very same act, however, archaeology confirms the ideological novelty and innovation of new media, by embracing the 'pastness' of the old. Furthermore, Elsaesser notes how media archaeology has located the many historical forms and technologies of analogue cinema within art galleries and exhibitions, thus withdrawing the medium from the formerly social milieu it has known (Elsaesser 2016, 206).

Elsaesser is right in pinpointing the potential preservationist aspects of media archaeology even if many adherents would point out that retrospection serves the aim of excavating potential, unrealised futures. It is also true that media archaeology has relegated moving image technologies to art institutions, or at least helped to turn analogue screenings into special events at cinematheques and festivals, as for instance, The Nitrate Picture Show festival at George Eastman Museum. Interestingly, these two observations would in turn warrant an 'archaeological' rereading of some of the canonical articles of film theory, for example, Bazin's understanding of cinema as a means to combat the passage of time through the trace of the past and Walter Benjamin's view of cinema as a transformation of the concept of art by embedding it in a popular context. However, as Elsaesser has claimed also on earlier occasions, the archaeological approach can be appreciated as a response to the rediscovery of early cinema and, no less, a critique of continuous and teleological models of film history (Elsaesser 2004).

The heterogeneous and diverse approaches of media archaeology attest to an attitude towards and a perspective on the past. Media archaeologists may be united in their critique of causal linear history and their dedication to material culture, but the theoretical underpinnings of different archaeological approaches are highly diverse. We are here at a similar position as the one outlined above: if we do not know what cinema is in the age of the digital, we do not really know what its symptom or remedy is either. However, within this heterogeneous and multifaceted field, among these methods, perspectives and practices, there are implicit or explicit theoretical positions that may tell us something about how digital media have affected film theory. I want to argue that there are two main, often opposing, strands of film theory responding to the challenge of the digital that may be outlined: one is more focused on the screen as interface and on spectator interaction, while the other is predominantly oriented towards the material conditions of media and the code level of information.

Screen Theory

British theorist Laura Mulvey has turned her attention from the interpellations of the spectator in an apparatus theory informed solely by the cinema theatre screening mode to issues of spectator interaction with digital screen interfaces in *Death 24x a Second* (2006). Mulvey identifies potentially liberating transgressions of the ideology of the sound and image in computer interfaces through freeze-frames, repetitions and slow motion. In a development starting with the television remote control, digital media facilitate a viewing process informed by individual choice and analysis. It must be asked, however, how much of a liberation and transgression these techniques really offer. The argument relies on the assumption that capitalism forms a stable background against which transgressive readings may unfold, when they may be exactly what capitalism in the digital age encourages. As Mary Ann Doane wrote in a review of Mulvey's book:

> Yet the acceleration and propagation of individualized ways of consuming images coincides with historically specific changes in commodity capitalism. Commodification now works through the promotion of notions of personal style and lifestyle, and training in consumerism masquerades as the proliferation of choices provided by 'interactivity'. Commodification no longer strives to produce homogeneity – in its objects and its consumers – but thrives on heterogeneity. (Doane 2007)

Doane's comment has far-ranging ramifications for any film theoretical attempt at equating spectatorial individual choice and interactivity in digital media with a liberated, transgressive or subversive spectatorship. The interpellations of the spectator in old screen theory may be present, in very different forms, in the new screens. Mulvey frames her engagement with new spectatorial modes in digital media as a reconsideration of

Screen theory of the 1970s and is, as such, representative for a return to the history of film theory to understand digital media.

The arguably most ambitious account of a reconfiguration of screen culture in the view of digital media is that of Anne Friedberg. *The Virtual Window; From Alberti to Microsoft* (2006) departs from digital screens to reposition concepts of windows, frames and screens from renaissance theory and the camera obscura to architecture debates and computer discourses. Both an excavation of material culture and an analysis of theoretical discourses subtending the concepts of window, frame and the virtual, she also revisits Eisenstein's discussions of architecture as montage and Bazin's concept of the window. The development from the window focus of her previous study of early cinema, *Window Shopping* (1993), to the much wider approach to screens demanded by digital technologies is telling of a historical explosion of scope and orientation demanded by new media.

The vast historical scope of the study illustrates the differences between screen theory and code level inflections of the key concept of convergence. The interrelations between the discourse of the window and frame in painting and architecture and its developments in screen media as photography and cinema to computer windows form a concept of convergence where one form of screen persists as it is incorporated into new ones. Friedberg claims: 'Once seen as the paradigmatic twentieth-century medium, the "cinema" has become embedded in – or perhaps lost in – the new technologies that surround it. Cinema now merely forms an originary visual system for a complexly diverse set of "postcinematic" visualities' (Friedberg 2006, 6). These remediations entail ruptures and breaks, but the computer screen still embeds photography and film on a phenomenological level – so, if cinema seems 'surrounded' by new technologies, it persists in this new constellation. Friedberg develops the concept of convergence in a reading of Paul Virilio's work:

> Virilio's screen: Is it a cinema, television or computer screen? Does Virilio parse the media specificity of these screens, or does he subtly elide their differences? More importantly: in an era of technological convergence, does it matter? If Virilio does not theorize the technological differences between film, television, and the computer, it is because, for him, the screen remains in a metaphoric register, a virtual surface that overrides any specificities of its media formation. (Friedberg 2006, 183)

Friedberg certainly doesn't ignore the technological and material properties of different kinds of screens, but they all seem to converge and persist on the computer screen. However, as I will return to shortly, the material properties of film, print and music are radically different from binary code; the computer convincingly simulates these media as what Friedrich Kittler calls 'surface effects'. As we all know, there are no words, sounds or images transmitted through the internet or stored on computer hard drives and servers, but the data can be experienced as separate media when they are run on any given program. When software is missing or outdated, we are reminded of the ever-converting materialities of media.

The convergence perspective also informs Lev Manovich's 'An Archaeology of a Computer Screen' (1995). Manovich outlines a historical development departing from the classical screen of still pictures, which by the end of the nineteenth century is complemented by the subcategory of the dynamic screen of moving images. The dynamic screen, in turn, opens for the new subcategory of real-time screens, those of radar, live video and computer screens around World War II, which again are complemented by the multiple windows of the computer screen as well as the explosion of the screen in the visual field of virtual reality (VR). The divergence of screen types as subsets to the classical screen is also a process of convergence in Manovich's view because the classical and real-time screens persist on the computer screens. The surprising exception to the model is the dynamic screen, which Manovich sees as ending a hundred years later. While the decomposition of the screen in VR and its fragmentation in the computer screen supposedly ends the age of the moving image screen, it leaves the still and real-time screens intact. Manovich understands the computer screen as a historical subset to the classical and real-time screens, even if it may have surpassed its ancestors in its ubiquity. This is a model of convergence based on continuity through fragmentation and adaptation, where previous media are embedded in new ones.

Acknowledging Marshall McLuhan's (1964, 23) proposition that 'the content of any medium is always another medium', a convergence model also informs Jay David Bolter and Richard Grusin's highly influential Remediation concept (Bolter and Grusin 1999). Remediation depends on a double logic of immediacy and hypermediacy, of erasing the impression of mediation while at the same time highlighting it. New media remediate the old by claiming greater transparency, liveness or interactivity and, in the process, they exhibit the medium itself. Remediation is a process of convergence insofar as new media contain the old, but rather than forming an ontology of media, the concept aims at an understanding of the logic of interface design, repurposing of content and the representation of other media as a conceived kind of competition and rivalry in the marketing of new media (Bolter and Grusin 1999, 339). Bolter and Grusin's concept aims at highlighting the rhetorical and, to employ an unfashionable term, ideological aspects of the convergence myth. McLuhan's idea of content was that of the piece of meat thrown to the watchdog by the burglar, a way to divert attention from the true operations of media. This piece of meat is often swallowed whole in content-based models of convergence, as in Henry Jenkins's book *Convergence Culture*: 'By convergence, I mean the flow of content across multiple media platforms, the cooperation between multiple media industries and the migratory behaviour of media audiences who will go almost anywhere in search of the kinds of entertainment experiences they want' (Jenkins 2006, 2–3). As one of the main approaches to the challenge of the digital mentioned above, screen theory is often prone to analyse the frames and windows as well as the content of these frames from an experiential viewpoint and thus to construct lines of convergence and persistence from old media to the new. The other approach gives priority to the materiality and functions of media over content and human experience.

Code Level Theory

A very different model of media shift appears if one devotes attention to the code level of the medium. Friedrich Kittler in his seminal *Gramophone, Film, Typewriter* (1999, 1–2) refers to the opposite condition, that 'content' consists really only of surface effects, while technology itself determines the workings of media. In binary code, there is no convergence of media in the sense of continuity. In digitization of analogue materials, the material base of media is instead *converted*: the analogue is what the digital may promise to simulate, but what it by definition never actually contains. The three analogue media of Kittler's book title do not converge into one in the digital; they are instead substituted by something materially different, the multimedium of the computer. The singular form highlights how the analogue media do not persist as digital multimedia but instead is supplanted by a very different medium. The theory of the conversion of media into a multimedium, the computer, upholds the idea that the analogue fully gives way to the digital and advocates a view of a clean break in a historical process from the one to the other. In this sense, both convergence and conversion theories, or screen and code approaches, propose a model of historical continuity for media change: one through a melding of technologies and the other through an absolute break.

The conversion of media is perceived as going steadily and unavoidably in a one-way direction. This idea may come easily to the cinema spectator, who has experienced a shift from 35mm projection to digital cinema packages (DCPs) and a huge accessibility of film files on the internet during the last decade or so. It is however complicated when attention is drawn to the material conditions of the institutions that subtend the existence of film history: the archive. Any linear account of convergence or conversion conflates the various orders of media in our current archival logic because it disregards the role of the analogue within digital files. The analogue film archival holdings, for example, are not just transformed into digital files. The analogue is rather complemented with a digital alias for its use online and for searching materials, while the analogue remains in the archive as the potential origin of future digitisations of the material in higher resolution or a different format. This means that archival work has not drifted into the digital altogether – there is no clear-cut conversion or convergence in the archive. There are other terms that try to escape the conflated landscape of film archival territory, as outlined in the important book by Giovanna Fossati, *From Grain to Pixel: The Archival Life of Film in Transition* (Fossati 2010). Fossati argues that 'transition' is not a phase that will end in a final result but should be understood as an ever ongoing process reforming archival practice and theory (Fossati 2010, 132–40). 'Transition' still suggests that we are moving from one situation to another, especially with the 'from–to' development in her book title. Nevertheless, Fossati's work is invaluable as a nuanced attempt to theorise archival work noting that most restoration and preservation techniques of film archives are hybrids between analogue and digital.

Perhaps a better way to understand media reconfigurations in the digital age would be to think in terms of ongoing processes than lines of convergence or absolute breaks and ruptures. Analogue cinema deployed a certain *connectivity* between media, which is dominated by thermodynamic machines and de-centralised networks. With the digitization of images, the media connectivity changes. The regime of the digital promotes different kinds of correlations, cybernetic machines and distributed networks. The distribution of moving images is predominantly taking place through the interconnectibility between autonomous computers. In the film archive, however, one network of media is not simply displacing the other. The born-analogue films persist as analogue masters or originals in the archives, and they require that we devote attention to how they are connected to other media at the time of their production as well as in the time of their interconnection with digital files. For this reason, I argue, only to speak of a conversion of media into a digital convergence is insufficient. Rather, one needs to approach the new archival situation as a *superimposition* of two intersected technological networks. The task for contemporary film theory is to think about the various ways that these correlations are construed and how the configurations between photochemical film and bits are coded.

The Index

Screen theories tend to understand the emergence of digital technologies as a process of convergence where the experiential dimensions of cinema persist in the new screens, while theories focused on techniques of inscription and storage often draw a clear line of divide between the analogue and digital. D. N. Rodowick's *The Virtual Life of Film* (2007) is an ambitious film theoretical attempt at identifying the ontology of the digital moving image. By identifying an absolute ontological break between analogue cinema and the digital image, Rodowick adheres to the conversion thesis discussed above. In accounting for changes in screen culture, he adheres to the principle of *code*: 'Fully analogical devices reproduce or amplify a signal that is spatially isomorphic with their source in an act of transcription temporally continuous with that source' (Rodowick 2007, 114). While the analogue film can produce blocks of space-time through its material bond to the profilmic event, the digital image disrupts this spatio-temporal relationship because it is a transcoding of light instead of a transcription. 'Digital capture involves a discontinuous process of transcoding: converting a nonquantifiable image into an abstract or mathematical notation' (Rodowick 2007, 117). This disruption of the integrity of time and space allegedly results in an inability to express duration. Duration is lacking because the composite quality of digital code breaks the continuous temporal and spatial connection to reality. The pixel is an individually addressable, and consequently manipulable, unit of the digital image, which results in a fragmentation of the temporal unity of the image.

This main argument of the book is argued through an analysis of Alexander Sokurov's *Russian Ark* (2002), which boasts to be composed of one single shot through the halls of the Eremitage and through Russian history. The material condition for this 93-minute shot is that the visual information is registered on a hard disc instead of on film reels, which for Rodowick disrupts its temporal duration. He sees it as '30,000 digital events' prone to manipulation in post-production, rather than as one continuous shot as established in the analogue film (Rodowick 2007, 165). It follows from Rodowick's argument that there can hardly be any shots at all in digital cinema, as this principle must apply to a three-second shot as well as 93-minute one. The only proof of this lack of duration Rodowick presents is, however, his own sensation when watching the film. This way, he argues along the same lines of subjective experience of technology as Roland Barthes and André Bazin, for whom the indexical bond to reality is verified in the punctum and the awareness of mechanical transfer of reality, respectively.[1]

Based on technological transformations not immediately accessible to human perception, Rodowick's argument remains phenomenological. Even if the movement of the digital image in cinema relies on the same phi-phenomenon as an analogue movement, Rodowick claims that *Russian Ark* is rather composed of an infinite number of fragmented frames. His counter-example from analogue cinema is Jean Eustache's *Numéro zéro* (1971), where the filmmaker conducts a 110-minute talk with his grandmother in continuous time through alternating shots by two 16mm cameras, where the second takes over when the first is running out of film and where film reels are changed for the next shot. It is thus by definition not a single-shot film, but according to Rodowick, it presents the integrity of time in a way the digital image can never achieve. It remains to ask if this lack of duration in the digital also applies to the intermediary medium of analogue video or any kind of electronic image. After all, there is also fragmentation of images into parts and pixels when light information is transcribed on magnetic tape or transmitted to the pixels of the television screen. One could also ask if this fractured time applies to shooting only, or if any analogue film converted to a digital code in today's DCP restorations is robbed of its duration as well.

Since Rodowick's thesis doesn't embark on these technologies, let us just note that his argument rests on the concept of the loss of the index in digital code. This has arguably been the predominant argument on the technological level for understanding the advent of the digital image as a rupture with analogue film by proponents and detractors of the digital alike. For Lev Manovich, it is a liberation of creativity from the constraints of outer reality, while for Rodowick and many others, it is the loss of the existential bond to this reality.[2] Of course, the existential bond to the outer world was a determining feature of photography from its early reception. In cinema, the French cameraman Bolesłas Matuszewski argued already in 1898 that films are 'a new source of history' and that society should maintain film archives in order to 'relive the past' as it really was (Matuszewski 1898). At the same time, the automatic inscription of outer reality was for these reasons conceived as an impediment to the medium's artistic possibilities.

In 1867, Charles Sanders Peirce coins the concept of the index that finds renewed treatment among film theorists of semiotic bent. While film theory has equated the index with photography and its material bond with the profilmic world, Peirce's understanding of the index was much broader and included demonstrative pronouns ('this, that'), shifters and hailing gestures like the pointed finger as almost perfect indexical signs.[3] Peirce's theory relies heavily on the relations expressed by signs, and Firstness (icon), Secondness (index) and Thirdness (symbol) are key tenets of his philosophy. Peirce's elaboration of the index draws on these relations of secondness, like the deictic dimensions and the trace aspect of signs, but only the latter aspect has been truly influential in film theory. Rodowick relies on a more sophisticated concept of the index in his reflection, distinguishing as he does between transcription and transcoding. He applies the trace aspect of the index not only to spatial dimensions but also to time, or better, to duration.

Still, even if we restrict the concept to its trace aspect, there is no reason why films shot with a digital camera should represent a break with the indexical sign. There is still a trace of the light patterns in front of the lens in digital cameras, even if these are recorded through a different material process ('transcoding', in Rodowick's words). Light receptors transcoding a signal into binary code still maintain an existential bond with the profilmic, even if there is another, intervening process compared to the patterns of light formed on the emulsion of analogue film. It is not quite clear in Rodowick's account why this process of transcoding should disable the image to form a material relation to the passage of time in a shot. The potential for tampering with this trace after shooting should not logically be a decisive factor, especially because analogue film was subject to post-production through colour grading and optical printing processes. Film theory has often mistaken digital video for computer-generated imagery, which is of course not indexical in the sense that it is programmed in the computer and not a trace of light from an exterior source. However, even a borderline case between CGI and digital video such as motion capture animation retains an indexical aspect as it traces a movement photographically (i.e. through the inscription of light). Film theory is in need of more finely granulated distinctions between different digital techniques.

In view of these generalizations and conflations, Tom Gunning is perhaps right in his call for moving away from the index as a theoretical concept defining cinema (Gunning 2007). Gunning argues that movement is a better candidate as the ontological placeholder for cinema, be it analogue and digital. The index may be an arresting concept in many film theoretical accounts, insofar as it equates cinema with still photography. However, movement is also a strong force in the work of Bazin, for whom the shot is a modulated trace, 'a mummy of change'. As we know that Bazin never invoked the concept of the index, but wrote of a 'transfer of reality', his realist ontology is not disqualified by Gunning's call for a move to movement. As Phil Rosen has underlined, Bazin's ontological aesthetics is key for an approach to cinema as a historiographical medium (Rosen 2001, 1–42). Without moving away from Bazin, Gunning suggests the early, phenomenological writings of Christian Metz on the reality effect of cinema as a starting point for reconceptualising movement as a media-specific trait of cinema that is able to bridge the technological divide between the analogue and digital. Metz sees movement, instead of the index, as the key agent in cinema's impression of reality which turns the pastness of the photographic index into present tense (Metz 1974). The force of movement lies in its strong participatory effect on the spectator, which Gunning understands as a basic phenomenological ontology of analogue and digital live action as well as animation cinema. Inscribed in its very name, this (re-)appraisal of movement as the core phenomenon of cinema is of course not new. Moreover, those who think that cinema is over and that we are in a post-cinematic age now tend to speak of moving images. Under this all-embracing rubric, some critical distinctions get lost. Gunning aims exactly to bridge these divisions between types of screens and inscription processes when he opts for movement as the basic phenomenological property of cinema, but in doing so, he shifts from a code level argument (the index) to a screen perspective.

Still, at the code level, there are different modes of movement and temporalities that also beg theoretical analysis. In analogue cinema, movement is produced through the succession of entire individual frames passing through the projector at a set rate of frames per second and their shift from one to the other are masked by the shutter producing an alternation between light and darkness. In analogue or digital video, there are no full frames nor darkness, but images continually evolving over the screen. Most digital video, however, will proceed through compression of the information: Motion Picture Experts Group (MPEG) standards divide the frame into blocks of pixels, which are in turn updated only when a significant change in colour graduation above a given threshold compared to the previous frame appears.[4] The rest of the frame, where no significant change has taken place, is retransmitted as the same as the previous frame. For the sake of the economy of files, movement results from partial updates of sections of the image in all digital video that can be seen on personal computers, pads and phones, accessed on DVD, Blu-Ray or the internet. In digital cinema projection, each frame is updated in full, as the system allows for huge data quantities in JPEG compression.

By arguing for a theoretical attention to critical distinctions between modes of movement, I am not bringing the index back into the discussion, as the trace aspect accounts for an existential bond to the source of the image. Instead, it is necessary to address different principles of movement internal to the movement itself, rather than their relation to an exterior reality, as Rodowick does through the concept of duration. It may be asked why we should theorize different modes of movement, as long as the phenomenological movement is intact, as Gunning argues. The answer is that different modalities of movement come with different distributions of power that facilitate surveillance and biopolitical measures. The standards of compression depend on the mathematical access to each pixel in an image, which in turn enables searches in digital image databases through not only written but also iconic metadata. This automated pattern recognition allows for searching images through other images, a process which has been implemented in biometric surveillance systems at airports, private corporations and in public space. For this reason, digital image compression is allied with new techniques of control and profiling of the population. A shift of movement in technologies of moving images also comes with shifting temporalities and power distributions that a film theory for the digital age cannot afford to ignore. At the same time, this implies that film theory needs to expand into a media theory ranging wider than the film object and be attentive to processes determining technological networks.

Process-Oriented Approaches

One way of approaching not only what is shown on screens but also the connectivity between files is to analyse the algorithms that inform what people actually watch on the internet. Watching films on the web always entails leaving trails of navigation that will establish links and connections between materials for others to follow. If the collective screening in the cinema theatre has been championed as a social activity, where the reactions and emotions of other spectators become part of the experience of cinema, watching film on the web is also profoundly social. The devotion to films on small, portable screens is often understood as an individual mode of consumption of moving images, but it always takes place in the setting of a social network. The surface effects of these links and protocols take the shape of suggestions for what to watch next on YouTube or Netflix, based on what other product consumers have been interested in watching. The algorithms forming these connections are self-learning entities and learn by experience from all other users' behaviours. Algorithms remember and modify their actions according to past navigations of the individual user and form a world wide web of trails and links.

This change of sociality in watching and browsing on the web has been theorised well over a hundred years ago by the sociologist Gabriel Tarde when he identified a shift in the framework of reception from the crowd to the *public* (Tarde 1989). Tarde's sociology identifies a trend going from the collective reception of meetings and spectacles to an individual reception where people were dispersed in space but congregated in time. The *public* depicts the capacity to affect and be affected over a distance but synchronized in time. Tarde's sociology is one of imitation and reflection, and hence of processes of propagation of ideas and opinions, but an imitation that promotes change at the intersections of imitative trends. Tarde proposed this shift of social reception in 1901, in the early years of cinema, but used the newspaper, the railway and the telephone as his main examples.[5] In this view, cinema is part of a network of technologies and media which disseminates ideas and sets off social memory according to a different spatial and temporal logic than that associated with the mass of the Frankfurt school. Television would probably have been a better example for Tarde, as it targets spectators who are dispersed in space through individual viewing but perfectly synchronized in time. We know that various televisual techniques predate cinema as an idea and existed as an imaginary technology in science-fiction works like Albert Robida's *Le vingtième siècle; La vie éléctrique* (1890), which portrays a device for transmission of image and sound called the *téléphonoscope*, from the late nineteenth century. Even if television became functional only decades later, it still existed as a horizon of expectation and could well have informed Tarde's concept of the public. However, the concept seems to come to full fruition with the advent of algorithmic indexation of materials on the internet, a process that provides metadata for analysing the interactions of the users.

Such an analysis of the connectivity between files on the internet is what Ute Holl calls for when she proposes traces, nodes and links as sources for excavation of behavioural patterns when watching films on the web. 'Cinema on the Web and Newer Psychology' (Holl 2012) argues for a mapping of perceptual patterns as an auto-analysis (where 'auto-' is both an automatic analysis and a self-analysis) of a new psychology of online film spectatorship. Holl departs from Maurice Merleau-Ponty's lecture at the French film school IDHEC in 1945, 'The Film and the New Psychology' (Merleau-Ponty 1964) to chisel out a 'newer psychology' emerging with algorithmic patterns formed by watching films online. These traces are accessible to users for charting their own pathways, cues and impulses in browsing and watching moving images. Web file navigation constructs logs of metadata that also provide media spectators and scholars with information that uncovers a reconfigured spectator psychology. Media scholars may approach these metadata with some unease, as it is well known that they primarily fulfil the goal of providing corporations with information for creating consumer profiles for targeting advertisement. Profiling users for commercial and political means is the main source of revenue for internet companies such as Google and Facebook, and using this information for personal and scholarly objectives may also be seen as an alternative use of these metadata to reveal the power structures behind the screens that circumscribe and inform spectatorship. Whether this mapping of behavioural and perceptual patterns qualifies as a subversive strategy is a point of discussion, but the metadata yield important information about the conditions of possibility for online spectatorship that is not to be found in the screens themselves.

To critically engage with the metadata of online viewing means 'following the actors' in technological networks. This entails charting the processes that take place in any local part of these networks. Bruno Latour's Actor-Network Theory (ANT) understands the actors (in French, *actants*) as the agents, human and non-human, in processes of transformation and translation. Algorithms and spectators, computer interfaces and TCP/IP are all agents in processes transforming materials and perceptions. In this respect, Latour makes an important distinction between 'intermediaries' and 'mediators'. An intermediary is for Latour 'what transports meaning or force without transformation: defining its inputs is enough to define its outputs', while with mediators, 'their input is never a good predictor of their output; their specificity has to be taken into account every time' (Latour 2005, 37). However, there are always transformations in the connective processes we are concerned with here, as metadata is always rewritten in any action. In order to address the connective networks between people and technologies, media theory must analyse the black boxes that are hidden and seem inconspicuous. The double-click is Latour's example of such an action where we do not have access to what is happening in a network, insofar as it only yields a result (the opening of a file). Instead of conveyors of information, media are networks where images, things and humans are mediated at the same level.

A turn to metadata in media theory also entails a turn to a process-oriented engagement with digital technologies. Wendy Chun argues that the computer's material specificity lies with dynamic temporal processing, electronic pulses and microtemporalities. Digital environments are always rewritten, updated, reconnected and disconnected and should be understood as dynamic processes of memory (Chun 2011, 137–40). Media theorist Wolfgang Ernst has also emphasised how digital archives substitute the storage priority of traditional archives with a focus on transmission and access (Ernst 2013, 85–101). Such a mobilization of archival materials is conditioned by the algorithmic memory encircling any interaction with web databases.

If Internet metadata allow for new reception research, as Holl argues, another material factor for a reorientation of film theory into media theory caused by digital technologies is the neuroscientific turn. 'Neurocinema' has gained considerable attention the last decade, due to new digital imaging techniques like functional magnetic resonance imaging (fMRI) that enable a charting of neural processes in large and also when an individual sees a film. Aiming at describing psychological processes 'directly', as they happen in the brain, these scanning techniques are far from the psychological properties that may be excavated from internet logs and protocols. Patricia Pisters argues that digital visualisation techniques of psychological processes and digital cinema showcase similarities that enable patterns of identification allowing the film spectator to enter into other minds. One of her examples is the opening ride through the brain of the protagonist(s) in *Fight Club* (Fincher 1999; Pisters 2012, 25). She understands this new form as an extension of Gilles Deleuze's (1985) time-image and even as a third regime of cinema that Deleuze could not address because it appeared after his books on cinema were published.

The announcement of a new cinema may be seductive at a time when so many speak of its death, but it also raises some serious questions. For one, it relies on very strong patterns of identification that have a closer kinship with the 1970s and 1980s apparatus theory than Deleuze's film theory. It also assumes that the sole representation of the brain in the case of *Fight Club*, or mental landscapes more generally, invariably lead to the spectator's entrance into other states of mind. Furthermore, having identified a brain-image outside spectatorial identification or representation in *The Time-Image*, it is doubtful that *Fight Club* and related films would have moved Deleuze to theorize a third regime of images. The historical development model structuring the break between the movement-image and the time-image is exactly what has been most often, and justly so, criticized in Deleuze's typology of images in cinema, and adding a third regime with the advent of digital imaging techniques merely skirts the issues at hand.

The charting of spectator activity in film reception is not new in film studies. For instance, more behaviourist members of the Filmology movement in France from the late 1940s to the 1960s aimed to measure viewers' psychophysiological response to specific films through electroencephalograms (EEG).[6] Instead of trying to assess the merits and shortcomings of a field of film theory under evolvement, it is perhaps more warranted to ask why the brain is so compelling in the digital age. New medical and cinematic visualization techniques are available, but this engagement with the brain far exceeds the visual domains. Pasi Väliaho suggests that the brain has become such a compelling topic because of biopolitical structures subtending neoliberal capitalism (Väliaho 2014, 16–25). Computer games and military simulation techniques are allied in targeting the reptilian dimension of the brain, in order to train useful military personnel for the so-called war on terror. Therapy for post-traumatic stress disorder (PTSD) has also become essentially oriented towards the visual pre-conscious mechanisms of the brain. This is a valuable reminder that theory should not only deploy the digital technologies at hand but also critically analyse the methods and ideas they enable.

Conclusion: How We Write

> I can hardly write a word these days if there isn't an image on the screen at the same time.
>
> —Harun Farocki, *Schnittstelle* (1995)

Harun Farocki's comment, taken from his film installation *Schnittstelle*, describes a reconfiguration of media in writing. The two-channel installation is focused around the editing table in analogue video, where two monitors are used, but digital video editing also employs a mode of editing with several windows on the computer screen. If Farocki has become accustomed to seeing an image while writing, this mode of writing has been facilitated by the multiple media windows of the computer. 'Our writing tools take part in our thinking', Friedrich Nietzsche observed when he acquired a typewriter (the Malling-Hansen *Schreibkugel*), and digital word processing is no exception.

When one asks how digital technologies have changed film theory, we do well to heed shifts and alterations in ways in which film theory is produced. Writing film theory has changed on a very material level. Writing in digital code means writing in the same medium as that of films. This is what Kittler pointed out when he observed that analogue media had been converted into one multimedium with the computer. Given that we can go seamlessly between texts, films, sounds and still images on the computer interface, this single medium situation enables a different approach to writing. The screen is determined by the code, as the perception of different media on the computer screen relies on the sameness of media on the code level. Anne Friedberg observes in her epilogue to *The Virtual Window* that we today write in different windows, cutting and pasting between files, checking journals and databases while we produce text (Friedberg 2006, 246–47).

The materiality of writing in the computer has in many ways facilitated an archaeological approach in film studies. We may check film files, still images and other sources in parallel windows while we write, which inadvertently breaks up the linearity of writing. If the non-linear approach is what for most theorists distinguishes media archaeology from historiographical chronology, it is in part, at least, a product of our writing tools. Of course, archaeological approaches have existed long before the personal computer, but it is symptomatic that many of these 'archaeologists' have lamented the limitations of the traditional book format. Eisenstein complained about the inaptness of the two-dimensionality of the book to purvey a theory of montage, and instead expressed the need for a three-dimensional, 'spherical' book (Somaini 2016, 90–92). It is perhaps no surprise that a theorist-director who understood the production of history as a matter of montage should opt for a non-linear and three-dimensional account of the past. Symptomatically, all his book projects remained unfinished or unpublished at his death, and *Notes for a General History of Cinema* consists of loose fragments describing the 'forerunners' of cinema in an anachronic manner. Other well-known examples of writers often described as 'archaeologists' who found the sequential linearity of the book to be a limitation are Walter Benjamin's *Arcades* project, which never found a fixed form between covers but existed as filing cards in boxes, and art historian Aby Warburg, who abandoned writing altogether and produced art history in images and montages in the iconographical archaeology of motives in *Mnemosyne Atlas*.

These examples tell us that there is an affinity between an archaeological approach and film montage. It is for this reason, and not an accident, if two of the contemporary film directors most preoccupied with the question of montage are also the ones who discuss the material properties of writing. Farocki, himself a film critic for many years in the German *Filmkritik*, identifies new medial conditions for writing in video editing. The other is Jean-Luc Godard, who throughout his career has deployed text fragments in his montagês, and in the first parts of *Histoire(s) du cinéma* (1988–98) sits at the semidigital typewriter to compose the core texts for his montage of cinema history. The materiality of writing is highlighted by the deferral between input and output of the machine: after the words are written on the keyboard, they are stored on the typewriter for correction and rewritings, upon which the message is released in writing. Both Farocki's and Godard's works are produced on, and display the machines of, analogue video, and it is perhaps from these intermediary technologies one can best interrogate the digital. Godard's proto-word processing machine and his video montages already depict the changing media environment for writing in the digital age.

Digitized or digital films facilitate a different analytical and theoretical engagement with them. They invite algorithmic analysis where features eluding human perception can be excavated and mapped as big data. Many of the digital tools for addressing huge numbers of images, through quantification of data sets and automated recognition techniques, are already present in software for image analysis and visualization. Cultural Analytics is one disciplinary initiative aiming at the historical analysis and visualization of huge quantities of visual (and other) data, which may be based on iconic search criteria instead of names of persons or of works.[7] For a film-specific approach to similar techniques of analysis and visualization, Frederic Brodbeck describes his project: 'Information such as the editing structure, colour, speech or motion are extracted, analyzed and transformed into graphic representations so that movies can be seen as a whole and easily interpreted or compared side by side'.[8] Each film analysed and visualized is given a *fingerprint* through a mapping of brightness, colour, movement and so on. The software enables a synchronic and spatial representation of the temporal structure of the film, in order to compare them side by side.

Most often, this work has been conducted as comparative analyses of individual films and historical mappings, but it also enables automated pattern recognition that may establish unexpected connections between very disparate materials. The results of this research for film theory is still to be established. However, it should be the task of a film theory for the digital age to investigate the software that enables these new kinds of historiographical and analytical forms, and to use them to explain how other forms of media connectivities are established algorithmically. For this investigation, film theory inadvertently turns into media theory. When these means for analysis and visualization exist within our writing tools, they also inevitably produce a technologically enabled mode of writing that is not only about digital technologies, but also a product of them. For this reason, digital technologies have changed film theory in very material ways.[9]

Notes

1 André Bazin positions this mechanical transfer as a phenomenological factor informing all reception of film in "Ontology of the Photographic Image" (Bazin 1958), and Roland Barthes identifies the subjective reception of the photograph conditioned by the 'ça-a-été' of the indexical bond to the past in *Caméra lucida* (Barthes 1981).

2 '[Cinema] is no longer an indexical media technology but, rather, a subgenre of painting' (Manovich 2001, 295).

3 Mary Ann Doane offers a valuable discussion of Peirce's theory in *The Emergence of Cinematic Time*, and concludes that the index is 'evacuated of content; it is a hollowed-out sign' (Doane 2002, 92).

4 I here simplify the movement technology of MPEG video compression somewhat, as there are reference frames, intermediate frames and bidirectional frames that anticipate and respond to changes in any block of pixels, but this is not essential for the theorization of the different principles of movement in analogue and digital moving images.

5 'Ainsi s'est formée, par un faisceau de trois inventions mutuellement auxiliaires, imprimerie, chemin de fer, télégraphe, la formidable puissance de la presse, ce prodigieux téléphone qui a si démesurément grossi l'ancien auditoire des tribuns et des prédicateurs' (Tarde 1989, 12). [Thus is formed, through a network of mutually auxiliary inventions—the printing press, the railroad, telegraph—the formidable power of the press, this prodigious telephone that has so outlandishly enlarged the former audience of tribunes and predicators.]

6 For an instructive discussion of Filmology as an ancestor to neuroscientific film theory, see D'Aloia and Eugeni (2014).

7 For an assessment of the achievements and the potential of Cultural Analytics a short decade after its formation, see Manovich (2016). http://manovich.net/index.php/projects/cultural-analytics-social-computing. Last visit 10 December 2016.

8 http://cinemetrics.fredericbrodbeck.de/. Last visit 10 December 2016.

9 On a personal footnote, I would like to add that this text was almost completed when the whole file was destroyed by the 'asterisk bug' of the Microsoft word program, rendering the whole text as only asterisks, and I had to write it all again as I had made no back-ups. This is a reminder not only to make back-ups, but also that there are no texts as such in digital files, and how our writing tools in a very material way impact 'film theory', if this entry qualifies as such.

Works Cited

Barthes, Roland. 1981. *Camera lucida*. New York: Hill and Wang.

Bazin, André. 1958 [1945]. 'Ontologie de l'image photographique'. In *Qu'est-ce que le cinéma? Vol. 1: Ontologie et language*, 11–19. Paris: Cerf.

Bolter, Jay David, and Richard Grusin. 1999. *Remediation: Understanding New Media*. Cambridge, MA: MIT Press.

Chun, Wendy. 2011. *Programmed Visions: Software and Memory*. Cambridge, MA: MIT Press.

D'Aloia, Adriano, and Ruggero Eugini. 2014. 'Neurofilmology: An Introduction'. *Cinéma & Cie* XIV, no. 22/23: 9–26.

Deleuze, Gilles. 1985. *Cinéma 2: L'image-temps*. Paris: Minuit.

Doane, Mary Ann. 2002. *The Emergence of Cinematic Time: Modernity, Contingency, the Archive*. Cambridge, MA: Harvard University Press.

———. 2007. 'Review: Laura Mulvey, Death 24x a Second: Stillness and the Moving Image. London: Reaktion Books 2006'. *Screen* 48, no. 1: 113–18.

Elsaesser, Thomas. 1998. 'Digital Cinema: Delivery, Event, Time'. In *Cinema Futures: Cain, Abel or Cable? Screen Arts in the Digital Age*, edited by Thomas Elsaesser and Kay Hoffmann, 201–222. Amsterdam: Amsterdam University Press.

———. 2004. 'The New Film History as Media Archaeology'. *Cinémas: revue d'études cinématographiques / Cinémas: Journal of Film Studies* 14, no. 2–3: 75–117.

———. 2016. 'Media Archaeology as Symptom'. *New Review of Film and Television Studies* 14, no. 2: 181–215.

Eisenstein, Sergei M. 1991. 'Laocoön'. In *Selected Works, Volume II: Towards a Theory of Montage, 1937–1940*, edited by Michael Glenny and Richard Taylor, translated by Michael Glenny, 109–202. London: BFI.

———. 2016. *Notes for a General History of Cinema*, edited by Naum Kleiman and Antonio Somaini. Amsterdam: Amsterdam University Press.

Ernst, Wolfgang. 2013. 'Archives in Transition: Dynamic Media Memories'. In *Digital Memory and the Archive*, edited by Jussi Parikka, 95–101. Minneapolis: University of Minnesota Press.

Fossati, Giovanna. 2010. *From Grain to Pixel: The Archival Life of Film in Transition*. Amsterdam: Amsterdam University Press.

Friedberg, Anne. 1993. *Window Shopping: Cinema and the Postmodern*. Berkeley: University of California Press.

———. 2006. *The Virtual Window; From Alberti to Microsoft*. Cambridge, MA: MIT Press.

Gaudreault, André, and Philippe Marion. 2015. *The End of Cinema? A Medium in Crisis in the Digital Age*. New York: Columbia University Press.

Gunning, Tom. 2007. 'Moving Away from the Index: Cinema and the Impression of Reality'. *Differences: A Journal of Feminist Cultural Studies* 18, no. 1: 29–52.

Hagener, Malte. 2008. 'Where Is Cinema (Today)? Cinema in the Age of Media Immanence'. *Cinéma & Cie* 11: 15–22.

Hediger, Vinzenz. 2012. 'Lost in Space and Found in a Fold. Cinema and the Irony of Media'. In *Screen Dynamics. Mapping the Borders of Cinema*, edited by Gertrud Koch, Volker Pantenburg, and Simon Rothöhler, 61–77. Wien: Filmmuseum/Synema.

Holl, Ute. 2012. 'Cinema on the Web and Newer Psychology'. In *Screen Dynamics. Mapping the Borders of Cinema*, edited by Gertrud Koch, Volker Pantenburg, and Simon Rothöhler, 150–68. Wien: Filmmuseum/Synema.

Huhtamo, Erkki, and Jussi Parikka. 2011. 'Introduction'. In *Media Archaeology: Approaches, Applications, and Implications*, edited by Erkki Huhtamo and Jussi Parikka, 1–21. Berkeley: University of California Press.

Jenkins, Henry. 2006. *Convergence Culture: Where Old and New Media Collide*. New York: New York University Press.

Kittler, Friedrich. 1999. *Gramophone, Film, Typewriter [1986]*. Stanford, CA: Stanford University Press.

Latour, Bruno. 2005. *Reassembling the Social – An Introduction to Actor-Network-Theory*. Oxford: Oxford University Press.

Manovich, Lev. 1995. 'An Archaeology of a Computer Screen'. Kunstforum International. http://manovich.net/index.php/projects/archeology-of-a-computer-screen.

———. 2001. *The Language of New Media*. Cambridge, MA: MIT Press.

———. 2016. 'The Science of Culture? Social Computing, Digital Humanities, and Cultural Analytics'. In *The Datafied Society. Social Research in the Age of Big Data*, edited by Mirko Tobias Schaefer and Karin van Es. Amsterdam: Amsterdam University Press. http://manovich.net/index.php/projects/cultural-analytics-social-computing. Last visit 10 December 2016.

Matuszewski, Bolesłas. 1995 [1898]. 'A New Source of History'. *Film History* 7, no. 4: 322–24.

McLuhan, Marshall. 1964. *Understanding Media: The Extensions of Man*. New York: McGraw-Hill.

Merleau-Ponty, Maurice. 1964 [1945]. 'The Film and the New Psychology'. In *Sense and Non-Sense*, translated by Hubert L. Dreyfus and Patricia Allen Dreyfus, 48–59. Evanston, IL: Northwestern University Press.

Metz, Christian. 1974 [1965]. 'On the Impression of Reality in the Cinema'. In *Film Language: A Semiotics of the Cinema*, translated by Michael Taylor, 3–15. New York: Oxford University Press.

Mulvey, Laura. 2006. *Death 24x a Second: Stillness and the Moving Image*. London: Reaktion Books.

Parikka, Jussi. 2012. *What Is Media Archaeology?* London: Polity Press.

Pisters, Patricia. 2012. *The Neuro-Image. A Deleuzian Film-Philosophy of Digital Screen Culture*. Stanford: Stanford University Press.

Robida, Albert. 1890. *Le vingtième siècle; La vie électrique*. Paris: Engel.

Rodowick, D. N. 2007. *The Virtual Life of Film*. Cambridge, MA: Harvard University Press.

Rosen, Philip. 2001. *Change Mummified: Cinema, Historicity, Theory*. Minneapolis: University of Minnesota Press.

Somaini, Antonio. 2016. 'Cinema as "Dynamic Mummification," History as Montage: Eisenstein's Media Archaeology'. In *Sergei M. Eisenstein: Notes for a General History of Cinema*, edited by Naum Kleiman and Antonio Somaini, 19–105. Amsterdam: Amsterdam University Press.

Souriau, Etienne. 1952. 'Filmologie et esthétique comparée'. *Revue internationale de filmologie* 10: 113–141.

Tarde, Gabriel. 1989 [1901]. *L'opinion et la foule*. Paris: Presses Universtaires de France.

Väliaho, Pasi. 2014. *Biopolitical Screens: Image, Power, and the Neoliberal Brain*. Cambridge, MA: MIT Press.

Chapter Thirteen

HOW JOHN THE BAPTIST KEPT HIS HEAD: MY LIFE IN FILM PHILOSOPHY

William Rothman

Thinking in the Dark (Pomerance and Palmer 2015), the excellent new anthology edited by Murray Pomerance and B. Barton Palmer, is a collection of lucid essays, each about a thinker whose theory of film the writer finds particularly enlightening. It is striking, though, that virtually every one of these thinkers is or was an outsider to academic film study. The field of film study, when it searches for theoretical insights, continues to look past its own members, including more than a few powerful thinkers whose achievements as theorists are rarely acknowledged. Indeed, a number of the writers who contributed essays to *Thinking in the Dark* are worthy of inclusion as theorists in their own right. I'm not thinking only of myself, but I am thinking of myself. After all, during the Film Philosophy workshop at the 2016 SCMS Conference, my friend David Rodowick called me "the John the Baptist of film philosophy." I trust that he didn't have in mind the ending to the Biblical story, but simply the fact that I began thinking philosophically about film—about the ways films think philosophically—before there was a field or subfield that could be called "film philosophy." I've perhaps earned the right, while I still have my head, to recount, however sketchily, my half-century of writing film criticism that is also philosophy.

It was in the late 1960s when I began writing the dissertation I was finally to submit to the Harvard Philosophy Department in 1973. It consisted of three interrelated essays: "A Theory of Artistic Expression," "Toward a Theory of Narrative Film," and "An Analytical Description of the Film *Notorious*"(Rothman 1973). That year, I began teaching in the NYU Cinema Studies Department, cutting my ties with academic philosophy and casting my lot with a field that was just starting—when will it finish?—to establish a legitimate place within American universities. In the decades since, I have sometimes felt that I was, like John the Baptist, "crying in the wilderness." But that's as far as the parallel goes. "Prepare the way of the Lord!" is what John the Baptist cried in a world that (as the New Testament tells the story) had not yet seen the Light Jesus was to bring into the world. John the Baptist was not the Light; he was only "sent to bear witness of that Light." I was not "sent" to say what I said in my dissertation. Nor did it prophesy that a marriage of film study and philosophy would one day come into the world. Whatever "film philosophy" is, I was already doing it. Of course, the same was true for Stanley Cavell, my mentor and dissertation advisor. If there's a "Light" my dissertation "bears witness of," it's the intuition, which guided Cavell in writing *The World Viewed*, that the marriage of film study and philosophy, exemplified by my own writings as well as his, is not only possible it is necessary—necessary no less for philosophy than for the study of film.

Cavell did not teach me how to think about film. What he taught me was that when I thought about film my way, I was doing philosophy. In the late 1960s, when he was writing *The World Viewed* (Cavell 1971), I arrived on my own at a number of ideas—about stardom and screen performance; about the viewer's outside-ness to the world on film; about the camera and the movie screen—that were akin to ideas Cavell's book articulated with a far more sophisticated understanding of their relation to the Western philosophical tradition. In writing *The World Viewed*, Cavell's goal was to achieve a philosophical perspective on the period of his life in which going to the movies had been a normal part of his week without it occurring to him to reflect philosophically on film. In writing my dissertation, my goal was different. There had been a shift in my experience of film from my childhood, when I, too, enjoyed what *The World Viewed* calls a "natural relation" to movies, to my high school and college years, when I was drawn to films widely accepted as art and looked down on popular American movies, old and new. The conjunction of two events precipitated a second shift. One was the attention Cavell gave to *Vertigo* in what in *The World Viewed* he called a "failed" graduate aesthetics seminar—it didn't fail me—that he allowed me to take although I was still an undergraduate. The other was the publication of an essay by Andrew Sarris on the auteur theory (Sarris 1962) that he was later to expand into his seminal book *The American Cinema* (Sarris 1968). In my dissertation, I sought a philosophical perspective on my experience of films by "auteur" directors for whom film was first and foremost a medium of self-expression. Given that films are composed of machine-made images, I asked myself how self-expression was even possible in the film medium. Sarris's claim was that an auteur film expressed its director's *personality*. I knew that this could not be right, since directors are invisible and silent, and outside the projected world, as the viewer is. Then what part or aspect of a director's "self" does an auteur film express and call upon us to acknowledge?

The first part of my dissertation reflected on a paradox inherent in expression. To express oneself is to change, I argued—to become other than who or what one had been. When an artist performs an act of self-expression by creating a work of art, what "self" is expressed? What "self" performs the act? Self-expression, I argued, reflects the fact that the human "self" is not unified; human identity is not fixed. In creating a work of art, the artist takes a step in the direction of realizing the "self," becoming more fully who he or she is.

The dissertation's second part took point-of-view cutting to be key to classical cinema's way of representing human being-in-the-world. Cutting from a character to his or her view and back to a "reaction shot" links our condition as viewers with that of the character, who is a viewer, too. It also separates the character from us, in that we cannot thrust ourselves into the projected world the way the character can—and must. Even when we view the character, in an "objective" shot, performing actions within the world he or she lives in with others, the character might at any moment withdraw, or be withdrawn, into the aloneness, the outside-ness, that is also the viewer's condition, and the director's—a condition that cannot ultimately be overcome or transcended apart from a metamorphosis equivalent, allegorically or metaphorically, to crossing the barrier-that-is-no-barrier of the movie screen, a barrier that is impossible to cross. The part or aspect of the "self" an author like Hitchcock expresses and calls upon us to acknowledge, I argued, is his aloneness, his condition as solitary, outside the human circle. What is expressed is thus a condition that sets him apart from all others, but outside-ness is also a condition he has in common with viewers, who are also outside the film's world. In the third part of my dissertation, which focused on *Notorious*, I dwelled on the condition of outside-ness that I took to be defining for Hitchcock's role as author. This part of the dissertation, as I revised it for publication in *The Georgia Review* and added numerous frame enlargements, provided the model for the readings in *Hitchcock—The Murderous Gaze* (Rothman 1982).

In my years at NYU, 1973–76, the NYU Cinema Studies Department was dominated by an ideology that privileged avant-garde cinema over "ordinary" movies, which students were encouraged to hold in contempt as "illusionistic." Like anyone who read *The World Viewed* with the kind and degree of attention it calls for, I knew it was philosophically naïve, and why it was naïve, to think of film images, or the worlds they project, as illusory. Had the department as a whole been prepared to acknowledge Cavell's philosophical seriousness, my years at NYU—not to mention the history of film study—might have been different. Be that as it may, during my years at NYU, the approach that prevailed within the Cinema Studies Department was being outflanked on the left by the theoretical frameworks that became prominent in France in the altered post-May 1968 cultural landscape. Semiology was all the rage, but offered little to anyone for whom writing about film was art, not science. The same was true for Saussurean linguistics, which for me had been blown out of the water by the Wittgenstein of *Philosophical Investigations*—and by Cavell. Christian Metz's "*Grande Sygmatique*," which claimed to establish the units of cinematic discourse, seemed to me an empty exercise. The so-called apparatus theory, which denied the viewer an active role, struck me as pernicious. Worse, to me, was the (1970) reading of *Young Mr. Lincoln* by the editors of *Cahiers du cinéma* published in translation by the British journal *Screen* (editors of *Cahiers du cinema* 1972). The essay claimed authority from both Althusserian Marxism, which enjoyed a brief heyday in American film study, and Lacanian psychoanalysis, which has proved to have a much longer shelf life.

Lacanian psychoanalysis also played a central role in "The Tutor Code of Classical Cinema" (Dayan 1974), an essay by Daniel Dayan published in *Film Quarterly* that presented Jean-Pierre Oudart's theory of suture to English-speaking readers. Going beyond Oudart, Dayan claimed that the fact that movies were pernicious ideological constructs—the thrust of the *Young Mr. Lincoln* piece as well—was an inevitable effect of the "system of the suture," AKA point-of-view cutting, which masked the real source of the film image's meaning-construction. This was a moment at which, in film study, it was *de rigueur* to invoke the Velasquez painting "Las Meninas" to buttress the theory that continuity editing in cinema was a system—analogous to linear perspective in painting—that made it impossible for classical movies to be anything but instruments of bourgeois ideology. (Laura Mulvey's widely anthologized "Visual Pleasure and Narrative Cinema" (Mulvey 1975) employed a variant of this approach by claiming that in classical movies the camera was an instrument of "the male gaze" (as if all men always do only one thing, or perhaps two, with their gaze), thus inevitably making such films instruments of patriarchal ideology.)

In "Against the System of the Suture" (Rothman 1975), which was published in *Film Quarterly* and itself was widely anthologized, I offered a painstaking critique of Dayan's argument, which especially ruffled my feathers because it flew in the face of the detailed analysis of point-of-view cutting in my dissertation. Looking back, it pleases me that I condemned so passionately Dayan's use of theory not as a companion to criticism, but as a justification for avoiding criticism as I aspired to practice it. Not that my response had any noticeable effect on the consensus, forming within the field, that to secure its legitimacy film study had to aspire to the condition of a science. In retrospect though, I regret that I avoided making any reference to my dissertation, which had predated Oudart's essay as well as Dayan's. Perhaps I was not completely immune at that time, stranded as I was in the philosophical wilderness of the NYU Cinema Studies Department, to the seductive but wrongheaded notion that breaking our attachment to movies was the first step we had to take if we are to think seriously about film. Or perhaps I was perversely withholding my thoughts from a field from which, at some level, I wanted to be outside of.

I lived in Cambridge between 1961, when I entered Harvard College, and 1973, when I started teaching at NYU. In 1976, that sentence was commuted when I was invited to return to Harvard to help to create a film program in which I would not be a voice "crying in the wilderness," a program with no walls separating filmmaking from film study, or film study from philosophy. Harvard's Carpenter Center was home to me; to Nick Browne; to Marian Keane; to Charles Warren; to Alan Cholodenko; to Vlada Petric and the Harvard Film Archive; to Robert Gardner and the Film Study Center he founded; to Gilberto Perez, for the year he was a Mellon Fellow at Harvard; to Alfred Guzzetti, whose 1975 film *Family Portrait Sittings* was the subject of one of my first published essays; to visiting filmmakers such as the great Dusan Makavejev; and to brilliant students, such as Richard Peña and Mira Nair; who took to heart the program's promise. And Stanley Cavell was across the street in Emerson Hall. In this environment, where thought-provoking conversations were an everyday occurrence, I published numerous essays that were later to find their way into *The "I" of the Camera* (Rothman 1988), my second book. In these writings, my commitment was, as it still is, to open myself to film's own ways of expressing thoughts; to let each film reveal itself—and myself—to me; to allow the film to help teach me how to view it, how to think about it, how to find what I had at heart to say about it.

My goal in writing *The Murderous Gaze*, my first book, was to achieve an understanding of Alfred Hitchcock's authorship and at the same time to investigate, philosophically, the *conditions* of film authorship. A premise and conclusion of the book is that Hitchcock's films express serious thoughts about their medium, about themselves, about such matters as the nature and relationships of love, murder, sexuality, marriage and theater. Thus the book rejects and contests the view, which was dominant within film study at the time, that on the basis of some theory or other we can rest assured that films cannot possibly be thinking—that we already know, without attending to what they have to say, that they have nothing to say, that they are in the repressive grip of ideology, a grip only theory can break. And the book rejects and contests the view, also dominant then within the field, that the concept of authorship had been discredited on theoretical grounds. No writing on Hitchcock goes further than *The Murderous Gaze* in keeping faith with the idea that he was an "auteur"—a master of what he called the "art of pure cinema" for whom film was first and foremost a medium of self-expression. But it is an auteurist study that is also a philosophical investigation of the *conditions* of authorship in the medium of film. *The Murderous Gaze* does not say everything there is to say about Hitchcock's films. Far from it. But what it does say is said in a singular way and in a distinctive voice, a voice I still recognize as my own. It is the voice of the writer I have always aspired to be. In *The Murderous Gaze*, I aspired to demonstrate something fundamental about Hitchcock's films and their place in the history of film, about film itself, and about the "art of pure cinema." To that end, I performed extended "readings," as I called them, of five characteristic Hitchcock films, following them moment by moment, shot by shot, line by line, as they unfold from beginning to end, putting into words—complemented by over six hundred frame enlargements—the thoughts inscribed in their successions of frames.

The method I followed was simply to attend to the films themselves, and to the experience of viewing them, with the degree and kind of attention required to follow one's own thinking. It is a central claim of the book that Hitchcock's films have a philosophical dimension. As I later put it,

> Within the world of a Hitchcock film, the nature and relationships of love, murder, sexuality, marriage, and theater are at issue; these are among Hitchcock's constant themes. His treatment of these themes, however, and his understanding of the reasons film keeps returning to them, cannot be separated from his constant concern with the nature of the camera, the act of viewing a film, and filmmaking as a calling. In demonstrating something about the "art of pure cinema," as he liked to call it, Hitchcock's films are asserting something about themselves, something about their medium, as well as something about our existence as human beings within the world. (Rothman 1982, xi)

The Murderous Gaze was published a year after Cavell's own *Pursuits of Happiness* (Cavell 1981b). Within film studies, both books were widely perceived, not wrongly, as incompatible with the agenda of a field that was increasingly marginalizing all alternatives to its then dominant practices. Flying under the field's radar, *The Murderous Gaze* was nonetheless widely read and has had an impact not readily measurable in terms of public recognition within the field of film studies. Innumerable strangers have introduced themselves at conferences to tell me, privately, how strongly they wish for the field to embrace, openly, the value of writing about films in one's own voice, in words accountable to one's own experience, as *The Murderous Gaze* does.

Between the mid-1970s and mid-1980s, the MIT Film Section, the world's premiere training ground for cinema-vérité filmmakers, sustained the countercultural, anti-MIT spirit envisioned by Edward Pincus and Richard Leacock, its founders. That spirit was snuffed out when it was subsumed in 1985 by MIT's new Media Lab. The demise of the MIT Film Section was virtually simultaneous with Harvard's decision, once grant support had run its course, not to fund the permanent positions its film study program needed. And so we went our separate ways. We all kept faith with the program's vision, even as we never stopped regretting that our collective voice had been silenced—a voice that might have made a difference within the debates that continued to forge the identity of film study, now all but unalterable, as a field. And so I journeyed on, to borrow a phrase from the signature song of Scottish music hall performer Harry Lawder.

I will skip over the years between 1985, when I left Harvard, and 1990, when I accepted my present position at the University of Miami, where I have been happily ensconced ever since. Those were adventurous, mind-expanding years when my wife and I traveled the world leading the International Honors Program on Film, Television and Social Change, even as we tried to put film projects together, leading to our writing and producing *Unni*, a 35mm feature film directed in South India by the great Indian director G. Aravindan, and signing a contract to coproduce a film with the Shanghai Film Studio, a project the Tiananmen Square massacre aborted. Although during those years I didn't expect I would ever again (or would ever again want to) be a film study professor, I continued to fulfill my responsibilities as editor of the Cambridge Studies in Film series. And I was moved to put together, for the series, a collection of my published and unpublished essays I called "The 'I' of the Camera," and to which I added a preface and pieces I wrote specifically for the book on *Birth of a Nation*, *True Heart Susie* and *City Lights*. Perhaps because I had cut my ties with academic film study, as I had earlier cut my ties with philosophy, I felt—and feel—that those essays, unencumbered by the wish to make an impression on the field, were the purest examples I had produced of the kind of writing I aspire to. I was not "crying in the wilderness." I was not "crying" at all. I was simply saying what I had at heart to say to any reader who might be moved to take an interest. And the Preface was my most lucid account of the way I write and why it is of value to me to write that way.

This Preface registered my conviction that the essays it contained challenged readers to think about film in ways responsive to the ways movies themselves think, and responsive as well to their own experience. It expressed the idea that films "speak to us in an intimate language of indirectness and silence," and thus that if we are to speak seriously about a film "we must speak about that silence, its motivations and depths; we must speak about that to which the silence gives voice; we must give voice to that silence; we must let that silence speak for itself" (Rothman 1988, xii). My point was that, as I put it with a nod to Wittgenstein, "It is not our words, but rather the silence they achieve when they reach the limits of what words can say—a silence within which echoes of the film's own silence can be heard—that gives voice to that which the film consigns to silence." I added, "The border that separates language from film is also where the two touch. It is when it reaches this border that film achieves its poetry. For writing about film to reach this boundary, the poetry of film must artfully be evoked by the writing itself, by its own voices and silences" (Rothman 1988, xii).

The time had come to be a film study professor again—only differently, this time, in the only city in the continental United States that looks like the South India my wife and I had fallen in love with. I have never regretted that decision. I came close, though, when the Society for Cinema Studies ("Media" had not yet been added its name) rejected the panel on Cavell that I proposed for its 1991 conference. I suspected that my proposal had not been judged on its merits, but had been rejected because Cavell's name had raised a red flag. I was well aware that his writings were not beholden, philosophically, to the field or its prevailing theories, and called radically into question views that had come to be treated as dogmas. My suspicion that panels on Cavell had been blackballed, in effect, was confirmed by a member of the conference committee who swore me to secrecy. I complained so vehemently that the Society for Cinema Studies (SCS) compromised, still rejecting the Cavell panel but accepting my paper ("Cavell's Philosophy and What Film Study Calls 'Theory'"), which it added to a panel with the innocuous title "Film Theory II." I was also added to a panel of speakers asked to make brief remarks at a plenary session devoted to the conference theme of "Multiculturalism." From that podium, I decried the hypocrisy of an organization that celebrated multiculturalism but pressured its members to speak in a single voice. Evidently, my intervention touched some nerves, as I was invited the following year to be on the SCS Dissertation Committee. Of the 15 dissertations I was given to read, 14 described their goal as developing a Lacanian approach to film study (the one holdout being a dissertation about films made from x-rays, a topic not amenable to a Lacanian approach, since only baby Superman could see his own mirror image with x-ray vision). No two dissertations explained the mirror phase in the same way. Just as the Freudian concept of the fetish had become fetishized by the field, the theory of the mirror phase had come to serve the same function within film study that, according to the theory, the mirror image serves for the baby: it helped enable the field to imagine itself as a unified subject, a reflection crafted according to its own desires.

This perfect validation of my critique of the field tickled my sense of the absurd, defused my anger and motivated two resolutions. One was that I would resume writing, without defensiveness, the way I valued. This led to my third book, *Documentary Film Classics* (Rothman 1997), published in 1997 in the Cambridge series I was still editing, in which I "read" five great documentaries in the manner of the readings in *The Murderous Gaze*. It also led me to produce for the series an expanded edition of *The "I" of the Camera* (Rothman 2004), doubled in size by adding essays I had written subsequent to 1988, and to edit and contribute introductions and essays to two new books on documentaries (*Jean Rouch: A Celebration of Life and Film* (Rothman 2007) and *Three Documentary Filmmakers: Errol Morris, Ross McElwee, Jean Rouch* (Rothman 2009).

The other resolution was to do whatever I could to make Cavell's writings, then still all but completely unacknowledged within film study, more accessible to the field. Film study had reached a point, my friend and comrade-in-arms Marian Keane and I both felt, at which it could not move forward without revisiting its own history. It was clear to us that at every juncture in film study's development, Cavell's work had blazed a path not taken by the field, a path leading to a territory that remained to be explored. Together, Marian and I wrote *Reading Cavell's* "The World Viewed" (Rothman and Keane 2000). By reading Cavell's book the way I read films in my own books, we hoped to open the field's eyes to a philosophical alternative to the theories that had caused film study and philosophy, happily married in Cavell's writings, to divorce. Wasn't it time for their remarriage?

In the course of writing "Bazin as Cavellian Realist" (Rothman 2008b), a review essay appreciating and responding to "Rethinking Bazin: Ontology and Realist Aesthetics"

(Morgan 2006), Daniel Morgan's brilliant revisionist reading, it dawned on me that Bazin's understanding of the role of reality in films was much closer to that articulated in *The World Viewed* than Cavell could have realized at the time, given how few of Bazin's writings were available to him. What I find surprising is not that Cavell was able to arrive at a position so close to Bazin's, but that Bazin was able to think about film in ways that anticipated *The World Viewed*, despite lacking the American philosopher's formidable intellectual advantages. Those advantages help explain why it is ultimately Cavell's work, not Bazin's, for all its extraordinary virtues and its historical importance, that provides a philosophical foundation for the study of film. Bazin's continual groping for metaphors bespeaks an awareness that his own words were inadequate or misleading, that they did not—could not—say what he meant. In order to articulate Bazin's ideas to his own satisfaction, Daniel Morgan often found himself reading *between* Bazin's lines. In *Reading Cavell's* The World Viewed, by contrast, Marian and I simply *read* Cavell's lines. Not that this was always a simple matter!

One of Cavell's advantages was his training in Anglo-American analytical philosophy at the time it was being radically challenged and extended by the Wittgenstein of *Philosophical Investigations* and the writing and teaching of Cavell's own professor of philosophy, J. L. Austin. Another was Cavell's inheritance of the philosophical concerns of Emerson, who, as Cavell later put it, "wrote comprehensively, brilliantly, with full literary and philosophical achievement, at a moment before the split between the Continental and Anglo-American traditions of philosophy was set" (Rothman and Keane 2000, 26). In his later writings, Cavell's intuition that Hollywood movies inherited the philosophical perspective of American transcendentalism, conjoined with his intuition that he too had inherited that perspective, led to the further intuition that his own philosophical procedures were underwritten by the ways American movies thought about society, human relationships and their condition as films. It was in the movies that were for so many years a normal part of Cavell's week that Emerson's ways of thinking remained alive within American culture, available *as* an inheritance. As Marian and I put it, "Apart from the role Hollywood movies played in Cavell's education, it would not have been possible for a philosopher who received his professional training within an analytical tradition that has never acknowledged Emerson as a philosopher to have 'inherited' Emerson's ways of thinking at all" (Rothman and Keane 2000, 27).

In a 1989 interview, Cavell observed that the ascension of French theory was to be welcomed because academic criticism in America "had been terribly undertheorized, much too dismissive and afraid of philosophy." Nonetheless, the fact that America "had to receive philosophy into the study of literature at the hands of the French" struck him as an irony and a pity, however understandable the historical forces at play may be, because "the price of this reception, in the context in which literary studies have shunned philosophy as practiced in America, is that what is called philosophy by departments of literature is not by American criteria simply to be called philosophy" (Cavell 1989, 32). Between Anglo-American analytical philosophy and Continental philosophy, which edges closer to literature than to science or mathematics, there was a history of mutual ignorance, incomprehension and distrust. By recognizing this rift within philosophy as a subject for philosophy, Cavell's aim was to achieve a perspective from which it becomes perspicuous how intimately they have been aligned, as if they were two halves of the same mind, not opposed positions between which to choose. For Cavell, the fact that Emerson (through his great reader Nietzsche and, through Nietzsche, Heidegger; but also through Bergson and, via Bergson, Deleuze) could be seen to underwrite the new French thought, conjoined with the fact that both traditions resist acknowledging their common ancestor and thus their kinship, intensified the irony that Americans turned to Europe to receive a philosophy that was American to begin with. And that philosophy, as received back in America, no longer recognized its American roots. "The tradition of philosophy it neglects is exactly our own," Cavell put it, registering that it neglected both the analytical tradition represented by American philosophy departments and Emerson's practice of philosophy (which American philosophy departments also neglected).

A recurring theme in our book is that *The World Viewed* takes its own writing to be inseparable from what the writing is about. In reflecting on the implications of the self-reflexive dimension of Cavell's writing, we invoked his observation, in the same 1989 interview, that "Philosophy at all moments answerable to itself. If there is any place at which the human spirit allows itself to be under its own question, indeed, that allows that questioning to happen is philosophy" (Cavell 1989, 36). The central thrust of our reading of *The World Viewed* as a whole is that its writing *is* at every moment "answerable to itself," that it is a "place at which the human spirit allows itself to be under its own question," that Cavell's book about film *is* philosophy.

Reading Cavell's "The World Viewed" promised a companion volume: a retrospective of Cavell's writings on film, apart from his books, in the years between the publication of *World Viewed* and our book about it. *Cavell on Film*, which I edited and for which I wrote the introduction, was that volume—and more, since it also contained many pieces written between 2000 and 2005. The idea of such a collection wasn't Cavell's; he had never chosen to isolate his writings on film in this way. Nor did I wish to suggest that Cavell's writings on film stood apart in their concerns, or in their standing as philosophy, from his other writings. In my introduction to the volume, I quoted Cavell's remark, in a 1999 Sorbonne colloquium organized by Sandra Laugier, that the study of film cannot be a "worthwhile human enterprise" if it "isolates itself"—as the academic field had largely done—"from the kind of criticism Walter Benjamin had in mind when he argued, as Cavell paraphrases him, that 'what establishes a work as art is its ability to inspire and sustain criticism of a certain sort, criticism that seeks to articulate the work's idea; what cannot be so criticized is not art'" (Cavell 2005, xxvi). In my introduction, I also quoted another of Cavell's remarks at the same colloquium (a remark I have since found myself quoting more than once) that thinking about film had an effect on his "ambitions for philosophical prose" and had left "permanent marks" on the way he writes. In particular, the "necessity to become evocative in capturing the moods of faces and motions and settings, in their double existence as transient and as permanent" (Cavell 2005, xxiii). This remark resonates with a passage from Cavell's (1983) essay "The Thought of Movies" that I have also quoted more than once:

> Every art, every worthwhile human enterprise, has its poetry, ways of doing things that perfect the possibilities of the enterprise itself, make it the one it is. I understand it to be a natural vision

> of film that every motion and station, in particular every human posture and gesture, however glancing, has its poetry, or you may say its lucidity. Any of the arts will be drawn to this knowledge, this perception of the poetry of the ordinary, but film, I would like to say, democratizes the knowledge, hence at once blesses and curses us with it. It says that the perception of poetry is as open to all, regardless of birth or talent, as the ability is to hold a camera on a subject, so that a failure so to perceive, to persist in missing the subject, which may amount to missing the evanescence of the subject, is ascribable only to ourselves, as if to fail to trace the implications of things requires that we persistently coarsen and stupefy ourselves. (Cavell 2005, xxvi)

I ended my introduction with this: "Marrying philosophy and film study, the writings gathered in the present collection do not miss the poetry of either subject, and thinking about film emerges as a worthwhile human enterprise, indeed. In these writings, the study of film achieves its own poetry, its own 'ways of doing things that perfect the possibilities of the enterprise itself, make it the one it is'" (Cavell 2005, xxvii). In thus defining Cavell's achievement, I was also defining my own aspiration as a writer. I do not wish to "coarsen and stupefy myself." (Do you?)

The foreword I wrote for the expanded edition of *The "I" of the Camera* expressed my hope that the book would no longer meet with the same kind, and degree, or resistance I had anticipated in the book's original Preface. After all, he reign of "theory" over film study had ended, I said in the new Foreword, hoping that I wasn't whistling in the dark. The Foreword, echoing the original Preface, registered my conviction that the essays it contained challenged readers to think about film in ways responsive to their own experience, and responsive as well to the ways films themselves think. How films think is a question every essay addresses.

In his essay on *North by Northwest*, Cavell writes, "What I found in turning to think consecutively about film a dozen or so years ago was a medium which seemed simultaneously to be free of the imperative to philosophy and at the same time inevitably to reflect upon itself—as though the condition of philosophy were its natural condition" (Cavell 2005, xxii). Film seemed to Cavell to be "free of the imperative to philosophy" insofar as it had been able to avoid for so long the fate of modernism—the situation in which, as he understands it, an art has no choice but to be, like philosophy, "answerable to itself," to be "under its own question." A traditional art like painting, for example, only brought itself "under its own question" when painters such as Manbet found that they could no longer make paintings they believed in, believed in *as* paintings, without breaking radically with the very traditions they wished to keep alive. It was no longer natural, as it were, for the art to be true to its nature. What enabled film to remain comfortable for so long with its own tradition, Cavell's essay suggests, is that being "under its own question" *is* film's tradition. That film is a "moving image of skepticism," as he put it in "More of *The World Viewed* (Cavell 1979, 188), opens one path to understanding why this is so. Another such path is opened by the idea, expressed in "What Becomes of Things on Film?" (Cavell 1978) that things and people filmed by the movie camera participate actively in the creation of their own film images.

In any case, if it is in the nature of the art of film, in effect, to be "under its own question," it is natural for a film's "idea" to be, at one level, an idea about its own art, about the conditions of its medium that make it possible for film to be an art. For writing to articulate a film's idea, it must be "under its own question," too. That is why it is necessary for film study to be married to philosophy if it is not to exclude the kind of criticism without which it cannot be a "worthwhile human enterprise." Criticism *is* philosophy when it achieves its own poetry by acknowledging the poetry of film.

Although it was far from my main focus after publishing *The Murderous Gaze*, I did write several new essays on Hitchcock. Two were included in *The "I" of the Camera* when it was published in 1988. Two more were among the essays added to the second edition. All these essays expanded on ideas articulated in *The Murderous Gaze*. This was also the case with "Blood is Thicker Than Water: The Family in Hitchcock" (Rothman 2008a). But then, quite unexpectedly, I found myself again thinking almost obsessively about Hitchcock, pushing my thoughts in a new direction. When I learned that *The Murderous Gaze* was going out of print, my friend and editor *extraordinaire* Murray Pomerance invited me to submit an expanded edition for the "Horizons of Cinema" series he edits for SUNY Press.

For the new edition (Rothman 2012), I wrote a chapter that follows *Marnie* from beginning to end in the manner of the five original readings. It turned out to be even longer than the *Psycho* chapter. One reason was that almost a half-century after its release *Marnie* still stood in need of defending. No one these days doubts the stature of *Vertigo* or *Psycho*. But although *Marnie* has supporters, it remains widely denigrated. A serious defense of *Marnie*, I felt, required establishing what is singular, unprecedented, about it. One way *Marnie* was unprecedented, I argued, resides in the altered role it accords the camera. As I put it in a new Foreword, "At every moment the camera is doing *something* to elucidate the characters' thoughts, feelings and moods even as it reminds us of the singular way the world on film is at once present and absent, real and unreal" (Rothman 2012, xiv). In *Marnie*, the camera's relationship to the characters "is at every moment so intimate that all its revelations of their thoughts and feelings and moods are also revelations about the camera, about the 'art of pure cinema'" (Rothman 2012, xv). Because in *Marnie* the camera is declaring itself in everything it does, and because it is doing something meaningful at every moment, I felt the need to attend closely to every sequence, not only the passages—surprisingly few—in which the camera performs the virtuoso gestures that abound in other Hitchcock films. It was a daunting challenge to convey in prose—even complemented by hundreds of frame enlargements—the poetry *Marnie* achieves at every moment, not least in its dialogue sequences. Take away its poetry, and the film would have little to say, little to teach, about the "art of pure cinema" or about anything else.

For my reading of *Marnie* to reach what in *The "I" of the Camera* I called "the border that separates language from film," the writing itself, its own voices and silences, had to artfully evoke the film's poetry. As I put it in that book's Preface, "Such writing perceives film—a medium limited to surfaces, to the outer, the visible—as also a medium of mysterious depths, of the inner, the invisible. The moods the writing expresses, and casts, are themselves colored by the moods of faces and motions and settings it evokes. When those moods resonate with the film's moods, writing about film attains its own poetry." Take away whatever poetry it has achieved, and my chapter would have little to say, little to teach, about *Marnie*.

In the introduction to the first edition of *The Murderous Gaze*, I observed that I could imagine the readings engendering the sense that Hitchcock's work ended where it began, that from *The Lodger* to *Marnie* and beyond, his philosophical position never changed, as if, to paraphrase the immortal words of Norman Bates, who knows whereof he speaks, Hitchcock was in his own private trap within which, for all he scratched and clawed, he never budged an inch. When I wrote *The Murderous Gaze*, I recognized that a tension between two incompatible worldviews ran through his work. *The Murderous Gaze* argued that the inevitability of being suspended between these positions *was* Hitchcock's position. And yet, in the original five readings, dark moods intensify until they climax in the last pages of the *Psycho* chapter and the melancholy Postscript I began writing the day I heard that Hitchcock had died. By the time I wrote the chapter on *Marnie*, I had become aware that I had favored the dark side of Hitchcock's split artistic identity, the aspect encapsulated in the Oscar Wilde line he loved to quote: "Each man kills the thing he loves." In my reading of *Marnie*, my intention was to balance the scales.

When I wrote *The Murderous Gaze*, I had no name for the affirmative side of Hitchcock's artistic identity, or a historical or philosophical context in which to place it. Enter Cavell's term "Emersonian perfectionism." For Cavell, Emersonian perfectionism as not a theory of moral philosophy comparable to Kant's view that there is a universal moral law by which we can rationally determine whether an action is right or wrong, or Mill's view that the good action is that which will cause the greatest good, or the least harm, for the greatest number. Instead, moral perfectionism, in general, is an outlook or register of thought, a way of thinking about morality expressed thematically in certain works of philosophy, literature and film, that takes it to be our primary task as human beings to realize our humanity within a world with other people in it. The questions that couples in remarriage comedies address in their witty give-and-take are *moral* questions, as Cavell argues in his magisterial late book *Cities of Words* (Cavell 2004). But they are "formulated less well by questions concerning what they ought to do, what it would be best or right for them to do, than by the question how they shall live their lives, what kind of persons they aspire to be" (Cavell 2005, 54).

The 39 Steps followed the lead of *It Happened One Night* by ending with the union of a man and woman that holds a hope of being in a relationship worth having. In turn, the films Hitchcock made in the few years remaining before his departure for Hollywood followed the lead of *The 39 Steps* by aligning themselves with comedies of remarriage—but only up to a point. Hitchcock could not bring himself simply to embrace the American genre's Emersonian outlook because he was equally attracted to the idea that we are fated to kill the thing we love. In *Must We Kill the Thing We Love?* my central thesis is that Hitchcock's ambivalence toward Emersonian perfectionism, and his ambivalence toward overcoming or transcending that ambivalence, was the driving force of his work. The book discerns, in the vicissitudes of his ambivalence, a progression from his British thrillers to his earliest American films (made when the Emersonian moral outlook was beginning to suffer repression in Hollywood); to his wartime films; to his postwar films; to his masterpieces of the 1950s, culminating in *The Wrong Man*, *Vertigo* and *North by Northwest*; to *Psycho*; to *The Birds*; and ultimately to *Marnie*, in which—I claim, recapitulating the argument of the reading of *Marnie* I wrote for the new edition of *The*

Murderous Gaze—Hitchcock overcame or transcended his ambivalence and embraced the Emersonian perfectionism he had always also resisted.

To embrace Emersonian perfectionism, as my new book claims Hitchcock finally did, means, in part, to abandon oneself to the view that, as Emerson puts it in "Circles," "Every action admits of being outdone," that "our life is an apprenticeship to the truth, that around every circle another can be drawn; that there is no end in nature, but every end is a beginning." It is a defining feature of the Emerson essay that it draws a circle around the essays that came before it, a circle around which another circle can be drawn (by another essay that succeeds it). *Must We Kill the Thing We Love?* argues that this is a defining feature of the Hitchcock film as well. Looking back from the Emersonian perspective that I believe *Marnie* achieves, it is possible to perceive the Hitchcock thrillers that preceded it as leading up to it. *Marnie* draws Hitchcock's largest circle.

"Everybody wants to be settled," Emerson writes, "but only insofar as they are unsettled is there any hope for them." Writing about *Marnie* for the new edition of *The Murderous Gaze* brought home to me how unsettled my thoughts about Hitchcock had become in the years since I wrote the original five readings. In those years, I was in almost daily conversation with Cavell. And yet, in retrospect, I could see that as much as I had been drawn to philosophy as practiced by Cavell and by Emerson before him, I had also been as drawn as Hitchcock was to the idea that we're in private traps from which we're powerless to escape, and that we're fated to kill the thing we love. In writing *Must We Kill the Thing We Love?*, which retraced the trajectory of Hitchcock's career in a manner meant to balance the scales, I found, happily, that, as I put it in the introduction, "the Moving Finger, having writ, tilted the scales in favor of the Emersonian perfectionism I find myself no longer resisting" (Rothman 2014, 30). I had become an Emersonian perfectionist. *Must We Kill the Thing We Love?* draws a circle around the circle I had drawn when I wrote *The Murderous Gaze*.

Must We Kill the Thing We Love? is about Hitchcock, not Emerson. The chapters that comprise the body of the book invoke Emerson's name only occasionally, and usually in the context of reflections on the Hitchcock thriller's relationship to the Hollywood genres Cavell has shown to be exemplary of Emersonian perfectionism, or in reflecting on the reflections, which run throughout Hitchcock's oeuvre, motivated by the question, "What, if anything, justifies killing another human being?" Hitchcock thrillers, in their darkness, may well seem—in a sense they *are*—further removed from Emerson's way of thinking—not that he was a stranger to dark thoughts—than comedies of remarriage. And yet, my guiding intuition was that *as authors* Hitchcock and Emerson had profound affinities. In the course of writing the book, I came to realize that I had to "pay the tuition" for this intuition, as Emerson would have put it. Thus I wrote a concluding chapter that complements the introduction by closely reading passages from several Emerson essays and tracing some of the implications, for the study of film, of my discovery that "the terms in which they speak about reality, about our 'flux of moods', about what it is within us that never changes, about freedom, about reading, about writing, about seeing and about thinking, are remarkably pertinent—almost uncannily so—to 'reading' films, to writing about them, and to thinking about their medium and the art that medium makes possible." Insofar as writing this book enabled me to discover that my practice of reading and writing about films was underwritten, philosophically, by Emerson's way of thinking about reading and writing, this concluding chapter makes the entire book "answerable to itself," brings it "under its own question," declares its writing to be philosophy.

In 2006, the first part of the "philosophical memoir" Stanley Cavell had begun appeared in *Critical Inquiry* under the title "Excerpts from Memory" (Cavell 2003). This was to be the subtitle of *Little Did I Know* (Cavell 2010), the book he completed and published four years later. In telling the story of his life, Cavell's aspiration was to compose "a philosopher's or writer's autobiography, which, like Wordsworth's *Prelude* (quality aside), tells the writer's story of the life out of which he came to be a (his kind of) writer." Wordsworth showed, the passage goes on, that his story of how he came to be his kind of poet "had to be told in poetry—or rather showed that the telling of that story was the making of poetry. To do something analogous to that work, I would have to show that telling the accidental, anonymous, in a sense posthumous, days of my life is the making of philosophy" (Cavell 2010, 5). Because our memories of movies are "strand over strand" with memories of our lives, as he put it in the opening sentence of *The World Viewed*, Cavell found it necessary, in undertaking to write the story of the life out of which he became the philosopher he is, to evoke every moment with such concrete particularity that the resulting memoir reads like a screenplay. How else could he have learned and taught that the story of a life *could* be written in a way that made philosophy?

For Wittgenstein, philosophy's goal is to bring philosophy to an end. For Cavell, too, philosophy is inescapably concerned with endings. In writing *The World Viewed*, he brought to an end the period of his life in which going to the movies was a regular part of his week. In *Little Did I Know*, he told the story of the period of his life that ended when he was reborn as the only kind of writer, the only kind of philosopher, who could have written such a book (or could have wanted to). In writing this book, too, Cavell brought to an end a period of his life—the period that began where the story the book tells ends, the period in which he fully yielded to his longing for philosophy. Writing the book that tells this story is inseparable from the story it tells. In this writing, Cavell was as committed as ever to "walking in the direction of the unattained but attainable self," but his way of moving forward was by looking back. In telling this story, he brought its meaning home. This "philosophical memoir" is not only "under its own question"; it finds the answer it is seeking. For Cavell, philosophy had achieved its end.

I'm still journeying on.

Works Cited

Cavell, Stanley. 1971. *The World Viewed: Reflections on the Ontology of Film*. Cambridge, MA: Harvard University Press.

———. 1979. "More of *The World Viewed*." In *The World Viewed Expanded Edition*. Cambridge, MA: Harvard University Press.

———. 1978. "What Becomes of Things on Film?" *Philosophy and Literature* 2, no. 2: 249–57 (reprinted in *Cavell on Film*).

———. 1981a. "*North by Northwest*." *Critical Inquiry* 7, no. 4: 761–76 (reprinted in *Cavell on Film*).

———. 1981b. *Pursuits of Happiness: The Hollywood Comedy of Remarriage*. Cambridge, MA: Harvard University Press.

———. 1983. "The Thought of Movies." *The Yale Review*, Winter.

"An Interview with Stanley Cavell (with James Conant)." In *The Senses of Stanley Cavell, Bucknell Review*, edited by Richard Fleming and Michael Payne, 1989 (reprinted in *Cavell on Film*).

———. 1999 Paris Colloquium on *La Projection du Monde* (French translation of *The World Viewed*), in *Cavell on Film*.

———. 2003. "Excerpts from Memory." *Critical Inquiry*, Summer.

———. 2004. *Cities of Words: Pedagogical Letters on a Register of the Moral Life*. Cambridge, MA: Harvard University Press.

———. 2005. *Cavell on Film*, edited by William Rothman. Albany: State University of New York Press.

———. 2010. *Little Did I Know: Excerpts from Memory*. Stanford: Stanford University Press.

Dayan, Daniel. 1974. "The Tutor Code of Classical Cinema." *Film Quarterly*, Autumn.

Editors of *Cahiers du cinéma*. 1972. "*The Young Mr. Lincoln*: An Ideological Analysis." *Screen*, Autumn.

Morgan, Daniel. 2006. "Rethinking Bazin: Ontology and Realist Aesthetics." *Critical Inquiry*, Fall.

Mulvey, Laura. 1975. "Visual Pleasure and Narrative Cinema." *Screen*, Autumn.

Pomerance, Murray, and R. Barton Palmer. 2015. *Thinking in the Dark: Cinema, Theory, Practice*. New Brunswick, NJ: Rutgers University Press.

Rothman, Willliam. 1973. *Three Essays in Aesthetics* (dissertation submitted to Harvard University Philosophy Department).

———. 1975. "Against the System of the Suture." *Film Quarterly*, Summer.

———. 1982. *Hitchcock—The Murderous Gaze*. Cambridge, MA: Harvard University Press.

———. 1988. *The "I" of the Camera*. Cambridge: Cambridge University Press.

———. 1997. *Documentary Film Classics*. Cambridge: Cambridge University Press.

———. 2004. *The "I" of the Camera Expanded Second Edition*. Cambridge: Cambridge University Press.

———, ed.. 2007. *Jean Rouch: A Celebration of Life and Film*. Paris: Schena Editore and Presses de l'Université de Paris-Sorbonne.

———. 2008a. "Blood Is Thicker Than Water: The Family in Hitchcock." In *A Family Affair: Cinema Calls Home*. London: Wallflower Press.

———. 2008b. "Bazin as Cavellian Realist." *Film International*, Spring.

———, ed.. 2009. *Three Documentary Filmmakers: Errol Morris, Ross McElwee, Jean Rouch*. Albany: State University of New York Press.

———. 2012. *Hitchcock: The Murderous Gaze Expanded Second Edition*. Albany: State University of New York Press.

———. 2014. *Must We Kill the Thing We Love? Emersonian Perfectionism and the Films of Alfred Hitchcock*. New York: Columbia University Press.

Rothman, William, and Marian Keane. 2000. *Reading Cavell's "The World Viewed": A Philosophical Perspective on Film*. Detroit: Wayne State University Press.

Sarris, Andrew. 1962. "Notes on the Auteur Theory in 1962." Film Culture 27: 1–8.

———. 1968. *The American Cinema: Directions and Directors 1929–1968*. New York: Dutton.

Part III

HOW WE UNDERSTAND SCREEN TEXTS

Chapter Fourteen

THE EXPRESSIVE SIGN: CINESEMIOTICS, ENUNCIATION AND SCREEN ART

Daniel Yacavone

The fact that must be understood is that films are understood.

If it is true that cinematic invention is inevitably a mixture of artistic inspiration and language-like fashioning, the fact remains that the film-maker is always foremost an artist.

—Christian Metz, *Film Language* (1974)

If film theory paradigms are stocks on the intellectual market, following their peak highs in the 1970s, shares in semiotics and allied conceptual frameworks have been in decline and past decades have seen a major sell-off in favor of cognitive, neo-formalist, affect-based, phenomenological and various other theoretical approaches. Yet like semiotics more generally, cinemasemiotics (for short) is far from a single unified corpus of theoretical works, one specific doctrine, or a position that is amenable to being either fully embraced or rejected. Within film theory, semiotics is an umbrella term of convenience covering many differently oriented theories of the basic units of filmic communication and/or films as wholes conceived as signs or symbol systems. As in other contexts, film signs are seen to compose messages. For some theorists, these are governed by the use of codes and sub-codes, historically variable conventions of signification often entwined with socio-cultural assumptions, beliefs and ideologies.

Christian Metz is rightly regarded as a founding father of film semiotics. His seminal work, rooted in the linguistic structuralism of Ferdinand de Saussure and several of his major followers, is a primary reference point for any discussion of it. For Metz and theorists favorably disposed to his general program (as laid out in his early essay collection, *Film Language*) cinema relies on some of the same design features that are productive of linguistic sense-making, as appropriately modified to fit the medium's primarily visual mode of address. These include a reliance on cinematic and extra-cinematic conventions (and related codes), the presence of syntagmatic relations (as may be found in both the spatial and temporal axes of the film form, and both within and among images and sequences) and cross-media intertextuality.

Metz's approach is centered on the causal, spatial-temporal structures in and through which cinematic stories and worlds are created and comprehended. Thus, rather than a semiotics per se, along the lines of Umberto Eco's writings on film or even Peter Wollen's *Signs and Meaning in the Cinema*, his pre-psychoanalysis informed work is at base a *structural narratology*. It draws on key concepts in the study of narrative such as *diegesis*, as well as structuralist concepts such as the originally Saussurean ideas of the *paradigmatic* ("vertical") and *syntagmatic* ("horizontal") organization of signs constituting a semiotic system, be it an entire language, a written text or a visual work understood as a text.

Paradigms, for instance, are sets of functionally equivalent signifying elements. Metz sees them at work in cinema on the micro-level of the image (shot) as consisting of sets of possible cinematic techniques in common use for representing objects: such as different types of shot scale (long shots, medium shots, etc.), types of lighting, types of camera movements, as well as edited transitions between images (straight cuts, wipes, dissolves, etc.). But there are also paradigms that function on a higher level in narrative terms and involve the combination of images into what are commonly referred to as sequences. For Metz, these rather than images, in the form of individual shots, are the smallest basic units of analyzable *narrative* meaning a film possesses. His "*grande syntagmatique*" is a paradigm set of different ways of combining, sequencing and editing images into such self-contained syntagma, or "autonomous segments" of a film (Metz 1974, 140–46). Each type of syntagmatic ordering is differentiated from others on the basis of the purely structural-formal relations among articulations of time, space and action it involves, irrespective of concrete story content. For instance, a parallel montage construction, where different story actions in different locations are presented as occurring at the same time, is differentiated from what Metz refers to as a "scene," where the continuity of a single space and time is strictly preserved (Metz 1974, 140–46). At its most general, this approach seeks to identify which specific paradigms are available options in cinematic storytelling and the common conventions governing their use. (Conventions rather than binding rules, since, unlike a language proper cinema lacks necessary rules of combination.) Thus Metz's scheme may be used to trace the historical evolution of narrative film form. But in syntagmatic terms, and as he demonstrates in detail, it also provides for a systematic analysis of the narrative structures of particular films and by extension individual styles, movements and modes of filmmaking (Metz 1974, 149–82).

As illuminating and influential as it has been, the particular conjunction of semiotics, structural linguistics and continental narrative theory focused on cinema to which Metz and others have given voice is only one of many ways of theorizing the visual narrative dimension of the fiction film. Others, such as David Bordwell's and Edward Branigan's respective narratologies of film, make no use of syntagmas, codes or other ideas derived from structuralist linguistics. Moreover, while Metz's account of "film language" is firmly anchored in Saussure's "*semiòlogy*," other cinesemiotic approaches are based on pragmatist philosopher C. S. Peirce's equally pioneering "*semiotics*," or on various combinations of these two foundational understandings of sign-based communication.

Semiotics was enthusiastically embraced by film theorists who for various sociohistorical and disciplinary reasons sought to move away from the traditional "ontological" and aesthetic questions which preoccupied classical realist and formalist film theory, as well as subsequent auteurist approaches. Beginning in earnest in the late 1960s, with the marked rise of ideological critique in more sophisticated film criticism and in film studies as an emerging academic discipline, certain debates concerning, for example, the physical materials and medium of cinema; it's unique artistic properties in comparison with other art forms; the personal style and expression of film directors; evaluative criteria for judging a film or filmmaker good or bad; and so on, were superseded by considerations of films (especially conventional or mainstream ones) as sociocultural artifacts mirroring extant social and political realities. Semiotics and related structuralist and poststructuralist perspectives on aspects of modern society and popular culture provided powerful conceptual and analytic tools to study the cinematic representation of class, gender, race and other sociocultural realties in a more precise fashion. These included the leading structuralist idea of signification working through prominent, culturally constructed binary oppositions, for example, culture/nature, male/female, white/black, West/East, to which value laden meanings are attached (Chandler 2007, 88–99). Also applied to the culturally shaped technology of filmmaking and viewing itself, semiotic analysis of some sort thus became an integral part of feminist film theory, Marxist-ideological film theory, "apparatus theory," "Screen theory" and other social praxis-centered approaches. As sometimes overlooked, however, some of the most influential semiotic frameworks have typically paid due regard to the specifically aesthetic as well as wider cultural-ideological dimensions of cinema. Moreover, they have partly evolved out of consideration of film as art. Metz's earlier writings were notably informed by a mid-twentieth-century French tradition of comparative aesthetics and the phenomenology of art, including the work of art theorist Étienne Souriau and philosopher Mikel Dufrenne's *Phenomenology of Aesthetic Experience*. Many of Metz's writings, like Wollen's *Signs and Meaning in the Cinema*, are among those in film semiotics that shed light on the profound copresence and enfolding of representation and expression in cinema, together with literal, fictional-narrative and what David Bordwell terms "artistically motivated" meaning (1985, 19: 21–23).

Against this general background and from the perspective of film as art as well as communication, this chapter will first revisit two major semiotic concepts as applied to cinema. The first is Peirce's famous tripartite taxonomy of signs. The second is the basic distinction of denotation/connotation, central in Saussurean semiology and linguistic structuralism but modified by Metz and others to suit the visual medium of film. However, some contemporary theorists have looked to alternative symbol-centered models of cinema that diverge from more familiar linguistic structuralist and Peircean frameworks alike. Such "proto-linguistic" views—as I will term them to contrast with linguistic structuralist perspectives—speak more directly to films not only as cognitive sign systems, or texts to be figuratively read but also as full perceptual and affective *experiences* with many of the attributes of artworks in general. In the past decade, theorists have turned to such conceptual frameworks in connection with the "poetic" aspects and uses of cinema (Sitney 2015, and earlier Orr 1998), films as reflective of processes of embodied thought and consciousness (Vaughan 2013) and the created and experienced "worlds" of films (Yacavone 2015), among other topics. Metz's last major writings, only recently translated into English, also valuably illuminate some of these and related subjects in perhaps unexpected ways. At the core of his late film theory is an original semiotic account of "impersonal enunciation," that is, filmic address or "speech" to viewers. This takes the form of extra-narrative and self-reflexive devices and related meanings, which I will enlist Wes Anderson's films, together with an advertisement he made in 2006 (for American Express), to explicate.

Peirce's Taxonomy of Signs, Referential Hybridity and Cinesemiotic Creativity

Discussions of cinema's especially close relationship to reality, but also its distance from it via creative stylization and the mediation of non-celluloid image-making technologies, have and continue to be framed with respect to a foundational semiotic concept. This is Peirce's classification of the major types of signs, or more precisely, different *modes* of signification (Peirce 1932; Chandler 2007, 36–47). Peirce observes that signs may be placed on a spectrum from those that are more natural and based on some physical relation to those that are more conventional and culturally instituted. In the alternative Saussurean terms adopted by many writers, this translates to the difference between "motivated" and "arbitrary" signs. On the most conventional (arbitrary) end of signification are *symbols*, of which the words of a language are often taken as the paradigm case but which also include such familiar cultural artifacts as traffic signals, flags, diamond rings and articles of clothing. A symbol bears no natural or necessary relation to whatever it represents. This is clearly not the case with *icons*, signs that work by virtue of a recognizable formal or structural *resemblance* between the material sign token (e.g., a representational picture) and its (absent) object. A visual icon looks like what it represents in some relevant way, as relative to an individual's perception and to cultural conditioning as this may also be (cf. Mitchell 1986). Finally, for Peirce, an *index* is a sign that refers the mind to the reference object or event on the basis of a natural (or "motivated") connection between the two that is physical, causal and regular. Although its basis is natural and objective, the indexical sign relation as such is, of course, unavoidably mediated by human awareness, intentions and beliefs. Some examples of indices in Peirce's original scheme include a pointing finger (e.g., the "index" finger), smoke indicating a fire, a footprint and the readings provided by scientific measuring instruments. Peirce also discusses the indexical aspect of photography as an especially instructive case (Peirce 1932, 2: 281; Chandler 2007, 43).

Unlike most non-photographic visual representations, the live-action celluloid film image is an actual physical trace of something that has existed before the camera. This is the basis for realist conceptions of cinema most famously associated with André Bazin, Siegfried Kracauer, and later, Stanley Cavell. In the spirit of Peirce's original discussion, however, for these theorists and more contemporary ones, cinema's indexical relation to reality is not a matter of physical fact alone but human psychological attitudes and beliefs. With these factors taken into account, the emergence of digital filmmaking technologies in the 1990s prompted a new wave of interest in the indexicality of celluloid cinema and its suggested lack, or at least weakening, in digitally shot and/or manipulated films. Theorists including Mary Ann Doane, returning to Peirce's writing on the index in detail, and Lev Manovich, with reference to how the "language of new media" overturns cinematic indexicality as a fact, concept and discourse, both argue that the transition from celluloid to digital is a radical ontological and psychological rupture in the history of cinema (Doane 2001; Manovich 2001). Viewing this development in either positive (Manovich) or negative (Doane) terms, like other theorists, they stress its profound epistemic, ethical, aesthetic and stylistic consequences. Yet, even if these accounts are accepted, Peirce's taxonomy and other semiotic concepts aid in better understanding of what has also fundamentally *remained constant* in the transition from celluloid to digital, including numerous transmedial representational and narrative processes. (Stephen Prince, among others, persuasively argues for continuity between the use of CGI in mainstream cinema—which *pace* Manovich may enhance rather than diminish cinema's perceived realism—and traditional Hollywood-style visual and narrative technique (Prince 2011).) More generally, semiotics' traditional focus on communicative processes functioning irrespective of their specific physical media is a prima facie argument for the continued, perhaps greater than ever usefulness of semiotic theory in contemporary film theory (Cobley 2010).

With reference to the photographic image's only technologically "*forced*" correspondence to "nature," Peirce recognizes that the three basic modes of signification are not mutually exclusive in important respects, not least in the interplay of the natural and the cultural (Peirce 1932, 2: 281; Chandler 2007, 43). In terms of medium alone, most digital film images are (still) marked by the powerful conjunction of indexicality and iconicity characteristic of most photographic representation. Yet films also have a multifaceted *symbolic* dimension, in Peirce's sense. This includes not only what most commonly are thought of as visual symbols in films—for example, "phallic symbols," *Citizen Kane*'s rosebud, the enigmatic monolith in *2001: A Space Odyssey*—but also the whole level of what film semioticians refer to as *connotation* in cinema. Likewise, symbolic in the relevant sense are the narratively "submerged" thematic deep structures of cultural binaries Wollen uncovers in classical Hollywood films, as well as the combined "semantic" elements and "syntactic" relations that Rick Altman argues comprise film genres, as paradigmatically conventional, cultural constructions (Altman 1984; Wollen 1998, 50–78). What Noël Carroll and Trevor Whittock respectively analyze as instances of visual metaphor and synecdoche in cinema have iconic (perceptual) *and* symbolic (cultural) *and* cognitive aspects (recalling Roman Jacobson's category of "symbolic icons") (Jacobson 1968, 702; Whittock 1990; Carroll 1996, 224–25). Daniel Chandler, following Umberto Eco and others, aptly observes that "the same sign may be treated as indexical by one person, iconic by another, and symbolic by a third" (2007, 44) and this is as true for cinematic signs as for those in other media.

In sum, what may be considered a high degree of indexical, iconic and symbolic overlap and copresence occurs throughout films, in virtually every image and sequence. Although irrespective of filmmaker intentions, in many cases, such semiotic richness and versatility (as it may be called) is clearly a major creative resource for filmmakers with artistic ambitions beyond crafting a comprehensible and entertaining story. Filmmakers may place these referential modes and processes—which correspond to modes of viewer attention—in creative relations of perceptual and cognitive tension, dynamic and sometimes dialectical in nature. The auditory and temporal dimensions of films along with the visual add significantly to this meaning and feeling-generating capacity.

The first image of Michelangelo Antonioni's *Identification of a Woman* is of a frame-filling, geometrically patterned surface. Watched on the vertical screen, it is initially perceived as a vertical plane, for example, an image of the side of a wall. Until, with the top of an opening door appearing at the bottom of the frame and a figure walking through it, viewers realize that they and the camera have been looking down at a marble floor from above. This is not only an iconic representation following on an indexical relation but also a symbol (as well as a metaphor) of a theme to be developed subsequently, vis-à-vis the film's title and plot, that not everything is what it appears to be. This particular choice and its effect are not motivated solely by the intention to create a purely perceptual shock, or so called de-familiarization, for its own sake, although it certainly achieves this result. Reflecting concerns found throughout Antonioni's work, it is also a metonymic representation of the film's exploration of the relativity and fallibility of our perceptions and the presumed truth that we derive from these, and its consequences for self-identity, knowledge of others and interpersonal relationships. These thematics are also visually exemplified in the film's bravura sequence in which the main characters become lost in a thick fog bank eventuating in a total, if temporary, loss of all perceptual bearings on their part and the viewer's. Both sequences highlight that a film may not only draw on but problematize any of the very means by which it conveys meanings, including with respect to Peirce's sign functions. By virtue of the deliberate creation of ambiguity on the level of the visual, camera-provided representation and viewer perceptual recognition that goes awry, a kind of meta-symbol is generated that is specific to Antonioni's film and its created world.

The literature of semiotics contains alternative schemes and taxonomies of signs. As part of his original synthesis of Peircean ideas and structural linguistics, Jacobson attempts to improve on the basic tripartite scheme with a fourfold one that is more closely related to an informal or context-based approach in general semantics. It hinges on relative degrees of "similarity" between signifier and signified as well as "contiguity" (Jacobson 1968, 700–705; Chandler 2007, 45). The latter spatial term refers to physical and causal proximity between signifier and signified. Ripe for application in film theory, Jacobson's classification of signs appears in many ways a more helpful way of thinking about the symbolic forms and functions at work in cinema. Of particular note in connection with film as art is Jacobson's fourth category of signification, absent from Peirce, of "imputed similarity" (Jacobson 1968, 700–705; Chandler 2007, 45). As an early champion of abstract art and an associate of the Futurist school, Jacobson was highly sensitive to both visual and specifically artistic symbolization. His fourth category refers us to "ostensibly non-referential signs which nevertheless generate emotional connotations—such as music and non-representational visual art" (Chandler 2007, 45). Converging with what philosopher Susanne K. Langer famously analyzes as the highly expressive "presentational" symbolism of art and film—as distinct from the "discursive" symbolism of language and logic—Jacobson's category of imputed similarity is based on neither representational likeness, per se, nor on wholly conventional, pre-established cultural attribution (Langer 1951, 1953). Instead, it speaks to perceptual and formal features of works, including films, which evince emotional tones or moods among other expressive qualities. Such features are an increasing object of interest on the part of cognitive, phenomenological, Deleuzian and other film theorists. For instance, the figuratively ambiguous (or non-figurative) images in some experimental and narrative films, which Laura U. Marks argues prompt a highly affective "haptic visuality" in so far as they bypass higher-order processes of imagination, reason and psychological control at work in conventional "optical" representations (Marks 2000, 164–76).

Connotation, Extra-Narrative Meaning and Artistic Invention

Contrary to strong realist and so-called perceptualist positions in film theory and the philosophy of film, semiotic approaches stress that although its technology allows cinema to *record* the visual appearance of existing physical objects rather than only *represent* things in the manner of other arts, complex, culturally mediated signification is always in operation in both the construction of film images and their comprehension. Despite certain and much discussed problems that emerge in its detailed application to (moving) images, apart from the signified/signifier distinction, that between *denotation/connotation* is the most fundamental in film semiotics (see Harman 1977).

Metz regards filmic denotation as the basic iconic reference by camera-generated images to the objects they represent, which is readily recognized by viewers on the basis of perceptual analogy between the two. Products of both nature and culture, as it were, film images and the narratives they comprise have this built-in level of literal reference, for example, in Robert Bresson's masterpiece *Au hasard Balthazar* iconic images *of* a donkey, the film being the story of said donkey's visually depicted abuse by a series of owners. But the self-same image or narrative may have substantial figurative meaning content, here in terms of the persecution of Christ or other spiritual martyrs. All such "surplus" meaning, which obviously comprises a very large category to say the least, has been labeled connotation by Metz and other film semioticians because like the connotative meanings of a word or longer expression in language and, most prominently, in literary and poetic writing, it is "parasitically" built upon but always exceeds denotation. Since for Metz, denotation in cinema is fundamentally a matter of perceptual analogy between the *signifier* (film image) and "*significate*" (the recognized object it presents), connotation is instead "symbolic" ("the significate motivates the signifier but goes beyond it") (Metz 1974, 108–9). As Jean Mitry also discusses in detail (including before Metz addressed the subject), film images are most typically not in the business of *merely* denoting their subjects in what some theorists call "neutral" images (Mitry 2000a, 2000b; Metz 2015, 135–40). Rather they routinely present them to convey multiple, often complex associative meanings that are tied to realities most often perceptually absent from what is actually seen on the screen or heard on the soundtrack, and hence that portion of actual reality that has been physically captured and recorded.

While cinematic denotation is within the capabilities of all viewers to grasp, basically at the level of untutored perception, the uptake of connotation is a much more variable matter. It is always conditioned by a given viewer's requisite background knowledge and cultural (including cinematic) experience. Setting a precedent for many subsequent theorists, in the 1950s (and starting *prior* to his discovery of Saussure's work on connotation), Barthes analyzed how certain manufactured and ideologically motivated "second order" meanings of objects and events in visual media—popular films, televised spectacles, magazines, advertisements, and so on—suppress many others. This is tantamount to an intentional closing down of the otherwise wide connotative field of signification in the interest of conservative political and consumerist agendas (Barthes, 1972). Although in reality constructed and contingent, such second order meanings, which Barthes terms cultural "mythologies," are erroneously (or in freedom-denying "bad faith") accepted as part of the "first order," that is, denotative, significance of the things to which they have been attached as an ostensible natural and necessary feature of them. Associative meanings working through cinematic representation in its literal register may be part of a larger ideological design as Barthes shows, or an artistic one, or neither. As in other forms and media, those connotations integral to a film's artistic function and experience, on thematic and conceptual levels as well as perceptual ones, may also be "second-order" realities; not only in the sense noted above vis-a-vis relation to denotation (alone), but as creatively built on top of other, preexisting cultural connotations.

Metz recognizes that one form of cinematic connotation, which unlike others is clearly under the control of filmmakers, is the figurative and strictly speaking extra-narrative meaning generated as a result of profilmic objects being framed, lit, edited or otherwise shown by filmmakers (like Bresson, in the example above) in unusual and often creatively stylized ways. For Metz, here drawing on Dufrenne's aesthetics, such deviations from perceptual norms are a major part of the distinctly artistic aspect of film signification rooted in style and aesthetic expressiveness (Metz 1974, 75–84). They are a primary means of drawing attention to something about denoted objects, or quite beyond them, in the pursuit of various and in principle unlimited meanings and feelings. Yet creative invention on the connotative plane is not confined to perceptual defamiliarization.

In Krzysztof Kieslowski's *Three Colors Trilogy*, a familiar, preexisting visual symbol with a host of connotations—the French tricolor flag and its component parts (blue, white and red)—are conjoined with the equally associative ideals of *liberty*, *equality*, and *fraternity*. Born of the 1789 Revolution, the latter were subsequently enshrined as the guiding principles and official motto of France's Third Republic. As a testament to the conceptual and expressive force of the Trilogy's combined visual, structural and thematic motif, many viewers and critics alike have simply taken the implied thematic connection of these principles with the tricolor's hues as a cultural-historical fact long predating the films. Far from a simple appropriation, however, their pairing with the flag in general—together with the matching of a specific color with an ideal (taking into consideration the conventional and natural symbolism of the colors and their potential resonances with multiple notions of liberty, equality and fraternity) was wholly the invention of Kieslowski and his accomplished screenwriter Krzysztof Piesiewicz (Kieslowski 1993, 312). Although it builds on the dual thematic/structural strategy at work in their earlier *Dekalog* cycle, ten films which are each free interpretations of one of the Biblical Ten Commandments, here a highly expressive visual component is added. In the Trilogy, this original, creative synthesis of two preexisting symbolic figurations, one visual and the other linguistic/conceptual is a platform for each film's dramatic, deeply humanistic exploration of the hopes, ambiguities and hypocrisies of the three idea(ls) in a late twentieth century European context. They are literally and figuratively filtered through the perceptual (iconic) corollary of color-coded objects, environments and images.

Alternative Proto-Linguistic Approaches and Film Worlds Theory

An alternative, loosely knit and symbol-centered tradition in film theory indicates the fertile territory outside of the boundaries of more familiar and established semiotic paradigms. Relatively closer to Peirce's semiotics than Saussure's semiology, given the former's primary attention to the non-linguistic sign, its best known proponents are two filmmakers as well as theorists, Jean Mitry and Pier Paolo Pasolini, and the major twentieth century philosopher Gilles Deleuze. Their stress on the full perceptual, audio-visual and dynamic temporal nature of the film image is reflected in Pasolini's account of "*imsegnia*" or "im-signs" (short for "image signs") as the basic semiotic materials of cinema; Mitry's detailed theory of the psychological-cum-aesthetic rather than linguistic sign in cinema; and Deleuze's elaborate, non-Saussurean taxonomy of vision-based "signs" and "images" in films (indebted to Pasoloni's ideas together with Peirce's and Henri Bergson's).

In spite of notable differences between them, Mitry's, Pasolini's and Deleuze's views of cinematic meaning and expression are aptly termed "proto-linguistic," based in the common experiential origins of *all* pictorial and linguistic symbolization. Unlike Saussure, who famously brackets off the psychological and behavioral dimensions of symbolic meaning generation, and the real world object (referent) of the sign itself, in his written rather than spoken language-centered semiology, these theorists stress the importance of both in cinema. They hold that both prior, and subsequent to, the artistic processes of filmmaking, the combined photographic and temporal nature of the moving image renders cinema especially close to the direct visual experience of objects and events that it simulates—and certainly much closer than any language. However, each also sees cinema as equally reflective of inner conscious life. It is intimately connected to the whole domain of mental imagery, encompassing the processes and contents of memory, dream, fantasy and pictorial imagination.

Mitry maintains that "we think in images, with images, long before we think with words," and this idea is the foundation for his understanding of the symbolic dimension of cinema in terms of an informal, vision-based and strongly contextual pragmatics of image relationships (2000b, 253). In his *Aesthetics and Psychology of Film,* he argues that the film image, as an intention-laden *analagon* of the object(s) it presents, always has a composite or dual character. Its immediate perceptual content provided by the camera (in the form of an image-object) is always concretely presented through filmic techniques and style in such a way as to call attention to a further dimension of narrative and extra-narrative meaning that is often highly specific to a given film (Mitry 2000a, 51, 72–88; see also Andrew 1976, Yacavone 2015; Lefebvre 2014). Thus Mitry asserts that in concrete experience, film images do not have denotation but *only* connotation. They are always and only encountered as an integrated part of a larger, highly expressive narrative, thematic and aesthetic totality (which he occasionally refers to as alternative "world" on the screen). More than the screenplay, for instance, or what a summary of a film in language could ever capture, this totality is the product of a filmmaker's style and expressed/expressive "vision," sequentially revealed as a film unfolds. For Pasolini, who emphasizes the filmmaker's creative *selection* among not just existing physical objects but also already existing transsubjective mental "images" with shared cultural or cross-cultural significance ("im-signs"), all filmmaking is rooted in the "common patrimony" of [non-linguistic] signs (Pasolini 1988, 171). Thus in artistic terms, the creation of the meaningful and expressive whole Mitry analyzes also necessarily involves filmmakers using and modifying all manner of symbolic associations already attached to profilmic objects to a work's own particular artistic ends (Metz 1974, 75–84; Pasolini 1988; Yacavone 2015, 75–83).

Deleuze writes in the preface to the English-language edition of *Cinema 1*: *The Movement-Image* that corresponding to a "pure semiotics," the images and signs comprising films are "pre-verbal intelligible content" (Deleuze 2001a, ix). With this focus, he idiosyncratically embraces aspects of Peirce's thought on signs that are not prima facie the creatures of language, using it as a foil for his well-known critique of structural, formal linguistics, including Metz's attempted application of it to cinema (Deleuze 2001b, 25–30). Following Bergson's metaphysics, Deleuze maintains that images as distinct from things, on the one hand, and ideas, on the other, are the primitive constituents of all direct experience. Cinema by virtue of the temporally dynamic properties of the medium and its technology as creatively employed has the ability to access and in effect replicate this primary level of awareness through moving images and their mental surrogates. Like Mitry and especially Pasolini—whose ideas concerning this reality, framed in terms of im-signs, Deleuze vigorously defends against the criticism of more orthodox semioticians like Eco and Metz—he regards films as an audiovisual product of distinctly cinematic thought (Deleuze 2001b). Based like all art (painting, literature, drama, etc.) in the "being of sensible," cinema has expressive rather than properly speaking rational and communicative significance (Deleuze 1994, 68). It thus stands wholly apart from the regime of the linguistic signifier and conceptual thought wedded to the a priori fixed categories of language.

Such proto-linguistic approaches are today particularly attractive given skepticism concerning films as conventionally signifying texts on the model of language and the abstraction from perception and concrete experience it entails. They speak to more sensory, affective and broadly speaking experiential dimensions of cinema many regard as historically neglected in film theory, whether in classical realist and formalist theory, or more recent cognitive approaches. These aspects are also clearly central to film as art and to film-viewing as an aesthetic experience. Yet Deleuze's antagonism notwithstanding, they ultimately compliment rather than necessarily replace a number of more orthodox semiotic ideas. In juxtaposition with phenomenological insights, Hunter Vaughan enlists Mitry's, Pasolini's and Deleuze's perspectives, as well as Metz's and Eco's understandings of cinematic connotation, to support his view that films may "think" about the world in new ways on the basis of cinema's audiovisual potential to both replicate, and reflect upon, objective and subjective poles of experience. This potential is fully actualized for Vaughan in the films of Jean-Luc Godard and Alain Resnais (Vaughan 2013). Similarly rejecting the idea that they are necessarily exclusive with respect to films *as wholes*, in my proposed model of a cinematic work as a multi-leveled "world," I have brought together a number of Metz's semiotic categories and distinctions—including his specific versions of the diegetic/non-diegetic and denotation/connotation dichotomies—with aspects of these more experientially and artistically focused proto-linguistic accounts (Yacavone 2015). More precisely, the total symbolic-cognitive and *experiential* reality of a cinematic work encompasses a film's significance on the levels of basic audiovisual representation and fiction (in the case of a narrative film), which together comprise what Metz and many other theorists term a film's "diegetic world" or what I alternatively call the "world-*in*" a film (Yacavone 2015). But as per both the more common understandings of the word, and specialized uses of the concept of "world" in philosophy, art and literary theory (stretching back to the eighteenth century), films are also best understood as worlds in others senses as well. These include as the singular narrative, semantic and stylistic wholes Mitry and Pasolini suggest. Both non- and extra-diegetic features and meanings (thematic, reflexive, intertextual, generic, parodic, allusive, etc.), as well as the concrete perceptual conveyance of all representational content through specific filmic techniques and styles are also part of films' singular, relatively self-enclosed and world-like character and experience. Finally, and no less importantly, these totalities involve individual feeling contents of various kinds as attached to each of these other four constitutive levels of a cinematic work (representational, narrative, extra-narrative and formal-stylistic), which share the affective stage of film experience with what I theorize (like Metz, with reference to Dufrenne's aesthetics) as a film's unique, overarching "cineaeshtetic world-feeling." As a "global," cumulative and emergent feature of a film's temporal experience, the latter supervenes on more temporally and spatially "localized" feelings (Yacavone 2015, 159–227). Including the represented world-in, the sum of the complex and work-constitutive relations among all of these interpenetrating levels or aspects in the form of an integrated cognitive and affective network is best described, in my suggested shorthand, as the created and experienced "world-*of*" a cinematic work, or simply "film world" (Yacavone 2015, 25–26, 31–34).

Some leading implications and consequences of this model in the present context are that no adequate understanding of a film as either an experience for the body and senses as well as the mind, or as an artwork, can ignore its semiotic dimension conceived in some of the ways discussed above. A narrative film is simultaneously and non-exclusively a mode of literal representation and communication, a form of storytelling and fictional world-making, a meeting point of wider cultural realities as well as all manner of cinematic, dramatic and narrative conventions (techniques, styles, genres, etc.), and in some instances a means of personal artistic expression. *All* of these modalities involve signification in one form or another. But films—both as films and as "virtual" worlds—also contain perceptual, affective and other first-person qualities that are not amenable to semiotic analysis. Moreover, as I have also argued in the context of worlds theory, the nature of cinematic art necessitates supplementing the Saussurean and Peircean semiotic frameworks most often discussed in film theory with other relevant theories of symbolization centered on art specifically. Prominent among these is philosopher Nelson Goodman's theorization of all art, including cinema, as a form of symbolic world-making (Goodman 1978). Rooted in referential relations of denotation and "exemplification," of which artistic "expression" and "allusion" are two category types, I have transposed Goodman's theory of symbolic form and function across all of the arts and the sciences to cinema in detail (Goodman 1976; Yacavone 2015, 86–157).

A "New" Pragmatics of Cinematic Enunciation, Style and Authorship

Continuing on the theme of more recent developments in semiotics and symbol theory that are of particular relevance to film art broadly defined, we come to Metz's in-progress return to the cutting edges of film theory discourse. Its occasion is the 2015 English-language publication of *Impersonal Enunciation, or The Place of Film* (a book only some sections of which were published before his death in 1993), which have prompted far-reaching comparisons with Derrida's and Barthes's poststructuralism, cybernetics, contemporary network and new media theory, and "media archaeology" (Metz 2015, ix–xxiii, 177–86). This last phase of Metz's work generally eschews the largely ahistorical (or "synchronic") approach of his early writing and Saussure's linguistics, together with the Lacanian psychoanalytic orientation of *The Imaginary Signifier*, in favor of a novel *textual pragmatics* of the moving image anchored in film and media history and style.

Beyond any suggested (informal) syntax and semantics of cinema, some film theorists, notably Francesco Casetti, a leading film semiotician, have stressed the importance of pragmatics in understanding filmic communication and especially a film's address of/to viewers, as at least a para-linguistic phenomenon. A corollary of the distinction within linguistic pragmatics between the content of an utterance and the act of its being spoken, the "énonciation/énoncé" distinction in literary theory (introduced by structural linguist and semiotician Émile Benveniste) draws attention to acts or processes of narration (énonciation) in contrast to narrated content (énoncé). Casetti's theory of enunciation in cinema centers on how films create the equivalent of those relations in speech that involve personal pronouns—I, you, me, she, it, etc. (Casetti 1999; Metz 2015). Speakers use these and other *deictic* markers in language in order to communicate meaning that is only fully comprehensible through shared knowledge of the specific spatial-temporal circumstances of the speech act. In films, on Casetti's analysis, depending upon the particular on screen dynamics with respect, for instance, to the tense of represented events, forms of narrative and character address, point of view and editing, these ever-shifting pronoun roles are filled by characters, the filmmaker and the film viewer. All three on this view are participants in the experience of film as a communicative conversation (see Casetti 1999 and Metz 2015, 13–16).

While acknowledging the originality of Casetti's models and retaining a number of his ideas, Metz finds this general approach via linguistic pragmatics, which he terms "humanoid enunciation," too anthropomorphic (2015, 3–24). Rather than an actual conversation between actual subjects, there is only one "speaker" in cinema—the film itself—whose "speech" is "uninterrupted" neither literally allowing nor acknowledging response (Metz 2015, 19). For this reason and others, film viewing is characterized by pronounced "textual closure" (Metz 2015, 19). Still wishing to retain enunciation as a fundamental part of filmic communication, Metz argues that it is instead a wholly "impersonal" semiotic process, "more *metadiscursive* than deicitic" (2015, 18). Making ample use of a wide range of relevant concepts in narrative theory, including Gerard Genette's categories of meaning which extend beyond the confines of diegesis ("extra-diegetic," "intra-diegetic," etc.), he maintains that films foreground both their own acts of narration and their filmic nature through a "semiological act by means of which certain parts of a text speak to us of that text as an act" (Metz 2015, 10). These acts take various concrete and coded forms that allow films to address viewers from a "place" (or "foyer") either completely or partly outside of their diegetic worlds (in the case of fictional films). Through a wealth of examples, Metz catalogs types and subtypes of the familiar devices used for this purpose. They include various forms of voice-over and "voice-in" narration; direct address of the camera; presentation of written text on screen (including inter-titles); the presence of objects signifying the filmic and/or theatrical apparatus (cameras, curtains, proscenium arches) in either literal or more figurative fashion; frames within frames; mirrors and other reflective surfaces within the mise-en-scene of films (and the *mise-en-abyme* figurations they may create) and various iterations of the *film-within-the-film* device. Consistent with the *world-in* and *world-of* distinction in film and the theoretical motivation behind it, as described earlier, on Metz's view all of these devices allow films to convey something to viewers on semantic and thematic planes which would not be possible from within the confines of their diegesis or fictional worlds. While originating in celluloid cinema, Metz's enunciative devices and categories are transmedial. He finds them at work in films shot on video, television programs and moving-image advertisements.

The relation of enunciation to style is the complex subject of one of the chapters in *Impersonal Enunciation*, "The Oriented Objective System: Enunciation and Style" (Metz 2015, 121–35) and this topic returns us to some of the issues addressed above under the heading of the stylistic and aesthetic aspects of filmic connotation. Metz insists on a clear distinction between enunciative devices and stylistic markers. Style is here understood as the personal, "auteur" style of filmmakers, which although it may make ample use of conventions and codes is by definition nonconventional. Enunciative devices, in contrast, acquire their basic meaning through repeated use and habitual recognition throughout the history of cinema and related moving-image media. They communicate to viewers extra-diegetically and extra-narratively, wholly irrespective of any significant creative originality which may or may not be present, and any notable personal style (another reason why Metz deems the enunciation he analyzes "impersonal"). When any of the devices in question are part of the work of a genuine auteur, however, as an element in the total artistic design of his or her film—for example, the *film-within-the-film* device in Godard's *Contempt*—its full significance in and for the film as a whole and its experience clearly exceeds its basic semiotic function. Enunciative convention in this instance is very "close" and in "exchanges […] numerous and ongoing" with all manner of intended personal meaning and expression within the context (in the above example) of Godard's artistic vision, style and world(s) (Metz 2015, 127). As borne out by film and televisual practice, it follows that a given enunciative device, for example, the direct address of the camera/viewer, may have many sorts of meaning—aesthetic, ideological (or counter-ideological), coercive (in the case of advertising), didactic (in the case of some documentaries)—depending on not only how it is employed, but *where* and *when* (given the temporal and cumulative nature of a film and its meaning).

With a demonstrable appeal well beyond the art cinema traditions of which they are also a part, Wes Anderson's films are chock-full of the enunciative devices Metz discusses. These include *The Royal Tenenbaums*' division into sections introduced by non-diegetic insert shots of the pages of a fictitious book. Implied to be telling the story of the film in chapters (complete with illustrations of the characters), its first sentences are read in voice-over by an unnamed narrator (Alec Baldwin). For Metz, enunciative devices may be either "reflexive" or "commentative" (i.e., commenting on the narrative fiction), or as in this case, both of these simultaneously (2015, 54). *The Life Aquatic* features a *film-within-the-film* being made by Captain Steve Zissou (Bill Murray) and his eccentric crew of explorers-cum-filmmakers, which reflects and refracts Anderson's filmmaking adventures with a now familiar and consistent roster of performers and off-screen collaborators. *The Life Aquatic* circularly ends at the world premiere of Zissou's film, and *both* represent a postmodern take on Jacques Cousteau's brand of staged underwater adventure documentaries filtered through Anderson's instantly recognizable visual style, tone and faux-naïve sensibility. Speaking to how enunciation may operate through certain represented objects by virtue of their inherent filmmaking and/or viewing associations, the frame-filling blue velvet curtains that open and close *Rushmore* are a conventional signifier of theatre and cinema presentation. Referring in "intra-textual" fashion forward and then back to the play-within-the-film written and directed by the precocious Max Fischer (Jason Schwartzman), this device also exemplifies the status of credit sequences in films as often simultaneously within and without the diegesis (as also discussed by Metz).

A final and particularly evocative act of cinematic enunciation is found in *Moonrise Kingdom*. Like Anderson's other films, it contains numerous highly stylized and "self-conscious" compositions of the sort Bordwell terms "planimetric" (1997, 168–69, 262–63). These are front-facing, symmetrically composed tableau, many featuring frames within frames provided by architectural features and other elements of mise-en-scene. The last of these compositions, in the film's final sequence, presents a centrally framed painting of a pivotal dramatic location from earlier in the film: the cove christened "Moonrise Kingdom" by Sam and Suzy, the two early teenage lovers who escape there, and which provides the setting for their proverbial coming of age. A now familiar *mise-en-abyme* situation of an image in a film *of* an image in the film—here paired with the "intermedial" gesture of representing a painting on screen—as if by fairytale magic the painting (made by Suzy) transforms into the place/location it represents via a slow dissolve to a wide shot of the cove. The film's last image is a fitting iconic (in the semiotic sense) microcosm of its expressive heart. On this affective note, although without recourse to the linguistic-semiotic term, Carl Plantinga has discussed some of the aforementioned enunciative devices and others in *The Royal Tenenbaums* as objects of "artifact emotion" on the part of viewers. Distinct but sometimes simultaneous with feelings generated by aspects of narrative, drama and character, such emotions are prompted by the viewer's attention to features of a film as a constructed work (Plantinga 2009, 89–93).

As a devout cinephile and professed lover of French New Wave cinema, in particular, it is difficult not to see Anderson's adoption of such extra-narrative and self-reflexive devices as general allusions to the films of Godard, Truffaut, Fellini, Bergman and other canonical European art film directors in which they are famously prevalent. Such allusion is certainly at work in Anderson's elaborate 2006 advertisement for American Express credit cards, comprising a continuous two-minute-long sequence shot. Produced by the major marketing firm of Ogilve and Mather and directed by Anderson, it is a direct homage to Truffaut's *Day for Night* and foregrounds the filmmaking process in many of the ways Metz analyzes.

In the manner of Truffaut's 1973 film in which he plays a celebrated director much like himself, the commercial depicts a fictitious film being shot by Anderson, who appears as himself alongside a number of his regular actors and crew. In the midst of chaotic and absurdly humorous on-set occurrences, Anderson periodically opines to the camera in tongue-and-cheek fashion concerning the process of filmmaking against the aural background of an extract of Georges Delerue's celebrated orchestral soundtrack to *Day for Night*. Shot in front of a French chateaux, the advertisement also contains the manufactured snow prominent in the last sequence of Truffaut's film, and otherwise inexplicable spoken references to a "Françoise" and "Jean-Pierre" (presumably New Wave icon and *Day for Night* star, Jean-Pierre Leaud). It ends on an appropriately self-reflexive note, with a dramatic rising-crane shot of Anderson and his cinematographer atop (another) crane rising high above the film set.

The commercial follows the enunciative conventions of American Express' "My Life. My Card" media campaign (begun in 2004), but in ways matching its subject also creatively deviates from this template. The series of advertisements in question feature creative artists in various media whose names and activities are relatively better known than their faces. Following a montage of scenes representing their working lives, all end with close-ups of American Express cards "revealing" their identities in the form of their signatures printed on the cards. This is accompanied by some version of the spoken motto "this is my life and this is my card." In this case, however, Anderson is introduced at the start of the advertisement as "Wes Anderson, Director" in his customary and by then already well-established titles design consisting of yellow text in a distinctive font. At its conclusion, rather than already printed on a credit card, Anderson's signature is invisibly hand signed before the viewer's eyes within an enlarged depiction of a card's signature box (as one side of a split screen composition with Anderson atop the aforementioned crane and facing the camera on the other). Calling to mind Derrida's exploration of the semiotics of the signature as a performative gesture, here the signature enlisted to sell the product is also a signifier of Anderson's "signature" style as a (then) rising auteur (Derrida 1988). It is couched in terms of inter-cinematic reference not only to *Day for Night* but through association with Truffaut, the famously auteur-centered French New Wave. However ironic in tone, and in addition to its extensive enunciative and reflexive signification in Metz's terms, viewed critically, the advertisement also exemplifies the contemporary cultural semiotics of film authorship. The auteur's name (be it a director's or screenwriter's) is now more than ever not only a signifier of a particular style and world or world-view, but as noted by Dudley Andrew and others, a brand and commodity; a marketing tool for selling cinema tickets and today more lucratively, DVD, Blu-ray and online streaming services (Andrew 2000).

In the advertisement and feature films mentioned, the "stock" reflexive and/or commentative devices employed are given new expressive and stylistic life by a creative filmmaker working on and with these conventional filmic signifiers. These examples clearly bear out Metz's suggestion that

> "postmodern" cinema [...] could be characterized in its entirety by systematic reproduction of old tics of enunciation that are reconditioned for extra-effect and transformed into tools of a style or markers of a manner. This evolution is even clearer in "trendy" advertising, which is to say, almost all advertising nowadays. (2015, 127)

A more detailed analysis of these and other such creatively recycled devices in Anderson's body of work, and their interaction with other narrative and extra-narrative features and techniques would clearly contribute to a better understanding of his particular "postmodern" brand of auteur filmmaking and its abiding critical and commercial popularity.

In another context, I have recently drawn attention to various phenomenological conceptions of artistic creation and aesthetic experience that have been marginalized or neglected in contemporary film theory mainly taking its cue from the phenomenology of ordinary, nonartistic perception and experience (Yacavone 2016). In a similar aesthetic vein and also departing from convention, here I have focused on some traditional (e.g., Metzian) and "alternative" semiotic frameworks and ideas that illuminate celluloid and digital film *as art*, as well as basic filmic communication and its sociocultural coding. A larger, meta-theoretical issue alluded to at the start of this chapter is a tendency in more recent film theory to treat semiotic accounts of cinema generally, and Metz's perpetually evolving work, in particular, as an all or nothing proposition to be accepted or as is now more common disowned *in toto*. Without going into more details, such absolutism, pro or con, is already suspect on a priori grounds. It runs counter to the powerfully hybrid, multisensory, audiovisual, dramatic, narrative and extra-narrative character and capacities of the fiction film form. And following from this, it risks denying that films are not only *understood* (as Metz stresses), but they successfully communicate and express on multiple levels, in multiple ways, and through multiple forms of reference. (Regardless of disagreement as to how many levels, their precise nature, the exact processes of reference in question, how these may or may not be shaped or determined by various media and their ontologies and so on.) With the benefit of distance in time and perspective from the hegemony of semiotics and structuralism in film theory—and a waning of the doctrinaire and proselytizing zeal with which it was first embraced—sign and symbol-centered approaches seem ripe for critical yet open-minded reassessment and revival.

Works Cited

Altman, Rick. 1984. "A Semantic/Syntactic Approach to Film Genre." *Cinema Journal* 23, no. 3: 6–18.

Andrew, Dudley. 1976. *The Major Film Theories*. Oxford: Oxford University Press.

———. 2000. "The Unauthorized Auteur Today." In *Film Theory: An Anthology*, edited by Robert Stam and Toby Miller, 20–29. Oxford: Blackwell.

Barthes, Roland. 1972. *Mythologies*. Translated by Annette Lavers. London: Paladin.

Bordwell, David, Janet Staiger and Kristin Thompson. 1985. *The Classical Hollywood Cinema, The Classical Film Style & Mode of Production to 1960*. London: Routledge.

———. 1997. *On the History of Film Style*. Cambridge, MA: Harvard University Press.

Carroll, Noël. 1996. *Theorizing the Moving Image*. Cambridge: Cambridge University Press.

Casetti, Francesco. 1999. *Inside the Gaze: The Fiction Film and its Spectator*. Translated by Nell Andrew with Charles O'Brien. Bloomington: Indiana University Press.

Chandler, Daniel. 2007. *Semiotics: The Basics*. London: Routledge.

Cobley, Paul, ed. 2010. *The Routledge Companion to Semiotics*. New York: Routledge.

Deleuze, Gilles. 1994. *Difference and Repetition*. Translated by Paul Patton. New York: Columbia University Press.

———. 2001a. *Cinema 1: The Movement-Image*. Translated by Hugh Tomlinson and Barbara Habberjam. Minneapolis: University of Minnesota Press.

———. 2001b. *Cinema 2: The Time-Image*. Translated by Hugh Tomlinson and Robert Galeta. Minneapolis: University of Minnesota Press.

Derrida, Jacques. 1988. "Signature Event Context." In *Limited Inc*, translated by Samuel Weber and Jeffrey Mehlman. Evanston, IL: Northwestern University Press.

Doane, Mary Ann. 2001. "Indexicality and Medium Specificity." *Differences: A Journal of Feminist Cultural Studies* 18, no. 7: 128–52.

Goodman, Nelson. 1976. *Languages of Art: An Approach to a Theory of Symbols*. Indianapolis, IN: Hackett.

———. 1978. *Ways of Worldmaking*. Indianapolis, IN: Hackett.

Harman, Gilbert. 1977. "Semiotics and Cinema: Metz and Wollen." In (2004) *Film Theory and Criticism*, 5th ed., edited by Leo Braudy and Marshall Cohen, 90–98. Oxford: Oxford University Press.

Jacobson, Roman. 1968. "Language in Relation to Other Communication Systems." In (1971) *Selected Writings, vol. 2, Word and Language*. The Hague: Mouton.

Kieślowski, Krzysztof. 1993. *Kieślowski on Kieślowski*, edited by Danusia Stok. London: Faber and Faber.

Lefebvre, Martin. 2014. "Symbol and Analagon." In *The Routledge Companion to Film Theory* edited by Edward Brannigan and Warren Buckland, 458–63. London: Routledge.

Langer, Susanne K. 1951. *Philosophy in a New Key: A Study in the Symbolism of Reason, Rite and Art*. New York: Mentor.

———. 1953. *Feeling and Form*. New York: Scribner.

Manovich, Lev. 2001. *The Language of New Media*. Cambridge, MA: MIT Press.

Marks, Laura U. 2000. *The Skin of the Film: Intercultural Cinema, Embodiment, and the Senses*. Durham: Duke University Press.

Mitchell, W. J. T. 1986. *Iconology: Image, Text, Ideology*. Chicago: University of Chicago Press.

Mitry, Jean. 2000a. *The Aesthetics and Psychology of Cinema*. Translated by Christopher King, edited by Benoit Pater. Bloomington: Indiana University Press.

———. 2000b. *Semiotics and the Analysis of Film*. Translated by Christopher King. Bloomington: Indiana University Press.

Metz, Christian. 1974. *Film Language: A Semiotics of Cinema*. New York: Oxford University Press.

———. 2015. *Impersonal Enunciation, or the Place of Film*. Translated by Cormac Deane. New York: Columbia University Press.

Orr, John. 1998. *Contemporary Cinema*. Edinburgh; Edinburg University Press.

Pasolini, Pier Paolo. 1988. "The Cinema of Poetry." In *Heretical Empiricism*, edited by Louise K. Barnett. Bloomington: Indiana University Press.

Peirce, Charles Sanders. 1932. *Collected Papers Vol. 2, Elements of Logic*, edited by Charles Hartshorne and Paul Weiss. Cambridge, MA: Harvard University Press.

Plantinga, Carl. 2009. *Moving Viewers: American Film and the Spectator's Experience*. Berkeley: University of California Press.

Prince, Stephen. 2011. *Digital Visual Effects in Cinema: The Seduction of Reality*. New Brunswick, NJ: Rutgers University Press.

Sitney, P. Adams. 2015. *The Cinema of Poetry*. Oxford: Oxford University Press.

Vaughan, Hunter. 2013. *Where Film Meets Philosophy: Godard, Resnais, and Experiments in Cinematic Thinking*. New York: Columbia University Press.

Whittock, Trevor. 1990. *Metaphor and Film*. Cambridge: Cambridge University Press.

Wollen, Peter. 1998. *Signs and Meaning in the Cinema*. London: BFI.

Yacavone, Daniel. 2015. *Film Worlds: A Philosophical Aesthetics of Cinema.* New York: Columbia University Press.

———. 2016. "Film and the Phenomenology of Art: Reappraising Merleau-Ponty on Cinema as Form, Media, and Expression." *New Literary History* 47, no. 1: 159–86.

Chapter Fifteen

NARRATOLOGY IN MOTION: CAUSALITY, PUZZLES AND NARRATIVE TWISTS

Warren Buckland

> *Over and over in the study of cinema the issue of narrative arises not simply because it has been the historically dominant mode of cinematic production, but because it is above all a tool for contextualizing, a logic for delimiting meaning. [...] In the representational cinema it can be flaunted, observed, or ridiculed, but narrative can never be absent. (Dudley Andrew 1984, 76)*

Dudley Andrew identifies two fundamental reasons film theorists study narrative: narrative cinema is the historically dominant mode of filmmaking, and narrative is a pervasive logic that delimits or organizes meaning. These two reasons are, of course, linked, for narrative cinema is dominant *because* it is a pervasive logic that organizes meaning. Andrew also notes the ways this dominant logic can and has been manipulated—flaunted and ridiculed—within representational cinema. Edward Branigan has similarly theorized the concept of narrative as a ubiquitous form of logic that "organizes data into a special pattern which represents and explains experience" (1992, 3; emphasis omitted). Yet, despite narrative's omnipresence, it is absent in extreme forms of nonrepresentational cinema. In the 1970s, modernist avant-garde filmmaker and theorist Peter Gidal developed a polemical critique of representational cinema because its narrative and processes of identification passively project viewers into an illusionistic fictional world. In his essays and films, Gidal promoted structural/materialist filmmaking, a radically nonnarrative, nonillusionistic, nonrepresentational, impersonal and reflexive practice that aims to destroy cinema's illusions and present nothing more than film's form, materiality and process on screen (Gidal 1989).

Rather than examine these extreme nonrepresentational antinarrative practices, this chapter focuses on the role of narrative in the popular and ubiquitous representational narrative cinema. Basic concepts of story, plot and medium are introduced, followed by three types of representational narrative cinema, introduced via examples: classical Hollywood (the opening of *Psycho*), art cinema (*The Weight of Water*) and "puzzle films" (*Lost Highway*), the latter designating a recent type of storytelling in contemporary representational cinema that manipulates and challenges (but does not eliminate) narrative.

The terminology of narrative theory is notoriously complex and contradictory. But the terminology is less important than the conceptual distinctions the terms try to identify, between (1) a chronological sequence of actions and events; (2) the arrangement or organization of those actions and events and (3) their manifestation in a particular medium. A sequence of actions and events is usually called story/narrative/*fabula*. The structure that arranges story elements is usually called plot/narration/*syuzhet*. These actions and events (story) and their arrangement (plot) are independent of media—although "narration" is sometimes defined as a combination of (2) and (3). Film manifests story and plot via a specific combination of materials of expression—filmic techniques such as camera placement and movement, shot framing, lighting, editing and sound design.

Story

At its simplest, story is a temporal sequence of actions and events linked together in such a way as to form a self-enclosed, unified whole. The task of narrative theory is to explain how such a self-enclosed unity is achieved. The starting point is to analyze the internal relations between actions. The dominant relation organizing story into a unified whole is cause-effect logic. A cause is "a single set of forces operating in such a way as to bring about the occurrence of the events comprising the sequence" (Jonnes 1990, 64). Cause-effect logic explains how stories progress in a sequential manner. But further elements are needed to constitute a story—especially characters, who make decisions that drive events forward. These decisions encounter obstacles and conflicts, but in classical stories, these are eventually transformed and resolved.

We can see cause-effect logic structuring the opening three scenes *Psycho* (Hitchcock, 1960):[1]

> Scene 1. The first scene, of Marion Crane (Janet Leigh) and Sam Loomis (John Gavin) in a seedy hotel room during lunch break, establishes a problem: Marion and Sam cannot be married because he has no money (he is not financially independent and so cannot support a wife), and she is no longer willing to continue an affair outside of wedlock.
>
> Scene 2. The second scene, of Marion returning to work, develops the theme of marriage further. The viewer learns that Marion's boss, George Lowery (Vaughn Taylor), a real estate agent, is lunching with a wealthy man, Tom Cassidy (Frank Albertson). Cassidy's daughter is to be married the following day, so he visits the office to buy a property as a wedding gift for his daughter. Cassidy hands over $40,000 in cash and Lowery asks Marion to take it to the bank. She asks Lowery if she can go home afterwards, since she has a headache and wants to sleep it off.
>
> Scene 3. The third scene opens with Marion in her apartment. When she turns her back to the camera, the camera dollies in to an envelope on the bed and the viewer sees that it contains the $40,000. The camera then pans right to show a suitcase, which Marion is in the process of packing. In a matter of seconds, this scene (within the context of scenes 1 and 2) establishes Marion's motives and also illuminates a chain of causality: in order to have the financial independence to be with Sam, she plans to steal the money and leave town.

The cause-effect logic in these three scenes is rigidly constructed. A productive way to analyze cause-effect logic is to conduct a thought-experiment, to imagine the scenes in a different order. If *Psycho* began with scene 3, a sense of mystery would be created because viewers would not have sufficient information to understand Marion's motives. Beginning the film with scene 3 is plausible, but would it be logical? It would raise many questions in the viewer's mind: whose money is this and what is this character planning to do with it? However, in the actual film, scene 3 is an effect of the previous two scenes. A lack (a financial obstacle) linked to two characters is established in scene 1—Sam's and Marion's penury; a surplus is established in scene 2—Cassidy hands over $40,000 in cash. Its surplus status is emphasized throughout the scene: Cassidy stresses that he only carries as much money as he can afford to lose and that he is rich because he does not pay taxes. Scene 3 then neatly ties up the lack and surplus—Marion decides to steal the money to overcome the financial obstacle preventing her from marrying Sam.

The film only presents actions relevant to its cause-effect logic, in order to guide and restrict the viewer's comprehension of those actions. The sequence is credible but has nonetheless been carefully designed. At first, scene 2 appears to put on hold Marion's problem presented in scene 1: whereas scene 1 focuses on her personal life, scene 2 is about her work environment. Scenes 1 and 2 seem to be loosely linked in terms of chronology. But a stronger causality is indirectly at work. Is it just a coincidence that the $40,000 is presented immediately after Sam and Marion talk about their inability to get married because of their lack of money? Is it a coincidence that Cassidy pays cash? And is it a coincidence that the money just happens to be for a wedding present? These events are not coincidences but are elements in a rigidly constructed cause-effect sequence.[2] The alternation between scene 1 and 2 (personal life/work life) is linked by an indirect causality in which the events in the work environment address the lack in Marion's personal life.

However, not all events are linked via cause-effect logic; they can be linked more loosely in descriptive sequences, which are common at the beginning of a film. Scene 1 of *Psycho* begins with a series of shots that describe the location of the story—Phoenix, Arizona. At this early stage in *Psycho*, causality is not at work. And not all cause-effect events are motivated by characters; instead, nature may act as the cause of an event—extreme weather, an earthquake or a volcano erupting. Nonetheless, these natural causes will prompt characters to initiate a series of cause-effect actions. Denis Jonnes defines a narrative as a series of significant cause-effect actions performed by characters interacting with each other—interactions defined primarily not only in terms of conflict but also alliance and cooperation (1990, 81–88).

Plot

Plot names a configuration, a form of authorial manipulation that selects, combines, filters, rearranges and deletes story actions and events. However, the classical plot is mimetic, for it appears to imitate story—it seems to follow a "natural" sequence of story actions without any authorial manipulation. The difference between story and classical plot is minimal. To paraphrase Emile Benveniste: the story seems to be telling itself.[3] The difference between story and plot is more pronounced in the two other types of narrative cinema discussed in this chapter—modernist art cinema and puzzle films, where the viewer perceives the authorial manipulation of plot.

Classical narrative cinema is so-named because it is based on the classical plot. Aristotle presented the first systematic account of plot in terms of classical principles over two thousand years ago in *Poetics*, chapters 7–14. Coherence and closure are the fundamental characteristics of the classical plot, which can only be achieved if the actions and events appear to be probable and even necessary rather than contingent and haphazard. Aristotle identified two forms of classical plot: simple and complex. A simple plot presents a character or small group of characters performing a single, continuous action organized and unified into a beginning (initiation of the action), middle (obstacles and conflicts) and end (the resolution of the obstacles and conflicts). A complex plot is a simple plot with added features—"reversal" and "recognition" (*Poetics*, ch. 11). A reversal is a negative element of a plot that transforms the hero's situation, leading to his or her decline. Recognition names the moment when the hero discovers that he or she is subjected to a reversal. Reversal and recognition introduce a line of causality that exists over and above the characters. Reversal and recognition are not obviously carried out by characters; they are imposed on the characters and radically alter their destiny. The addition of a second line of causality that introduces reversal and recognition is what, for Aristotle, makes the complex plot complex. Yet, the complex plot is nevertheless classical, for it still gives the appearance of having internal unity. (I will return to Aristotle's definition of the complex plot when discussing puzzle films, which challenge the internal unity of the classical plot.)

Aristotle's study of the plot's actions was developed and refined in the twentieth century in Vladimir Propp's study of Russian fairy tales (1968). Propp reduced the potentially infinite number of actions to a finite system of 31 action types, or abstract functions ("absentation," "interdiction," "violation of interdiction," "reconnaissance," etc.). Functions are actions defined in terms of their significance: "Function is understood as an act of a character, defined from the point of view of its significance for the course of the action" (Propp 1968, 21). Propp later defined significance in terms of *consequences* of an action for the rest of the plot (67). He organized his 31 functions into a fixed, invariant sequence, suggesting that each fairy tale follows the same sequence of actions (although not all tales manifest all the functions) and grouped them further into seven spheres of activity organized around characters (the villain, the dispatcher, the helper, the princess/prize and her father, the donor, the hero, the false hero). Like Aristotle, Propp privileged action over character; characters are simply agents of functions—they are defined in terms of what they do; they are not defined mimetically, in terms of some human "essence."[4]

In the 1970s, film and cultural theorists considered the viability of Propp's morphology as a universal model of narrative structure. Although constructed from the analysis of 100 Russian fairy tales, the functions and spheres of activity are not necessarily limited to that corpus of texts. Peter Wollen analyzed *North by Northwest* (Hitchcock, 1959), concluding that "I was surprised how easy Propp's functions and method of analysis, in general, could be applied to *North by Northwest*. [...] The basic structure described by Propp is present" in the film (1982, 31). Part of Wollen's surprise was no doubt because the film (generally) fits into Propp's rigid linear sequence of actions, suggesting that the Russian fairy tales and Hitchcock's film share common narrative functions and characters. Wollen also highlighted the moments where Propp's model only fits problematically and concluded that his essay represents a starting point, the first steps in on new avenue of film analysis. Although the application of Propp to film has attracted strong criticisms (John Fell, David Bordwell), we should nonetheless consider what insights such an analysis can reveal about film narrative, however partial and fragmentary the analyses may be.

Film Style and Techniques

Film viewers encounter story and plot via specifically filmic techniques, including framing, camera movement and editing. In representational narrative cinema, these filmic techniques control the viewer's access to the story. One option of control is to limit access to the film's story by filtering it through the experiences of just one character. This technique is typical in detective films, in which story information is limited to what the detective knows, creating mystery. Another option is to create suspense by revealing to the viewer story action and events the main character is unaware of (e.g., Norman approaching Marion in the shower in *Psycho*: the viewer sees Norman approaching with a large knife while Marion is oblivious to his presence). More generally, viewers can be granted access to story events via several characters—a typical trait of melodramas, in which the viewer knows more about the story than any single character.

Sometimes the camera will disengage itself completely from all characters; access to the story is then directly controlled by an agent outside the story—the "director" (conceived within narratology not as a real life person but as an "implied author," a construct inferred by the viewer from textual traces in the film). In the first two scenes of *Psycho,* the camera is filtered through Marion (except for the descriptive shots of Phoenix opening scene 1). But in scene 3, the camera disengages itself from Marion and begins to represent the director's vision directly. In the first few seconds of the scene, the director keeps the money off-screen, giving the viewer the fleeting impression that Marion may have gone to the bank and deposited the money. But when Marion turns her back to the camera, the director moves the camera to reveal the money on the bed. The camera then pans to the half-packed suitcase. The camera is not simply showing what is on the set but is telling the story by carefully controlling what is on and off-screen second by second. The non-diegetic music also plays a role in narrating the events; it begins as soon as the stolen money appears on screen, supporting the camera in creating a menacing mood in the scene.

Narrative Cognition

In *Narration in the Fiction Film* (1985), David Bordwell developed a cognitive theory of film focused on story, plot and film style. The viewer's key activity when watching a film involves constructing the story—which, crucially, is not a pre-given entity. This activity is not open and free, but takes place within a series of constraints: *cues* in the film's *plot* and *style* interact with the viewer's cognitive *schemata*, guiding them to generate inferences or *hypotheses* in order to construct a coherent mental representation of the story.[5]

The process of hypothesis generation is common to all forms of communication and expression. In Bordwell's theory, hypotheses are assumptions or inferences viewers generate about the film's story. Following narratologist Meir Sternberg (1978), Bordwell identified several types: curiosity hypotheses (in which viewers are encouraged to generate inferences about past events in the story); suspense (or anticipatory) hypotheses (inferences that anticipates forthcoming events); probable and improbable hypotheses (concerning the level of credibility of inferred events); exclusive/non-exclusive hypotheses (the viewer is encouraged either to generate one or several inferences at a particular point in the plot); and micro-level (moment by moment) or macro-level (large scale) hypotheses, in which an inference is confirmed or rejected either within a short span of the plot or a long span, respectively.

These hypotheses are generated with the aid of cues in plot and schemata in mind. Schemata are cognitive structures that organize experiences into mental representations. One schema in particular guides the generation of hypothesis formation when watching a narrative film—the Aristotelian-based canonical story format: "Nearly all story-comprehension researchers agree that the most common template structure can be articulated as a 'canonical' story format, something like this: introduction of setting and characters—explanation of a state of affairs—complicating action—ensuing events—outcome—ending" (Bordwell 1985, 35). Filmic narration is carefully constructed to guide or cue viewers to generate a series of specific inferences that form a coherent story. These cues include gaps. Following Sternberg, Bordwell identifies several types of gap: temporary/permanent (most are temporary—that is, resolved by the end of the film); flaunted/suppressed (a gap is flaunted when viewers are made aware that there is some information they need to know about the story, whereas a suppressed gap does not call attention to itself); diffused/focused (a diffused gap is open-ended, leading viewers to generate a series of non-exclusive hypotheses, whereas a focused gap is clearly defined and leads viewers to generate an exclusive hypothesis. A diffuse gap introduced at the beginning of a film can be gradually brought into focus as the film progresses). A film may deliberately lead viewers to generate incorrect hypotheses and/or deliberately challenge the canonical story format, a trait more common in art cinema. This is also the case with puzzle films, which I will discuss in the final section, complete with a sample analysis that employs many of these types of gaps and hypotheses.

Art Cinema

David Bordwell has outlined the characteristics of another mode of filmmaking, art cinema, in his well-known essay "Art Cinema as a Mode of Film Practice" (2008). Art cinema is located between the classicism of dominant cinema and the nonnarrative avant-garde. Cause-effect logic still structures art cinema, but that logic is loose, for the story is populated with aimless characters that lack motivation and direction. Art cinema, therefore, privileges what Bordwell calls "subjective realism" (the interior lives of characters, often revealed through dialogue) rather than action. It also privileges "objective realism," or a sense of place and the values embedded in that place (values that may make it stable and secure, or complex, conflicting and unpredictable). As one would expect, art cinema challenges the mimeticism of the classical plot structure outlined by Aristotle and also overturns the prominence of plot over character. Crucially, for Bordwell, art cinema is characterized by marks of "authorial expressivity," in which the director's presence becomes noticeable due to unusual film style, or unusual plot structure: "In the art cinema, the puzzle is one of plot: who is telling this story? How is this story being told? Why is this story being told this way?" (2008, 155). The conflict between the realism and authorial expressivity creates ambiguity, a conflict between characters and events in the film motivating the story and the director outside the film manipulating those events. In a classical narrative, all actions and events function to advance the story either directly or indirectly. The narrative elements of an art film are linked together more loosely, and they may end on ambiguity and lack resolution.

We can consider the art cinema's plot structure, specifically how its story is being told, by briefly analyzing Kathryn Bigelow's art house film *The Weight of Water* (2000), which has a distinct style and plot. The film alternates between two story worlds (the 1870s; the present day) but is set in the same location (Isles of Shoals). The action is narrated by two women who also appear in the film (Maren (Sarah Polley) from the 1870s, Jean (Catherine McCormack) in the present day). This 1870s story revolves around a murder on the Isles, and the present day story follows Jean as she investigates the murder and tries at the same time to save her marriage. The film's plot is distinct: it begins in the 1870s with the arrest of a murder suspect, and then switches to the present day, to Jean and her husband travelling to the Isles. The present day events are regularly interrupted by fragments of the 1870s story. Whereas the present day story is chronological, the 1870s story is presented out of sequence (after opening with the arrest of the murderer, it moves back and forth in time to Maren's move to the Isles, to her life in Norway, to her first introduction to the murderer, to his trial, and so on). When returning to the 1870s, viewers do not necessarily see the next chronological action.

As the film progresses, Jean, in particular, begins to identify with Maren's repressed rage and appears to "see" her on the Isles (via a point of view shot; Jean on the island in the present day looks off screen; cut to Maren in the same location in the 1870s). The plot is structured to draw parallels between the two women in different temporal periods, and it is this parallelism that motivates this specific plot structure. Film style is also distinct: in this color film, the 1870s story contains a number of black and white images, although their status is ambiguous (are they memories? fantasies? false images?). The contemporary story also contains freeze frames, plus a number of black and white images when Jean takes photographs. All these stylistic elements draw attention to the narrator outside the film.

In sum, while the 1870s story consists of a distinct series of actions (presented out of sequence), the contemporary story involves little action (except a storm at the end), or even dialogue. Instead, it relies on indirect, non-verbal interaction between characters (especially furtive looks between characters, reaction shots), typical of art cinema, and many of its lacunae—or gaps in narrative clarity—can or must be attributed to the artistic sensibility of the filmmaker.

Puzzle Films

> How strange it is to hear people speak, and not without insisting sometimes, about the "breakdown of the narrative" at a time when a new generation of cinematographic narrators has come to the fore. (Metz 1974, 227)

In the remainder of this chapter, I present my formulation of the concepts of the "puzzle film" and the "Hollywood puzzle film," and comment on several revisions and expansion of the concept. Puzzle films "flaunt" and "ridicule" narrative, to use Dudley Andrew's terms, but this does not mean that they reject it. When Metz claimed that "a new generation of cinematographic narrators has come to the fore," he was referring specifically to European art cinema, and to its renewal and enrichment of storytelling. Puzzle films, like modern art films, also enrich and renew storytelling, but they go further: they challenge deep-seated cultural conventions that regulate and try to stabilize consciousness and representation, plus the attendant concepts that support these conventions—such as agency, discrete identity, memory, temporal linearity and singularity. Puzzle films are distinctive in that they carry out a filmmaking task that cannot be conveyed in classical or even art cinema. *Lost Highway* (David Lynch, 1997), to be discussed below, is centered on a schizophrenic character's nonlinear journey, and involves character duplication and transformation, faulty memory and so on, which cannot be manifest in the canonical narrative structure, yet does not completely reject story and plot the way Peter Gidal and other avant-garde filmmakers do.

In the Introduction to *Puzzle Films* (Buckland 2009b), several narrational properties of puzzle films are listed:

> Puzzle films embrace nonlinearity, time loops, and fragmented spatio-temporal reality. These films blur the boundaries between different levels of reality, are riddled with gaps, deception, labyrinthine structures, ambiguity, and overt coincidences. They are populated with characters who are schizophrenic, lose their memory, are unreliable narrators, or are dead (but without us—or them—realizing). (2009b, 6)

This definition ranges over three distinct categories—(1) order, (2) different levels of reality and (3) character psychology—and identifies subtypes within these categories.

We have seen in the section on plot that Aristotle's *Poetics* provides a definition of the complex plot, to complement his simple plot. Yet, Aristotle's complex plot (like his simple plot) remains classical and mimetic. To understand puzzle films, the Introduction to *Puzzle Films* argues that we need to go beyond Aristotle's understanding of complex:

> The term Aristotle uses for complex is *peplegmenos*, which literally means "interwoven." In a successful complex plot, the second line of causality (which introduces recognition and reversal) is interwoven into the first, the characters' plotline. By using the term "interwoven" Aristotle understands that, while the second plot initially disrupts the first by radically altering the hero's destiny, the second plot is eventually integrated into the first, resulting in a unified, classical plot once more, in which reversal and recognition appear to be probable and even necessary actions. (2009b, 2–3)

An interweaving of two narrative plots is not sufficient to characterize contemporary puzzle films:

> The use of the term "complex" in *Puzzle Films: Complex Storytelling in Contemporary Cinema* extends far beyond Aristotle's term *peplegmenos*. The "puzzle plot" is, I would argue, the third type of plot that comes after the complex plot. A puzzle plot is intricate in the sense that the arrangement of events is not just complex, but complicated and perplexing; the events are not simply interwoven, but *entangled*. (2009b, 3)

"Complicated," "perplexing," and "entangled" all imply a higher level of disorganization and confusion than the more straightforward term "complex."

The introduction also states where the complexity lies:

> The complexity of puzzle films operates on two levels: narrative and narration. It emphasizes the complex *telling* (plot, narration) of a simple or complex *story* (narrative). (2009b, 6)

Lost Highway is an exemplary puzzle film based on this third type of plot. The film begins with Fred Madison (Bill Pullman) at home.[6] The front-door intercom buzzes, and he hears the message "Dick Laurent is dead." He goes over to the window in another part of the house to look out, but he sees no one. In the penultimate scene of the film, we see that Fred Madison was *also* outside pressing the intercom and delivering the message. The intercom message at the beginning of the film leads the viewer to generate at least two hypotheses, focused around the questions: Who rang the bell? And, who is Dick Laurent? These two hypotheses are generated in response to the gaps in the story that the plot has constructed. In this opening scene, the gaps in the story are, firstly, spatial. The viewer does not see the identity of the person outside. This spatial gap is evident to viewers, and is therefore a flaunted (rather than a suppressed) gap. It is also a clearly delineated gap, and is therefore specific (rather than diffuse). It is also temporary (rather than permanent) because it is eventually filled in at the end of the film. The hypotheses generated about this spatial gap are a suspense, non-exclusive hypotheses operating at the film's macro level—suspense because we assume the gap will be resolved in the future (so we anticipate the filling in of this gap at a later time in the film's unfolding); it is non-exclusive because it could have been anyone (we cannot generate an hypothesis suspecting a particular person); and it operates on the macro level because it spans the entire film. The scale of probability–improbability usually refers to the hypotheses we generate. But in this case, the way the plot fills in this gap at the end of the film is highly improbable. Although our hypotheses were non-exclusive, it is highly unlikely that any viewer would generate the hypothesis that Fred Madison is *also* outside the house pressing his own doorbell! The lack of information on Dick Laurent's identity is a temporary, flaunted, focused gap that leads the viewer to generate an exclusive, curiosity hypothesis that operates on the macro level (for his identity is not immediately resolved).

The key to Lynch's puzzle film is, therefore, the trick ending, which I have characterized very precisely in terms of the narratological theories of Sternberg and Bordwell. Other scholars have also written about the same phenomenon under the name of "twist ending" (see Eig 2003; Lavik 2006; Flory 2010), "mind trick films" (Klecker 2013), while Garrett Stewart frequently uses the synonymous term "trick ending" within his broader theory (see 1999, 102, 361; 2007, 17, 63, 82, 103, etc.).

Extending the Puzzle Film

Since the publication of *Puzzle Films* (2009a), the notions of "puzzle films" and "complex storytelling" have been developed via innovative revisions, expansions and new directions. Gabriele Weyand (2011) and Maria Poulaki (2014) separately attempt to rethink puzzle films in terms of systems theory. Poulaki persuasively argues that

> it is no longer enough to show how complex films are *not* conventional narratives; the need for a positive definition and description of their processes has become apparent. In films characterized as "complex narratives," such as the puzzle films, it is more the "complex" than the "narrative" that can bring fresh insight into their structure, through the introduction of an alternative theoretical framework: not the one of narratology but that of complex systems theory. (2014, 37)

Poulaki proposes a systems theoretical framework (based on sociologist Niklas Luhmann's theory of self-reference) to examine the complexity of puzzle films. This theory of self-reference is not the same as modernist techniques of alienation; instead, from a systems theory perspective, the process of self-reference adds complexity to puzzle films.

Similarly, Pepita Hesselberth successfully argues that we need to identify "ordering principles other than (or at least in addition to) narrative if we want to come to grips with the complexity of contemporary cinematics and the kind of viewer engagement it demands" (2012). She returns to concepts such as presence and deixis and uses the new term "tangibility" to supplement the narratological approach to puzzle films (see Hesselberth 2012, 2014). Weyand, Poulaki and Hesselberth (amongst others) generate new insights on the puzzle film phenomenon. In "Mind-Tricking Narratives: Between Classical and Art-Cinema Narration," published in *Poetics Today* (Klecker 2013), Cornelia Klecker joined the debate promoting a new term, mind-trick films. These films, she claims, are dominated by characters with mental illnesses; they feature an ending that takes viewers by surprise; the surprise or twist at the end always resettles or resolves the film; and she attempts to define these films in terms of who deceives, how is it done, and when does the audience find out about the deception (see Klecker 2013, 119, 130, 133).

Klecker's essay presents many problems, for her mind-trick film is simply the puzzle film under another label. Mental illness motivating the characters is a common assumption stated time and again by film scholars writing on both puzzle films and what Elsaesser (2009) calls mind-game films. We have already seen in the *Lost Highway* analysis that the surprise revelation at the end of a puzzle film is a commonplace assumption. Klecker further stipulates that this surprise or twist at the end always resettles or resolves the film; yet, this is not relevant to at least two key examples, *Memento* and *Lost Highway*, for the twists at the end do not definitively resolve the films' plots: viewers do not come out of either film thinking everything has been settled. (Moreover, both *Memento* and *Lost*

Highway consist of several twists rather than one major twist at the end.) Klecker, therefore, needs to leave out *Memento* and *Lost Highway* from her definition of mind-trick films. To define the mind-trick film according to who deceives, how is it done, and when the audience finds out about the deception is not identifying anything new, for these three "insights" are in fact just fabricated from the research of other scholars writing about puzzle films.

Klecker also misrepresents the definition of the puzzle film presented in the Introduction to *Puzzle Films* (2009a): "it appears," she writes, "that the term *puzzle film* does little more than replace the vague concept of complex storytelling. […] It seems that puzzle films comprise more or less everything that is in some way(s) 'out of the ordinary'" (2013, 128–29). Here Klecker simply ignores several pages of the Introduction to *Puzzle Films* that identify puzzle films in terms of the three distinct categories of (1) order, (2) different levels of reality and (3) character psychology (plus the subtypes within those categories). Furthermore, nowhere does the Introduction present the idea that puzzle films simply name everything that seems "out of the ordinary"—despite the fact that Klecker has put quotation marks around it. Klecker is setting up her own caricature to criticize.

The Hollywood Puzzle Film: Ontological Pluralism and Cognitive Dissonance

The 2009 puzzle film volume (focused on international art cinema) was followed by *Hollywood Puzzle Films*, focused around Hollywood filmmakers from the 1990s onward who have appropriated some of the narratological innovations of the puzzle film.[7] This volume also develops from the 2009 volume the discussion of the puzzle plot as complicated, perplexing and entangled by introducing the concepts of "ontological pluralism" and "cognitive dissonance."[8]

Film reviewers were quick to notice the encroachment of the puzzle plot into mainstream Hollywood films. Referring to *Inception*, Patrick Goldstein noted, "I was dazzled by the movie's originality, but also so confused by its dense, video-game narrative style that, by the last 40 minutes of the film, I'd pretty much lost track of the story" (Goldstein 2010, 12), while Cosmo Landesman asked, "Are mainstream Hollywood films becoming too smart for their own good, or at least too smart to make sense? There was a time when only obscure art-house films with subtitles left you wondering, 'What the hell was that?' Not now. *Source Code* is the latest in a line of supersmart sci-fi works, such as *Inception* and *The Adjustment Bureau*, whose plotting is so complex, whose big ideas are so big, you'll find you're still in the dark when the cinema lights go on" (Landesman 2011, 15). Hollywood filmmakers have not passively embraced en masse puzzle film conventions: instead, a small number of filmmakers appropriate its conventions in an attempt to adapt to new technological, historical and social circumstances (while other, more conventional filmmakers nostalgically look back to traditional, stable forms of storytelling). Puzzle film techniques inject novelty but also unpredictability and uncertainty into the stringent economic conditions of Hollywood filmmaking. But what are the "new technological, historical and social circumstances" to which puzzle filmmakers are the "answer?" A number of accounts have been offered, particularly involving technological circumstances. Hayles and Gessler argue that the art of storytelling has dramatically changed, due to "the flow of information and the technologies of interconnectivity [that] have increased exponentially across the globe with the advent of the microcomputer, distributed processing, the Internet and the World Wide Web" (Hayles and Gessler 2004, 497). The implicit premise here is that new media digitally (that is, numerically) codes data, which are open to algorithmic manipulation, unlike analogue media (see Manovich 2001, 27–31). The numeric coding and algorithmic manipulation make digital media malleable, variable, scalable and contingent, serendipitous, rather than fixed and permanent, allowing for increased combination and fragmentation. Hayles and Gessler imply that storytelling is reacting to this new media environment.

We can go further and speculate about the desires, fears and fantasies puzzle films address. Employing puzzle film techniques in Hollywood blockbusters is risky because these techniques challenge deep-seated cultural conventions that regulate and try to stabilize consciousness and representation, plus the attendant concepts that support these conventions (agency, discrete identity, memory, temporal linearity, singularity, etc.). One prevalent way in which consciousness and representation are destabilized is through the entanglement of the actual (realized) world and unrealized possible worlds, an interaction that codifies the actual world as contingent and malleable, rather than permanent and fixed. This possible world theme in puzzle films adds complexity by entangling actual and potential (different ontological levels), sometimes blurring the boundaries between levels, making it difficult to distinguish between them. Yet, such entangling is usually motivated by the counterfactual desire to change the past or alter the direction of the future ("what if" or "what might have been" scenarios). The manifestation of this counter factual world on screen can be rationalized via psychology (the protagonist's desire to change the past, which invariably relates to his/her dysfunctional childhood, based on loss and trauma); or via history (to a nation's historical trauma and guilt); or it can be rationalized as a fantasy to foil a terrorist attack that has already taken place, made possible via science fiction genre conventions (in which the possible world is actualized via new forms of technology or via time travel). We also find a series of sub-themes involving the artificial manipulation of identity and a technological refiguring of the human/nonhuman and the self/other boundaries. These fantasies, desires and themes are found in many Hollywood puzzle films, from *Source Code* to *Shutter Island*, *Déjà vu*, *Premonition*, *Inception* and numerous Philip K. Dick adaptations (*Total Recall*, *Minority Report*, *A Scanner Darkly* and *The Adjustment Bureau*).

Finally, from the perspective of information theory, the complex structure of puzzle films (inside and outside Hollywood) carries more informational content because it is more disorderly and unpredictable (or innovative) than a classical film, which has less information content because it is more orderly and predictable. One consequence of this increase in informational content is that puzzle films encourage repeat viewing and a cult following. They create an active fan base that interprets the films in all their minutiae, unpacking the films' ambiguities, improbabilities and plot inconsistencies on blogs or dedicated web pages.

This chapter has presented several types of cinematic storytelling, ranging from classical Hollywood cinema, puzzle films (international cinema), Hollywood puzzle films, art house cinema to nonrepresentational non-narrative avant-garde. When discussing Metz's work I emphasized the differences between the modernist European art cinema and puzzle films. But, clearly, there is considerable overlap between them. Both art cinema and puzzle films (Hollywood/international cinema) do not so much reject narrative, but instead open it out, making it flexible and multi-faceted. In this respect, at least, Metz's comments on modern cinema apply equally well to puzzle films, when he argued that "the modern film is more narrative, and more satisfyingly so, and that the main contribution of the new cinema is to have enriched the filmic narrative" (1974, 208).

Notes

1 This example expands the analysis of *Psycho* presented in Buckland (2015), chapter 2.

2 Stories use coincidence only on rare occasions. Its overuse leads to a loss in credibility and unity, because the film's events seem to happen by chance; that is, they are not causally interrelated and psychologically motivated.

3 In "Correlations of Tense in the French Verb," Benveniste introduced the distinction between *histoire/discours*, subsequently taken up by narratologists. In this essay he quoted three examples of historical writing, written in the third person with no reference to the act of narration. He comments: "The events are set forth chronologically, as they occurred. No one speaks here; the events seem to narrate themselves" (1971, 208).

4 A. J. Greimas (*Structural Semantics*, and elsewhere) reduced Propp's narrative agents (or actants) to six roles, which he organized into binary oppositions (subject/object, sender/receiver, helper/opponent), and reorganized Propp's 31 functions into 20 functional categories (including binary oppositions). This more abstract model conceives the actants and functions in terms of an underlying paradigmatic system of logical relations rather than a syntagmatic sequence (plot). Greimas also inverted Propp's priority by privileging the actants over functions.

5 Bordwell uses the Russian Formalist terms *syuzhet* for plot and *fabula* for story.

6 The following analysis of *Lost Highway* appears in my chapter in *Puzzle Films* (Buckland 2009c).

7 The following comments are reworked from my Introduction to *Hollywood Puzzle Films* (Buckland 2014).

8 Cognitive dissonance can be theorized as one cultural cause of puzzle films—puzzle films are expressing the contemporary Zeitgeist feeling of dissonance (but which, in turn, is caused in part by the proliferation of new media technologies).

References

Andrew, Dudley. 1984. *Concepts in Film Theory*. New York: Oxford University Press.

Benveniste, Emile. 1971. *Problems in General Linguistics*. Coral Gables: University of Miami Press.

Bordwell, David. 1985. *Narration in the Fiction Film*. London: Methuen.

———. 2008. "Art Cinema as a Mode of Film Practice." In *Poetics of Cinema*. New York: Routledge: 151–69.

Branigan, Edward. 1992. *Narrative Comprehension and Film*. London: Routledge.

Buckland, Warren. ed. 2009a. *Puzzle Films: Complex Storytelling in Contemporary Cinema*. Oxford: Wiley-Blackwell.

———. 2009b. "Introduction: Puzzle Plots," in Buckland (2009): 1–12.

———. 2009c. "Making Sense of *Lost Highway*," in Buckland (2009): 42–61.

———. 2014. "Introduction." In *Hollywood Puzzle Films*, edited by Warren Buckland, 1–14. New York: Routledge.

———. 2015. *Film Studies: An Introduction*, 5th ed. London: John Murray.

Eig, Jonathan. 2003. "A Beautiful Mind(Fuck): Hollywood Structures of Identity." *Jump Cut* 46: http://www.ejumpcut.org/archive/jc46.2003/eig.mindfilms/text.html.

Elsaesser, Thomas. 2009. "The Mind-Game Film," in Buckland (2009): 13–41.

Flory, Dan. 2010. "Cinematic Presupposition, Race, and Epistemological Twist Films." *Journal of Aesthetics and Art Criticism* 68, no. 4: 379–87.

Gidal, Peter. 1989. *Materialist Film*. London: Routledge.

Ghislotti, Stefano. 2009. "Narrative Comprehension Made Difficult: Film Form and Mnemonic Devices in *Memento*," in Buckland 2009: 87–106.

Goldstein, Patrick. 2010. "The Older You Get. The Age of Inception: Gamers Generation Get It, Geezers Don't." *The Hamilton Spectator* (August 4): 12.

Hayles, N. Katherine, and Nicholas Gessler. 2004. "The Slipstream of Mixed Reality: Unstable Ontologies and Semiotic Markers in *The Thirteenth Floor, Dark City*, and *Mulholland Drive*." *PMLA: Publications of the Modern Language Association of America* 119, no. 3 (May): 482–99.

Hesselberth, Pepita. 2012. "From Subject-Effect to Presence-Effect: A Deictic Approach to the Cinematic." *Necsus: European Journal of Media Studies* 2: http://www.necsus-ejms.org/from-subject-effect-to-presence-effect-a-deictic-approach-to-the-cinematic/.

———. 2014. *Cinematic Chronotopes: Here, Now, Me*. London: Bloomsbury.

Jonnes, Denis. 1990. *The Matrix of Narrative: Family Systems and the Semiotics of Story*. Berlin: Mouton de Gruyter.

Klecker, Cornelia. 2013. "Mind-Tricking Narratives: Between Classical and Art-Cinema Narration." *Poetics Today* 34, no. 1–2: 119–46.

Landesman, Cosmo. 2011. "Source Code. Bold Concepts and a Hot Hero on a Mission Make the Slightly Silly Sci-Fi of Source Code a Hit." *The Sunday Times* (April 3): 15.

Lavik, Erlend. 2006. "Narrative Structure in *The Sixth Sense*: A New Twist in 'Twist Movies'?" *Velvet Light Trap* 58: 55–64.

Manovich, Lev. 2001. *The Language of New Media*. Cambridge, MA: MIT Press.

Metz, Christian. 1974. "The Modern Cinema and Narrativity." In *Film Language: A Semiotics of the Cinema*, 185–227. New York: Oxford University Press.

Poulaki, Maria. 2014. "Puzzled Hollywood and the Return of Complex Films." In *Hollywood Puzzle Films*, edited by Warren Buckland, 35–53. New York: Routledge.

Propp, Vladimir. 1968. *Morphology of the Folktale*, 2nd ed. Austin: University of Texas Press.

Sternberg, Meir. 1978. *Expositional Modes and Temporal Ordering in Fiction*. Baltimore: Johns Hopkins University Press.

Stewart, Garrett. 1999. *Between Film and Screen: Modernism's Photo Synthesis*. Chicago: University of Chicago Press.

———. 2007 *Framed Time: Toward a Postfilmic Cinema*. Chicago: University of Chicago Press.

Weyand, Gabriele. 2011. "Order from Chaos—Re-Orientation in Complex Cinema," paper presented at the Disorienting Media Conference, December 8. Presentation available online: http://www.rubcast.ruhr-uni-bochum.de/index2.php?id=882.

Wollen, Peter. 1982. *Readings and Writings: Semiotic Counter-Strategies*. London: Verso.

Chapter Sixteen

HE(U)RETICAL FILM THEORY: WHEN COGNITIVISM MEETS THEORY

William Brown

In this essay, I shall offer a historical overview of cognitive approaches to film, before putting forward what to cognitive film theory might be an 'heretical' argument, in that I shall try to find ways in which cognitive film theory can work with, rather than against, more 'classical' film theory in order to enrich our understanding of cinema. I shall do this by looking at the concept of *heuretics*, as discussed by Christian Keathley in his book, *Cinephilia and History, or The Wind in the Trees* (2006). Before reaching this point, though, let us look at the history of cognitive film theory.

From *The Photoplay* to *Post-Theory* and Beyond

For the uninitiated, cognitive film theory has as perhaps its central principle the idea that viewers are active while watching a film; that is, viewers constantly are carrying out cognitive/conscious labour in order to recognise what they see, make sense of a story, make evaluations about situations and characters, have an emotional response to films and so on. In some senses, to assert as much should be self-evident: of course, viewers engage actively with films when they watch them. Nonetheless, this claim was perhaps a big one when cognitive film theory began to emerge in the mid-1990s through the development of the Society for Cognitive Studies of the Moving Image (SCSMI) and, in particular, the publication of David Bordwell and Noël Carroll's edited collection, *Post-Theory: Reconstructing Film Studies* (1996a). For, as various authors make clear in that collection, cognitivism marks a break from the older, more 'classical' film theory that had psychoanalysis and Marxism at its theoretical core.

Emerging most prominently out of the journal *Screen* in the 1970s, the 'classical' or 'Grand' film theory argued that viewers of films were passive in that they unwittingly were prey to the ideologies peddled by mainstream cinema. Laura Mulvey (1975) famously suggested, for example, that mainstream cinema reinforced a specifically masculine way of looking both at the world and at women in particular, since in most mainstream narrative films, women are reduced to spectacles that are to be looked at, rather than being active agents or rounded characters. For this reason, mainstream narrative cinema was deemed to peddle a patriarchal ideology, and viewers watching mainstream films would have consciously to resist this misogynistic ideology, to which otherwise they might unconsciously be exposed and, by proxy, might irrationally condone or, worse, adopt (with Mulvey going on to suggest that female viewers identifying with men is a process characterised by 'sadness' – since only in youth and before socialisation into a patriarchal society do women get to be active; see Mulvey 1990). In contrast to such arguments, then, Noël Carroll writes that cognitivism has a

> tendency to look for alternative answers to many of the questions addressed by or raised by psychoanalytic film theories, especially with respect to film reception, in terms of cognitive and rational processes rather than irrational or unconscious ones. (Carroll 1996, 62)

While making clear that cognitive film theory is not unified, it is useful, so Carroll might suggest, for addressing not invisible processes, but visible ones. That is, the 'classical' *Screen* theory appeals to the invisible because mainstream cinema does the invisible work of making me a misogynist unless I consciously resist when watching it. A cognitive approach to cinema looks only at what empirically can be measured – as a result of being visible. As Carroll says, 'cognitivists can readily acknowledge that film has a political dimension, and they can and have studied it. Though, of course, insofar as they are cognitivists, they will attempt to discover the role that *cognitive* processes play in the dissemination of ideology' (Carroll 1996, 48–49) – and not the role that unconscious, irrational and invisible processes play. Indeed, because invisible, the very existence of those unconscious processes is up for question; cognitive film theory concentrates on that which definitely exists and about which we can, therefore, reach solid conclusions.

While cognitive film theory seems to have emerged in the mid-1990s as, in Carroll's terms, a *stance*, however, it in fact has a significantly longer history. Bordwell and Carroll say in their introduction to *Post-Theory* that cognitive science includes work in linguistics, anthropology, psychology, aesthetics and philosophy of the mind (1996a, xvi) – and approaches to film that incorporate one or more of these frameworks are as old as the study of film itself. For example, psychologist Hugo Münsterberg's *The Photoplay: A Psychological Study* (1916) is possibly the first book-length study of the cinema, and in it, Münsterberg argues that attention, memory and the emotions constitute a key part of the film experience. That is, Münsterberg is concerned with how we process films, as opposed to with what effects films might have on us. Indeed, part of the rationale for writing the book seems to have been to counter the prevailing view at the time that 'cinematic escapism violated the work ethic, and by extension, national goals' as a result of the medium's overpowering of the unsuspecting and helpless viewer (see Mitchell 1982). Given that this rationale is not so dissimilar to Carroll and Bordwell's opposition to *Screen* theory, which similarly voiced concerns that mainstream cinema makes reactionary parrots out of its viewers, we might even say that in film studies, *plus ça change, plus c'est la même chose*! Nonetheless, Münsterberg's argument that the viewer plays a key role in the construction of a film (e.g. by seeing continuous movement and depth in what are ultimately flat and still images projected on to a wall) means that *The Photoplay* remains an important and influential text today.

Beyond Münsterberg, I might also mention how Soviet filmmakers like Sergei M. Eisenstein, Lev Kuleshov, Dziga Vertov and V. I. Pudovkin were in the 1920s all interested in the role that human cognition plays in the film viewing experience, and thus were all to a certain extent active cognitive film scientists. To offer two clear examples, we can first take Kuleshov's fabled experiment, whereby he took footage of actor Ivan Mozzhukhin and placed it alongside various shots – for example, of a bowl of soup, of a girl in a coffin – and, even though the Mozzhukhin footage was the same, viewers supposedly read into his performance either great hunger (looking at the soup) or great grief (looking at the coffin). Dubbed the Kuleshov effect, this experiment clearly demonstrates Kuleshov's interest in how editing (the order in which we put images and content) produces different psychological effects/emotional responses in viewers (we might perhaps note both that Pudovkin claimed to have been involved in this experiment and that it was not particularly rigorous, in that no details of how it was conducted actually remain).[1] Secondly, as a growing number of scholars become interested in the cinematic experience as a multimodal one that involves more than just the senses of vision and hearing, many refer back to Eisenstein's own understanding that cinema is a medium that one *feels* (see Eisenstein 1957, 71; see also Laine and Strauven 2009, 252). As a result, we can see how these filmmakers were also making movies that in some respects were psychological experiments – as Tim J. Smith (2014) makes clear through his investigation into Eisenstein's writings on his own film, *Alexander Nevsky* (USSR, 1938).

We should also mention various other figures who have played a prominent role in the 'pre-history' of cognitive film studies, including Rudolf Arnheim, who wrote not only about cinema (1983) but also about art and perception more generally (e.g. 1974). Edgar Morin (2005) pioneered in the 1950s an anthropological approach to cinema, arguing that film and viewer merge during film viewing, in that the film shapes how the viewer sees, while the viewer also shapes what the film shows. Meanwhile, Jean Mitry (2000) wrote the expansive *Aesthetics and Psychology of the Cinema* in 1963, before Christian Metz (1977) introduced psychoanalysis in the 1970s as a theoretical framework through which to understand film. Even though Metz would heavily influence the theorists writing for *Screen*, he also is a key figure in the history of cognitive film theory, as is made clear by a reference to Metz ('"What must be understood," Christian Metz famously noted, "is how films are understood"') on the 'What is the history and purpose of SCSMI?' page of the SCSMI website (n.d.). And so, while in the 1980s psychologists like James J. Gibson (1986) and Julian Hochberg (2007) were respectively writing about and carrying out experimental investigations into film perception, scholars working within film studies tended themselves to move away from such psychological approaches, preferring instead the afore-mentioned *Screen* approach – until *Post-Theory* emerged in 1996.

As mentioned, cognitivists are not unified in their outlook on film. Fittingly, then, around the publication of *Post-Theory*, a raft of monographs emerged, each looking at different aspects of film from the cognitive perspective. David Bordwell (1985) and Edward Branigan (1992), for example, gave cognitivist explanations of film narrative and narration, while Murray Smith (1995) and Ed S. Tan (1995) explored the role that emotion plays in the film viewing experience. Joseph D. Anderson (1998) provided an 'ecological' conception of cinema, drawing on a psychological understanding of perception, identification and comprehension to explain how films interact with the mind of the human viewer, while Torben Grodal (1999) provided an evolutionary account for why humans watch films. At around this time, the SCSMI began to meet more often, with regular attendants contributing also to Carl Plantinga and Greg M. Smith's edited collection, *Passionate Views: Film, Cognition, and Emotion* (1999). By 2006, the SCSMI had begun to channel its work through the journal, *Projections: The Journal for Movies and Mind*, with the 2000s and 2010s also seeing important cognitive approaches to, *inter alia*, Indian cinema (Hogan 2009), Mexican cinema (Aldama 2013), Hollywood cinema (Plantinga 2009), various genres (Grodal 2009) and the films of Bernardo Bertolucci (Serra 2013). In other words, cognitive film studies has come to be in rude health, with two methodological developments also worth mentioning. The first is the development and refining of eye-tracking studies of film, which allow scholars to understand precisely where a viewer looks while watching a movie, thus giving great insights into how and why films capture and keep our attention. Foremost among those working in this field is Tim J. Smith, whose 'Attentional Theory of Cinematic Continuity' was published in *Projections* (2012), as was 'Neurocinematics: The Neuroscience of Film', written by Uri Hasson and colleagues (2008b), and the neuroscientific framework of which constitutes the second important development that I wish to mention. Where Smith looks at where eyes go during film viewing, Hasson uses functional Magnetic Resonance Imaging (fMRI) technology to look at what happens in the brain during film viewing.

I shall engage at greater length with both Hasson and Smith below. But beforehand, I should like to point out how the potted post-1996 history offered above highlights the development of specifically Anglophone cognitive film studies. As Warren Buckland reminds us in *The Cognitive Semiotics of Film* (2000), there has also been a non-Anglophone (mainly Italian and French) tradition of cognitive film studies, too. What is more, while Christian Metz clearly remains a landmark figure in Anglophone cognitive film studies (hence the reference to him on the SCSMI website), he seems nonetheless to mark a point of rupture, from which Anglophone film theory strayed 'unproductively' into *Screen* theory and from which cognitive film studies set itself the task of rescuing film studies more broadly. Meanwhile, in the non-Anglophone tradition theorists like Francesco Casetti and Roger Odin work far more productively with Metz, 'transforming Metz's semiotics by means of theories of pragmatics, cognitive science and transformational generative grammar (which is in fact one of the main research programs in cognitive science)' (Buckland 2000, 2). In other words, Buckland suggests that the non-Anglophone (or what he terms 'European') tradition offers a more productive marriage of the ideas, including the psychoanalytic ones that inform Metz's work, as opposed to the basic rejection of psychoanalysis that the Anglophone cognitive film theorists have undertaken.[2] In a similar spirit, then, I wish now to put together recent work in Anglophone cognitive film theory, in particular on neurocinematics, and work aligned with the more 'classical' *Screen* school, in particular on cinephilia, in order to generate what hopefully is a productive discourse between the two, as per the non-Anglophone theorists that Buckland identifies.[3] Let us turn our attention, then, to a 'heuretical' approach to film, even if this risks constituting a 'heretical' gesture towards Anglophone cognitive film theory.

Heuretics and Film

There is a tension within film studies between the intensely personal (and positive) response that film can elicit as well as the collective, matching effects that movies can have on and across their audiences. Cognitive approaches to film have tended to consider the latter, collective responses to movies. For example, David Bordwell opens an essay on *Mildred Pierce* (Michael Curtiz, USA, 1945) by suggesting that '[b]y and large, audiences understand the films they see' (2007, 135) and that film scholars should concern themselves with how films are understood. Meanwhile, the personal, subjective response to film has been theorised only in a more abstract manner.

As a result of cognitive film theory's emphasis on the general – an emphasis built into the field as a result of, for example, its insistence upon statistically significant results in experiments – the argument that I shall propose here is in some senses 'heretical'. That is, I shall be making a case for idiosyncratic responses to film rather than the general results confirmed via experimentation. However, inherent to the 'heretical' theory of film that I wish to propose here is the process of heuretics. Heuretics denotes a process of trial and error or a second form of experimentation. Rather than experimentation as a means of confirming or denying a hypothesis, experimentation here signifies a kind of journey into the unknown – experimenting not to confirm a hypothesis, but to see without knowing in advance where it will lead to (i.e. to experiment without hypothesis). Given the heretical and heuretical nature of the theory I shall put forward here, I have coined the parenthetical neologism, he(u)retical film theory, to try to encapsulate my argument.

In his monograph on cinephilia, Christian Keathley uses the term heuretics in contrast to hermeneutics. Hermeneutics for Keathley signifies 'the interpretation or decoding of that which has been encoded', while heuretics signifies 'not *re*covery, but rather a process of *dis*covery ("Eureka! I have found it!")' (Keathley 2006, 143). Heuretics is, for Keathley, far closer to cinephilia than hermeneutics. That is, the love of cinema lies not in finding a meaning in the film that exists *a priori* and which has been inserted into the film in advance; rather, the love of cinema emerges at moments when one discovers something new, when one makes new connections or has new thoughts that may, in fact, have little to do with the filmmakers' intentions.[4] The example given is the role played by hats in Fritz Lang's film *M* (Germany, 1931), specifically bowler hats. Keathley reports that one of his students discovered that bowling at pins originated in Germany as a religious rite representing society cleansing itself: the ball rolls down the alley and knocks over the pins, which symbolise the heathens (the *Heide*) in a given community. *M* is subsequently read as a film involving a society purging itself of its unwanted elements, with Peter Lorre's murderer 'hiding' down 'alleys' and being 'toppled' (see Keathley 2006, 144).

I can imagine that such an ingenious reading of *M* would not be to everyone's taste; it is not a verifiable interpretation of the movie – if one feels compelled to measure interpretations against the intentions of a film's author(s) – and it is unlikely that many/any other viewers would come up with the same interpretation independently. Nonetheless, we have a sense here of heuretics: novel connections are made, and *M*, in conjunction with the viewer, suddenly means something slightly different and new compared to more traditional readings of the film.

The method that Keathley describes is experimental in the second sense of the word described above. As he himself puts it, '[i]f the cinephiliac moment is the starting point, and this starting point has a variety of features, then how can one know in what direction to proceed? One cannot know for sure in advance what direction will be fruitful, so the best answer might be this: intuition' (Keathley 2006, 144). Keathley goes on to discuss intuition in light of Stanley Cavell's understanding of that term. However, the important point to get across here is that cinephilia, the love of cinema, is defined as without a specific *telos* or goal; it is an open-ended experience ('[o]ne cannot know for sure in advance what direction will be fruitful'). Furthermore, while the bowler hat reading of *M* involves research on the part of the student who came up with it (looking up the history of bowling in the *Encyclopaedia Britannica*), this need not be the case: '(h)eureka' moments can take place during the watching of a film without the need for input via external sources. But it is the moment during film viewing or while thinking about a film when a new detail is noticed and a new meaning discovered in the film.

Neurocinematics

I shall eventually argue for a neurological basis for 'heuretics' in both cinephilia and life more generally, but first we should consider how neuroscience has been used to influence our understanding of film, looking primarily at the phenomenon of 'neurocinematics', a term coined by Uri Hasson and colleagues to define the study of what happens in the human brain during film viewing (see Hasson et al. 2004, 2008a, 2008b). Hasson, first of all, showed that a film like *The Good, the Bad and the Ugly* (Sergio Leone, Italy/Spain/West Germany, 1966) produces a noticeable level of what he terms 'intersubject correlation' (ISC). In other words, the same parts of the brain fired across viewers when watching Leone's film – leading Hasson to conclude that 'individual brains "tick together" in synchronised spatiotemporal patterns when exposed to the same visual environment' (Hasson et al. 2004, 1635). Where in that first paper, Hasson claimed that we '"tick collectively" during natural vision' (Hasson et al. 2004, 1634), he later refined this argument to suggest that certain film styles induce greater rates of ISC than others and that the film style perhaps most close to natural vision (an absence of cinematic techniques like cuts, and an absence of a clear narrative) in fact involves the lowest amount of ISC. That is, we perhaps tick less collectively during natural vision than during film viewing.

Hasson and his colleagues showed clips from *The Good, the Bad and the Ugly*, an episode of *Alfred Hitchcock Presents* called *Bang! You're Dead* (Alfred Hitchcock, USA, 1961), an episode of the Larry David comedy show *Curb Your Enthusiasm* (USA, 2000) and images of a concert in Washington Square Park, New York. The amount of ISC varied across the four clips, with the Hitchcock eliciting 'similar responses across all viewers in over 65 per cent of the cortex', *The Good, the Bad and the Ugly* with 45 per cent similarity, *Curb Your Enthusiasm* 18 per cent, and the park scene, described as an 'unstructured segment of reality', eliciting less than 5 per cent similarity (Hasson et al. 2008b, 14). It seems, then, that films made using the rules of continuity editing (Hitchcock, to a lesser extent Leone) evoke greater ISC than films made using a quasi-documentary style (*Curb Your Enthusiasm*, which regularly involves both long takes and long shots – even if these techniques are relatively unusual for television, which tends to favour faster cutting and more close-ups as a result of smaller screen size and image resolution) and certainly more than films involving an 'absence' of style (no camera movement on the Washington Square Park bench).

There are several reasons for presenting this review of Hasson's work. Firstly, the favouring of clear, as opposed to messy, statistics suggests the way in which psychology as a discipline works towards understanding the general, as opposed to the idiosyncratic, even if psychology has at its heart individual case studies of people with brain disorders, as so famously written about by the likes of Oliver Sacks (1986). This relates to a second point, which is the fact that Hitchcock's evocation of a 65 per cent cortical correlation across subjects is presented as the key finding of Hasson's paper. In effect, Hitchcock is presented as the purveyor of real cinema, while the Washington Square Park sequence is described as 'unstructured' and as being 'without […] any cinematic devices such as pans, cuts, and close-ups' (Hasson et al. 2008b, 7). And yet, while admittedly 'extreme', the Washington Square Park sequence cannot be devoid of cinematic devices, especially framing and modifications in colour as a result of design decisions in the hardware and software used to record, place onto a timeline, and then to present the footage recorded. That is, while few filmmakers present films like that of the Washington Square Park concert, there is a tradition in cinema, typically art house cinema, of static cameras, long takes and long shots – a style that comes closer to the Washington Square Park sequence than it does to the Hitchcock film. It is likely, then, that certain film styles elicit little ISC – but that these are *equally cinematic* to the techniques adopted by filmmakers like Alfred Hitchcock, even if Hasson's essay implicitly suggests that the latter is 'more' cinematic.

I shall return to the relationship between ISC and film style later, linking a lack of ISC to a greater possibility for 'heuretical' thought. However, before making such a link, I should continue my analysis of Hasson. Hasson and his cowriters speculate that 'part of the mesmerising power of movies stems from their ability to take control of viewers' minds' (Hasson et al. 2008b, 17). However, they also admit that 'the possibility to achieve a tight grip on the viewers' minds can be used for creating an unethical form of propaganda or brainwash' (Hasson et al. 2008b, 18). In an endnote, Hasson et al. make reference to Leni Riefenstahl as an exemplar of someone having 'a tight aesthetic control over the viewer' (Hasson et al. 2008b, 24) – even though there is no statistical analysis of whether Riefenstahl actually achieved this through her films.

Ultimately, I am going to share Hasson's suggestion that films can 'control' the minds of viewers – but I think that some clarification needs here to be made – and we can do this through a brief consideration of Riefenstahl. Riefenstahl is considered a great filmmaker, her *Triumph of the Will* (Germany, 1935) and *Olympia* (Germany, 1938) being classics of documentary cinema. The reason they are classics is because the technical accomplishments achieved by Riefenstahl have been widely imitated since – **without** *Olympia,* sports coverage might look wholly different to how it does today. However, Riefenstahl is considered a propaganda filmmaker because she used those techniques to present to viewers pro-Nazi messages.

In a similar vein, D. W. Griffith, to whom Hasson et al. could and perhaps should also make reference, is considered the founding father of narrative/fiction cinema. That is, it is the techniques devised by Griffith that have been adopted and 'improved upon' by the likes of Alfred Hitchcock, and which techniques Hasson identifies as being most effective at controlling audiences. And yet, we know that Griffith's *Birth of a Nation* (USA, 1915) is a pro-Ku Klux Klan tract that conveys a deeply racist ideology. That is, Griffith's political outlook is abhorrent – anachronistic even for the time of the film's production – and, precisely, propagandistic.

I discuss Riefenstahl and Griffith for two reasons. First, by discussing only Riefenstahl as a propagandistic filmmaker, Hasson seems to suggest that propagandistic filmmaking only exists 'over there' (in Germany, and not in the USA). And yet, if Griffith is the founding father of narrative cinema, and if Griffith is a propagandistic filmmaker, then propaganda equally exists not just 'over there', but also 'here'. More than this, though, is the fact that the same techniques used by Riefenstahl and Griffith are used today. In other words, if Riefenstahl could control the minds of her audience, and if the techniques that Griffith devised elicit greater levels of ISC in contemporary audiences, then the conclusion that we might and perhaps should draw is that all narrative and even documentary cinema is propaganda of one form or another – and expressly not something 'over there'.

There is an important paradox for us to work through here. For, to name as propaganda only the cinema with which one disagrees (Hasson et al. dismiss Riefenstahl as propaganda because pro-Nazi) is to create a syllogism: propaganda controls our minds, but we label as propaganda that with which we disagree, meaning that propaganda does not control our minds. If propaganda does not control our minds (it is 'over there'), then propaganda as such does not exist. However, Hasson et al.'s findings would suggest that cinema can and does control our minds, meaning that cinema is propagandistic. And yet the cinema that best controls our minds is celebrated by Hasson et al. not as propaganda, but as successful entertainment – with propaganda being relegated precisely to 'over there' (Riefenstahl, as opposed to Griffith, who is the forefather of the cinema that Hasson and colleagues celebrate).

Moving beyond this contradiction, we might nonetheless conclude that all cinema is to a greater or lesser extent propaganda, in the sense of conveying messages via the use of certain techniques, regardless of whether we agree or disagree with them. Rather than dismiss that with which we disagree as propaganda, then, we might consider the propagandistic elements in even the cinema that we enjoy. That is, propaganda does not lie in the message of a film *per se* (I find *Triumph of the Will* to endorse fascism; I find *Birth of a Nation* racist), but in the techniques that a film uses. That the techniques of supposedly/precisely 'propagandistic' filmmakers like Riefenstahl and Griffith continue to be so influential would seem only to reaffirm as much. In other words, even though cognitive film studies as a whole, with *Post-Theory* standing as its figurehead, was born as a reaction against ideological criticism of films, particularly along Marxist lines ('classical' *Screen* theory), then neurocinematics, which is born out of the post-theoretical moment in film studies, seems logically to demand that we come full circle and engage with films once again on the ideological level, in order to tease out the messages that films present to us (see also Brown 2011).

Flicker: Your Brain on Movies

Jeffrey M. Zacks recently authored a neuroscientific approach to the film entitled *Flicker: Your Brain on Movies* (2014). Zacks presents a comprehensive understanding of how film engages our brains, although he perhaps overlooks to a large extent the role that sound, especially dialogue and music, plays in engaging us as viewers of films. Without wishing to rehearse his arguments in detail, I wish to highlight how Zacks also claims to have settled the issue of whether film can influence behaviour, saying with certainty that exposure to violent films can lead to a more violent lifestyle (Zacks 2014, 79), and that, after fellow psychologist Deborah Prentice, '[w]hen we experience a story, our default is to accept what it tells us as true. We have to do extra work to override that default and question what we are reading [or viewing]' (Zacks 2014, 70). Zacks presents various arguments as to why people might not take more seriously the potentially damaging effects of film and the media more generally, saying that a 'reason why it may be hard to convince people that violent media are bad for them is this: they may not like hearing that something they enjoy is bad for them. And finding that smoking or violent movies is bad for you might invite policies that restrict what we can consume. This sort of thing gives many of us the heebie-jeebies. Particularly in the United States, the threat of restricting our personal freedoms taps into a deep vein of antipathy' (Zacks 2014, 83).

It is the final sentence of this quotation that is worth picking apart. For, Zacks seems to suggest here that people from the United States understand freedom better than members of any other nation. Why this would be so is not clear to me. Or rather, if Americans do understand freedom better than others, then it is because the United States is what Benedict Anderson (2006) would term an 'imagined community' that possesses its own ideology, which itself is a product at least in part of the national media. This complicates the belief, expressed by Noël Carroll, that all humans are fundamentally the same. Carroll argues in *Post-Theory* that 'surely, the perception of the cinematic image, and the comprehension of narrative will have the same biological, psychological, and cognitive foundations in any humanly imaginable, non-repressive, classless egalitarian utopia that those perceptual and cognitive processes have in present-day Los Angeles' (1996, 51). And yet, Zacks seems to suggest that while universally the media shape our attitudes towards violence and our likelihood to be violent, antipathy towards limiting one's freedom of expression is a particularly American phenomenon (people could indeed be different in a utopia from Los Angeles). In other words, Zacks acknowledges the media's influence with one hand, while with the other he overlooks the way in which his self-professed 'American' outlook is itself an ideological construct that is shaped at least in part by the media, and which has become naturalised to such an extent that he can make pronouncements about American specificity without stopping to think twice about them.

To return to neurocinematics, Zacks reinforces Hasson et al.'s argument that films can be propagandistic (exposure to violence makes us violent), while not acknowledging how ideology informs his nationalist outlook regarding freedom. Again, it is not the propaganda is 'over there', but that unthinking ideological beliefs (Americans are special in thinking this way about that thing), themselves partially formed in response to the media, inform every aspect of our lives. In other words, all media are propagandistic.

Neuronal Activity and Thought

While Hasson makes the suggestion that films might function as a means of controlling the minds of viewers, he and his colleagues are clear that this assertion is speculative. In addition, Hasson does make reference to the work of Ludwig Wittgenstein when he and his cowriters suggest that neurocinematics could be a tool for measuring how there might be a neurological basis for groups from different ethnic, sexual, gendered, age and cultural backgrounds to respond to the same films in different ways. In other words, Hasson acknowledges, after Wittgenstein (and Lev Vygotsky) the 'central role that the external environment plays in shaping our thoughts, intentions, and behaviours under different circumstances' (Hasson et al. 2008b, 20) – another assertion that would seem to contradict Carroll's claim that utopians and Angelinos view images in the same way.

However, I would also like to evoke Wittgenstein in order to challenge Hasson. For, in his *Philosophical Investigations*, Wittgenstein suggests that 'psychology treats of behaviour, not of the mind' (Wittgenstein 2009, 188) – and the same accusation might be levelled against neurocinematics. In other words, demonstrating what happens on a brain-behavioural level does not necessarily take us any closer to understanding what happens during film viewing on a mental level. It may well be that Hitchcock can get the brains of 65 or more per cent of film viewers to be 'ticking together', but this does not mean that those 65 per cent of film viewers thought about the same thing. Cinema may not literally control our minds such that we all think about the same thing(s) in the same way(s).

Nonetheless, I wonder that there is a case to be made for this being so. With regard to film technique, it seems that a strong link has been established between the techniques of mainstream narrative cinema, especially continuity editing or what is referred to more generally as the classical style, and a greater level of ISC. Across a range of publications, Tim J. Smith has established that there is a similar correlation in terms of eye activity and what he terms 'attentional synchrony' (Smith 2006, 2012, 2013). That is, the direction of viewers' gaze is the same, particularly when watching films that are made using the techniques associated with continuity editing. As with the cortical responses to films measured by Hasson et al., the less the film was made with the techniques associated with continuity editing, the more idiosyncratic the responses of viewers. Hasson and colleagues also found the same result (Hasson 2008b, 5). If movies made using continuity editing techniques capture our gaze in a more uniform fashion, then mainstream narrative cinema functions as a tool for arousing and capturing our attention. And as Zacks says, '[i]f we can't attend to something we almost might as well be blind to it' (Zacks 2014, 132).

Now, Zacks here is referring to change blindness, and humans' capacity to miss very obvious features of the visual field (e.g. a woman dressed in a gorilla suit), if their attention is taken up by something else (counting passes made by a basketball team). What is true literally about cinema, though, might well be true in a more metaphorical way. That is, if our attention is diverted such that we miss other things happening before our eyes – a basic principle involved in the magician's sleight of hand – then maybe we also miss the ideological messages being passed on to us in conjunction with the story when we are immersed in a narrative film. At the very least, Hasson and Zacks's speculations would imply this, since it is the techniques of immersive storytelling that are the same techniques that might be (or rather, are) used for propaganda purposes.

What is more, this line of argument is supported by the suggestion of Nobel prize-winning neuroscientist Gerald M. Edelman, who with Giulio Tononi suggests that our conscious thoughts arise as a result of neurons in our brains firing in clusters. A big enough cluster of neurons fires and the signal in our brain becomes strong enough that we think consciously about it/its source (see Edelman and Tononi 2001, 120–34). If neurocinematics demonstrates that films can control the way in which our brains do fire, then truly cinema might be a means for controlling our thoughts, for getting us to think about certain things – and perhaps in a certain way – and not about other things, since cinema can control which clusters of neurons fire when and in response to what. When films repeatedly associate characters of certain ethnicities and/or nationalities with criminal traits, or when films repeatedly suggest that violence does solve problems, or when films repeatedly suggest that happiness can only be achieved through material wealth, then our brains in conjunction with those films lay down neuronal pathways evoked by the images conveying those messages in such a way that they become habitual for us. As Donald Hebb so famously said of the human brain: what fires together, wires together (a phrase Hasson et al. echo when they speak of film viewers 'ticking together'). And so we begin to think certain thoughts as a result of our repeated exposure to those things in the media that surround us.

Perhaps I should take a moment to clarify briefly what I mean by ideology before developing the final strands of my argument. When I say that we are prone to ideological messages and that all films are propaganda, this does not mean that all films are *de facto* 'bad', in particular, films made in the continuity style (though I do want to challenge the assumption that such films are 'better'). For, one cannot be without ideology, or thought patterns that have become natural as a result of repeated exposure to, or practising of, certain ideas. For example, it is as much an ideological assertion to be against racism as it is to be a racist, even if we think of movies conveying racist messages as propaganda (*Birth of a Nation*) and movies that are more politically correct as being more even. The Wittgenstein-inspired argument by Hasson earlier – that our thoughts, intentions and behaviours are shaped by the external world – would suggest as much. For, if the world cannot but shape our thoughts, intentions and behaviours, then we can never get away from external influence, including the ideas that surround us and which are conveyed through our media. It would be precious (but a natural by-product of a capitalist ideology that puts so much emphasis on the autonomy of the individual) to think that we can achieve a state where we are free of all ideology and where we somehow achieve autonomy of thought or thought that is not shaped by the outside world. Indeed, this would be antithetical to what is potentially neuroscience's chief discovery, namely that we are not Cartesian beings whose thoughts are disembodied and whose bodies are not connected to, or are fundamentally entangled with the world (see Damasio 1994; Brown 2013). We are entangled with the world and our thoughts are embodied; as such, everything shapes us.[5] So the aim is not to be outside of ideology as I am defining it here; rather, the aim is as much as we can to be conscious of and thus participate actively in the formation of our own ideology and/or thoughts, rather than simply passive consumers thereof.[6] Cognitive film studies may have sought to reject passivity in film viewers; however, its possibility still lingers.

He(u)retical Film Theory

This is where my he(u)retical film theory becomes important. For, here I shall make a heretical gesture by suggesting that idiosyncratic responses to film are key to understanding one of the things that cinema can do when put in conjunction with viewers. It is not that any single, idiosyncratic response to a film is important; it is that idiosyncratic, rather than clustered, responses to film might be statistically important, rather than 'noise' in comparison to the 'clear' results that brain scanning achieves when looking at audiences of mainstream narrative/continuity editing cinema.

Idiosyncratic responses to film, both in terms of eye movement and in terms of cortical activity, are greatly increased when a film is made not via the techniques associated with continuity editing, but instead via the techniques associated more with art house cinema: long takes, long shots, minimal camera movement. Although this view has precursors in the work of, for example, André Bazin, who similarly suggested that deep focus and a concomitant stillness of the camera 'implies [...] a more active mental attitude on the part of the spectator' (Bazin 1967, 50), it remains somewhat speculative in the sense that ISC, or a lack thereof, does not necessarily imply an 'active mental attitude.' For this reason, I call 'heretical' the theory that if mainstream narrative cinema induces synchronised thought, art house cinema allows viewers more to think 'for themselves' – they decide or choose what to look at/for in the image that they see (with the sound perhaps also guiding their sight, with sound being a key aspect of cinema that should not be overlooked).

This heretical film theory is also one attuned to heuretics as outlined earlier. For, if thought pursues an idiosyncratic trajectory when a viewer watches a film made with a certain set of techniques (there is little ISC), then thought takes on a dimension of 'experimentation', a willingness to pursue avenues that do not have a pre-set destination. This would indeed tie in with David Bordwell's (1979) view that the 'art house' film – involving long takes, long shots and minimal camera movement – is one defined by ambiguity; were the 'meaning' clear, the film would presumably involve strong ISC, while a lack of ISC implies ambiguity, with the ambiguous film inducing varied as opposed to shared responses. The ambiguous 'art film' may thus tell the same story as the film made in the continuity style, but by being able to choose – not wholly, but to a greater extent (we must always acknowledge that the filmmaker has framed her images, chosen and developed acting styles with her actors, designed the set, chosen film stock, and so on) – what to look at and what therefore to attend to and think about, the viewer is more likely to see different, unexpected patterns in the film, to achieve a position of cinephilia – even if Bordwell (cynically?) implies at times that the 'art film' is a somewhat cynical exercise in deliberate 'meaninglessness'. The subtitle to Keathley's book is *The Wind in the*

Trees: sometimes cinema need not tell us an exciting story; it can simply open our eyes to see as if for the first time the way in which leaves dance when stimulated by the wind resulting from changes in air pressure.

The final question becomes, then: what is the benefit of such an experience? Film is considered by some to be a means of communication, and so, efficient story-telling *à la* Hitchcock is surely 'better' than the kind of film I am describing (and which many viewers, put simply, find boring). However, film is not simply a means of communication. Humans adapt their environment and adapt to their environment; in adapting, they survive. However, no one knows what the future holds, nor what kinds of skills – physical or mental – will be important in order to survive. Art house cinema, as I am defining it here (and I am not proposing that this is the only definition of art house cinema), and perhaps art more generally (with not all cinema necessarily qualifying as art), function therefore as a means of shaking us out of the naturalised way in which we see the world, to make us see the world anew, by making us have new thoughts and making new connections.[7] Cinema can build a community by solidifying beliefs via ideological messages – whether or not we like the idea of this; but cinema can also help an individual to begin to think for themselves, to begin to think differently. Being able to think differently may even be useful in an ever-changing environment in which the old and seemingly rigid rules begin no longer to apply. Heuretics may seem heretical from the perspective of mainstream cinema, then, but he(u)retical film theory provides a novel framework through which we can consider the benefits of, and perhaps the need for, art house/'heretical' cinema – not instead of but in addition to mainstream narrative cinema. By bringing together (Anglophone) cognitive film theory and a more 'classical'/*Screen*-like approach to film (itself an Anglophone reading of predominantly French film theory), we perhaps can learn how art, as a means for helping us to think differently, potentially also becomes a means to enable our very survival.[8]

Notes

1 Subsequent attempts to reproduce the Kuleshov effect have on the whole been unsuccessful, or at the very least have not confirmed Kuleshov's proclaimed results (see Prince and Hensley 1992; Mobbs et al. 2006).

2 Buckland's use of the term 'European' is problematic, since many of the Anglophone cognitive film theorists hail from Britain, Denmark, Germany and the Netherlands, among other European places. For this reason, I distinguish Anglophone (work published in English) from non-Anglophone (work not published in English) – even if this is still a problematic distinction because, for example, work along this vein continues also to be published in German.

3 In a gesture that is anathema to some members of the SCSMI (I have seen people leave the room at the mention of Gilles Deleuze's name), I might even contend that some Anglophone theorists who adopt a Deleuzian framework are already providing such a synthesis of Anglophone and non-Anglophone cognitive approaches, because Deleuze himself was latterly influenced by neuroscience, as made clear in his book *What is Philosophy?* (Deleuze and Guattari 1994). Examples of such work might include Paul Elliott (2011), Patricia Pisters (2012) and William Brown (2013).

4 Jacques Rancière presents a similar argument when, in a discussion of Kenji Mizoguchi's *Sanshô dayû/Sansho the Bailiff* (Japan, 1954) in *Les Écarts du Cinéma*, he suggests that the film enacts that

of which cinema as a whole is capable. Having freed some slaves, Zushiô (Yoshiaki Hanayagi) simply goes home to his mother, meaning that the slaves must now decide for themselves what to do. Similarly, cinema itself can free (or to borrow a term from another text by Rancière, emancipate; see Rancière 2009) its spectators, such that they, too, can decide how to engage with the text. For Rancière, this is linked precisely to cinephilia (see Rancière 2011, 7–22).

5 I do not have space to engage fully with her work here, but Karen Barad's (2007) concept of entanglement, which takes its inspiration from physicist Niels Bohr's understanding of the world, suggests that we can never separate ourselves from the world.

6 For one of the key explorations of how ideology works, readers might consult Louis Althusser's writings on ideological state apparatuses (Althusser 1971, 127–86). Furthermore, Roland Barthes's (1976, 32–33) notion that all ideologies are 'dominant' also reflects my suggestion that, whether 'good' or 'bad,' it is difficult if not impossible to escape ideology.

7 As already suggested in note 3 above, I might nonetheless add how this process is akin to Gilles Deleuze's argument, following Henri Bergson, that the human brain is a machine that can help us to 'triumph over mechanism' (i.e. unthinkingness/seeing the world automatically and not anew; see Deleuze 1991, 107). Since, as Deleuze argues elsewhere (2000), 'the brain is the screen,' in the sense that the cinema screen is akin to and has a direct relationship with the brain, then to offer up an unusual as opposed to an easy cinema ('triumphing over' the 'mechanism' of mainstreaming filmmaking) might have a similar effect on the brain. Furthermore, in 'The Ecocinema Experience,' Scott MacDonald (2013, 19–20) has more recently suggested that long takes and 'slow' images of nature can offer 'new kinds of film experience' that train us in a 'patience and mindfulness' that might then help us to act similarly in our real lives. Both might find support from he(u)retical film theory.

8 The author would like to thank the editors for their very helpful comments on an early draft of this essay.

References

Aldama, F. L. 2013. *Mex-Cine: Mexican Filmmaking, Production and Consumption in the Twenty-First Century*. Ann Arbor: University of Michigan Press.

Althusser, L. 1971. *Lenin and Philosophy and Other Essays*. Translated by B. Brewster. New York: Monthly Review Press.

Anderson, B. 2006. *Imagined Communities: Reflections on the Origin and Spread of Nationalism*. London: Verso.

Anderson, J. D. 1998. *The Reality of Illusion: An Ecological Approach to Cognitive Film Theory*. Carbondale: Southern Illinois University Press.

Arnheim, R. 1974. *Art and Visual Perception*. Berkeley: University of California Press.

———. 1983. *Film as Art*. London: Faber and Faber.

Barad, K. 2007. *Meeting the Universe Halfway: Quantum Physics and the Entanglement of Matter and Meaning*. Durham, NC: Duke University Press.

Barthes, R. 1976. *The Pleasure of the Text*. Translated by R. Miller. London: Cape.

Bazin, A. 1967. *What is Cinema? Volume 1*. Translated by H. Grey. Berkeley: University of California Press.

Bordwell, D. 1979. 'The Art Cinema as a Mode of Film Practice'. *Film Criticism* 4, no. 1 (Fall): 56–64.

———. 1985. *Narration in the Fiction Film*. Madison: University of Wisconsin Press.

———. 2007. *Poetics of Cinema*. London: Routledge.

Bordwell, D., and N. Carroll. 1996a. 'Introduction'. In *Post-Theory: Reconstructing Film Studies*, edited by D. Bordwell and N. Carroll, xiii–xvii. Madison: University of Wisconsin Press.

Bordwell, D., and N. Carroll, eds. 1996b. *Post-Theory: Reconstructing Film Studies*. Madison: University of Wisconsin Press.

Branigan, E. 1992. *Narrative Comprehension and Film*. London: Routledge.

Brown, W. 2011. 'Rejecting the Psycho-Logic of Intensified Continuity'. *Projections: The Journal for Movies and Mind* 5, no. 1 (Summer): 69–86.

———. 2013. *Supercinema: Film-Philosophy for the Digital Age.* Oxford: Berghahn.

Buckland, W. 2000. *The Cognitive Semiotics of Film.* Cambridge: Cambridge University Press.

Carroll, N. 1996. 'Prospects for Film Theory: A Personal Assessment'. In *Post-Theory: Reconstructing Film Studies*, edited by D. Bordwell and N. Carroll, 37–68. Madison: University of Wisconsin Press.

Damasio, A. 1994. *Descartes' Error: Emotion, Reason and the Human Brain.* London: Vintage.

Deleuze, G. 1991. *Bergsonism.* Translated by H. Tomlinson and B. Habberjam. New York: Zone Books.

———. 2000. 'The Brain is the Screen', translated by M. T. Guirgis. In *The Brain Is the Screen: Deleuze and the Philosophy of Cinema*, edited by G. Flaxman, 365–73. Minneapolis: University of Minnesota Press.

Deleuze, G., and F. Guattari. 1994. *What is Philosophy?* Translated by G. Birchill and H. Tomlinson. London: Verso.

Edelman, G. M., and G. Tononi. 2001. *Consciousness: How Matter Becomes Imagination.* London: Penguin.

Eisenstein, S. M. 1957. *Film Form: Essays in Film Theory.* New York: Meridian Books.

Elliott, P. 2011. *Hitchcock and the Cinema of Sensations: Embodied Film Theory and Cinematic Reception.* London: I.B. Tauris.

Gibson, J. J. 1986. *The Ecological Approach to Visual Perception.* Hillsdale, NJ: Lawrence Erlbaum Associates.

Grodal, T. 1999. *Moving Pictures: A New Theory of Film Genres, Feelings, and Cognition.* Oxford: Oxford University Press.

———. 2009. *Embodied Visions: Evolution, Emotion, Culture, and Film.* Oxford: Oxford University Press.

Hasson, U., O. Furman, D. Clark, Y. Dudai and L. Davachi. 2008a. 'Enhanced Intersubject Correlations During Movie Viewing Correlate with Successful Episodic Encoding'. *Neuron* 57, no. 3: 452–62.

Hasson, U., O. Landesman, B. Knappmeyer, I. Vallines, N. Rubin and D. J. Heeger. 2008b. 'Neurocinematics: The Neuroscience of Film'. *Projections: The Journal for Movies and Mind* 2, no. 1: 1–26.

Hasson, U., Y. Nir, I. Levy, G. Fuhrmann and R. Malach. 2004. 'Intersubject Synchronisation of Cortical Activity During Natural Vision'. *Science* 303, no. 5664: 1634–40.

Hochberg, J. 2007. *In the Mind's Eye: Julian Hochberg on the Perception of Pictures, Film, and the World*, edited by M. A. Peterson, B. Gillam and H. A. Sedgwick. Oxford: Oxford University Press.

Hogan, P. C. 2009. *Understanding Indian Movies: Culture, Cognition, and Cinematic Imagination.* Austin: University of Texas Press.

Keathley, C. 2006. *Cinephilia and History, or The Wind in the Trees.* Bloomington: University of Indiana Press.

Laine, T., and W. Strauven. 2009. 'The Synaesthetic Turn'. *New Review of Film and Television Studies* 7, no. 3: 249–55.

MacDonald, S. 2013. 'The Ecocinema Experience'. In *Ecocinema Theory and Practice*, edited by S. Rust, S. Monani and S. Cubitt, 17–41. London: Routledge.

Metz, C. 1977. *The Imaginary Signifier: Psychoanalysis and Cinema.* Bloomington: Indiana University Press.

Mitchell, George. 1982. 'The Movies and Münsterberg'. *Jump Cut* 27 (July): 57–60. Available at: http://www.ejumpcut.org/archive/onlinessays/JC27folder/Munsterberg.html (accessed 9 November 2015).

Mitry, J. 2000. *The Aesthetics and Psychology of the Cinema.* Translated by C. King. Bloomington: Indiana University Press.

Mobbs, D., N. Weiskopf, H. C. Lau, E. Featherstone, R. J. Dolan and C. D. Frith. 2006. 'The Kuleshov Effect: The Influence of Contextual Framing on Emotional Attributions'. *Social Cognitive and Affective Neuroscience* 1, no. 2: 95–106.

Morin, E. 2005. *The Cinema, or the Imaginary Man.* Translated by L. Mortimer. Minneapolis: University of Minnesota Press.

Mulvey, L. 1975. 'Visual Pleasure and Narrative Cinema'. *Screen* 16, no. 3: 6–18.

———. 1990. 'Afterthoughts on "Visual Pleasure and Narrative Cinema" Inspired by *Duel in the Sun* (1946)'. In *Psychoanalysis and Cinema*, edited by E. A. Kaplan, 24–35. New York: Routledge.

Münsterberg, H. 1916. *The Photoplay: A Psychological Study.* London: D. Appleton.

Pisters, P. 2012. *The Neuro-Image: A Deleuzian Film-Philosophy of Digital Screen Culture.* Stanford: Stanford University Press.

Plantinga, C. 2009. *Moving Viewers: American Film and the Spectator's Experience.* Berkeley: University of California Press.

Plantinga, C., and G. M. Smith. 1999. *Passionate Views: Film, Cognition, and Emotion.* Baltimore: Johns Hopkins University Press.

Prince, S., and W. E. Hensley. 1992. 'The Kuleshov Effect: Recreating the Classic Experiment'. *Cinema Journal* 31, no. 2: 59–75.

Rancière, J. 2009. *The Emancipated Spectator.* Translated by G. Elliott. London: Verso.

———. 2011. *Les Écarts du Cinéma.* Paris: La Fabrique éditions.

Sacks, O. 1986. *The Man Who Mistook His Wife for a Hat.* Basingstoke: Picador.

Serra, S. 2013. *Emotion and Cognition in the Films of Bernardo Bertolucci.* Kibworth Beauchamp: Troubador.

Smith, M. 1995. *Engaging Characters: Fiction, Emotion, and the Cinema.* Oxford: Clarendon Press.

Smith, T. J. 2006. An Attentional Theory of Continuity Editing, PhD thesis submitted to the University of Edinburgh, UK.

———. 2012. 'The Attentional Theory of Cinematic Continuity'. *Projections: The Journal for Movies and Mind* 6, no. 1: 1–27.

———. 2013. 'Watching You Watch Movies: Using Eye Tracking to Inform Cognitive Film Theory'. In *Psychocinematics: Exploring Cognition at the Movies*, edited by A. P. Shimamura, 165–91. New York: Oxford University Press.

———. 2014. 'Audiovisual Correspondences in Sergei Eisenstein's *Alexander Nevsky*: A Case Study in Viewer Attention'. In *Cognitive Media Theory*, edited by T. Nannicelli and P. Taberham, 85–105. London: Routledge/American Film Institute.

Society for Cognitive Studies of the Moving Image. n.d. 'What Is the History and Purpose of SCSMI?' http://scsmi-online.org/faq/what-is-the-history-and-purpose-of-scsmi (accessed 19 December 2014).

Tan, Ed S. 1995. *Emotion and the Structure of Narrative Film: Film as an Emotion Machine.* London: Routledge.

Wittgenstein, L. 2009. *Philosophical Investigations.* Translated by G. E. M. Anscombe, P. M. S. Hacker and Joachim Schulte. Oxford: Blackwell.

Zacks, J. M. 2014. *Flicker: Your Brain on Movies.* Oxford: Oxford University Press.

Chapter Seventeen

PHILOSOPHY ENCOUNTERS THE MOVING IMAGE: FROM FILM PHILOSOPHY TO CINEMATIC THINKING

Robert Sinnerbrink

After the moving image was neglected by much of twentieth-century philosophy, philosophy of film has emerged in recent decades as an independent field of inquiry.[1] Since the decline of so-called Grand Theory (Bordwell and Carroll 1996), film theory has diversified in different directions, from historicism and media theory to phenomenology and cognitivist approaches. One of the most interesting developments – and the subject of this entry – is the philosophical turn in film theory and the rise of what is described as 'film and philosophy'. The latter comprises a number of strands of philosophical film theory, encompassing both philosophy of film (often indebted to analytic aesthetics and/or cognitivist approaches) and film-philosophy (often aligned with a range of Continental and post-Continental thinkers, as well as phenomenological and critical theory approaches).[2] In what follows, I explore key elements of the film and philosophy relationship, focusing on the work of Deleuze and Cavell, examining the idea of 'film *as* philosophy', and some concluding reflections on the possibilities of cinematic thinking.

Image, Movement, Time: Deleuze

Gilles Deleuze published the first of his two books on film and philosophy in 1983, *Cinema 1: The Movement Image* (trans. 1986), followed by the 'sequel' in 1985, *Cinema 2: The Time-Image* (trans. 1989). In their ambitious attempt to conceptualize the 'essential' concepts of cinema, Deleuze seeks to respond to problems shared by both film and philosophy. His project begins with a critical commentary on Henri Bergson's metaphysics of movement, which we may summarize in the three theses mentioned below:

Movement is Distinct from the Space Covered

Bergson's first thesis, according to Deleuze, holds that movement as such is qualitative, and so cannot be divided up without changing qualitatively (1986, 1). Space, on the other hand, is quantitative and so can be divided indefinitely. Space is homogeneous, movement heterogeneous (Deleuze 1986, 1). This implies that movement cannot be recomposed out of individual positions in space or instants in time; static sections (positions and instants) can only be synthesized in succession to create an 'illusory' movement. This is what happens in cinema, according to Bergson, which synthesizes static images, passing in rapid succession, in order to generate a 'false movement': the illusionistic impression of movement on the screen. However, what we experience in film, Deleuze claims, is not illusory movement but rather a 'mobile section of duration': a 'movement-image' that moves in itself, enabling movements to be captured and extended over time through the cinematic devices of framing, editing, cutting, montage and so on (1986, 2–3).

Ancient versus Modern Conceptions of Movement

According to Deleuze/Bergson, there are two ways of composing 'illusory' forms of movement (recomposing movement from static instants or 'poses'). For the Greeks, movement was composed via intelligible elements or eternal Forms; for the moderns, following modern science, movement refers to generic temporal instants or the 'any-instant-whatever' (Deleuze 1986, 3–4). Time is taken as an independent variable, which allows movement to be measured and quantified. Cinema inherits this quantitative conception of movement and of time, and can, therefore, be defined as 'the system which reproduces movement by relating it to the any-instant-whatever' (Deleuze 1989, 6).

Movement Expresses a Qualitative Change in the Whole

According to Bergson/Deleuze, what we take to be temporal instants are only 'immobile sections' of movement; movement itself, however, is a 'mobile section' expressing qualitative change in the Whole (Deleuze 1989, 8). From this holistic perspective, movement is an expression of qualitative change, an expression of what Bergson called *duration* [*durée*]. What we take to be static images are really 'immobile sections' of movement or frozen moments of *durée* (Deleuze 1989, 8–9). A key distinction comes into play here: that between mobile sections of duration (*movement-images*) and direct images of duration (*time-images*) in which time is no longer subordinated to movement.

The key points that Deleuze derives from his analysis of Bergson are these: (1) that cinema produces movement-images depicting a plurality of movements *within* the image, (2) that film also expresses movement *between* composed images (montage), and (3) that this composed series of images expresses duration *across the Whole* of the film as well as beyond it (1986, 11). These three Bergsonian theses on movement provide Deleuze with a conceptual framework for classifying cinematic image-signs (namely as varieties of movement-image and time-image).

Movement-Image

Deleuze's ontological project is to define the specificity of cinema as depicting movement in relation to generic instants (the 'any-instant-whatever'), which allow for the measuring of movement against a succession of equidistant temporal instants (t_1, t_2, t_3, ...). Deleuze follows Bergson in arguing that movement cannot be deduced from pre-existing 'transcendental poses', static positions, or privileged moments (1986, 4). Rather, cinema is a mechanical system of *animating* images that enables the reproduction of movement 'as a function of the any-instant-whatever' (equidistant temporal instants), which are selected and combined in order to 'create the impression of continuity' (Deleuze 1986, 5). Once the technical apparatus of creating movement-images via generic instants is taken over 'as a machine of synthesis for purposes of art and entertainment', we have, according to Deleuze, the cinema (1986, 6).

More specifically, once an image is related to a 'static' point of view – what Bergson calls a 'centre of indetermination' in the image nexus – we have a *perception-image*, which can take 'objective' and 'subjective' forms (the establishing shots that open many films, or the shot-countershot format depicting dialogue, respectively). Perception, however, is linked to action, both in the sensory-motor schema of human cognition and in the image nexus composing narrative film. Once an image is related to a perception-image and to an encompassing milieu, we have the *action-image*: the familiar medium shots, for example, of characters expressing their perception of a situation through action (like the Mexican standoff scene in Tarantino's *Reservoir Dogs* (1992)).

The link between perception and action, however, is a *complex* rather than reflex movement; the 'gap' or 'interval' between perception and action – whether in cognition or in narrative film – is filled by *affect* or *affection* (the ways in which our bodies are affected by movement). This yields the *affection-image*, which expresses bodily affect or emotion but also qualities and powers in an ontological sense (as pure singularities). Affection-images are most familiar as the close-up of the face or of affectively charged objects, which express affect but also qualities by sensuous means (the 'dancing bag' sequence in Mendes's *American Beauty* (1999), or the bright pool of blood that so fascinates Ricky Fitts [Wes Bentley] in the same film). Affection-images gain intensity, moreover, when the perception-action nexus is interrupted, thereby opening up an affective space for the expression of pure qualitative states or 'non-subjective' affects. For Deleuze, affects are not simply the expression of a subjective feeling or sensation on the part of a human subject; rather, they express 'pure qualities' manifested between subjects, in relation to objects, or even via places and landscapes.

Again following Bergson, Deleuze takes this perception-affection-action circuit to articulate the basic mechanism of action-driven narrative film. The latter is governed by the 'sensory-motor action schema' (Deleuze 1986, 155ff.): the linking of perception-, affection- and action-images within an encompassing milieu. The action-image is typically associated with *realism*, which Deleuze defines via the relationship between a milieu and behaviour: a milieu that actualizes various qualities and powers and modes of behaviour expressing individuated responses to this milieu (1986, 141). Realist action-image cinema, in turn, is defined by two major forms: the 'large form' (1986, 142ff.), found in genres such as the documentary, the Western, psycho-social drama, *film noir* and the historical drama, in which an initial situation (S) leads to action (A) that modifies the situation (SAS_1) and the 'small form' (1986, 160ff.), in which action (A) discloses a partially obscure situation (S), which leads to new action (ASA_1), found in genres such as melodrama and comedy.

Crisis of the Action-Image

The sensory-motor action schema, for Deleuze, provides the framework for the major traditions of narrative film (not only Hollywood but Soviet, French, German and Japanese). Drawing on an historical account of film (Burch, Ropars, Schefer), Deleuze claims that the ascendancy of the sensory-motor action schema undergoes a crisis in the postwar period: a rupturing of the sensory-motor link, a loosening of plot, a dispersion of space and self-consciousness concerning clichés, signs which herald the emergence of the *time-image* (1986, 205–15; 1989, 1–13). The latter inverts the primacy of movement over time, interrupting the link to sensory-motor action in order to express time on its own account. Such images are no longer sensory-motor in orientation but reveal 'pure optical and sound situations', a cinematic innovation that first appears, for Deleuze, with Ozu (1989, 13). These are pure audio-visual descriptions that are no longer extended into action, that express a new way of depicting the world, opening up intensive dimensions of time, affect and thought. A new cinema of 'the seer' replaces the old cinema of the agent (Deleuze 1989, 2). With this shift from sensory-motor action to pure optical and sound situations, and the subsequent development of time-images, the transition to cinematic modernity is achieved (Deleuze 1989, 5). Film thus realizes its 'essence' – its vocation expressing time, affect and thought – in a post-War chronology roughly tracking the appearance of Italian neo-realism (from 1948), the French *nouvelle vague* (from 1958), New German cinema (from 1968) and American independent film during the 1970s (1986, 211).

The 'crisis of the action-image' afflicting post-war cinema involves a breakdown in the sensory-motor action schema, affecting both large (SAS) and small (ASA) forms of action-image narrative. This crisis, moreover, is driven by a *historical* dynamic: the traumatic effects of the experience of WWII, and a related scepticism towards overarching cultural-political ideologies (revolutionary Communism, the American vision of a democracy of equals). Deleuze identifies here a plurality of relevant historical factors: shared cultural crises in meaning, new social movements, the shift towards an image-centred culture, the crossover with modernist literature and the crisis in traditional Hollywood genres (1986, 206). His focus, however, remains with Italian neo-realism, whose distinctiveness lies in the way in which it disrupts the sensory-motor action schema by blocking the link between perception and action. The resulting images no longer refer to an encompassing or determinate situation but to a reality that has become elliptical and dispersive (Deleuze 1986, 207). The sensory-motor action schema is replaced by a meandering 'trip' narrative, which Deleuze calls 'the stroll' or urban voyage and return journey (1986, 208) defined by loosely connected episodes with multiple characters occurring in generic urban spaces or the 'any-space-whatever' (like the rubble-strewn urban landscapes in Rossellini's *Rome, Open City* (1945)).

This disconnected and dispersed world is no longer sustained by a shared conception of history, a vision of the future or sense of social solidarity. Rather, they are sustained only by optical, auditory and psychic *clichés* or the 'sensory-motor images' of things: floating, anonymous images that substitute for a disconnected reality that scarcely fosters or sustains belief. The crisis in the action-image – encompassing the dispersive situation, deliberately weak narrative links, the voyage form, the consciousness of clichés and condemnation of plot – is also an expression of a broader crisis afflicting the 'American Dream' (the vision of individual liberty and fulfilment of historical destiny within a diverse community of equals) (Deleuze 1986, 210). Post-War cinema thus begins with a critical reflection on the dominant model of narrative film (Hollywood) but also questions the shared belief in the power of individual action to transform (historically meaningful) situations.

'Two Ages' of Cinema?

As critics have noted, there seems to be a tension between Deleuze's conceptual taxonomy of image types and his recourse to a historical account of the shift from movement- to time-image narrative. Jacques Rancière (2006, 107–23), for example, criticizes Deleuze's attempt to contrast 'two ages' of the cinema – a classical movement-image cinema, and a modern time-image cinema – for positing a 'fictive' distinction between movement-images and time-images and relying on 'allegorical' interpretations of film examples to support these claims. For Rancière, there are two key questions for Deleuze's analysis: (1) How to explain the relationship between 'a break in the art of images and the ruptures that affect history in general' (2006, 108) and (2) how to recognize, in actual films, the evidence of this break between image-regimes, as well as the distinction between the movement-image and the time-image in specific cases. Rancière's response is to question Deleuze's reliance on a historical account to explain a shift of a conceptual order and to argue that the distinction between movement-images and time-images collapses once submitted to critical scrutiny.

To take up the latter point, the distinction between movement-image and time-image begins to blur within the course of Deleuze's analyses. The affection-image, for example, already expresses pure qualities that articulate a virtual power of the image independent of sensory-motor narrative (see, e.g., Dreyer's silent masterpiece, *The Passion of Joan of Arc* (1928)). Moreover, this blurring of the distinction between movement- and time-images appears in the very examples that Deleuze adduces in order to show the differences between them. Bresson is praised for his use of the affection-image to construct any-spaces-whatever (Deleuze 1986, 108–11), an account that is repeated in *Cinema 2* in relation to the theme of 'thought and cinema' (Rancière 2006, 112). The same film examples (Dreyer or Bresson) can be used either to illustrate the role of affection-images or to exemplify the breaking of the sensory-motor link that defines time-image cinema (Rancière 2006, 112). This equivocation renders doubtful Deleuze's distinction between movement-images and time-images and his claims concerning the break with sensory-motor action schemas in post-War cinema.

Moreover, to support his claims, Deleuze uses film examples that function *allegorically*: films whose *narrative content* is supposed to demonstrate the crisis of the action image. Rancière cites a number of pertinent examples: Hitchcock's *Rear Window* (1954), with its immobilized photographer-protagonist 'Jeff' Jeffries [James Stewart], and *Vertigo* (1959), with its famous shot of Scotty [Stewart] hanging over the abyss by his fingertips; Bresson's *Au hasard Balthazar* (1966), with its linking of hands caring, working and exploiting the eponymous donkey; or *Pickpocket* (1959), whose thieves caress, rather than seize, their booty (2006, 114–19). All of these examples are supposed to serve as allegorical figures expressing a generalized 'crisis in the action-image'.

For Rancière, this ambiguity between image-type and narrative content suggests that the distinction between movement-images and time-images is artificial: a 'fictive rupture' (2006, 119) that cannot be sustained in the face of cinema's dialectic between intentional and automatic elements, narrative and spectacle, representational form and aesthetic experimentation. Indeed, what Deleuze presents is less a shift from one discrete image regime to another than a 'dual perspective' model in which the same images/films can be analysed either from the perspective of movement-image or from that of time-image cinema (Rancière 2006, 114). The (Deleuzian) story of film, Rancière concludes, is thus a thwarted one, much like the 'film fables' defining cinema, forever divided between narrative content and visual spectacle that undo each other continuously (2006, 1–18). Deleuze's 'fictive' opposition between the 'two ages of cinema' (classical and modern) does not do justice to the hybrid character of film, and rests upon an essentializing 'ontology of the cinema argued for with bits and pieces gleaned from the entire *corpus* of the cinematographic art' (2006, 5). We can add to Rancière's critique another observation: the appearance of hybrid forms of narrative cinema in which sensory-motor action and pure optical time-image narrative become indiscernible. Deleuze's historicist thesis looks doubtful given the flourishing of cinema that affirms the play of *mythos* (narrative) and *opsis* (spectacle), classical action-narrative and modern optical and sound situations, in culturally diverse, aesthetically hybrid forms.

Viewing Worlds: Cavell

The shared *problemátique* that unites Deleuze and Cavell centres on the *relationship* between film and philosophy. For both thinkers, philosophy and film engage with problems – above all, *scepticism* and *nihilism* – that cut across cultural, aesthetic and ethico-political domains. Both thinkers also argue that philosophy cannot merely be 'applied' to film as its object; rather, film and philosophy enter into a *transformative* relationship that opens up new ways of thinking. As Rodowick observes, Deleuze's work on cinema (like that of Cavell), is concerned with a single question: 'How does a sustained meditation on film and film theory illuminate the relation between image and thought?' (1997, 5). We might thus regard Deleuze and Cavell as exemplifying two paths for the film-philosophy relationship to pursue: conceptualizing cinema in response to the historico-philosophical problem of a 'loss of belief in the world' (Deleuze); and overcoming scepticism via the engagement between film and philosophy, elaborating how film and philosophy think together in ways yet to be explored (Cavell).

First published in 1971, Cavell's *The World Viewed* (1979) is a landmark work, one of the first philosophical studies dedicated to film ontology. Why is this encounter between film and philosophy important? Cavell's answer is that the experience of film affords us a way of contending with *scepticism* – arguably, *the* problem of modern thought – thereby helping restore meaning in a culture that struggles with philosophy's disenfranchisement of the ordinary. With scientific revolution, transition to secularism, and Enlightenment emphasis on rational autonomy, the ancient problem of scepticism takes on a renewed urgency in the modern age, mutating into the broader cultural-philosophical problem of *nihilism* so important for Deleuze. Modern scepticism – the view that we can have no certain knowledge of the world, that we remain metaphysically isolated from reality/being – has troubled philosophy since at least Descartes. Modern philosophy tried to vanquish scepticism by showing that objective knowledge *is* possible (mathematics, logic, science), that we can attain *certainty* about ourselves and the world in some respects, but that such claims always remain open to sceptical doubt. Despite the success of modern rationalism, the knowledge that really matters to us – about the self, morality or our relations with others – remains frustratingly uncertain.

What do these ruminations on scepticism and metaphysics have to do with cinema? Film, for Cavell, literally (cinematically) 'stages' this sceptical concern. Film can present a visual world of movement and time that not only captures aspects of our experience of reality but which also remains separate from it; a world that is present to me, but from which I am absent. Film shows the interplay of presence and absence in the image; showing objects, figures and events that are absent, yet which enjoy a ghostly presence in the image-world. It also shows how this image-world – what Cavell calls 'the world viewed' – is nonetheless *meaningful*, a restoring of the sundered link with the world that has been lost in modernity. From this point of view, film can be viewed as 'a moving image of skepticism' (Cavell 1979, 188). Echoing Bazin, Cavell remarks that cinema is motivated by our desire for metaphysical connection with the world, 'the wish for self-hood', like all art (1979, 22); yet it shows how we can find this retrieval of meaning in ordinary experience, however much the spectre of scepticism still haunts it.

Following classical film theory, *The World Viewed* commences with an inquiry into the ontology of the cinematic image. Inspired by Panofsky (1977 [1934]) and Bazin (1967), who claimed that the medium of movies refers to 'physical reality as such', or that it 'communicates by way of what is real' (Bazin 1967, 110), Cavell turns to the relationship between photography and film. What Panofsky and Bazin mean, Cavell explains, is that the medium of film has a *photographic* basis and that photographs are *of* a world (1979, 16). When applied to film, their question becomes, 'What happens to reality when it is projected and screened?' (1979, 16). This question is linked with the question of how we experience reality more generally, not only how we perceive it but how we interpret, remember or imagine it. As any filmgoer will attest, we recollect films as well (or as poorly) as we do events in our past, or even our dreams. We can be haunted by images from films seen many years past; some images, scenes or characters can become more familiar or significant than one's own memories. So what are we experiencing when we watch a film?

Unlike painting, photography and film, for Cavell, do not represent so much as 'capture' things; they present us, 'we want to say, with the things themselves' (Cavell 1979, 17). We recognize here Cavell's version of what has been called the 'transparency thesis': that cinematic images are not representations but presentations of what they depict, a view based on the claim that (pre-digital) photography is a realist medium that retains an ontological link between image and referent (Scruton 1981; Walton 1984). A photograph of a landscape is clearly not the same thing as a landscape painting. A portrait of me is a likeness or visual representation, but a photograph is *of* me (not just *like* me). So what is the ontological link between a photograph and what it depicts? It is not a likeness nor is it like a replica, according to Cavell; it is something more ontologically mysterious – a trace of the past, of a presence that is no longer present for us. The photo is present to me, but what it depicts is not. According to Cavell, photographs do not reproduce a 'sight' (or 'look') of something no longer present; rather, they present something that is hard to name, for which a word appears lacking in our language (1979, 19). Is a photograph, as Bazin suggests, therefore like a 'visual mold' of an object? Not really, because the original, Cavell observes, remains *present* in the image. Photographic images, to be sure, are manufactured or 'constructed' images of the world; but what they capture, mechanically and automatically, is the world itself, not a mere likeness of it. It is this mechanism or *automatism* in photography's capturing and reproduction of images that finally satisfies, as Bazin put it, 'our obsession with realism' (quoted in 1979, 20).

Indeed, photography, Cavell remarks, satisfied a wish, growing in the West since the Reformation, 'to escape subjectivity and metaphysical isolation – a wish for the power to reach this world, having for so long tried, at last hopelessly, to manifest fidelity to another' (1979, 21). After the advent of nihilism or what Nietzsche called 'the death of God', painting and photography – and later, film – aimed to re-establish our sense of connection with the world. These were arts that aimed a sense of presentness: not just of the world's presence to us, but a sense of our presence to it (Cavell 1979, 22). During the course of Western modernity, despite (or perhaps due to) the rise of science and technology, consciousness becomes increasingly estranged from reality, interposing 'subjectivity between us and our presentness to the world' (Cavell 1979, 22). When subjectivity became what is most properly present to us, individuality became metaphysical isolation; hence the route taken to connect with the world is via *subjectivity*. This is the path of *romanticism*, whether in art/literature (Blake, Wordsworth) or in philosophy (Kant, Hegel, Heidegger, Wittgenstein); a movement that Cavell sums up as 'the natural struggle between representation and the acknowledgment of our subjectivity' (1979, 22).

Visual art, for Cavell, is precisely a response to scepticism, a human expression of selfhood against metaphysical isolation, and thus a way of restoring our connection with the world. Photography overcomes subjectivity in a manner unavailable to painting, namely through *automatism*: 'by removing the human agent from the task of reproduction' (Cavell 1979, 23). Photos depict a world that I can know and see but to which I am not present, and which I cannot control; and such a world is a 'world past', a past world (Cavell 1979, 23). The art of moving images inherits and projects this world: a *screened world* or 'world viewed' that is present to us but for which we *are not*. With this insight into the modern condition – the age of the 'world-image' (as Heidegger puts it) or 'the world viewed' (as Cavell does) – we have an answer to the question as to why movies matter philosophically.

Moving pictures, moreover, screen photographic images of the world: a world that is *screened*, supporting nothing but a projection of light, which Cavell takes in at least two senses. The silver screen both 'screens' me from that world (I am not present to it), and it 'screens' the world from me (removes its physical existence) (Cavell 1979, 24). As far as defining the medium is concerned, Cavell proposes that film is '*a succession of automatic world-projections*' (1979, 73): film captures movement (and time) in the world, within the image and between images composing a film ('succession'), and it does so 'automatically', without direct human intervention, thanks to its photographic character. Film captures the ontological reality of a 'world', even a fictional one, by presenting it to us, who remain absent to it, photographically. And it does so via a 'projection' on screen, projecting human figures in a world from which we remain forever absent, thus creating a phenomenological and aesthetic rupture, but also continuity, with experience (Cavell 1979, 73).

Cinematic Mythmaking and the 'End of the Myths'

As is well-known, Cavell has written two books on classical Hollywood of the 1930s and 1940s, the first on the genre of 'remarriage comedy' (1981) and the second on the 'melodrama of the unknown woman' (1996). His shorter pieces on film, video and television, moreover, have been collected in another volume edited by William Rothman and Marian Keane (2005). Already in *The World Viewed*, however, one finds reflections on the end and future of Hollywood that resonate with Deleuze's remarks on pre- and post-War cinema. Cavell too notes the shift in cinematic practice since the War, commenting on the 'end of the myths' and 'loss of conviction' that sustained classical Hollywood narrative and genres:

> I assume it is sufficiently obvious that these ways of giving significance to the possibilities of film – the media of movies exemplified by familiar Hollywood cycles and plots that justify the projection of types – are drawing to an end. And this means [...] that they no longer naturally establish conviction in our presentness to the world. (Cavell 1979, 60)

Like Deleuze, the crisis signalled by the exhaustion of genres and 'end of the myths' is also a crisis of belief: the loss of a sense of connection with the world. Deleuze describes this phenomenon as a 'loss of belief in the world'; Cavell as a loss of 'conviction in our presentness to the world'. They amount to the same cultural-cinematic diagnosis, which we can express as an acknowledgment of *nihilism* or *scepticism*. For both thinkers, however, this is not a cause for despair so much as an occasion for thought: to understand the source and significance of this crisis in narrative and genre and to explore the possibilities that contemporary cinema opens up in its attempts to question the (mutating) medium of film.

Narrative film since the 1960s and 1970s, according to Cavell, has moved away from the traditional Hollywood emphasis on genres and types (from the expression of generic types or culturally resonant individualities). Indeed, Cavell comments on the recycling of traditional narratives, the hyperbolic inflation of received techniques and the seeming 'interchangeability' of film actors, characters and plots (1979, 69–72). It is as though film had lost conviction in its own aesthetic and mythmaking power, had become estranged from its own history and thus from its future – Cavell's version of Deleuze's complaint against the ubiquity of cinematic and cultural *clichés*. Again, for both Deleuze and Cavell, the future of the art of film turns on *belief*: belief in the possibilities of the medium, in inheriting and renewing its own traditions, in having something meaningful to offer to a cultural milieu afflicted by a diffuse and inarticulate scepticism (Cavell 1979, 62).

Like Deleuze, Cavell also identifies a post-War break with the belief in individual and collective agency. Following the traumatic historical experience and moral disorientation brought about by WWII, the Cold War and Vietnam, many of the myths of cinema – as of history, politics and morality – have been shattered:

> These beliefs flowered last in our films about the imminence and the experience of the Second World War, then began withering in its aftermath – in the knowledge, and refusal of knowledge, that while we had rescued our European allies, we could not preserve them; that our enemies have prospered; that we are obsessed with the ally who prospered and prepared to enter any pact so long as it is against him; that the stain of atomic blood will not wash and that is fallout is nauseating us beyond medicine, aging us very rapidly. (Cavell 1979, 63)

Some of this historical loss of belief, however, is also due to a more positive shift in social mores and cultural sensibilities: we no longer believe, for example, in chauvinist depictions of women, which opposed beauty and intelligence, intimacy and demonstrativeness (1979, 63–64), nor in the demand for the bullish machismo of men who must be strong and silent, or else outspoken and heroic (Cavell 1979, 67). The possibilities of the body, again anticipating Deleuze, open up new expressions of selfhood that promise a reinvention of types – both male and female – via the cinematic 'myth of youth', the 'vanity of personal freedom', and the democratic athleticism of the body (Cavell 1979, 68). Despite these signs of renewal, the waning of film's conviction in its own aesthetic possibilities, in its capacity to deploy the 'automatisms' of the medium, signals its belated entry into the condition of *modernism*.

Here one might ask whether such signs of modernist cinematic self-reflection are really so recent. For film has always been 'modern', concerned to reflect on its own history ('movies come from other movies', as Cavell observes), and thus able to renew itself in relation to its own historical traditions. It has always been modern and pre-modern at once, synthesizing traditional narratives with reflections on the genre, the history of film, on the medium itself and on cultural mythologies. As Rancière puts it, cinema is an expression of the modern *aesthetic regime* of the arts, which combines an ethical concern with the social-cultural use of images, an emphasis on representational narrative and an egalitarian aesthetic of experimentation across all possible styles and subject-matters (Rancière 2004; 2006, 7–11). In short, contemporary cinema, in its troubled self-consciousness, cannot avoid asking the (philosophical) question, 'What is film?' Or better, 'What becomes of film in a sceptical age?' It must reinvent the possibilities of its evolving medium, now turned digital, and in doing so, will be 'asking exactly whether, and under what conditions, it can survive' (Cavell 1979, 72).

Both Cavell and Deleuze ground their respective paths of film-philosophy in the cultural-philosophical crises in meaning that go by the names of scepticism or nihilism. Both thinkers see cinema as responding to this shared problem, whether through the invention of new images and narrative forms or through film styles and genres in which scepticism is both enacted and defused. Both also point to the shift in film during the previous century, from a classical to a post-classical phase in which film 'exists in the condition of philosophy': a modernism in which film 'has lost its natural relation to its history'

(Cavell 1979, 72), and thus strives to invent new artistic uses of the medium. Where both thinkers differ is in their approach to the film-philosophy relationship: Deleuze's taxonomy of images draws on a plurality of film-examples to instantiate a conceptual framework articulating the shift from movement-image to time-image cinema. Cavell's philosophical readings of films undertake a form of criticism that aims to show or perform, rather than say or state, what the film-philosophy relationship means, in light of film's vocation to both project and work through scepticism. As film-philosophers par excellence, Cavell and Deleuze thus leave us with a tantalizing question: can films 'do philosophy' in a distinctively cinematic way?

'Bold' Film-Philosophy (Mulhall)

A number of contemporary philosophers have responded to this question by exploring the idea of film *as* philosophy: that film can contribute to philosophical understanding via cinematic means. Inspired by the work of Cavell, Stephen Mulhall's *On Film* (2002, 2008) offers one of the more contentious versions of this thesis. In his 'Introduction' (2002, 1–11), Mulhall outlines his reasons for selecting the *Alien* quadrilogy – *Alien* (Ridley Scott, 1979), *Aliens* (James Cameron, 1986), *Alien³* (David Fincher, 1992) and *Alien Resurrection* (Jean-Pierre Jeunet, 1997) – as a case study demonstrating the idea of 'film as philosophy'. Far from being trivial, for Mulhall, these films treat identity and embodiment with a 'sophistication and self-awareness' that suggests they are 'making real contributions' to our philosophical understanding (2002, 2). In an oft-quoted passage, Mulhall restates this claim as follows:

> I do not look to these films as handy or popular illustrations of views and arguments properly developed by philosophers; I see them rather as themselves reflecting on and evaluating such views and arguments, as thinking seriously and systematically about them in just the ways that philosophers do. Such films are not philosophy's raw material, nor a source for its ornamentation; they are philosophical exercises, philosophy in action – film as philosophizing. (2002, 2)

This passage has provoked a storm of debate, with both critics and defenders arguing over its meaning and implications. Many have taken it as defining Mulhall's 'position' as a film-philosopher, treating his remarks as representative of a general methodology for the study of cinema (see Baggini 2003; Smith 2006). Mulhall has since defended his approach, stressing that the real argument is to be found in his philosophical interpretations of the *Alien* films, a point mostly ignored by his critics (2008, 130–34).

Mulhall presents this passage following a discussion of the *Alien* films' philosophical interest in the problem of 'the relation of human identity and embodiment' (2002, 2). These films' thematic exploration of 'the bodily basis of human identity', in turn, raises the question concerning the conditions of cinema, for it is a medium dependent upon 'the projection of moving images of embodied human individuals presented to a camera' (Mulhall 2002, 3). These two issues, for Mulhall, suggest that a film like *Alien* explores questions about 'the nature of the cinematic medium' which one might otherwise expect to find in the philosophy of film (2002, 3–4).

This Cavellian insight leads Mulhall to specify three senses in which film can be said to 'philosophize' (2002, 3–6). The first is akin to the *philosophy of film*, where a film explores issues that theorists might consider (like 'the nature of the medium'). The second is *film as philosophizing*, where films explore recognized philosophical ideas, themes or problems (like human identity and embodiment). The third is *film in the condition of philosophy*, where films reflect upon their own conditions of possibility or the presuppositions of their own practice (the dialectic of 'originality and inheritance', for example, inherent to cinematic sequels). These are overlapping perspectives and the distinctions between them are not always sharp, but they provide an illuminating conception of the different ways in which we might define 'film as philosophy'.

There are some ambiguities, however, in Mulhall's account. He cites *Alien*'s concern with human embodiment and identity as suggesting that it engages in 'film as philosophizing' (2002, 2) but also as what relates it to the 'philosophy of film' (2002, 4). Reflection upon the nature of the cinematic medium, by contrast, is a sign that the *Alien* films emulate the 'philosophy of film' (2002, 3–4) but also that they are instances of 'cinematic modernism' (2002, 6), which he then identifies with 'film in the condition of philosophy' (2002, 6). Moreover, 'art in the condition of modernism' is identified with art that exists 'in the condition of philosophy' (Mulhall 2002, 6), which would exclude non-modernist cinematic works from philosophical status. Conversely, any work that exhibits elements of self-reflection – like episodes of *The Simpsons* or recent horror movie franchises – would count as modernist and so as philosophical. Film-philosophy, however, need not be tethered to modernist self-reflection, nor should self-reflection be assumed as the hallmark of a philosophically significant cinematic work.

'Moderate' Film-Philosophy (Wartenberg)

Thomas Wartenberg has addressed these criticisms and defended what he calls a 'moderate' version of film-philosophy (or cinematic philosophy). In *Thinking on Screen* (2007), Wartenberg questions whether there are good reasons to accept the Platonic 'philosophical disenfranchisement of film' that underpins most common criticisms of film-philosophy: 'a priori criticisms' that 'do not refer to actual films, but make general claims about what films cannot do' (2007, 16). As a consequence, critics have tended to posit 'a fundamental theoretical problem' at the heart of film-philosophy, rather than questioning their own assumptions about the relationship between philosophy and film (2007, 16).

Wartenberg summarizes these as the *explicitness*, *generality* and *imposition* objections (2007, 16–31). The first turns on the claim that film, as a visual rather than linguistic medium, 'lacks the explicitness to formulate and defend the precise claims that are characteristic of philosophical writing' (2007, 16). Films are either taken to be ambiguous, rhetorical and, hence, epistemically inferior to philosophy or they are taken as making implicit philosophical claims that critics must make explicit (Russell 2006, quoted in Wartenberg 2007, 19). The idea that only interpreters make arguments in relation to film, however, is misguided. As Wartenberg points out, although viewers or critics may make such arguments explicit, this does not mean that they (rather than the film) are the source or bearers of these arguments. Even if arguments are implicit in films, they do not necessarily have to be imprecise (as critics suggest); many philosophical arguments are ambiguous, so 'ambiguity' is not a sound criterion for distinguishing between the claims of film and those of philosophy (Wartenberg 2007, 19–20).

The generality objection challenges this idea: philosophy deals with issues characterized by 'abstractness and generality', whereas narrative film deals with the particularity of characters, situations and events (2007, 21). Wartenberg responds by pointing to non-fiction or documentary films, which can make important contributions to our understanding of historical events or social issues (2007, 22–24). What of fictional film? Here Wartenberg underlines the significance of narrative film as a way of screening complex 'thought experiments' involving hypothetical narrative situations that prompt us to reflect upon the plausibility and coherence of our beliefs, moral assumptions or philosophical commitments (2007, 24–25; Chapter 4).

The third and most common complaint about film-philosophy is the 'imposition of objection': that film theorists are often guilty of 'imposing' inappropriate or unintended theoretical meanings upon their chosen films. This can be reformulated, however, as a maxim to guide philosophical interpretation: avoid imposing inappropriate interpretations on a cinematic work and ensure that any interpretation attributed to it could have been intended by its author (Wartenberg 2007, 26). Wartenberg distinguishes, moreover, between *creator*-oriented and *audience*-oriented interpretations: reconstructing the meaning that an author of a work could have intended, versus that which audiences might find relevant to understanding or appreciating a work. Only the former, Wartenberg claims, 'can justify the claim that the film itself is philosophical', a point he takes up in his Aristotelian interpretation of Carol Reed's *The Third Man* (1948) as an exploration of the concept of friendship (2007, 26).

So how can films 'do philosophy'? There are two ways in which philosophers have sought to show this: a global or 'universalist' approach, which posits an intrinsic connection between film and philosophy (Cavell on film and scepticism) and a local, particularist or empirical approach, which 'investigates the question of film's relationship to philosophy by paying attention both to individual films and specific philosophical techniques' (Wartenberg 2007, 28). Along with other film-philosophers, Wartenberg champions the latter approach, examining what philosophical questions or issues a film raises, and how, in specific terms, films screen these philosophical issues (2007, 28).

Such an approach implicitly raises the meta-philosophical question concerning one's conception of philosophy. According to Wartenberg, three distinct conceptions are pertinent here: philosophy as a discipline addressing basic human concerns or 'eternal questions'; philosophy as a discipline that asks questions of other disciplines; and philosophy as a distinctive mode of discourse involving 'the argument, the counterexample, and the thought experiment' (2007, 30). There are, moreover, many ways in which films can 'screen' philosophy: they can illustrate philosophical ideas in innovative ways; they can make arguments concerning philosophical and moral issues; they can reflect upon the medium of cinema; and they can stage cinematic thought experiments that serve as philosophical counterexamples provoking reflection on our assumptions and beliefs. From this perspective, a 'moderate' film-philosophy can be defended against the standard objections and can show how films make creative contributions to our philosophical understanding using cinematic means.

Wartenberg thus rejects 'bold' versions of film-philosophy, which risk assuming a conception of philosophy that is either too encompassing (anything counts as philosophy) or too esoteric (assuming a 'controversial' definition of philosophy). Mulhall's claim that films can philosophize in 'just the ways philosophers do', for example, is criticized for failing to explain 'how a cultural form other than philosophy itself can make a substantial contribution to the specifically philosophical discussion of an issue such as that of human embodiment' (2007, 37). In a similar vein, radical film-philosophers are criticized for claiming that film's expressive capacities sometimes outstrip what can be readily articulated in standard philosophical discourse, which means we require a new kind of idiom – perhaps a new kind of thinking – in order articulate what film enables us to experience (see Frampton 2006; Sinnerbrink 2011).

Can a more bold or radical conception of the idea of 'film as philosophy' be defended? Arguments over the relationship between film and philosophy always assume a given conception of what counts as philosophy, and hence how cinema may (or may not) contribute to philosophical understanding. In short, this is both an aesthetic and a meta-philosophical debate: one that not only challenges us to think through the philosophical significance of cinema but to entertain the possibility that cinema may also enlarge our conception of philosophy. The idea of film as philosophy, I suggest, thus invites us to explore the novel ways in which our communication and understanding of philosophical experience might be transformed through our encounter with film. The question of what counts as a philosophical contribution, and the manner in which such thinking can be communicated, are precisely what film forces us to consider. This experience, both aesthetic and philosophical, is what brings film and philosophy together in a mutually illuminating encounter. This is especially so in cases where films enact a 'resistance to theory', which makes them challenging test cases to explore the hypothesis of *cinematic thinking* – a non-conceptual or affective thinking in images that resist cognitive closure or theoretical subsumption (Sinnerbrink 2011, 139; see also Vaughan 2013).

It is still important, of course, to explain how films can philosophize, and to clarify the ways in which films *do not* always philosophize 'in just the ways philosophers do': how they express thought in non-philosophical ways (by aesthetic means, through affect, sensation or emotion; via cinematic style, using visual ideas or aesthetic abstractions; and through narrative form, deploying all the devices of the narrative arts). Indeed, it might be better to speak of films 'thinking' or expressing thought in ways that embrace *both* philosophical and non-philosophical means of expression. This openness to the 'non-philosophical' manner of cinematic thinking might make us more attuned to transforming our horizons of meaning, questioning what was hitherto familiar, and opening up new paths for thinking – all of which are part of the creative practice of film-philosophy, or of what it might become.

To end with a speculative remark, the recent surge of interest in cinephilia, I suggest, might be understood as a cultural-cinematic renovation of the ancient (but also romantic, existentialist and perfectionist) idea of 'philosophy as a way of life' (Hadot 2005). This is not to subsume film into a 'traditional' conception of philosophy but to learn from the encounter with cinema that philosophy can be experienced and expressed differently. From this perspective, film-philosophy has the potential to become a richly experiential mode of shaping our existence both ethically and aesthetically through the thoughtful engagement with film. It can become a form of cultural practice defined by a love of cinema (and of philosophy), but also by a commitment to the idea that cinema can reveal the world anew, disclosing the everyday in new ways, bringing it to our attention under different aspects, or wiping away, as Bazin once wrote, 'that spiritual dust and grime with which my eyes have covered it' (1967, 15). Cinema opens up an aesthetically intensified experience of reality, expressing a love or care for existence – for nature and spirit – that includes whatever exceeds our habitual ways of knowing. It brings film and philosophy together as complementary ways of understanding and transforming ourselves thanks to the virtual worlds that cinema reveals. The film-philosophy relationship, in short, is a cross-medial dialogue or 'thinking encounter', at once creative and conceptual, in which the relations between thought and image are explored in a manner that can transform our ways of thinking.

Notes

1 See Allen and Smith (1997), Carel and Tuck (2011), Colman (2009), Freeland and Wartenberg (1995), Livingston and Plantinga (2009), Read and Goodenough (2005) and Wartenberg (2011). I have drawn on material in Sinnerbrink (2011) for this entry, which has been revised and reworked for publication here.

2 Compare the different approaches in the volumes edited by Livingston and Plantinga (2009), Read and Goodenough (2005) and Carell and Tuck (2011). See Sinnerbrink (2014) for a discussion of film-philosophy.

Bibliography

Allen, Richard, and Murray Smith. 1997. *Film Theory and Philosophy*. Oxford: Oxford University Press.

Baggini, Julian. 2003. 'Alien Ways of Thinking: Mulhall's *On Film*'. *Film-Philosophy* 7, no. 24 (August). http://www.film-philosophy.com/vol-2003/n24baggini (accessed 1 May 2008).

Bazin, André. 1967. *What Is Cinema? Volume I*. Translated by Hugh Gray. Berkeley: University of California Press.

Bordwell, David, and Noël Carroll. 1996. *Post-Theory: Reconstructing Film Studies*. Madison: University of Wisconsin Press.

Carel, Havi, and Greg Tuck, eds. 2011. *New Takes in Film-Philosophy*. London: Palgrave Macmillan.

Cavell, Stanley. 1979. *The World Viewed: Reflections on the Ontology of Film*. Enlarged Edition. Cambridge, MA: Harvard University Press.

———. 1981. *Pursuits of Happiness: The Hollywood Comedy of Remarriage*. Cambridge, MA: Harvard University Press.

———. 1996. *Contesting Tears: The Melodrama of the Unknown Woman*. Chicago: University of Chicago Press.

———. 2005. *Cavell on Film*, edited by William Rothman and Marian Keane. Albany: State University of New York Press.

Colman, Felicity, ed. 2009. *Film, Theory and Philosophy*. Durham: Acumen Press.

Deleuze, Gilles. 1986 (1983). *Cinema 1: The Movement-Image*. Translated by Hugh Tomlinson and Barbara Habberjam. Minneapolis: University of Minnesota Press.

———. 1989 (1985). *Cinema 2: The Time-Image*. Translated by Hugh Tomlinson and Robert Galatea. Minneapolis: University of Minnesota Press.

Frampton, Daniel. 2006. *Filmosophy*. London: Wallflower Press.

Freeland, Cynthia A., and Thomas E. Wartenberg, eds. 1995. *Philosophy and Film*. London: Routledge.

Hadot, Pierre. 2005. 'There Are Nowadays Professors of Philosophy but no Philosophers', translated by J. Aaron Simmons, *Journal of Speculative Realism* 19, no. 3: 229–37.

Livingston, Paisley, and Carl Plantinga. 2009. *The Routledge Companion to Philosophy and Film*. London: Routledge.

Mulhall, Stephen. 2002. *On Film*. New York: Routledge.

Panofsky, Erwin. 1997 (1934). 'Style and Medium in the Motion Pictures'. In *Film and/as Literature*, edited by J. Harrington, 283–94. New York: Prentice Press.

———. 2008. *On Film*, 2nd ed. New York: Routledge.

Rancière, Jacques. 2004. *The Politics of Aesthetics*. Translated by Gabriel Rockhill. London: Continuum.

———. 2006. *Film Fables*. Translated by Emiliano Battista. Oxford: Berg Books.

Read, Rupert, and Jerry Goodenough, eds. 2005. *Film as Philosophy: Essays on Cinema after Wittgenstein and Cavell*. Basingstoke: Palgrave Macmillan.

Rodowick, D. N. 1997. *Gilles Deleuze's Time Machine*. Durham: Duke University Press.

Russell, Bruce. 2006. 'The Philosophical Limits of Film'. In *Philosophy of Film and Motion Pictures: An Anthology*, edited by Noël Carroll and Jinhee Choi, 387–90. Malden MA: Blackwell.

Scruton, Roger. 1981. 'Photography and Representation'. *Critical Inquiry* 7, no. 3 (Spring): 577–601.

Sinnerbrink, Robert. 2011. *New Philosophies of Film: Thinking Images*. London: Continuum.

———. 2014. 'Film-Philosophy'. In *The Routledge Encyclopedia of Film Theory*, edited by Warren Buckland and Edward Branigan, 207–13. Abingdon: Routledge.

Smith, Murray. 2006. 'Film, Art, and Ambiguity'. In *Thinking through Cinema: Film as Philosophy*, edited by Murray Smith and Thomas E. Wartenberg, 33–42. Malden, MA: Blackwell.

Vaughan, Hunter. 2013. *Where Film Meets Philosophy: Godard, Resnais, and Experiments in Cinematic Thinking*. New York: Columbia University Press.

Walton, Kendall L. 1984. 'Transparent Pictures: On the Nature of Photographic Realism'. *Critical Inquiry* 11, no. 2 (December): 246–77.

Wartenberg, Thomas E. 2007. *Thinking on Screen: Film as Philosophy*. London: Routledge.

———. 2011. 'Philosophy of Film'. *Stanford Encyclopedia of Philosophy*. http://plato.stanford.edu/entries/film/.

Chapter Eighteen

SCREEN PERCEPTION AND EVENT: BEYOND THE FORMALIST/ REALIST DIVIDE

Nadine Boljkovac*

Here, too, Bazin can come to the rescue, since his belief that the cinema has yet to be invented must mean today that the cinema – neither as reality's copy nor its illusory opposite, but its ever-present potential *– always already 'knew' what it knew, as well as what it could not have 'known'.*

—Elsaesser (2010, 11; emphasis mine)

There will always be gaps, fissures, eruptions of the anarchy.

—Rombes (2014)

Tell me, why are you filming me like that?

Because I want to show that there is no distance in the world.

—Natalia and Chantal Akerman (2015), *No Home Movie*, dir. C. Akerman

At six minutes, five seconds into Chantal Akerman's *No Home Movie* (2015), the film cuts from a handheld high-angle shot of a backyard to a close-up shot from behind Natalia Akerman, the filmmaker's mother. Natalia pushes a door screen left and enters the living space. A camera – Chantal – follows Natalia before stopping at the doorway. While the camera records this modest entry into an apartment's open space, the relation between subject/*mother* and camera/*daughter* reveals both the comfort of a family home and a hesitant urgency to fully witness, capture and hold dear. The camera's sway in Akerman's hands suggests at once the immediacy of home movie footage, and the ephemerality of an always already lost present. Such felt proximity to transient subject, space and time in these early moments of Akerman's final film, with its Akermanesque rhythm of extended long take and sudden break, enacts a flow between intimate 'real life' duration and the insistent minimalism of an artist devoted throughout her career to an ethics of a 'very frontal gaze', as Adrian Martin and Cristina Álvarez López suggest, among others. The seeming formalist/realist juxtaposition of *No Home Movie*'s opening sequence, in fact, offers a subtle microcosmic mapping of a fundamental dichotomy in classic film theory, a distinction and opposition that corresponds, as Dudley Andrew writes, 'to the cliché that all cinema has roots in either Méliès or Lumière'(1976, vi), in either formal experimentation that foregrounds the medium's distinctiveness (*formalism*) or an 'objective' documentation that reveals an indexical link with the real (*realism*).

As Thomas Elsaesser and Malte Hagener note, 'by far the most common way of building a classification system of theoretical approaches to the cinema has been to take the influential distinction between formalist and realist film theories as a starting point' (2010, 3). This common distinction opens to questions of digital cinema and intermediality, what Martin describes as an 'intermedial phenomena' with 'traces of so many diverse media (film, theatre, radio, installation, fiction, documentary) [that] are set in relation to each other like so many levels, panels, screens or computer windows, not fused but held distinct and resonating precisely via their intervals' (Martin 2011). These pervasive shifts towards postproduction and 'post-cinema' in a post-photographic age give way to contemplations of multi-sensorial potentials and the cinema itself as a 'state' of *becoming* and an *event* of perception. Via simultaneous yet bifurcating movements between former and contemporary directions in screen theory, this essay will repeat that realist and formalist positions both diverge and interconnect, as Akerman's cinema evinces. The realist/formalist split, useful for categorizations and film theory classes, is a divide too readily maintained, and a task of the following will be to outline specific contributions of each position to then turn towards productive future intersections.

To counter any loss or fetishization of the indexical or, conversely, overt celebrations of the digital,[1] the following embraces certain cinematic concepts as advocated for instance by Elsaesser and Hagener's alternative question: '*What is the relationship between the cinema, perception, and the human body?*' (2010, 4). Such an approach acknowledges affects and effects, sensations and variations deriving from lights and sounds, interstices and cuts, rhythms and textures of the filmic image – those 'small, seismic disturbances' Álvarez López and Martin sense (2011), and the 'rifts and folds' Tom Conley discerns (Conley 2011, 33) – that prompt and inform our perceptions of our durations, subjectivities and the world. Conley addresses the heart of the matter: 'A point of departure is found in the writings of André Bazin in which philosophy and criticism inform questions concerning the nature of filmic space. The question, "What is cinema?" has as its corollary "What is the *event* that we call cinema?" ' (Conley 2007, 207). Accordingly, the following will also consider insights pertaining to nothing less than the 'very existence of the world [as] an event of perception' (Conley 2007, 20) that 'cuts through the perceiving subject' (Conley 2011, 39). As a 'pure conscience' unto itself (Conley 2005, 13), the event that we call cinema indeed bespeaks a simultaneous process of perceiving and being perceived, or *auto-perception* (Boljkovac 2013, 133).

As an art of neither pure artifice nor definitive representation, the cinema often pursues means of expressing the ineffable. With reference to what he terms 'oxymoronic' theories regarding the medium's own demise or rebirth, Elsaesser discerns an opposition between an 'anxiety about the loss of distance and alterity', what he describes as ' "negative" definitions of the new audiovisuality', and the 'positive connotations associated with the label "New Hollywood," "Post-classical," or "Post-Film Cinema," where the cinematic experience is typified quite differently, with metaphors centred on space, on embodiment, on sensation rather than visual perception' (Elsaesser 1998, 8). In any event, Elsaesser concludes that 'the movies emerge above all as an event' that is 'experienced as a second skin or total perceptual surface by which to dress rather than be addressed as subject' (1998, 9).Through ever-emergent sub-genres and technologies, twenty-first century cinema and proliferating practices in multi- and digital media encompass both experimentation and testimony, formalist and realist practice, seemingly divergent yet allied strategies imbued with inherent potential for sociopolitical effect. As these new filmic and multimedia works trace lived experiences their explorations are permeated at once by relations of visibility and invisibility, actuality and virtuality, exteriority and interiority, history and memory, associations which forever fragment binary divisions.

Inasmuch as filmic practice increasingly obscures realist and formalist categorizations, borders likewise become indistinct necessitating a 'new rationality' of the 'obvious and obscure' of which Jacques Rancière writes. Such might contemplate the 'history of material life', of 'lowly actions and commonplace objects', that stands 'in opposition to the histories of great names and events' (Rancière 2004, 37). As it addresses thoughts of André Bazin (1918–1958) and Sergei Eisenstein (1898–1948) in relation to other thinkers whose thoughts do not simply fit into a binary, this discussion of filmic realism and formalism in theory and practice strives for movement and thought beyond considerations of adequate or inadequate resemblance, or the primacy of 'reality' and original source over art and secondary reproduction. Which is to say, the cinema as an experiential and sensory persistence that often does not mimic or represent but directly affects and affronts will be assessed and contextualized within our contemporary moment.

***

> Between the originating object and its reproduction there intervenes only the instrumentality of a nonliving agent.
>
> —Bazin (2005, 13)

> The real was no longer represented or reproduced but 'aimed at'. [...] fragmentary, ephemeral, piecemeal, missed encounters.
>
> —Deleuze (1989, 1)

Designations of formalism and realism convey an uneasy divide that exists at the crux of classic film theory in that the cinema cannot preclude both tendencies. Likewise, most feature-length films cannot but include both movement- and time-images although, as will be discussed, the time-image's post-war emergence realized a shift from pre-war action montage to a wandering image caught by a headless, inhuman camera in the act of perceiving itself in time and space. Formalism maintains that the cinema must be juxtapositional and that its language must create and manipulate, refashion and transform reality through montage. Realism, on the other hand, is believed to apprehend an organic, seamless photographic link to the physical world that the cinema ought to record in all its ambiguity. Most broadly stated, formalists propose that the cinema achieves artistic status when humans intelligently shape and transform its raw material, as expressed via Eisenstein's belief that montage is the 'essential, meaningful and sole possible language of cinema' (Eisenstein 1998, 41), while Bazin's writings stress the ontological basis of the medium that exists without and beyond the human. As Elsaesser and Hagener once more observe, 'whereas formalist theories look at film in terms of construction and composition, realist theories emphasize film's ability to offer a hitherto unattainable view onto (non-mediated) reality. In other words, "formalists" focus on cinema's artificiality, whereas "realists" call attention to the (semi-)transparency of the filmic medium, which ostensibly turns us into direct witnesses' (2010, 3). This essay will assess this seeming realist/formalist binary by, again, thinking beyond subjective or objective accounts of the cinema given to examinations of interior experience or to any objective world respectively. Rather, alongside thoughts articulated by Hunter Vaughan and others, this essay considers a cinematic approach 'based not on the camera as a perceptive vehicle but on the flow of cinematic meaning as a dialogic openness between different subjective positions, an immanent field where the content of the image and the human manipulation behind its production meet […]: the image is neither objective nor subjective but a process of transformation that structures itself according to subjective or objective systems of reference' (Vaughan 2013, 38). The 'image's collusion between these two' positions, to repeat Vaughan's insight (38), most particularly concerns these pages.

In an interview, Nicholas Rombes reflects upon the formalist/realist opposition, 'a binary that privileges so-called artifice ("art") over so-called naive representations of reality', as he discusses Eisenstein's essay, 'Dickens, Griffith, and the Film Today' (Gallix 2014). Rombes suggests a correspondence in the Soviet formalist filmmaker's thought between 'Dickens-era realism' and montage; between the '"story" (events, content) and "discourse" (expression)'; 'between the ever-present affective experience of watching a film […] and the internal world of narrative time' (Gallix 2014). Whether films reveal, obscure or construct reality, or necessarily perform all, their associations of content and form conjoin with what Rombes terms a 'messy correlation between the informational mode of a film still and [its] affective mode' (Gallix 2014). However, before discovering such complementarities between heightened realist and formalist compositions in this essay, it will be helpful to ever briefly summarize the positions.

Bazin argues that 'photography and the cinema […] are discoveries that satisfy, once and for all and in its very essence, our obsession with realism' in that their 'production by automatic means' renders photography and the cinema qualities of credibility and objectivity (2005, 12–13). Without human intervention, the cinema, Bazin maintains, presents a 'natural' world image 'in all its virginal purity' through an 'impassive lens' (15). As Elsaesser states, 'Bazin is useful today because he can bridge the often fatal divide between photographic and post-photographic cinema simply by the fact that he did not know it existed' (2011, 4). Contra to readings of Bazin's writings that focus primarily upon mimesis and indexicality, a term, Elsaesser reminds us, that was never used by Bazin, Bazin's thoughts anticipate modern materialist readings of the moving image, despite accusations of the very opposite.

In a sensitive and thorough review of Bazin's contributions, Vaughan traces Bazin's concept of ontology through Louis Delluc and Jean Epstein's 'common debt to Marcel l'Herbier' with respect to the cinema's propensity to produce an 'imprint of life', a 'phenomenal truth' and reality transmitted, again, without human intermediary (Vaughan 2009, 103). This 'inhuman portrait of the world', as Andrew stresses, 'makes of cinema and photography not the media of man [*sic*] but the media of nature' (1976, 138). A photograph's origin stems from direct contact with the objects it reveals; for Bazin, this presence of the referent and essence of the real, this record that exposes, embalms and transcends a raw material's brute reality, is not an aesthetic style but a function and commitment to a 'natural' continuity of time and space in cinema, a preservation of life achieved via the reproduction of life. This then is not a *representation* as Conley further illuminates:

> The long shot, the plan-séquence (or long take) and deep-focus photography make the very existence of the world *an event of perception*. For Bazin the cinematic image is endowed with simultaneously visible, tactile, and material qualities. It is in dialogue with the players and objects that move within it, and for that reason an image – at least an image worthy of its name – is not a representation but the world itself. (2007, 20, emphasis mine)

Famously, Bazin distinguishes between 'directors who put their faith in the image and those who put their faith in reality' (2005, 24). The latter, according to Bazin, demands an active spectatorship prompted by revelations of reality's inherent ambiguity as exposed, again, via a particular perspective to its filming. 'Writing in the 1940s and 1950s', as Vaughan states, 'Bazin condemns the very style of manipulating reality that is central to Eisenstein's model' (2013, 49); indeed, Bazin sought means for salvaging humanity via a true faith and a return to 'the real'. Through post-war Italian neorealist cinema, Deleuze discovers further depths to Bazin's humanist thought as he writes of revelatory time-images that 'put thought into contact with an unthought, the unsummonable, the inexplicable, the undecidable, the incommensurable' (Deleuze 1989, 214). Horrors of the war and its lingering affects and effects found onscreen expression through filmic projections of corporeal and incorporeal realities. Writing from within the immediate post-war period, Bazin, and years later, Deleuze, observed a 'new type of character for a new cinema' (Deleuze 1989, 19), a visionary mutant overcome by forces too powerful, unjust or beautiful, in any case 'too great for us, like too strong a pain', 'a limit-situation [...] but also the most banal, a plain factory, a wasteland' (18). This encountering of the intolerable and unbearable in 'its excess of horror or beauty' (20) fragments the self and its psychology, beliefs and memory, and from this new cinema of the post-war emerges both Bazin's writing and Deleuze's concept of the time-image.

This breaking down precipitated by the war during which, again, Bazin wrote and through which Deleuze locates a 'cinema of the seer' with characters who become viewers themselves as their situations outstrip their motor capacities, results in the visionary sleepwalkers both Bazin and Deleuze identify, who lose themselves to the violence and intensity they witness, but who have 'learnt to see' because they have been 'struck to the core by the simple unfolding of images [...] [and] something unbearable' (Deleuze 1989, 2–3). A non-human film-eye haunts the buildings and streets of shattered cities whose survivors, premonitory ghostly figures, endure at the 'pace of a dream or a nightmare' (3), ever in trepidation of the future unknown. As Andrew discerns, both Bazin and Deleuze 'track the crucial shift' from classic to modern cinema by their regard for the cinema as an evolutionary becoming whose 'power lies in the extremes of life and death' (Andrew 1997, 88–89).

The putting of 'faith in the image', however, corresponds with Eisenstein's belief in the cinema as a means for montage to forcefully influence and stimulate an audience perceptually, emotionally and intellectually. Significantly, as Vaughan notes,

> Eisenstein's theories are ideologically attributable to a particular moment in history – the birth of Soviet communism and the promise of industrial utopia embraced by formalist artistic movements of the interwar period – that, in the wake of World War II, generated much skepticism as a result of how such rhetoric played out in the arena of global destruction and genocide. Illustrating a historical, intellectual shift toward rejecting the technocracy of fascism, film theorists after the war abandoned a certain idealism of what film expression could do to surpass the meaning inherent in nature and moved toward an argument that cinema was essentially meant to offer a nonbiased depiction of reality. (Vaughan 2013, 49)

Eisenstein strove for a unity of practice and theory through his films and passionately written works as he sought means to most directly affect spectators, hence the significance of his 'montage of attractions'. As in Eisenstein's 1925 films *Strike* and *Battleship Potemkin*, editing creates a dynamic didacticism for propagandist, agitational and aesthetic effects: 'there is, or rather should be, no cinema other than agit-cinema' (Eisenstein 1998, 41). The dialectical materialism as proposed by Eisenstein combines stylization with naturalism to destroy and reconstruct reality as a filmic system capable of generating powerful effects upon spectators.

Alternatively, Bazin expresses his commitment to a democratization of viewer perception via a nuanced approach that in fact supports both realism and artifice in representation so long as such artifice supports realism's illusion of transparency. As noted, while Eisenstein eschews the notion of perfectly recorded reality in his pursuit of maximum shock, tension and conflict within and between shots, Bazin affirms the cinema's ability to preserve time and space in their pure states through long takes, depth of field, certain uses of montage and whatever other 'techniques' that represent reality without further contrivance, dissection and meaning.

Eisenstein's *techne*, the devices he exploits through each shot's own compositional possibilities as a singular montage cell within a violently juxtapositional superimposition of several cells and associations, expresses the revolutionary spirit of 1920s and 1930s Russian formalism, Marxism, the Moscow Linguistic Circle and figures including Siegfried Kracauer, Walter Benjamin, Victor Shklovsky and Bertolt Brecht. Shklovsky's concept of *ostrenai*, a strategy of defamiliarization or *making strange* first foregrounded in his 1917 essay 'Art as Technique', seeks to impart the 'sensation of things as they are perceived and not as they are known' (Shklovsky 1965, 12). The consequences of such thought permeate Eisenstein's own prolific art and writing. And yet, despite differences in method and enunciation, might we in fact even locate the life-forces and heartbeats of both Bazin and Eisenstein's thoughts in the very exploration of filmic sensation and perception?[2]

***

> It remains for me to point out that Chris Marker does not restrict himself to using documentary images filmed on the spot, but uses any and all filmic material that might help [...].

> There is only one common denominator in this firework display of technique: intelligence. Intelligence and talent.
>
> —Bazin (2003, 45)

> These books will not […] claim to offer an exhaustive geography and geology of cinema, but merely to draw the reader into a succession of soundings, explorations, and overviews practiced when films are put forward for the critic's daily reflection.
>
> —Bazin (2005), as quoted by Conley (2007, 6)

> Is materiality a matter of the reality registered within the film frame, or the reality of the frame […] itself?
>
> —Martin (2011)

This essay cannot claim to offer a thorough summary of formalist and realist theories.[3] It does aim to touch upon certain filmic theories that provocatively and at times poetically and passionately assess evocations of human activity, experiences and perceptions of this world and its temporality in the aftermath, and persistence, of our great feats of self-abolition. Here Bazin's thought resonates as deeply with the cinematic past as it does with a future that will witness Bazin's particularly favoured strategies, such as deep focus, diminish with digital imaging while other technological means and aesthetic results emerge. In 2011, Adrian Martin writes that 'it is precisely *materiality* – the ways in which we define it, and deploy it, in relation to cinema – which is at stake, and in flux, today'. Martin turns again towards Bazin, and to '[Nicole] Brenez's challenge to produce a "Bazinian exigency maintained at the heart of a type of non-Bazinian analysis"' (Martin 2011). In our time, if questions occasioned by a 'materiality-effect' supersede thoughts of the 'reality-effect', does this, again, demand a conjoined formalist-realism so that we might, as Laura Mulvey muses, 'continually rediscover the beauty, that Bazin compared to the flower or snowflake, of the indexical sign' (Mulvey 2009, 193, quoted in Martin 2011)?

Of such beauty and formalism in the real itself, whether in moments of extreme simplicity, banality or violence, it is useful to consider Pier Paolo Pasolini's claim that '*reality is, in the final analysis, nothing more than cinema in nature*' (Pasolini 1972, 198). By this, and a critique of Saussurean semiotics arising from Pasolini's belief in the possibility of *directly* revealing or expressing the real, Pasolini proposes life itself as *cinema*, and a specific work as a *film* within an infinite network of films. To this extent,

> Cinema expresses reality with reality. […] In any moment reality is 'cinema in its natural state'; it only lacks a camera to reproduce it, that is, to write it through the reproduction of what it is. Cinema is therefore virtually an endless 'sequence shot', endless as the reality which can be reproduced by an invisible camera. (Pasolini 1972, 133)

If then, cinema reproduces reality with reality itself, directly and without translation or intercession as via other media, cinema reproduces reality as a 'natural semiology',

Pasolini argues (228). Bazinian associations with Pasolini's thought seem striking in that both arguments stress a realism that is at once inevitably formalist. Pasolini nor Bazin reject editing *outright* despite conventional recapitulations of the formalism/realism debate whereby, again, the former corresponds to stylistic strategies of the medium while the latter advocates for a direct and untampered recording of reality as it unfolds. Interestingly, with respect to filmmaker/multimedia artist Chris Marker's (1957) *Lettre de Sibèrie*, Bazin observes:

> Chris Marker brings to his films an absolutely new notion of montage that I will call 'horizontal', as opposed to traditional montage that plays with the sense of duration through the relationship of shot to shot. Here, a given image doesn't refer to the one that preceded it or the one that will follow, but rather it refers laterally, in some way, to what is said. Better, it might be said that the basic element is the beauty of what is said and heard, that intelligence flows from the audio element to the visual. The montage has been forged from ear to eye. (2003, 44)

Bazin proceeds to uncharacteristically claim that 'this time we are way beyond cleverness and irony, because what Marker has just demonstrated is that objectivity is even more false than the two opposed partisan points of view; that, at least in relation to certain realities, impartiality is an illusion. The operation we have observed is thus precisely dialectic' (Bazin 2003, 44).

Bazin's comments regarding objectivity and impartiality by way of Marker's work reaffirm Bazin's openness to certain formalist strategies of directly depicting or rendering reality through, as Pasolini also maintains, the use of any means necessary to convey that real. With regard once more to his distinction between cinema and film, Pasolini suggests that cinema, or reality itself, becomes audiovisual technique and nothing other than '*human action in reality*' (1972, 198) that can and does give rise to both propagandist and emancipatory techniques of ideology. A *film*, however, necessarily edits and reconfigures that slice of life, and for Pasolini as much as for Eisenstein, a film's editing can offer an explicit sociopolitical critique that violently provokes and agitates its spectator. 'We are lay humanists or, at least, nonmisologist Platonists [i.e. those in favour of critical thought and debate], and we must, therefore, fight to demystify the "innocence of technique" to the last drop of blood' writes Pasolini, with a fervour that can only be qualified as Eisensteinian. At the same time, 'realist' proponents diverge from formalist filmmakers and theoreticians by their perspectives pertaining to editing for poetic or didactic ends respectively.

Discrepancies between Pasolini and Bazin's thoughts manifest, however, in relation to the natural realism Bazin so admires through the cinema's photographic essence, that very flower or snowflake, as Mulvey reminds above, which Bazin captures, 'Photography affects us like a phenomenon in nature, like a flower or a snowflake whose vegetable or earthly origins are an inseparable part of their beauty' (Bazin 2005, 13). Pasolini alternatively challenges such adoration:

> I avoid the sequence shot: because it is naturalistic and therefore […] natural. My fetishistic love of the world makes it impossible for me to consider them natural. Either it consecrates them or it desecrates them violently, one by one; it does not bind them in a correct flow, it does

> not accept this flow. But it isolates them and adores them, more or less intensely, one by one. In my cinema, therefore, the sequence shot is completely substituted by editing. (1972, 227)

Via means reminiscent of Akerman, Pasolini's frontal framings and stylized long takes do not aim, then, for the natural flow of Italian neorealist cinema. Although revelatory of worlds equally beset with anguish and despair, the filmic strategies of Pasolini's (1962) *Mamma Roma* and Vittorio De Sica's (1952) *Umberto D*, for instance, produce radically differing temporal and spatial images. Pasolini's impassioned and complex commitment to realism – as Deleuze might suggest, 'around', 'behind', 'even inside the image', and beyond (Deleuze 1989, 125) – demands, seemingly paradoxically, a non-naturalist approach to time and montage, much akin to formalist theorizations.

While appreciating moments wherein the seventh art speaks for itself, Bazin, in fact, also values fragmentation and breakage in the service of naturalistic depiction, as between one shot and another through effective montage, and as indicated by above thoughts on Marker's cinema, as well as in the exposure of broken characters and terrains themselves. As noted in relation to neorealist cinema, here all lost wanderers, survivors and charred remnants become seers themselves of a post-apocalyptic world.

***

> In *Umberto D* one catches a glimpse [...] of what a truly realist cinema of time could be, a cinema of 'duration'. [...] I have no hesitation in stating that the cinema has rarely gone such a long way toward making us aware of what it is to be a [hu]man. (And also, for that matter, of what it is to be a dog.)
>
> —Bazin (2005, 76)

> Neo-realism therefore invented a new type of image [a formal or material 'additional reality'], which Bazin suggested calling 'fact-image'. [...] However, we are not sure that the problem arises at the level of the real, whether in relation to form or content. Is it not rather at the level of the 'mental', in terms of thought?
>
> —Deleuze (1989, 1)

> When our apprehension of space comes forward through the immutable duration of the landscape, we realize what Bazin implies wherever he writes of the 'event' of cinema.
>
> —Conley (2011, 38)

These pages have reviewed formalist and realist contentions to affirm their inseparability. In its final moments, this essay more fully considers singular images that expose duration (Henri Bergson's *durée*) through landscapes and geological layers that effect a film's *living* form. In his introduction to *Cartographic Cinema*, following Bazin and Deleuze, Conley as perceptive cartographer attests to a film's 'fluid and shifting spaces' and their potentially affective force.

> At the outset of his work on cinema, Gilles Deleuze asserted that the 'great authors' of cinema could be compared to painters, architects, and philosophers. Often destroyed, silenced, or left to decay, their lives and creations bear witness to the force and fragility that mark the great works of art and thought in general. Notwithstanding the global production and circulation of cinematic rubbish, these authors have invented 'irreplaceable

> autonomous forms' (1983, 7–8) that, we can add, mark the lives of all of us who live with them. (Conley 2007, 21)

As writes Elsaesser with regard to questions of cinema and media convergences and ever multiplying emergent terms relating to our 'new audiovisuality', 'one of the more accessible metaphors' acknowledges that 'the movies emerge above all as an event' (1998, 8). In lieu of a 'theoretical fix' betwixt, so to speak, celluloid and digitization or realism and formalism, what if, to repeat Elsaesser's thought, 'the status of authenticity and proof of a photograph or moving image had never resided in its indexical relation to the real at all'? (14). Elsaesser suggests rather a *trust* for both spectators and theorists whose task is to 'think both sound and image's pseudo-indexicality within the cultural crisis of record, imprint, evidence and the institutional crisis of accountability and public trust' (14). Prior to our 'digital age', Deleuze already proposed that the cinematic medium could be assessed more inclusively, and thus, rather than posit a divide between the screen itself and spectator, or reality and artifice, an 'either this or that', as in 'to go out or stay in' (Deleuze 1997, 153), 'disjunction [...] become[s] inclusive; everything divides, but into itself' (Deleuze 1997, 153), 'this and then that' (Deleuze 1989, 180). As Deleuze explains with regard to cinema of the time-image, this is 'the method of BETWEEN, "between two images"' (Deleuze 1989, 180), that corresponds to a crisis indeed in life and for possibilities of its onscreen evocation. When life faces its greatest dangers, those to which Deleuze and Guattari so often refer – threats of cruelty, stupidity, war – filmic images respond with always-new revelations of time and space.

As we are painfully reminded in an age of fear and xenophobia greater than ever possibly anticipated, the heart of the matter is not one of authenticity or proof of *fixed identity* but rather one of incessant self-realization and perception, a gift that the cinematic medium has always had the potential to impart by exposing ourselves to ourselves. For both the future of the medium and ourselves, this seems the only route of survival. With regard to the very event of cinema itself that folds us within its folds, we might speak of a coupling or doubling process. Inasmuch as a film replays or redoubles the actual events of our lives, as well as their underlying intensities and affective significances, our increasing perception of any 'greater picture' or life itself becomes externalized. At the same time, such perception is also at once enfolded and internalized into a larger collective fold of universal memory and future (see also Boljkovac 2013, 101).

Conley observes that 'an event is what causes us to perceive the conditions and actions of perception in what we are seeing and perceiving (and often, we discover, what sees and perceives *us*)' (2007, 207; emphasis mine). Moreover, Conley reminds us that '[a]n event is not what takes place or is framed by a cause, an effect, or what would have the appearance of a datum [...]. It is rather what is endowed with duration' (2000, 312). The screen and spectator become both perceiver and perceived at once. Such a processual act of *auto-perception* (Boljkovac 2013, 133), of perceiving and being perceived, unfolds in relation to experiences of 'auto-affection', of affecting and being affected, and expresses haptic and sensual qualities of a movie and its articulations of space, time and, as Elsaesser urgently reminds us, sound (Elsaesser 1998). Yet what of this in relation to contemplations of formalism and realism?

Once more, we might propose paradox upon paradox: both perceiver/perceived and realist/formalist. The more 'you' are one, the more 'you' are the other; the more realist, the more formalist 'you' are. As Pasolini's art and writing reiterates, alongside Bazin and several others, one cannot be realist without being formalist. In an essay that thoughtfully and thoroughly questions whether 'materiality [is] a matter of the reality registered within the film frame, or the reality of the frame' as it richly traces and contextualizes the concept of a *dispositif* vis-à-vis an *apparatus*,[4] Martin stresses, among others, the 'dual-edged nature' of Bazin's thought:

> In truth his position (as clearly stated in his unfinished book on Jean Renoir) was that 'realism does not at all mean a renunciation of style' – going on to stake his ethical-aesthetic preference that 'cinematic expression must be dialectically fused with reality and not with artifice' (Bazin 1986: 106). Yet this opens the possibility of precisely the opposing option: that cinematic expression can also be dialectically fused with artifice. Moreover, Bazin spoke with equal passion and conviction of the vocation of an impure cinema (Bazin 2009), and it is to this idea that [Raymond] Bellour returned at the dawn of our new, digital 21st century. (2011)

If a film cannot be deemed realist without also requiring formalist strategies, to rephrase this paradox at the heart of the formalist/realist 'cliché', where does the film image exist? Deleuze asserts another paradox: 'it is we who are internal to time, not the other way round. That we are in time looks like a commonplace, yet it is the highest paradox. Time is not the interior in us, but just the opposite, the interiority in which we are, in which we move, live and change' (1989, 82). This particular paradox may seem beside the point. Yet, a filmic image's potential to directly reveal this immensity of time and extended duration in which we exist corresponds at once with this essay's preoccupation with perception and attendant questions of realism, time, ontology and the very potentials of the medium.

This 'time [that] is always actual and virtual' and 'a beyond of psychological memory' (Deleuze 1989, 109) continually 'corresponds to the most fundamental split in time': the 'passing of the present, and the preservation of the past' (Deleuze 2002, 151). When Deleuze explains this process of becoming conscious of this continual duplicating of one's present into perception and recollection, he suggests that one will 'compare himself to an actor playing his part automatically, listening to himself and beholding himself playing' (1989, 79). Again, the subject's perception of perception facilitated through the cinematic time-image (Boljkovac 2013, 147), finds expression particularly through the time-image's crystal-image, a 'mobile mirror' through which cinema exposes time's ceaseless division, this virtual-actual doubling or folding of all events, time, memory and the self. Bazin's influence once more for Deleuze, and here vis-à-vis Deleuze's conception of the crystal-image, is striking. In an illuminating text that 'explore[s] Deleuze as a visionary reader of Bazin', Diane Arnaud writes, 'Bazin opens the way for Deleuze's *image-cristal* thanks to his own rich metaphors. In the 1948 manuscript on Wyler, when he metaphorically compares the invisible stratification process of the sea shell – which can be seen only if broken – to the aesthetic structure of the mise-en-scène, Bazin introduces the visionary notion of "*cristallographie*"' (Arnaud 2011, 85, 92).

If, then, strategies of formalism and realism forever coexist, line and serve one another, alongside images of both movement and direct time (movement- and time-images), just as 'remembering [...] is not the opposite of forgetting, but rather its lining' (Marker 1982, *Sans Soleil*), might we discern, again, a productive association between such presupposed divides? From 'the moment in which editing enters the picture' Pasolini states, 'when we pass from the cinema to a film [...] it happens that the present becomes past [...]; a past that, for reasons immanent in the cinematographic medium, and not because of an aesthetic choice, always has the qualities of the present (*it is, in other words, a historical present*)' (Pasolini 1972, 236). Deleuze's second cinematic volume, *Cinema 2: The Time-Image*, continues the lineage from Bazin to Deleuze and reveals a new image of thought, a time-image that seeks not a 'realistic' image of movement in parcelled, chronological, rational time but that exposes an image of multiple pasts. While unearthing Deleuze's debt to Bazin with respect to 'where geography and geology bear on Bazin's notion of *evolution* and their impact, correlatively, on that of the *event* of cinema', Conley contends 'that where Bazin writes of evolution and event, he anticipates what, in strong political and aesthetic senses alike, Deleuze calls "stratigraphy"' (Conley 2011, 32).

Montage of the time-image then 'takes on a new function: instead of being concerned with movement-images from which it extracts an indirect image of time, it is concerned with the time-image and extracts from it the relations of time on which aberrant movement must now depend' (Deleuze 1989, 23). The stratigraphic time as noted previously wherein landscapes 'see' in the absence of humans, those that 'have passed into the landscape and are themselves part of the compound of sensations' as Deleuze and Félix Guattari write (1994, 169), reveals a bifurcating time that launches at once towards a future as it delves beneath ashes, 'geological sections' and 'archaeological layers' to unearth regions and stratums of harrowing pasts (Deleuze 1989, 254). And through these filmic responses to devastation and despair across geologic layers we can locate Bazin's past and future influence not only for Deleuze's thought but also contemporary media practices and post-cinematic considerations of realism and formalism across various screens.

As Mulvey suggests in interview, key directors of neorealism such as Roberto Rossellini and other 'great protagonist[s] of cinema as a realist mode [...] also loved the magic of cinema, as something as fantastic as it was realist, and also more fantastic because of the image's credibility' (Mulvey 2017). Mulvey's fascination with 'the irrational in human life, mixed in with the struggle to find certainty through the cinematic image' speaks to the ineluctable interconnection of filmic fantasy and reality and that 'something powerful left over, some aesthetic force', of which Martin also writes, that is 'left for the theorist to define' (Martin 2011). Contemporary screen theorists take this challenge of defining the wondrous osmotic quality of *cinema*, now '*post-cinema*', in multiple productive directions that connect with questions of new perceptions and sensations of time that affect our self-awareness, perceptions of others, our environments and planet itself in a perilous time of 'post-truth'.

***

> I am interested in the presence of reality in cinema but the question of truth seems to me to be more loaded and more subjective. Whose truth?
>
> —Mulvey (2017)

> We set all sorts of nets and traps but reality is what evades them, becoming the impossible object of our desire for possession, for pleasure, and the passion for order that underlies our lust for knowledge and command.
>
> —Sean Cubitt (2013, 281)

Stephen Rust and Salma Monani commence their introduction to *Ecocinema Theory and Practice* with the following:

> From an ecocritical perspective, environment is not just the organic world, or the laws of nature to which Kant counterposed the powers of human reason in the struggle for freedom, or that Nature from which Marx thought we were condemned to wrest our survival; it is the whole habitat which encircles us, the physical world entangled with the cultural. It is an ecology of connections that we negotiate to make our meanings and our livings. In this habitat, cinema is a form of negotiation, a mediation that is itself ecologically placed as it consumes the entangled world around it, and in turn, is itself consumed. (2013, 1)

In this Trumpian era, when damage has been done to our illusionary world of truths, how might questions of truth, fact and reality find effective post-cinematic realizations and theorizations that can effect any act of resistance to a world beset with bigotry and authoritarianism? How can contemporary cinema and media work to unsettle the preconceived and overcoded and discover life? If, as Deleuze writes, 'the less human the world is, the more it is the artist's duty to believe and produce belief in a relation between [hu]man[ity] and the world' (1989, 171), if the truthful man wants 'nothing other than to judge life' (137) and impose morality as a truth and right to self-appointed justice and repressive sovereignty, the cinema must seek to shatter censoring 'truths' in our actual world and so produce and embrace new differences and other worlds 'capable of restoring our belief' in *this* world (181). Along these lines are works of ecologically motivated films.

'It is only recently, most notably since the mid-1990s', write Rust and Monani, 'that a growing number of scholars have begun to critically interrogate cinema's ecological dimensions and their implications for us and the more than human world in which we live' (2013, 2). Scott MacDonald adjoins, 'The job of an ecocinema is to provide *new kinds of film experience* that demonstrate an alternative to conventional media-spectatorship and help to nurture a more environmentally progressive mindset' (2013, 20), and here again across certain works of ecocinema we might locate formal means advocated by Bazin, such as uses of extended durations, long takes and slow pacing so as to 'allow the apparatus of cinema a moment to stand before nature and before us' (33), as well as a breaking down of an object/subject divide. While assessing twenty-first century post-cinema and the 'emergence of ecology as a dominant way of understanding the human–Earth relationship' (Ivakhiv 2013, 87), Adrian Ivakhiv stresses that 'film, like other forms of world-making, is "subject/object-omorphic": it produces a world for us that is at once subjective and objective' (96).

With respect to an 'exclusive claim to knowledge and power that marks the objective political frame surrounding populist environmentalism', Cubitt asserts the 'difficult, strictly unimaginable leap required to include "nature" as a political subject', and the need for ecocriticism to 'contest the boundaries between (human) subjects and (environmental) objects' (2013, 284). While writing on 'traditionally eco-themed films' including Roland Emmerich's *Godzilla* (1998), *The Day After Tomorrow* (2004) and *2012* (2009), Cubitt's recollection of a Walter Benjamin contention that might serve as a 'general criticism of these films' is apropos: 'Mankind, which in Homer's time was an object of contemplation for the Olympian gods, now is one for itself. Its self-alienation has reached such a degree that it can experience its own destruction as an aesthetic pleasure of the first order' (285).

Perhaps most movingly, and in ways reminiscent of Bazinian thought, MacDonald writes of ecocinema as 'a cinematic experience that models patience and mindfulness – qualities of consciousness crucial for a deep appreciation of and an ongoing commitment to the natural environment' (2013, 19) in our far more than and too human world. I am again reminded of the prescient urgency of Chris Marker's oeuvre and the significance of animals as well, most notably cats and owls, across his works. Recall the burning World Trade Towers image superimposed, with its cloud of devastation evocative of Hiroshima's, against a Paris skyline in Marker's (2004) *Chats perchés*. A voiceover reminds us that there was talk in November 2001 of a 'new age' of 'Us against Them', 'the Killers'.[5] Dualist positions withstand in our world, as embedded in self-destructive, aggrandising notions of difference. With hope, our post-cinema will continue, in moments, to prompt belief in this world.

Notes

* I am deeply indebted to the wonderful editors of this volume, Tom Conley and Hunter Vaughan. Dedicated to Hanjo Berressem with much love.

1 Repeatedly Elsaesser has examined a 'something-both-more-and-less of cinema at the threshold of the digital age' (2013, 14) that identifies a 'revolution and a renaissance at the same time' (40) in relation to an increasing recognition that the two positions, 'often opposed as realist and formalist, resemble each other more than is generally assumed' (Elsaesser and Hagener 2010, 8), and that 'there may *not* be a "before" and "after" the digital in the way we speak of before and after Christ' (see Elsaesser 2004, 78)!

2 See Vaughan's clear assessment: 'Polarized representatives of the duality between shot and montage, Eisenstein's and Bazin's respective theories are constructed around particular beliefs in film's capacity for simulating aspects of human subjectivity, be it as consciousness (Eisenstein) or perception (Bazin)' (2013, 46).

In his reflections on the May 1968 period and the years that followed, Anthony Easthope also usefully asserts that

> *Both* [formalist and realist] positions support that cinema, based as it is in the photographic process, must be assessed as in part a mechanical reproduction, whether feeble or convincing. It was not until the 1960s that this view—the naturalist, or reflectionist, fallacy—began to be finally overthrown in film theory. (1998, 52)

With regard to the three theoretical interventions, 'the encounter of Marxism and psychoanalysis on the terrain of semiotics' (Stephen Heath 1985, 511), that enabled film theory to 'develop into a fully fledged account of cinema,' Easthope notes that semiotics arrived first on the scene, as it were (52). The consequence, Easthope explains, of 'semiotic attention to cinema was to weaken concern with the issue of realism and strengthen attention to the cinema as a particular kind of textuality' (53). Following the emergences of semiotics, Altusserian film criticism from the late 1960s and Christian Metz's contributions, realism in the cinema was entirely reassessed in this period, leading in 1974 to Colin MacCabe's 'Realism and the Cinema: Notes on Some Brechtian Theses'. Famously, MacCabe proposes, following Roland Barthes and Bertolt Brecht, that the classic realist text of the nineteenth-century literary novel is typified by an internal hierarchy of discourses (1974, 7–8); this analysis of realism looks not, that is, to an external reality but to the construction of reality as 'an effect [that] the text produced through a specific signifying organization' (Easthope 1998, 55).

3 Reassessments and revisitations of Bazin's contributions are ongoing and will so remain it seems, from Daniel Morgan's 'Rethinking Bazin: Ontology and Realist Aesthetics', to the more recent hyperrealist theories of object-oriented ontology.

4 Martin writes: 'The *dispositif* [...] is instantly and necessarily more of a social machine for Baudry, a set-up, arrangement or disposition of elements that adds up to the cinema-going experience: body in a chair, dark room, light from the projector hitting a screen. Baudry posed the movement between the two terms [*apparatus* and *dispositif*] in this way: where the basic cinematic apparatus already includes the fact of projection, the *dispositif* adds in the spectator and all this implies (Baudry 1978)' (2011).

5 For analysis of Marker's *Chats Perchés*, see Boljkovac (2013, 163–64).

References

Filmography

De Sica, Vittorio. 1952. *Umberto D.*

Eisenstein, Sergei. 1925. *Strike.*

———. 1925. *Battleship Potemkin.*

Emmerich, Roland. 1998. *Godzilla.*

———. 2004. *The Day after Tomorrow.*

———. 2009. *2012.*

Marker, Chris. 1957. *Lettre de Sibèrie.*

———. 1982. *Sans Soleil*, Chris Marker (conception and editing), Sandor Krasna/Chris Marker (camera).

———. 2004. *Chats Perchés*, Chris Marker (video), Michel Krasna (soundtrack).

Pasolini, Pier Paolo. 1962. *Mamma Roma.*

Works Cited

Álvarez López, Cristina, and Adrian Martin. 2011. 'Philippe Garrel: Portraits'. Transit (14 December 2011). http://cinentransit.com/philippe-garrel-retratos/#one (accessed 1 May 2016).

———. 2015. 'Chantal Akerman: A Primer'. *Sight and Sound*, 54–57.

Andrew, Dudley. 1976. *The Major Film Theories*. London: Oxford University Press.

———. 1997. 'André Bazin's "Evolution"'. In *Defining Cinema*, edited by Peter Lehman, 73–96. New Brunswick, NJ: Rutgers University Press.

Arnaud, Diane. 2011. 'From Bazin to Deleuze: A Matter of Depth'. In *Opening Bazin: Film Theory and Its Afterlife*, edited by Dudley Andrew with Hervé Joubert-Laurencin, 85–94. New York: Oxford University Press.

Bazin, André. 2003 and 1983. 'Chris Marker, *Lettre de Sibérie*'. In *Le Cinéma français de la Libération à la Nouvelle Vague (1945–1958)*, 179–81. Paris: Cahiers du Cinéma. Republished 2003 in *Film Comment*, Dave Kehr (trans.), 44–45.

———. 2005. *What is Cinema? Volume I.* Jean Renoir (foreword), Dudley Andrew (new foreword), edited and translated by Hugh Gray. Berkeley: University of California Press.

Boljkovac, Nadine. 2013. *Untimely Affects: Gilles Deleuze and an Ethics of Cinema*. Edinburgh: Edinburgh University Press.

Conley, Tom. 2000. 'The Film Event: From Interval to Interstice'. In *The Brain Is the Screen: Deleuze and the Philosophy of Cinema*, edited by Gregory Flaxman, 303–26. Minneapolis: University of Minnesota.

———. 2005. 'The Desert Island'. In *Deleuze and Space*, edited by Ian Buchanan and Gregg Lambert, 207–19. Edinburgh: Edinburgh University Press.

———. 2007. *Cartographic Cinema*. Minneapolis: University of Minnesota Press.

———. 2011. 'Evolution and Event in *Qu'est-ce que le cinéma?*' In *Opening Bazin: Postwar Film Theory and Its Afterlife*, edited by Dudley Andrew with Hervé Joubert-Laurencin, 32–41. New York: Oxford University Press.

Cubitt, Sean. 2013. 'Everybody Knows This Is Nowhere: Data Visualization and Ecocriticism'. In *Ecocinema Theory and Practice*, edited by Stephen Rust, Salma Monani and Sean Cubitt, 279–96. New York: Taylor & Francis.

Deleuze, Gilles. 1989. *Cinema 2: The Time-Image*. Translated by Hugh Tomlinson and Robert Galeta. Minneapolis: University of Minnesota Press. [*Cinéma 2, L'image-temps* (Paris: Minuit, 1985).]

——— 1997. *Essays Critical and Clinical*, Daniel W. Smith and Michael A. Greco (trans.). Minneapolis: University of Minnesota Press.

——— 2002. 'The actual and the virtual', in *Dialogues II*, Eliot Ross Albert (trans.), 148–52. New York: Columbia University Press.

Deleuze, Gilles, and Félix Guattari. 1994. *What Is Philosophy?* Translated by Hugh Tomlinson and Graham Burchell. New York: Columbia University Press. [*Qu'est-ce que la philosophie?* (Paris: Minuit, 1991).]

Easthope, Anthony. 1998. 'Classic Film Theory and Semiotics'. In *The Oxford Guide to Film Studies*, edited by John Hill and Pamela Church Gibson, 51–57. Oxford: Oxford University Press.

Eisenstein, Sergei. 1998. *The Eisenstein Reader*, edited by Richard Taylor, translated by Richard Taylor and William Powell. London: British Film Institute.

Elsaesser, Thomas. 1998. 'Truth or Dare: Reality Checks on Indexicality, or the Future of Illusionism'. In *Cinema Studies into Visual Theory?* edited by Anu Koivunnen and Astrid Soderbergh Widding, 31–50. Turku: D-Vision.

———. 2004. 'The New Film History as Media Archaeology'. *Cinémas* 14, no. 2–3: 75–117.

———. 2011. 'A Bazinian Half-Century'. In *Opening Bazin: Postwar Film Theory and Its Afterlife*, edited by Dudley Andrew with Hervé Joubert-Laurencin, 3–12. New York: Oxford University Press.

———. 2013. 'Digital Cinema: Convergence or Contradiction?' In *The Oxford Handbook of Sound and Image in Digital Media*, edited by C. Vernallis, A. Herzog and J. Richardson, 13–44. New York: Oxford University Press.

Elsaesser, Thomas, and Malte Hagener. 2010. *Film Theory: An Introduction through the Senses*. New York: Routledge.

Gallix, Andrew. 2014. 'Interview with Nicholas Rombes'. *Bomb* (8 May). http://bombmagazine.org/article/1000132/nicholas-rombes (accessed 1 April 2016).

Heath, Stephen. 1985. '*Jaws*, Ideology and Film Theory'. In *Movies and Methods: Volume II*, edited by Bill Nichols, 509–16. Berkeley: University of California Press.

Ivakhiv, Adrian. 2013. 'An Ecophilosophy of the Moving Image: Cinema as Anthrobiogeomorphic Machine'. In *Ecocinema Theory and Practice*, edited by Stephen Rust, Salma Monani and Sean Cubitt, 87–106. New York: Taylor & Francis.

MacCabe, Colin. 1974. 'Realism and the Cinema: Notes on Some Brechtian Theses'. *Screen* 15, no. 2 (July): 7–27.

MacDonald, Scott. 2013. 'The Ecocinema Experience'. In *Ecocinema Theory and Practice*, edited by Stephen Rust, Salma Monani and Sean Cubitt, 17–42. New York: Taylor & Francis.

Martin, Adrian. 2011. 'Turn the Page: From Mise en scène to Dispositif'. Screening the Past (July). http://www.screeningthepast.com/2011/07/turn-the-page-from-mise-en-scene-to-dispositif/ (accessed 1 February 2016).

Morgan, Daniel. 2006. 'Rethinking Bazin: Ontology and Realist Aesthetics'. *Critical Inquiry* 32, no. 3 (Spring): 443–81.

Mulvey, Laura. 2009. 'Some Reflections on the Cinephilia Question'. *Framework* 50, no. 1–2 (Spring/Fall): 190–93.

———. 2017. 'Death 24x a Second: In Conversation with Laura Mulvey'. four by three magazine. http://www.fourbythreemagazine.com/issue/death/laura-mulvey-interview (accessed 1 May 2017).

Pasolini, Pier Paolo. 1972. 'The Written Language of Reality'. In *Heretical Empiricism*, edited by Louise K. Barnett, translated by Ben Lawton and Louise K. Barnett. Washington: New Academic, LLC.

Rancière, Jacques. 2004. *The Politics of Aesthetics.* Translated by Gabriel Rockhill. London: Continuum.

Rust, Stephen, and Salma Monani. 2013. 'Introduction: Cuts to dissolves—defining and situating ecocinema studies'. In *Ecocinema Theory and Practice*, edited by Stephen Rust, Salma Monani and Sean Cubitt, 1–14. New York: Taylor & Francis.

Shklovsky, Victor. 1965. 'Art as Technique'. In *Russian Formalist Criticism: Four Essays*, edited and translated by Lee T. Lemon and Marion J. Reis, 3–24. Lincoln: University of Nebraska Press.

Vaughan, Hunter. 2009. 'André Bazin'. In *Film, Theory and Philosophy: The Key Thinkers*, edited by Felicity Colman, 100–108. Montréal: McGill-Queens University Press.

———. 2013. *Where Film Meets Philosophy: Godard, Resnais, and Experiments in Cinematic Thinking.* New York: Columbia University Press.

POSTFACE

Tom Conley

Composed and written with force and conviction, the essays in this collection attest to the continued pertinence and promise of film theory. Born of cinema itself, whether in view of the Lumière Brothers's *Workers Exiting a Factory* or Bill Morrison's *Dawson City: Frozen Time*, theory begs us to consider how and why we commit ourselves to study cinema and visual media. And for what ends: examining at a gamut of cinemas from the origins of the seventh art to the digital age, each of the authors in the pages above discerns issues that make theory contemporary. Mindful of film history, they show how the moving image remains a compelling forum for dialogue and exchange over issues of a first magnitude: what it means to live in a world that by and large we experience on screens or through moving images; but also, on how visual media might shape the future of cognition as such. The authors remind us that with theory, we are enabled to consider the force and fragility of cinema: in what ways the medium is endowed with uncanny power and yet, how ephemeral and passing it can be. Demonstrating that theory rescues cinema from itself without the promise of redemption, the authors employ a variety of concepts and methods that turn films into unsettling critical objects.

At the risk of repeating what Hunter Vaughan notes cogently in the Preface, and what in different ways the authors have shown in their contributions: the foundations of theory are strong, and the directions it is taking bear untold promise. Several major of lines of inquiry draw their way through the sum of the essays. First, as historians of the present are quick to remind us, since 2007, following the implementation of the cell phone and the iPad, the advent of Facebook and the growth of the internet, we live in the world in ways inalterably other than those we had known even a decade ago. We can posit that the great tradition of 'going to the movies' is long gone and that the movie palace is now either a museum or a photographic image. Distant are memories of the pleasure of purchasing a ticket from an irascible vendor enclosed in a glass booth under a marquise illuminated by neon lights; so also, much as Truffaut had shown in *The Four Hundred Blows*, are those of the children we once were, browsing by windows at the wings of the entry, ogling at glossy stills of scenes from current and forthcoming features soon to be seen. The nature of cinema as an *event* has changed. We watch movies in bits and pieces and in formats of different proportion. Using flash drives and DVDs (already an antiquarian item), we stop and start our image-streams at will. When we 'work' on a film, the computer screen becomes what had once been a Moviola or a Steenbeck flatbed table.

Today, with theory everywhere around us, the pleasures of our viewings are in concert with our labours of editing.

Thus today, as Francesco Casetti underscores in the inaugural essay to this volume, how we think about – how we make visible – our relation with cinema and new media has altered what he calls our *experience* of them. It now seems as if, contrary to how theory developed 40 years ago, when much was made from little, or when intense and detailed speculation derived from patient scrutiny of segments taken from 16mm copies of films, we now proceed in patchwork ways. We shuttle from site to site; scan over films on YouTube, and download and copy sequences as we wish; we buzz from film to film like bees in clover. Given a plethora of material at our fingertips, often at the risk of losing the devil from detail, we shape our speculations from the experience of moving over and across many films and images. We see films in their entirety, it seems, when we attend festivals or, far from multiplexes, we find ourselves in the urban or academic milieus of archives or art theatres.

New modes of viewing inspire us to think afresh about what, already 15 years ago, Mary Ann Doane famously called the *emergence* of cinematic time and, by extension, about its correlative of cinematic space. Theory has turned in the direction of what we make of how they play in our experience of cinema. The ostensive 'return' to the phenomenological underpinnings of film indicates that what we 'do with' the ambient world comes through the ways our eyes and ears process moving images – in other words, of what we 'make' of the world through the filter of cinemas and new medias. Having turned away from a psychoanalytical tradition that confers a privilege upon the unconscious, in which study had been made of originary or traumatic events that determine a person's being and mediated quality of life, theory now takes up how we deal with the conscience and consciousness of cinema. Film theory enables us to grasp and even to nurture the effects of that experience and to understand it from the standpoint of conditions that determine the character and fabric of our lives.

As a consequence, we can appreciate the role cinema plays in elaborating different ways of treating matters of gender, race and sexual difference. What Freud had equated with the irreversibility of anatomical destiny or sexual difference is no longer so. Outside or beyond what plots or storylines are said to 'represent', through cinema we can discern how untenable distinctions, forces of exclusion and ideology (that Louis Althusser had called the imaginary relation we hold with real conditions of the production of consciousness) come to us in the shape of received ideas. Now, more than ever calling those ideas in question, the new strains of theory in this volume carry strong political latency. Contributors note that from its very beginnings cinema has been an industrial medium and that it remains an ideological engine as such. Working with and against the drive of the latter, in what might be another concern of the essays, theory studies political issues through their evidence or absence in both old and new visual media. It is here, as Hunter Vaughan makes clear in his introductory essay, that in the context of new fields of study that include posthumanism, object-oriented ontology, actor network theory and others, we do well to see how cinema informs and even manages their expression and content.

Especially notable here and now, because it entails how we live with the world at large, is ecology and its relation to cinema, a field where the stakes of politics and aesthetics could not be greater. A collective project of theory might entail discerning its operative principles in the context of what Jussi Parikka calls a 'geology' of media. Rooted in the excavation and refinement of precious metals amidst the detritus of the past, he contends that the history of contemporary media begins in the earth itself.[1] Here, too, as he predicted in 1955, in the melancholy of *Tristes Tropiques,* Claude Lévi-Strauss proposed an ecology of the human sciences. Prior to becoming an ethologist and venturing into Brazil in the 1930s, Lévi-Strauss found inspiration in three muses or 'mistresses': Marx, Freud and Geology. The line of demarcation Marx had drawn between infra- and super-structure, he noted, also cut a path along a fault line that Freud had traced between conscious life and the unconscious or the manifest and latent content of human actions, while the same line could be found in landscapes evincing duration and metamorphosis over duration of time far beyond the limits of our imagination. In its current labours, theory works along similar traces of rift and shift. As a consequence of the emergence of new media, in the dynamics of viewership and circulation of critical discourse, theory has become processual, open-ended, tentative, hardly dogmatic or blaring, free from the culture wars or quarrels of Ancients and Moderns of times past. By addressing the changing nature of experience, as Hunter Vaughan shows in the Preface, we are taking it along unforeseen lines of inquiry. First and foremost, the knots that tied Marx and Freud to film have loosened. Enthusiasts of the *Critique of Political Economy* who had shown how cinema engaged alienation to consider human plight now realize that in the world of digital spectacle, alienation, having been all but elided from representation, becomes a critical tool that permits gainsay on cinema in a global sphere – that is, on how digital technologies have spawned an eighth art, an art related to the logic and logistics of positioning systems, that now moves effortlessly over and about the globe.[2]

Now situated in greater environmental awareness, Marxian and Freudian models of analysis find themselves refashioned in studies of cinema and its relation to sentience and cognition. Where psychogenesis is tied to sensation and perception, theorists of recent vintage use the concept of an errant or haptic eye to examine how old and new media relate to how we touch and are touched by the ambient world. When taken as dictionaries tell us, 'the mental action or process of acquiring knowledge and understanding through thought, experience and the senses', cognition implies a subject's give-and-take with sensation itself. Now a function of technologies that far exceed human limits, knowledge and experience cannot be done without 'sensors' and sensory apparatus whose purchase on the world is greater than ours. They lead us to wonder if cinema is itself a cognitive machinery from which we can continue to gain knowledge.[3]

And yet, although Marx and Freud have become history, in media studies, we do well not to forget the profound social and personal role that desire continues to play in our inquiry. By way of conclusion, a fragment from pre-history shows why. Inaugurating 'De l'experience' [Of Experience], the last of the *Essais* that he published four years before his death in 1592, laying a foundation for cognitive theory that could apply to film theory, pilfering Aristotle, Montaigne writes,

> Il n'est desir plus naturel que le desir de connoissance. Nous essayons tous les moyens qui nous y peuvent mener. Quand la raison nous faut, nous y employons l'experience, (c) *Per varios usus artem experiential fecit: Exemplo monstrante viam.*[4]
>
> [There is no desire is more natural than the desire of knowledge. We essay all the means that can lead us to it. When reason fails, we employ experience, *By various means experience gives birth to art, and the example leads the way*].

In what a media theorist might call a grammatical lap-dissolve, unlike its source in Greek or Latin, the partitive construction, *desir de connoissance,* suggests that the one and the other are mixed: that we exude desire for knowledge as much as knowledge extends its own force of attraction to us. *Cognition* would take place where the one and the other converge and meet. The effect would be a continuous apprehension and appreciation of film that continues to be an object of speculation.[5] Where, as Vaughan aptly notes above, contemporary film theory embraces cognition in the coextensive desire of and for knowledge of cinema and media. Such is what the contributors to this volume take up in the pages above. We thank them for their selfless and generous contributions and hope that our enthusiasm will be collectively shared.

Notes

1 Jussi Parikka, *Media Archeology: Approaches, Applications* (Berkeley: University of California Press, 2011) and *A Geology of Media* (Minneapolis: University of Minnesota Press, 2015).

2 See William Rankin, *After the Map: Cartography, Navigationand the Transformation of Territory in the Twentieth Century* (Chicago: University of Chicago Press, 2016).

3 Mark B. N. Hansen, *Feed-Forward: On the Future of Twenty-First Century Media* (Chicago: University of Chicago Press, 2015).

4 Michel de Montaigne, *Essais,* ed. M. Rat and A. Thibaudet (Paris: Éditions Gallimard/Pléiade, 1950), 1194. (Translation mine.) The intercalated '(c)' indicates that the citation (from Manilius) was penned into the 1588 copy and printed in the first posthumous edition of 1595. I am indebted to Dominique de Courcelles, author of an unpublished essay, 'Coup d'essai(s) et coiup de maître ès arts: La philosophie artistique des *Essais* de Montaigne, un art cinématographique?' in a forlorn copy of the *Bulletin de la Société des Amis de Montaigne.*

5 For Randle Cotgrave, in his *Dictionarie of the French and English Tongues* (London, 1611), 'Cognoissance' is 'Knowledge; acquaintance, familiaritie with, cunning, experience in; a notice, or notion; an intelligence, understanding, or apprehension of; also, a deed or scedule of acknowledgement, or confession of a debt; also, a badge, or cognisaunce'. But also, proverbially, with an almost Freudian inflection: 'Chose perduë est lors cogneuë: prov: *The worth of things known is when they be lost*'.

NOTES ON CONTRIBUTORS

Nadine Boljkovac is a senior lecturer in the School of Film and Television at Falmouth University. From August 2018, she is a visiting fellow of the Center for Transformative Media, Parsons School of Design, The New School, and from October 2018–19, a research fellow of the Morphomata International Center for Advanced Studies, University of Cologne. Boljkovac has recently co-edited and contributed to 'Materialising Absence in Film and Media' (*Screening the Past* Special Dossier with Saige Walton, 2018). Her monograph in progress, *Beyond Herself: Feminist (Auto)Portraiture and the Moving Image*, follows *Untimely Affects: Gilles Deleuze and an Ethics of Cinema* (2013; 2015).

Elisabeth Bronfen is professor of Anglo-American literature and culture at the University of Zürich and Global Distinguished Professor at New York University.

William Brown is senior lecturer at the University of Roehampton. He is the author of *Non-Cinema: Global Digital Filmmaking and the Multitude* (2018) and *Supercinema: Film-Philosophy for the Digital Age* (2013), as well as numerous essays. Brown is also a maker of zero-budget films, including *En Attendant Godard* (2009), *The New Hope* (2015), *Circle/Line* (2016) and *This Is Cinema* (2018). He is currently working with David H. Fleming on a book about cephalopods and cinema, provisionally entitled *Kinoteuthis Infernalis: The Rise of Chthulucinema.*

Warren Buckland is reader in Film Studies at Oxford Brookes University. His recent publications include *Conversations with Christian Metz: Selected Interviews on Film Theory* (co-edited with Daniel Fairfax, 2017), *The Routledge Encyclopedia of Film Theory* (co-edited with Edward Branigan, 2014), *Film Theory: Rational Reconstructions* (2012) and *Puzzle Films: Complex Storytelling in Contemporary Cinema* (ed. 2009).

Francesco Casetti is the Thomas E. Donnelly Professor of Humanities and Film and Media Studies at Yale University. Among his books are *Inside the Gaze; Theories of Cinema, 1945–1995* (1998); *Eye of the Century: Film, Experience, Modernity* (2008); and *The Lumière Galaxy: Seven Key Words for the Cinema to Come* (2015). Casetti currently works on fears that cinema raised in the first decades of its life, and on the increasing interdependence of media and environment.

Tom Conley teaches in the Departments of Visual and Environmental Studies and Romance Languages and Literatures at Harvard University, and has recently co-edited *Falso movimento: Ensayos sobre escrita e cinema* (with Clara Rowland, 2016) and *The Wylie-Blackwell Companion to Jean-Luc Godard* (with T. Jefferson Kline, 2014).

Mary R. Desjardins is professor of Film and Media Studies at Dartmouth College where she also teaches Women's, Gender, and Sexuality Studies. She is author of *Recycled Stars: Female Film Stardom in the Age of Television and Video* (2015) and *Father Knows Best* (2015), and co-editor of *Dietrich Icon* (2007).

Camilla Fojas is a professor of American Studies and Media Studies at the University of Virginia. Her most recent books are *Zombies, Migrants, and Queers: Race and Crisis Capitalism in Pop Culture* (2017) and *Migrant Labor and Border Securities in Pop Culture* (2017).

Theresa L. Geller is a Scholar-in-Residence with the Beatrice Bain Research Group at the University of California, Berkeley. Before moving to the Bay Area, Geller was professor of film theory and history at Grinnell College, and a Whitney Humanities Fellow at Yale University in 2015–16. Geller is the author of *The X-Files* (2016) and co-editor of *Reframing Todd Haynes: Feminism's Indelible Mark* (forthcoming).

Brendan Kredell is an assistant professor at Oakland University, where his work focuses on the intersection of urban and media studies. Kredell is the editor, with Marijke de Valck and Skadi Loist, of *Film Festivals: History, Theory, Method, Practice* (2016).

Trond Lundemo is an associate professor in Cinema Studies at the Department of Media Studies at Stockholm University. He is co-editor of the book series "Film Theory in Media History" at Amsterdam University Press, and was a member of the NECS steering committee, 2011–15.

Laura U. Marks is full professor and Grant Strate University Professor at Simon Fraser University. She works on media art and philosophy with an intercultural focus. Marks's most recent book is *Hanan al-Cinema: Affections for the Moving Image* (2015).

Codruţa Morari is associate professor of French and Media Studies at Wellesley College. She is the author of *The Bressonians. French Cinema and the Culture of Authorship* (2017).

William Rothman received his PhD in philosophy from Harvard, where he taught for many years. He was founding editor of the Harvard Film Studies and Cambridge Studies in Film series and is the author of many books. Rothman is currently a professor in Cinema and Interactive Media at the University of Miami.

Robert Sinnerbrink is Australian Research Council Future Fellow and associate professor of Philosophy at Macquarie University, Sydney. He is the author of *Cinematic Ethics: Exploring Ethical Experience through Film* (2016), *New Philosophies of Film: Thinking Images* (2011), *Understanding Hegelianism* (2007/2014), and is a member of the editorial board of the journal *Film-Philosophy*.

James Tweedie is associate professor of Comparative Literature, Cinema and Media at the University of Washington. He is the author of *The Age of New Waves: Art Cinema and the Staging of Globalization* (2013) and *Moving Pictures, Still Lives: Film, New Media, and the Late Twentieth Century* (2018).

Pasi Väliaho is professor in History of Art at the Department of Philosophy, Classics, History of Art and Ideas, University of Oslo. He is the author of *Biopolitical Screens: Image, Power, and the Neoliberal Brain* (2014) and *Mapping the Moving Image: Gesture, Thought and Cinema circa 1900* (2010).

Hunter Vaughan is associate professor of Cinema Studies at Oakland University, and a 2017 Rachel Carson Fellow. He is the author of *Where Film Meets Philosophy* (2013), *Screen Life and Identity: A Guide to Film and Media Studies* (with Meryl Shriver-Rice, 2017), and *Hollywood's Dirtiest Secret: The Hidden Environmental Costs of Our Screen Culture* (forthcoming 2019), and is co-editor of the *Journal of Environmental Media.*

Daniel Yacavone is lecturer in Film Studies at the University of Edinburgh, where he has been director of the Film Studies Programme within the School of Literatures, Languages, and Cultures. Yacavone is the author of *Film Worlds: A Philosophical Aesthetics of Cinema* (2015) and is currently writing a book on reflexivity in the moving image.

FILMOGRAPHY

INDEX

Bold numbers indicate figures.